INDIAN FINANCIAL SYSTEM

Dr. S.B. Deodhar
Economist, (Retd.),
Maharashtra State Financial Corporation,
Visiting Faculty, Management Institutes,
Mumbai.

Aditi A. Abhyankar
Head, Associate Professor,
Department of Economics,
Ramnarain Ruia College,
Matunga, Mumbai.

HPH
Himalaya Publishing House
ISO 9001 : 2015 CERTIFIED

First Edition	:	**2001**
Second Revised Edition	:	**2003**
Third Edition	:	**2005**
Fourth Revised Edition	:	**2007**
Fifth Edition	:	**2008**
Sixth Revised Edition	:	**2012**
Edition	:	**2018**
Edition	:	**2021**
Edition	:	**2025**

ISBN No. : 978-93-5051-012-4

Published by : Mrs. Meena Pandey
for **Himalaya Publishing House Pvt. Ltd.,**
"Ramdoot", Dr. Bhalerao Marg, Girgaon, Mumbai - 400 004.
Phone: 022-23860170, 23863863; **Fax:** 022-23877178
E-mail: himpub@bharatmail.co.in; **Website:** www.himpub.com

Branch Offices :

New Delhi : "Pooja Apartments", 4-B, Murari Lal Street, Ansari Road, Darya Ganj, New Delhi - 110 002. Phone: 011-23270392, 23278631; Fax: 011-23256286

Nagpur : Kundanlal Chandak Industrial Estate, Ghat Road, Nagpur - 440 018. Mobile: 09325409992, 09325908881

Bengaluru : Plot No. 91-33, 2nd Main Road, Seshadripuram, Behind Nataraja Theatre, Bengaluru - 560 020. Phone: 080-41138821; Mobile: 09379847017, 09379847005

Hyderabad : No. 3-4-184, Lingampally, Besides Raghavendra Swamy Matham, Kachiguda, Hyderabad - 500 027. Phone: 040-27560041, 27550139

Chennai : No. 34/44, Motilal Street, T. Nagar, Chennai - 600 017. Mobile: 09380460419

Pune : "Laksha" Apartment, First Floor, No. 527, Mehunpura, Shaniwarpeth (Near Prabhat Theatre), Pune - 411 030. Phone: 020-24496323, 24496333; Mobile: 09370579333

Cuttack : Plot No 5F-755/4, Sector-9, CDA Markat Nagar, Cuttack - 753 014, Odisha. Mobile: 09338746007

Kolkata : 3, S.M. Bose Road, Near Gate No. 5, Agarpara Railway Station, North 24 Parganas, West Bengal - 700109. Mobile: 09674536325

DTP by : Sunanda

Printed at : Geetanjali Press Pvt. Ltd., Nagpur. On behalf of HPH.

PREFACE TO THE SIXTH REVISED EDITION

In bringing out the present edition of the book, due care has been taken to make the presentation more analytical along with the updating of information. Besides this, a new chapter on Financial Inclusion – Microfinance has been included.

We express our thanks to Shri K.N. Pandey, Himalaya Publishing House Pvt. Ltd. and hope that this edition also receives favourable response from the students and other readers.

AUTHORS

PREFACE TO THE FIRST EDITION

We are sure you would, soon after initial reading, agree that this is not just one more book on the subject of Indian Financial System. What takes it apart is it's attempt to present in a clear, simple language, devoid of jargon, the subject which is generally considered as difficult and complex. The potential readers of the book kept in view are mainly the students pursuing this subject for their studies at the level of graduation. Of course, anyone interested in reading on the financial system would find the book absorbing and informative.

The field of finance has been always dynamic. The financial system in the country has gone through in the recent years quite rapid and radical changes and, presently, poised for further and even innovative transformation. Efforts have been made in the book to put together these developments and sketch the Indian Financial System as it was and as it is.

The authors have preferred to build up their analysis in the book, backed up by the latest and suitable data drawn from different sources including RBI publications like Reports on Currency and Finance, Report on Trends in Banking in India etc. The contributions made by other writers on the subject have been acknowledged as and when drawn in the book.

We hope the book gets due attention of all those concerned with the subject and receives their favourable response. We would look forward to constructive suggestions for improving the contents.

We express our deep gratitude to Shri D.P. Pandey and Shri K.N. Pandey, Himalaya Publishing House, who played pivotal role in seeing that the book is released.

AUTHORS

CONTENTS

BRIEF CONTENTS

1

Financial System: Definition and Meaning, Constituents and Functions

INTRODUCTION

A well developed financial system performs very crucial role in the smooth functioning of an economy and its future growth prospects. It intermediates to mobilise and to effectively allocate the scarce resources of the economy.

Financial system facilitates flow of funds between different surplus spending entities (savers) and the productive or deficit spending units (*i.e.,* investors) who borrow funds. Indian financial system today is one of the well developed and diversified financial systems particularly in the developing world.

In this chapter, we will discuss the following aspects of the Financial System:

1.1 Financial System and Economic System

1.2 Financial System: Definition and Meaning

1.3 Constituents of the Financial System

[A] Financial Institutions, [B] Financial Markets and [C] Financial Instruments

1.4 Structure and Interrelationships in a Financial System

1.5 Role of the Financial System

1.6 Functions of the Financial System

1.7 Financial System and Economic Development

1.8 Interconnection between Finance and Growth in India

1.1 FINANCIAL SYSTEM AND ECONOMIC SYSTEM

An economic system is responsible and functions for the production and distribution of goods and services meant for attaining welfare of the people. These economic activities, *i.e.,* production and distribution of goods and services belong to the *'real'* sectors of the economy, but require funds or finance for their effective working. Those engaged in production and distribution of goods and services seek arrangements by which their need for funds will be met adequately and timely. The financial system consists of the arrangements devising ways and means whereby it would render this service to the real sectors for their operations and growth.

In economies at the low level of development, the production of goods and services relies on capital mobilised from within, *i.e.,* on self-financed investment, and the distribution or exchange of goods and services is effected through a simple payment system supported mainly by cash transactions.

In a modern economy, which is in the process of changing or which has transformed its set-up to speed up the pace of development, these earlier arrangements for the provision of funds and for the payments with regard to transactions fall short, giving place to a much broader network, acting as the bridge between the savers and investors and providing mechanisms for transfer of funds.

Those who save do so out of the *'surplus'* of their incomes over what they spend. Those who invest for undertaking production, particularly on a larger scale, are likely to incur more by drawing upon the surplus available with others. An effective interrelationship between the two — the savers and investors in the form of mechanism for extending credit and the arrangements for transfer of funds is essential to the modern economy so as to facilitate mobilisation and allocation of financial resources in the socially desirable and productive channels.

The tasks of allocation of funds and meeting credit needs of the real sectors of production and distribution of goods and services have the dimensions of both time and space. These tasks consist of fulfilling adequately the needs of funds for various time-lengths and wherever required.

1.2 FINANCIAL SYSTEM: DEFINITION AND MEANING

In the literature on Systems Analysis, the word *'system'* is described as an aggregate of elements considered together with the relationships holding among them. As such, financial system consists of parts or constituents which in combination with one another form a structure for rendering an essential service of providing funds towards the attainment of goals of development and welfare.

> "The financial system consists of a variety of institutions, markets and instruments related in a systematic manner and provide the principal means by which savings are transformed into investments."
>
> *Prof. Prasanna Chandra*

> "The financial system of any country consists of specialised and non-specialised financial institutions, of organised and unorganised financial markets, of financial instruments and services which facilitate transfer of funds. Procedures and practices adopted in the markets and financial interrelationships are also parts of the system."
>
> *Prof. L.M. Bhole*

> "The financial system is a set of institutional arrangements through which financial surpluses available in the economy are mobilised."
>
> *Prof. S.B. Gupta*

The above descriptive explanations of the term 'Financial System' draw our attention to:

(i) Constituents;

(ii) Structure and its aspects;

(iii) Interrelationships and arrangement/mechanism; and

(iv) Role played or functions performed by the system.

Besides these points, the *raison d'être* or significance of the Financial System lies in the extent and quality of service it renders towards the pursuit of goals of rapid economic development and maximum social welfare.

Before proceeding ahead to deal individually in details with the above aspects of the financial system, it is relevant to note certain points highlighted in the above explanations:

1. Constituents: With regard to constituents, it is mentioned that the financial *institutions*, financial *markets* and financial *instruments* are the three main constituents of the system.

2. Structure: The constituents are varied in nature and form a structure having linkages or interrelationships among the parts and sub-parts of the system.

3. Role: The role is mobilisation of financial resources by way of transfer of funds through transformation of savings into investment.

Further to this, it may be mentioned that —

- Financial system renders an essential service to the 'real' sectors of the economy.
- The service rendered consists of extending credit and provision of funds.

The system has its relevance in any modern economy in so far as it helps the 'real' sectors engaged in the production and distribution of goods to achieve acceleration in economic development and enhancement in social welfare.

1.3 CONSTITUENTS OF FINANCIAL SYSTEM

The constituents of financial system are —

(A) Institutions

(B) Markets

(C) Instruments

The system is meant to render *financial 'services'*: Certain basic points to be recorded in respect of the constituents of the financial system are:

1. The constituents are varied in nature: The financial institutions, markets and the instruments are varied and diverse and the extent of their diversity or varied nature reflects the level of services rendered by the financial system in accordance with the progress achieved for meeting the growing needs of credit and funds in the course of economic development.

2. The constituents of the financial system, *i.e.,* financial institutions, markets and instruments are *interrelated* and not mutually exclusive. The financial system denotes financial institutions operating in markets dealing with financial instruments.

Financial markets exist wherever financial transactions, *i.e.,* dealing in financial instruments takes place between all those including institutions which serve as links between those who need and hence borrow funds and those who provide or lend funds.

A. FINANCIAL INSTITUTIONS

> "Financial institutions are business organisations that act as mobilisers and depositories of savings and as purveyors of credit or finance."
>
> *Prof. L.M. Bhole*

As could be seen from the above explanation, financial institutions as business organisations are distinct from other organisations such as industrial and commercial organisations engaged in manufacturing and/or trading activities. The financial institutions by themselves neither create economic values in products nor trade them against money.

The financial institutions render financial services of dealing in financial assets, *i.e.,* mobilise savings against financial claims, *i.e.,* commitment of future payment and pool these savings for being transferred and allocated among different productive uses. The term 'financial assets' is further clarified under the heading 'Financial Instruments.'

It is necessary to classify the financial institutions in regard to the nature or type of their activities.

Banking and Non-banking

Banking: The banking institutions in a country mobilise savings by accepting monetary deposits from the people, participate in payments mechanism for the exchange of goods and services and extend credit while lending money. The typical feature of the banking institutions is that they not only supply credit, but also create credit. The banks create credit in the form of promises to pay and lend to their borrowers as facilities to draw funds. The money deposits accepted from the people by the banks form a major part of the money supply and their credit creation by way of promises to pay enhances money supply. The banks lending funds by way of drawal facilities extended, advances made to the customers constitutes credit creation.

The Reserve Bank of India (RBI), commercial banks and the co-operative banks are the banking institutions.

Non-banking: The non-banking financial institutions also mobilise financial resources directly or indirectly from the people and lend to the extent of resources made available. These institutions lend funds but do not create credit. The Insurance Companies — Life Insurance Corporation (LIC) and General Insurance Corporation (GIC), the Mutual funds including Unit Trust of India (UTI), Development Financial Institutions (DFIs), Organisations of Pension, Provident Fund (PF) fall under this category.

Intermediaries and Non-intermediaries

Financial intermediaries intermediate, i.e., serve as a link between the savers, *i.e.,* 'surplus' spenders among the people and the deficit spenders who borrow funds for investment purposes. The banking institutions are necessarily intermediaries as they act as *bridges* between the people by mobilising their saving as monetary deposits in terms of financial claims against themselves, and the real sector production units, who borrow funds for investment. In addition to the banks, the non-banking institutions like LIC, GIC, including UTI, Pension and PF funds are financial intermediaries as they channelise funds from the savers under their schemes and take up lending for investment.

The restructuring of DFIs like IDBI, ICICI has been dealt with later in the separate chapter on DFIs.

The Development Financial Institutions (DFIs) like Industrial Development Bank of India (IDBI), Industrial Credit & Investment Corporation of India (ICICI), Industrial Financial Corporation of India (IFCI) etc., are non-banking institutions and are non-intermediaries. The DFIs have been set up for specific purposes of promoting development of certain sectors like industry, agriculture, etc. and of backward regions, and engage themselves in long-term lending.

These *DFIs are non-intermediaries* or rather cannot be called as intermediaries in the real sense as their resource-base does not consist of funds drawn directly from the *'surplus'* spenders or the people but from other sources including subscriptions and borrowing from the government, RBI and other financial institutions. The DFIs are specialised institutions.

It is being argued that the distinction between the banks as financial intermediaries and the DFIs as non-intermediaries is getting blurred as the DFIs have resorted to raising of funds from the people, directly or indirectly, through their bonds/debenture issues. Those who subscribe to these issues of DFIs are UTI, insurance companies and banks. As such, the DFIs generate funds through mostly an indirect link with the savers.

It is also relevant to note here the Narasimham Committee's observation that the banks and DFIs are moving closer to each other in terms of convergence of their activities.

B. FINANCIAL MARKETS

For the common man, the markets are places where he engages himself in exchange of goods and services against money. These are 'real' transactions as these pertain to goods and services.

As against these real transactions, the financial transactions are those under which financial assets are created and/or transferred. When the common man goes to a bank and makes his savings available for the creation of say, fixed deposit, the deposit 'Receipt' is a financial asset for the holder and a financial liability for the bank. What the common man has got out of this transaction is a financial claim of future income in respect of which the bank has involved itself into a financial liability of promise to pay.

Financial markets exist wherever financial transactions — as the one illustrated earlier — occur. The financial transactions could be by way of a creation of a financial asset and/or through transfer involving buying and selling of a financial asset. The common man having converted his savings for acquiring financial securities say equity shares can meet his need of *'liquidity'*, *i.e.,* the need of funds by reaching the stock market for the sale of financial assets in his possession.

As such, financial markets are the centres which provide facilities for financial transactions, *i.e.,* for the creation and transfer of financial assets or claims.

Capital Market and Money Market

We are familiar with terms like money market and capital market. When we mention these terms, we are referring to financial markets and classifying these into money market and capital market. The money market and capital market deal in financial assets and yet the distinction between the two arises as the transactions in these markets pertain to claims of different time-lengths, *i.e.*, periods of maturity. The money market deals in short-term, *i.e.,* one year or less and the capital market deals in medium and long-term assets/claims. *"Money market is the centre for dealings in monetary assets of a short-term character."*

The participants in money market are individuals, including even moneylenders and brokers, the institutions like the Reserve Bank of India (RBI), the banks — the commercial and co-operative banks, non-banking financial institutions, including even insurance companies, UTI etc. and the government. Money market is a short-term credit market, and the instruments dealt with are Hundis, Commercial bills, Treasury bills etc. The borrowers of funds in the money market include the traders, industrial units — corporate and small, the banks and government requiring short-term finance — for short periods like less than a week, a month, three/six months and upto one year. The lenders in the money market consist of moneylenders, indigenous bankers, the banks, the non-banking financial institutions parting with their command over liquid funds for short time-lengths. RBI as an apex institution in the money market, plays the role of monitoring, directing and co-ordinating the performance of other participants and hence viewed by them as the ultimate or the last source of money and credit in the country. The sub-parts of the money market are such as call money market, commercial bills market and treasury bills market.

The capital market gets distinguished from the money market mainly in respect of the time-lengths or the periods of maturity of the financial assets dealt with. The participants like banks and even the indigenous bankers function in both, *i.e.,* money market as well as the capital market as they deal with short-term as well as medium and long-term assets. The capital market has to meet medium and long-term requirement of funds of the real sector units engaged in the production and distribution of goods and services by way of transfer of financial resources to the deficit spenders. Apart from the banks, the capital market consists of financial institutions including Development Financial Institutions (DFIs) like IDBI, IFCI etc., investment institutions like insurance companies — LIC, GIC and the Mutual Funds including UTI, and the stock market which handles the creation of financial claims for raising fresh capital and also trading in such claims already issued.

Primary Market and Secondary Market

The other way in which the financial markets are classified is *Primary market* and *Secondary market.*

The primary market is also called 'New Issues' market, as it provides the principal mechanism by which savings of the people are transformed into investment in terms of new financial assets — shares and debentures — issued. The 'real' sector units, *i.e.,* companies or corporate units raise fresh capital by issuing financial securities or assets, *i.e.,* equity shares and debentures. The savings of the people flow directly to the real sector units when these issues are created in favour of the *'savers'* and flow indirectly when the institutions like banks, financial institutions and mutual funds subscribe to these issues.

The secondary market extends facilities for trading in the financial assets already issued. These facilities provide access to general public, *i.e., savers* for the conversion of their savings into financial securities, *i.e.,* equity shares and debentures and *vice versa* granting *'liquidity'* to their asset holding. The stock market has a primary component in the form of 'New Issues' market and a secondary component in stock exchanges.

Financial Markets — Organised and Unorganised

Keeping in view the structure of financial system and its diversity in a wide variety of institutions, it is quite relevant to distinguish financial markets as *'Organised'* and *'Unorganised'.* Both the components of financial markets, *i.e.,* money market and the capital market have the organised and the unorganised segments. The distinction between these two markets relates to the individuals and institutions operating in these markets, their activities and the extent to which their activities could be co-ordinated and monitored. The commercial banks and the co-operative banks are the main components of the 'organised' money market and their activities are amenable to direction and control by the Reserve Bank of India (RBI). As against this, the moneylenders, shroffs and indigenous bankers constitute the unorganised money market. The activities and the practices of those who operate in the unorganised segment are not necessarily in the broader interests and yet remain beyond the purview of co-ordination and control. The organised segment of the capital market consists of the banks, the non-banking financial institutions including Development Financial Institutions (DFIs, IDBI, IFCI etc.), investment institutions like insurance companies and Mutual Funds including Unit Trust of India (as mentioned earlier) and the stock market including New Issues component and Stock Exchanges. The unorganised capital market exists in Nidhis, Chit Funds and Finance Companies — which play an informal and often personalised role.

C. FINANCIAL INSTRUMENTS

Financial instruments are the financial assets or claims which form an important constituent of the financial system and the developed status and maturity of the financial system is indicated by the wide range of instruments dealt with for mobilising and allocating savings for productive and effective use.

In the financial transactions, those who need borrow funds and those who have a 'surplus', lend funds by creating and/or transferring financial assets or securities in the form of claims on future income. As the financial assets or securities are created for certain time-lengths or periods of maturity — short, medium and long-terms, the 'liquidity' aspect of the financial assets is significant. In this regard, it is relevant to note whether the financial assets are tradable or not.

The financial assets like deposits with the banks, companies — corporates, and Post offices, Insurance Policies, the NSCs (National Savings Certificates), Provident Funds and Pension funds are not tradable. The financial assets or securities, *i.e.,* equity shares of companies — debentures, government securities and bonds are viewed as *'liquid',* being tradable and hence transferable. The units/shares of mutual funds including UTI could also be tradable.

Primary Securities and Secondary Securities

Primary securities are the financial claims issued to actual savers for mobilising their savings. These securities are created by real sector units, *i.e.,* companies-corporates engaged in the production of goods and services as borrowers of funds in the form of equity shares, preference shares and debentures.

These primary securities are also created by the Government for mobilising savings of the people by issuing bonds. The banks, financial institutions and mutual funds which act as financial intermediaries also subscribe to these primary securities. As dealers in securities, the banks, financial institutions and other intermediaries buy primary securities.

	Issued by	*Subscribed by*	*Remark*
Primary Securities	Real sector units like companies corporates: requiring finance and the government	1. Actual savers with surplus 2. Banks and financial institutions	*Direct finance* as funds flow directly from actual savers to borrowing real sector units *Indirect finance* as the funds flow from the savers to the borrowing real sector units through intermediaries
Secondary Securities	Banks, financial institutions and other intermediaries	Actual savers with surplus	These are claims created by the financial intermediaries against themselves.

Secondary Securities

The banks, the financial institutions including investment institutions like Insurance companies and Mutual funds collect savings of the people in the form of bank deposits, units and insurance policies by issuing financial claims against themselves, called 'Secondary Securities'. As dealers in securities, the financial institutions and mutual funds acting as intermediaries sell secondary securities and buy primary securities.

The financial intermediaries create secondary securities against themselves which enable them to generate resources out of which they direct funds for subscribing to primary securities. Their significance in financial transactions/markets lies in this transformation by way of selling secondary securities on one side and buying primary securities on the other, thereby facilitating mobilisation and allocation of funds from savers to the investors.

It is proposed to furnish further details individually in respect of these three constituents of the financial system under separate chapters.

1.4 STRUCTURE AND INTERRELATIONSHIPS IN A FINANCIAL SYSTEM

A structure is formed of the elements or parts and sub-parts of the system which have an arrangement of interrelationships between them so as to co-ordinate their activities and role towards the attainment of the goals of the system. The structure has to integrate the part processes into the total or overall working of the system.

The financial system in the context of a broader economic system of a country has the goal of helping rapid economic development through effective mobilisation and allocation of financial resources for productive uses. As discussed earlier under 1.2 on 'Constituents', the financial system operates through financial institutions which perform in financial markets by dealing in financial instruments/assets.

It is interesting to note that the financial system helps economic development in a country and alongwith the development the system undergoes growth, giving rise to a complexity of structure in the wide diversity of constituents — parts and sub-parts and the gamut of their interrelationships. The structure of the financial system is simple and narrow in scope in the economies at low levels of development as it offers limited choice to both suppliers and users of funds. The suppliers of funds or *'savers'* show preference to convert their savings into real physical assets and partly lend funds for creating financial assets like bank deposits. Those who require funds either on short-term or long-term basis have to depend on own funds or on borrowings from informal sources. In a modern economy, the structure of the financial system gets complex in terms of a broad network of institutions offering a wide array of financial instruments, *i.e.,* assets or securities for the choice of those who borrow and lend funds. In a developing economy like India, the financial system has a structure having a mixed set-up of 'tradition and modernity' in its financial institutions, markets and assets. In other words, the structure of the financial system has the 'organised' and the 'unorganised' components, representing a scenario of what it had in the past and what has emerged in the later period. The unorganised component has individuals like moneylenders and shroffs and institutions like indigenous bankers, finance companies, Nidhis and chit funds operating, on an informal and personalised basis and handling instruments like Hundis.

The 'organised' component of the structure consists of diverse institutions offering a wide choice or options to 'savers' to lend their funds in regard to several considerations of future income, risk and liquidity etc. and also to the users of funds in the form of sources of funds, avenues of credit, borrowing and/or equity financing. The diversification of the structure takes place in terms of options made available in financial instruments for the mobilisation and allocation of funds.

The institutional set-up offers choice to savers, *viz.,* bank deposits, P.O. deposits, corporate sector deposits, insurance policies, units of UTI, equity shares or debentures etc. and to those who need funds an access to alternatives consisting of different credit facilities, debt capital, equity finance etc.

The extent of facilities provided and services rendered by the banks, non-banking financial institutions, stock markets etc. have not only helped savers but induced them, and has not only helped capital formation but also led to effective allocation. The duality of structure in having organised and unorganised components has, however, been viewed as its limitation for the lack of co-ordination.

Interrelationships

The structure of the financial system is relevant for the interrelationships within the system and the interrelationship the system has in the context of the broader economic system.

It is necessary to mention here certain interrelationships as illustrations:

The commercial banks which are the *'core'* institutions in money market also operate in capital market. The banks accept deposit of funds from the people, create and supply credit and grant short and medium term loans. As the financial intermediaries, the banks play a significant role in transforming the short-term funds into long-term funds and *vice versa.* As such, there exist close interrelationships between the interest rates in respect of provision of funds for different time-lengths.

There are close linkages between the new issues market and the secondary market at stock exchange where the primary securities already issued are traded. The companies-corporates proposing to raise fresh capital as equity are quite likely to be influenced by the trend — volume and pricing of new issues in the secondary market. Likewise, the people — the investing public are likely to get induced to subscribe to new issues by the favourable conditions prevailing in the stock market.

The interdependence of financial markets and the financial assets dealt with arises on account of the options exercised by the suppliers and users of funds. The savers or suppliers of funds have a wide choice as between bank account, insurance policy, P.O. savings, company deposit, purchase of primary securities — equity shares. The users of funds like corporates can opt for accepting deposits, borrowing from the Development Financial Institutions and/or raising funds through capital issues — equity shares and debentures. Apart from the interrelationships within the financial system illustrated above, the financial system is influenced by the broader aspects of the economic system.

The financial system has to induce 'savers' — saving public to convert more of their surplus into financial assets. In this regard, it is quite relevant to note that the people exercise options of holding cash, holding unproductive assets like gold and ornaments, converting into physical assets like housing and buying financial assets. These considerations for their relative *'holdings'* and the changes in their respective shares influence the flow of funds either directly by way of subscription to capital issues or to financial intermediaries for being made available to the final users of funds.

As a main constituent of the money market, the commercial banks play a crucial role of *'creating credit'* in relation to the extent of deposits mobilised. The credit created by the banks is a significant factor monitored by the monetary authority like Reserve Bank of India (RBI) while regulating the money supply in an inflationary situation.

The interest rates for the financial assets of different time-lengths have to correspond with each other. Likewise, the interest rates have to be low or high to match with the general prices, *i.e.*, level of inflation.

During the last decade or so, particularly after the introduction of economic reforms towards liberalisation and globalisation, the capital markets in India have developed closer links with the capital markets abroad. This aspect is dealt with later in other chapters.

1.5 ROLE OF THE FINANCIAL SYSTEM

The essence of the role played by the financial system could be described as mobilise savings and thereby generate and *allocate* financial resources into investment channels for productive use. For undertaking and stimulating their activities, the real productive units need, along with other inputs, an easy access to the enhanced flow of funds, *i.e.*, capital for investment.

The decision to save is a decentralised decision as it lies with the people having a surplus out of their incomes. The financial system has to co-ordinate these decisions of savers and offer them opportunities or alternative options for converting their savings into financial assets. On the other hand, the financial system has to provide for the mechanism or arrangement for the transfer of these resources into investment channels.

The decision to invest for *'production'* is also a decentralised decision as it is taken by all those who are engaged in the production and distribution of goods and services. The financial system has to facilitate the provision and allocation of funds among those productive units who need resources for investment.

The financial system acts as the conduit for the transfer of financial resources or for the transformation of savings into investment. The effectiveness of the financial system lies in inducing savers to save more as attracted by the wide range or the diversified portfolio of financial assets and in transforming these resources into higher quantum of capital accumulation needed for rapid economic development.

The decisions to save and to invest funds are guided by several considerations including the returns, liquidity, safety — the risks and uncertainty etc. It is for the financial system to provide mechanism or arrangement which will ensure enhanced flow of funds by matching these considerations or expectations of those who borrow and lend funds.

To play the above-mentioned crucial role, the financial system has to perform different, and yet interrelated functions. In any modern economy, the functions of the financial system are key to more effective and productive use of the real physical resources as *the finance is viewed as the 'prime mover' for the production, development and well-being.*

1.6 FUNCTIONS OF THE FINANCIAL SYSTEM

The financial system:

(1) helps distribution or exchange of goods and services by providing *credit related payment system.*

(2) helps in the *mobilisation of funds and their transformation into accumulation of capital* required for production.

(3) provides arrangements for the transfer of financial resources across time and space.

(4) provides ways and means for managing uncertainty and controlling risk.

(5) helps in co-ordinating decentralised decision-making, by generating and disseminating information.

As you are aware, the technological developments in a modern era have given rise to revolutionary changes in respect of communications and payments system among those who perform in the financial system across the world.

(a) Facility for distribution or exchange of goods and services

Facilitates Exchange: When the exchange transactions take place, the settlements can be in terms of payments in cash or by way of promises to pay in future and backed up by credit instruments like Hundi, Bills of exchange etc. Those who are engaged in exchange transactions, *i.e.,* buying and selling of goods and services, seek access to bank credit which helps them in overcoming the constraints of cash settlements and allows them to perform more freely by widening their activities. The commercial banks play a significant role in helping exchange transactions by granting credit facilities in terms of allowing their borrowers to draw amounts for the settlement of payments.

The commercial banks, as the prime constituents of the money market, supply and also create credit. The banks serve the borrowers engaged in exchange transactions by extending facilities in different forms of credit against commercial bills and drawing facilities of amounts under credit limits to make payments.

(b) Mobilisation of funds for being transferred into capital accumulation and allocation

Promoting Savings and Investment: For capital formation, the funds or the financial resources have to flow from the savers to the investors engaged in production. It is the function of the financial system to ensure that the savers are induced to direct the surplus available with them for being transformed into financial securities and assets to meet the short-term and long-term capital needs of real sector production units. There is a need for pooling of financial resources to meet the requirements of production units diverse in time-lengths and scattered over places. The banks and financial institutions including financial intermediaries acting as link mobilise savings, pool the financial resources and effect the transfer and allocation of resources into investment channels for production.

(c) Mechanism or arrangements for transfer of resources

Transfer of Resources: The people sell their productive factors and services and earn incomes which they spend partly on buying current output to meet their present needs and set aside the other part, *i.e.,* surplus as savings. The savings are the prime source of finance required by the real sector production units for covering the deficit with regard to the provision of funds they have and what they spend on the conduct of their activities.

The financial system has to perform a role of transferring funds from those who have a surplus and hence can lend to those who expose themselves to deficit and hence borrow funds. The financial system consists of a structure arranging for both the *'direct'* and *'indirect'* transfer of resources, *i.e.,* directly when the savers having surplus, buy securities released as capital issues — equity shares and debentures by the production units; and 'indirectly' through, banks, financial institutions acting as intermediaries which deal in financial assets, *i.e.,* mobilise resources from the savers by selling secondary securities against themselves and provide resources for investment either as loan finance and/or by subscribing to primary securities issued by the production units.

The financial system through institutional set-up helps not only in the transfer of financial resources, but promotes savings by offering the savers wide options of financial assets, and encourages investment by production units in terms of an access to the alternative channels of finance.

(d) Ways and means of managing uncertainty and controlling risk

Risk and Uncertainty: The terms *'risk'* and *'uncertainty'* pertain to future which remains unknown for everyone, *i.e.,* for savers expecting future incomes and investors expecting returns in future. The savers with surplus show a general preference for converting their part incomes in financial assets influenced by considerations like convenience, less risk, liquidity etc. It is more convenient for the people to go to a bank or a Post office and open a bank account or buy a saving certificate. Their preference is also for short-term lending as they would like to have easy conversion in money and are reluctant to take more risk. The borrowers of funds, *i.e.,* production units need funds for different time-lengths, *i.e.,* short- and long-term funds and hence look for a combination of financial assets which will help them in reducing costs and minimising the risks.

The financial system, in its constituents like banks and financial institutions including financial intermediaries dealing in the wide range of financial assets, attempts to reconcile these considerations and preferences of borrowers and the lenders of funds.

(e) Generating and disseminating information for co-ordination

Flow of Information: The financial markets and their operations were localised and narrow when, in the past, the financial transactions were conducted between individuals and agencies on the informal and personalised basis. The financial markets have enlarged their scope with the emergence of a variety of institutions dealing in diverse — an array of assets giving rise to closer links between the borrowers and lenders of funds whereby the financial transactions in the markets are in a better position to meet the expectations and preferences of both.

The decisions to save and invest are the decentralised decisions and hence have to be co-ordinated by the creation and dissemination of information pertaining to opportunities and options available for lending and borrowing of funds so that the savers can exercise their choices of financial assets and the production units can suitably channelise their investments.

In the present-day world, the developments in the field of information technology have extended the dimensions of financial markets to the global level. It has been possible for those who operate in the domestic financial markets to have closer links with the international markets and *vice versa* through the electronic communication system and achieve cross-border mobility of funds.

1.7 FINANCIAL SYSTEM AND ECONOMIC DEVELOPMENT

An economic system of a country has to undergo varied and comprehensive changes so as to achieve rapid economic development and result in the sustained increase in incomes (per capita or per head) of people, enabling them to lead better life. Changes in the course of economic development take place in all aspects like social, technological and even attitudinal — apart from the economic aspects with a view to bring about stimulated performance for the effective and productive utilisation of physical resources in men and natural endowments in soil, above the soil and beneath the soil.

The financial system, as a part of the economic system, has to gear up to meet the prime need of economic development of a continuous and increased flow of funds by way of capital for investment. The financial system, which plays a role of mobilising savings, generating pool of financial resources and their transfer for investment purposes, could be viewed as a key factor in strengthening the pace of economic development. The financial system in a modern economy contributes significantly through its structure of a variety of financial institutions including banks operating in active financial markets and dealing in an array of financial assets, by attracting increase in volume and rate of savings and by bringing about enhanced flow of funds for capital accumulation and allocation to be more effectively used by the productive sectors of the economy.

It is obvious that financial resources by themselves cannot bring about economic development and yet, it has to be acknowledged that they are a crucial factor as the financial system with arrangements for the production units to have sustained and increased command over capital is likely to promote their activities and produce greater output of goods of services.

One significant aspect of the financial system is that it has a mechanism to facilitate both production and exchange of goods and services by not only transferring resources for lending funds and supplying credit but also by creating credit. The commercial banks help exchange of goods and services and extend markets for them by granting credit facilities, *i.e.,* facilities to draw for settlements of payments against future claims. The financial institutions like banks when they create credit, they do so in anticipation of savings mobilised in deposits. As such, the financial system is able to accelerate economic development by pooling and the transfer of financial resources through increased mobilisation of savings and also by creating credit in anticipation of savings. In developing countries, these efforts of providing to production units increased command over capital even in anticipation of savings are done with an expectation that economic development would lead to increased incomes giving rise to higher savings in future.

An active and broad-based financial system is essential for economic development and economic development, in turn, nourishes further progress in activities and performance of the financial system. The growing requirements of finance, *i.e.,* funds for investment in the course of economic development, act as a stimulus to the financial system. The financial markets widen as different new institutions come up and the financial transactions increase both in number and volume, as a wide range of financial assets are introduced and are dealt with. A wide variety of services are rendered by the financial institutions to the lenders of funds with surplus and to the borrowers for raising capital for productive use. The effectiveness of the financial system in serving the priorities and needs of economic development is reflected in the extent to which it copes up with the challenges of enhanced capital formation and suitable capital allocation.

Interconnection between Finance and Development

Two contrary views are expressed in regard to the relationship between financial development and economic growth. One view regards an efficient financial system effectively mobilising and allocating resources as a necessary pre-condition for economic growth. The other view is that economic growth created demand for financial services and hence financial development follows growth.

The relationship between finance and development could be viewed as a *'virtuous circle'* of interdependence between the two. The relationship between financial development and economic growth is a two-way relationship with positive feedback between them. Availability of finance encourages growth and growth, in turn, facilitated financial development. The process of growth fosters participation in financial markets, thereby facilitating financial development. The financial development, in turn, enables selection of efficient investment projects, stimulating investment and thereby growth.

Finance influences growth through the links provided through processes of saving and investment. Saving rate is one basic channel of influence of financial development on growth. The saving rate when enhanced through financial intermediation, *i.e.,* in terms of the role played by financial intermediaries like banks and others could promote investment and result in higher growth depending on the extent to which savings get channelised into investment, particularly into projects with higher productivity by harnessing improved modern technology.

Financial development may be viewed as a crucial determinant of the growth. Still it has to be realised that finance would be only one of the ingredients of growth as the financial development has to be accompanied by other complementary inputs like formation of human capital with new skills and capabilities, the widening base of technological innovations and overall macro economic stability.

The importance of financial development in regard to promoting economic growth relates to the extent to which financial markets mitigate risks, reduce uncertainty and enable resources to flow towards projects which raise efficiency of investment and result in higher productivity.

For mobilising financial resources effectively and allocating them efficiently, the question comes up about the type of financial system which would be more conducive to economic growth. The key aspects of financial markets and infrastructure for enhancing and channelising savings and their conversion into productive investments are: (i) maximising the quality of information among those who save and those who direct these resources among alternative uses (ii) minimising the transaction costs.

The two mechanisms operating under the financial system are: (a) the financial intermediaries like the banks and other financial institutions and (b) the stock markets which facilitate mobilisation and allocation of resources. Whether the bank-based or the market-based financial system could be the choice for achieving economic growth? In USA and UK, the financial markets have played an important role in the development. As against this, there is a dominance of bank-based system in Germany and Japan.

Apart from the relative advantages and disadvantages of the two systems of finance, *i.e.,* bank-based and market-based, the type of financial system for mobilising and allocating resources has some bearing with the stage of economic development in the country. In the early stages of development, the banking system carrying out screening and monitoring of firms and their projects acts as an effective conduit for channelising financial resources by being a bridge between the borrowers' and lenders' interests. As markets develop, the stock markets gain in importance as they provide companies and firms an access to capital with long-term commitment and thereby facilitate economic growth. To the extent the stock markets become liquid, the investors who are otherwise reluctant to part with control over their funds for long periods turn to stock markets having overcome their fears associated with market uncertainties.

Provision of credit and allocation of resources is claimed to be better under bank-based system as the banks/FIs perform screening and monitoring of firms on behalf of the investors whose funds the institutions mobilise. The market-based system has an advantage of lower transaction costs but suffers from information deficiencies and risks of equity capital. These limitations are corrected when the stock markets follow higher disclosure standards and better protection to investors is offered.

It is desirable that both the systems — financial intermediaries based and market-based — coexist to impart greater efficiency to the financial system in regard to mobilisation and allocation of resources.

1.8 INTERCONNECTION BETWEEN FINANCE AND GROWTH IN INDIA

The financial development in the country has been to a large extent a state-induced activity and the government has played a significant role in fostering the process.

To cater to the emerging financial needs of rapid industrialisation under the Five year plans, the government played the role of an 'encourager' by creating a diversified base of financial institutions. The other aspect of the role of government is reflected in the frame of the regulations and administrative mechanism evolved for ensuring that the functioning of the financing agencies/ markets shapes in conformity with the broader goals and priorities of economic growth. Besides this, the government resorted to direct intervention in terms of nationalisation of banks in 1969 meant to shift the emphasis in allocation of credit in favour of those sectors to which the credit flow remained nearly denied on account of commercial consideration.

The fiscal factors which influenced the growth of financial system in the country include rising fiscal deficit, accumulation of debt and the saving-investment gap of the public sector. The combined Gross Fiscal Deficit (GFD)/GDP ratio of the Central and State Governments averaged 9.4 per cent during the second half of 1980s and stood at 10 per cent in 1990-91. The combined debt/GDP ratio of Central and State Governments touched a high of 61.7 per cent in 1990-91. The saving-investment gap for the Public Sector had risen to 8.7 per cent of GDP in 1990-91. To cover up budgetary deficit, short-term finance was raised by Government through the sale of *'ad hoc'* 91-days Treasury bills. The practice of automatic monetisation of Central Government Budget deficit through the sale of *'ad hoc'* Treasury bills has been discontinued since 1997. The government securities market which has to ensure availability of relatively long-term funds to government on an ongoing basis, remained less developed till 1990s. The gilt market has been transformed through corrective measures taken like broadening of participation, introduction of auction system and introduction of innovative debt instruments.

The saving-investment gap for the public sector — the 'deficit' public sector has taken recourse to heavy draft on the savings of the 'surplus' household sector by getting it channelised through the banks.

The other important feature is the major role of banks as the financial intermediaries in catering to the requirements of industry and trade. The Development Financial Institutions were set up to meet the medium and long-term needs of industry, trade and agriculture. The financial development in India has given rise to a financial intermediation based system where banks, DFIs and other intermediaries have played a dominant role. Though India has a long history of capital markets, the resources mobilisation through stock markets remained limited until 1990s.

Significance of Stock Markets *vis-a-vis* Banks and FIs

The relative significance of stock market *vis-a-vis* banks is expressed as a ratio of market capitalisation to scheduled commercial banks (SCBs) and Financial Institutions (FIs).

Table No. 1.1
Financial Intermediation and the Capital Market
(As per cent of GDP at current prices)

As at end of March	Financial assets of SCBs	Financial assets of FIs	Market capitalisation as % of SCB's	Market capitalisation assets
1981	31.0	11.6	3.8	12.2
1991	39.2	21.6	16.0	40.8
1996	41.2	23.5	47.5	115.3
2000	43.5	25.6	46.7	107.3

Source: Report on Currency and Finance, RBI 2000-01.

During 1970s and 1980s, the resources mobilised by the capital market amounted to about 0.6 per cent of GDP. Till the 1990s, the term lending by DFIs was the prime source of industrial finance. The overall activity in the stock market improved with the introduction of several measures under the reforms' process of 1990s.

Table No. 1.2
Sources of Resources Mobilisation

(per cent of GDP)

	Item	Period	
		1971 to 1992	1992 to 2000
A	Credit by banks	3.3	3.2
B	Credit by DFIs	0.6	1.1
	A + B	3.9	4.3
C	Resource Mobilisation from capital market	0.6	1.7

Source: Report on Currency and Finance, RBI 2000-01.

In the recent years, the financial system has witnessed transformation and provides for complementary coexistence for financial intermediation and equity market in the context of a wider and deeper financial structure in the country.

KEY TERMS

Financial System, Financial Institutions, Financial Markets, Financial Instruments

REVIEW QUESTIONS

1. What is a financial system? Explain the components of a financial system.
2. Discuss the structure and interrelationships in a financial system.
3. What functions are performed by a financial system?
4. Discuss the relationship between financial system and economic development.

REFERENCES

1. Allen, Franklin and Douglas Gale (2000), Comparing Financial System, MIT Press, Cambridge, Mars.
2. Bhole L.M. (1999), Financial Institutions and Markets, Structure, Growth and Innovation, Tata McGraw-Hill, New Delhi.
3. Gurley J.G. and Shaw E.S. (1955), 'Financial Aspects of Economic Development', American Economic Review, Vol. 45, pp. 515-38.
4. Jalan Bimal (2000), 'Finance and Development – Which Way Now', RBI Bulletin, June 2000, pp. 29-45.
5. Levine, Ross and Sara Zervos (1996), 'Stock Markets Banks and Economic Growth', The World Bank Policy Research, Working Paper No. 1582, March 1986.
6. Reserve Bank of India, Annual Reports.
7. Reserve Bank of India, Reports on Currency and Finance.
8. Singh Ajit (1997), 'Financial Liberalization, Stock Markets and Economic Development', The Economic Journal, Vol. 107 (May), pp. 771-82.

❑❑❑

2

Macro Economic Dimensions of Financial System

INTRODUCTION

Macro economic dimensions of the financial system draw our attention to the very fact that the financial system forms part of the broader economic system in any country. There are certain *'macro'* or the *'aggregative'* aspects of the economic system which influence the past and present status as well as the functioning of the financial system. The interlinkages between the parts, *i.e.,* between financial system and other 'macro' aspects of the economy are the subject-matter of this chapter.

As you are aware, the 'macro' as differentiated from the 'micro' aspects, are really a matter of approach of viewing the economic system. In other words, the 'macro' and the 'micro' view-points are not mutually exclusive. In any economy, the decisions to spend a part of money income on meeting day-to-day needs and to set aside the other part as a provision for future needs is taken by the individuals. Likewise, there are several other economic decisions made by the individuals *viz.,* decision to offer labour or render services for remuneration, decision to undertake investment by mobilising finance, any activity to produce output. It is possible to consider and view these decisions and the activities at the 'individual' level and also as decision taken and activities carried out at the 'total' or 'aggregative' level. The former viewpoint is 'Micro' and the latter is called 'Macro' approach. In the 'macro' approach, the above decisions and activities would be termed as 'consumption' expenditure and 'savings' as aggregates out of total money incomes of all the members of the economic system. Likewise, it is the 'micro' view to study the person earning wages for the work performed and the 'macro' view when the wage-incomes are examined as a part of the total factor incomes accruing in the economy as a whole. The 'investment' as a macro economic variable relates to the decisions and activities of all those, taken together, who prefer to direct and utilise financial resources for acquiring physical assets for the production of output of goods and services. When the macro economic aspects are being dealt with, the focus is on the aggregates of say, savers, the producers, the investors etc. The decisions and activities of the savers as an aggregate, of the investors and the producers at the total level give rise to savings, investment and the output in the economy as a whole.

The chapter is divided into following sections:

2.1 Sector of an Economy –

Sectors

(i) Household Sector

(ii) Private Corporate Sector

(iii) Public or Government Sector

(iv) External or Foreign Sector

2.2 Macro Economic Dimensions –

(i) Distinction between Saving and Investment

(ii) Credit and Financial System

(iii) Saving Rate and Forms of Saving

(iv) Household Saving

(v) Investment: Volume and Rate

2.3 Sectors of Economy and Financial System –

(i) Household Sector and Financial System

(ii) Private Corporate Sector and Financial System

(iii) Government or Public Sector and Financial System

(iv) External or Foreign Sector and Financial System

2.1 SECTORS OF AN ECONOMY

It is conventional and also convenient to adopt a 'sectoral' approach for examining the functioning of the economic system by aggregating the decisions and activities of the individual members as grouped under *'Sectors'*. Certain expressions like the household sector and corporate sector are being commonly used by all of us, without necessarily knowing that these terms relate to the standard classification adopted by the Central Statistical Organisation (CSO), Government of India, to facilitate the analysis of our economic system and its operations.

(i) Household Sector

The term *'household'* denotes a family formed of a number of individuals bonded together by certain considerations. The households or the families are not alike as they differ in several respects like size, sex and age composition, means of livelihood, lifestyle etc. and yet, they together form the 'household' sector as the households have similarities in that their members are engaged in activities of earning money incomes, spending the same on meeting current family needs and, if possible, partly saving for the future. It is necessary to clarify that the household sector as per the CSO classification includes:

(i) the individuals/families;

(ii) the small enterprises or units engaged in trade, industry and agriculture. These are privately run proprietary units of single persons or partnership organisations. As such, these are non-government entities; and

(iii) the non-profit making institutions, including Trusts. Being non-profit making, these institutions are run for charitable, religious and other purposes.

(ii) Private Corporate Sector

The units belonging to this sector are privately owned corporate entities engaged in the production and distribution of goods and services and other activities like financial services. These corporate bodies organise themselves as private limited companies, public limited companies and co-operatives. The private limited companies are often closely held in regard to ownership, control and other aspects of decision-making. The public limited companies are more broad-based and hence, give rise to a wider scope for the separation of ownership, control and management.

The units in this sector are non-government entities and could be financial organisations rendering financial services and/or non-financial units engaged in production, trading etc. As against the small enterprises in trade, industry and agriculture which are covered under the household sector, the units in the corporate sector are often, organised as large-scale units. To initiate, conduct and expand their activities, these units are unable to generate adequate funds-support from within and hence seek the supply of funds from others within the sector and/or from other sectors such as the household sector and from financial intermediaries like banks and financial institutions.

The 'co-operative' institutions engaged in a variety of activities including banking, trade, and manufacturing etc. are also included in this sector.

(iii) Public or Government Sector

In any modern economy, the Government is not in a position to limit its role to minimum traditional functions of administration, defence, maintenance of internal law and order etc. but take up, particularly in the context of developing countries, other functions which are critical for the pursuit of rapid economic development and welfare of the people. The Government undertakes the responsibility of formulating policies and plans and of pushing their implementation for accelerating the pace of economic development and also ensuring that the gains of development get more equitably shared and benefit the society.

The Government at the Centre and the State governments are the significant constituents of this sector. Certain activities are conducted by the Government as the departmental undertakings — Ordnance Factories, Mint etc. To cope up with the challenges of rapid economic development, the Government diversified its activities into production and services by setting up government companies and corporations etc., forming corporate bodies under the public sector. The widening of functions performed led to the trend of ever increasing public expenditure and the Government emerged as the *'deficit'* spender. The Government took recourse to the borrowing of funds as advances from the Reserve Bank of India (RBI) — being the apex monetary authority in the capacity of the Banker to the Government and by way of *'market'* borrowing against 'treasury bills' and 'gilt-edged' securities. [The details on these two are given in the chapter on financial instruments.] The public sector undertakings including companies and corporations being unable to create any significant 'savings' on their own, have to rely on borrowing from the market against 'bonds' issues.

'External' or 'Foreign' Sector

The external sector draws its significance from the interrelationships between the economy of a country and the rest of the world in regard to imports and exports, *i.e.,* inflow and outflow of goods and services and also the inflow and outflow of resources including human and capital resources. The developing countries are at a disadvantage or rather, not favourably placed in regard to their trade relations with others, particularly the advanced countries, as these developing countries have relatively slow-moving exports and show a high preference for imports of both the consumption items and capital goods. This aspect has a close bearing on the reserves and the flow of foreign exchange resources of these countries.

The capital-starved developing countries look forward to receiving inflow of capital from abroad in the form of aid, loans, equity funds etc. and from sources including individuals, corporate bodies and institutions inclusive of international agencies. In the wake of liberalisation policies adopted in the recent years, the external trade relations scenario is getting transformed with the removal of barriers and restrictions. The corporates or companies have increased access to the inflow of funds from abroad and also move out and mobilise funds externally against the issue of financial instruments like Global Depository Receipts (GDRs), Foreign Currency Bonds etc. (discussed separately later).

After getting acquainted with the 'macro' aspects of the economy and its classification into sectors like household, private corporate, government or public and the external sector, it is now proposed to consider these:

(1) ***Macro economic Dimensions:*** Describe the interrelationship between 'macro' aspects like saving, investment, etc., at the aggregative level and the financial system.

(2) ***Financial System and the Sectors:*** Describe the mutual links the financial system has with the different sectors — the household, corporate, government and the external.

2.2 MACRO ECONOMIC DIMENSIONS

In the earlier chapter, the nature, constituents and the functions of the financial system have been described.

To recapitulate,

- The financial system denotes mechanism or arrangements for the mobilisation of funds, their transfer and allocation.
- The funds are mobilised from the 'savers' having a surplus.
- The financial assets act as vehicles for mobilising and transfer of financial resources from the savers to the investors.
- The investors are the real sector production units which require funds for production and distribution of goods and services.

The funds required for investment in the real sector production units have a prime source in the 'savings' of the public which are mobilised, transferred and allocated by the financial markets wherein the financial institutions perform financial transactions of dealing with the creation and purchase and sale of financial assets.

(i) Distinction between Saving and Investment

The savers lend funds in exchange of financial assets exercising their option between equity, deposits etc. influenced by several considerations like convenience, safety, returns etc.

Those who need funds for investment in production units obtain these funds to meet their short-term and long-term requirements in different forms like bank credit, loans, equity finance etc. against financial assets like bills — commercial and treasury bills, equity shares, debentures and bonds.

In other words, the financial assets or instruments which are dealt with in the financial markets are the vehicles separating the act of saving from the act of investment. In the production units which are self-financed, the act of saving coincides with the act of investment as the investment is made of funds drawn mostly from own savings. Finance acts as a limit for the growth in the size of production units.

In any modern economy, the prominent performers in production are the large-scale enterprises which initiate investment out of own funds but seek the major financial support from others, *i.e.,* either directly from the savers in equity issues and/or indirectly from the banks and other financial institutions. The act of saving and the act of investment being separated, the function of establishing an effective link or a bridge between the two acquires 'critical' significance. The mechanism or the arrangement which functions as a link or bridge has to promote both the savings and investment by matching the interests and considerations of the savers, *i.e.,* the public and the investors — the production units — to their maximum possible satisfaction. The financial system offers an impressive outlet to the 'savers', *i.e.,* enable the people to convert their surplus out of money incomes into various financial assets. The financial system creates through mobilisation of savings, a pool of funds from which the investors or the production units can draw to meet their requirements.

In a less developed economic set-up, the act of saving would coincide with the act of investment, leaving limited scope for the financial transactions. The separation of the act of saving from the act of investment in the course of economic development gave rise to a 'felt-need' of linking the two, which is served by the financial system.

(ii) Credit and Financial System

Access to credit facilities helps in making payments and thereby widens and enhances the scope of exchange transactions involved in the distribution of goods and services. In a less developed economic set-up, the exchange transactions pertaining to goods and services as against money remain limited in scope, being settled mainly by making cash payments. As the economy progresses, these exchange transactions grow rapidly in number and volume alongwith the increased flow of output. The settlements in exchange transactions are often made in terms of promises of future payments, using monetary assets/instruments like Hundi, Bills of exchange etc. The Commercial Banks as the prominent constituents of the money market in a country, play a significant role of providing funds for settlement of payments involved in exchange transactions by extending credit facilities, *i.e.,* facilities to draw amounts and/or against the claims or IOUs, *i.e.,* promises of future payments. The commercial banks as financial institutions engaged in creating and supplying credit help the deficit *'spenders', i.e.,* the real sector units in production and distribution of goods and services to enhance their activities by crossing the limitations of financial constraints.

To put it in other words, the extent or the level of credit supplied by the banks is closely associated with what is required, *i.e.,* demand for credit in accordance with the level of and changes in economic activity in the country. It may also be pointed out the Reserve Bank monitors the flow of credit inputs in production and other activities and between the private sector needs and government priorities.

(iii) Saving Rate and Forms of Saving

Saving by an individual is the part of his income which he sets aside and does not spend on meeting current consumption needs. In this regard, the aspects of both the magnitude and the rate are relevant. The magnitude of saving is the volume of saving expressed in actual monetary terms, and the rate is its percentage share in money income received. In simple words, ₹ 200 saved out of ₹ 1000 as his personal income is the magnitude and 20 per cent is the saving rate.

Savings at the national level are expressed as arising in relation to aggregate variables such as national income, and its difference over aggregate consumption expenditure.

Savings at the national level arise as an aggregate of savings by the household sector, business or private corporate sector and the Government. As explained earlier, both the aspects of volume and the rate of savings at the national level are important. The volume of saving is expressed by Gross Domestic Savings (GDS) as a sum total of private sectors savings, *i.e.,* household savings plus corporate savings and public sector, *i.e.,* government savings. The saving rate denotes the relationship of percentage share of gross domestic saving in national income expressed as Gross Domestic Product (GDP).

Domestic: The word *'domestic'* refers to the resources generation within the country, *i.e.,* the financial resources for capital formation coming up by way of savings from the above three sectors within the country, as distinct from the inflow of capital from abroad originating in foreign savings.

Gross and Net: Gross domestic savings denote a sum total of savings by the three sectors — the household, the private corporate sector and the government or public sector. Apart from what they spend on current consumption, these three sectors from their residual incomes, have to make provision by way of "capital consumption allowance" for the fixed capital assets used, *i.e.,* for the repairs, maintenance and replacement etc. of fixed capital assets. When the capital consumption allowance or provision for the consumption of fixed capital assets is deducted from the gross domestic savings, we get net domestic savings.

The measures of savings like volume or magnitude of gross and net domestic savings and the saving rate expressed as gross domestic savings as percentage of GDP and their trends are the macro economic aspects, which are quite significant from the point of view of promotion of savings by the financial system in a country. (refer Table 2.1).

From the point of view of mobilisation of savings, the sourcewise or sectorwise distribution of savings is quite relevant. (see Table 2.2).

Table No. 2.1

Gross Domestic Savings as % of GDP

(At current prices)

(₹ in Crores)

	1980-81	*1984-85*	*1985-86*	*1990-91*	*1994-95*	*1995-96*	*1996-97*	*1997-98*
Gross Domestic Savings (GDS)	27136	46063	54167	131340	251463	296747	317261	352178
Gross Domestic Product (GDP)	143764	245515	277991	568674	1012770	1188102	1366209	1522547
% Share	18.9	18.8	19.5	23.1	24.8	25	23.2	23.1

	1998-99	*1999-00**	*2000-01*	*2001-02*	*2002-03*	*2003-04*	*2004-05*	*2005-06*	*2006-07*	*2007-08*	*2008-09*
Gross Domestic Savings (GDS)	374659	487301	496272	537966	648994	797512	997873	1228028	1475108	1779614	-
Gross Domestic Product (GDP)	1740985	1958814	2107661	2281305	2449736	2760224	2877701	3282385	3779364	4320892	4933183
% Share	21.5	24.9	23.6	23.6	26.5	28.9	31.7	34.2	35.7	37.7	-

Source: Economic Survey, Government of India, 2008-09.

* 1999-2000 onward — as per new series: base year 1999-2000

During the decade of 1980s, the % share of GDS in GDP was less than and around 20 per cent. The same moved up during 1990s and beyond.

Table No. 2.2

Sectorwise Distribution of Gross Domestic Savings

(1999-2000 series)

(₹ *in Crores*)

Sector	*1980-81*	*1985-86*	*1990-91*	*1991-92*	*1992-93*	*1993-94*	*1994-95*	*1995-96*	*1996-97*
Household sector	19868	39796	109897	110736	131073	158310	199358	216140	233252
(% share)	(73.2)	(73.5)	(83.7)	(76.9)	(80.4)	(81.8)	(79.3)	(72.3)	(73.5)
Public Sector	4929	8946	6279	12868	11865	5445	16845	24065	22197
(% share)	(18.2)	(16.5)	(4.8)	(8.9)	(7.3)	(2.8)	(6.7)	(8.1)	(7.0)
Private Corporate Sector	2339	5426	15164	20304	19968	29866	35260	58542	61092
(% share)	(8.6)	(10.0)	(11.5)	(14.2)	(12.3)	(15.4)	(14.0)	(19.6)	(19.2)
Gross Domestic Saving	27136	54167	131340	143908	162906	193621	251463	298747	317261

Sector	*1997-98*	*1998-99*	*1999-00*	*2000-01*	*2001-02*	*2002-03*	*2003-04*	*2004-05*	*2005-06*	*2006-07*	*2007-08*	*2008-09*
Household sector	268437	326802	416726	446317	502674	565408	648634	716874	864653	994898	1150135	--
(% share)	(76.2)	(87.2)	(85.5)	(89.9)	(93.4)	(87.1)	(81.3)	(71.8)	(70.4)	(67.4)	(64.6)	
Public Sector	20255	–17169	–16659	–37062	–46377	–16181	28026	68951	86823	137926	212543	--
(% share)	(5.8)	(–4.6)	(–3.4)	(–7.5)	(–8.6)	(–2.5)	(3.5)	(6.9)	(7.1)	(9.4)	(11.9)	
Private Corporate Sector	63486	65026	87234	87017	81689	99767	120852	212048	276550	342284	416936	--
(% share)	(18.0)	(17.4)	(17.9)	(17.5)	(15.2)	(15.4)	(15.2)	(21.3)	(22.5)	(23.2)	(23.4)	
Gross Domestic Saving	352178	374659	487301	496272	537966	648994	797512	997873	1228026	1475108	1779614	--

Note: Figures in brackets indicate % share in the total *Source:* Economic Survey, Government of India, 2005-06.

1999-2000 onwards — as per new series, base year 1999-2000. Between 1998-99 and 2002-03, Public Sector gave rise to 'dissaving'

The Household Sector's Share in GDS has fallen in the recent years and that of Public Sector has risen significantly.

As it is widely known, the predominant share in gross/net domestic savings originates in the household sector. The difference of incomes over current consumption yields a surplus which acts as a prime source of saving. In this regard, it is also necessary to distinguish between the gross and net savings of the household sector. The household sectors while spending incomes follow, particularly in advanced countries and in an urban setting in other developing countries, certain practices like hire purchase, instalment buying, use of credit cards etc. Besides this, the members of household sector also borrow funds from other sectors and constituents like banks, financial institutions, co operatives etc. These could be termed as household sector financial liabilities. The net household savings would arise from the gross savings after deducting the household sector's financial liabilities. The household sector emerges as a 'net surplus' sector to the extent the sector has limited financial liabilities. (refer Table 2.3).

The private corporate or business sector and the Government or public sector do not account for any significant shares in the gross domestic savings. Actually, these two sectors emerge as 'deficit spenders' and look upto inflow of finance from others — particularly from the household sector. The 'retained profits' of the private corporate sector could be considered as the prime source of their investments from within. The issue like 'retained profits' vs higher dividend pay-out influenced by several considerations is a main factor limiting the scope for business savings. The Government or the public sector has a relatively low share in domestic savings, as for the sector expenditure, *i.e.,* revenue and capital expenditure — as a whole exceeds the receipts of government and of public sector undertakings, though some undertaking may be yielding a surplus.

The above pattern of the distribution of gross domestic savings among the sectors directs us to focus our attention further on the analysis of the household sector savings — in terms of inducing factors, trends in volume and rate of savings over the years and form of savings as distributed between the financial assets and real physical assets. (refer Table 2.4).

(iv) Household Savings

The household sector enjoys an option of holding its savings in a wide variety of forms including currency, partly in gold and ornaments and in real physical assets like construction (including residential construction), plant — equipment and machinery and stocks or inventories and in different financial assets other than holding currency. The form of household savings or the composition of savings of the household sector is a significant influence on the extent to which household savings are available for being mobilised for capital formation or investment (refer Table 2.5).

The portion of household sector savings held in currency and also that part which gets converted into gold and ornaments serves no purpose of mobilising savings into channels of investment. The next point is the percentage shares or distribution of household sector savings into holding real physical assets and the financial assets. The portion of household sector savings directed to real physical assets results in addition to fixed assets including construction, machinery and equipment and inventories. It is important to note that the percentage distribution of household sector savings shifts, along with the economic development, in favour of financial assets and the *financialisation of savings* or savings in the form of financial assets other than currency is viewed as the prime change necessary for stimulating mobilisation of savings and thereby the pace of overall changes in investment and production in the economy. Besides this, there are certain advantages in holding financial assets as against holding physical assets.

Table No. 2.3
Savings of the Household Sctor: Gross and Net Savings
(At Current Prices)

(₹ in Crores)

Year	*Gross Savings (in Financial Assets)*	*Financial Liabilities*	*Net Savings (in Financial Assets)*
1980-81	12117 (8.4)	3508	8609 (6.0)
1985-86	25662 (9.2)	6983	18579 (6.7)
1990-91	58907 (10.0)	9267	49640 (8.4)
1991-92	68045 (10.4)	5997	62048 (9.5)
1992-93	80354 (10.7)	15056	65298 (8.7)
1993-94	109618 (12.8)	14859	94759 (11.0)
1994-95	145501 (14.4)	24770	120731 (11.9)
1995-96	124331 (10.5)	18620	105717 (8.9)
1996-97	158519 (11.6)	16857	141662 (10.4)
1997-98	171740 (11.3)	24919	146821 (9.6)
1998-99	207103 (11.9)	26773	180330 (11.4)
1999-00*	236214 (12.0)	35275	200939 (10.3)
2000-01	248394 (11.8)	31779	216615 (10.3)
2001-02	296581 (13.0)	51727	244854 (10.7)
2002-03	322583 (13.2)	60305	262278 (10.7)
2003-04	377387 (13.8)	69982	307405 (11.2)
2004-05	434318 (15.0)	120586	313732 (10.9)
2005-06	597867 (18.2)	183434	414443 (12.6)
2006-07	650412 (17.2)	176767	473645 (12.5)
2007-08	715994 (16.6)	173135	542859 (12.6)
2008-09	746864 (15.1)	165656	581208 (11.8)

Source: (i) Economc Survey, Government of India, 2005-06.
(ii) Handbook of Statistics on Indian Economy, RBI 2005-06.

Note: Figures in brackets indicate % to GDP

* 1999-2000 onwards — as per new series

Financial liabilities include bank advances, loans and advances from other institutions, loans and advances from Government, loans and advances from co operative and, non-credit societies.

Table No. 2.4

Household Sector Savings: Financial Assets and Physical Assets (At Current Prices)`1

(₹ in Crores)

Year	Household Sector Savings	Financial Assets (Net)	Physical Assets
1980-81	19868	8610 (43.3)	11258 (56.7)
1985-86	39795	18538 (46.6)	21257 (53.4)
1990-91	109897	49640 (45.2)	60257 (54.8)
1991-92	110736	62101 (56.0)	48635 (44.0)
1992-93	131073	65367 (49.9)	65706 (50.1)
1993-94	158310	94738 (59.8)	63572 (40.2)
1994-95	199358	120733 (60.6)	78625 (39.4)
1995-96	216140	105719 (48.9)	110421 (51.1)
1996-97	233252	141661 (60.7)	91591 (39.3)
1997-98	268437	146777 (54.7)	121660 (45.3)
1998-99	326802	180346 (55.2)	146456 (44.8)
1999-2000*	416726	206602 (49.6)	210124 (50.4)
2000-01	446317	215219 (48.2)	231098 (51.8)
2001-02	502674	247476 (49.2)	255198 (50.8)
2002-03	565408	253256 (45.7)	312152 (55.3)
2003-04	664064	307405 (46.3)	356659 (53.7)
2004-05	716874	313732 (43.8)	403142 (56.2)
2005-06	864653	414443 (48.0)	450210 (52.0)
2006-07	994898	473645 (47.6)	521253 (52.4)
2007-08	1150135	542859 (47.2)	607276 (52.8)

Source: Handbook of Statistics on Indian Economy, 2008-09.

Note: Figures in brackets indicate % to the Household Sector Savings.

* 1999-2000 onwards as per new series 1999-2000

During second half of 1990s, there was a higher preference for financial assets, but in the recent years, there has been a switch in favour of physical assets.

One simple advantage is that of convenience, *i.e.,* it is more convenient to hold financial assets as these can be easily stored and are more liquid. The other advantage is that the financial assets do not need supervision and management as is necessary in respect of holding physical assets. For any common man as a saver, it is likely to be more convenient to have his savings converted into financial assets like bank deposits than being in the possession of physical assets like machinery/equipment which would require more supervision and management.

Besides holding currency, the household sector converts savings in a wide variety of financial assets such as bank deposits, other (non-banking) deposits, *i.e.,* corporate deposits, P.O. deposits LIC policies, Units of UTI, provident fund, pension fund, claims on government in the form of small savings, shares and debentures etc. The ample choice or the wider portfolio of financial assets acts as an inducing factor in regard to the household sector savings as the savers are open to making combinations of holding financial assets by harmonising considerations of safety, liquidity, yield etc. The other aspect of the shifting composition of the household sector savings is the institutionalisation of savings in terms of the preference of the household sector in favour of financial intermediaries like banks, UTI, Insurance companies by opting for financial assets like bank deposits, units, LIC policies and others rather than diverting the savings directly to primary securities by subscribing to the corporate equity issues. These broader trends of growing significance of financial intermediaries and/or the emergence of *'equity culture'* by way of participation of the public in subscribing to equity issues and also in trading of shares, are also significant in the mobilisation of savings and in making savings increasingly available for investment in productive uses.

Table No. 2.5
Household Sector Savings: Composition
(At Current Prices)

(₹ *in Crores*)

	1980-81	*1985-86*	*1990-91*	*1991-92*	*1992-93*	*1993-94*	*1994-95*	*1995-96*	*1996-97*	*1997-98*
Gross Savings in Financial Assets	12118	25502	58908	68045	80354	109618	145501	124337	158519	171740
1. Currency	1625	2220	6251	8167	6562	13367	15916	16525	13643	12780
	(13.4)	(8.7)	(10.6)	(12.0)	(8.2)	(12.2)	(10.9)	(13.3)	(8.6)	(7.4)
2. Bank deposits	5550	10603	18777	17848	29518	36236	55835	39941	50902	74099
	(45.8)	(41.5)	(31.9)	(26.2)	(36.7)	(33.0)	(38.4)	(32.1)	(32.1)	(43.1)
3. Non-bank deposits	378	1423	1286	2218	6035	11654	11547	13198	25980	6733
	(3.1)	(5.6)	(2.2)	(3.3)	(7.5)	(10.6)	(7.9)	(10.6)	(16.4)	(3.9)
4. Life Insurance Fund	915	1779	5599	7003	7114	9548	11370	13894	16121	19410
	(7.6)	(7.0)	(9.5)	(10.3)	(8.8)	(8.7)	(7.9)	(11.2)	(10.2)	(11.3)
5. P.F. and Pension	2122	4188	11155	12501	14814	18323	21414	22343	30390	32267
	(17.5)	(16.4)	(18.9)	(18.4)	(18.4)	(16.7)	(14.7)	(18.0)	(19.2)	(18.8)
6. Claims on Government	712	3413	7883	4845	3885	8908	13186	9588	11783	22162
	(5.9)	(13.4)	(13.3)	(7.1)	(4.8)	(8.1)	(9.0)	(7.7)	(7.4)	(12.9)
7. Shares & Debentures	412	1394	4972	6800	8212	10067	13473	8839	6631	4464
	(3.4)	(5.5)	(8.4)	(10.1)	(10.2)	(9.2)	(9.3)	(7.1)	(4.2)	(2.6)
8. Units of UTI	31	586	3438	9087	5612	4705	3908	262	3776	595
	(0.3)	(2.3)	(5.8)	(13.3)	(7.0)	(4.3)	(2.7)	(0.2)	(2.4)	(0.3)
9. Trade deposits	373	–44	–453	–414	–1398	–1190	–1148	–252	–708	–770
	(3.1)		(–0.8)	(–0.6)	(–1.7)	(–1.9)	(–0.8)	(–0.2)	(–0.4)	(0.4)

Table No. 2.5 (Contd.)

	1998-1999	1999-00	2000-01	2001-02	2002-03	2003-04	2004-05	2005-06	2006-07	2007-08	2008-09
Gross Savings in Financial Assets	207103	236214	248394	296581	322583	377387	434318	597867	650412	715994	746864
1. Currency	21822	20845	15632	28156	28632	42675	36977	53071	66274	81278	93056
	(10.5)	(8.8)	(6.3)	(9.5)	(8.9)						
2. Bank deposits	79433	82802	94703	112936	123462	141967	158259	274864	311347	360993	409611
	(38.4)	(35.0)	(38.1)	(38.9)	(38.3)						
3. Non-bank deposits	7670	3844	6911	7912	8788	3803	3370	6130	1516	3751	13453
	(3.7)	(1.6)	(2.8)	(2.7)	(2.7)						
4. Life Insurance Fund	23428	28644	33861	41237	52009	52240	67986	63540	114851	128930	150337
	(11.3)	(12.1)	(13.6)	(14.2)	(16.1)						
5. P.F. and Pension	46408	53907	47882	46609	48441	48952	56552	62581	72106	70878	70891
	(22.4)	(22.8)	(19.3)	(15.7)	(15.0)						
6. Claims on Government	28220	28985	39007	51938	56087	87372	106420	87168	19198	–28315	–23479
	(13.6)	(12.3)	(15.7)	(17.5)	(17.4)						
7. Shares & Debentures	5105	16308	11148	9834	7122	9078	8113	31179	58907	89458	22086
	(2.5)	(6.9)	(4.5)	(3.3)	(2.2)						
8. UTI	1887	1811	–934	–1857	–1618	–8586	–3148	–444	–310	–324	–2737
	(0.9)	(0.8)	(–0.4)	(–0.6)	(–0.5)						
9. Trade deposits	–6870	–1023	183	–183	–341	–114	–213	–222	6523	9345	13446
	(–3.3)	(–0.4)	(0.07)	(–0.06)	(–0.1)						

Source: Handbook of Statistics on Indian Economy, 2008-09.

Note: Figures in brackets % indicate % to the total.

(v) Investment: Volume and Rate

It is generally seen that the common man understands by the term *'investment'* his purchases of financial assets like equity shares, debentures, bonds etc. Actually, these purchases are that part of his savings which are held in financial assets. Hence, it is necessary to stress and make it clear that 'investment' denotes what is devoted for the purchase of new real physical assets.

The domestic savings arise in the household, private corporate and government sector, by way of a surplus of what they earn as incomes over what they spend by way of expenditure. As the savers are not necessarily the investors, the domestic savings are mobilised and transformed into a pool of funds, which supports the process of capital accumulation or investment by the production units in the economy. Investment is defined as *"that part of current output of goods and services which is devoted to adding to the stock of capital and hence to raising the future income flow."*

Let us understand the above-mentioned income flow process. Incomes are earned by those who contribute to the production of current output of goods and services. The current output of goods and services consists partly of goods and services for consumption and partly of those which add to productive capacity. Out of the incomes, a part is spent on consumption of goods and services and the surplus of incomes over consumption forms *'domestic savings'*. As such, this part of income supports investments, *i.e.,* adding to the stock of capital or physical assets for producing more output and thereby generating incomes.

At the aggregate level, the domestic savings and domestic investment should match as the two sides of the same coin and give rise to an accounting identity.

Investment is made by the production units as capital formation for producing more output of goods and services. The capital formation or investment is by way of adding to stock of real physical assets by the household, private corporate or business and the government or public sector. The additions to the stock of physical assets or capital formation could be in:

(a) Fixed Assets

(i) construction, *i.e.,* plants, factories etc. (including even residential construction of the household sector) and

(ii) machinery, equipment.

(b) Inventories

Stocks of finished and semi-finished goods and raw materials.

The producing units in the private corporate sector and the the government or public sector, being unable to mobilise funds for investment from within emerge as the *'deficit spenders'* and obtain capital in different forms like equity, loans, working capital etc. from the public directly and from the banks and the financial institutions against a wide range of financial liabilities like bills, shares and debentures, bonds etc.

Some concepts related to Investment are as follows:

(a) Domestic Investment

The investment or capital formation in a country may be partly out of funds drawn from savings abroad and the domestic savings may partly flow to support investments abroad. An overall position in this regard is called *Net Investment Abroad*. Domestic investment is when net investment abroad is deducted from gross investment.

(b) Gross and Net Investment

Gross Investment or Gross Domestic Capital (GDC) formation consists of: (i) the production and addition to the stock of fixed assets — construction, plant, machinery and equipment and (ii) addition to inventories. To get net domestic investment, the *'depreciation'* is deducted from gross domestic investment, to account for the part of fixed assets produced for replacement of the existing stock.

The important measures indicating the trend in investment is the 'investment rate' or the Gross Domestic Capital formation expressed as a percentage of measure of national income, *i.e.,* Gross Domestic Product (GDP). The saving rate expressed as a percentage of gross domestic savings to GDP and the investment rate as a percentage of gross domestic capital formation to GDP when viewed side by side would show the relevance and adequacy of both for increasing the pace of economic development.

The macro economic aspects relevant in this regard are that the domestic savings and domestic investment do not match, giving rise to, particularly in the developing countries, a saving-investment gap accounted for by the net capital inflow from abroad. The other important macro economic aspect is the composition of investment. As pointed out earlier, the gross domestic investment consists of: (i) production of and additions to fixed assets and (ii) changes in stocks or inventories. A certain level of inventories is necessary in the given state of technology in production. Still, it is more important for the development process that investment takes place more in the additions to fixed assets rather than having undue level of inventories.

2.3 SECTORS OF ECONOMY AND THE FINANCIAL SYSTEM

The sectoral approach in macro economics is meant to have a more detailed analysis of the behaviour of the economy as a whole by forming sub-categories as household, business, government and the external or foreign sector.

A brief description of these sectors has been already given earlier in the chapter. It is now intended to explain the mutual links of the financial system with the four sectors.

(i) Household Sector and Financial System

As explained earlier, the household sector is diverse in composition as it includes alongwith the individuals and their families, the small enterprises in trade, industry and agriculture and non-profit making institutions including trusts. The act of saving lies with the large number of members of the household sector. Their savings large and small, arise as a surplus of their incomes over what they spend on current consumption. The household sector saving accounts for a major share in the aggregate savings in the country. For mobilising savings, a prime function of the financial system, the significant factors are changes in the volume of household sector savings and its rate as a percentage of the GDP. Apart from the volume and the rate of household sector savings, the *form* in which the savings are held is important.

There are two main components of household sector savings. A portion of household savings is devoted to holding physical assets including construction, machinery and equipment and stocks and the other part is converted to acquire financial assets including holding currency and other financial assets like bank deposits, non-bank deposits, LIC policies, units of UTI, claims on government, *i.e.,* small savings, shares, debentures etc. (see Table 2.5).

Table No. 2.6 (A)

Gross Domestic Saving and Gross Domestic Investment

(at current prices)

(as % of GDP)

	1993-94	1994-95	1995-96	1996-97	1997-98	1998-99	1999-00	2000-01	2001-02	2002-03	2003-04	2004-05	2005-06	2006-07	2007-08
Gross Domestic Saving	22.5	24.8	25.1	23.2	23.1	21.5	24.9	23.5	23.6	26.5	28.9	31.7	34.2	35.7	37.7
Public Sector	0.6	1.7	2.0	1.7	1.3	-1.0	-0.9	-1.8	-2.0	-0.7	1.0	2.2	2.4	3.3	4.5
Private Sector	21.9	23.2	23.1	21.5	21.8	22.5	25.8	25.3	25.6	27.2	27.9	29.5	31.8	32.4	33.2
of which															
Household sector	18.4	19.7	18.2	17.0	17.6	18.8	21.3	21.2	22.0	23.1	23.5	22.8	24.1	24.1	24.4
Private Corporate Sector	3.5	3.5	4.9	4.5	4.2	3.7	4.5	4.1	3.6	4.1	4.4	6.7	7.7	8.3	8.8
Gross Domestic Investment@															
(i) Adjusted Total	23.1	26.0	26.9	24.5	24.6	22.6	26.0	24.2	23.0	25.3	27.2	32.1	35.5	36.9	39.1
(ii) Total of Public plus private	21.3	23.4	26.5	21.8	22.6	21.4	26.1	24.3	24.3	25.3	26.3				
Pubic sector	8.2	8.7	7.7	7.0	6.6	6.6	7.5	6.9	6.9	6.2	6.5	6.9	7.8	8.0	9.1
Private Sector	13.0	14.7	18.9	14.7	16.0	14.8	17.9	16.7	16.8	18.5	18.9	23.4	26.1	27.2	28.5
Saving-Investment Gap	– 0.6	– 1.2	– 1.8	– 1.4	– 1.5	– 1.1	– 1.1	– 0.6	0.6	1.2	1.6				
Public Sector	– 7.6	– 7.0	– 5.7	– 5.3	– 5.3	– 7.6	– 8.3	– 8.7	– 8.9	– 6.8	– 5.5	– 4.7	– 5.2	– 4.6	– 4.6
Private Sector	8.9	8.5	4.2	6.8	5.8	7.7	7.8	8.6	8.8	8.6	9.0	6.1	5.7	5.2	4.7

@ Adjustment arises due to Errors and Omissions.

Source: Economic Survey, Government of India, 2005-06.

The saving-investment gap was negative as the investment rate exceeded the saving rate.

Table No. 2.6 (B)

Sectorwise Rates of Capital Formation Gross Domestic Investment

(as % to GDP at current prices)

Sector	*1999-2000*	*2000-01*	*2001-02*	*2002-03*	*2003-04*	*2004-05*	*2005-06*	*2006-07*	*2007-08*
(i) Household Sector	10.7	11.0	11.2	12.7	12.0	13.9	13.5	13.5	13.8
(ii) Public Sector	7.5	6.9	6.9	6.2	6.5	7.5	8.3	8.7	9.9
(iii) Private Corporate Sector	7.2	5.7	5.6	5.8	6.9	11.8	15.0	16.2	17.4
* Gross Domestic Investment	26.0	24.2	23.0	25.3	27.2	34.6	38.0	39.8	42.3
	(25.4)	(23.6)	(23.7)	(24.7)	(25.4)	(33.2)	(36.8)	(38.4)	(41.1)

* Adjusted for Errors and Omissions

Note: Figures in brackets indicate sum total of (i), (ii) & (iii).

In regard to household sector savings, the measures like gross and net indicated that from the gross domestic savings, the liabilities like bank loans, hire purchase, instalment buying, credit cards have to be deducted. The difference of incomes over current consumption in the household sector devoted to financial assets activates the financial system, and in turn, the financial set up which offers a wide spectrum or portfolio of financial assets induces the savers in the household sector to mobilise more funds for being transferred to channels of productive use.

In regard to the mobilisation of savings to meet investment requirements, the developing countries give rise to saving-investment gap, showing their dependence on the inflow of capital from abroad. Among the sectors, the household sector generates a surplus, *i.e.,* net saving, as against the deficits arising in the private corporate sector and the Government or public sector. The strong and increasing net saving of the household sector held in the variety of financial assets facilitates the transfer of funds by the financial system to the deficit sectors and thereby help in reducing the saving-investment gap at the aggregate level.

In brief, the household sector saving and the financial system are interlinked in regard to their progress and growth.

(ii) Private Corporate Sector and Financial System

The private corporate sector consists of non-government corporate entities organised as private limited companies and public limited companies and co-operatives. These units are relatively large-scale enterprises engaged in different economic activities including production, trading and financial services. These units emerge as 'deficit' spenders as they are unable to raise adequate finance from internal sources and hence look up to outside sources for funding their activities and projects. The financial requirements of the private corporate sector differ in time-lengths, *i.e.,* short-term and long-term requirements and they also need working capital.

These units are exposed to saving-investment gap as the funds mobilised by them from within fall short of their requirements of investment. The internal sources for private corporate sector units consist of promoters' capital in new units and the 'reserves and surplus' out of plough back of profits. The private corporate sector units need access to outside finance and reach the financial system, *i.e.,* the constituents of the system like the commercial banks, the financial institutions including development financial institutions and new issues market etc. The private corporate sector units have to adopt a measure of striking combination of different modes of financing like equity issues public deposits, debt financing or borrowing and facilities for the provision of working capital. The short-term loans and the working capital facilities are provided by the commercial banks, the term loans are granted by the development financial institutions and for raising finance through equity issues and debentures, the private corporate sector units depend on the new issues market and on the other institutions, rendering specialised financial services of promotional nature like underwriting and credit rating etc.

(iii) Government or Public Sector and Financial System

In a modern economy, particularly in the developing countries, the government performs a wide range of functions and involves in various economic activities to serve the priorities of rapid development and also ensure meeting the welfare ends of society at large. The Government, the public sector undertakings including government companies and the corporations have to step beyond the frame or limits of balancing the budget, *i.e.,* of matching the receipts and expenditure — on the revenue and the capital account and emerge as 'deficit' spender. The internal sources of funds, for government surplus generation by way of public sector savings prove quite low and inadequate to meet the investment requirements. The public sector gives rise to the saving-investment gap which the sector attempts to cover by obtaining funds from the financial system consisting of domestic and external sources.

The large-scale and growing public sector investment may be viewed as useful in pursuing rapid economic development and yet it is necessary to examine as to how the public investment is financed. As a 'deficit' spender, the public sector takes recourse to internal and external borrowing. For the short-term internal borrowing, the government receives advances from the RBI as the banker to government and produces financial liabilities like treasury bills with maturity period upto one year. The long-term borrowing by the government and by the public sector undertaking is in the form of market borrowing against the gilt-edged securities and bonds. To a certain extent, the long-term funds from the external sources flow to the public sector as aid or assistance. The prominent aspect of the external inflow of funds to the public sector is the borrowing from international capital markets and the agencies like World Bank etc.

It may be mentioned that though public investment by the 'deficit' spender, *i.e.*, public sector through debt financing is considered necessary for rapid development, it is likely that the large burden of servicing and repayment of debt could record lower growth.

(iv) External or Foreign Sector and Financial System

The external sector has two aspects: (i) trade relations of a country with the rest of the world in terms of exports and imports of commodity items and services giving rise to an overall position of receipts and payments in foreign exchange, and (ii) inflow and outflow of capital as assistance, borrowings and non-debt creating investment. The role of the external or foreign sector in the developing countries is influenced by the regulatory mechanism monitoring both the aspects of trade relations and the inflow-outflow of capital. The present trend is towards open economies adopting liberalisation policies in terms of withdrawal of restrictions/barriers and deregulation which has offered more operational freedom for those engaged in external trade and foreign exchange market and those associated with capital flows overseas.

The external or foreign sector is viewed by the developing countries as the key factor in their development in terms of being a source of capital to cover up the gaps such as in the receipts (exports) and payments (imports) in the external trade and the saving-investment gap. The developing countries are capital-starved and depend on external sources of capital arising out of savings abroad — for inflow of funds in aid and assistance, borrowings and non-debt investment — direct as well as portfolio investment.

As mentioned earlier, the private corporate sector and the public sector are the sectors which are deficit sectors, as these sectors are unable to mobilise from within the funds required for investment. These sectors give rise to the saving-investment gap and look to the household sector and the external or foreign sector for getting access to capital both by the transfer of resources effected through the financial system and the net inflow of funds from abroad. The significance of foreign aid or assistance in regard to the capital formation for the public sector is limited when compared, particularly, with the rapidly increasing requirements of investment. The loans from the international agencies and the commercial borrowings including Non-resident Indian (NRI) deposits having a high burden of servicing and repayment has to be relied upon for financing to cover the deficits suffered by the public sector and the private corporate sector. The policies of liberalisation have facilitated the raising of funds abroad by the private corporate sector against the financial instruments like Global Depository Receipts (GDRs) including American Depository Receipts (ADRs), Convertible Bonds etc. The non-debt creating foreign investment inflows are being welcomed as Foreign Direct Investments (FDIs) and by allowing Foreign Institutional Investors (FIIs) to participate in the new issues and secondary capital market and create portfolio investment. The recent development is in terms of private corporate sector units listing themselves with the stock exchanges in the advanced countries for mobilising funds through equity/debentures issues.

The 'deficit' sectors are the public sector and the private corporate sector as they give rise to saving-investment gap, being unable to self-finance their investments. The household sector is a 'net surplus' sector and offers its savings held in financial assets as the prime source of capital formation and helps in the reduction of aggregate saving-investment gap. The other mode of reducing saving-investment gap in the developing countries is allowing the debt-creating as well as non-debt creating foreign capital inflows.

KEY TERMS

Household Sector, Private Corporate Sector, Government or Public Sector, External or Foreign Sector, Saving and Investment – Domestic, Gross, Net, Credit.

REVIEW QUESTIONS

1. Discuss the different macro economic sectors and their significance for the financial system of an economy.
2. Explain the importance of and the forms of household sector savings in Indian Financial System.
3. Explain the nature and role of investment in the financial system of a country.
4. Explain how the acts of savings and investment are co-ordinated in modern economy.

REFERENCES

1. Government of India, Economic Survey – 2008-09, 2009-10.
2. Handbook of Statistics on Indian Economy 2005-06, 2008-09.

❑ ❑ ❑

3

Flow of Funds and Financial Development

INTRODUCTION

In the preceding two chapters, we have discussed various aspects of financial system such as Concept, Constituents, Structure, Functions, Relation between financial system and economic development, Macro economic Dimensions and Sectors. It is now proposed to deal with flow of funds and financial development.

Financial Development

3.1 Flow of Funds

(i) What is Flow of Funds Analysis?

(ii) Flow of Funds: Significance for Financial System

(iii) Flow of Funds and Financial Intermediation

3.2 Financial Development

(i) Indicators of Financial Development

(ii) Financial Development Ratios

(iii) Financial Development: Qualitative Aspects.

3.1 FLOW OF FUNDS

(i) What is Flow of Funds Analysis?

It needs to be clarified that flow of funds analysis and the statement or matrix arising thereof could be prepared at: (i) the firm or company level as a useful tool for financial management and, (ii) the aggregate level or for the economy as a whole designed to depict the changes in the total financial activities. It is proposed to describe in this chapter the flow of funds analysis at the aggregate level or for the economy as a whole so as to focus further on its significance with regard to the working of the financial system.

It is desirable for the firm or a company to prepare a flow of funds statement to know its level of financial operations during a given period, apart from ascertaining its financial status at a point of time as revealed by the balance sheet of a company. However, to know the level of total operations, *i.e.,* financial transactions in the financial system, it is necessary that the flow of funds statement is prepared for the economy as a whole.

Funds denote stock of monetary resources and their transfer results in a flow. The transfer of resources could pertain to *real* transactions, for instance a person buys a pen in exchange of money, and in *financial* transactions when he creates a bank deposit. Lending of funds by a person to the bank has given rise to a financial asset. If the person had borrowed from say a bank, he gets funds by incurring a financial liability. The financial activities or flows arise when the financial operations or transactions take place in the form of borrowing and lending at different levels, say at the individual level between two persons, at the company level between say the firm and the bank and between sectors like household, private corporate and the government sector.

Certain terms like sources and uses of funds, financial flows and non-financial flows need to be clarified to understand the flow of funds analysis. As the flow of funds statement is prepared as a record of transactions between different sectors of the economy, the above terms are explained as mainly pertaining to the sectors.

Sources of Funds: Along with the saving, the borrowing is viewed as sources, which involves incurring of financial liabilities.

Any addition to equity or reduction in physical/financial assets could also be sources of funds.

Uses of Funds: Consists of investment and lending, *i.e.*, acquiring physical assets (investment) and financial assets in respect of lending. Uses of funds could be for reduction in equity holding and decrease in liabilities.

Uses	*Sources*
Change in Δ	Change in Δ
(i) Financial Assets, *i.e.,* lending	(i) Financial Liabilities, *i.e.,* borrowing
(ii) Physical Assets, *i.e.,* investment	(ii) Saving, *i.e.*, net worth

For more fuller understanding, certain terms like negative uses and negative sources are also clarified.

Negative Uses

- *Disinvestment in real assets: Increase in assets is:* Uses, the disinvestment in real assets which is in fact sources of funds is viewed as negative use.
- *Sale of Securities:* In fact, it is sources of funds. It is viewed as negative uses.

Negative Sources

- *Dissaving:* Saving is source, dissaving is negative source or in fact use of funds.
- *Debt repayment:* Increase in liability is Sources, repayment of debt, *i.e.,* decrease in liability which is, in fact, use of funds is viewed as negative sources.

Financial Flows and Non-financial Flows

Financial Flows — Borrowing and Lending: Financial transactions involving transfer of resources by way of *borrowing* creating financial liabilities and *lending* giving rise to financial claims.

Non-financial Flows: Saving and Investment

This pertains to transactions involving changes in saving (net worth) and investment, *i.e.,* changes in physical assets.

As a record of transactions, the flow of funds statement includes both financial flows and non-financial flows involving saving, investment, lending and borrowing. A flow of funds statement is a record of transaction among different sectors, on the basis of a *'sources and uses of funds'* statement prepared for each sector like household, private corporate and the government.

Balance Sheet of a Sector

The balance sheet of a sector in form of sources and uses of funds by way of net changes in assets, liabilities and net worth provides the basis for preparing an overall record of inter-sectoral transactions over a certain period.

Let us understand the process. The balance sheet, *i.e.,* stock statements of assets and liabilities position of different sectors at the beginning and at the end of the period are prepared. By examining these two statements, for different sectors at two different points of time, an overall statement showing inter-sectoral, *i.e.,* between the sectors, flow of funds is prepared for the economy as a whole for a certain period — say a year.

While preparing a balance sheet for a sector, the focus of attention is on sources and uses of funds, *i.e.,* on changes in assets, liabilities and net worth. As such, items like household consumption expenditure and government expenditure financed by tax revenues are ignored.

While preparing the flow of funds statement for the economy as a whole, the basis is the inter-sectoral, *i.e.,* between the sectors' transactions over a period, ignoring the intra-sectoral transactions, *i.e.,* transactions within a sector. The loans from one household to the other is intra-sectoral and hence gets excluded due to consolidation.

Balances Sheet Identity

The balance sheet identity, *i.e.,* between assets and liabilities must hold for a sector and also for the economy as a whole.

Uses		*Sources*
Investment + Lending	=	Saving + Borrowing

Net changes in physical assets + Financial assets = Net worth + Financial liabilities.

The word 'Net' changes on both sides of identity indicates that negative uses and sources described above have been taken into account. The sources and uses of funds are shown balancing in theory. In practice, they often do not balance.

To simplify, the above balance sheet identity could be explained with the help of an illustration.

Suppose the household income is ₹ 10 lakh. The household spends ₹ 8 lakh on consumption and saves ₹ 2 lakh and invests ₹ 1 lakh in physical assets. The borrowing of the household from the bank is ₹ 5 lakh.

For the balance sheet identity.

Investment + Lending = Net worth + Borrowing

1.00 + ? = 2.00 + 5.00

The above equality shows that the household has created financial assets by lending ₹ 6 lakh.

The household emerges net lender of ₹ 1 lakh as the lending is ₹ 6 lakh and the borrowing is ₹ 5 lakh.

Flow of Funds

It is a report not as a statement of financial position at a point of time, but rather a report on financial operations — a profile of financial activities carried on during a given period. Flow of funds accounts describe the changes in financial activity.

The flow of funds is a *matrix* that depicts the balanced sources and uses of funds for each sector, the interrelationships among the sectors and the saving, investment, borrowing and lending and the funds flow total. (refer Table 3.1)

The interrelationships between the different sectors have been analysed in the earlier chapter. Let us understand the interrelationships and the flow of funds between sectors as expressed in the terminology of the flow of funds analysis.

The excess of investment over saving is the *resources gap* for the sector. The financial uses are acquiring financial assets, *i.e.,* lending. The financial sources is creating financial liabilities, *i.e.,* borrowing. The financial balance is a position with regard to financial assets and financial liabilities. If investment by a sector exceeds its own saving, the position could be expressed as:

Resources Gap = Financial Balance
Investment – Saving = Borrowing – Lending

In other words, the sector becomes a net borrower and allows net transfer of resources or funds from other sectors to cover up the resources gap of the excess of investment over own savings. The private corporate sector and the Government sector are the deficit sectors as they give rise to resources gap in terms of investments exceeding financial resources internally available within the sector.

As against this, the household sector emerges as a net surplus sector as the sector's savings exceeds investments, *i.e.,* increase in physical assets, enabling the sector to be a net lender of funds to the other sectors.

The above equation for the household sector turns out as:

Saving – Investment = Lending – Borrowing.

The flow of funds accounts are prepared in India as yearly statement by dividing the economy into six sectors.

Household
Private corporate business
Government
Rest of the world
Banking
Other financial institutions

The complexity of the flow of funds matrix lies in the number of sectors and the variety of assets and liabilities included. In USA, the flow of funds statements are prepared by dividing the economy in nine sectors.

(ii) Flow of Funds: Significance for the Financial System

What is contained in the flow of fund accounts? These accounts depict sectoral and aggregate sources and uses of funds and show the financial interrelationships among different sectors of the economy.

Table No. 3.1
Financial Flows: Sectorwise: 1995-96

(₹ in Crores)

Sector / Financial Transactions with other sectors	*Banking*		*Other Financial Institutions*		*Private Corporate Sector*		*Government*		*Rest of the World*		*Household*		*Total*	
	Sources	*Uses*	*Sources*	*Uses*	*Sources*	*Uses*	*Sources*	*Uses*	*Sources*	*Uses*	*Sources*	*Uses*	*Sources*	*Uses*
Banking	—	—	11,909	7,091	54,694	4,450	30,823	4,290	– 10,001	– 2,066	22,642	56,615	1,10,067	70,380
Other Financial Institutions	11,274	– 1,337	—	—	45,673	– 457	8,384	2,344	– 9	5,128	2,207	42,197	67,529	47,875
Private Corporate Sector	2,156	22,082	– 754	62,736	—	—	1	2,319	—	11,978	342	5,976	1,745	1,05,091
Government	7,587	39,959	3,304	48,912	7,372	7,935	—	—	324	1,169	275	20,198	18,862	1,18,173
Rest of the World	4,850	– 5,953	11,990	4,226	4,549	389	12	97	—	—	—	—	21,401	– 1,221
Household	56,615	22,642	42,197	2,207	5,976	342	20,198	275	—	—	—	—	1,24,986	25,466
Sectors not elsewhere classified	6,709	45,145	21,279	13,025	28,395	28,607	31,010	5,849	1,725	– 5,851	—	—	89,718	86,775
Total	89,191	1,22,558	89,925	1,38,197	1,46,659	41,266	91,028	15,174	7,961	10,358	25,466	1,24,986	4,34,308	4,52,539
Sources — Uses	– 33,367		– 48,272		1,05,393		75,834		– 18,319		– 99,520		– 18,231	

Financial Deficit (–)

Financial Surplus (+)

Financial balance, *i.e.,* Sources of funds, *i.e.,* borrowing – Uses of funds, *i.e.,* lending is negative in case of household sector as it is borrowing less and lending more to other sectors like Banking, other Financial institutions including Insurance Companies and Mutual Funds (UTI) and Government.

Financial balance, *i.e.,* Sources of funds, *i.e.,* borrowing – Uses of Funds, *i.e.,* lending is positive in case of private corporate sector and Government sector as these sectors borrow more than what they lend.

Financial System: The real production sectors need financial resources for investment. These sectors are deficit sectors as their investment requirements exceed their savings available from within. The savings arise substantially as a surplus of incomes over consumption expenditure in the household sector. The financial system consists of arrangement to promote both savings and investment by mobilising savings, pooling and allocating resources in terms of transfer of funds from the surplus lenders to the deficit borrowers.

From the flow of funds accounts prepared as a matrix for the economy as a whole on the basis of the balance sheets or sources and uses of funds statements for the different sectors, it is possible to read and understand —

The financial behaviour of the sectors in creating asset structure and including financial liabilities, their resources gap and the interrelationships by way of inter-sectoral flow of funds and capital movements.

As the flow of funds statement is meant to depict the change in financial operations or activities over a period, it could reveal the nature and the extent of financial development as expressed in the increase in size and type of the total financial claims issued at the aggregate level.

The balance sheet or the sources and uses statement of a particular sector reveals the financial balance — say the financial deficit (liabilities – financial assets) in case of the private corporate sector and government sector and flow of funds statement at the aggregate level would show how these deficits are financed by the financial flows from other sectors, mainly by way of transfer of resources as direct financing and by financial intermediaries.

(iii) Flow of Funds and Financial Intermediation

For the transfer of resources, the flow of funds takes place from the surplus sector — the household sector to the deficit sector units in private corporate sector and the public sector either directly when these units issue primary securities like shares, debentures and bonds and these are subscribed by the public and indirectly when the financial intermediaries like banks and the non-banking institutions including mutual funds, insurance companies etc., play the role of facilitating the transfer of resources. As explained in earlier chapters, the financial intermediaries obtain funds from the public by issuing secondary securities drawn on themselves like Bank deposits, Units of UTI, insurance policies etc., and transfer these resources for the purchase of various primary securities, issued by the deficit sectors.

The public or the members of the household sector are more familiar with institutions like the banks, insurance companies, Unit Trust of India etc., and find it more convenient to make their savings available to them. The public carries a general impression that a greater degree of risk is associated with direct subscription to equity issues. On their own, the members of the household sector are not adequately informed and equipped to build up a diversified portfolio of assets.

The financial intermediaries serve a purpose of facilitating transfer of resources by: (i) mobilising savings — large and small — under different schemes and facilities from a large number of savers, (ii) rendering the services of professionally managing the funds and allocating the funds in a variety of suitable channels, and (iii) building up portfolio diversification, *i.e.,* transforming the pool of resources into a variety of channels of financial investment and thereby reducing the risk.

3.2 FINANCIAL DEVELOPMENT

(i) Indicators of Financial Development

(ii) Financial Development Ratios

(iii) Financial Development: Qualitative Aspects.

(i) Indicators of Financial Development

In any economy, the pace of economic development and the growth of the financial system strengthens each other. The acceleration in the pace of economic development relies heavily on the changes in the financial system of a country which will stimulate both savings and investment and generate the pool of funds for increased capital formation. The insufficiently developed financial infrastructure in the developing countries leaves them capital-starved due to the low level performance of their financial system, *i.e.,* in their financial institutions and financial markets. Any economy which gathers momentum gathers it through an initial step up in capital formation. For this initial and subsequently enhanced needs of financial resources for investment, the contribution has to flow from the active financial system having larger numbers of participants, say savers and investors, a wide array of financial institutions rendering different services, various financial market segments dealing in a variety of financial instruments. In the words of Schumpeter,* *"Thus, the main function of the money or capital market is trading in credit, for the purpose of financial development. Development creates and nourishes this market. In the course of development, it becomes the market for sources of income themselves."*

The financial system has three constituents — the financial institutions, the financial markets and financial instruments. As such, financial development has to be viewed as growth and improvement in the operational performance of the financial institutions and the financial markets, leading to the maturity and sophistication of the financial system as reflected in the growing volume and diversity of the financial assets offered.

This trend of increase in volume or stock of financial assets and their diversity is termed as "Financial deepening."

The financial development or the developed status of the financial infrastructure in a country is indicated by the effectiveness and efficiency of the financial system in the functions performed and the services rendered.

Certain concepts or terms like efficiency, diversification, integration, innovation etc., are used in the context of financial development.

Efficiency: The term *'efficiency'* refers to the operations and the working of various financial market segments like money market, capital market including new issues market and stock exchanges. As the financial markets deal with financial transactions, the efficiency lies in the reduction of transaction costs, and in the transfer of resources from the savers to the investors by matching to maximum mutual interests like convenience, liquidity, safety etc., for the savers and the cost, returns etc., for the investors and yielding a reasonable return for the financial intermediaries. The Report on Currency and Finance, RBI (1998-99) has highlighted the allocational aspect of efficiency by stating that, *"Financial markets perform an important function of mobilisation of savings and channelising them into the most productive uses," i.e.,* the productive activities and projects with higher returns. In regard to the working of capital market — New issues and Secondary market, certain aspects like valuation of securities, reduction of risks etc., are relevant for the efficiency of the markets. The prices of securities in the stock market

* As quoted by Prof. L.M. Bhole: Financial Institutions and Markets, p. 12.

should reflect intrinsic value. On the basis of information generated and disseminated, the transactions should be so transparent as to leave little scope for undue speculative gains out of purchase/sale of securities.

Diversification: A well developed financial system is one which has a diversified structure in the financial institutions and financial markets and provides a variety of financial instruments and renders various related financial services. This aspect indicates financial development as it offers to the savers wide options for converting their funds set aside into financial assets in accordance with their considerations of liquidity, safety and yield etc., and to the production units, the alternative channels of equity finance, loan finance etc., for obtaining funds for investment, weighing the factors like cost, returns etc.

Integration: Integration refers to the extent of cohesion between different constituents or parts of the financial system in terms of linkages giving rise to effective interrelationship in their working. In the Indian context, the cohesion between different constituents of the financial system is affected by the existence of a dualistic set-up consisting of organised and unorganised markets. These market segments differ significantly in regard to their practices, services rendered and the volume, cost and purpose of fund flows.

As the financial system develops, new institutions come up to perform specialised functions, new financial instruments are introduced to meet short-term and long-term fund requirements, the existing institutions take up new tasks say, commercial banks setting up their mutual funds. A closer link between the financial institutions participating in the money market and the capital market and in sub-parts of these markets can evolve a better integration and give rise to increased flow of funds among them.

The prominent aspect of the close link between the money market and the capital market is that the commercial banks and also the co operative banks are significant participants in both the markets. The commercial banks in terms of their subsidiaries and mutual funds are allowed to render financial services like merchant banking, equipment leasing, venture capital etc., and also channelise funds to participate in the stock market. The participation of investment institutions like insurance companies — LIC, GIC and mutual fund — UTI and the financial institutions like The Industrial Development Bank of India (IDBI) as the lender in the 'call money' market is an advantageous linkage between the markets for short-term and long-term funds.

One significant feature of integration is the 'internationalisation' in terms of close linkage between domestic and international capital markets. It is most realistic to say that the recent technological developments in the electronic payments system and communications system has facilitated the cross-border mobility of funds and brought about the growing integration of global capital markets. By adopting liberalisation policies, it has been possible for the developing countries like India to attract more capital from abroad as foreign direct investment and/or foreign institutional investment. The corporate sector units have been able to raise capital in international markets against the financial instruments like Global Depository Receipts and American Depository Receipts and foreign currency bonds. Further development is the access to the international stock markets acquired by the corporate units and financial institutions by way of listing for their participation in the foreign capital markets.

Innovation: Innovations in the financial system take place in a wide variety of ways and give rise to the structural and operational changes as a result of the introduction of 'new' elements in any dimension or part of the system like financial institutions, markets, instruments, practices, techniques, services etc. It is necessary to clarify that certain developments by way of changes or introduction of something 'new' takes place in the financial infrastructure of the developing countries like India on the lines of or rather as replication of what already exists and operates abroad. For the domestic financial system, these changes in the budding stage may not amount to innovations in the global context, but are significant for maturity and sophistication and for giving results towards specified goals and objects.

The most significant changes in the financial system of developing countries like India are the emergence and growth of financial institutions for long-term financing and the transformation in the role played by the commercial banks. The conventional form of bank credit has been cash credit, overdraft and bills discounting. The banks have now shifted their lending in favour of those who need their credit most, *i.e.,* the rural sector, small-scale units, units in backward areas and also participate in term lending by adopting a 'consortium' approach with development financial institutions. The commercial banks have begun allocation funds for money market instruments like Commercial Papers (CPs) and subscribe to the corporate equity/debenture issues either through their mutual funds and/or directly as participant in the capital market. The specialised institutions have come up for specific functions like merchant banking, credit rating and stock holding etc., and the development financial institutions engaged in the term-lending have set up their own banks, have diversified by being lenders in the call money market. The public sector undertakings raise funds by way of bonds and deposits directly from the capital market. The extension of the domestic capital market in terms of linkages with the overseas capital market for raising of funds through Euro issues and the corporate units and financial institutions listing on the stock markets abroad and participating to offer of equity shares for subscription and acquiring equity base in foreign companies needs to be viewed as a significant development towards internationalisation.

(ii) Financial Development Ratios

Besides describing financial development in terms of certain terms like efficiency, innovation, diversification, integration etc., it is relevant to express financial development in a quantitative manner, *i.e.,* in terms of Financial Development Ratios (FDRs).

It is necessary to make it clear that the present discussion restricts itself to cover ratios indicating financial development or the development of the financial system in a country. It is not intended to deal with the 'Ratio Analysis' including liquidity ratios, profitability ratios, activity ratios, leaverage ratios etc., reflecting the financial health/status of production units and guiding the management decisions. To make it more clear, it could be said that the Financial Development Ratios are the quantitative expression of how far or to what extent the financial system has progressed in performing its task of promoting savings and investment for more productive uses in a country and the 'ratio analysis' is the quantitative reflection of the financial status using accounting data for the guidance of management of production or commercial units in their decision-making.

Financial Development Ratios are:

(i) Finance Ratio (FR)

(ii) Financial Interrelations Ratio (FIR)

(iii) New Issues Ratio (NIR), and

(iv) Intermediation Ratio (IR)

(i) Finance Ratio (FR): This ratio indicates the relationship between financial development and economic development. In the course of economic development, the prime requisite of stimulating production is the increased investment or capital formation. In this regard, the financial system has to perform a crucial role of promoting both savings and investment and facilitate capital formation by transferring resources from those who save to those who make investment in production units. The transfer of resources takes place in terms of financial transactions directly between the savers and the production units creating *primary issues* and indirectly when the savers lend to financial intermediaries which create *secondary issues* against themselves and transfer funds to the non-financial real sector production units.

The total financial transactions in a year creating financial claims in favour of lender of funds and the liabilities for the borrowers indicate the level of financial activities in the financial system. The level of financial activity expressed as the total financial claims (sum total of primary issues + secondary issues) during a year is the numerator for the finance ratio. This is related to the national income which acts as a measure of the value of the final output produced during the year.

Finance Ratio is expressed as percentage relationship between total financial claims and national income for the year being considered.

$$\text{Finance Ratio} = \frac{\text{Total finance claims}}{\text{National income}}$$

(expressed as %)

The finance ratio going up indicates that the financial activity of mobilising and transferring resources for capital formation or investment is rapidly rising with the economic development. The savings have been increasingly mobilised by the financial institutions.

(ii) Financial Interrelations Ratio (FIR): The financial system mobilises funds from the savers so as to channelise these into investments, *i.e.,* adding to stock of physical assets or capital formation. Hence this ratio expresses a relationship between what the financial system does and the financing of investment.

While transferring funds in the form of financial transactions, the system gives rise to total financial claims consisting of primary issues when the funds are transferred directly from the savers to the real sector production units and the secondary issues which are created by the financial intermediaries working as links between the savers and the production units. As a result of the financial activity during a year, there comes about an increase in the stock of financial assets or claims.

The level of investment is the total stock of physical assets at a point of time and the increase in investment is addition to the stock of physical assets during a year expressed as net physical capital formation, *i.e.,* making provision for capital consumption or depreciation (for replacement of existing stock).

The extent to which the financial system has been able to promote investment is expressed by way of relationship between the level of financial activity, *i.e.,* total financial claims and the level of investment, *i.e.,* net physical capital formation.

$$\text{Financial Interrelations Ratio (FIR)} = \frac{\text{Total finance claims}}{\text{Net physical capital formation}}$$

This ratio could be expressed at a point of time as the ratio of total stock of financial assets to the total stock of physical assets or as an incremental relationship between increase in stock of financial assets to the increase in the stock of physical assets. The higher value of ratio indicates relatively quicker growth in the financial infrastructure as compared with increase in the stock of physical assets.

(iii) New Issues Ratio (NIR): New Issues Ratio indicates the extent to which the investment or net physical capital formation is financed by the primary issues, *i.e.,* the primary securities issued by the real sector production units. The non-financial or the real sector production units finance their investment, *i.e.,* net physical capital formation to a certain extent as 'equity finance' through primary issues, *i.e.,* issue of primary securities. The investment by the non-financial or real sector production units could be said to be financed directly when the primary issues are subscribed by the savers and indirectly when these primary issues are subscribed by financial intermediaries obtaining and pooling funds from the savers as against secondary securities issued by them.

The New Issues Ratio (NIR) indicates the extent to which the investment or net physical capital formation by the non-financial or real sector production units is financed by them through primary issues, *i.e.,* primary securities issued or the financial claims created.

$$\text{New Issues Ratio (NIR)} = \frac{\text{Primary issues}}{\text{Net physical capital formation}}$$

The ratio expresses the relationship as a percentage and indicates how for investment has been financed by the direct issues to the savers rather than through financial intermediaries. The non-financial or real sector production units have the option of raising funds such as equity finance and/or debt finance.

(iv) Intermediation Ratio (IR): The financial institutions intermediate or act as the link/bridge between the savers and real sector production units raising funds for investment. The financial institutions buy primary securities by subscribing to primary issues of the real sector production units and obtain funds from the savers by selling secondary securities, *i.e.,* by creating secondary issues against themselves.

The primary securities are issued by the non-financial real sector production units. The secondary securities are issued by the financial institutions. The primary securities and secondary securities together as a sum total would be the total financial issues during a year.

Intermediation Ratio (IR) provides a measure of financial intermediation or the extent of financial activity, *i.e.,* financial transactions which take place through the financial institutions acting as intermediaries.

This ratio is expressed as —

$$\text{Intermediation Ratio} = \frac{\text{Secondary issues}}{\text{Total financial issues}}$$

and indicates the extent or how far the financial transactions through the financial institutions account for in the total financial activity.

Intermediation Ratio expressed as:

$$\text{Intermediation Ratio} = \frac{\text{Secondary issues}}{\text{Primary issues}}$$

indicates the relative importance of the financial intermediaries in the mobilisation, pooling and transfer of funds as compared with the direct flow of funds from the savers to the real sector production units.

Table No. 3.2
Financial Development Ratios

	1980-81 to 1984-85	*1985-86 to 1989-90*	*1990 to 91*	*1991 to 92*	*1992 to 93*	*1993 to 94*	*1994 to 95*	*1995 to 96*
(i) Finance Ratio (FR)	0.34	0.4	0.4	0.5	0.38	0.47	0.52	0.49
(ii) Financial Interrelation Ratio (FIR)	2.42	2.40	1.75	2.92	2.18	2.83	2.43	2.26
(iii) New Issues Ratio (NIR)	1.42	1.40	1.0	1.62	1.19	1.49	1.16	1.33
(iv) Intermediation Ratio (IR)	0.69	0.72	0.74	0.81	0.84	0.9	0.91	0.7

Source: Report on Currency and Finance, RBI 1999-2000.

Finance Ratio = Total Financial Claims/National Income
FIR = Total Financial Claims/Net Physical capital formation
NIR = Primary Issues/Net Physical Capital Formation
IR = Secondary Issues/Primary Issues.

(iii) Financial Development: Qualitative Aspects

The views expressed on financial development relate to the question — Does financial development indicate the changes or increase in quantitative terms — or there are certain qualitative aspects which are equally important? Along with certain measures like increase in the number of participants, increase in the number and volume of financial transactions, increase in the number of financial institutions and their level of operations, the wide range of financial markets and their financial instruments, increase in number and variety of financial services, the flow of funds statements and the financial development ratios reveal trends in the quantitative aspects of financial development.

There are certain points which could be discussed as relevant for the qualitative aspects of financial development.

The developments in the financial system take place in the form of spurt or boom by way of new institutions coming up, new roles being taken up by the existing institutions, new services being introduced and new financial claims being offered. This results in undue multiplication. There is a need to ascertain the capacities of the markets and the felt-need should justify the developments in the financial infrastructure.

The financial system and its constituents remain insufficiently developed in an environment of controls and government regulation. The working and operations of financial institutions including commercial banks are influenced by factors other than commercial consideration and circumscribed by government interferences. The policies of liberalisation implemented through the withdrawal of controls and deregulation provides for the structural changes in the financial system and allows more operational freedom to the financial institutions.

The household sector savings, a prime source of funds for capital formation, are influenced by considerations like safety, liquidity, yield etc. One important influence on the household savings flowing for conversion in different financial assets or claims is the tax concessions. This consideration for availing tax concessions often becomes an overwhelming or decisive factor in the distribution of household savings in different institutions and among financial claims.

In developing countries like India, there is among the people an element of fear associated with the financial investment, *i.e.,* in directing the funds to acquire financial assets. The fear of default and capital loss arises on account of their lack of confidence in the financial markets and in the operations of financial institutions including commercial banks which, the people know, suffer from mounting bad debts, political influence and fraudulent practices.

The operations of the financial institutions including commercial banks are afflicted by the widespread 'sickness' prevalent in nearly all sectors of the economy — private and public, corporate and small-scale segments of the industry and also in agriculture. This critical situation creates a pressing need for the financial institutions to be more concerned and guided by the norms of financial discipline with a view to attain both operational and allocational efficiency.

Financial development signifies that the deficiencies or weaknesses in the financial infrastructure like absence of secondary markets for certain assets are removed and the operations of various financial institutions including banks are better co-ordinated by avoiding contradiction and overlapping in their roles.

KEY TERMS

Flow of Funds, Sources and Uses of Funds, Balance Sheet, Financial Intermediation, Indicators of Financial Development, Financial Development Ratios – Finance Ratio, Financial Interrelation Ratio, New Issues Ratio, Intermediation Ratio.

REVIEW QUESTIONS

1. Discuss the various aspects of the flow of funds analysis.
2. Explain the significance of the flow of funds analysis for a financial system.
3. What is financial development? What are the indicators of financial development?
4. Discuss the financial development ratios in the context of the Indian Financial System.

REFERENCES

1. Reserve Bank of India, Report on Currency and Finance.
2. Reserve Bank of India, Bulletin, Nov. 2007.

❑ ❑ ❑

4

Indian Financial System: Past and Present

INTRODUCTION

The study of the Indian financial system as it existed in the past has been divided into two periods, *i.e.,* pre-independence (prior to 1947) and post-independence period. The political independence of the country in 1947 is marked by a significant change in the attitude and the role of the government with regard to economic activities including financial activities. This change was distinctly reflected in the choice of 'mixed economy' as a path for economic development in future. The path of 'mixed economy' envisaged three specific aspects of the role of government *vis-a-vis* economic activities. These three aspects pertain to government as: (a) encourager (b) participant, and (c) controller or regulator. These aspects of the changed role of the government could be seen in terms of certain developments pertaining to the financial system immediately after independence in the country. These steps were taken by the government by way of remedial action to overcome certain deficiencies or weaknesses as they existed on the eve of independence. The rapid growth of industries needed provision of long-term funds. As the financial set-up lacked in this regard, the Industrial Finance Corporation of India (IFCI) was set up under the Act of Parliament in 1948 to provide long-term financial assistance to industries. The Reserve Bank of India (RBI) which started its operations in 1935 became fully state owned in 1949 and has been vested since then with extensive regulatory powers under the Banking Regulation Act 1949 of supervision and control over commercial banks. This regulatory measure was taken to prevent the recurring bank failures, particularly of small banks under unscrupulous managements, during the immediately preceding period, *i.e.,* 1937-48 when 620 banks failed. The other significant regulatory measure was the Capital Issues (Control) Act, 1947 which had the objects of: (i) protecting the interests of the investors, (ii) promoting growth of the private corporate sector on sound lines and (iii) preventing diversion of funds to non-essential activities.

The developments in the Indian Financial System in the post-independence period had their roots in the progress and deficiencies of the financial set-up during the pre-independence period.

This chapter is devoted to the study of Indian Financial System under the following heads:

Indian Financial System:

4.1 Pre-independence Period
- (i) Upto Mid 19th century (Upto 1850s)
- (ii) Mid 19th Century to World War I (1914-18)
- (iii) World War I to Mid 20th Century (1950s)

4.2 Post-independence Period
- (i) Broader Relevant Aspects:
  - (a) Environmental Aspects: Economic Planning, Phase of Control and Regulation
  - (b) Saving-Investment Trends
- (ii) Major Developments in Indian Financial System
  - (a) Financial Institutions
  - (b) Financial Markets
  - (c) Financial Instruments
  - (d) Financial Services
- (iii) Growth of Indian Financial System
  - (a) Quantitative Indicators
  - (b) Qualitative Changes and Reforms

4.3 Current Scenario in the Indian Financial System
- (i) Financial Institutions
- (ii) Financial Markets and Financial Instruments

As could be seen from above, the developments with regard to the financial system in the country in the post-independence period have their roots in the progress and deficiencies in the financial set-up during the pre-independence period.

I. INDIAN FINANCIAL SYSTEM:

4.1 PRE-INDEPENDENCE PERIOD

For the sake of suitable presentation and clarity, the study of Indian financial system in the pre-independence period is divided into certain periods as under:

- (i) Upto middle of the 19th century, *i.e.,* 1850s;
- (ii) Middle of 19th century to World War I; and
- (iii) World War I to the middle of 20th century (1950s)

The above division into three periods is around landmarks which are actually extraneous factors like advent and stronghold of the British Rule in India, Swadeshi Movement (1905) onwards and World War I (1914-18). The decade of 1850s has a unique significance in terms of the introduction of the modern means of transport — the Railways, and communications, *i.e.,* Post & Telegraph services. These developments helped trading activities and thereby the growth of banking. The Swadeshi Movement enthused people to take initiative in diverse fields including starting industries, establishing joint-stock companies to run banking business etc. The war gives rise to a temporary boom in economic activities. The World War I provided a stimulus to industrial activities in the country and in turn, encouraged trade and banking.

(i) Financial Set-up upto the Mid of 19th Century (upto 1850s)

Though modern banking made a beginning in India in the early part of the 19th century, the indigenous financial agencies formed the core of the financial system in the country till the period of the 1850s. Modern banking began in India with the establishment of three banks (named later as Presidency Banks) — the Bank of Bengal in 1806, followed by the Bank of Bombay in 1840 and the Bank of Madras in 1843. The indigenous financial agencies consisted of the moneylenders, agency houses and the indigenous bankers and dominated the scene by providing credit to small farmers and artisans in rural areas and to the traders, producers and even to the government.

The financial set-up in the country upto to the middle of 19th century could be described as, 'dualistic' in that it had two main constituents of the 'traditional' sector of indigenous agencies and the 'modern' of banking business. Among the indigenous financial agencies, the role of moneylenders dates back to the ancient period. The agency houses came up in the period when the East Indian Company enjoyed monopoly trading rights in the country. The agency houses could be viewed as the forerunners of joint-stock banking in India. Initially, the East India Company conducted its external trade from Calcutta Port. The agency houses came up mainly to act as agents for the planters and merchants in the region. Besides this, the agency houses performed the banking business, accepted deposits and made advances on shipments and to the producers of indigo, opium, yarn, saltpetre, cotton and silk. These early agency houses were promoted by few British merchants and acted as bankers to the East India Company for the civil and military services as the company began acquiring administrative powers.

As distinct from the moneylenders, who were engaged in lending funds, relying mainly on their own resources, the indigenous bankers conducted banking business, in combination with other activities such as being goldsmith, merchants etc. by both receiving deposits and advancing loans. They financed trade by dealing in short-term credit instrument known as Hundi, made remittances of money or the transfer of funds from one trading centre to the other. The indigenous bankers were individuals or small private firms formed usually by the members of certain castes or communities such as Multanis, Marwaris and Chettiars etc. The moneylenders operated primarily in rural areas and the indigenous bankers to a large extent were urban-based, *i.e.,* located in industrial and trading centres and port towns. The indigenous bankers encouraged trade through financing by discounting 'hundis' and also by endorsing the hundis issued by the traders. They also financed small manufacturers and the units in cottage industries like Handlooms. Through their brokers, the indigenous bankers ascertained the creditworthiness of borrowers and provided personal guarantees for the loans. The most important feature of indigenous bankers as the financing agencies was that they conducted business on the basis of informal and personalised relationships. The services rendered were relatively prompt as the procedural formalities were not involved. The borrowers had to pay higher rate of interest for the credit extended by the indigenous bankers who did not concern themselves with the purpose or end-use of credit and included even the speculative activities in commodity trade.

This could be described as the long period of slow progress of banking on modern lines in the country. Besides the three banks which were set up during the first half of 19th century at the port towns of Calcutta, Bombay and Madras, some banks were started but soon failed. The joint-stock banks established after 1860 organised themselves on the basis of principle of limited liability under Joint-stock Companies Act and were made applicable to banking.

(ii) Developments during Middle of 19th Century to the beginning of the 20th Century, *i.e.,* before World War I

Soon after the applicability of the principle of limited liability in 1860, a number of banks along with other joint-stock companies were promoted. A number of these banking companies were short-lived and soon collapsed being involved in speculation. Still between 1865 and the early years of the 20th century, a few joint-stock banks and some exchange banks were set up. These included Allahabad Bank set up in 1865 and Punjab National Bank in 1894. By the year 1900, there were 9 joint-stock banks, eight exchange banks and three presidency banks which were set up earlier.

The other two developments relevant for the progress of the financial set-up during this period are: (i) establishment of stock exchanges at Bombay in 1887, Ahmedabad in 1894 and at Calcutta in 1908. It was only a beginning and the paid-up capital of joint-stock companies amounted to only ₹ 24 crore in 1890 and (ii) impact of 'Swadeshi Movement' during 1906-1913. The uprising of people took a shape of a movement after 1905 and resulted in starting of new industries and the setting up of joint-stock banks. The number of commercial banks with a share capital of ₹ 5 lakh and more doubled to 18 by 1913. Some of the banks established during the years have grown into some prominent banks of today such as Bank of India, Central Bank of India, Bank of Baroda, Canara Bank, Corporation Bank, Indian Bank and the Bank of Mysore.

Though the 'modern' sector of the financial scene in India consisted primarily of the banking business, it is necessary to mention the beginnings made in insurance field and the issues of government securities. In this period, the Life Insurance and General Insurance business made a beginning. The Indian Life Insurance Companies Act 1912 was enacted, giving a way for life insurance business to run on sound lines. The other development pertains to the early efforts of the central and provincial governments to raise amounts through the issues of government securities. The gross amount raised through the issues of government securities was ₹ 2 crore in 1890. During World War I, treasury bills were also first issued in 1917 and the amounts of treasury bills sold was ₹ 87 crore in 1919.

The progress of the banking business was slow in this period, particularly till the beginning of the 20th century. The reasons for the slow progress of banking in this period lie partly in the overall economic conditions and also in the banking activities. There were recurring bank failures as the banks engaged in speculative pursuits and collapsed due to the mismanagement of funds. Even after the introduction of modern means of transport and communications such as Railways and Post and Telegraph, the pace of economic changes in this period remained slow. Modern factories came up on the scene and certain industries like cotton textiles, jute textiles and also coal mining were started. Initially, the industrial activities were at centres like Bombay and Calcutta and could spread to the other regions towards the end of the 19th century. Still, the growth of industries was slow and the total number of factories in the country by 1914 was less than three thousand. The progress of banking during the period could be slow in view of the slow speed of transformation in economic scene on modern lines. The changes gathered speed during and after World War I.

(iii) World War I to the Middle of the 20th Century (1950s)

The tempo of economic activities in the country increased and was maintained high during this period, except for those years of 1930s when there was worldwide economic slow-down or a crisis known as Great Depression. As it is widely known, the main factor which raised the tempo of economic activities and gave a stimulus to rapid growth of industries was the 'World Wars'. The characteristic feature of wars as stimulus to economic activities is that the World Wars created a short-period, temporary rush of activities in the form of a boom, which was invariably followed by an aftermath of a slow-down. After World War I, the pace of industrial activities increased as a sequel to the *'protection'* granted to certain industries.

Growth of Banking: These features of the short-period rush in activities followed by the crisis as an aftermath are seen in respect of the progress of banking in this period. The banking activities witnessed rapid growth and yet it is said that this period is marked by recurrent bank failures. The short period of rapid growth in the banking business in the early years of the past century was followed by a crisis of bank failures, mainly among small banks. Between 1913-19, 98 banks failed, of which 87 banks were with a capital of less than ₹ 2 lakh.

- There were significant structural changes in the banking set-up as under:
  (i) The three presidency banks were amalgamated to form Imperial Bank of India in 1921. The Imperial Bank of India acted like a Central bank and as a banker for other banks.
  (ii) As a result of the Act of 1934, the Reserve Bank of India was set up in 1935 as a central bank of the country and was at the apex of the monetary system. The establishment of a central bank to overview and monitor the banking activities, particularly in view of the recurring bank failures, was a felt-need and a long awaited measure.
- The characteristic feature of the progress of banking during this period is the significant growth in activities juxtaposed with recurrent bank failures.

The growth in banking business could be described as significant in terms of increase in the bank deposits:

Year	*Deposits (₹crores)*
1910	82
1939	263
1945	1031

For the years 1948 and 1950, the bank deposits amounted to ₹ 957 crore and ₹ 1,304 crore respectively.

In the inter-war period, during Second World War and the years immediately after, there were periodic failures, particularly among small banks under unscrupulous managements. During the years 1913-36, 480 banks failed and during and immediately after Second World War, 620 banks failed. The main causes for these bank failures were mismanagement, speculative investment of funds, insufficient capital base of paid-up capital and reserves, neglect of proper liquidity of assets etc. Still, it could be said that the small banks rendered a useful service of taking banking activities to distant areas in the country. This is significant in view of the limited geographical spread of banking facilities by the bigger banks in cities and port towns.

The commercial banks were granting advances mainly to trade and commerce and provided short-term credit to industries. The financial set-up in the country did not have any institutional arrangement for meeting the long-term funds requirements of industries. There were seven *industrial banks* operating in a limited manner during this period.

The share of commercial banks in rural credit was low. The moneylenders were the prime source of funds as they provided both personal loans as well as short-term and long-term loans for the agricultural sector. Though the efforts to make the rural scene in India free from the exploitative hold of moneylenders were being made by promoting co-operative credit institutions since the early years of the 20th century, *i.e.,* 1904, the progress achieved in the field of *co-operative banks* could not make the desired impact. The prime importance assigned to agricultural sector financing could be noticed in the creation of the Agricultural Credit Department of the Reserve bank of India, established in 1935. Still, the progress in this regard was limited as by the middle of the 20th century, out of the total debt outstanding of cultivator households, only 3.7 per cent was owed to co-operative societies.

By 1947, the banking scene in the country consisted of the Reserve Bank of India (fully state owned in 1949), the Imperial Bank of India and co-operative banks — 14 banks at the states level, nearly 500 central co-operative banks at the districts level, a few exchange banks and Indian Joint-stock Banks. There were 640 commercial banks, of which only 96 were scheduled banks in being listed with the Reserve Bank of India. The commercial banks were categorised as A, B, C and D with regard to their paid-up capital and reserves. Class A: ₹ 5 lakh and more, Class B: More than ₹ 1 lakh and less than ₹ 5 lakh, Class C: More than ₹ 0.5 lakh and less than ₹ 1 lakh and class D: Less than ₹ 0.5 lakh.

The characteristics features of the banking scene in India were:

- The banking facilities were mainly available in bigger cities and port towns. The small banks were geographically somewhat more scattered.
- The banking business was concentrated with a few leading joint-stock banks and the Imperial Bank of India. Among the joint-stock banks, 63 per cent of the deposits were accounted for by class 'A' banks. Of these, a major portion of deposits was with only five to seven banks.
- A high proportion of bank advances were granted to trade. The most common forms of bank credit were cash credit, overdrafts and loans. Nearly fifty per cent of bank advances were for commerce, of which nearly half were given to wholesale trade.

An Overview of the Modern Banking Scene by the Middle of the 20th Century

- By the middle of the 20th century, modern banking had traversed a long path of nearly a century and half, *i.e.,* between 1806 and 1947.
- Till the early years of the 20th century, the progress of banking business on modern lines was slow and the financial scene in the country was dominated by agency houses, indigenous bankers and moneylenders.
- The developments in the banking activities were as a matter of rush or a boom to respond to the raising of overall economic activities during periods of the two world wars.
- There were recurring bank failures, caused due to speculative pursuits, mismanagement, irregularities in lending, inadequate capital base etc.
- There was no arrangement for monitoring the banking activities till 1935 when the Reserve Bank of India was established.
- The modern banking business progressed and yet had a number of lacunae or limitations such as: (a) high degree of concentration, (b) functioning restricted to major cities, port towns and to financing of trade and commerce and (c) neglect of credit needs of other prominent sectors like long-term finance for the industry and different types of credit provisions for agriculture.

It is necessary to mention other aspects of the financial set-up in the country by the middle of the 20th century, *i.e.,* by 1947.

Public Deposits: The practice of raising funds directly from the public by way of deposits prevailed among companies engaged in industrial activities like textile mills in Bombay and Ahmedabad.

Stock Market: Between 1887 and 1937, there were four stock exchanges established: Bombay: 1887, Ahmedabad: 1894, and Calcutta: 1908, Madras: 1937. The funds raised on the stock markets through capital issues by the private sector companies — industrial units increased significantly during the first half of the 20th century. As mentioned earlier, the world wars were the main factor or stimulus for the raising of overall economic activities in form of a rush or a boom followed by a slow-down or a slump. The industrial activities and also the new issues market or the new capital issues activities were exposed to the ups and downs on the similar lines, *i.e.,* high amount of capital issues during and immediately after war, followed by a sharp fall in capital issues. The capital was raised mainly by the issue of ordinary shares, as the debentures were not popular. As observed by Prof. L.M. Bhole, "the capital issues of joint-stock companies, on an average, amounted to ₹ 70 crore per year during the inter-war period."

Small Savings: The people, belonging to different income groups, and engaged in different occupations have found since long, *i.e.,* second half of 19th century, post office saving banks deposits, a suitable and convenient method for directing their savings. Post offices also attracted small savings by offering certificates of specific maturities. The post office saving bank deposits which amounted to ₹ 3.66 crore in 1896 increased to nearly ₹ 99 crore by the middle of the 20th century.

Gilt-edged (Government) Securities and Treasury Bills: The main subscribers to government securities issued from time to time with different maturity periods were the banks, insurance companies, princely state governments. Treasury bills with maturities upto and less than one year were first introduced during the World War I period. Though the treasury bills were issued by both the Central Government and the provincial governments, the banks did not much prefer subscribing to these issues. By the middle of 20th century, treasury bills sold amounted to only ₹ 85 crore.

Insurance Companies: The Life Insurance Companies and their functioning was significant in that they mobilised savings of the people and utilised their funds mainly for subscribing to government securities.

4.2 POST-INDEPENDENCE PERIOD

In this part of the chapter, it is proposed to mention the developments in the Indian financial system during the second half of the 20th century, *i.e.,* after Independence in 1947 and upto 1990s when the phase of economic reforms including financial reforms speeded up in the country. During this post-independence period of forty and odd years, there has been a significant growth in the Indian financial system in terms of the size or the quantitative indicators as well as in diversification and innovations.

The financial system has financial institutions, financial markets and the financial instruments as the main constituents and it performs in terms of financial services rendered. The details of the growth in the Indian financial system as spelt out individually in respect of these three constituents — their parts and sub-parts and the services rendered is dealt with separately in different chapters of the book. It is now intended to present an overview of the development in the financial system in the post-independence period upto 1990s as under:

(i) Broader relevant aspects:
   (a) Environmental aspects: Economic planning. Phase of control and regulation;
   (b) Saving-Investment trends.

(ii) Major Developments in Indian financial system:
   (a) Financial Institutions;
   (b) Financial Markets;
   (c) Financial Instruments;
   (d) Financial Services.

(iii) Growth of Indian financial system:
   (a) Quantitative indicators;
   (b) Qualitative changes and reforms.

(I) BROADER RELEVANT ASPECTS

(a) Environmental Aspects

Phase of State Participation: In the context of economic planning accepted as a path for achieving rapid economic development, this post-independence period could be described as a phase of the active role of the government in both stimulating and regulating the processes of change in all dimensions of the Indian economy including the financial system. The prime focus of measures taken by the government by way of participation in the financial system was on: (a) creating institutions to build up financial infrastructure for the provision of funds to those sectors like industry, agriculture etc. which remained neglected and (b) directing or monitoring the flow of financial resources in accordance with the priorities of development by acquiring control through 'nationalisation' and regulation with powers contained in the enactments. The economic planning laid emphasis on bringing about a structural change in the country in the form of the rapid growth of industries. The government took up initiatives by promoting specialised financial institutions for the provision of assistance of long-term funds to industries such as Industrial Finance Corporation of India (1948), Industrial Credit & Investment Corporation of India (1955) and Industrial Development Bank of India (1964). The Reserve Bank of India which was established in 1935 as the apex monetary institution, became fully state-owned in 1949. Apart from this, the other measure of acquiring control by the Government was the formation of State Bank of India by nationalising the Imperial Bank of India in 1955. The early regulatory measures included Capital Issues (Control) Act, 1947, Banking Regulation Act, 1949, Securities Contract (Regulation) Act, 1956, empowering the apex bank under Bank Regulation with supervision and control over banks, and the other two enactments authorising the government to regulate the stock markets in regard to new issues as well as trading on the stock exchanges.

These are some of the early measures which persisted throughout the phase of active state participation in the form of setting up of new institutions, acquiring control through nationalisation and regulation by way of amendments and/or new provisions under enactments. These are discussed in details in subsequent chapters.

Government Deficits — Monetary Expansion: The other aspect of government participation in the process of economic development having a significant relevance to the financial system is that the system had to face the continuously mounting pressure of raising finance to meet the excess of government disbursements over receipts and to take up the public sector projects. Since the 1950s, the Reserve Bank as the banker to the Government has to provide short-term credit and manage public debt by coping up with the challenge of meeting the growing requirements of funds by the government and yet monitoring the impact of monetary expansion and thereby inflation.

The Central Government borrows from the RBI through treasury bills to meet the short-term funds requirements and the RBI grants ways and means advances to central and state governments for this purpose. Every year, the budgets make a mention of the amount of funds to be raised through the new issue of government securities. Funding or rather refunding of government debt resorted to for the extension of maturity periods results in short-term treasury bills becoming a source of long-term funds and the maturing and near-maturing securities giving a way for the new securities with extended maturity. Over the years, the RBI has brought about reduction in the proportion of its holding of government securities by making it obligatory for commercial banks, co operative banks, LIC, GIC and the PF organisation to comply with the specified requirement of the holding of government securities. Still, the financing of government deficit through these financial instruments leaves a built-in pressure of resulting in monetary expansion and the consequential inflation.

(b) Saving-Investment Trends

The prime function of the financial system is to promote savings and investment in the country and thereby help in speeding up economic development. As such, it is relevant to know the trends in aggregate savings and aggregate investment expressed in both volume and rate. The trend in volume is expressed as Gross Domestic Savings ad Gross Domestic Capital formation over the years 1951-2000 and rate as the percentage of national income or Gross Domestic product over the same period.

The word 'domestic' refers to the financial resources generation for investment within the country as distinct from the inflow of capital from abroad. The 'gross' and 'net' differ with regard to the provision by way of capital consumption allowance for the fixed capital assets used.

The trend in aggregate savings and aggregate investment are expressed at current prices The trends have been presented as disaggregated in three sectors — household, private corporate and public sector and also the totals.

The trend in *Gross Domestic Savings* reveals that —

- The increase in the total was slow in the decade of 1950s, but picked up in 60s, 70s and 80s and slowed in second half of 1990s.
- Sectorwise

Household:	Slow in 1950s maintained high since then.
Private Corporate:	Slow in 1950s and 1980s picked up since then.
Public:	Very slow in 1950s picked up in 1960s and 1970s and fallen significantly since then.

Sectorwise shares in total

Household:	The share of household sector in total saving has been high between 69% and 75% and has gone above 81% in recent period.
Private Corporate:	The share of private corporate sector has ranged 9% and 14% and shot up to 18% by the end of 1990s.
Public Sector:	The share of public sector has ranged between 15% and 22% and fallen significantly in the recent period. The public sector has indicated dissaving.

The trend in gross domestic capital formation:

- Gross Domestic capital formation showed a slower increase during 1950s. It has maintained a high level since then.

Sectorwise:

Public Sector:	Slowed down during 1960s. It has moved up duing 1970s and 1980s and slowed again in 1990s.
Private Sector:	Initially slow increased faster during 1970s and 1980s.

Saving and Investment (as % GDP)

Gross Domestic Saving (GDS)

- As GDS has fluctuated over the years in respect of % to GDP the trend has been shown as Average % for the decade.

  There has been persistent increase in regard to GDS as % of GDP for the total as well as for household sector.

  The increase in GDS as % of GDP in case of private corporate sector has remained low. It shows a rise during 1990s for private corporate sector and a decline in case of public sector.

Gross Domestic Capital Formation

- Gross Domestic capital formation as % GDP at the total level shows a persistent increase and reached a peak level of 26.9% during 1995-96.
- As % of Gross Domestic Capital formation to GDP for both private and public sector flucuated over the years, the trend has been indicated in terms of average % for the decade.

Saving and Investment as % of GDP (see Table 4.2)

Gross Domestic Saving

- There has been a persistent increase in respect of gross domestic saving as % of GDP for the total as well as in the household sector, the increase being on higher side during the decade of 1970s.
- The increase in gross domestic saving as % of GDP has not been consistent and has remained low or even negative in case of the private corporate and the public sector.

Table No. 4.1
Gross DomesticSaving and Investment in India
(at current prices)

(₹ in Crores)

Period	Gross Domestic Saving							Gross Investment (Domestic Capital Formation)							
	Household Sector	% increase	Private corporate sector	% increase	Public sector	% increase	Total*	Household sector	% Increase	Private Corporate sector	% increase	Public sector	% Increase	Total	% increase
1970-71	4634		672		1343		6649	3263		1045		2919		7227	
	(69.7)		(10.1)	257	(20.2)	289			225		195		316		257
		243	2398		5226		24314								
1979-80	16690				262		1748	10609		3078		12137		25824	
	(74.4)		(10.6)		(15.0)										
1980-81	19868		2389		4929		27136	11258		3505		12105		26868	
	(73.2)		(8.6)		(18.2)										
		348		406		66			335		461		283		328
1989-90	86955		11845		8179		106979	48957		19673		46405		115035	
	(81.9)		(11.1)		(7.6)										
1990-91	109897		15164		6279		1313401	60257		23498		53099		136854	
	(63.7)	268	(11.5)	456	(4.8)				230		432		153		191
1999-2000	404401		84329		–20049		468681	198658		125120		134484		458262	
	(86.3)		(18.0)		(-4.3)										

Note:% increase is over the decade. For GDS — Figures in brackets indicate % to the total as per new series 1999-2000

Period	Household Sector	% increase	Private corporate sector	% increase	Public sector	% increase	Total*	Household sector	% Increase	Private Corporate sector	% increase	Public sector	% Increase	Total	% increase
1999-2000	416726		87234		–16659		487301	210124		140088		146483		512214	
	(85.5)		(17.9)		(–3.4)										
2000-01	446317		87017		–37062		496272	231098		119993		145775		511590	
	(89.9)		(17.5)		(-7.4)										
2001-02	502674	54.5	81669		–46377		537966	255198	74.3	127503	89.8	157580	53.8	554488	344
	(93.4)		(15.2)	73.0	(–8.6)										
2002-03	565408		99767		–16181		648994	312152		141659		151246		619914	
	(87.1)		(15.4)		(–2.5)										
2003-04	648634		120852		28026		797512	332190		188728		180228		725630	
	(81.3)		(15.1)		(3.5)										
2004-05	716874		212048		68591		997873	399328		338755		216962		996099	
	(71.8)		(21.2)		(6.9)										
2005-06	864653		276550		86823		1228026	443679		491983		271835		1248889	
	(70.4)		(22.5)		(7.0)										
2006-07	994898		342284		137926		1475108	512076		611044		329679		1502508	
	(67.4)		(23.2)		(9.4)										
2007-08	1150135		416936		212543		1779614	596846		749894		429014		1829346	
	(64.6)		(23.4)		(11.9)										

Source: (i) Economic Survey, Government of India 2005-06. (ii) Handbook of Statistics on Indian Economy, RBI 2005-06.
The % increase is for 2000 to 2005 period.

Table No. 4.1(A)

Gross Domestic Saving and Gross Investment

(at current prices)

(₹ *in Crores*)

Year	*Household Sector*			*Private Corporate Sector*			*Public Sector*			*Total*		
(1)	*S*	*I*	*Gap*	*S*	*I*	*Gap*	*S*	*I*	*Gap*	*S*	*I*	*Gap*
1970-71	4634	3263	1371	672	1045	–373	1343	2919	–1576	6649	7227 (7043)	–394
1980-81	19868	11258	8610	2339	3505	3505	4929	12105	–7176	27136	26868 (29230)	–2094
1990-91	109987	60257	49730	15164	23498	23498	6279	53099	–46820	13140	136854 (149536)	–136396
1999-2000	404401	198658	384533	84329	125120	125120	–20049	134484		468681	458262 (490669)	–21988

Note: Figures in brackets indicate the 'adjusted' total. 'Gap' is negative when the investment rate exceeded the saving rate.

As per new series 1999-2000

Year	*Household S*	*Household I*	*Household Gap*	*Private Corporate S*	*Private Corporate I*	*Private Corporate Gap*	*Public S*	*Public I*	*Public Gap*	*Total S*	*Total I*	*Total Gap*
1999-2000	416726	210124	206602	87234	140088	–52834	–16659	146483		487301	512214	–24913
2000-01	446317	231098	215219	87017	119993	–32976	–37062	145775		496272	511590	–15318
2001-02	502674	255198	247976	81669	125703	–44004	–46377	157580		537166	554488	–16522
2002-03	565408	312152	253256	99767	141659	–41892	–16181	151246		648994	619914	29080
2003-04	648634	332190	316444	120852	188728	–67896	28026	180228	–152202	797512	725630	71882
2004-05	716874	399328	317546	212048	338755	-126709	68951	216962	–148011	997873	996099	1774
2005-06	864653	443679	420974	276550	491983	-215433	86823	271835	–185012	1228026	1248889	–20863
2006-07	994898	572076	482822	342284	611044	-268760	137926	329679	–1981753	1475108	1502508	–27400
2007-08	1150135	596846	553289	416936	749894	-332958	212543	429014	–216471	1779614	1829346	– 49732

P: Provisional

Note: Investment under column. 'Total' may not be equal to sum total of sectorwise investment as the same is 'adjusted' total.

Table No. 4.2

Gross Domestic Saving and Gross Investment in India

(as % of GDP at current prices)

Period	*Gross Domestic Saving*								*Gross Domestic Investment*					
	Household Sector	*average % for decade*	*Private corporate sector*	*average % for decade*	*Public sector*	*average % for decade*	*Total*	*average % for decade*	*Public sector*	*average % for decade*	*Private sector*	*average % for decade*	*Total*	*average % for decade*
1970-71	10.1		1.5		2.9		14.6		6.4		9.4		15.8	
		12.0		1.6		2.4		17.5		8.1		10.0	(15.4)	17.6
1979-80	13.8		2.0		4.3		20.1		10.0		11.3		21.6	
													(20.6)	
1980-81	13.8		1.6		3.4		18.9		8.4		10.3		18.7	
		14.6		1.8		3.0		19.4		10.0		12.0	(20.3)	21.2
1989-90	17.9		2.4		1.7		22.0		9.5		14.1		23.7	
													(24.5)	
1990-91	19.3		2.7		1.1		23.1		9.3		14.7		24.1	
		18.9		2.7		0.9		23.1		7.8		15.2	(20.3)	22.2
1999-2000	20.9		4.4		–1.0		24.2		6.9		16.7		29.7	
													(25.3)	

Note: % average for the decade.

as per new series — 1999-2000

Period	Household Sector	Private corporate sector	Public sector	Total	Public sector	Private sector	Total
1999-2000	21.3	4.5	–0.9	24.9	7.5	17.9	26.1
							(26.0)
2000-01	21.2	4.1	-1.8	23.5	6.9	16.7	24.3
							(24.2)
2001-02	22.0	3.6	-2.0	23.6	6.9	16.8	24.3
							(23.0)
2002-03	23.1	4.1	-0.7	26.5	6.2	18.5	25.3
							(25.3)
2003-04	23.5	4.4	1.0	28.9	6.5	18.9	26.3
							(27.2)
2004-05	22.8	6.7	2.2	31.7	6.9	23.4	30.3
2005-06	24.1	7.7	2.4	34.2	7.6	26.1	33.7
2006-07	24.1	8.3	3.3	35.7	8.0	27.2	35.2
2007-08	24.4	8.8	4.5	37.7	9.1	28.5	37.6

Source: Economic Survey, Government of India, 2005-06.

Note: Figures in brackets indicate adjusted total.

Gross Domestic Capital Formation

- There has been a persistent increase in respect of gross domestic capital formation as % of GDP at the total level.
- Between 1950-51 and 1969-70, the increase was only 5 percentage points. As against this, during the subsequent two decades, there has been increase of 10 percentage points from around 15% to earlier 25% by the end of 1980s.
- The percentage of gross domestic capital formation to GDP has fluctuated over the years in case of both public and private sectors, with the increase being on the higher side during 1970s.

(II) MAJOR DEVELOPMENTS IN THE INDIAN FINANCIAL SYSTEM

It is proposed to put together the major developments in respect of the constituents of the financial system during the post-independence period, *i.e.,* from 1947 to 1990. The post-reform developments, *i.e.,* developments in the financial system during the decade of 1990s are separately mentioned under the heading *'Indian Financial System at Present'*. Likewise, further details about the constituents, *i.e.,* financial institutions, financial markets and financial instruments are recorded separately in the book.

(a) Financial Institutions

Development Financial Institutions (DFIs)

One of the most significant and a major development in the Indian financial system since independence is the creation of a wider financial infrastructure in the country in terms of the setting up of Development Financial Institutions (DFIs) as specialised financial institutions by the Government. As an active participant, the Government took this initiative to cater to the various financial requirements of certain sectors which had remained largely unattended. Though the DFIs are alternatively called as 'Development Banks', they are really non-banking financial institutions. The DFIs differ from commercial banks as the latter are necessarily financial intermediaries and the DFIs are not financial intermediaries in the real sense of the term. The commercial banks mobilise savings of the people by accepting monetary deposits and pool these resources for their transfer to meet the short/medium term financial needs of real sector *'deficit'* spenders. As against this, the resource-base of the DFIs consists of the subscriptions and the borrowings from the government and the RBI, and their activities, primarily revolve round extending long-term financial assistance. As discussed in the earlier chapter, the difference between the banks and DFIs as the financial institutions has become less distinct, as they are coming closer to each other in their activities and the DFIs are also mobilising financial resources from the market by way of their bonds/debenture issues. The banks undertake financing for meeting working capital needs. In the recent years, the DFIs have diversified by entering into working capital financing. The banks have broadened their role and take up financing industrial projects which has been the domain of the DFIs.

At this stage, it is intended to note certain broad features of the financial institutions categorised as DFIs, the details regarding the working and growth of these institutions individually are mentioned separately in the book.

Broad Features of DFIs

The DFIs present a wide array of financial institutions which differ in regard to the level at which they operate, the type or a mix of activities/functions performed and the beneficiaries or sectors served.

Level — All India or States: There are all-India level institutions such as DFIs serving industrial sector — IDBI, ICICI, IFCI, IRBI (now IIBI), NSIC, SIDBI, DFI for agricultural/rural sector — NABARD and DFI for External Trade — Export-Import (EXIM) Bank. The *states level* institutions include SFCs, SIICs for the industries sector and Land development banks for agriculture.

Activities / Functions: The DFIs are mainly term lending institutions extending medium and long-term finance. As the development institutions, the other two prominent aspects of their role is the promotional role and consultancy service. The DFIs as development agencies take up other tasks such as encouraging new entrepreneurs and the new enterprises in the industrially backward regions. There are also specialised institutions operating in the fields like risk capital, lease finance, capital provision for specific requirements like Rural Electrification Warehousing, Tourism, Housing, Rehabilitation of sick units etc.

The promotional activities and the technical services of DFIs include —

- Underwriting of new issues and direct subscription to shares and debenture issues. This function is meant to encourage the coming up of new industrial units and thereby activate the capital market.
- Arranging for foreign currency loans.
- Extending guarantees for term loans
- Identification of new industrial projects, preparation and evaluation of project reports.
- Feasibility studies — technical advice, market information.
- Conduct entrepreneurship development programmes and help entrepreneurs in project formulation and implementation.

Beneficiaries or Sectors Served

Refinance and Rediscounting: Refinancing of loans and rediscounting of bills are the facilities provided to the financial institutions, commercial banks and co operative banks by IDBI and NABARD respectively for industry and agricultural sectors. IDBI and NABARD are apex financial institutions providing support through these facilities to other institutions, DFIs and banks are engaged in direct financing of both industries and agricultural sectors. As the apex financial institution, IDBI extends support to other financial institutions, also by way of subscription to equity capital and bond issues and NABARD through subscription to debenture issues of land development banks.

Industries Sector	Large Scale:	All India Financial Institutions, IFCI, IDBI, ICICI
	Small Scale:	NSIC/SIDBI: All India level SFC/SIIC/SIDC: State Level SIDBI is All India level, apex institution
	Rehabilitation of Sick Units	IRBI (now IIBI)

Agricultural Sector	Refinance to co operative banks and states level land development/banks for their loans and advances to agricultural sector by NABARD. — Warehousing Corporations
External Trade	Export-Import (EXIM) Bank
Infrastructure (Transport, Communication, Power etc.)	Infrastructure Leasing and Financial Services Ltd., Infrastructure Development Finance Company, Rural Electrification Corporation.

There are specialised DFIs catering to financial and related needs of specific sectors like shipping, Tourism, Housing, Co operative Development etc. This listing is only illustrative and not exhaustive.

Development Financial Institutions: Growth Details

Since the late 1940s when the Development Financial Institutions (DFIs) appeared to fill the gap in the capital market with regard to the provision of long-term finance for the growth of the industries sector, the DFIs have increased in number and grown significantly in terms of the volume of financial assistance extended in diverse fields like industry, agriculture, external trade etc. The feature that makes DFIs distinct is the role played by the government in building up this institutional infrastructure to gear up the supply of long-term capital required for pursuing rapid development envisaged under strategic economic planning.

Over the years, the number of DFIs has increased manifold, their activities have also increased and diversified and yet the overall scene of DFIs remains a constantly changing scenario. New institutions are added, institutions are reorganised when their activities tend to overlap, they are reconstituted and even renamed to provide for changes in their activities. A few cases to illustrate this feature could be mentioned:

Agricultural Finance Corporation (1968)	: Reconstituted to form Agricultural Finance Consultant Ltd. (1988-89)
Agricultural Refinance Development Corporation (1963)	: Taken over by NABARD in 1982.
Industrial Reconstruction Corporation of India (1971)	: Renamed Industrial Reconstruction Bank of India (IRBI) (1985) : Converted into Industrial Investment Bank of India (IIBI) (1997)
Shipping Credit & Investment Corporation of (SCICI) (1986)	: Merged with ICICI (in 1996)
Infrastructure Devt. Finance Co.	: Started operations in Jan. 1997.

As a result, the total number of DFIs keeps on changing making it difficult to make a specific and correct mention of their total number operating in different fields and at different levels — national and state levels.

The growth in the volume of DFIs assistance expressed in sanctions and disbursement is given in Table 4.3.

Chart 4.1
Development Financial Institutions

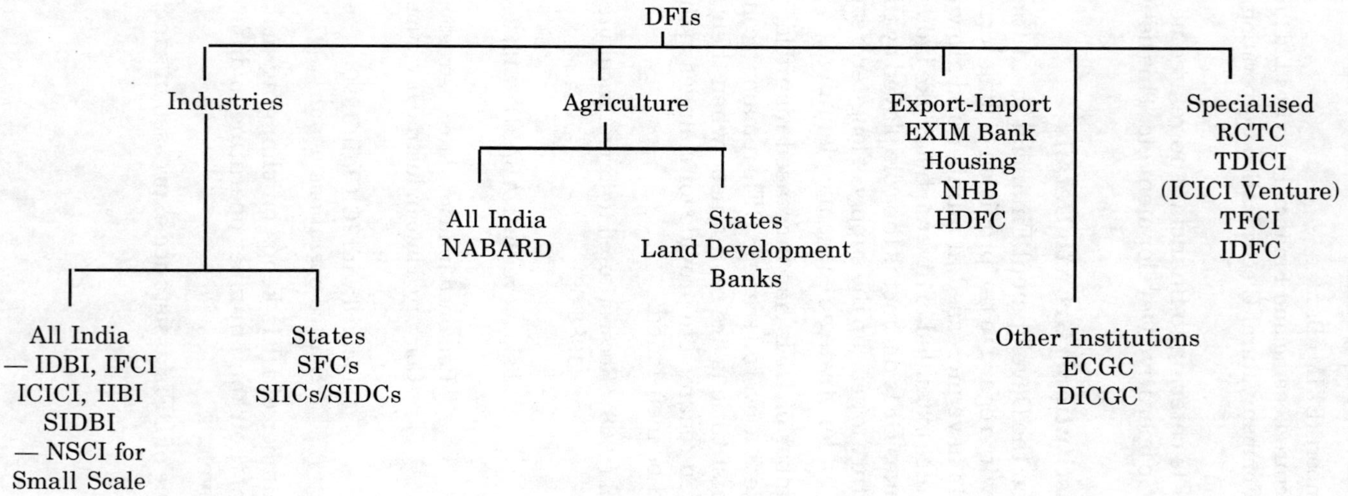

Note: RCTC: Risk Capital and Tech. Finance Corporation Ltd.
TFCI: Tourism Finance Corporation Ltd.
IDFC: Infrastructure Development Finance Company.

Table No. 4.3

Financial Assistance Sanctioned and Disbursed by All Financial Institutions

(*₹ in Crores*)

Period	*Sanctions*	*Disbursement*	*Disbursement to Sanctions (%)*
1948-51	8.13	5.79	71.1
1951-56	37.47	15.22	40.6
1956-61	212.24	142.02	66.9
1961-66	471.91	422.84	89.6
1966-69	374.78	335.93	89.6
1969-74	1452.61	984.20	67.7
1974-79	4737.90	3092.10	65.3
1979-84	18153.80	12476.40	68.7
1984-85	5550.7	3627.9	65.4
1985-86	6532.6	4940.0	75.6
1986-87	8118.4	5709.1	70.3
1987-88	9554.5	7061.1	73.9
1988-89	11286.7	7700.8	68.2
1989-90	14400.9	9639.7	66.9
1990-91	19202.4	12810.1	66.7
1991-92	22394.6	16260.0	72.6
1992-93	33196.1	23150.3	69.7
1993-94	40987.0	26624.3	64.9
1994-95	59275.3	33568.1	56.6
1995-96	64162.7	38649.5	60.2
1996-97	54641.2	42656.5	78.1
1997-98	77091.8	53647.9	69.6
1998-99	83695.6	58329.5	69.7
1999-00	101917.8	68594.2	67.3
2000-01	120548.1	75363.6	62.5
2001-02	75088.5	58734.7	78.2
2002-03	28310.9	26704.6	94.3
2003-04	40758.6	30172.7	74.0
2004-05	30403.9	21505.8	70.7
2005-06	27665.4	21145.5	76.4
2006-07	31259.4	38652.6	123.7
2007-08	58692.7	46008.4	78.4
2008-09	99967.2	88973.7	89.0

Source: Handbook of Statistics on Indian Economy, 2008-09.

Sources of Finance and Forms of Assistance

Sources of Finance: Besides the internal resources like repayment and reserves, the resource base of the DFIs consists of subscriptions to share capital and borrowings from the Government and RBI and other financial institutions including foreign currency borrowings. The other sources of funds are raising finance from the market through the bonds/debenture issues and now even in the form of public deposits. This has helped in broadening the resources base of DFIs. For the direct assistance by DFIs in the form of term loans, the DFIs get these refinanced from the apex institutions — IDBI, NABARD and SIDBI.

Form of Assistance

The DFIs provide both fund-based and non-fund based assistance. They extend financial assistance directly to industries and also help them in raising funds from other sources in terms of underwriting of new issues and the guaranteeing of term loans.

The financial assistance is extended by the DFIs in the form of term loans (rupee loans), foreign currency loans, underwriting of shares and direct subscriptions to equity and guarantees. The main component of the financial assistance from DFIs is the debt capital or the term loans extended on a security basis. Though the 'convertibility' clause forms part of the terms and conditions while granting term loans, and provides option for the conversion of loans into equity, the actual exercise of option by the DFIs is quite limited. The assistance is provided by the DFIs to private, public sector, joint sector and also co operative sector units. They prefer to provide debt capital as term loans and their subscriptions to debenture issues are less. The trends in the DFIs' financial assistance in the form of underwriting of shares and direct subscription to equity show a rise over the years indicating increased institutional support to the capital market, and the emergence of DFIs as important owners of industrial securities.

As described earlier, the DFIs extend fund-based and also non-fund based assistance in the form of promotional activities including underwriting of new shares, merchant banking services, guaranteeing of loans and advisory and consultancy services like identification of new industrial projects, preparation and evaluation of projects, project formulation, technical advice, project implementation, feasibility studies and market information.

Further Details of DFI's Assistance

As Development institutions, the DFIs in extending their assistance, are expected to foster the growth of industries and also ensure that considerations like growth of entrepreneurship, reducing concentrated ownership and regional distribution for balanced growth are pursued.

Composition of Financial Assistance

The rupee loans, foreign currency loans, underwriting and direct subscription and guarantees are the main types of financial assistance extended by the DFIs.

The rupee loans form the major part of the financial assistance from all financial institutions. Still, it could be seen from the Table 4.4 that the share of rupee loans in the total financial assistance has come down in the recent years from over 80 per cent in 1980s. There has been a distinct rise in the percentage shares of foreign currency loans and underwriting and direct subscription respectively from around 5 per cent to over 10 per cent and from around 10 per cent to over 20 per cent.

Regional Distribution

From the point of view of achieving balanced regional growth, the DFIs were expected to focus their attention on encouraging industrial activities in the backward areas. It has been noticed that the financial assistance of DFIs has substantially led growth of industries in those areas which were already developed and thereby accentuated regional disparities.

Table No. 4.4
Financial Assistance by All Financial Institutions
Break up as per Type of Assistance

(*₹ in Crores*)

Year	*Rupee Loans*		*Foreign Currency Loan*		*Underwriting and Direct Subscription*		*Guarantee*		*Total*	
	S	*D*	*S*	*D*	*S*	*D*	*S*	*D*	*S*	*D*
1983-84	3254.8	2437.8	281.2	134.7	437.1	287.1	80.4	4.7	4053.5	2864.3
	(80.3)	(85.11)	(6.9)	(4.7)	(10.8)	(10.0)	(2.0)	(0.2)		
1989-90	12342.5	8161.5	1562.9	556.8	2002.8	1259.5	840	23,9	15992.2	10001.7
	(77.2)	(81.6)	(9.8)	(5.6)	(12.5)	(12.6)	(0.5)	(0.2)		
1990-91	14111.5	9711.9	2493.2	1079.9	2295.4	1091.3	135.8	93.3	19035.9	11976.4
	(74.1)	(81.1)	(13.1)	(9.0)	(12.0)	(9.1)	(0.7)	(0.8)		
1993-94	24994.2	18701.1	2807.1	1857.1	11178.2	5633.2	2342.9	408.2	41322.4	265996
	(60.4)	(70.3)	(6.8)	(7.0)	(27.0)	(21.0)	(21.2)	(5.7)	(1.5)	
1997-98	46336.2	34229.4	8468.9	6804.2	17399.1	125662	9385.2	232.4	81598.4	53832.0
	(56.8)	(63.6)	(10.4)	(12.6)	(21.3)	(23.3)	(11.5)	(0.4)		

S: Sanctions

D: Disbursements

Note: Figures in parenthesis are percentage to the total.

Diffusion of Ownership

The trend of *ownership* in the private sector has been in the past, towards concentration in the hands of large business houses. To counter this trend, the DFIs were guided by the objective of evolving diffusion of ownership through their financial assistance. They could do little to resist this trend and the financial assistance did flow significantly in favour of relatively larger units belonging to large business houses. Over the years, this pattern has undergone a change and financial assistance is somewhat more scattered in favour of not so big units belonging to the new generation of entrepreneurs. The DFIs have now engaged themselves in entrepreneurship development and DFIs at the states level particularly endeavour to promote small-scale industries and even the tiny sector.

The other non-banking financial institutions which form part of the capital market are mentioned below and will be dealt with separately in the book.

Insurance Cos. **LIC:** Life Insurance Corporation of India (1956)

GIC: General Insurance Corporation set up 1971 took over subsidiaries in 1974.

The pattern of their investment of funds is laid down under the Act —

Central and State Government Securities, lending for socially desirable projects, *viz.,* housing, semi-government bonds, loans to companies, invest in shares/debentures of companies etc.

LIC and GIC set up their Mutual Funds in 1989-90 and also participate as lenders in the call money component of the money market.

Mutual Funds: UTI: Unit Trust of India set up in 1964 to mobilise savings from the low and middle income groups and provide them assured income by channelising these savings into productive investment.

Other Mutual Funds

1986: Public sector banks allowed to set up their mutual funds.

1989-90: LIC and GIC Mutual Funds.

Regulatory Institution

SEBI: Securities and Exchange Board of India.

Capital Issues (Control) Act, 1947 repealed in 1992.

SEBI was set up in 1988, but was granted statutory powers under the Act of 1992.

To protect the interest of investors, promote healthy growth of the securities market.

Control and regulate stock exchanges.

Other Services

Holding Custody and Transfer of Shares (SHCIL): Stock Holding Corporation of India Ltd. (1988).

Introduced book entry system for the quick transfer of shares.

Holding custody of securities.

Credit Rating (CRISIL): Credit Rating and Information Services of India Ltd. (January 1988).

To guide the investors by assigning rating to debt instruments of companies like debentures, deposits, preference shares and Commercial Papers (CPs).

It is now intended to turn to the major developments in respect of the financial institutions forming part of the money market like the Reserve Bank of India (RBI), the commercial banks, the co operative banks and Discount and Finance House of India (DFHI).

Reserve Bank of India (RBI)		**Early Developments**
Deposit Insurance	:	Deposit Insurance Corporation set up in 1962. To inspire greater public confidence in banks and thereby substantiate the banking habit.
Rural Credit	:	Agricultural Refinance and Development Corporation: (ARDC) Subsidiary of RBI, 1963. To strengthen Co operative credit structure: increased amount of RBI refinance.
Credit Guarantee	:	Credit Guarantee Scheme for small-scale industries, 1960.
Credit Authorisation Scheme	:	Introduced in 1965 to regulate the flow of bank credit to large borrowers.
Selective Credit Control, Credit Allocation and Credit Planning	:	*Macro level:* Credit planning Credit allocation. *Credit Control:* to change the composition of credit.
		Later Developments
Deposit Insurance & Credit Guarantee	:	**Credit Guarantee Corporation established in 1971.** To provide guarantee cover to banks in respect of loans to small borrowers. Credit Guarantee Corporation merged with Deposit Insurance Corporation in 1978. New institution was formed — Deposit Insurance and Credit Guarantee Corporation (DICGC).
Rural Credit	:	**Regional Rural Banks set up in 1975.** To develop rural economy. To provide credit and other facilities to agriculture and other production activities in rural areas. NABARD: took over ARDC in 1982.
Credit Authorisation	:	Withdrawn in 1988, replaced by post-sanction scrutiny under the credit monitory arrangement.

Commercial Banks: Major Developments

- **Nationalisation** 1969: 14 banks

  1980: 6 banks

  1955: SBI formed by conversion of Imperial Bank of India.

  1959: Conversion of state-associated banks as the subsidiaries of SBI making total of 8 banks in the SBI group.

- **Shift in Approach of Commercial Banks:**

Prior to Nationalisation:
- Liquidation approach
- Bank lending guided by — safety, liquidity and profitability
- With emphasis on security, the banks looked to assets of the borrowers.

Post-nationalisation:
- 'Going concern' approach
- Bank lending on the basis of:

  — needs of the borrowers

  — their ability to repay.

- Branch Expansion: 1962: RBI followed a programme of branch expansion particularly in semi-urban, rural and other unbanked areas.

  1978: focus shifted from branch expansion to consolidation.

- Social control of Banks: 1968: allocation of commercial bank credit — to priority sectors:
  - Earlier 3 sectors: agriculture, small-scale industries and exports
  - as recommended by National Credit Council

    Subsequently added:
  - road and water transport operators
  - Professional and self-employed persons
  - Retail trade and small business, Education

    — prescribed CRR and SLR requirements.

- Lead Bank Scheme (1969): Scheme of RBI —
  - Emphasising 'area approach'
  - District Credit Plans to be prepared.
  - Major scheduled banks to play the lead role and co-ordinate the activities of other financial institutions in respective districts.

- Consortium Approach : Introduced by RBI in 1974.
  - Large credit limits: more than one bank can finance a single borrower.

- New Instruments:
  - Participation certificates, Inter-bank Participation.

Co operative Banks

The co operative credit institutions are agricultural and also non-agricultural. The agricultural segment of co operative credit has a 3-tier structure:

	Agricultural	Non-agricultural
State level:	State Co operative Banks (SCBs)	Urban Co operative Banks
Districts level:	Central Co operative Banks (CCBs)	
Village level:	Primary Agricultural Credit Societies (PACS)	

These institutions are engaged in financing rural and agricultural development.

Efforts to Strengthen Co operative Credit Structure

1963: Agricultural Refinance and Development Corporation (ARDC) set up as subsidiary of the Reserve Bank of India to increase refinance provision.

1969: Nationalisation of 14 commercial banks: Shift in the role in terms of emphasis on the provision of credit to priority sectors including agriculture.

1975: Regional Rural Banks — created to operate exclusively in rural areas.

1982: NABARD: an apex institution to strengthen the rural credit structure.

The contribution of institutional sources in rural credit which was less than 4 per cent in 1954 increased to 62 per cent in 1990.

Discount and Finance House of India (DFHI)

The DFHI was set up by the RBI in April 1988 and it is jointly owned by the the public sector commercial banks and the all-India financial institutions.

It has been set up to deal in the call money market both as lender and borrower and also in other money market instruments like treasury bills (182 days Treasury Bills), Commercial bills, and others like Commercial Papers (CPs) and Certificates of Deposits (CDs) etc.

DFHI plays both a developmental and a stabilising role. The development role lies in stimulating activity in the money market instruments particularly in the secondary markets. The stabilising role relates to the DFHI playing as a money market intermediary to even out the demand for and supply of short-term finance.

(b) Financial Markets

The major developments in financial markets, *i.e.,* Money Market and Capital Market during 1947-1990 are now recorded. The features of financial markets in India indicate that they remained less developed during the said period. The financial markets were subject to tight regulations, had limited number of participants and dealt with limited number of financial instruments. The financial reforms initiated during 1980s as applied to the financial markets consisted of measures taken up for broadening and deepening of the markets.

Money Market

The money market consisted of sub-parts such as call money market, treasury bills market and commercial bills market till the end of the decade of 1980s when the markets came up to deal with new instruments introduced like commercial paper (as in January 1990), Certificate of Deposits (CDs in June 1984).

The developments took place towards the end of the decade of 1980s by way of certain measures introduced in accordance with the recommendations of the Chakravarty Committee (1985) and the Vaghul Working Group (1987).

- **Call Money Market**

The participants in the call money market were commercial banks, co-operative banks and foreign banks:

1970:	Participation by financial institutions (other than banks) like LIC and UTI was allowed as lenders.
1973:	A ceiling on the call rate was fixed.
April 1988:	Discount and Finance House of India (DFHI) was set up by RBI. DFHI operations activate and also stabilise the call money market as it participates both as lender and borrower.
May 1989:	Ceiling on call money rate removed.
May 1990:	The participation by the financial institutions — GIC, IDBI and NABARD as lenders was permitted.
October 1990:	All participants in the bills rediscounting market were allowed to operate as lenders.

With effect from May 1990, the number of participants in bills rediscounting market has been increased to include —

All-India Financial Institutions	:	IDBI, ICICI, IFCI, IRBI (now IIBI), SCICI, IFCI, SIDBI, NABARD, ECGC.
Mutual Funds	:	UTI, SBI Mutual Fund, LIC Mutual Fund, Canbank Mutual Fund
Insurance Companies	:	LIC, GIC.
Other Institutions	:	Select urban co-operative banks, National Housing Bank EXIM Bank DFHI.

- **Treasury Bills Market**

91 days Treasury Bills

Earlier	:	Sold by tender at weekly auctions.
July 1965 onwards	:	Available throughout the week 'on tap.'
182 days Treasury Bills	:	Introduced by RBI in November 1986. These are sold through auction. The auctions are held fortnightly with effect from July 1988. These bills cannot be purchased by the state governments and PF organisations.
Refinance facilities	:	April 1987 The refinance to the holders of these bills (other than DFHI) available from are RBI. The Refinance facilities extended to DFHI in April 1988.

		The secondary market has developed as the refinance facilities are available to DFHI and other holders of these bills.

● Commercial Bills Market

To develop the commercial bills market, the RBI introduced the following schemes —

1952 Scheme	:	Bills could be used as security by the banks for the loans from the RBI.
1970 Scheme	:	Commercial banks are eligible for offering bills to the RBI for rediscounting. Discounting of genuine Trade Bills.
June 1974	:	RBI permitted scheduled commercial banks to rediscount genuine trade bills with other commercial banks, LIC, GIC, UTI and ICICI.
Earlier	:	A ceiling on the rate at which bills could be discounted by banks with other banks.
May 1989	:	Ceiling has been withdrawn by the RBI.
May 1990	:	The number of participants in the bills rediscounting market was increased to include All-India Financial Institution Mutual Funds, Insurance Companies — LIC, GIC and other institutions including DFHI, select urban co-operative banks, NHB and EXIM Bank.

Capital Market

The real sector production units in the private and public sector approach the capital market for meeting their long-term funds requirements in the form of debt finance and/or equity finance. The gilt-edged securities market is a subsidiary of the capital market which enables the governments — central and state and the semi-government authorities to raise long-term funds for financing development projects.

Institutionalisation of Capital market is a significant development during this period which has helped in widening of the market. In regard to the debt finance, the development of prime importance is the setting up of an array of *development financial institutions* at the All-India and the states level. The other type of institution is the *investment institutions* including LIC, GIC and UTI which mobilise savings through their schemes and participate in the capital market — the new issues market — by subscribing to industrial securities, *i.e.,* new issues of shares, debentures/bonds and also to government securities.

There was a sudden spurt in the institutionalisation of capital market when nearly 16 Mutual Funds were set up by the banks and the financial institutions towards the end of the 1980s. Of these 16 mutual funds newly set up between 1986 and 1990, seven were overseas funds for collecting subscriptions from residents abroad.

This period of 1980s signifies the setting up of new institutions which provided the necessary infrastructure for the capital market —

CRISIL (1988) : Credit rating: assigning rating to debt instruments.

SCHIL (1988) : Holding custody of securities, facilitating transfer of shares.

SEBI (1988) : To promote healthy growth of the securities market.

Merchant Banking

The other facet of development by way of facilitating services for the new issues market is the appearing of merchant banking services after the 1970s. Merchant banking institutions came up as either separate divisions/subsidiaries of the banks and the financial institutions. SBI Capital Markets Ltd. (1972) and ICICI Merchant Banking division (1974) were followed by other banks like Bank of Baroda, Bank of India, Canara Bank, Punjab National Bank, Central Bank of India and the separate divisions of IDBI and IFCI among financial institutions. The private consultancy firms have also set up their organisations to offer these services. The services offered by merchant bankers are meant for marketing corporate and other securities inclusive of 'underwriting', *i.e.,* guaranteeing sales and distribution of shares. The merchant bankers now take up other services like project counselling, issue management etc.

Stock Exchanges: The stock market has a *'secondary'* segment in 'stock exchanges' which expanded in number to eight stock exchanges in 1980-81 and to 18 in 1988-89. The number of companies listed at various stock exchanges grew from 3883 at December-end 1984 to 5841 in 1988 and to 6229 at March-end 1991 — at an average annual growth of 10.6 per cent. The market capitalisation of all listed stocks increased from ₹ 11,636 crore at December-end 1983 to ₹ 1,10,279 crore by March-end 1991 — at an average annual rate of 38.5 per cent.

(c) Financial Instruments

The different segments of the financial market remained less developed and a prominent feature reflecting the low level of development was the limited financial instruments dealt with. The state of financial markets continued to be insufficiently developed upto the 1980s when some reforms were introduced in accordance with the recommendations of the Chakravarty Committee (1985) and the Vaghul Working Group on the money system.

Money Market Instruments: The money market instruments consisted mainly of call (overnight) and short notice (14 days) money, inter-bank term money, commercial bills and treasury bills. Among these, call and short notice money and treasury bills were significant as the commercial bills market played only a limited role inspite of various efforts made by the Reserve Bank to develop its operations.

The developments with regard to both call and short notice money, commercial bills and treasury bills have been recorded separately under financial markets. It is now intended to make mention of other financial instruments, particularly Commercial Paper (CP) and Certificate of Deposit (CD) introduced newly during 1989-90. The prominent players in the money market are banks, financial institutions and primary dealers (PDs).

Long-term Bills: The long-term bills with maturity upto five years were introduced in 1965 to finance transactions arising out of the sale of machinery on the deferred payment basis. These bills are eligible for refinance under the IDBI scheme.

Participation Certificates and Inter-bank Participation

Participation Certificates (PCs) were introduced by Reserve Bank in 1970, making it possible for the bank to sell a part of the loans granted. The use of PCs declined after 1980.

Inter-bank Participating (IBP): IBPs are inter-bank instruments either on risk-sharing and on non-risk sharing basis. The interest rate ceiling on inter-bank participation certificates was withdrawn in May 1989 along with those on rediscounting of bills and inter-bank term money.

Commercial Papers (CPs): Commercial Paper as a money market instrument was introduced by the apex bank in January 1990.

Commercial paper is to be issued by the companies with specified net worth (earlier ₹ 10 crore reduced to ₹ 4 crore) for working capital purposes.

The issue of CP should be for a minimum of ₹ one crore (later reduced to ₹ 25 lakh) and for the maturity period of 91 days to 6 months (later modified to 30 days to one year).

The maximum permissible bank finance for the company in respect of working capital requirements should not be less than ₹ 25 crore (later reduced to ₹ 4 crore).

During the 1990s, the requirements for issue of CPs were progressively relaxed:

— delinking of CP from the cash credit component of maximum permissible bank finance.

— extent of CP that can be issued was raised to 100 per cent of the working capital credit limit.

Certificate of Deposit (CD): The Certificate of Deposit was introduced in June 1989. Only banks can issue CDs. All-India financial institutions like IDBI, ICICI, IFCI have been allowed to issue CDs since 1991-92.

CDs are issued by banks against deposits kept by individuals, companies and institutions.

Limit on Issue of CDs: 1% of average aggregate deposits raised to 10% subsequently abolished in October 1993.

Minimum Amount for CD: ₹ one crore reduced to ₹ 50 lakh lowered to ₹ 10 lakh and now to ₹ 5 lakh.

Tenure of CD: 91 days to one year minimum lock-in period was reduced to 30 days and further to 15 days.

Money Market Mutual Funds

April 1992: Allowed to be set up by scheduled commercial banks and All-India financial institutions. The progress is quite limited as only three funds are operational by the end of decade of 90s.

Capital Market Instruments

The major instruments issued by the private corporate sector are equity shares, preference shares and debentures, those issued by government, quasi government bodies are government securities and those by public sector undertakings and financial institutions are the bonds.

New Developments

Preference shares

- Cumulative Convertible Preference shares (CCPs).
- CCPs were introduced in August 1985.
- Public Ltd. companies can issue CCPs for setting up new projects, expansion and diversification of existing activities, for normal capital expenditure and working capital needs.

- Fully convertible into equity shares between 3rd and 5th years of issue.

Debentures:

1970s : Issuing of convertible debentures and rights debentures.

Convertible debentures:

As per specified terms and conditions converted into ordinary shares.

Rights debentures:

- These are issued on a right basis to the existing shareholders.
- Issued to raise finance for long-term working capital requirements.

January 1989 : Partly Convertible Debentures (PCBs), buyback facility is provided relating to the non-convertible portion.

Bonds:

1980s : Public Sector Undertakings issuing bonds (PSU Bonds).

These bonds are not redeemable. These bonds are transferable.

Capital Gains Bonds: issued by financial institutions like IDBI, NHB.

NRI Bonds: Offered by SBI to NRIs

- The first series of bonds issued in 1988.

Purpose: Remitting dollar denominated funds of NRIs.

Railway Bonds: Issued by Indian Railway Finance Corporation in 1991.

III. GROWTH OF INDIAN FINANCIAL SYSTEM

It is proposed to describe the growth in Indian Financial System in the recent years in terms of both: (a) the quantitative indicators as well as (b) the qualitative changes and performs.

(a) Quantitative Indicators of Growth in Financial System

The growth in Indian financial system is explained with the help of quantitative indicators of financial development:

1. Broad Indicators

(i) Flow of funds: Extent of Financial Intermediation

(ii) Contribution of finance-related activities in real GDP.

(iii) Financial development ratios.

(i) Flow of Funds

As discussed in the Chapter 2 under flow of funds analysis for the Indian economy, the flow of funds statement is prepared by dividing the economy into six sectors: Private Corporate business, household, government, rest of the world, banking, other financial institutions.

In the Table 4.5 and Table 4.6, the financial flows in India for the years 1987-88 and 1995-96 have been presented. The tables indicate intersectoral transactions in the form of 'Sources', *i.e.,* increase in liabilities and 'Uses', *i.e.,* increase in assets and also the overall total level of financial activities for the economy as a whole. The creation of liabilities and acquisition of assets is expressed in the tables in the form of –

Table No. 4.5 : Financial Flows: Sectorwise: 1987-88

(₹ in Crores)

Sector/Financial Transactions with other sectors	Banking		Other Financial Institutions		Private Corporate Sector		Government		Rest of the World		Household		Total	
	Sources	Uses	Sources	Uses	Sources	Uses	Sources	Uses	Sources	Uses	Sources	Uses	Sources	Uses
1	2	3	4	5	6	7	8	9	10	11	12	13	14	15
1. Currency & deposits	21,121	40	990	3,529	697	598	4,815	– 73	– 181	1,421	—	19252 (54.8)	27,442 (24.12)	25,258 (23.06)
2. Investments	351	14,736	4,428	4,683	3,215	121	14,684	496	– 859	– 91	—	2,777	21,819 (19.18)	22,722 (20.75)
(a) Government securities	—	12,264 (10.0)	—	1,894	—	61	14,327	—	—	– 114	—	34	14,327 (12.59)	14,139 (12.91)
(b) Other Government securities	—	501	—	393	—	—	357	—	—	—	—	228 (0.65)	357 (0.31)	1,122 (1.02)
(c) Corporate securities	—	383	—	25	3,215	—	—	176	—	23	—	804 (2.29)	3,215 (2.82)	3,323 (3.03)
(d) Bank securities	351	—	—	25	—	1	—	139	—	—	—	95	351 (0.30)	260 (0.30)
(e) Other financial institution securities	—	1126	4,428	—	—	—	—	138	—	—	—	1616 (4.6)	4,428 (3.89)	2,880 (2.63)
(f) Foreign securities	—	34	—	26	—	–6	—	—	–859	—	—	—	–859	54
(g) Others	—	428	—	408	—	65	—	43	—	—	—	—	—	944 (0.86)
3. Loans and Advances	– 504	9999 (22.0)	3,025	8,296	3,798	1,684	6,610	795	– 204	3,323	7,915	—	20,040 (17.61)	24,096 (222.0)
4. Small savings	—	—	—	—	—	—	—	3633	—	—	—	3633 (10.34)	3,633 (3.19)	3,633 (3.31)
5. Life Fund	—	—	2,047	—	—	—	—	549	—	12	—	2584 (7.36)	2,596 (2.28)	2,596 (2.37)
6. PF	—	—	3,580	—	—	—	—	2676	—	—	—	6256 (17.8)	6,256 (5.49)	6,256 (5.49)
7. Compulsory Deposits	– 50	—	—	—	—	—	—	—	—	—	—	– 50	– 50	– 50
8. Trade debit and credit	—	—	– 10	—	62	—	28	1500	—	—	—	161	80 (0.07)	1,661 (1.5)
9. Foreign claims not elsewhere classified	2071	– 384	2	—	—	—	—	1070	– 636	706	—	—	1,437 (1.26)	1,392 (1.27)
10. Other items not elsewhere classified	26,212	21,051	1,232	487	1,453	– 80	1,601	466	—	—	—	—	30,498 (26.81)	21,924 (20.02)
Total	49,201	45,442	15,294	16,955	8,625	2,323	34,596	4254	– 1,880	5,361	7,915	35,113	1,13,751	1,09,488

Table No. 4.6 : Financial Flows: Sectorwise: 1995-96

(₹ in Crores)

Sector/Financial Transactions with other sectors	Banking		Other Financial Institutions		Private Corporate Sector		Government		Rest of the World		Household		Total	
	Sources	Uses	Sources	Uses	Sources	Uses	Sources	Uses	Sources	Uses	Sources	Uses	Sources	Uses
1	2	3	4	5	6	7	8	9	10	11	12	13	14	15
1. Currency & deposits	76,825	1,416	12,494	8,999	2,887	12,588	7,674	3,968	255	3,683	—	69,718 (55.78)	1,00,135 (23.05)	1,00,372 (22.18)
2. Investments	2,765	34,835	9,338	56,482	39,574	1,230	46,858	1,078	– 10,001	16,283	—	9,546	88,534 (20.38)	1,19,454 (26.4)
(a) Government securities	—	38,090 (31.08)	—	40,648	—	– 442	46,441	—	—	9	—	28	46,441 (10.7)	78,333 (17.39)
(b) Other Government securities	—	–1,192	—	–1,699	—	—	417	—	—	—	—	581 (0.46)	417	– 2,310
(c) Corporate securities	—	466	—	16,342	39,574	—	—	886	—	16,274	—	5,083 (4.06)	39,574 (9.1)	39,051 (8.63)
(d) Bank securities	2,765	—	—	3,055	—	239	—	– 467	—	—	—	112	2,765 (0.6)	2,939 (0.65)
(e) Other financial institution securities	—	–1,851	9,338	—	—	– 457	—	726	—	—	—	3,742 (2.99)	9,338 (2.15)	2,160 (0.48)
(f) Foreign securities	—	– 625	—	96	—	389	—	—	– 10,001	—	—	—	– 10,001	–140
(g) Others	—	– 53	—	– 1,960	—	1,501	—	– 67	—	—	—	—	—	– 579
3. Loans and Advances	9,621	51,200 (42.4)	32,206	66,256	85,488	26,839	11,282	9,301	45	– 3,757	25466	—	1,64,108 (37.8)	1,49,659 (33.070
4. Small savings	—	—	—	38	—	—	9,187	—	—	—	—	9,149 (7.32)	9,187 (2.1)	9,187 (2.03)
5. Life Fund	—	—	12,768	—	—	—	1,170	—	—	44	—	13894 (11.1)	13,938 (3.2)	13,938 (3.08)
6. PF	—	—	13,498	—	—	—	8,794	—	—	—	—	22,292 (17.8)	22,292 (5.1)	22,292 (4.9)
7. Compulsory Deposits	—	—	—	—	—	—	—	—	—	—	—	–7	– 7	– 7
8. Trade debit and credit	—	—	534	—	– 140	—	388	– 501	—	—	—	394	782	– 107
9. Foreign claims not elsewhere classified	—	– 5,308	—	—	—	—	—	509	1,740	– 5,895	—	—	1,740	– 10,694
10. Other items not elsewhere classified	– 13	40,595	9,087	6,422	18,850	609	5,675	819	—	—	—	—	33,599	48,445
Total	89,191	1,22,558	89,925	1,38,197	1,46,659	41,266	91,028	15,174	– 7,961	10,358	25466	124987	434308	4,52,539

Currency and deposits
Investments
Loans and Advances
Small Savings
Life Fund
Provident Fund
Compulsory deposits
Trade debts and credits

Though it would be interesting to compare and analyse the tables in fuller details, some observations have been recorded to show the trends in financial activities in the country.

The figures in brackets indicate percentages of columnwise totals.

Column-wise: The place of the item in the particular sector's total liabilities (sources) and total assets (uses).

Row-wise: The share of the sector holding of a particular asset or liability in the overall total of assets/liabilities.

These tables could be analysed and understood as under:

During the period: *1987-88 to 1995-96:*

Column-wise: Banking Sector: The shares of investment in government securities in total assets of the sector has increased from 10% to over 31%.

The shares of loans and advances in total assets has increased from 22% to over 42%.

Household sector: The share of investment in corporate securities in total assets of the sector has increased from 2.29% to over 4%.

The shares of currency and deposit in total assets of the sector have remained nearly the same at around 55%.

Row-wise: Private corporate business: The shares of loans and advances in the overall total liabilities have increased from 18.9% to over 52%.

Rest of the world (External sector): The shares of investment in corporate securities in the overall total assets have increased from 0.7% to nearly 42%.

The above examples have been mentioned by way of illustration.

During the period, the total financial flows have increased nearly four times from ₹ 1,13,751 crore to ₹ 4,34,308 crore.

- The shares of loans and advances corporate securities in the overall total liabilities have significantly increased.
- The share of government securities in the overall total liabilities has fallen from 12.6% to 10.7%.
- The share of investments in the overall total assets has gone up from 20.75% to 26.4%.

The asset-wise distribution of the financial saving of the household sector shows that bank deposits, PF, Life Insurance Policies, Small Savings, Corporate Securities, other financial institution securities like units (UTI) are important.

Extent of Financial Intermediation: The flow of funds from the surplus sectors, mainly the household sector to the deficit sectors such as government, corporates takes place either directly or through intermediaries like banks and other financial institutions (OFIs). Primary issues arise when funds flow directly and secondary issues denote funds flowing through the financial intermediaries, *i.e.,* banks and OFIs. The distribution of Total issues between Primary issues and Secondary issues and particularly increase in the share of secondary issues shows the extent of financial intermediation.

Table No. 4.7
Primary and Secondary Issues

(₹ in Crores)

Year	*Primary Issues*	*Secondary Issues*	*Total Issues*
1970-71	3,541 (60.3)	2,336 (39.7)	5,877
1980-81	21,452 (59.3)	14,731 (40.7)	36,183
1985-86	42,006 (57.9)	30,558 (42.1)	72,564
1990-91	96,508 (57.6)	71,016 (42.4)	1,67,524
1991-92	1,31,916 (55.4)	1,06,386 (44.6)	2,38,302
1992-93	1,13,990 (54.3)	95,790 (45.7)	2,09,780
1993-94	1,59,200 (52.7)	1,42,897 (47.3)	3,02,097
1994-95	2,08,182 (52.3)	1,89,96 (47.7)	3,98,178
1995-96	2,55,192 (58.8)	1,79,116 (41.2)	4,34,308

(ii) Contribution of finance-related activities in real GDP

It is expressed in terms of the contribution of banking and insurance in GDP.

Table No. 4.8
Real GDP Originating in Banking and Insurance

(Per cent)

Period	*Share of Banking and Insurance in GDP*	*Share of Banking and Insurance in Service Sector*
1970-71 to 1974-75	2.2	5.7
1975-76 to 1979-80	2.7	6.8
1980-81 to 1984-85	3.1	7.5
1985-86 to 1992-93	4.9	11.2
1993-94 to 1998-99	4.7	11.8

Source: Report on Currency and Finance, RBI 1999-2000.

As could be seen from the above Table, the real GDP originating in banking and insurance has steadily increased from 2.2 per cent to 4.7 per cent during the period. The share of finance-related activities — banking and insurance has also gone up from 5.7 per cent to 11.8 per cent in regard to services sector.

(iii) Financial Development Ratios

In the earlier chapter, the following ratios and their significance in regard to indicating the financial development have been explained in full details.

Finance ratio (FR)

Financial Interrelation Ratio (FIR)

New Issues Ratio (NIR)

Intermediation Ratio (IR)

Table 4.9

Financial Development Ratios

Ratio to	*80-81 to 84-85*	*85-86 to 89-90*	*1990 to 91*	*1991 to 92*	*1992 to 93*	*1993 to 94*	*1994 to 95*	*1995 to 96*
1. Finance Ratio (FR)	0.34	0.40	0.40	0.5	0.38	0.47	0.52	0.49
2. Financial Interrelation Ratio (FIR)	2.42	2.40	1.75	2.92	2.18	2.83	2.43	2.26
3. New Issues Ratio (NIR)	1.42	1.40	1.0	1.62	1.19	1.49	1.16	1.33
4. Intermediation Ratio (IR)	0.69	0.72	0.74	0.81	0.84	0.9	0.91	0.7

Source: Report on Currency and Finance RBI, 1999-2000.

$$\text{Finance Ratio (FR)} = \frac{\text{Total financial claims}}{\text{National income}}$$

Total Financial claims *i.e.,* primary issues + secondary issues

Financial Interrelation Ratio (FIR)

$$= \frac{\text{Total financial claims}}{\text{Net physical capital formation}}$$

$$\text{New Issues Ratio (NIR)} = \frac{\text{Primary issues}}{\text{Net physical capital formation}}$$

$$\text{Intermediation ratio (IR)} = \frac{\text{Secondary issues}}{\text{Primary issues}}$$

Over the years, there has been an increase in the values of all the four ratios indicating financial development. As you are aware, the development of financial system lies in mobilising more savings and channelising these into the real physical productive investment. An increase in FR indicates that the financial system is more effective in creating financial assets alongwith the economic development in the country. Similarly, the increase in FIR indicates the effectiveness of financial system in creating financial assets for funding of investment. NIR indicates the extent to which real sector production units fund their investment by going directly to the public. IR shows the effectiveness of the role of financial intermediaries.

2. Specific Indicators of financial development

- **Credit based aggregate deposits/GDP ratio:** role of intermediation played by banks.
- **Liquidity-based:** M_3/GDP ratio

Period	*Aggregate Deposits*	M_3
	(as per cent of GDP at market prices)	
1980-81 to 1984-85	30.0	39.1
1985-86 to 1989-90	36.1	45.4
1990-91 to 1994-95	39.6	49.3
1995-96 to 1999-2000	43.8	53.8

Source: Report on Currency and Finance, RBI 1999-2000.

- **Banking-based Indicators**

Per capita deposit :	1969 : ₹ 88	Per capita credit 1969	: ₹ 68
	1999-2000 : ₹ 8247	1999-2000	: ₹ 4705

- **Financial Indicators Relating to Non-banking Financial Sector**

Disbursement by	*Period*	*Per cent*
Financial Institutions	First half of 1970s	0.5
(as percentage of GDP)	First half of 1980s	1.4
	First half of 1990s	2.9
	Second half of 1990s	3.3

Resources Mobilisation by	*Period*	*Per cent*
Mutual Funds	1970-71 to 1974-75	0.04
(as percentage of GDP)	1990-91 to 1992-93	1.59
	1994-95	1.12

(b) *Qualitative Changes and Reforms*

The growth of Indian financial system viewed in terms of the qualitative changes or improvements in the recent years when the reform process has been initiated and gathered momentum lies in: (i) the extent to which and how effectively the financial sector of Indian economy acts as a conduit for mobilisation and transfer of funds from the net savers (say household sector) to the net borrowers (*i.e.,* deficit sectors like private corporate and public sector). How far the real productive sectors of the economy would gain depends on the quantitative increase and the qualitative improvement in the performance of the financial sector. In the present context of economic liberalisation under overall economic reforms, the need for a strong and viable financial sector (system) is even greater, and (ii) the transformation of the system by removing structural weaknesses inhibiting/limiting the functioning of its constituents, *i.e.,* financial institutions, financial markets and instruments, with a view to evolve a vibrant financial system.

The main thrust or focus of changes or reforms in the financial sector in the first half of decade of 1990s was on liberalisation, *i.e.*, deregulation — such as lowering of statutory pre-emptions, dismantling of administered interest rates structure and operational autonomy. There has been in the second half of 1990s, a greater concern for prudential measures like increase in capital to risk-weighted assets ratio (CRAR) to 10%, stricter NPA norms and provisioning requirements and adherence to asset-liability management and risk management guidelines.

The details of changes witnessed in regard to the structure, the participants and their interrelationships have been described separately under different chapters. It is intended here to put together some aspects of changes in these financial system in relation to certain yardsticks indicating maturity, diversity and sophistication of the system.

Information Technology: In recent times, information technology and the communications networking systems have virtually transformed the domain of operations of banks and other financial institutions all over the world. Recently, in India the advances in information technology have made inroads in the banks and other components of the financial sector.

- In the banking field, since the introduction of MICR cheques in mid-1980s, RBI has proceeded to make significant improvements in the functioning with respect to the application of information technology such as — introduction of electronic funds transfer, introduction of automated teller machines (ATMs), introduction of inter-bank electronic payments system etc.
- The technological developments in electronic payments systems and communication systems have given rise to closer linkage between the domestic and international capital markets.
- The open outcry trading system prevalent in our stock exchanges has been replaced by online screen-based electronic trading. The electronic trading and order matching system has been introduced in all 23 stock exchanges which have nearly 8,000 trading terminals spread all over the country.
- The 'dematerialisation' of shares is at the top of several measures undertaken by SEBI to promote efficiency and investor protection in the stock exchanges. Between March 1998 and Dec. 1999, the number of 'demat' shares has increased from 1.8 billion to 12.7 billion shares. The list of scrips for compulsory dematerialised trading now consists of 200 scrips. The proportion of 'demat' shares in the total delivery value at NSE increased from 2.5% in April 1998 to 79.3% in Dec. 99.

Certain changes with regard to the constituents of the financial system are now recorded.

Institutions

Towards the end of the decade of 1980s, new institutions were set up such DFHI in money market with a prime role in call money market and SHCIL, CRISIL and SEBI for rendering specific services in the capital market.

In decade of 1990s, new institutions were set up — over-the-counter-exchange (OTCEI) — a stock exchange for small companies, National Stock Exchange (NSE) as a complementary to existing exchanges, (STCI) — Securities Trading Corporation of India for promoting secondary market in Government securities, (IDFC) — Infrastructure Development Finance Company for financing projects in power, telecommunications etc.

One significant aspect in regard to the institutional set-up is the 'role transformation' as between the activities and operations of DFIs and the banks. A working group appointed by RBI under the chairmanship of Shri S.H. Khan in this regard submitted its report in May 1998. Economic survey 1999-2000 records this change as "Recent years have witnessed a blurring of the barriers between banks and AIFIs (All-India Financial Institutions). While the banks have entered the domain of project financing, AIFIs have entered the areas of working capital financing."

In regard to investment institutions like insurance companies and mutual funds, the significant change during 1990s is the introduction of competition. As many as 31 mutual funds were set up in the private sector during 1990s. The insurance sector has been thrown open to the private sector with the passing of Insurance Regulatory and Development Authority Act, 1999.

In regard to the structural aspects of Indian financial system, it is said, that it is 'dualistic' having organised ad 'unorganised' components considered as an obstacle for an integrated growth of the system. The Non-banking Financial Companies (NBFCs) have recorded a rapid growth in the recent years and yet remained unregulated till recently, except for the directives issued by RBI from time to time. The NBFCs like finance companies, hire purchase finance companies, chit funds, nidhis etc. belong to unorganised sector, raise funds from the public in the form of deposits and also lend. As only 20 per cent of NBFCs submitted their returns to RBI, their activities remained exposed to limited degree of regulation. To ensure that NBFCs function on healthy lines and to safeguard the depositor's interest, RBI Act was amended in Jan. 1997 under which RBI acquired powers to register NBFCs and regulate their working so that they align themselves suitably with the overall functioning of the system.

Financial Markets and Instruments

Financial Markets: Several developments during 1990s have: (a) helped in broadening, deepening of markets, (b) have led to closer integration between different segments of the market and between domestic and the international capital markets and (c) have ensured maintaining integrity with enhancement in the levels of transparency of financial statements and standards of disclosures, and ensuring safety of the markets through risk containment measures.

Money Market: The core segment of money market, *i.e.,* call money market broadened to a considerable extent with the entry of non-bank participants, *i.e.,* all participants in the bills rediscounting market and mutual funds as lenders.

With a view to deepening the money market, RBI in July 1999, introduced guidelines on interest rate swaps (IRS) and forward rate agreements (FRAs) to enable banks, the primary dealers and financial institutions to hedge interest rates.

To influence short-term liquidity, RBI introduced in December 1992 'Repos' transactions.

Repos: repo operations refer to selling government securities to repurchase later: usually 14 days. The time-length reduced to 3-4 days to absorb very short-term liquidity and further to daily Repos.

Repo operations by means of government securities is conducted by RBI. Besides this, RBI has allowed Repo transactions among banks and other select institutions in PSU Bonds and private corporate sector debt securities.

Reverse Repos: This facility was started by RBI in 1994-95 to provide liquidity support to the primary dealers including DFHI, STCI etc. The RBI intervenes the market to arrest excess liquidity.

Government Securities Market

Several measures have been taken to bring about qualitative changes in different aspects like settlement practices, maturity structure etc. in terms of introduction of delivery vs. payment system, shifting maturity structure in favour of medium or short-term borrowing. The investor base in government securities market has been broadened allowing even FIIs to invest in government securities. The secondary market in government securities has grown significantly since 1994.

Capital Market

New Issues Market: The infrastructure of market has become diversified with the setting up of a number of merchant bankers, investment consultancy agencies and registrar to issue etc. The market has widened and deepened as the public sector banks, financial institutions and PSUs are raising resources from the market.

Secondary Market:

- risk containment measures including trade/settlement guarantee funds set up by 10 stock exchanges.
- disclosure standards strengthened to protect investor's interests.
- settlement cycles shortened from 14 days to 7 days.

Integration of domestic capital market with international capital market:

- FIIs allowed to invest in both equity shares and debt instruments.
- Indian corporate units allowed to raise capital from International capital markets through issues of GDR/ADR FCCBs, external commercial borrowings.

Introduction of 'Derivatives':

The derivatives trading in stock indices has been introduced in two stock exchanges (BSE and NSE) which would provide investors a hedging instrument of international standards to manage risk and help in improving the depth and liquidity of secondary capital markets (BSE: Bombay Stock Exchange; NSE: National Stock Exchange).

The capital markets in India have in the recent years, but in practice several reform measures aiming to achieve international standards in trading practices and ensure investor protection.

Foreign Exchange Market:

- Foreign Exchange Management Act, 1999 replaced FERA. The provisions of FEMA are in conformity with the liberalised market for foreign exchange.
- Risk management strategies for corporates, risk management guidelines for banks, internationally accepted documentation standards.
- Automatic approval for FDI, automatic route for issue of GDR/ADR by Indian companies.

Financial Instruments

The financial markets in the country remained for long insufficiently developed with low volume of transactions due to limited number of participants dealing in limited number of instruments. During 1990s, as a result of various reform measures the number of participants and instruments dealt with in various segments of financial markets have increased giving rise to broadening and deepening of markets. As various segments of markets have become better integrated, there has been increase in the size of and turnover in different market segments.

In the early 1990s, the certificates of deposits (CDs) and commercial papers (CPs) were introduced in money market along with the setting up of Money Market Mutual Fund (MMMF). One significant development was the introduction of Repo transactions by RBI to influence short-term liquidity. In 1999, RBI introduced delivery vs. payment in regard to Repos and allowed access to short-term liquidity through Repos to non-bank participants in money market.

The treasury bills of different time-lengths 14-day, 28-day, 364-day were introduced and 182-day treasury bills were reintroduced.

In field of 'Bonds' several new types like discount bonds, deep discount bonds, zero coupon bonds, zero coupon convertible bonds have appeared. Secured premium notes (SPNs) are issued by companies for raising debts. The SPN could be with detachable warrants for conversion into equity. The other debt instrument offered is non-convertible debentures with detachable equity warrants. Preference shares fully convertible, cumulative, redeemable were introduced.

The 'Derivatives' as securities have come up on the scene in the form of stock index futures.

The Indian corporates raise funds in the international capital markets in Euro issues and in terms of instruments like GDR/ADR, FCCBs, ECBs etc.

4.3 CURRENT SCENARIO OF THE INDIAN FINANCIAL SYSTEM

In this part of the chapter, the state of the financial system in India during the past two decades has been described. As mentioned earlier, some reforms in accordance with the recommendations of the Chakravarty Committee (1985) and Vaghul Working Group (1987) were introduced in the second half of decade of 1980s. In continuation of these efforts, major policy initiatives have been taken up as a part of financial reforms from the year 1991-92 with a view to remove structural weaknesses and overcome deficiencies in the financial system of the country. It is, therefore proposed to describe the present state of the Indian financial system in terms of the major developments in the post-reform period, *i.e.,* during the decade of the 90s. In line with the overall trend towards liberalisation in economic reforms introduced during the 1990s, the key element in the financial sector reforms was withdrawal or reduction in regulatory and control mechanisms and allowing more flexibility like free pricing of financial assets. What was meant was not the total absence of regulation, but rather modernisation or rationalisation of controls such as introduction of prudential norms in view of the alarming increase in sickness in the financial system. The financial system, which had remained insufficiently developed for long, has been going through the process of transformation towards a more diversified — broader and deeper — structure and improved operational effectiveness and efficiency. The policy initiatives undertaken as a part of the financial reforms during the 1990s are in the form of a continuing efforts to further strengthen the financial system in regard to viability, competitiveness and internal as well as global integration. The financial reforms are an ongoing process of change through which the financial system is keeping pace with the overall changes in the economy. The overall changes in the economy are as a result of economic reforms inclusive of fiscal reforms, industry trade reforms, external sector reforms etc.

It is now intended to record the recent developments during the 90s, *i.e.,* post-reform period in respect of the constituents of the financial system — financial institutions, financial markets and financial instruments.

(i) Financial Institutions

Securities and Exchange Board of India (SEBI) :

- Capital Issues (Control) Act 1947 was repealed in May 1992.
- Prior consent for floating and pricing of issues to raise capital from the market not required.
- Though set up in 1988, SEBI was given statutory powers under the Act in 1992.

Over the Counter Exchange of India (OTCEI) :

- Promoted in Oct, 1990 (started in October 92) jointly by ICICI, IDBI, IFCI, UTI, LIC, GIC and the Merchant banking subsidiaries of SBI and Canara bank.
- Fully automated exchange.
- Extending the operations of exchange to the country as a whole
- 70 companies listed (December 1995).

National Stock Exchange (NSE):	• Set up by IDBI in 1992. • Started operations in June 1994. • Completely automated system. • Only medium size companies and PSUs are listed: 600 companies listed.
Credit Rating	
Investment Information and Credit Rating Agency of India Ltd. (ICRA)	• Sponsored by public financial institutions in 1991. • Delhi-based. • Rating of debt instruments as rating is compulsory for all debt instruments.
Credit Analysis and Research Ltd. (CARE)	• Set up in private sector in November 1993.
Government Securities	• Securities Trading Corporation of India (STCI) set up by RBI in 1994. • To promote secondary market in government securities. This work STCI took over from DFHI.
Money Market Mutual Funds	• Set up in 1992 by commercial banks and financial institutions.

Banking Sector

A major thrust of financial reforms initiated during the 1990s pertain to the banking sector with *'deregulation'* as the central feature, and thereby granting greater operational autonomy. Prior to 1990s, the banking sector functioned amidst controls and restrictions in several aspects of operations like ceiling on interest rates, quantitative restrictions on credit flows etc. The main theme of reforms was to open up the banking sector to more freedom along with the introduction of prudential norms to tone up their working.

The phase of administered interest rate structure ended as the ceiling on interest rates on loans were either removed or the banks were granted freedom along with the reduction in the categories of lending rates. The regulation relating to the concentration of bank credit was operative under the Credit Authorisation Scheme. It was abolished in 1988 and replaced by Credit Monitoring Arrangement (CMA). The CMA was discontinued during 1997-98. The quantitative restrictions on credit flows were put in practice through preferences for the priority sector lending and statutory requirements of investment in government securities under SLR specifications. These restrictions have been lowered on the one hand and on the other, the restrictions on project financing by banks have been increasingly liberalised to enable banks to extend term loans.

In an environment of greater autonomy and freedom, the banks and financial institutions are undergoing substantial role transformation and the distinction between the banks and non-banking financial institutions is getting blurred, and their activities are converging towards more integration. It is also quite significant to note the risk management strategies adopted by the banks by allocating funds as per capital adequacy requirements and reducing non-performing assets. The Reserve Bank issued guidelines in this regard in 1999.

(ii) Financial Markets and Financial Instruments

The main elements of reforms pertaining to different segments of financial markets have been increasing the number of participants, introduction of new financial instruments and also allowing free pricing, *i.e.,* withdrawal on ceiling on the pricing of financial assets like government securities, capital issues etc.

The Commercial paper as a money market instrument showed a steady increase initially in amount outstanding, but has risen faster in the recent period.

Money Market

Call money	● The participation was limited upto 1987 to commercial banks, co operative banks, foreign banks and LIC and UTI as lenders. ● 1988: DFHI was set up with a prime role in the call money market. ● 1989: Ceiling on call money rate removed. ● 1990: IDBI, NABARD, GIC were permitted to participate as lenders. ● Present: All participants in the bills rediscounting market and mutual funds allowed to operate as lenders.
Inter-bank Term Money, Commercial bills	● All-India financial institutions permitted to borrow in October 1993. ● Interest ceiling withdrawn on — rediscounting of commercial bills, inter-bank term money, and inter-bank participation certificates in October 1997. ● The banks were advised by RBI that at least 25% of inland credit purchases of borrowers should be through bills.
Treasury Bills	91-days treasury bills on tap; 91 days ad hoc treasury bills replaced by ways and means advances.
New instruments	364 days treasury bills: Since April 1992, through Auction. — 14 days treasury bills: June 1997 182 days treasury bills discontinued in April, 1992 and reintroduced in May 1999. 91 days treasury bills: Sale through auction from January 1993. Earlier 364 days treasury Bills had replaced 182 days Treasury Bills.
Commercial Paper	Introduced in January 1990. Over the years, the requirements for issue of CPs have been progressively relaxed — Minimum amount: reduced from ₹ 1 crore to ₹ 25 lakh. Maturity period: 91 days to 6 months modified to 30 days to 1 year linking with working capital credit limit. Oct. 1997: Delinking from the cash credit component. Nov. 1996: Extent of CP: upto 100 per cent of the working capital credit limit.
Certificate of Deposits (CDs)	● Introduced in June 1989. ● Minimum amount reduced to ₹ 5 lakh. ● Minimum lock-in period reduced from 30 days to 15 days. ● Bank-wise limit on issue — a certain percentage of the fortnightly average of outstanding bank deposits. Oct 1993: bank-wise limits abolished.

Commercial Papers (CPs)

Year (March-end)	*Amt. Outstanding (₹ Crore)*	*Year (March-end)*	*Amt. Outstanding (₹ Crore)*	*Year (March-end)*	*Amt. Outstanding (₹ Crore)*
1993	577	2002	7224	March 31, 2007	17838
1994	3264	2003	5749	July 31, 2007	30631
1995	604	2004	9131	Oct 31, 2007	42183
1996	76	April 2004	9706	March 31, 2008	32592
1997	646	May 2004	10328	July 31, 2008	51569
1998	1500	June 2004	10910	Oct 31, 2008	48442
1999	4770	July 2004	10848	March 31, 2009	44171
2000	5663	July 31, 2006	21110	June 15, 2009	67239
2001	5846	Oct 31, 2006	23171		

The trend in respect of Certificate of Deposits (CDs) has indicated fluctuations in amount outstanding as per liquidity conditions in the economy.

Certificate of Deposit (CDs)

Year (March-end)	*Amt. Outstanding (₹ Crores)*	*Year (March-end)*	*Amt. Outstanding (₹ Crore)*	*Year (March-end)*	*Amt. Outstanding (₹ Crore)*
1992	5682	2001	771	March 30, 2007	93272
1993	9803	2002	1576	July 20, 2007	105317
1994	5571	2003	908	Oct 26, 2007	124232
1995	8017	2004	4461	March 28, 2008	147792
1996	16316	April 2004	4725	July 18, 2008	164892
1997	12134	May 2004	4880	Oct 24, 2008	158562
1998	14296	June 2004	5438	March 2009	192867
1999	3717	July 21, 2006	59167	July 19, 2009	221491
2000	1227	Oct 27, 2006	65764		

Government Securities Market

Repo Transactions : Dec. 1992: *Repo:* Selling government securities to repurchase later.

Repos: Repurchase Agreements between the RBI and commercial banks.

Period of Repos: 14 days
3-4 days repos since Nov. 1996.

Reverse Repos: In the form of reverse Repos, RBI provides liquidity support.

July 1999: Non-bank participants were allowed access to liquidity through Repos, on par with banks

Introduction of Auction System : Auction system for the sale of government securities introduced in June 1992.

Secondary Market : The primary dealers (PDs) were allowed to operate in 1995 in government securities — Securities Trading Corporation of India (STCI) set up in May 1994 to promote secondary market in government securities.

- RBI to extend liquidity support to mutual funds working exclusively for investments in government securities.
- Reverse Repo facility with the RBI extended to DFHI and STCI.

Capital Market

Primary Market or New Issues Market

- Withdrawal of Controls : All controls relating to pricing of equity issues and the time when they could be issued have been removed.
- Disclosure standards : The companies raising finance through capital issues have to disclose information on various aspects including risk factors, track record at the time of issue and are also required to make continuing disclosure.

The withdrawal of controls and introduction of free pricing of issues led to an upsurge in activity and a significant increase in resource mobilisation. The sharp increase in resource mobilisation was mainly due to equity issues with premium. The primary market has also witnessed the introduction of a variety of new instruments such as secured premium notes, non-convertible debentures, fully convertible redeemable preference shares etc.

- Integration of Indian capital market with international capital markets:
- The Foreign Institutional Investors (FIIs) such as mutual funds, pension funds etc. are allowed to operate in Indian capital market. Initially, they were given permission to invest in the equity shares and were later allowed to invest in the debt market.
- Indian companies allowed to raise capital from the International capital market through issues like Global Depository Receipts (GDRs), American Depository Receipts (ADRs), Euro Issues, Foreign Currency Convertible Bonds (FCCBs) and External Commercial Borrowings (ECBs).

Secondary Market or Stock Exchanges

- The open outcry trading system replaced by the screen-based computerised trading system. 23 stock exchanges have nearly 8000 trading terminals spread all over the country.
- The settlement period shortened from 14 days to 7 days. Trade/settlement guarantee funds have been set up in 10 stock exchanges.
- 1992: Insider Trading prohibited by SEBI.

Foreign Exchange Market or External Financial Market

In the chapter on *'Macro Economic Dimensions of the Financial System,* the role of external or foreign sector has been discussed as a part of sectorwise analysis. The imports and exports, *i.e.,* external trade gives rise to trade-based transaction and the inflow and outflow of capital, *i.e.,* capital transfers give rise to financial transactions. These transactions take place in the foreign exchange market at an exchange rate between the national money units and foreign money units. In India, we had during the period 1975-92, basket-linked (pegged) exchange rate and the pound sterling was the intervention currency. All exchange transactions in the foreign exchange market were regulated under exchange control regime under Foreign Exchange Regulation Act (FERA) and RBI prescribed the exchange rate and performed market-clearing role on day-to-day basis to maintain the external value of the rupee.

During the 1990s the exchange control being relaxed, the pegged exchange rate was transited to flexible exchange rate system, *i.e.,* dual exchange rate during 1992-93 and then to market determined exchange rate from March 1, 1993. The other significant development was the rupee being made convertible on current account, *i.e.,* pertaining to trade transactions in respect of imports and exports. To facilitate capital flows, the FERA of 1973 has been replaced recently, by the Foreign Exchange Management Act. The Committee on Capital Account Convertibility — Tarapore Committee 1997 made certain recommendations. The measures to implement the recommendations with a view to move towards capital account convertibility are being taken. These developments have led to a considerable increase in the foreign exchange market turnover in recent years.

INDIAN FINANCIAL SYSTEM: STRUCTURE (BY MARCH-END 2004)

(₹ in Crores)

Institutions	*No. of Institutions*	*Outstanding Asset*	*Assets % to Total*
Financial Sector (A + B)		3,124,427	100
A. Banking Sector (1 + 2)		2,347,337	75.1
1. Commercial Banking (a + b)	291	2,045,948	65.5
(a) Scheduled Comm. Banks	286	2,045,748	65.5
Public Sector Banks	27	1,471,428	47.1
State Bank Group	8	549,257	17.6
Nationalised Banks	19	9,22,171	29.5
Private Sector Banks	30	3,67,276	11.8
Old Private Banks	20	1,20,700	3.9
New Private Banks	10	2,46,476	7.9
Foreign Banks	33	1,36,316	4.4
Regional Rural Banks	196	70,728	2.3
(b) Non-scheduled Comm. Banks	5	200	0.01
2. Co operative Banks	3111	301589	9.7
(a) Rural Co operative Banks	1185	1,78,984	5.7
Short-term Structure	397	1,72,595	5.5
Long-term Structure	788	6389	0.2
(b) Urban Co operative Banks	1926	1,22,605	3.9
of which scheduled	55	58,256	1.8
B. Broader Financial Sector (3 to 7)		7,77,090	24.9
3. Term lending Institutions	8	2,00,089	6.4
IDBI	1	66921	0.4
IFCI	1	20293	0.6
Exim Bank	1	15,552	0.5
NABARD	1	55889	1.8
NHB	1	13108	0.4
IIBI	1	3073	0.1
SIDBI	1	19327	0.6
IDFC	1	5926	0.2
4. Investment Institutions	7	4,66,306	14.9
UTI	1	57,946	1.9
LIC	1	3,46,119	11.1
IIC	1	16,441	0.5
Four Subsidiaries of GIC	4	45,800	1.5
5. State Level Institutions	46	25012	0.8
SFCs	18	12712	0.4
SIDCs	28	12300	0.4

6. Other Institutions	2	10477	0.3
DICGC	1	8740	0.28
ECGC	1	1737	0.06
7. Non-banking Financial Companies	892	75,206	2.4
NBFC	870	37709	1.2
RNBC	5	20362	0.7
Primary Dealer	17	17135	0.5
C. Capital Markets (8 to 9)		1,340,823	100
8. Equity		1,201,207	89
9. Mutual Funds		1,39,816	11
Public		34,624	3
Private		104992	8

Source: Report on Currency and Finance, RBI 2003-04.

The above Table presents at a glance picture of Indian Financial System and its constituents.

KEY TERMS

Agency Houses, Indigenous Bankers, Development Finance Institutions, Insurance Company, Mutual Fund, Credit Rating, Nationalisation of Commercial Banks, Co-operative Banks, Financial Markets – Money Market, Capital Market, Government Securities Market, Foreign Exchange Market, SEBI, OTCEI.

REVIEW QUESTIONS

1. Discuss the progress of India Financial System in the pre-independence period.
2. Explain the major developments in the Indian Financial System in the post-independence period (1947-2000).
3. What are the quantitative indicators of the growth of the Indian Financial System?
4. Discuss the qualitative changes and reforms in the Indian Financial System.
5. Give an outline of the current scenario of the Indian Financial System.

REFERENCES

1. Avadhani V.A., Studies in Indian Financial System, Jaico, Bombay 1978.
2. Government of India, Economic Survey, Various Issues.
3. RBI – Annual Reports, Various Issues.
4. RBI – Handbook of Statistics on Indian Economy, 2008-09.
5. RBI – Report on Currency and Finance, Various Issues.

❑ ❑ ❑

5

Major Issues in the Indian Financial System: Narasimham Committee Report (1991)

INTRODUCTION

After having taken an overview of the main features of the Indian financial system in the pre-independence and post-independence period and as at present, attention is now focussed on recording major issues in the Indian financial system. In the context of Indian financial system, the decade of 1980s could be described as the period of gradual transition in the form of reform measures taken up to implement the recommendations of the Chakravarty Committee and Vaghul Working Group, which examined the working and problems of monetary system in the country. In 1991, a high level committee was appointed under the chairmanship of M. Narasimham, which examined all aspects relating to the structure, organisation, functions and procedures of the financial system and submitted its report in November 1991. During the decade of 1990s, the major initiatives have been undertaken by way of financial system reforms in accordance with the recommendations made in the Narasimham Committee Report. As such, alongwith the analysis of major issues in the Indian financial system, it is quite necessary to study the main contents and the recommendations made in the Narasimham Committee report.

This chapter therefore, is divided into three sections:

5.1 Major Issues in the Indian Financial System;

5.2 Narasimham Committee Report on the Indian Financial System; and

5.3 Progress of Reforms During Last Two Decades (1991-2010)

5.1 MAJOR ISSUES IN THE INDIAN FINANCIAL SYSTEM

The major issues are:

(i) *The system is politicised* giving rise to political interference with harmful influence on policies and its day-to-day working also.

(ii) *The financial health of the system has deteriorated* and there is an alarming sickness in the financial system reflected in *the erosion of profitability*.

(iii) There has been a perceptible *decline in productivity and efficiency* of the system affecting customer service and its integrity.

In 1991, a major thrust of economic policy changes in the form of liberalisation, privatisation and globalisation was introduced in India. As an integral part of the broader economic system, it became compulsive that the issues of financial system are identified along with their causal factors and adverse effects so that the reform measures could be undertaken to make the system vibrant enough to meet the challenges of the changing environment in the country. Let us analyse these major issues of the Indian Financial System in more details.

(i) The financial system is politicised giving rise to excessive political interference: The political interference has its source in state ownership and it operates in practice through government control. This aspect could be traced back to the late 1960s when the policy of social control over banks was adopted and 14 major scheduled commercial banks were nationalised. Apart from nationalised banks, the *'public'* ownership applied to Development Financial Institutions (DFIs) set up as initiated by the Government to fill the gaps in the capital market segment of the financial system. In terms of nationalisation, public ownership and through the policies of social control, it was possible for the government to acquire control over the pool of financial resources and their allocation. The institutions functioned in a regulated framework which directed their investments and credit programmes.

The political interference nearly distorted every aspect of the financial institutions working from lending to the recycling of funds. The quality of lending deteriorated as the cases were common where the political influence overturned the sound norms of financing. The political influence extended further towards the other end when loan repayments were pursued. The culture of repaying loans was adversely affected by the political pressures insisting on the widespread write-offs. Inspite of rising sickness among the loanee units, the closure of sick units was discouraged by the government guided by several other considerations including socio-economic aspects and political pressures.

Apart from the contamination of loan portfolio, the other adverse facets were *'financial repression'* under the regime of government control and regulation and the administrative interference in internal management and day-to-day working of the banks and financial institutions. The term 'financial repression' denotes the virtual lack of freedom for the banks and financial institutions in their investments and credit programmes. The administered interest rate structure inclusive of concessional credit to certain sectors and the pre-emptive allocation of bank funds for investment in government securities could be mentioned as the main features of financial repression, which put banks under serious strain in their performance. The political interference through 'public', *i.e.,* state ownership spilled over the internal management and day-to-day working including *'personnel'* aspects like recruitment, transfer/promotions and internal controls.

If the state ownership and regulated framework led to political interference and its ills, what was needed by way of reforms was depoliticisation and deregulation to give rise to a financial system with more freedom.

(ii) Deterioration in Financial Health: Erosion of Profitability: The health of the financial system deteriorated in terms of reduction of capital base due to the growing imbalance between income generation and enhancement of capital funds on the one hand and rising expenditure by institutions on the other. The issue of capital inadequacy or weak capital base has been more prominent among banks, but relevant for Development Financial Institutions, particularly the state-level institutions like SFCs whose working suffered from loan portfolio contamination. The deterioration in the quality of loan portfolio led further to the high incidence of loan losses or loan defaults, affecting both recycling of funds and income generation. As a result, banks and financial institutions could not enhance their capital and also could not make adequate provision for loan losses/defaults. The capital inadequacy and the falling profitability reached that stage when the viability of banks and financial institutions was at stake. This unhealthy state of financial system was a combined effect of several factors which influenced the growth of institutions in the past and their operations over the years. In the phase of social banking and nationalisation, the banking sector expanded rapidly through massive branch expansion irrespective of being to a certain extent, remunerative or not. This was accompanied by massive recruitment, resulting in overstaffing or excess manpower which delayed the acceptance and progress of updated technology in operations. The regime of government control and regulated framework exposed the banking sector to excessive pressures and strains. The pressures were due to political interference and the strains were due to economic constraints of directed investments and directed credit programmes. These pressures and strains also affected the operations of the development financial institutions in terms of lack of autonomy in loan sanctioning and the lack of operational flexibility. The directed credit programmes of the banking sector under regulation included:

— administered interest rate structure,

— concessional credit to the 'priority' sector upto specified limits in the total bank lending,

— regulation relating to concentration of bank credit in favour of large business groups,

— subsidisation of credit by charging higher interest rates on lending to non-priority sectors, and the

— immobilisation of credit — affecting recycling of funds due to concessions, delays and defaults in the repayment of loans.

The directed investment pertained to investments in government securities as statutory requirements under SLR (Statutory Liquidity Ratio) by way of a pre-emptive hold on bank resources.

The directed investment and directed credit programmes deployed bank funds at low or below market rates of interest and hence affected bank profitability adversely.

(iii) Decline in Productivity and Efficiency of the System: The effectiveness of the financial system lies in rendering customer service timely and adequately by minimising the transaction costs and the administrative expenses of the operating institutions. The productivity and efficiency of the financial system declines when customer service is poor and yet the transaction costs are high and the administrative expenses soar up. The Indian financial system suffered from a perceptible decline in the productivity and efficiency caused due to organisational inadequacies and management weaknesses. The situation worsened further due to undue political interference which affected functional autonomy and operational flexibility of banks and financial institutions. The operations of banks and financial institutions could be flexible to the extent these institutions enjoyed functional autonomy. A crucial question that comes up in regard to functional autonomy is whether greater degree of autonomy is compatible with public ownership. The characteristic feature of any set-up under public ownership is *'centralisation'* reflected in the limited delegation of authority and stringent controls from the top. The fear associated with this trend is that the institutions under public ownership should be exposed to regulations, lest they may cease to be accountable. The other aspect is that the greater degree of functional autonomy is taken to mean the absence of regulation and supervision.

The low level of functional autonomy in the financial system has been caused due to management weaknesses, and due to excessive administrative and political interference in the internal management of the institutions. In view of the public ownership of banks and financial institutions, the Government engages itself not only in direct regulation, through policy directives/guidelines but also involving in day-to-day working. Under such conditions of insufficient delegation of authority, the management weaknesses such as absence of work culture, inadequate internal controls system appear and harm the functioning of the banks and financial institutions. It is not necessary that the regulation has to be through framework which would restrain the working of financial institutions to compliance in accordance with the rules. To enhance the productivity and efficiency of the financial system, it is imperative that financial institutions are granted greater degree of autonomy of functional freedom, and yet ensuring their accountability through a framework of purposive, prudential regulations supported by the effective internal control systems, along with the delegation of authority. It is said that the functional autonomy is a prerequisite for operational flexibility of the financial institutions to achieve improved performance in terms of productivity and efficiency. In a regulated framework providing for direct government controls, the operations of the financial institutions are confined to spheres, specified under the rules and are segmented as per the structural rigidities. The banks and the financial institutions have to be given greater degree of flexibility of operations to gain in competitiveness by enhancing efficiency, productivity and profitability.

The lack of operational flexibility for the financial institutions and the tight regulations on financial markets have given rise to distortions in the allocation of resources by the financial system. The direct regulations imposed through several measures like directed investment, directed credit programmes, administered interest rates structure, prior approval for capital issues and their pricing etc. had put restraint on the operations of the institutions and the functioning of markets. The financial institutions were left with little choice to introduce any flexibility in their operations for tackling the problems like low capital base, alarming sickness rates and their own viability.

The effectiveness of the financial system in rendering efficient services was hampered as the different segments of the financial market such as money market, government securities market, capital market and foreign exchange market remained less developed and suffered from deficiencies like limited number of participants, limited number of financial instruments, tight regulations, low coupon rates, lack of efficient market practices including trading and settlement practices etc. Well developed financial markets having a large number of participants and more options in the number of financial instruments available at market determined pricing are viewed as the crucial factor in making the financial system more efficient in the allocation of resources and more productive in terms of the increased turnover or the volume of transactions performed.

The deteriorating financial health as reflected in the erosion of profits, declining productivity and efficiency of the financial system gave rise to the problem of loss of the system's integrity. The operations of the banks and financial institutions suffered from the problems like low capital base, poor quality of loan portfolio and hence low income generation and additions to capital funds. As a result, adequate provisioning for bad assets — non-performing assets could not be made. In this regard, the banks and financial institutions adopted certain accounting practices which did not show their realistic picture. The income recognition, *i.e.*, reckoning interest income was done on the *'accrual'* basis and not on *'realisation'* basis. The banks and financial institutions adopted accounting practices which would enable them to avoid full disclosure in respect of their operations, particularly the bad and non-performing assets and provisioning against such assets. The lack of transparency in the statements of accounts as in the case of the balance sheets raised the problem of integrity with regard to the financial system.

In the post-independence period of fifty years, the decade of 1990s stands out for the realisation that the extensive involvement of the government in ownership and by way of direct regulation was not any further relevant and also for the introduction of distinct shift in economic policies in favour of more, liberated market-oriented 'mixed economy' having primarily indirect and prudent regulation. The main theme of the financial system reforms initiated in response to the recommendations made in the Narasimham Committee Report in 1991 was on transformation on the same lines from the system with financial repression to a more free and market-related system having the protecting and facilitating prudential regulations.

5.2 NARASIMHAM COMMITTEE REPORT ON THE INDIAN FINANCIAL SYSTEM

The report of the Committee on the financial system known as the Narasimham Committee was submitted in November 1991.

M. Narasimham, former Governor of the Reserve Bank of India was the chairman of this committee, which was appointed by the Government of India in August 1991.

The Narasimham Committee drew attention to the progress made and the achievements of the Indian financial system, and at the same time, made diagnosis of the ill-health of the system suffering from certain issues which required urgent consideration and stringent remedial action.

The Committee expressed that a competitive and more effective financial system was also necessary to suitably meet the requirements of ongoing real sector changes under the New Economic Policy initiated in 1991.

The *terms of reference* of the Committee were as follows:

(i) To examine the existing structure of the financial system and its various components and to make recommendations for improving the efficiency and effectiveness of the system with particular reference to the economy of operations, accountability and profitability of the commercial banks and financial institutions;

(ii) To make recommendations for improving and modernising the organisational system and procedure as well as managerial policies;

(iii) To make recommendations for infusing greater competitive vitality into the system so as to enable the banks and financial institutions to respond more effectively to the emerging credit needs of the economy;

(iv) To examine the cost, composition and adequacy of the capital structure of the various financial institutions and to make suitable recommendations in this regard;

(v) To review the relative roles of the different types of financial institutions in the financial system and to make recommendations for their balanced growth;

(vi) To review the existing supervisory arrangements relating to the various entities in the financial sector, in particular the commercial banks and the term lending institutions and to make recommendations for ensuring appropriate and effective supervision.

(vii) To review the existing legislative framework and to suggest necessary amendments for implementing the recommendations that may require legislative change;

(viii) To make recommendations on any other subject matter as the Committee may consider germane to the subject of enquiry or any related matter which may be specifically referred to the committee by the Government of India.

In recommending the financial sector reforms, the *focus of the committees' approach* was on ensuring that the financial services industry operates on the basis of operational flexibility and functional autonomy with a view to enhancing efficiency, productivity and profitability.

The two main elements of the committee's terms of reference are:

(A) Review; and

(B) Recommendations.

(A) Review

The Committee proposed to review —

(i) The *existing structure of the financial system* and its various components,

(ii) The *cost, composition and adequacy of the capital structure* of various financial institutions.

(iii) The *relative roles of the different types of financial institutions.*

(iv) The *existing supervisory arrangements* relating to the various entities in the financial system, in particular the commercial banks and the term lending institutions;

(v) The existing *legislative framework.*

(B) Recommendations

(i) For improving the *efficiency* and *effectiveness* of the system with particular reference to the economy of operations, accountability and profitability of the commercial banks and financial institutions;

(ii) For improving and *modernising the organisational systems and procedures.*

(iii) For infusing greater *competitiveness and vitality* into the system.

(iv) For *balanced growth of different types of financial institutions.*

(v) For ensuring *appropriate and effective supervision.*

(vi) Suggest necessary *amendments in the legislative framework* for implementing the recommendations.

The Committee decided to undertake diagnosis of the existing financial system by: (a) examining the *existing structure* and the different components of the system such as financial institutions, financial markets and financial instruments; (b) reviewing the cost, composition and adequacy of the capital structure of different financial institutions and their relative roles and (c) by studying the specific aspects like supervisory arrangements and legislative framework for the system.

The goals of the committee while making recommendations for the financial sector reforms could be mentioned as under:

The reforms were aimed at improving the *efficiency, effectiveness, competitiveness* and *vitality* of the financial system. The improvement was to be brought about with particular reference to the economy of operations, accountability, modernising the organisational systems and procedures and profitability of the banks and financial institutions.

The other objects of the financial sector reforms were achieving the balanced growth of different financial institutions, ensuring effective supervision, pursuing the necessary amendments in the legislative framework of the system.

In the context of the broader, real sector economic reforms of liberalisation, privatisation and globalisation introduced since the early 90s, the financial sector reforms also aimed at other goals like:

- Deregulation of the system so as to eliminate *'financial repression'* which existed in the form of administered interest rate structure, pre-emptive hold over financial resources.
- To develop a competitive, market-oriented *'free'* system by dismantling the direct controls to give way to the indirect and prudent controls.
- To achieve more rational allocation of financial resources so as to effectively serve the needs of rapid economic development.

Though the Committee identified the *'public'* ownership of the banks and financial institutions as the causal factor which politicised the financial system, the committee in recommending reforms expressed more concern for ensuring integrity and autonomy of the financial system than the question of ownership.

The Narasimham Committee in its report has referred to the progress made and the achievements of the Indian financial system on the following lines:

(1) Progress in extending geographical spread and functional reach by banks.

Geographical Spread

	1969	*1989*
No. of branches	8187	57811
No. of rural branches	1443	32873
Rural to Total %	18	57

Functional Reach
Sp. to Borrowers in Agriculture and Small-scale Industries

(*₹ in Crores*)

	Credit to Priority Sectors				
	Agriculture	*Small-scale industries*	*Others*	*Total*	*Gross Bank Credit*
1972	439	597	172	1208	5480
	(8.0)	(10.9)	(3.1)	(22.0)	
1980	2,767	2635	1328	6730	21235
	(13.0)	(12.4)	(6.3)	(31.7)	
1990	16612	15615	8248	40475	1,02,783
	(16.2)	(15.2)	(8.0)	(39.4)	

Note: Figures in brackets indicate % of the Gross Bank Credit.

(2) Progress in financial intermediation and growth of financial savings.

In India, the household sector savings account for a major share in the total savings. The share has increased from nearly 72% in 1970-71 to 81 per cent in 1988-89. The banks are necessarily financial intermediaries which mobilise savings by creating secondary assets in the form of bank deposits and transferring these resources to the private corporate sector and government/public sector which issue primary securities like equity shares, bonds/debentures for obtaining funds.

Household Sector Savings
(at current prices)

(₹ in Crores)

	1970-71	*1980-81*	*1988-89*
Gross savings	4873	22030	66222
Gross financial savings	2110	12118	40516
Bank deposits	754	5550	16367

(3) The Development Financial Institutions as the term lending institutions have offered significant financial assistance for investment, *i.e.,* the creation of fixed capital assets in the private sector.

(4) The diversification of money market and capital market in terms of increase in participants and introduction of new financial instruments.

(5) New financial services are being offered — merchant banking, mutual fund, leasing companies, venture capital companies, hire purchase companies, factoring companies. These services are rendered by the non-banking financial companies and by the banks and the financial institutions through their subsidiaries.

The details of the developments in the Indian financial system in regard to above aspects have been separately dealt with in respective chapters.

NARASIMHAM COMMITTEE REPORT (1991)

Problems diagnosed:

(1) Erosion of profitability
(2) Decline in productivity and efficiency
(3) Erosion of profitability on expenditure side
(4) Deterioration in the quality of loan portfolio
(5) Structure of rural credit
(6) Capital market regulation
(7) Foreign Banks: policy aspects
(8) Policy regarding new institutions rendering financial services.

1. Erosion of Profitability

Factors responsible:

(i) Directed investments at low rates of interest. Pre-emptive allocation of bank funds for investment in government securities as SLR requirement.

Reforms proposed:

- SLR be brought down to 25 per cent over a period of about 5 years.
- CRR may be progressively reduced.
- Interest rates paid to banks on their SLR investments and on CRR in respect of impounded deposits above the basic minimum should be raised and be fixed at the level of bank's one-year deposit rate.

(ii) Directed credit programme:

— Allocation of bank credit to priority sectors target: 40 per cent of the total bank credit.

— Administered interest rates:

— Lending to priority sectors at concessional rates of interest; non-priority sectors may be charged higher interest rates.

Reforms proposed:

- Directed credit programme should be phased out.
- Priority sector be redefined to include weaker sections such as —

  Small and marginal farmers
  Tiny sector of industries
  Small business and Transport operators
  Village and cottage industries
  Rural artisans.

- The credit limit for the redefined priority sectors should be 10 per cent of the aggregate credit.
- For the provision of bank credit to the erstwhile constituents of the priority sector, RBI and other refinancing agencies should institute a preferential refinancing scheme.
- Interest rates: present interest rate structure is complex and rigid. *The interest rates should be deregulated.* The concessional interest rates should be phased out.
  It is desirable to provide a prime rate — a floor of the lending rates of banks and DFIs.

(iii) Deterioration in the quality of loan portfolio. This has caused adverse effect on banks income generation and enhancement of capital funds and resulted in low capital base and inadequate provision for bad debts.

Reforms proposed:

- The assets of the banks should be evaluated on the basis of their realisable values.
- In regard to income recognition, the banks and FIs should follow 'realisation' system and not the 'accrual' system of accounting. No income should be recognised in the accounts in respect of Non-performing Assets (NPAs).
- **NPA:** An asset would be considered non-performing if interest on such assets remains past due for a period exceeding 180 days at the balance sheet date.
- Capital adequacy ratio:

Basle Committee norms:

March 1993 : 4 per cent capital adequacy in relation to risk-weighted assets (CRAR).

March 1996 : 8 per cent CRAR.

- Asset classification as per health code

  Standard
  Substandard
  Doubtful
  Loss

- Provisioning for bad/doubtful debts:

Substandard	: 10 per cent of total outstanding.
Doubtful	: 100 per cent of security shortfall.
Loss	: to be written off or 100 per cent provision.

4 year's period for the banks and FIs to conform to these provisioning requirements. As an incentive to banks to make provisions, the specific provision made by the banks and FIs should be given consideration by making such provisions tax deductible.

2. Decline in Productivity and Efficiency

Lack of operational flexibility

Lack of functional autonomy

Factors responsible - insufficient delegation of authority
- inadequate internal controls
- weaknesses in the internal organisation structure
- duality of control over banks: RBI and Ministry of Finance.

Reforms proposed:

- Various guidelines and directions issued by the Government or the RBI in regard to internal administration should be reviewed to examine their continuing relevance in the context of the need to ensure the autonomy of banks.
- Depoliticising the appointment of the chief executives CMD and ensuring security of tenure for the CMD.
- The internal organisation of banks should be left to the judgement of managements of the individual banks.
- Functional autonomy:

  Recruitment of officers: Instead of having a common recruitment system for officers, individual banks should be free to make their own recruitments.

3. Erosion of Profitability on Expenditure Side

Factors responsible – massive expansion of branches
– overstaffing
– inadequate progress in updating work technology.

Reforms proposed:

- Branch Licensing should be abolished.
- Opening or closing of branches should be left to the commercial judgement of the individual banks.
- To evolve policies aimed after 'rightsizing'; redeployment of the surplus staff either by retaining them.
  – giving them appropriate alternative employment or by introducing a voluntary retirement scheme (VRS) with appropriate incentives.

- Computerisation:
  - urgent need for a far greater use of computerised systems;
  - computerisation to be recognised as an indispensable tool for improvement in customer service, better control systems, better work environment and greater efficiency.

4. Deterioration in the Quality of Loan Portfolio:

Factors responsible:
- True picture of the state of affairs of banks and FIs does not get reflected in their statement of accounts, *i.e.*, the balance sheets on account of accounting and disclosure practices adopted.
- Low recoveries of loans and difficulties faced in the enforcement of security charged.

Reforms proposed

- Balance sheets of the banks and FIs should be transparent and full disclosures be made.
- Special Tribunals to be set up to speed up the process of recovery so that the dues to the credit institutions could be realised without delay.
- Asset Reconstruction Fund (ARF):
  - With special powers of recovery.
  - Bad and doubtful debts of the banks and FIs to be taken off their balance sheets. ARF to take over from banks and FIs bad and doubtful debts at a discount. The banks and FIs have to write off the amounts to the extent of discounts. The Government of India plans to provide loan to the banks and FIs in this regard.

5. Structure of Rural Credit

Improving viability of Regional Rural Banks (RRBs)

Reforms proposed:

- Each public sector bank should set up one or more rural banking subsidiaries which would take over its rural branches.
- RRBs should be allowed to engage in all types of banking business with a focus on lending to target groups.
- Interest rate structure of RRBs should be in line with those of commercial banks.

6. Capital Market

Capital Market Regulation

Development Financial Institutions

Capital Market Regulation:

Reforms proposed:

The capital market should be gradually opened up to foreign portfolio investment. Efforts should be initiated to improve the depth of market by facilitating issue of new types of equity/debt instruments.

DFIs: Reforms proposed:

- Consortium lending should be dispensed with.
- DFI should increasingly engage in providing core working capital and the commercial banks should be encouraged to provide term finance to industry.
- The infected portion of the DFI's portfolio should be handed over to the ARF.
- DFIs should seek to obtain their resources from the market on competitive terms.
- In the matter of appointment of chief executives and the Board, the system recommended for banks should apply to DFIs.

  State Level Financial Institutions:
- The committee felt it necessary to distance them from the State Governments and ensure that they function on sound business principles, based on prudential norms.

Policy Reforms in the Indian Financial System

1. Deregulation of the interest rates; system of administered interest rates dismanted, interest rate structure simplified and market interest rates applicable to government securities.
2. SLR brought down from 38.5 per cent (1991) to 25 per cent; reduced preemption of banks' resources through SLR.
3. Reduction in CRR from 15 per cent (1991-92) to 10 per cent (1995-96); gradually further reduced.
4. The Basle Committee framework of capital adequacy adopted and made compulsory to all banks, financial institutions and all kinds of market intermediaries.
5. A new Supervisory Reporting System introduced in Feb.1995 to focus attention on critical areas such as capital adequacy asset quality, management, earning and liquidity.
6. Recovery of debt due to Banks and Financial Institutions Act 1993 passed to set up Special Recovery Tribunals to facilitate quicker recovery of loan arrears.
7. The system of *ad hoc* treasury bills was abolished and replaced by ways and means advances from April 1, 1997.
8. Capital Issues (Control) Act, 1947 repealed and the office of Controller of Capital Issues abolished.
9. Securities and Exchange Board of India has been made a statutory body in Feb.1992 and has been given the necessary authority and powers for regulation and reform of the capital market.
10. The RBI (Amendment) Act 1997 passed to compel all Non-bank Financial Companies (NBFCs) with net owned funds of ₹ 25 lakh and more to register with the RBI.
11. Liquidity Adjustment Facility (LAF), Repos and Reverse Repos auctions introduced.
12. Primary dealers introduced in Government Securities Market, Securities Contract Regulation Act has been amended.

7. Foreign Banks

Reforms proposed:

More Liberal Policy with regard to —

- Allowing foreign banks to open offices in India.
- Joint ventures between foreign banks and Indian banks.
- Foreign operations of Indian banks need to be nationalised. Indian banks could jointly set up one or more subsidiaries to take over their existing branches abroad.

8. New Institutions

Rendering Financial Services: Merchant banks, Mutual Funds, Leasing companies, Venture capital companies, Factoring Companies.

Recommendations:

- There is need to lay down prudential norms and guidelines governing the functioning of these institutions.
- Prudential guidelines relating to capital adequacy, debt-equity ratio, income recognition, provisioning against doubtful debts, adherence to sound accounting and financial policies, disclosure requirements and valuation of assets.
- Supervision of these institutions: a new agency to be set up. SEBI to have jurisdiction over these institutions to the extent their activities impinge on market operations.

5.3 PROGRESS OF REFORMS DURING THE LAST TWO DECADES (1991-2010)

The progress of reforms during the 1990s decade has been separately dealt with in respect of the different constituents of the Indian financial system in the respective chapters.

At this stage, the progress of reforms is mentioned in terms of:

(i) Report of the Committee on banking sector reforms chaired by M. Narasimham which submitted its report in April 1998.

(ii) An overview of the progress of reforms during the 1990s.

(i) Report of the Committee on Banking Sector Reforms (April 1998)

Capital adequacy	Recommendations
	• Capital adequacy requirements to take into account market risks in addition to the credit risks. • Government securities and other approved securities are subject to zero risk weight. There should be 5% weight for market risk. • Norms for capital adequacy: to be increased from 8% to 10% minimum capital to risk-weighted assets CRAR ratio/in phases: 9% in 2000 10% by 2002 • RRBs and co-operative banks should reach a minimum of 8% of CRAR over a period of 5 years. • There should be no recourse to any scheme of debt waiver. • No further recapitalisation of banks be undertaken from the government budget. • Alternatives to ARF proposal:

(i) Assets Reconstruction Company (ARC): Loan assets in the doubtful and loss categories should be transferred to ARC which would issue to banks NPA swap bonds representing the realisable value of the assets transferred.

(ii) Banks to issue bonds.

NPAs: Introducing the norm of 90 days in place of 180 days by 2002.

Standard Assets: provision of 1%

- *Government Guarantee Advances:* Income recognition, asset classification and provisioning norms should apply.

Methods in Banks — Recommendations

- Revised manuals for internal control systems: Computer Audit.
- Independent loan review mechanism to identify potential NPAs.
- To introduce a system of recruiting skilled manpower from the open market.
- Chief Executive: Minimum tenure should be three years.
- Assessing training needs to offer specialised training.
- External vigilance and investigative agencies.
- Advisory Board for bank frauds for various levels.
- Requisite success in the application of ongoing revolution in information and communication technology has not been achieved.

Structural Issues

- Banks and FIs are moving closer to each other in the scope of their activities.
- *Mergers*

  Weak banks whose accumulated losses and NPAs exceed its net worth or

  whose operating profits less its income on recapitalisation bonds is negative for three consecutive years. Mergers should be the solution.
- *Functional autonomy*
  - Public sector banks should be encouraged to go to the market to raise capital.
  - Minimum shareholding by the government/RBI should be brought down to 33 per cent.
- *NBFCs*

  Non-banking financial companies are required to have a minimum net worth of ₹ 25 lakh, which should be progressively raised to ₹ 2 crore.

  Deposits with NBFCs should not carry any insurance.
- *Deposit Insurance*

  In place of flat rate premiums the 'risk-based' or variable premiums on the basis of CAMELS's ratings to banks.

  C: Capital Adequacy;
  A: Assets Quality
  M: Management Quality
  E: Earning Quality
  L: Liquidity.
  S: Systems

- *Money Market*

— Inter-bank call and notice money market and term money market should be, with the exception of primary dealers (PDs), restricted to banks.

- Non-banking financial institutions — can have access to Bills rediscount, Commercial Paper (CPs), Certificate of Deposits (CDs), Treasury Bills and MMMFs.

— Minimum lock-in period of CPs, CDs and MMMF should be reduced from 30 days to 15 days.

— 91-day Treasury Bills — RBI should withdraw from the primary market for 91-day Treasury Bills.

— FII should be given access to Treasury Bills Market.

Regulation and Inspection

Integrated system of regulation and inspection.

Board for Financial Regulation and supervison to be set up to regulate and supervise the activities of banks, FIs and non-banking firms, Finance companies including Rural Credit Institutions and Urban co-operative banks.

Legal and Legislative Framework

The legal implications of the recommendations should be examined. It is proposed that an expert committee representing Ministry of Law, Banking Division, Ministry of Finance, RBI and experts from external firms should be set up to formulate specific legislative proposals.

Progress of Reforms: An Overview

It is intended to present an overview on the progress of reforms during the 1990s, particularly in terms of the progress pertaining to the reforms proposed by the Narasimham Committee (1991). The developments including policy changes that have taken with regard to the constituents of the Indian financial system, *i.e.,* financial institutions, financial markets and instruments during the 1990s decade have been mentioned in the chapter on the Indian financial system. An account of full details of these changes has been given individually for the financial institutions, market segments and instruments in separate chapters in the book. The changes, including even the normal policy changes in response to the dynamic economic conditions is an ongoing process and hence may not be treated as reforms in the context of the financial system.

1. Administered interest rates: *Reform proposed:* *Interest rate deregulation*

(a) Lending Rates

During the period 1975-76 to 1994-95, when the administered interest rates were in operation, there were distinct three phases:

1975-76 to 1980-81	:	The minimum lending rate as well as the ceiling rate was prescribed by the RBI.
1981-82 to 1987-88	:	The ceiling rate was fixed.
1988-89 to 1994-95	:	RBI switched over to prescribing minimum lending rate.

Deregulation: The lending rate was deregulated for loans above ₹ 2 lakh, effective October 18, 1994.

In April 1998, the banks were given freedom (not exceeding PLR) in respect of interest rates as on loans upto ₹ 2 lakh. The PLR or the prime lending rate was between 12 per cent to 14 per cent during 1998-99.

(b) Deposit Rates

April 1992	:	A single prescription of not exceeding 13 per cent was prescribed for 46 days to three years and above.
October 1995	:	Rates for Deposit over two years freed.
July 1996		• Minimum maturity period was reduced from 46 days to 30 days. • Rates of deposit over 1 year freed.
Oct. 1997	:	Banks were given freedom to determine their own interest rates on deposits of 30 days and over.
April 1998	:	Minimum maturity period was reduced from 30 days to 15 days.

2. *Direct investments:* *Reform Proposed* *Rationalising i.e., lowering the prescriptions of SLR / CRR (Statutory Liquidity Ratio, Cash Reserve Ratio)*

Under the statutory SLR requirement, the bank funds were pre-emptively allocated for investment in government securities at low rates of interest. At the onset of the reforms process in 1991, the statutory pre-emptions under CRR and SLR on an incremental basis, reached a level of 63.5 per cent. This together with compulsory priority sector lending left very little resources at the disposal of banks for earning profits.

CRR (Cash Reserve Ratio): reduced in phases from 15 per cent to 10 per cent between April 1993 to January 1997 (incremental 10 per cent CRR was withdrawn in 1992). The CRR was raised to 11 per cent in October 1998 and then cut to 9 per cent in November 1999.

SLR: With a view to rationalising the prescription of SLR, all scheduled commercial banks, effective from October 1997, are required to maintain a uniform SLR of 25 per cent on their net demand and time liabilities.

This has brought down the statutorily pre-emption of bank resources to 34 per cent from the earlier high level reached of 63.5 per cent.

- The maximum coupon rate on central government securities has been raised to near-market rates.
- The scheduled commercial banks have been granted exemption from maintaining CRR and SLR on their inter-bank liabilities, *i.e.,* their liabilities to the banking system.

3. *Deterioration in the quality of loan portfolio*

- Low capital base
- Inadequate provision for bad debts
- Low recoveries of loans
- Accounting and disclosure practices

Reforms proposed

- Prudential norms regarding capital adequacy, income recognition, provisioning against doubtful debts, sound accounting policies and disclosure practices, valuation of assets.
- Setting up special tribunals.
- The instructions have been issued by the RBI to commercial banks in respect of the prudential norms on income recognition, assets classification and provisioning for bad debts. These norms are applicable to the RRBs and financial institutions also.

- Recovery of debts due to Banks and the Financial Institutions Act, 1993 passed to set up special recovery tribunals to facilitate quicker recovery of loan arrears.
- Move towards full disclosure, transparency and effective supervision of banks.

The banks were advised to make the following disclosures in the *'Notes on Account'* to the balance sheet for the year ended on

March 31, 1997: (i) Per cent of net NPA to net advances.
(ii) Provisions made towards NPA, depreciation in the value of investments.
(Net NPA is the provision adjusted NPA)

March 31, 1998: (i) Capital adeauacy ratio.
(ii) Interest income as % of working funds.
(iii) Non-interest income as % of working funds.
(iv) Operating profits as % of working funds.
(v) Return on assets.
(vi) Business per employee.
(vii) Profits per employee.

March-end 2000: (i) Maturity patterns of: (a) loans and advances, (b) investments in securities, (c) deposits, (d) borrowing; (ii) foreign currency assets and liabilities'; and (iii) movements in NPAs; and (iv) lending to sensitive sectors like real estate, capital market and other sectors as defined by the RBI from time to time.

It has been decided to assign the risk weight of 2.5 per cent to all investments, including investments in approved securities and non-SLR securities with effect from March 31, 2001.

- *Inspection:* A Board for Financial Supervision (BFS) with an advisory council has been set up in RBI. The Board has to focus on critical areas such as capital adequacy, assets quality, management, earnings and liquidity and systems (CAMELS). BFS would supervise banks, all-India financial institutions and non-banking financial companies NBFCs.
- The performance obligations and commitments (PO&C) obtained by RBI from banks. The (PO&C) are meant to ensure a high level of portfolio quality so that problems such as heavy losses, low profits and erosion of equity do not recur.
- The detailed guidelines on asset-liability management and risk management systems have been issued by the RBI.

4. *Public Ownership: Banks and Financial Institutions*

- Public sector banks permitted diversified ownership subject to 51 per cent holdings of government/RBI.
- SBI, IFCI, IRBI converted themselves into public limited companies.
- IDBI allowed to raise capital upto 49 per cent of its paid-up capital from the public and to induct private participation in its Board of directors.

5. *Rural Credit: Co-operative Banks and RRBs*
- Instructions of RBI in respect of the prudential norms on income recognition, asset classification and provisioning are applicable to RRBs.

Kisan Credit Cards (KCC)

- KCC introduced in 1998-99 to improve credit delivery to farmers so that they can purchase agriculture inputs and meet their production needs.
- The scheme operated by scheduled commercial banks, co operative banks and RRBs.
- By March-end 1999, number of KCC issued were 6.11 lakh. The scheme has progress well and the number of KCCs issued by March-end 2004 were 413.8 lakh of this, 58.6% or bulk of the cards were issued by co operative banks, public sector banks: 32% and RRBs: 9.4 per cent. To assess the impact, RBI entrusted on survey to NCAER which conducted study in 11 states covering 54 districts.

Development Financing Institutions (DFIs) Deregulation Reforms:

- Convertibility clause is no longer obligatory in the case of assistance sanctioned by All-India Financial Institutions (DFIs).
- Floating interest rates introduced on financial assistance by All-India Financial Institutions (DFIs).

Foreign Banks: The policy of permitting foreign banks to open branches liberalised.

Capital Markets: Deregulation

- Capital Issues (Control) Act, 1947 repealed.
- Office of the Controller of Capital Issues abolished.
- Securities and Exchange Board of India (SEBI) made a statutory body, having regulatory powers.
- Abolition of capital issues control and the introduction of free pricing of issues.

Non-banking Financial Companies (NBFCs)

The Reserve Bank of India Act was amended in 1997, giving regulatory and supervisory powers for strengthening the NBFCs.

To register with the RBI, NBFCs required net-owned funds of a minimum of ₹ 25 lakh.

The requirement of minimum net owned funds for any company seeking a certificate of registration has been raised from ₹ 25 lakh to ₹ 2 crore with effect from April 21, 1999.

The ceiling on bank credit to NBFCs has been abolished in respect of registered NBFCs.

On January 2, 1998, a new regulatory framework for NBFCs, was announced to protect the interests of the depositors and provide more effective supervision over NBFCs, particularly those which accept public deposits.

External Financial Market

Reforms

- Flexible Exchange rate system introduced.
- Exchange controls relaxed: rupee made convertible on current account.
- Foreign Institutional Investors (FIIs) allowed access to the Indian Capital market.
- Indian companies permitted access to international markets through various instruments.

A Hundred Small Steps: Report of the Reghuram Rajan Committee on Financial Sector Reforms

The Committee on Financial Sector Reforms was tasked with proposing the next generation of reforms for the Indian Financial System. The main areas of focus of the committee were as given below.

A. The Macro Economic Framework and Financial Sector Development.

B. Broadening Access to Finance.

C. Levelling the playing field for all kinds of financial institutions.

D. Creating more efficient and liquid markets.

E. A Growth Friendly Regulatory Environment

- changes in legislation (regulations).
- changes in the process of evaluation and compensation.
- changes in the regulatory architecture.

F. Creating A Robust Infrastructure for Credit.

G. Special Topics

The main proposals of the committee were as follows:

A. The Macro Economic Framework

Proposal 1: The RBI should formally have a single objective, to stay close to a low inflation number, of within a range, in the medium term, and move steadily to a single instrument, the short-term interest rate (repo and reverse repo) to achieve it.

Proposal 2: Steadily open up investment in the rupee corporate and government bond markets to foreign investors after a clear monetary policy framework is in place.

B. Broadening Access to Finance

Proposal 3: Allow more entry to private well-governed deposit-taking small finance banks offsetting their higher risk from being geographically focused by requiring higher capital adequacy norms, a strict prohibition on related party transactions, and lower allowable concentration norms (loans as a share of capital that can be made to one party). Make significant efforts to create the supervisory capacity to delivery the greater monitoring these banks will need initially, and put in place a tough prompt corrective action regime that ensures these banks do not become public charges.

Proposal 4: Liberalise the banking correspondent regulation so that a wide range of local agents can serve to extend financial services. Use technology both to reduce costs and to limit fraud and misrepresentation.

Proposal 5: Offer priority sector loan certificates (PSLC) to all entitles that lend to eligible categories in the priority sector. Allow banks that undershoot their priority sector obligations to buy the PSLC and submit it towards fulfillment of their target.

Proposal 6: Liberalise the interest rate that institutions can charge, ensuring credit reaches the poor, but require: (i) full transparency on the actual effective annualised interest cost of a loan to the borrower, (ii) periodic public disclosure of maximum and average interest rates charged by the lender to the priority sector, and (iii) only loans that stay within a margin of local estimated costs of lending to the poor be eligible for PSLCs.

C. Levelling of the Playing Field

Proposal 7: Sell small underperforming public sector banks, possibly to another bank or to a strategic investor, to gain experience with the process and gauge outcomes.

Proposal 8: Create stronger boards for large public sector banks, with more power to outside shareholders (including possibly a private sector strategic investor), devolving the power to appoint and compensate top executives to the board.

Proposal 9: After starting the process of strengthening boards, delink the banks from additional government oversight, including by the Central Vigilance Commission and Parliament, with justification that with government controlled boards governing the banks, a second layer of oversight is not needed. Further ways to justify reduced government oversight is to create bank holding companies where the government only has a direct stake in the holding company. Another is to bring the direct government stake below 50 per cent, perhaps through divestment to other public sector entities or provident funds, so that the government (broadly defined) has control, but the government (narrowly defined) cannot be considered the owner.

Proposal 10: Be more liberal in allowing takeovers and mergers, including by domestically incorporated subsidiaries of foreign banks.

Proposal 11: Free banks to set up branches and ATMs anywhere.

Proposal 12: Allow holding company structures, with a parent holding company owning regulated subsidiaries. The holding company should be supervised by the Financial Sector Oversight Agency (see later), with each regulated subsidiary supervised by the appropriate regulator. The holding company should be well diversified if it owns a bank.

Universal banking should thus be possible in India through holding company structures. Some legislative and tax change is required to make these structures viable, and these are outlined in the report.

D. Creating More Efficient and Liquid Markets

Proposal 13: Bring all regulation of trading under the Securities and Exchange Board of India (SEBI).

In areas where multiple regulators share concerns about a market (for example, RBI has a legitimate interest in the government bond market), regulators will have to co-operate even after the supervision of trading moves to SEBI. The rest of the Committee's main market-related proposals are self-explanatory.

Proposal 14: Encourage the introduction of markets that are currently missing such as exchange traded interest rate and exchange rate derivatives.

Proposal 15: Stop creating investor uncertainty by banning markets. If market manipulation is the worry, take direct action against those suspected of manipulation.

Proposal 16: Create the concept of one consolidated membership of an exchange for qualified investors (instead of the current need to obtain memberships for each product traded). Consolidated membership should confer the right to trade all the exchange's products on a unified trading screen with consolidated margining.

Proposal 17: Encourage the setting up of 'professional' markets and exchanges with a higher order size, that are restricted to sophisticated investors (based on net worth and financial knowledge), where more sophisticated products can be traded.

Proposal 18: Create a more innovation-friendly environment, speeding up the process by which products are approved by focusing primarily on concerns of systemic risk, fraud, contract enforcement, transparency and inappropriate sales practices. The threshold for allowing products on professional exchanges or over-the-counter markets should be lower, so that experimentation can take place.

Proposal 19: Allow greater participation of foreign investors in domestic markets. Increase participation of domestic investors by reducing the extent to which regulators restrict an institutional investor's choice of investments. Move gradually instead to a 'prudent man' principle where the institutional investor is allowed to exercise judgement based on what a prudent man might deem to be appropriate investments. Emphasise providing access to suitable equity-linked products to the broader population as part of the inclusion agenda.

E. Creating a Growth Friendly Regulatory Environment

Proposal 20: Rewrite financial sector regulation, with only clear objectives and regulatory principles outlined.

Proposal 21: Parliament, through the Finance Ministry, and based on expert opinion as well as the principles enshrined in legislation, should set a specific remit for each regulator every five years. Every year, each regulator should report to a standing committee (possibly the Standing Committee on Finance), explaining in its annual report the progress it has made on meeting the remit. The interactions should be made public.

In addition, to ensure there are more direct checks on the regulator in a system that is less rule-bound, the Committee recommends Proposal 22.

Proposal 22: Regulatory actions should be subject to appeal to the Financial Sector Appellate Tribunal, which will be set up along the lines of, and subsume, the Securities Appellate Tribunal.

To enhance the quality of regulatory staff, the Committee suggests that regulators continue their ongoing attempts to give recruits higher, remuneration as well as responsibilities, but also that every effort should be made to allow mobility to and from the private sector. Each individual organisation will, however, have to take reasonable precautions against conflicts of interest arising out of prior or subsequent employment.

Proposal 23: Supervision of all deposit taking institutions must come under the RBI. Situations where responsibility is shared, such as with the State Registrar of Co operative Societies, should gradually cease. The RBI will have to increase supervisory capacity to take on this task. The Committee recognises this involves constitutional issues but nevertheless recommends a thorough overhaul of the system of shared responsibility.

Proposal 24: The Ministry of Corporate Affairs (MCA) should review accounts of unlisted companies, while SEBI should review accounts of listed companies.

Proposal 25: A Financial Sector Oversight Agency (FSOA) should be set up by statute. The FSOA's focus will be both macro-prudential as well as supervisory; the FSOA will develop periodic assessments of macroeconomic risks, risk concentrations, as well as risk exposures in the economy; it will monitor the functioning of large, systemically important, financial conglomerates; anticipating potential risks, it will initiate balanced supervisory action by the concerned regulators to address those risks; it will address and defuse inter-regulatory conflicts.

Proposal 26: The Committee recommends, setting up a Working Group on Financial Sector Reforms with the Finance Minister as the Chairman. The main focus of this working group would be to shepherd financial sector reforms.

The Committee also notes the consumer faces an integrated portfolio of services. It is increasingly important for the consumer to have a 'one stop' source of redress for complaints, a financial ombudsman. Also, an integrated ombudsman is needed to enhance financial literacy and financial counselling, issues that span regulators. The ombudsman can also monitor the selling of different products, the degree of transparency about their pricing, and their suitability for targeted customers. Finally, given that household debt loads are increasing, the ombudsman can provide a neutral forum (and possibly act as an arbitrator) for out-of-court negotiated settlement of debt.

Proposal 27: Set up an Office of the Financial Ombudsman (OFO), incorporating all such offices in existing regulators, to serve as an interface between the household and industry.

Finally, the Committee noted that a large number of undercapitalised deposit-taking entities continued to survive in the system. Regulatory forbearance should be the exception, especially when there is more rapid entry into the system.

The Committee recommends strengthening the capacity of the Deposit Insurance and Credit Guarantee Corporation (DICGC) to both monitor risk and resolve a failing bank, instilling a more explicit system of prompt corrective action (see Proposal 3), and making deposit insurance premia more risk-based.

Proposal 28: The combination of the proposed changes to legislation, regulatory incentive structures, and regulatory architecture, should help create a far more enabling regulatory framework, which will provide for greater stability, higher growth and innovation, and more inclusion.

F. Creating a Robust Infrastructure for Credit

Proposal 29: Expedite the process of creating a unique ID number with biometric identification.

Proposal 30: The Committee recommends movement from a system where information is shared primarily amongst institutional credit providers on the basis of reciprocity to a system of subscription, where information is collected from more sources and a subscriber gets access to data subject to verification of 'need to know and authorisation to use' of all subscriber by the credit bureau. This will also require rethinking the incentives of providers to share information, and a judicious mix of payments as well as mandatory requirements for information sharing will have to be developed.

Proposal 31: Ongoing efforts to improve land registration and titling – including full cadastral mapping of land, reconciling various registries, forcing compulsory registration of all land transactions, computerising land records, and providing easy remote access to land records – should be expedited, with the Centre playing a role in facilitating pilots and sharing experience of best practices. The Committee also suggests the possibility of special law courts to clear the backlog of land disputes be examined.

Proposal 32: Restrictions on tenancy should be re-examined so that tenancy can be formalised in contracts, which can then serve as the basis for borrowing.

Given clear title to an asset, let us now turn to the process of registering a creditor's interest in the asset. In order for creditors to establish they have a secured claim to an asset, and in order that prospective lenders or purchasers be made aware of prior claims, a well-organised system to register and publicise security interests is essential. The current system of registration in India is fragmented and neither fully computerised nor easily accessible. The Committee offers some suggestions in the report on how this can be remedied.

Proposal 33: The powers of SARFAESI that are currently conferred only on banks, public financial institutions, and housing finance companies should be extended to all institutional lenders.

Proposal 34: Encourage the entry of more well-capitalised ARCs, including ones with foreign backing.

Finally, while secured creditors have been empowered, unsecured creditors still have little protection. If India is to have a flourishing corporate debt market, corporate public debt, which is largely unsecured, needs to have value when a company becomes distressed. This means a well functioning bankruptcy code, that neither protects the debtor at the expense of everyone else including employees, as our current system does, nor one that allows secured creditors to drive a well-functioning firm into the ground by seizing assets. A good bankruptcy code is especially needed for large complex infrastructure projects, which typically have many claimholders.

Proposal 35: The Committee outlines a number of desirable attributes of a bankruptcy code in the Indian context, many of which are aligned with the recommendations of the Irani Committee. It suggests an expedited move to legislate the needed amendments to company law.

In the final chapter, the Committee offers views on three important topics, the financing of infrastructure, the financing of old age pensions, and the generation of information in the economy.

KEY TERMS

Productivity and Efficiency of Financial System, Directed Investment, SLR, CRR, Directed Credit, Priority Sector, Administered Interest Rates, Capital Adequacy Norms.

REVIEW QUESTIONS

1. What were the major issues of the Indian Financial System on the eve of the Financial Sector Reforms 1991?
2. Discuss the terms of reference and the recommendations of the Narsimham Committee 1991.
3. What were the problems diagnosed and reforms proposed by the Narsimham Committee 1991?
4. Discuss various policy reforms in the Indian Financial System.
5. Discuss the main aspects of the Narasimham Committee Report on Banking Sector Reforms 1998.
6. Comment on the Financial Sector Reforms in the Indian Financial System in last two decades (1990-2010).
7. Discuss the main proposals of the Reghuram Rajan Committee Report on Financial Sector Reforms.

REFERENCES

1. Bhole L.M. (1992), 'Proposals for Financial Sector Reforms in India' – An Appraisal, Vikalpa, July-Sept.
2. Chakraborty L. (2008), Analysing the Reghuram Rajan Committee Report on Financial Sector Reforms, Economic and Political Weekly, June 21.
3. Jalan Bimal, (2001), 'India's Economy in the Twenty-first Century: A New Beginning or a False Dawn', RBI Bulletin, Feb. 2001.
4. Rangarajan C., (1997), 'The Financial Sector Reforms: The Indian Experience', RBI Bulletin, July, 1997.
5. Rajan Reghuram, (2008), 'A Hundred Small Steps: Report of the Committee on Financial Sector Reforms'.

❑❑❑

6

Financial Institutions — Reserve Bank of India: Monetary Policy of RBI

INTRODUCTION

It is proposed to describe in details the 'Financial Institutions' as the constituents of Indian Financial System under two separate headings:

(i) Banking Institutions

(ii) Non-banking Institutions.

The chapters devoted to the Banking Institutions are:

(i) Reserve Bank of India. (Chap. 6)

(ii) Commercial Banks. (Chap. 7)

(iii) Co-operative Banks. (Chap. 7), and

The chapters on Non-banking Institutions are:

(iv) Non-banking finance Companies (NBFCs). (Chap. 8)

(v) Development Financial Institutions (DFIs), IDBI, ICICI, IFCI, SFCs and others. (Chap. 9)

(vi) Investment Institutions — Insurance Companies: LIC, GIC, Mutual Funds including UTI. (Chap. 10)

(vii) Contractual Savings Institutions — Small Savings, Provident Funds (PF) (including Post-office Savings). (Chap. 11)

Some of the non-banking financial institutions like LIC, GIC, UTI are financial intermediaries like commercial banks and co operative banks. The DFIs as non-banking financial institutions are not financial intermediaries in the real sense of the term.

In the recent years, the distinction between the banks and the financial institutions other than banks is getting blurred. They are converging in regard to their activities as the term lending financial institutions have entered into the area of working capital financing and the banks have made entry into the domain of project financing.

In this chapter, following aspects of the Reserve Bank of India and the Monetary Policy are discussed:

6.1 Functions of the Reserve Bank of India

6.2 Techniques of Monetary Control

6.3 Monetary Policy:

(i) An Appraisal

(ii) Recent Developments

(iii) Interest Rate Channel and Credit Channel

6.4 Monetary Policy Developments:

(i) Objectives

(ii) Framework of Monetary Policy

(iii) Operating Procedure

RESERVE BANK OF INDIA

The Reserve Bank of India (RBI) was established on April 1, 1935 as a shareholders' bank. It was nationalised on January 1, 1949 and it then became a state-owned institution under the Reserve Bank (Transfer to Public Ownership) of India Act 1948. As the central bank of the country, the RBI is the apex institution in the Indian monetary system.

6.1 FUNCTIONS OF THE RESERVE BANK OF INDIA

The Reserve Bank of India is one of the oldest and strongest apex banks among the central banks in the developing countries. Apart from the traditional central banking functions, the bank also performs various developmental and promotional functions.

Reserve Bank of India was established on the model of the Bank of England and therefore its general central banking functions are similar to those of the Bank of England.

Issue of Currency Notes

As a central bank, the Reserve Bank has the sole right or authority of issuing currency notes other than one rupee notes and coins and coins of smaller denominations. One rupee coins and notes and coins of smaller denominations are issued by the Government of India and they are put into circulation only through the RBI. The currency notes issued by the RBI are legal tender in India without any limit. All the currency notes are issued through the Issue Department.

In India, the proportional reserve system of note issue existed till 1956. Under this system, the RBI was required to keep 40 per cent of assets in the form of gold coin, gold bullion and foreign securities subject to the condition that the value of gold (coin and bullion) should not be less than ₹ 40 crore. Later on in 1956, the proportional reserve system was replaced by the minimum reserve system. Under this system, the Reserve Bank is required to ensure that the value of gold coin and bullion should not be less than the value of ₹ 115 crore. Along with this, there should be foreign securities of the minimum value of ₹ 85 crore so that together with gold (coin and bullion) the minimum value of these assets is ₹ 200 crore. This system is less restrictive and provides larger scope for the regulation of currency.

Banker to Government

The RBI acts as a banker to the Central and State Governments. The RBI is under obligation to transact the banking business of the government and it provides to the government all banking services such as accepting deposits or money on account of the government, withdrawal of funds by cheques, receipts and collection of payments on behalf of the government and so on. It also undertakes transfer of funds and management of public debt. It floats rupee loans in the form of stock certificates and promissory notes.

The Reserve Bank can make *"ways and means advances"* to the government. These temporary advances are made to bridge the temporary gap between receipts and payments.

The gap in the receipts and payments of state governments is met by these ways and means advances and the gap or deficit in the central government account with the RBI is managed by creation of treasury bills, *i.e.,* the *ad hoc* treasury bills on behalf of the central government and thereby provides short-term finance. This operation also helps to absorb any excess liquidity in the money market.

In addition to the ways and means advances, the state governments heavily depend upon the overdrafts given to them by the apex bank.

The RBI also acts as an adviser to the government on banking and financial matters. It acts as an agent of the transactions on account of India's membership of the International Monetary Fund and the World Bank.

Banker's Bank

The Reserve Bank enjoys extensive powers to control the commercial banking system in the country. Banks are required to maintain a certain percentage of their deposits with the RBI. All scheduled banks (included in the second schedule of RBI) can borrow from the RBI on the basis of eligible securities. They are under a statutory obligation to maintain a certain minimum of cash reserve with the RBI against their demand and time liabilities. The apex bank determines this Cash Reserve Ratio (CRR) between 3 per cent and 15 per cent of aggregate demand and time liabilities as per the amendment of 1962 to the Banking Regulation Act.

The scheduled commercial banks are required to submit weekly statements of their transactions to the RBI. Various activities such as licensing of banks branch expansion, liquidity of the assets of the commercial banks, their management and working, reconstruction, liquidation and amalgamation, are under supervision and control of the RBI. It undertakes inspection of the commercial banks and recommends measures to improve their operations. The RBI is known as the lender of the last resort as it lends funds to the commercial banks in the times of their needs.

Controller of Credit

As a Controller of credit, the RBI regulates both, the extent of credit and the rate at which it is made available. It makes use of various quantitative methods of credit control such as Open Market Operations, Cash Reserve Ratio and the Bank Rate and also the selective or qualitative methods of credit control.

Through the Open Market Operations, the cash or reserve position of the banks is augmented by the RBI which influences the credit capacity of the banks. The purchase of securities increases the resources and the sale of securities reduces the resources of the commercial banks which respectively results in the expansion and contraction of credit.

The RBI has been using two ratios — Cash Reserve Ratio (CRR) and Statutory Liquidity Ratio (SLR) as potential instruments of credit control.

Bank Rate as an instrument of credit control is used to change the volume of lendable resources of the banks. In addition to this, the selective credit control methods are used to allocate credit to different priority sectors and to deny it to others.

Exchange Management and Control

The apex bank has to maintain stability in the external value of rupee. For this, the Reserve Bank relies upon various fiscal and monetary tools. However, persistent Balance of Payments (BoP) problem has forced RBI to resort to direct methods of exchange control. In 1947, the Foreign Exchange Regulation Act (FERA) was passed, which empowered the RBI to exercise control over foreign securities, foreign payments and transfer of currency, bullion and securities to foreign nationals. This Act was replaced by a more comprehensive Foreign Exchange Regulation Act 1973.

It is necessary to regulate the demand by the nationals for foreign exchange and also the disposal of foreign exchange earned by them. Therefore, all the dealings in the foreign exchange are required to be transacted only through authorised dealers. In India, the foreign exchange earnings have always been far less than the demand for the same. Therefore, they had to be rationed to maintain exchange stability. This is done through exchange control imposed on both receipts and payments of foreign exchange on trade, invisible on capital accounts.

The RBI performs the foreign exchange control function, it fixes (or manages) the exchange rate between the rupee and other currencies and co-ordinates its activities with the International Monetary Fund and the World Bank. The exchange rate of rupee has been fixed in terms of the *'basket of currencies'* since, 1975. This basket of currencies includes five currencies, *i.e.,* US dollar, pound sterling, Mark, Yen and Franc.

Promotional and Developmental Functions

In addition to the traditional central banking function, the RBI has taken up various promotional and developmental functions in the developing Indian economy. It includes mobilisation of savings by spreading over the banks and other financial institutions in different parts of the country, developing banking habits among people, resorting to branch banking in rural, semi-urban areas and thereby reducing the dependence of the people on the indigenous bankers and moneylenders. With an objective of providing security to the depositors, the RBI took an initiative in establishing the Deposit Insurance Corporation in 1962.

The provision of institutional credit to agriculture has been one of the major contributions of RBI. It actively participated in the establishment of Agricultural Refinance and Development Corporation (ARDC) in 1963 and the National Bank for Agricultural and Rural Development (NABARD) in 1982. The RBI also extended its assistance to the co operative credit movement in agriculture.

After 1947, to meet the long standing credit requirement of the industrial sector, the RBI also actively participated in the establishment of various specialised institutions such as Industrial Finance Corporation of India (IFCI) and the State Finance Corporations. The Industrial Development Bank of India also was established as a subsidiary by the RBI and later on it was made autonomous.

The RBI has strengthened the banking and financial structure of the Indian economy and has helped in the mobilisation of savings, and their allocation to productive channels for the achievement of economic development.

Promoter of the Financial System

The Reserve Bank has been responsible for the widespread growth of the banking and non-banking financial institutions in the country. It has been instrumental in strengthening the money market and the capital market and in providing short and medium-term credit to the priority sectors and long-term credit to the industrial sector. It has played a major role in strengthening and giving a boost to the Indian financial system.

6.2 TECHNIQUES OF MONETARY CONTROL

The Reserve Bank has been using traditional as well as specially designed and adopted methods of monetary control in India. The apex bank has used several means at its disposal to influence three aspects of money, *i.e.,* the supply of money or the quantity of money, access to the demand for money and the price of money or the rate of interest.

The following measures have been used by the RBI from time to time:

(a) Open Market Operations (OMOs)

(b) Bank Rate

(c) Discretionary Control of Refinance

(d) Cash Reserve Ratio (CRR)

(e) Statutory Liquidity Ratio (SLR)

(f) Direct Regulation of Interest Rates

(g) Direct Credit Allocation and Credit Planning

(h) Selective Credit Controls

(i) Moral Suasion.

(a) Open Market Operations

Open Market Operations is a widely used tool of monetary control in many developed countries such as the USA & UK. By undertaking purchases and sales of government securities, the RBI can affect the reserve position of the banks, volume and cost of bank credit and also the yield on government securities. There is no restriction on the quantity and maturity of government securities which it can buy or sell or hold. The Reserve Bank can operate effectively its treasury bills and central government securities of all maturities. At the time of issue of loans, the securities directly bought by the RBI are excluded from the definition of OMOs. RBI is continuously in the market, selling government securities on tap and buying them mostly in switch operations, and it generally does not purchase them against cash. In India, since government securities are predominantly held by institutional investors, *i.e.,* banks, IDBI, NABARD, Insurance companies etc., the dealings of the RBI in regard to OMOs are mostly confined to them.

In India, OMOs have mostly been used for the purpose of debt management and this has undermined their effectiveness as a tool of monetary policy. As the Government securities market in India is not broad-based, well organised and as the interest rates on them are very low and administered, this reduced the efficiency of OMOs.

Prior to the Second World War Open Market Operations were conducted on a very limited scale. But during the World War II, the RBI conducted open market purchase operations on a large scale in order to support gilt-edged security market and to meet the government's defence requirements. After the war was over the RBI engaged itself in the sale and purchase of securities to meet the seasonal variations in the reserves of the banking system and to provide greater strength in the banking structure and the money market. In November 1951 along with raising the bank rate from 3 per cent to 3.5 per cent, the RBI announced that except in some exceptional circumstances, it would not buy securities from the commercial banks in order to augment their reserves. In October 1956, the RBI conducted open market purchase operations for supporting the government securities and for meeting the increased demand for funds.

Open Market Operations have indirectly helped in the regulation of supply of bank credit to the private sector in two ways. Firstly, the Reserve Bank has often conducted switching operations of sale of long-term scrips in exchange for short-term ones to ensure harmonious maturity and yield to investors. Secondly, the Reserve Bank's net sales (sales-purchases) of government securities has increased over the years. In addition to this, Open Market Operations have been undertaken to prevent unchecked expansion of liquidity through monetisation of government debt in the recent years. The demand for the government securities has been kept up by imposing a statutory condition on various financial institutions to invest a portion of their income or deposits in the government and other approved securities. This also has helped in preventing unrestricted increase in liquidity.

(b) Bank Rate

The technique of bank rate is used to regulate the cost and availability of refinance and to change the volume of lendable resources of banks and other financial institutions. The bank rate is the basic cost of refinance and rediscounting facilities.

As a central bank of the country, the Reserve Bank of India is empowered to use bank rate as an instrument of credit control. The effectiveness of the bank rate policy depends on following factors: (i) commercial banks in the country should not be averse to availing the rediscounting facility from the central bank, (ii) banks do not maintain any excess cash reserves against deposits and if extraordinary demands are made by the depositors, they should have no option but to rediscount bills from the central bank, and (iii) banks must hold adequate quantity of such credit instruments which will be rediscounted by the Central bank. Last two conditions are not fulfilled in India. Firstly, the commercial banks in India are no much dependent on the Reserve Bank for financial assistance, and secondly, in absence of well-organised bill market, they lack adequate quantity of eligible bills which can be rediscounted from the RBI.

Upto 1951, the RBI followed the cheap money policy and the bank rate was only 3 per cent. This resulted in large expansion of credit which encouraged speculative activities and substantial deficit in the balance of payments. In 1951, the bank rate was raised to 3.5 per cent and to 4 per cent in 1957. Due to growing inflationary pressure, it was again raised to 4.5 per cent in 1963. Cheap money policy was considered inappropriate as the inflationary pressure was mounting and to arrest unwarranted credit expansion, the bank rate was again raised to 5 per cent in 1964. Within six months again, it was raised to 6 per cent and it continued at that level upto 1968 when in March 1968, it was brought down to 5 per cent. Later on, it was fixed at 9 per cent in July 1974 and it remained so for next seven years. It was raised upto 10 per cent in 1981. After ten years, in 1991, it was first raised to 11 per cent and then was fixed at 12 per cent during the same year.

During the forty years (from 1951 to 1991), the bank rate was changed only nine times and it remained static during some periods. There seems to be some hesitation regarding altering the bank rate rapidly and as many times as desired. During the decade of the 1980s, interest rates on bank deposits and loans were changed without changing the bank rate.

The traditional technique of bank rate was simple to operate. But the hesitancy of the central bank to change the bank rate frequently to protect the market for and yield on the government securities, has brought in multiple and differential refinance rates chargeable to different banks. The new techniques of control of refinance resulted in the loss of '*announcement effect*' of the bank rate. Therefore, the rehabilitation of bank rate as a major tool of monetary policy and simplification of the refinance policy is urgently required

(c) Discretionary Control of Refinance

Although the bank rate was not frequently altered during 1951 to 1991, the Reserve Bank experimented with some new techniques of control of refinance. In October 1960, a new system of raising cost of refinance, *i.e.,* quota-cum-slab-rate system was introduced. It linked the availability of cost of refinance to the maintenance of required cash reserves by the banks. Under this system, the Reserve Bank used to fix borrowing quotas for banks with the graded cost of refinance. The basic quota used to be fixed at some percentage, say 25 per cent as 50 per cent of the average required statutory cash reserves and it used to be available at the bank rate. For the use of the second, third or fourth quotes, the RBI interest rate used to be increased by certain percentage points. The availability of refinance beyond the basic quota was at the discretion of the RBI and was not automatic. This system was abandoned in September 1964.

The quota-cum-slab system was soon replaced by a new system known as Net Liquidity Ratio system (NLR). Under this system, the cost of refinance came to be linked with the ratio of bank's net liquid assets (cash and balances with the RBI and other notified banks plus balances in the current account with other banks plus investments in government and other approved securities minus borrowings from the RBI, SBI and IDBI) to the aggregate demand and time liabilities of the bank.

NLR = SLR – bank's borrowings from the RBI, SBI and IDBI.

Under this system, if the NLR declined by a given percentage point (say 1%) below a given prescribed minimum level (say 28 per cent), the RBI would charge a stipulated additional rate of interest (say 1 per cent) over and above the bank rate. Under this system, the RBI could increase the cost of refinance by increasing the minimum NLR, by increasing the penal interest rate, by increasing the bank rate and by reducing the extent of drop in NLR for applying the penal interest rate. The NLR was raised from 28 per cent in 1964 to 39 per cent in 1974.

The Reserve Bank had been providing refinance at the bank rate or concessional rate on a selective basis in respect of bank loans to preferred sectors such as exports, agriculture, food procurement and small industries. Over a period of time, even to these sectors, less and less refinance was made available and that also at an increasing cost.

In the general category, refinance normally used to be available on automatic basis for a long period of time. But in November 1973 refinance facilities were made available on a semi-discretionary basis and quantitative ceilings were imposed on it. The RBI started using discretion in respect of volume, maturity and cost of refinance on the basis of credit deposit ratio of the banks, the extent of its fulfillment of credit allocation targets, general compliance with RBI's policy objectives and directives, efforts to mobilise deposits, difficulties faced in the respect of operations in backward areas and so on. In addition to this, the virtually automatic refinance came to be restricted to a stipulated ceiling known as *basic refinance quota* with its two components: (a) the basic borrowing limit of one per cent of bank's demand and time liabilities and (b) the basic bills rediscounting quota of 10 per cent of total bills purchased and discounted, both as on a prescribed date. This refinance quota used to be provided at the rate of interest different (above) from the bank rate.

In May 1977, the basic automatic rediscount quota was discontinued and the rediscount facility was placed entirely on a discretionary basis.

Since June 1978, RBI began giving refinance only in very special situations of extreme need. In March 1979, the access to refinance and rediscounting facilities for banks defaulting on CRR and SLR was discontinued and a system of penal rate of interest of 3 per cent over and above the bank rate on the outstanding refinance equivalent to shortfall in CRR and SLR was introduced. During 1980s, the refinance policy concentrated on raising the cost of refinance.

The RBI, not intending to influence credit creation, indiscriminately avoided a general increase in the bank rate and resorted to a system of differential rates. The purpose of the introduction of this technique of credit control was to check the commercial banks' indulgence in excessive borrowings from the Reserve Bank.

(d) Cash Reserve Ratio (CRR)

The Cash Reserve Ratio (CRR) is a very effective instrument of credit control. It refers to the cash which the banks have to maintain with the Reserve Bank as a certain percentage of their demand and time liabilities. Under the RBI Act 1934, scheduled banks were required to maintain with the RBI a minimum cash reserve of 5 per cent of their demand liabilities and 2 per cent of time liabilities. These ratios could be raised upto 20 per cent and 8 per cent for the demand and time deposits respectively as per the 1956 amendment of the RBI Act. This Act also empowered the RBI to direct the scheduled banks to maintain with them a certain percentage of their liabilities created after a specified date in cash. This marginal CRR could not exceed 100 per cent. In 1960, when the commodity prices recorded a steep rise in March and May 1960, the marginal CRR of 25 per cent and 50 per cent respectively was imposed. This provision was later suspended in two stages as the demand for credit increased.

The 1962 Amendment of the RBI Act removed the distinction between the demand and time liabilities for the purpose of reserve requirement and also empowered the apex bank to determine CRR in the range of 3 per cent to 15 per cent. The rules regarding the marginal CRR were not changed. The CRR is applicable to all scheduled banks including the scheduled co-operative banks, the Regional Rural Banks (RRBs) and the non-scheduled banks. The non scheduled banks, co-operative banks and the RRBs have to maintain CRR only at 3 per cent.

The RBI has powers to impose penal interest rates on banks if they fail to maintain the prescribed CRR, which is normally 3 per cent above the bank rate for the first week of default and 5 per cent for the subsequent weeks till the default is made good.

To control inflation, CRR has been widely used. On June 29, 1970, CRR was raised from 3 per cent to 5 per cent and it was further raised to 7 per cent on September 22, 1973.

This restricted the credit creation capacity of the banks. There was rapid growth of deposits in early 1980s, which resulted in excess liquidity in the banking system. Therefore, the CRR was raised in August 1983. Commercial banks were also directed to maintain a marginal CRR of 10 per cent of the increase in net demand and time liabilities. In October 1987, CRR was raised up to 10 per cent. With effect from July 1, 1989, CRR was raised by 4 percentage points upto 15 per cent from 11 per cent in 1988.

The Narasimham Committee in its report did not favour the use of CRR to control inflationary pressures. It mentioned that a high CRR adversely affected the profitability of the banks and forced them to charge high rates of interest on their advances to the commercial sector. Therefore, the CRR was to be reduced to a level below 10 per cent. It was initially brought down to 14.5% in April 1993 and to 14 per cent in May 1993.

It was brought down to 13 per cent in April 1996. Again in April 1998, it was brought down to 10 per cent which raised the lendable resources of the commercial banks. In November 1999, CRR was brought down to 9 per cent mainly to facilitate adequate supply of credit to the industrial sector and ensure industrial recovery.

(e) Statutory Liquidity Ratio (SLR)

In addition to the CRR which enables the Reserve Bank to impose primary reserve requirements on the banks, SLR enables it to impose secondary or supplementary reserve requirements. The SLR empowers the Reserve Bank to restrict expansion of bank credit and augment investment of the banks in government securities. Banks are prevented from disinvesting government securities for expanding commercial credit.

The SLR, like CRR, is applicable to co operative banks, non-scheduled banks and the RRBs at a constant level of 25 per cent for the scheduled commercial banks and it can be raised upto 40 per cent.

Under the RBI Act 1949, the commercial banks were required to maintain a liquidity ratio of 20 per cent against their demand and time liabilities. Cash in hand, cash balances with the RBI and other banks, gold and unemcumbered approved securities constituted liquid assets. This provision would allow commercial banks to liquidate their government security holdings whenever the RBI would raise the CRR. The Amendment Act 1962 provided for maintaining a minimum statutory liquidity ratio of 25 per cent by the banks against their demand and time liabilities over and above the minimum reserve requirements.

Therefore, SLR is the ratio of cash in hand (exclusive of cash balances maintained by banks to meet required CRR, but not the excess reserves), balances in current account with the SBI, its subsidiaries, other nationalised banks and the RBI, gold, and unemcumbered approved securities, *i.e.*, central and state government securities, securities of the local bodies and the government guaranteed securities to total demand and time to abilities of banks.

The SLR was raised upto 30 per cent in 1972, upto 35 per cent in 1982 and finally upto 38.5 per cent in 1990.

The SLR may not be considered as an effective technique of monetary control as it only distributes bank resources in favour of the government sector. An increase in SLR may restrict only the private sector expenditure while helping to increase the government expenditure.

The Narasimham Committee did not favour a high SLR and therefore it was to be brought down to 25 per cent over a period of time as a part of the financial sector reforms.

(f) Direct Regulation of Interest Rates

Considering the fact that the bank rate was not very effective in bringing about appropriate changes in market rates of interest, the RBI was compelled to regulate directly interest rates on bank deposits and credit. The apex bank began to fix all deposit rates of the co operative banks and their lending rates were brought under control by the RBI in 1974 and 1980 respectively. Till 1975, the deposit and the lending rates of the banks and the bank rate, both were changed together. But thereafter, bank rate was not necessarily altered along with the changes in other interest rates. A system of differential interest rates or fixing either the maximum or minimum or dual interest rates has evolved in India in the recent years. The interest rates of the banks on deposits and credit have been changing very frequently.

(g) Direct Credit Allocation and Credit Planning

Various quantitative credit controls and credit ceilings have been introduced by the Reserve Bank from time to time.

The distribution and allocation of credit among different sectors, borrowers and users has been achieved by resorting to fixation of quantitative credit ceilings or credit targets. Regarding allocation of credit to agriculture and the priority sector, quantitative targets were fixed for the banks. It also aimed at achieving rural, urban and regional and geographical balance in respect of credit disbursal. For example, in 1980, following instructions were given to the banks: (i) priority sector advances should constitute 40 per cent of aggregate bank advances by 1985, (ii) advances to the agricultural sector should be 40 per cent of the priority sector advances or at least 16 per cent of total bank advances by 1985, (iii) direct advances to the weaker sections in agricultural sector should be at least 50 per cent of total direct lending to agriculture by 1983 and (iv) advances to rural artisans, village craftsmen and cottage industries should be 12.5 per cent of the total advances to the small-scale industries by 1985.

(h) Selective Credit Controls (Qualitative Credit Control)

Selective Credit Control is the most effective technique of credit control in India. In a developing economy like India, the quantitative techniques of credit control cannot be used frequently as they may adversely affect the productive activity and the development effort. Therefore, selective credit controls can be used to check misuse of the borrowing facilities and allocate credit for productive purpose. It is used to prevent speculative hoarding of essential commodities and check the undue rise in prices.

The selective credit controls are used by the RBI in three forms:

(i) the determination of margin requirement for loans against certain securities.

(ii) determination of maximum amount advances or their financial accommodation.

(iii) charging of discriminatory interest rates on certain types of advances.

In addition to these, the RBI also gives direction to the banks regarding the purpose for which loans may or may not be given.

Selective credit controls prevent speculative hoarding of essential commodities by traders but the credit for production, movement of commodities and exports is not denied. Advances against the security of foodgrains such as paddy and rice, cotton textiles, sugar, oilseeds etc. were brought under selective credit control in late 1950s by fixing the margin requirements. It helped in overcoming the artificial scarcities of these commodities in the market and their rising prices.

To restrict the stock market speculative activities, margin requirement for loans against the security of ordinary shares were fixed at 50 per cent.

Advances against five broad categories of commodities, *viz.,* foodgrains, oilseeds, sugar, gur and khandsari and vegetable oil were brought under strict selective controls and since 1973-74, the margin requirements for loans against the stocks of these commodities varied from 20 per cent to 75 per cent. The interest rates on advances against the security of these commodities also were kept higher.

Under the Credit Authorisation Scheme introduced by the RBI in 1965, the Bank regulates the amount and the terms of credit flows. It ensures that credit is directed to genuine productive purposes and not monopolised by a borrower or a group of borrowers.

The Selective Credit Controls on bank advances against a large number of price-sensitive commodities such as pulses, grains, oilseeds, sugar, cotton were liberalised in 1996-97.

Selective Credit Control not only tries to regulate the availability but also the cost of credit.

(i) Moral Suasion

The Reserve Bank has used moral suasion as a technique of monetary control to regulate the supply of credit. For the first time, this technique was tried out by the RBI in September 1949 when it sent a circular letter to commercial banks urging them to exercise restraint in giving advances for speculative purposes. In 1957, the RBI advised commercial banks to avoid advances against the security of agricultural products. The method of moral suasion was more effectively implemented by the RBI after the nationalisation of 14 commercial banks in 1969.

In addition to all this, the RBI has been giving important guidelines and instructions to banks regarding the drawbacks in their operations and credit management. The issuing of specific micro level inventory norms and introducing new methods of bank lending for credit appraisal and determining the volume of credit, the follow-up of bank credit were some major developments in the area of credit management. It has tried to reduce the bias towards the industrial sector in extending bank credit.

To match the demand for and the supply of bank credit, policy measures and credit planning also has been undertaken by the RBI. Each bank is expected to check out its credit budget every year after taking into consideration its deposit mobilisation, its growth and other resources and submit it to the apex bank, so that the banks do not overextend their credit and face any liquidity problem.

To achieve the goals of Five year plans, estimates of required credit expansion are worked out. The provision is made for allocation of funds for pre-empted purposes such as investment in government securities, financing food procurement and distribution etc. Aggregative estimates of the credit needs of the priority and key sectors are also made, separately for the busy and slack seasons. Taking into consideration the deposit growth, growth in the RBI refinance etc., its allocation of bank credit to different sectors purposes and pertaining to regions is worked out.

6.3 MONETARY POLICY OF THE RBI

In developing economies like India, the monetary policy cannot remain confined only upto controlling the supply of money as in the case of the developed economies. In India, it has been structured to meet the particular development requirements of the planned economy. In a growing economy, there has to be continuous expansion of money supply and credit to meet the credit requirements of different potential sectors of the economy such as industry, agriculture, exports and so on. At the same time, the rate of inflation has to be contained within reasonable limits.

The Reserve Bank of India tries to regulate the money supply by controlling bank credit. Variations in the bank credit is the major factor which influences economic activity in India. It tries to influence the cost, volume and the direction of credit in the economy and pays special attention to seasonal requirements of credit. The sectors which have received special attention are core industries (coal, iron steel and engineering); foodgrains (rice, wheat etc.); priority sectors (agriculture small-scale industry etc.) and the weaker sections of the population. The monetary policy of the apex bank (RBI) has encouraged sectoral and overall development and has supported the programmes aiming at social justice.

The statement of the monetary policy of the RBI used to be announced twice a year in April for April to September and in October for October to March. Now it has become an annual affair as the policy statement is now announced in the month of April and only to be reviewed in the month of October.

The Monetary policy had a difficult role to play in India as on one hand, it had to facilitate achieving of basic objectives of planning and on the other act as a countervailing force.

After 1951, the quantitative measures of monetary control, *viz.,* bank rate, CRR and SLR were frequently raised and later lowered to tackle the inflationary pressures.

But the monetary controls to arrest inflation have been used only moderately so as to prevent its adverse effects on the growth performance of the economy. The monetary policy has not only performed a limited role of regulating money supply and checking the price rise but had directly influenced the allocation of credit, especially after the nationalisation of the commercial banks.

Along with the traditional instrument of bank rate, quota-cum-slab system, net-liquidity-ratio etc. were introduced for providing refinance. The selective credit controls also were introduced to curb speculative and unproductive activities. The Credit Authorisation Scheme was introduced to prevent large lending to big borrowers. In the decade of 1970s, to fight inflation, fiscal measures also were introduced along with the monetary measures. Credit norms regarding provision of credit to priority sectors such as agriculture, small-scale, exports etc. and also to the weaker sections of the society were laid down from time to time.

An Appraisal of the Monetary Policy

To mention some of the achievements of the monetary policy, one can say that the overall requirements of a growing or developing economy have been met adequately. Credit to the priority sector has been upto the prescribed norms. The financing of the development programmes for the weaker sections has been satisfactory. As far as controlling the growth of money supply and arresting of inflationary pressures is concerned, the efforts have been remarkable.

However, there are some important areas where the performance of the monetary policy has been that of serious failures. One of the most prominent problems has been in respect of the expansion of the supply of money which has been much larger than the growth of the real output. This has led to large inflationary pressures throughout the planning period.

With regard to the distribution of credit, a much larger share has always gone in favour of urban areas and developed states and regions. The dependence of the agricultural sector and the small-scale industry on the unorganised sector has still not been adequately covered by the institutional credit. Large-scale industries in the organised sector and the services sector have received much larger share in the institutional and bank credit.

The effectiveness of the monetary policy largely depends upon the overall policy framework in the economy and also upon the fiscal policy of the state.

The predominance of currency in the Indian economy inhibits the credit creating capacity of the banking system and restricts the effectiveness of the monetary policy.

Compulsory holding of the government securities by the banks, provision of a specified percentage of credit to the priority sectors, administered rates of interest etc. indicate lack of independence of the RBI in pursuing its monetary affairs.

The large unorganised segment of the money market also restricts the scope of the monetary policy and therefore modernisation of the money market can alone be a foundation for an effective monetary policy.

In April 1985, the RBI had appointed a Committee to review the working of the monetary system headed by Sukhomoya Chakravarty. The Committee was asked to review the monetary system and recommend measures for making the existing monetary policy more effective.

The recommendations made by the Sukhomoya Chakravarty Committee were as follows:

(i) Although price stability is one of the major objectives of the monetary policy, this objective should not come in the way of other socio-economic goals of the Five year plans. The Committee recommended that an appropriate framework is necessary to regulate the credit of the Reserve Bank to the government as it had been a major factor causing large increases in money supply, leading to inflation.

(ii) The Committee suggested a change in the definition of budgetary deficit. The budgetary deficit of the Central Government which was measured in terms of an increase in treasury bills overstated the extent of the monetary impact of fiscal operations as no distinction was made between the absorption of the treasury bills and the increase in the holdings of the treasury bills by the RBI.

(iii) The Committee felt that the banks should have greater freedom in determining their lending rates. It said that this would prevent the misuse of cheap credit.

(iv) It did not favour the continuance of cash credit as the predominant form of bank credit. It mentioned that loans and bill finance forms of bank credit should be encouraged.

(v) The Committee recommended restructuring of the Indian money market wherein the treasury bill market, call money market and commercial bill market will play an important role in the allocation of short-term resources.

Subsequently, the main recommendations of the committee were accepted and were implemented.

Monetary Policy Developments in the Recent Years

The monetary policy developments in the post-reform period, *i.e.,* since mid-1980s and particularly during 1990s reflect the overall shift from the controlled economy to market-determined economy in terms of a transition from the administered framework to the one which is liberalised and yet open to 'prudent' regulation. The current slow-down in economic performance recorded in the decline in the growth rate since 1998-99 has prompted the need for measures initiating growth revival. As such, the task for the monetary policy is to stimulate growth process towards attaining the 'desired' growth rate balanced by the tolerable rise in prices which accompanies these efforts to step up growth rate. The monetary policy transmits its influence on the real sectors of the economy such as output, employment and also over the prices to the extent of a gap it leaves between aggregate demand and supply movements. The gap arises say, when the supply-side lags behind in spite of the policy of 'monetary easing' pursued. This challenge of reconciling between twin objectives of 'Growth and Stability' could be noticed in the objectives spelt out in the recent Monetary and Credit Policy announcements. The policy stipulates that it would facilitate adequate flow of credit for supporting higher GDP growth and ensure that there is no emergence of inflationary pressure on this account. This reveals the monetary stance of RBI in the recent years of meeting adequately all legitimate requirements of credit consistent with the objective of price stability.

The two dimensions of the mechanism through which the monetary impulses travel are the financial market prices such as interest rates, asset prices, equity prices, and the quantities like money supply, aggregate credit, funding of government expenditure etc. Though the monetary policy operates through both the channels of influence, *i.e.,* 'interest rate' channel and 'credit channel,' the interest rates as an instrument of monetary policy has been activated in 1990s. The changes during 1990s indicate the policymakers concern to make the monetary policy framework operationally effective in producing money effects on the real activity through credit flow channel running alongside the interest rate channel, which was earlier administered and inflexible. The faith in the working of credit channel could be noticed right from 1950s when the expansionary monetary policy was pursued. Upto 1980s, the fiscal policy was accorded prime importance in stepping up investment, and the credit flow was directed for financing government expenditure, but monitored or curbed in respect of the commercial sector to guard against inflationary consequences. The period of 1970s was marked by the quantitative credit planning and the measures like credit rationing, selective credit control and the credit authorisation scheme meant for influencing the level and composition of aggregate demand. The restrictions on the credit creation by raising reserve requirements of cash reserve ratio (CRR) and statutory liquidity ratio (SLR) together had reached a peak level of around 60 per cent.

The latter half of the decade of 1990s is however, marked by the phases of monetary policy measures taken — such as hardening and softening of interest rates and raising and cut in reserve requirements — to tackle volatility in money markets by tightening or easing liquidity conditions for containing the impact of volatility in foreign exchange scene due to a drop or rise in the capital inflows and, in turn, a reduction in or accretion to foreign exchange reserves.

Interest Rate Channel and Credit Channel of the Monetary Policy of the RBI

Interest Rate Channel: The emergence of interest rate channel as an important transmission mechanism of monetary policy in 1990s could be seen mentioned in policy objective of maintaining stable interest rate environment with preference for softening and in the successive cuts in key interest rates advocated since 1997.

Bank Rate

Though it indicates the cost at which the banks have access to liquidity by approaching RBI, the bank rate had limited role to play till it was activated in April 1997. The bank rate remained unchanged for 7 years between mid-1970s and 1980s and for 10 years between 1981 and 1990 at respectively 9 per cent and 10 per cent. It was firstly raised to 11 per cent and then to 12 per cent during 1991. By March-end 1999, the bank rate was reduced to 8 per cent. Since activated in April 1997, the bank rate has acted as a reference rate and provides an indication of the trend-softer interest rates — prevailing in the different segments of financial market. By March-end 2001, the bank rate was at 7 per cent which was reduced to 6.5 per cent in Oct. 2001 and further lowered to 6.25 per cent in Oct. 2002, touching the lowest level mark since mid-1970s.

Deposit and Lending Rates

As against the administered interest rates regime which existed between 1975-76 and 1994-95, the scheduled commercial banks (SCBs) have now considerable flexibility in regard to both, the deposit and lending rates. Under the administered interest rates regime, RBI initially prescribed both minimum lending rate and the ceiling rate, then switched over to prescribing only the ceiling rate and between 1988-89 and 1994-95 prescribed only the minimum lending rate. In Oct. 1994, the lending rate was deregulated in respect of loans up to ₹ 2 lakh. In 1994, RBI prescribed prime lending rates (PLRs) as the minimum lending rates for the SCBs. The norms regarding PLRs have been liberalised as banks are now free to prescribe their respective PLRs linked with different tenors. Banks have been allowed to lend at interest rates below PLRs to exporters and other creditworthy borrowers including PSUs. The banks have been granted flexibility in the composition of working capital as between cash credit and loan components of the facilities extended to the clients. On the deposit side, the banks are free to offer fixed/floating rates. The stipulation of minimum lending rates being withdrawn, the co-operative banks are now free to determine their lending rates.

Credit Channel

Guided by the goal of revitalising the growth process, the monetary management in 1990s has been geared up to ensure that all legitimate requirements of credit are adequately met through the availability of loanable funds, viewing the bank credit flow as a financial accelerator. The other policy development is conducting of liquidity operations under Liquidity Adjustment Facility (LAF) under which liquidity in the system is managed since June 2000 by absorbing injecting liquidity on day-to-day basis through repos and reverse repo transactions.

CRR: To enhance the availability of lendable resources with banks, the cash reserve ratio or CRR maintained by banks as specified percentage of their net demand and time liabilities (NDTL) has been reduced as under:

Month and Year	*CRR (in % of NDTL)*
Aug. 1998	11.0
Nov. 1999	9.0
May 2001	7.5
Oct. 2001	5.5
June 2002	5.0
Nov. 2002	4.75

(Statutory minimum for CRR is 3 per cent.)

The mode of maintaining CRR has also been revised. During the reporting fortnight, the banks may maintain 50 per cent of requirements for first 7 days and 65 per cent for next 7 days. The inter-bank term liabilities have been exempted from maintaining minimum CRR of 3 per cent.

On all eligible cash balances maintained by the banks with RBI, interest at the Bank rate will be paid.

Liquidity Adjustment Facility (LAF)

LAF is operated through daily repo and reverse repo transactions, *i.e.*, auctions to meet the liquidity requirements of the system, by injecting and absorbing liquidity. This facility has helped in smoothening volatility in the short-term money market rates.

The Repo/reverse repo transactions are conducted between RBI and the banks. RBI absorbs liquidity through repo transactions and injects liquidity through reverse Repos. These transactions are also effected among the banks and between banks, PDs and financial institutions.

There are a number of recent changes in the operational procedures of LAF.

- Minimum bid size reduced from ₹ 10 crore to ₹ 5 crore.
- Clearing Corporation of India (CCIL) has been set up by RBI on April 30, 2001 registered under the Companies Act, 1956. CCIL has become operational on Feb. 15, 2002. All repo transactions have to be put through CCIL.
- Negotiated Dealing System (NDS) has been made operational from Feb. 15, 2002. The system provides for online electronic bidding facility and the paperless settlement of transactions in government securities, money market instruments including repos. Since Feb. 15, 2002, the members of NDS submit their LAF bids through the system, facilitating thereby the daily operations of the LAF. Banks, PDs, and financial institutions having Subsidiary General Ledger (SGL) Accounts and current accounts with RBI are eligible to participate in NDS. It is proposed to move towards full-fledged LAF and do away with sectorwise standing liquidity facilities from RBI.
- Repo rate: Auctions under LAF conducted on uniform price basis. A multiple price auction, *i.e.,* variable rate repos was introduced in May 2001. Repo rate was 5.75 per cent by June-end 2002. Repo rate reduced by 0.25 per cent for LAF on Oct. 30, 2002.

Policy Developments Regarding Financial Markets

In line with the objectives of monetary policy of improving the functioning and orderly development of the different segments of the financial markets, there are a number of policy developments pertaining to call/notice money market, government securities market, repo market and foreign exchange market.

The developments in the recent period in regard to repo market and foreign exchange market have been dealt with under respective headings.

Call/Notice Money Market

Inter-bank Market: As the repo market develops further for managing liquidity in the system, it is indicated that the call money market would move towards being a pure inter-bank (including PDs) call/notice money market, by phasing out the non-bank participation. The participants in the call/notice money market upto 1987 were the banks as both borrowers and lenders and LIC and UTI as lenders. As recommended by the Vaghul Working Group in 1987, the number of participants in the call/notice money market was enlarged by allowing the entry of non-banking institutions as lenders. The phasing out of the non-bank participants would be in four stages by limiting their lending as under:

Stage I : 85 per cent of their average call money lending: with effect from May 5, 2001.

Stage II : lending limit reduced to 70 per cent from Feb. 15, 2002, *i.e.,* the date when CCIL has become operational.

Stage III : three months after stage II, the lending limit reduced to 40 per cent.

Stage IV : three months after stage III, the lending limit, reduced to 10 per cent and then disallowed to lend.

Prudent limits: The other aspect of the policy development regarding call/notice money market is the prudent limits put on the extent to which the banks may rely on the call/notice money market for their lending and borrowing on a fortnightly basis.

Prudent Limits on SCBs
(lending and borrowing on fortnightly basis)

		Lending	*Borrowing*
Stage 1	:	Oct. 2002: not exceeding 50% of their NOF	not exceeding 150% of their NOF.
Stage 2	:	Dec. 2002: not exceeding 25% of their NOF	not exceeding 100% of their NOF.
[*NOF*	:	Net Owned Funds: paid-up capital + reserves]	*OR* 2% of their aggregate deposits, whichever is higher.

The limit on borrowing from call/notice money market of 2 per cent of aggregate deposits is also applicable in case of Primary Dealers (PDs), Urban Co operative Banks (UCBs), State Co operative Banks StCBs and District Central Co operative Banks (DCCBs).

Government Securities Market

In the last few years, the limiting factors which worked as constraints on the development of Government securities market have been corrected. The discontinuation in April 1997 of the practice of automatic monetisation of central government budget deficits through *'ad hoc'* treasury bills and the switch over to market-related interest rates for government market borrowing from the earlier low coupon rates offered are the measures which have led to the genuine development of government securities market.

Banks are fairly active in dealing in government securities and have set up subsidiaries for acting as primary dealers (PDs) for government securities such as SBI Gilts, PNB Gilts and Gilt Securities Trading Corporation set up jointly by Canara Bank and Bank of Baroda.

The measures like introduction of Negotiated Settlement System (NDS) and the setting up of Clearing Corporation of India Ltd. (CCIL) are meant for enlarging the number of participants, by providing country-wide access to government securities by way of online electronic bidding facility in the primary auctions, screen-based electronic dealing and reporting of transactions, and paperless settlement of transactions in government securities. CCIL has commenced its operations from Feb. 15, 2002 and NDS has also been operational from the same date.

All transactions in Government Securities upto ₹ 20 crore have to be settled through CCIL while those above ₹ 20 crore would have the option for settlement through RBI or CCIL.

Demat form: All SGL holders/stock certificate holders with the Public debt office of RBI, *i.e.*, PDs, RRBs, UCBs, SCBs should hold their investments in government securities in either SGL (with RBI or constituent SGL (with SCB/StCBs/PDs/FIs/sponsor banks in case of RRBs) and SHCIL or in a dematerialised form with depositories — National Security Depository Ltd. (NSDL) or Central Security Depository Ltd. (CSDL).

Policy Developments Regarding Banks

1. Statutory Liquidity Ratio (SLR):

- There has been no change in the requirement of SLR of 25 per cent of NDTL of commercial banks.
- UCBs: The urban co operative banks have to maintain the entire prescribed 25 per cent SLR holding in Government and other approved securities from April 2003.

- RRBs: Earlier, the fixed deposits of RRBs with their sponsor banks were considered towards maintenance of SLR. Now, RRBs are required to maintain their entire SLR holdings in Government and other approved securities and hence convert their deposits with sponsor banks into Government Securities by March-end 2003.

Cash Reserve Ratio (CRR)

Earlier

- Statutory minimum: 3% of NDTL
- RBI (amendment) Act 2006

  RBI can prescribe CRR without any ceiling on floor rate

  RBI cannot pay interest on any portion of CRR balances held by banks. Earlier RBI paid interest on CRR balances above 3% and upto 5%. No interest was payable since September 2004.

2. Collateral Lending Facility (CLF): The liquidity support available to banks against the collateral of Central Government Securities/Treasury Bills held in excess of SLR. With the progressive development of inter-bank Repo Market, the Collateral Lending Facility has been withdrawn effective from Oct. 2002. Now the Standing Liquidity Facilities of RBI to SCBs consists of: (i) export credit refinance and (ii) liquidity support to PDs.

3. Exposure Limits: The exposure limits in respect of bank for single borrower have been reduced from 20 per cent to 15 per cent of capital funds from March-end 2002. The exposure limits for groups have been reduced from 50 per cent to 40 per cent. The limits for infrastructure projects are extendable upto 50 per cent.

4. Composition of Working Capital: Banks have been given freedom to change the composition of working capital by increasing cash credit component beyond 20 per cent *OR* the loan component beyond 80 per cent in case of working capital limits of ₹ 10 crore and above.

5. NPA Norms:

- Non-performing assets (NPAs) consists of assets under three categories: substandard, doubtful and loss.
- The norms for recognition, identification and classification have been changed with effect from March 31, 2001.
- *Earlier* (Effective from March 31, 2001).

NPA is an advance where interest and/or instalment of principal remain overdue for more than 180 days in respect of term loans. [For overdraft/cash credit — the account remains 'out of order' for a period of more than 180 days.]

- The duration of treating an asset as NPA reduced from 180 days to 90 days with effect from March 31, 2004.
- Banks are advised to make additional provisions from the year ending March 31, 2002.

  Earlier (Effective from March 31, 2001)

  A *substandard asset* is one which remains NPA for a period less than or equal to 18 months.

  A *doubtful asset* is one which remains NPA for more than 18 months.

- With effect from March 31, 2005, an asset would be classified as doubtful if it remained in substandard category for 12 months.

Banks have been permitted to phase the additional provisioning consequent upon the reduction in transit period from substandard to doubtful from 18 months to 12 months over a four year's period, commencing from the year ending March 2005.

— To deal effectively with the NPAs of the banking sector:

— RBI issued guidelines in July 2000 on *Settlement Advisory Committees* (SACs) for recovery of NPAs with outstanding balances upto ₹ 5 crore. As on June 30, 2001, PSBs recovered ₹ 2,600 crore from 3,65,000 accounts.

— Recovery of Debts due to Banks and FIs Act 1993 was amended in Jan. 2000 to enhance the effectiveness of Debt Recovery Tribunals (DRTs) in recovery of NPAs. As of March-end 2002, there are 22 DRTs and 5 Debt Recovery Appellate Tribunals.

Cases dealt with by DRTs

	2001	(as on March-end)	2002
No. of Cases	8625		13520
Recovery effected (₹ crores)	1,657	2,864	
	2003 (Dec.)	**2004** (June-end)	**2006** March
No. of Cases filed	61301	63600	73999
Involving amount	₹ 88,876 cr.	₹ 91,926 cr.	₹ 1,11,293 cr.
No. of Cases Adjudicated	25510	25358	38803
Involving amount	₹ 23,273 cr.	₹ 25,359 cr.	₹ 42,792 cr.
Recovery effected	₹ 6,874 cr.	₹ 7,845 cr.	₹ 14,992 cr.

Securitisation and Reconstruction of Financial Assets and Enforcement of Security Interest Ordinance 2002

(Promulgated on Aug. 22, 2002).

Though there has been a decline in their recent years in Gross and Net NPAs of commercial banks expressed as percentage of their advances and assets, the NPAs of SCBs have increased (as over the previous year) in absolute terms. It became as a policy aspect necessary that the issue of stock of NPA is tackled.

The ordinance empowers secured creditors, *i.e.,* lenders as under:

The secured creditor may require the borrower to discharge his liabilities within 60 days from the date of notice, failing which the secured creditor is entitled to take possession or management of the secured assets, including right to transfer by way of lease, assignment on sale or appoint any person to manage the secured asset.

The acquisition of financial assets by the securitisation/reconstruction company would be through the issuance of debentures/bonds or agreements with banks/FIs. The notice of acquisition may be sent by banks/FIs to the concerned borrower who, in turn, is to make payment to the concerned securitisation/reconstruction company.

A securitisation/reconstruction company with owned funds of not less than ₹ 2 crore or not exceeding 15 per cent of total financial assets to be acquired can commence business after obtaining Certificate of Registration from RBI.

The Supreme Court had stayed the operations of the ordinance to the extent that the secured assets can be seized but cannot be leased or assigned.

Securities and Reconstruction of Financial Assets and Enforcement of Security Interest Act (SARFAESI Act) 2002

In view of the Supreme Court Judgement, certain amendments have been made in the ordinance promulgated earlier.

The Certificate of Registration (COR) has been granted by RBI to 3 Asset Reconstruction Companies (ATRs)

Asset Reconstruction Company of India Limited (ARCIL).

Assets Care Enterprise Limited (ACEL).

ASREC (India) Limited

Of these 3, ARCIL has commenced operations and acquired assets of book value of ₹ 9,631 crore. The requirement of minimum NOF for commencement of business by these companies has been increased RBI to not less than 15 per cent of the assets acquired or to be acquired or ₹ 100 crore whichever is less, on an agreeable basis. The Act permits ARC to commence operations with a minimum NOF of ₹ 2 crore.

As on June 30, 2004, public sector banks had issued 61,263 notices involving outstanding amount of ₹ 19,744 crore and recovered an amount of ₹ 1,748 crore from 24,092 cases. IDBI has transferred 11 cases with aggregate outstanding of ₹ 239 crore to ARCIL. IFCI has made an offer to ARCIL to acquire 4 cases with outstanding of ₹ 173 crore.

By March 2006, public sector banks had issued 1,33,665 notices involving an amount of ₹ 41,053 crore and recovered ₹ 7,206 crore in 72,178 cases.

The 'compromise' proposals dealt with were 35,090 involving an amount of ₹ 4,410 crore. The banks/FIs had sold their NPAs to APCIL valued at ₹ 15,343 crore in 2004-05.

Lok Adalat

By March 2006, the commercial banks filed 8,16,068 cases involving ₹ 4,263 crore with ***Lok Adalat.*** 30,7189 cases were decided involving ₹ 1,574 crore. The 'recoveries effected' amounted to ₹ 649 crore in 2,40,819 cases.

6.4 MONETARY POLICY DEVELOPMENTS

(i) Objectives

It was said earlier that monetary policy is exposed to a dilemma in regard to the pursuit of twin objectives "Growth with stability." For supporting economic growth the availability of adequate and timely finance is a prime factor which requires provision of appropriate credit to government and the private sector. At the same time, the authorities need to ensure that the prices do not rise unduly.

The economic reforms initiated in our country in 1990s, have opened up the economy alongwith environment changes which have brought into prominence the additional objective of 'financial stability', *i.e.,* ensuring orderly conditions in the financial markets.

As such, the objectives for the conduct of monetary policy relate to:

(a) price stability

(b) supporting investment requirements of economic growth

(c) financial stability.

(a) Price Stability

The price stability implies low and stable inflation. The prices rise due to both demand pressures as well as shocks and shortages on the supply side.

The pressures on the demand side were the persistent feature of the decades of 1970s and 1980s when the government expansionary fiscal policies. On the supply side, there were shocks caused due to unfavourable conditions like oil crisis and recurring droughts.

Even in the first half of 1990s, the inflationary pressures continued due to high fiscal deficit as well as current account deficit leading to balance of payments crisis. Since mid-1990s, the monetary authorities have faced a new challenge of controlling excessive liquidity, *i.e.,* expansionary effect of an upsurge in the capital (foreign exchange) flows. In the recent years, the inflation rate has however averaged at around 5 per cent in response to the measures taken to offset this effect and contain inflation.

(b) Supporting Economic Growth

For supporting economic growth, the expansionary fiscal policies were pursued and the widening fiscal deficits were covered by enhanced borrowing from RBI and the support from the banking system. Apart from direct borrowing from RBI, the Central Government fiscal deficits were financed by way of automatic monetisation against the sale of *ad hoc* Treasury bills. The banking system supported government borrowing by investing in government securities to meet the pre-emptive SLR requirements (raised to 38.5 per cent in early 1990s). Under Control regime, the interest rates were administered and the credit flows were regulated. In 1990s, as a part of the broader policies of liberalisation, the interest rates have been halved. The credit delivery system being liberalised, the flow of bank credit may get guided by the considerations of efficiency gains, but has to be monitored towards provision in favour of certain sectors like agriculture, rural poor etc.

(c) Financial Stability

With the opening of Indian economy, the reforms in the external sector replaced the administered exchange rates by a system of market-determined flexible exchange rates. The system provided intervention if and when necessary as the foreign exchange market in India is characterised by uneven flow of demand and supply over different periods.

The conduct of monetary policy came to be influenced by the capital (foreign exchange) flows in India in recent years — *i.e.,* by the upsurge in the capital inflows created large surplus in the balance of payments and increases in foreign exchange reserves. Due to increase in net foreign exchange assets of RBI, steps had to be taken to tackle the excess liquidity conditions caused due to expansionary impact of external flows.

(ii) Framework of Monetary Policy

The major change in respect of the framework of monetary policy was when it moved away from control-oriented regime to a liberated but regulated set-up. Arising out of this change, there have been modifications in the conduct of monetary policy — the fiscal dominance of the earlier years has given place to the monetary fiscal co-ordination by improving the interface between the two. In the face of expansionary fiscal policies of the earlier years, the effectiveness of monetary policy in regard to containing inflation was limited. The standard mix of instruments of conducting monetary policy, *i.e.,* open market operations and changes in the bank rate proved ineffective. Besides this, the changes in reserve requirements like CRR were brought about to monitor the monetary, *i.e.,* liquidity conditions.

The steps taken to improve monetary-fiscal interface included phasing out of automatic monetisation through *ad hoc* Treasury bills and the recent regulatory measure — Fiscal Responsibility and Budget Management Act 2003 which granted more operational flexibility to RBI in the conduct of monetary policy.

The Fiscal Responsibility and Budget Management Act: (FRBM Act 2003) FRBM rules July 2004. The Act prohibits direct borrowings by the centre from RBI from the year 2006-07 except by way of ways and means advances (WMA).

The Act stipulates appropriate measure by the central government to reduce the fiscal deficit and eliminate revenue deficit by March 31, 2008.

FRBM rules have set annual targets for the phased reduction in key deficit indicators over the period ending March 31, 2008.

RBI (Amendment) Act 2006

The Amending Act will provide RBI with greater flexibility in the conduct of monetary policy.

The Act empowers RBI:

- to deal in derivatives
- to lend and borrow securities
- to undertake reverse repo and repo operations.

RBI can prescribe CRR without any ceiling or floor rate. RBI carried pay interest on any portion of CRR balances.

The Act has granted powers to RBI to regulate money market and government securities market.

(iii) Operating Procedure

The other aspect of change in the conduct of monetary policy is the recasting of operating procedure and shifting from direct instruments like bank rate, variations in the reserve requirements etc. to indirect instruments and more particularly market-based instruments.

The Repo/reverse repo operations enabled RBI to influence short-term interest rates and monitor liquidity in the system. These operations are carried out under new window introduced in the form of Liquidity Adjustment Facility (LAF). With the surge in the capital flows in the recent years, a combination of measures like open market operations, repo/reverse repo operations under LAF and Market Stabilisation Scheme (MSS) introduced in April 2004 to modulate the monetary conditions by 'sterilising' the expansionary impact of large capital (foreign exchange) inflows.

Second LAF

Second LAF was introduced on November 28, 2005. Substantial recourse to second LAF has been with effect from November 28, 2005.

Market Stabilisation Scheme (MSS)

As recommended by RBI working group on the instruments of sterilisation, a Market Stabilisation Scheme (MSS) was introduced on April 1, 2004. To maintain stability in foreign exchange market, the MSS intends to strengthen RBI's ability to sterilise foreign exchange inflows. Under the scheme, Treasury Bills and dated securities of the Central Government are issued for conducting stabilisation operations.

An increase in RBI's net foreign assets (NFAs) have to be matched by an accretion in Government balance under MSS, driving down the RBI credit to Government. Money raised under MSS is held by Government in a separate account maintained and operated by RBI. The amount held in this account would be appropriated for the redemption and/or buyback of the Treasury Bills and/or dated securities.

The ceiling on outstanding amount under MSS of ₹ 60,000 crore was enhanced to ₹ 80,000 crore.

April to June 2004:

Proposed to issue:	₹ 35,500 crore
Actually issued:	₹ 39,370 crore

July to Sept. 2004

Proposed to issue	₹ 36,500 crore

Outstanding amount of securities under MSS

On Nov. 13, 2004:	₹ 55,686 crore
of which	
91 days TBs.	: ₹ 16,705 crore
364 days TBs.	: ₹ 13,981 crore
dated securities	: ₹ 25,000 crore

Outstanding issuance under MSS on Dec. 10, 2004: ₹ 1,334 crore.

Under MSS, Treasury bills and/or dated securities are issued by Government in addition to the normal borrowing requirement. Securities held under MSS are matched by an equivalent cash balance held by the Government with RBI, offsetting the monetary impact of accretion to RBI's net foreign assets. This issuance of securities under MSS enables RBI to improve liquidity management, to maintain stability in the foreign exchange market and suitably conduct monetary policy.

RBI continued to manage liquidity using a combination of instruments:

- repo and reverse repo operation under LAF
- open market operation
- operation under MSS

March to October 2005:

Liquidity conditions comfortable

- absorption through issuance under MSS
- liquidity absorbed through LAF reverse repo

October 2005 to March 2006:

Liquidity conditions: tight

MSS: suspended issuance of Treasury Bills and dated securities under LAF

LAF: injection through Repo operations

March to August 2006:

Liquidity conditions comfortable

MSS: issuance reintroduced LAF: reverse repo operations

MMS was introduced in April 2004. The Scheme provided another tool of liquidity management of RBI to undertake liquidity absorption, with the introduction of MSS, the pressure on LAF window has to some extent come down.

	LAF	MSS
Outstanding Balances	(₹ *crores)*	
March 2005	19,330	64,211
March 2006*	7,250	29,062
March 2009	1,485	88,077

* reflects IMD redemption of about ₹ 32,000 crore
(IMD : India Millennium Deposit)

KEY TERMS

Open Market Operations, Bank Rate, Interest Rate Channel, Credit Channel, Liquidity Adjustment Facility, Collateral Lending Facility (CLF), Non-performing Assets (NPAs), Market Stabilisation Scheme (MSS).

REVIEW QUESTIONS

1. What are the different financial institutions functioning in the Indian Financial System?
2. Discuss the central banking, promotional and developmental functions of the Reserve Bank of India.
3. Discuss the techniques of Monetary Control of the Reserve Bank of India.
4. Explain the quantitative and qualitative methods of credit control of the RBI.
5. What methods of selective credit control are used by the RBI?
6. What is Monetary Policy?
7. Discuss the S. Chakravarty Committee Reforms (1985) for effectiveness of the Monetary Policy.
8. Discuss the recent developments in the Monetary Policy of the RBI and present an appraisal of the monetary policy.

9. Explain the Interest Rate Channel and the Credit Channel of the monetary policy.
10. Discuss the major aspects of monetary policy framework and the RBI (Amendment) Act, 2006.

REFERENCES

1. Bhole L.M. and Sebastian V. (1996), 'Determinants of Interest Rates in a Deregulated Open Economy', Indian Journal of Economics, Oct. Issue.
2. Mohanty, Deepak and Others, 'Perspectives on Monetary Developments and Policy in India', RBI Occasional Papers, June-Sept., 1997.
3. Mohan, Rakesh (2004), "Challenges to Monetary Policy in a Global Context", RBI Bulletin Jan. 2004.
4. Reserve Bank of India, Annual Report, Various Issues.
5. Reserve Bank of India, Report on Currency and Finance, Various Issues.
6. Reddy Y.V. (2007), 'Evolving Role of Reserve Bank of India: Recent Developments', RBI Bulletin, Dec.

❑ ❑ ❑

7

Commercial Banks: Assets and Liabilities of Commercial Banks and Co operative Banks

INTRODUCTION

Commercial banks are the oldest and the most prominent financial intermediaries in India. In the financial structure of every modern economy, the commercial banks occupy a unique position and they primarily deal in money and credit. Their major task is to mobilise the savings of the community in the form of a variety of deposits and to give loans and advances to borrowers for varied purposes. In terms of the banking policy and operations, commercial banking in India is very unique. It has to work within the constraints of social goals and public ownership. All the public sector, private sector and even the foreign banks have to operate within the prescribed framework and meet the targets both sectoral and regional.

In this chapter, following aspects have been discussed –

7.1 Theoretical Aspects of Banking

7.2 Functions of Commercial Banks

7.3 Progress of Commercial Banking in India Prior to Nationalisation

7.4 Nationalisation of the Commercial Banks, Lead Bank Scheme, Performance in Post Nationalisation Period, Regional Rural Banks

7.5 An Appraisal of Banking since Nationalisation and Recent Reforms and Developments in the Banking Sector

7.6 Assets and Liabilities of Scheduled Commercial Banks

7.7 Co operative Banking in India — Structure and Performance

7.8 Banking Sector Reforms

7.1 THEORETICAL ASPECTS OF BANKING

Commercial banks are basically business concerns guided by the objective of profit making. In India, they have to seek a proper balance between this objective and the other social goals.

The commercial banks also have to maintain a proper balance between profitability and liquidity. Banks deal in other people's money and a substantial part of it is repayble on demand. Therefore along with profitability, management of liquidity is equally important. The commercial banks are expected to hold a part of their deposits in the form of liquid cash, *i.e.,* the cash reserves and the ratio of cash reserves to deposits is known as the cash reserve ratio. The Reserve Bank prescribes this reserve ratio which all the commercial banks have to maintain.

Unlike the other financial institutions, banks can create money. Every loan given by banks creates a deposit. Currency and demand deposits of the banks are the main constituents of money supply. Advances given by the banks lead to the creation of chequable deposits and hence they add to the supply of money in the economy. All the banks have to maintain a reserve ratio specified by the Central Bank say of 10 per cent. Suppose a bank receives a fresh inflow of ₹ 1,000 either as a deposit or as proceeds of sale of government bond to the central bank or in some other form.

Therefore, ₹ 1,000 is bank money out of which ₹ 900 can be utilised for undertaking investment or giving loans as the reserve requirement is 10 per cent. Let us further assume that the bank gives loans worth ₹ 900. The borrower who takes the loan either deposits the amount in the same bank or in some other bank. The total amount of bank money created at this stage will be ₹ 1,000 + ₹ 900 = ₹ 1,900. This process may continue till all the banks maintain only the required reserves of 10 per cent. The total money supply created in the economy will be ₹ 10,000 (₹ 1,000 × 10). The ratio of new deposits to the original increase in reserves is called the *credit multiplier,* money multiplier or deposit multiplier. As the required reserve ratio is 10 per cent, this multiplier is reciprocal of it, *i.e.,* $^{1}/_{10}$.

In practice, however, banks may maintain a higher reserve ratio than the required reserve ratio. When banks give loans, there may be some leakages in the form of cash holding. Therefore, the process of creation of bank money may not work upto full capacity. Commercial banks perform a very crucial role in the business, trade and the industry of modern economies. They mobilise the inactive savings of the community and put them to productive uses and help the capital formation process in the economy.

7.2 FUNCTIONS OF THE COMMERCIAL BANKS

Banking is *accepting* for the purpose of lending. The two most important functions of the commercial banks are:

(i) Accepting deposits, and
(ii) Advancing loans

By performing these functions, they facilitate the mobilisation of savings and putting them to productive uses. In addition to these functions, banks also render some valuable services to their customers.

(i) Accepting Deposits

Commercial banks accept deposits from individuals, business firms and other institutions. They allow to operate three types of accounts to their customers belonging to different sections of the society having different needs, *viz.,* the fixed deposit account, the current account and the saving bank account.

In the fixed deposit account, money is deposited for a specified period and it cannot be obtained by the depositor before the expiry of that period. Earlier withdrawal is permitted by the bank only in exceptional cases. This account particularly suits the needs of the people who have some excess money to be spared for the fixed period and earn some interest on it.

Most business firms prefer to operate the current account. They can make any number of deposits and withdrawals every day. These deposits are chequable deposits earning no rate of interest. But banks provide other services to the holders of these accounts indirectly by giving a preferential treatment to their loan applications and by reducing their service charges etc.

Savings deposits are mostly operated by individuals. They are highly liquid and also earn some interest.

(ii) Advancing Loans

Out of the money received from the depositors, banks give loans. This is the most important function of the banks in modern economies. Commercial banks have been giving loans for productive purposes and usually for short term. Nowadays, banks also give consumer's credit. It is the credit given by the banks to purchase consumer durables. Such a credit is not only safe but also lucrative to the banks as they get high returns on these loans. It also helps in keeping the level of effective demand in the economy very high. After the nationalisation of the banks, their role has undergone drastic change. To bring them in line with the objectives of economic planning and to achieve economic development, banks also have to give a large share of their credit to the priority sectors, *i.e.,* agriculture, small-scale industry and even exports. Banks usually give loans against easily marketable securities.

7.3 PROGRESS OF COMMERCIAL BANKING IN INDIA PRIOR TO NATIONALISATION

A beginning in modern banking in India was made by the British in the seventeenth century. The agency houses used to perform the banking business as an adjunct to their main business. Later, in early nineteenth century, three presidency banks were set up namely, the Bank of Bengal (1806), the Bank of Bombay (1840) and the Bank to Madras (1843). Indian Exchange banks and some exchange banks also were set up during the second half of the nineteenth century. Stagnant economic conditions, falling prices and high rate of bank failures were responsible for the slow rate of growth of banking till the beginning of the twentieth century.

During the twentieth century, the progress of banking was faster. In 1920, the Imperial Bank of India was set up with the merger of three presidency banks.

The Reserve Bank of India (RBI) was established in 1935 as the central bank of the country. In 1949, the Banking Regulation Act was passed and the RBI was nationalised and acquired extensive regulatory powers over the commercial banks.

In 1950, the Indian banking system comprised of the Reserve Bank of India, the Imperial Bank of India, co operative banks, exchange banks and Indian joint stock banks. According to the amount of paid-up capital and reserves held by them, Indian joint stock banks were divided into four classes, *i.e.,* class A, B, C and D. Class A had ₹ 5 lakh and over, class B (₹ 1 lakh and over but less than ₹ 5 lakh), class C (₹ 50,000 and over but less than ₹ 1 lakh) and class D with rupees less than 50,000.

Later on, the banks were divided into two categories of scheduled and non-scheduled banks. The class A banks became the scheduled banks and were known as class A_1 banks and others came to be known as class A_2 banks.

In 1955, on the recommendations of the Rural Credit Survey Committee, the Imperial Bank of India was converted into the State Bank of India and was nationalised. In 1959, the State Bank of India (Associate Banks) Act was passed and a State Bank of India group was created with the nationalisation of eight regional banks.

The SBI group under statutory obligations was required to open new offices in rural and semi-urban areas and modern banking was taken to these unbanked remote areas.

The Deposit Insurance Corporation was set up in January 1962 in order to provide some protection to the depositors. It enhanced the confidence of the people in banks and helped in the mobilisation of more and more deposits.

The nationalisation of fourteen commercial banks in 1969 was a turning point in the history of commercial banking in India. In July 1969, 14 commercial banks in the private sector, each having deposits worth ₹ 50 crore and above were nationalised. Subsequently in 1980, six more banks with deposit liability of not less than ₹ 200 crore were nationalised. In 1969, the Lead Bank Scheme was introduced to extend banking facilities to every corner of the country. Later in 1975, the Regional Rural Banks were set up to supplement the activities of the commercial banks and to especially meet the credit needs of the weaker sections of the rural society.

The Lead Bank Scheme played crucial role in transforming the profit-oriented commercial banks into institutions of development — both sectoral and geographical.

The nationalised banks are banks in which the Government of India is a major shareholder. There was a merger of two nationalised banks in 1993 and now there are 19 nationalised banks. The SBI group includes the State Bank of India and seven associate banks. Therefore, 19 nationalised banks and the eight banks in the SBI group together are known as the public sector banks. Their share in the total banking business is over 90 per cent.

As at the end of March 2002, 97 commercial banks, 196 Regional Rural Banks (RRBs), 52 scheduled Urban Co operative Banks (UCBs) and 16 scheduled State Co operative Banks were operating in the country as scheduled banks.

The Structure of Banking System in India (March-end 2002)

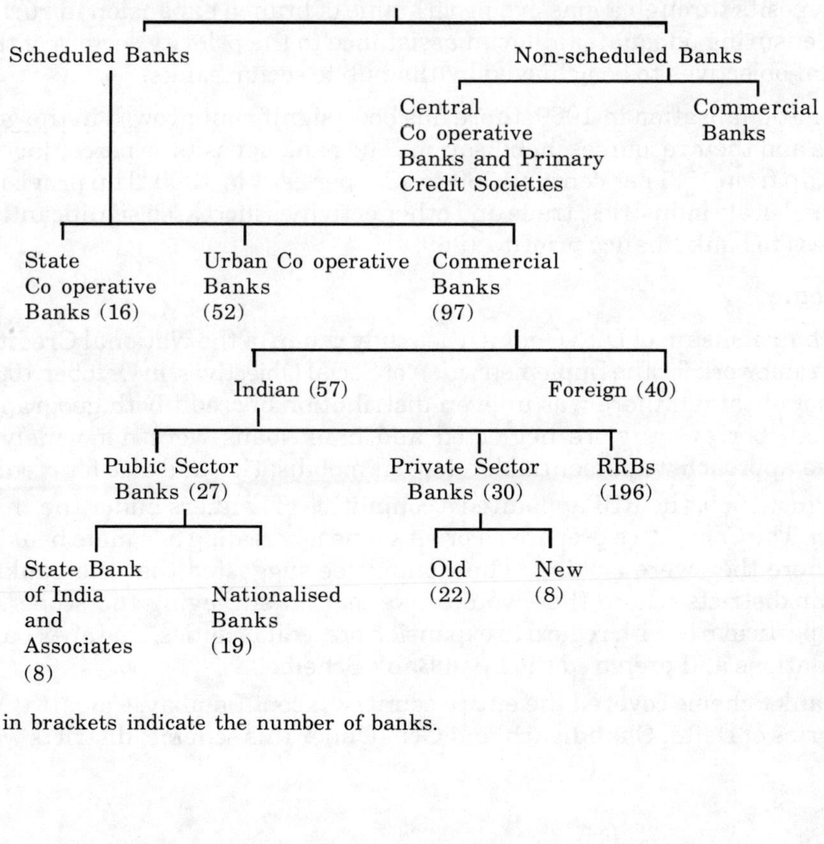

Note: Figures in brackets indicate the number of banks.

The public sector banks dominated the entire banking sector. The 1980s was a period of gradual transition and decontrol.

The Reserve Bank is the apex level bank, *i.e.,* the Central Bank of the country. The scheduled banks are those which are included in the second schedule of The Banking Regulation Act 1965. A scheduled Bank should have paid-up capital and reserves of not less than ₹ 5 lakh. It must also satisfy the RBI that its affairs are not conducted in a manner detrimental to the interest of its depositors. They have to maintain a certain amount of reserves with the RBI. Other banks are the non-scheduled banks.

The early 1990s, guided by the recommendations of the Committee on Financial System (Chairman Shri M. Narasimham 1991) marked the reforms of the banking sector in terms of deregulation and liberalisation. But the second half of the decade saw an increased awareness of the dangers associated with inadequate regulation and supervision of banks. Therefore, banks will have to reap economies of scale in order to cut cost, raise profitability, bring in more transparency in their operations as a move towards international best practices.

7.4 NATIONALISATION OF THE COMMERCIAL BANKS (1969)

The decision of nationalisation of commercial banks was a major turning point in the history of commercial banking in India.

In July 1969, fourteen major commercial banks in the private sector, each having deposits of ₹ 50 crore and above were nationalised. The focus was on social banking for meeting the needs of a developing economy. It aimed at making banking facilities available to all the people even in the remote areas and the provision of adequate credit to agriculture, small industry and exports. It was to encourage new entrepreneurs and development of the backward areas. Mobilisation of deposits through a massive programme of branch expansion in rural and semi-urban areas and ensuring adequate financial assistance to the priority sectors of the economy were the two main objectives to be achieved by the public sector banks.

Since bank nationalisation in 1969, there has been significant growth in the geographical coverage of banks and their resources mobilisation. The bank deposits as percentage to national income has gone up from 15.5 per cent in 1969 to 48.7 per cent in 1999. The provision of credit to agriculture, small-scale industries, trade and other activities increased significantly as against their limited access to bank finance prior to 1969.

Lead Bank Scheme

Under the chairmanship of D.R. Gadgil, the study group of the National Credit Council on 'Organisational Framework for the Implementation of Social Objectives' in October 1962, observed that prior to nationalisation, there was uneven distribution of credit both geographically and purposewise. Small borrowers were neglected and bank loans were not widely dispersed. Therefore, an area approach was essential for deposit mobilisation and also for credit dispersal.

Later in August 1969, the RBI appointed a committee of bankers under the chairmanship of F.K.F. Nariman. The Committee prepared a programme for creating adequate banking facilities in the regions where they were lacking. The Committee suggested that the banks should be allotted particular districts where they would take lead in surveying the scope for banking development and particularly with regard to expansion of credit facilities. The apex bank accepted these recommendations and prepared the Lead Bank Scheme.

The Lead Bank Scheme covered the entire country except Bombay, Calcutta, Madras and the Union territories of Delhi, Chandigarh and Goa. Under this scheme, districts were allotted to State Bank group, 14 nationalised banks and three private Indian banks. The SBI group was allotted 69 districts. Different banks were allotted districts on the basis of their resources and the number of their branches already existing in those districts except some small states, and each state was to have at least two lead banks.

As at the end of March 2002, the Lead Bank Scheme covered 580 districts in the country.

The lead banks were expected to get familiarised with the socio-economic conditions prevailing in the districts and take up the responsibility of major development in the allotted districts. They were required to undertake a survey to obtain information regarding resource endowment, economic and social infrastructure, patterns of different types of production activities, possibility of introducing different development schemes and also the deposit potential and credit gaps in these allotted districts.

Accordingly, the lead banks prepared phased programmes for banking development which are being implemented with the co-operation of other commercial banks and financial institutions.

Before nationalisation, offices of the commercial banks were concentrated in urban areas and industrial and trade centres. Post-nationalisation, out of the total number of new offices, nearly 60 per cent were established in the rural and areas without any banking branch expansion was faster in the backward states of Assam, Orissa, Bihar, Madhya Pradesh etc. compared to the developed states like Maharashtra. The bank branches in the rural areas increased from 1,860 in 1969 to 32,918 in 1998.

The total number of branches of commercial banks in the country was 65933 at June-end 2001 and 66186 at June-end 2002. The share of rural branches was 49.4 per cent in 2001 and 49.1 per cent in the year 2002.

Performance of Commercial Banks in Post-nationalisation Period

There has been a spectacular expansion of bank offices after 1969. The total number of offices of the commercial banks increased from 8,262 in 1969 upto 65,538 in 1997 and 66,137 in June 1998.

Table No. 7.1
Progress of Commercial Banking in India

Indicator	*June 1969*	*June 1975*	*June 1980*	*June 1985*	*March 1990*	*March 1995*	*March 2000*
No. of Scheduled Commercial Banks (SCBs)	73	74	148	264	270	281	297
of which							
RRBs			73	183	196	196	196
Other SCBs			75	81	74	85	100
No. of Bank Offices	8262	18730	32419	51385	59752	62367	67339
Population per office (in '000s)	64	32	21	15	14	15	15
Per capita deposit (₹)	85	208	494	1026	2095	4242	8247
Per capita credit (₹)	68	148	327	675	1275	2320	4705

Table No. 7.1 (A)

Total No. of Commercial Banks : 2004-06

	2004 (June-end)	*2005 (June-end)*	*2006 (June-end)*
SBI	1	1	1
Associates of SBI	7	7	7
Nationalised banks	19	19	19
Other Public Sector Banks	—	1	1
Private Sector Banks	30	29	28
Foreign Banks	32	31	29
RRBs	196	196	130
(Local Area Bank)	5	4	4
Total	290	288	219

Year	*2003*	*2004*	*2005*	*2006*	*2007*	*2008*	*2009*
(a) Total No. of bank branches	66535	67188	68355	69471	71839	76061	79722
(b) No. of Rural branches	32303	32121	32082	30579	30551	31069	31682
(c) % share of rural branches in the total	48.5	47.8	46.9	44.0	42.5	40.8	39.7
(d) Population per office (in 000s)	16	16					

The total number of branches of commercial banks in the country as at June-end 2009 was 79722. The share of rural branches were 40.8% in 2008 and 39.7 in 2009. The lower shares of rural branches in recent years show the impact of the branch rationalisation policy.

Deposit Mobilisation: After nationalisation, there has been massive rise in the deposits of the scheduled commercial banks. Total outstanding deposits of the scheduled commercial banks on March 31, 1999 were ₹ 7,37,003 crore as against ₹ 4,665 crore in July 1969. Of the total deposits of ₹ 12,45,919.42 crore in the year 2001-02, the nationalised banks accounted for the largest share of nearly 50 per cent, followed by the SBI and its associates with a share of 28.2 per cent; other private sector banks 13.6 per cent, foreign banks 5.2 per cent and RRBs with a share of 3.4 per cent.

As far as the statewise ownership pattern of the deposits of the scheduled commercial banks is concerned, Maharashtra is the leading state with nearly one-fifth share in total bank deposits in the country. It is followed by Uttar Pradesh, West Bengal, Delhi, Gujarat and Tamil Nadu.

Bank Lending: After nationalisation, there has been a spectacular rise in the bank credit. Total advances of the scheduled commercial banks increased from ₹ 3,399 crore in 1969 to ₹ 3,21,813 crore on March 27, 1998. This phenomenal growth in credit was due to massive deposit mobilisation on one hand and on the other due to the inflationary expansion of money supply. But the bank deposits have grown much faster in the recent years than the bank credit. As a result of this, the credit deposit ratio touched to 53.5 per cent on March 27, 1998.

Since 1998, *i.e.,* between 1998 and 2002 the average annual growth rate in aggregate deposits was 17.2 per cent and the average annual growth in the bank credit was 17 per cent, leaving credit-deposit ratio around 53 per cent.

Sectoral Deployment of Bank Credit: At the initial stage, *i.e.,* beginning of economic planning in 1951, commerce and industry received major shares in bank credit. The agricultural sector was not taken into consideration at all.

After nationalisation, there was remarkable change in the credit policy of the banks. Credit to the priority sectors especially agriculture and the small industry was given more importance by the policymakers.

On March-end 1997, the outstanding gross bank credit was ₹ 2,49,408 crore of which large and medium industries received ₹ 1,00,025 crore. The share of the priority sectors was 32 per cent of the total bank credit.

On March 28, 1997, the outstanding bank credit to agriculture was ₹ 30,874 crore. Various innovative schemes such as village adoption, agricultural development branches and equity funds for small units etc. were introduced for the potential disbursement of bank credit.

For making the banking sector an integral part of the planning process in the country, credit planning was introduced. Banks have to prepare quarterly credit budgets to bring about more correlation between the demand for and supply of credit.

Regional Rural Banks (RRBs)

The Working Group on rural banks under the chairmanship of Shri M. Narasimham recommended the setting up of regional rural banks as part of a multi-agency approach to rural credit. It was realised that the commercial banks and co-operative credit societies were not adequately meeting the credit needs of small and marginal farmers, agricultural labourers and artisans in the rural areas. The small income groups required low cost credit. The regional rural banks staff were to be recruited from the neighbouring areas to understand the local needs and problems of the people.

Table No. 7.2

Outstanding Loans and Advances of RRBs

(at March-end)

(₹ in Crores)

Purpose	*2000*	*2001*	*2002*	*2003*	*2004*	*2005*	*2006*	*2007*	*2008*	*2009*
1. Crop loans (short term)	2865	3670	4883	6495	7664	10980	14690	18707	22748	24986
2. Term loans for agriculture	3339	3547	3522	3766	4058	5730	6704	8745	10486	11480
3. Other advances	23	—	—	—	—	—	—	—	—	—
I. Total agricultural (1 + 2 + 3)	6227 (47.5)	7217 (45.7)	8405 (45.2)	10261 (46.3)	11722 (44.9)	16170 (50.8)	21394 (54.0)	27452 (56.6)	33216 (56.3)	36466 (52.8)
4. Rural artisans (Village Cottage Industries)	773	561	671	695	715	713	702	736	671	820
5. Other Industries	664	246	226	330	433	580	824	880	1227	1400
6. Retail Trade etc.	2073	1951	2984	3264	3607	4364	3925	3677	4531	5015
7. Other Purposes	3372	5819	6343	7608	9638	10504	12868	15748	19339	25329
II. Total Non-agricultural (4 + 5 + 6 + 7)	6882 (52.5)	8517 (54.3)	10224 (54.8)	11897 (53.7)	14393 (55.1)	16161 (49.2)	18319 (46.0)	21041 (43.4)	25768 (43.9)	32564 (41.2)
Total (I + II)	13109	15794	18629	22158	26115	32871	39713	48493	58984	69030

Source: Report on Trends and Progress of Banking in India: 2008-09.

Between 2000 and 2009, the loans and advances by RRBs have gone up nearly 5 times.

Note: Figures in brackets indicate % share in total.

In 1975, only 5 RRBs were set up. There were 196 RRBs in 2005. The RRBs can be set up when a public sector bank sponsors them. The branches of RRBs increased significantly from 17 in 1975 to 14,516 in 1996. Earlier, the authorised capital of every RRB was ₹ 1 crore and the issued capital was ₹ 25 lakh. In this, the shares were Central Government: 50 per cent, the concerned State Government: 15 per cent and the sponsor bank: 35 per cent. Later, the authorised capital of RRB was raised to ₹ 5 crore and the issued capital to ₹ 1 crore.

These banks have played on important role in mobilising rural savings. Advances to the weaker sections account for more than 40 per cent share in the total direct advances of RRBs. The RRBs now conduct all types of banking business generally within one to five districts.

Distribution of Total Advances of RRPs (in percentage)

March-end 2000:			
	Agriculture Advances	:	47.5
	Non-agricultural Advances	:	52.5
Total			100
March-end 2006:			
	Agricultural Advances	:	54.0
	Non-agricultural Advances	:	46.0
Total			100

Distribution of Agricultural Advances of RRBs (in Percentage)

	March 2000	*March 2006*
Crop loan	46	69
Term loan	54	31

Between 2000 and 2006, the share of crop loans in agricultural advances has increased and that of term loans declined. There has been 6.5% increase in the share of advances to agriculture in the total advances during 2000-2006.

Table No. 7.3

Performance of RRBs
(as at March-end)

(*₹ in Crores)*

Item	*1999-2000*	*00-01*	*01-02*	*02-03*	*03-04*	*04-05*	*05-06*	*06-07*	*07-08*	*08-09*
Aggregate Deposits	30051	35995	42494	47644	53390	58286	64195	81620	94412	113828
Of which										
Demand Deposits	5105	6098	7305	8513	10727	12757	17355	20003	21022	24353
Term Deposits	24946	29897	35183	39131	42663	45529	46840	61617	73390	83475
Bank Credit	12663	15211	18033	21359	25057	31651	36050	48420	57417	64011
Investment	6009	7489	6871	12008	17532	20213	19050	22424	25387	29414
of which										
(a) Government Securities	1224 (20.3)	1642	1970	7673	13324	16970 (54.0)	16787	20249	23411	27118 (92.0)
(b) Other Approved Securities	4786 (79.7)	5847	4901	4335	4208	3242 (16.0)	2263	2175	1976	2296 (8.0)

Source: Handbook of Statistics on Indian Economy: 2008-09
Report on Trends and Progress of Banking in India: 2008-09
Note: Figures in bracket indicate % share to the total.

Between 1999-2000 and 2008-09, aggregate deposits of RRBs have gone up 3.8 times and the increase in bank credit has been more than 5 times.

During 2000-09, the share of Government securities in investment of RRBs has gone up from over 20 per cent to nearly 92 per cent, indicating a distinct shift in favour of government securities.

The RRB have been suffering from various organisational and recovery problems.

(i) Multi-agency control of RRBs (*i.e.,* Central and State Governments and the sponsor banks) has resulted in many problems in their functioning in terms of lack of support and proper monitoring.

(ii) Expansion of these RRBs and their branches has resulted in lack of control and management.

(iii) The recovery position of RRBs has been very bad due to defective loaning policies, weaks supervision and monitoring, political interference and lack of legal and administrative support from the state government in their recovery of loans.

Majority of RRBs incurred huge losses and became unviable. The losses of RRBs wiped off their share capital and eroded even a part of their deposits.

Inadequate attention to the recruitment and training of the staff and non-competent management also resulted in a number deficiencies in the functioning of RRBs.

In 1991, Narasimham Committee had recommended that RRB may be given a choice to maintain a separate identity or to get merged with the sponsor banks as rural subsidiaries.

In the recent years, there has been a significant improvement in the performance and the asset quality of RRBs.

The asset quality improvement could also be noticed in terms of reducing level of Non-performing assets (NPAs) of RRBs.

In February 2005, RBI appointed Working Group on RRBs. It submitted report in June 2005. On September 12, 2005, 28 RRBs were amalgamated into 9 (nine) new RRBs.

August 2006, 132 RRBs have been amalgamated to form 41 new RRBs.

October 2006: 137 RRBs have been amalgamated to form 43 new RRBs.

Total no. of RRBs

March 2005	:	196
March 2006	:	133
March 2007	:	90
March 2008	:	90
March 2009	:	86
(P)		

As at the end of March 2009, there were 86 RRBs including 45 amalgamated and 41 stand-alone RRBs.

Table No. 7.4

RRBs — (1) Profit/Loss: Operating and Net

(2) Growth in Total Assets

(₹ in Crores)

	2000-01			*2001-02*			*2002-03*		
No. of RRBs	*Loss making* (26)	*Profit making* (170)	*RRBs No.* (196)	*Loss making* (29)	*Profit making* (167)	*RRBs No.* (196)	*Loss making* (40)	*Profit making* (156)	*RRBs No.* (196)
(1) Profit/Loss									
(i) Operating	–59.90	790.10	730.20	-63.59	637.67	774.08	-149	863	715
(ii) Net	-75.84	676.48	600.64	-92.05	699.93	607.88	-215	739	525
(2) Total assets	5235.70	44405.69	49641.39	6169.30	50634.54	56803.54	10282	53332	63614
	2003-04			*2004-05*			*2005-06*		
No. of RRBs	*Loss making* (33)	*Profit making* (163)	*RRBs No.* (196)	*Loss making* (30)	*Profit making* (166)	*RRBs No.* (196)	*Loss making* (22)	*Profit making* (111)	*RRBs No.* (133)
(1) Profit/Loss									
(i) Operating	–94	1149	1055	– 102	1110	1008	-104	891	787
(ii) Net	-184	953	769	– 154	902	748	-170	681	510
(2) Total assets	8892	61386	70278	9780	68086	77866	11747	77898	88652
	2007-08			*2008-09*					
No. of RRBs	*Loss making* (8)	*Profit making* (82)	*RRBs No.* (90)	*Loss making* (6)	*Profit making* (80)	*RRBs No.* (86)			
(1) Profit/Loss									
(i) Operating	– 43	1902	1859	– 24	2651	2627			
(ii) Net	– 56	1083	1027	– 36	1405	1369			
(2) Total assets	4548	1206465	125194	3250	142574	145824			

The total assets of RRBs have increased from ₹ 49641 crore in 2000-01 to ₹ 88652 crore in 2005-06 and to ₹ 145824 crore in 2008-09. The net profit was over ₹ 600 crore in 2000-01, but declined to over ₹ 500 crore in 2005-06 and increased to ₹ 1369 crore in 2008-09.

Table No. 7.5
NPAs of RRBs
(As per cent to total loans)

(as at March-end)

Assets	*1997*	*1998*	*1999*	*2000*	*2001*	*2002*
Standard Assets	63.2	67.2	72.2	76.9	81.2	83.9
Non-performing Assets	36.8	32.8	27.8	23.1	18.8	16.1
Substandard	8.2	8.5	8.1	7.0	5.3	N.A.
Doubtful	24.0	20.4	17.0	14.0	12.0	N.A.
Loss	4.6	3.9	2.7	2.1	1.5	N.A.

Table No. 7.5(A)
NPAs of RRBs
(as % to total loan)

(at March-end)

	2004-05	2005-06
Gross NPA	8.5	7.3
Net NPA	5.15	3.96

Source: Report on Trends and Progress of Banking in India: 2005-06.

7.5 AN APPRAISAL OF BANKING SINCE NATIONALISATION AND RECENT REFORMS AND DEVELOPMENTS IN THE BANKING SECTOR

After nationalisation of the commercial banks, their branches and their deposits increased considerably. Along with the total bank credit, the priority sector credit also increased upto nearly 34 per cent of the total bank credit. Although the performance of the banking system was very impressive, it suffered from many weaknesses, mainly due to the inadequacies of the banking system and their unsatisfactory performance. The directed investment and the directed credit programmes along with rising expenditures completely eroded the profitability of the banks. The SBI and its subsidiaries declared small profits, whereas some public sector banks and foreign banks reported net losses in the early 1990s. The overall profitability of the commercial banks is still low. The major causes of low profitability of the Indian banks and the measures introduced to improve them recommended by the Narasimham Committee (1991) and implemented by the authorities are as given below:

Directed Investment

The cash reserve ratio was initially introduced as an instrument to limit the liquidity of the banks and the statutory liquidity ratio was meant for imposing financial discipline on banks and to provide some protection to the depositors.

In the post-nationalisation period and particularly during the 1980s, rising fiscal deficit forced the government to borrow from the Reserve Bank and external sources. The inflationary pressure generated due to the government borrowing from the RBI led to rising cash reserve ratio. The pressure to borrow from external sources resulted in increasing statutory liquidity ratio. As a result of this, the banks were required to make heavy investments in the government securities carrying low interest rates and the securities of the public sector financial institutions also.

In October 1985, the CRR and SLR stood at 9 per cent* and 37 per cent respectively. In 1991, the statutory pre-emptions under CRR and SLR, on an incremental basis, reached a level of 63.5 per cent. On the balance of 36.5 per cent, there were pre-emptions under the priority sector of 40 per cent, export credit, food credit and other formal and informal, pre-emptions. Such financial repression due to pre-emptions on account of high CRR and SLR coupled with administered rates of interest severely undermined the profitability of commercial banks.

Note: *The 9 per cent CRR was on outstanding net demand and time liabilities (NDTL). There was also a 10 per cent CRR on incremental NDTL.

The Narasimham Committee therefore recommended a reduction in the SLR to 25 per cent by 1996 and also an unspecified reduction in the CRR.

The SLR was maintained at 25 per cent on November 25, 1999. The CRR was brought down step by step from 13 per cent in May 1996, then to 10 per cent and in November 1999 it was brought down to 9 per cent. The incremental 10 per cent CRR was withdrawn in 1992.

Therefore, the statutory pre-emption of bank resources was brought down from 63.5 per cent to 34 per cent, releasing about 20 per cent of the resources for deployment at the bank's discretion.

There has been no change in the statutory minimum requirement of SLR of 25 per cent of NDTL (Net Demand and Time Liabilities).

A policy of reducing CRR (cash reserve ratio) has been pursued further towards the objective of reducing it to its statutory minimum of 3 per cent.

Nov. 1999 : 9.0 per cent.

Nov. 2002 : 4.75 per cent.

Between May 2001 and Nov. 2002, the CRR has been reduced from 7.5 per cent to 4.75 per cent.

Directed Credit Programme

One of the major objectives of bank nationalisation in 1969 was to make the bank credit available to the priority sector to facilitate economic growth and achieve social justice. To some extent, this objective also was achieved but at a very high cost, as a result of the shift from security-oriented credit to purpose-oriented credit. Fixation of targets for credit to the priority sectors such as agriculture, small-scale manufacturing units, export sector, food procurement operations and so on, neglect of the qualitative aspect of lending, accumulation of overdues considerably deteriorated the quality of loan portfolio of the banks. A further damage was done by political and administrative interference in credit decision-making.

All this not only badly affected the profitability of the banks but also failed in achieving any efficiency and equity. In the agricultural sector, for example, medium and large farmers mostly benefited from such credit and also received large subsidies for a number of years.

The Narasimham Committee in 1991, recommended phasing out of such directed credit programmes. However, some credit support in the medium term was recommended to the (redefined) priority sector and the credit target was to be reduced from 40 per cent to 10 per cent of the total credit.

But the government will to implement these recommendations was almost lacking. Large farmers, small industrialists and transporters, who have greatly benefited from such directed credit programmes did not permit the phasing out of these programmes so easily.

In 1985, the share of the priority sector in gross bank credit was 38.4 per cent and it rose upto 39.4 per cent in 1990. In the 1990s, this share fell to 34.4 per cent in 1994 and then to 31.6 per cent in 1996. In 1999, the share of the priority sector was 33.5 per cent.

In addition to this, concessional interest rates on the bank credit to the priority sector further reduced the profitability of the banks. The Narasimham Committee in 1991 recommended phasing out of concessional interest rates for the priority sectors. In the opinion of this Committee, easy and timely availability of credit was more important than its cost.

Administered Interest Rates

Under the administered interest rate system, the interest rates on both bank deposits and bank loans used to be fixed by the Reserve Bank. In the opinion of the Narasimham Committee, the main function of the interest rates is that of allocating the scarce loanable funds among alternative users and therefore , the interest rates must be determined by the market forces. At present, the banks are allowed to decide the interest rates on all term deposits of maturity of over one year and on all advances greater than two lakh.

Income Recognition, Asset Classification and Provisioning

In April 1992, the Government accepted the recommendations of the Narasimham Committee and adopted Basel Capital adequacy standards.

The RBI issued guidelines for income recognition, and asset classification and provisioning.

Non-performing assets (NPAs): The Narasimham Committee for the first time defined the concept of non-performing assets.

Non-peforming loan was defined as credit facility in respect of which interest has not been received for 180 days.

Asset classification: These non-performing loans are classified as substandard, doubtful and loss depending on how long they have been non-peforming.

Substandard asset: One which remains NPA for a period less than or equal to 18 months.

Doubtful asset: One which remains NPA for more than 18 months.

- The duration of treating on asset as NPA reduced from 180 days to 90 days with effect from March 31, 2004.
- From March 31, 2005, an asset would be classified as doubtful if it remained in substandard category for 12 months.

Income recognition: Accrued income from the non-performing loans could no longer be treated as income by the banks.

Provisioning: Provisioning had to be made at 10% for substandard loans, 20% to 50% for doubtful loans and 100% for loss loan.

Standard assets: The provision requirement for standard assets was 0.25%. In November 2005, the provisioning for the standard assets was raised from 0.25% to 0.4% excluding direct advances to agricultural and small and medium enterprises (SMEs) sectors. The general provisioning requirement for banks (excluding RRBs) on standard assets has been increased from 0.4% to 1.0% in May 2006 in respect advances to certain sectors — personal loans, loans and advances qualifying as capital market exposures, residential housing loans beyond ₹ 20 lakh, commercial real estate loans.

Substandard and doubtful

The provisioning requirements in respect of substandard and doubtful assets are:

Substandard assets	:	Secured advances: 10%
		Unsecured exposure: 20%
Doubtful assets	:	Secured: 20% to 100%
		Unsecured portion: 100%

Non-Performing Assets (NPAs)

Between 2000 and 2002, the NPAs of SCBs showed an increase over the previous year

Table No. 7.6
NPAs of Scheduled Commercial Banks
(as of March-end)

(₹ in Crores)

Year	*Gross NPA*	*% increase*	*Net NPA*	*% increase*
1999-2000	60408	2.9	30073	7.3
2000-2001	63741	5.5	32461	7.9
2001-2002	70861	11.2	35554	9.5
2002-2003	68717	– 3.0	29692	– 10.5
2003-2004	64812	– 5.7	24396	– 17.8
2004-2005	59373	– 8.4	21754	– 10.8
2005-2006	51097	– 13.9	18543	– 14.8
2006-2007	50486	–1.2	18543	8.4
2007-2008	56435	11.8	24734	23.0

There has been a decline in Gross NPA during and after 2002-03 and up to 2006-07. In regard to Net NPA, the decline has been during and after 2002-03 and up to 2005-06.

Public Sector Banks

Year	*Gross NPA*	*% increase*	*Provision*	*Net NPA*	*% increase*
1999-2000	53033	—	—	26187	—
2000-2001	54672	3.0	9476	27077	6.8
2001-2002	56473	3.3	13611	27958	0.07
2002-2003	54090	– 4.2	25876	24877	– 11.0
2003-2004	51537	– 4.7	29649	19335	– 22.3
2004-2005	48399	– 6.1	—	16904	– 12.6
2005-2006	41358	– 14.5	—	14566	– 13.8
2006-2007	38968	–5.8	—	15145	4.0
2007-2008	40595	4.2	29307	17836	17.8

There has been a decline in Gross NPA of Public Sector Banks during and after 2002-03 and up to 2006-07. In regard to NPA of Public Sector Banks, the decline has been during and after 2002-03 and up to 2005-06.

TABLE No. 7.7
Gross and Net NPAs of Scheduled Commercial Banks Expressed as % to Gross and Net Advances and Total Assets

(₹ *in Crores*)

Year	*Gross NPA*				*Net NPA*			
	Gross Advances	*Gross NPA Amount*	*% to Goss Advances*	*% to Total Assets*	*Net Advances*	*Net NPA Amount*	*% to Net Advances*	*% to Total Assets*
1998-1999	399436	58722	14.8	6.2	367012	28020	7.6	2.9
1999-2000	475113	60408	12.7	5.5	444292	30073	6.8	2.7
2000-2001	558766	63741	11.4	4.9	526328	32461	6.2	2.5
2001-2002	680958	70861	10.4	4.6	645859	35554	5.5	2.3
2002-2003	778043	68717	8.8	4.0	740473	32671	4.4	1.9
2003-2004	902026	64812	7.2	3.3	862643	24396	2.8	1.2
2004-2005	1152662	59373	5.2	2.5	1115663	21754	2.0	0.9
2005-2006	1551378	51097	3.3	1.8	1516851	18543	1.2	0.7
2006-2007	2012510	50486	2.5	1.5	1981237	20141	1.0	0.6
2007-2008	2507885	56435	2.3	1.3	2477039	24734	1.0	0.6
2008-2009	3038254	68973	2.3	1.3	3000906	31424	1.1	0.6

By March-end 2009, Gross NPAs of SCBs were at 2.3% of Gross advances and 1.3 per cent of total assets and Net NPAs were at 1.1 per cent and 0.6 per cent of net advances and total assets respectively.

During 1998-99 and 2008-09, there has been a persistent decline in the percentage of Gorss NPA, to Gross Advances and total assets and in the percentage of Net NPAs to net advances and total assets.

Table No. 7.8

NPAs: Bank Groupwise Distribution

(Per cent)

Bank Group	*Gross NPA to Gross Advances*									
	1998 to 1999	*1999 to 2000*	*2000 to 2001*	*2001 to 2002*	*2002 to 2003*	*2003 to 2004*	*2004 to 2005*	*2005 to 2006*	*2006 to 2007*	*2007 to 2008*
Public Sector Banks	15.89	13.98	12.37	11.09	9.4	7.8	5.5	3.6	2.7	2.2
Old Private Sector Banks	10.81	8.17	8.37	9.65	8.9	7.6	6.0	4.4	3.1	2.3
New Private Sector Banks	—	—	—	—	7.6	5.0	3.6	1.7	1.9	2.5
Foreign Banks	7.59	6.99	6.84	5.38	5.3	4.6	2.8	1.9	1.8	1.8
Bank Group	*Gross NPA to Total Assets*									
	1998 to 1999	*1999 to 2000*	*2000 to 2001*	*2001 to 2002*	*2002 to 2003*	*2003 to 2004*	*2004 to 2005*	*2005 to 2006*	*2006 to 2007*	*2007 to 2008*
Public Sector Banks	6.71	5.95	5.31	4.89	4.2	3.5	2.7	2.1	1.6	1.3
Old Private Sector Banks	4.48	3.61	3.65	4.83	4.3	3.6	3.1	2.5	1.8	1.3
New Private Sector Banks	—	—	—	—	3.8	2.4	1.6	1.0	1.1	1.4
Foreign Banks	3.10	3.16	3.04	2.43	2.4	2.1	1.4	1.0	0.8	0.8
Bank Group	*Net NPA to Net Advances*									
	1998 to 1999	*1999 to 2000*	*2000 to 2001*	*2001 to 2002*	*2002 to 2003*	*2003 to 2004*	*2004 to 2005*	*2005 to 2006*	*2006 to 2007*	*2007 to 2008*
Public Sector Banks	8.13	7.42	6.74	5.82	4.5	3.1	2.1	1.3	1.1	1.0
Old Private Sector Banks	7.41	5.41	5.44	5.72	5.2	3.8	2.7	1.7	1.0	0.7
New Private Sector Banks	—	—	—	—	1.5	1.7	1.9	0.8	1.0	1.2
Foreign Banks	2.94	2.41	1.82	1.89	1.7	1.5	0.8	0.8	0.7	0.8
Bank Group	*Net NPA to Total Assets*									
	1998 to 1999	*1999 to 2000*	*2000 to 2001*	*2001 to 2002*	*2002 to 2003*	*2003 to 2004*	*2004 to 2005*	*2005 to 2006*	*2006 to 2007*	*2007 to 2008*
Public Sector Banks	3.14	2.94	2.72	2.42	1.9	1.3	1.0	0.7	0.6	0.6
Old Private Sector Banks	2.83	2.30	2.27	2.49	2.5	1.8	1.4	0.9	0.6	0.4
New Private Sector Banks	—	—	—	—	0.7	0.8	0.8	0.4	0.5	0.7
Foreign Banks	1.10	1.03	0.77	0.82	0.8	0.7	0.4	0.4	0.3	0.3

During the period 1999-2002, there has been an increase in the percentage share of standard assets in the loan assets of SCBs and the shares of substandard, doubtful and loss assets have declined.

Table No. 7.8 (A)

NPAs of SCB: Bank Groupwise

(Per cent)

	Gross NPAs									
Bank Group	*Gross NPA to Gross Advance*					*Gross NPA to Total Assets*				
Year	*2001*	*2002*	*2003*	*2004*	*2005*	*2001*	*2002*	*2003*	*2004*	*2005*
Public Sector Bank	12.4	11.1	9.4	7.8	5.7	5.3	4.9	4.2	3.5	2.8
(Old) Private Sector Banks	10.9	11.0	8.9	7.6	6.0	5.1	5.2	4.3	3.6	3.2
(New) Private Sector Banks	5.1	8.9	7.6	5.0	5.0	2.1	3.9	3.8	2.4	2.4
Foreign Banks	6.8	5.4	5.3	4.6	2.8	3.0	2.4	2.4	2.1	1.4
	Net NPAs									
	Net NPA to Net Advances					*Net NPA to Total Assets*				
Year	*2001*	*2002*	*2003*	*2004*	*2005*	*2001*	*2002*	*2003*	*2004*	*2005*
Public Sector banks	6.7	5.8	4.5	3.0	2.1	2.7	2.4	1.9	1.3	1.0
(Old) Private Sector Banks	7.3	7.1	5.5	2.7	3.8	3.3	3.2	2.6	1.8	1.4
(New) Private Sector Banks	3.1	4.9	4.6	2.4	1.9	1.2	2.1	2.2	1.1	0.8
Foreign Banks	1.8	1.9	1.8	1.5	0.9	0.8	0.8	0.8	0.7	0.4

Table No. 7.9

Scheduled Commercial Banks: Classification of Loan Assets

Year	*Standard Assets*	*Substandard Assets*	*Doubtful Assets*	*Loss Assets*
1988-99	85.3	5.0	7.8	1.9
1999-00	87.2	4.1	7.1	1.6
2000-01	88.6	3.3	6.8	1.4
2001-02	89.6	3.1	6.1	1.2
2002-03	91.2	2.6	5.1	1.2
2003-04	92.8	2.3	4.0	0.8
2004-05	94.9	1.2	3.3	0.6
2005-06	96.7	1.0	2.0	0.4
2008	97.7	1.1	1.0	0.2
2009	97.7	1.2	0.9	0.2

During the period 1998-99 and 2005-06, there has been a consistent increase in the percentage share of standard assets in the loan assets of SCBs, and the shares of substandard, doubtful and loss assets have fallen.

NPA Management by Banks

The option now available to banks for resolving their non-performing assets (NPAs) include—

Channels for recovery of due

- Approaching Debt Recovery Tribunals (DRTs) set up under *Recovery of debts due to Bank and FIS Act 1993.*

  The Act has been amended in 2000 and 2003

Cases filed by banks with DRTs	No. 71 399 cases
	Amount ₹ 1,11,203 cases
Cases adjudicated	No. 38803 cases
	Amount involved ₹ 42,792 crore

  Amount recovered so far through adjudicated case ₹ 14,992 crore.

- Securitisation and Reconstruction of Financial Assets and Enforcement of Security Interest Act (SARFAESI Act 2002)

Under the Act, banks have issued notices to 133665 cases with outstanding amount ₹ 41,053 crore and banks have recoverd ₹ 7,296 crore in 72,178 cases. The compromise proposed were reached in 35,090 cases involving an amount of ₹ 4,410 crore.

- Forum of 'Lok Adalats'

By March-end 2006, 8,16,068 cases were filed by the commercial banks with Lok Adalats, involving an amount of ₹ 4263 crore. The cases decided were 3,07,189 involving ₹ 1574 crore. The recoveries amounted to ₹ 649 crore in 2,40,819 cases.

- Restructuring: Corporate Debt Restructuring Mechanism (CDRM)

For extending support through restructuring in genuine cases facing difficulties, CDRM was evolved and guidelines were issued by RBI in August 2001 for implementation by the banks.

The guidelines were revised in February 2003 and further revised in November 2005 on the basis of the recommendations of the Special Group constituted by RBI.

The CDRM scheme covers cases with outstanding exposure of ₹ 10 crore and more.

One-time Settlement Scheme

For recovery of NPAs below ₹ 10 crore for SME (Small and Medium Scale Enterprise) sector. The detailed guidelines on debt restructuring mechanims for units in SME sector were issued by RBI in September 2005. The scheme covers all NPAs of the SME sector which have become doubtful or loss as on March 31, 2004 and also NPA assets which were classified as substandard on March 31, 2004 but subsequently became doubtful or loss amount recovered under the scheme: ₹ 608 crore.

Scheme for Small Borrowers/NPA Accounts

Small borrowers: Where principal amount is equal to and less than ₹ 25,000.

NPA accounts: Which have become doubtful or loss accounts as on September 30, 2005.

Banks were advised to provide simplified mechanism.

Asset Reconstruction Companies under SARFAESI Act 2002

Out of 18 applications received by RBI, Certificate of Registration (COR) has been granted to 4 Companies

1. Asset Reconstruction Company (India) Ltd. (ARCIL)
2. Asset Care Enterprises Ltd.
3. ASREC (India) Ltd.
4. Pegasus Assets Reconstruction Private Ltd.

By 2004-05, banks/FIs have sold their NPAs amounting to ₹ 15343 crore to ARCIL. By March-end 2006, ARCIL acquired financial assets from SCBs and FIs amounting to ₹ 21,126 crore. Foreign Direct Investment (FDI) in equity of Reconstruction Companies was permitted in November 2005.

Securitisation of Standards Assets

RBI issued draft guidelines in April 2005 and final guidelines on securitisation of standard assets in February 2006.

Securitisation of standard assets is a two-stage process.

First stage: Assets are sold to a special purpose vehicle (SPV) in return for immediate cash payment.

Second stage: A liquidity facility is provided to SPV which on one hand receives cash flows from the underlying assets and has to make payments to third party investor to whom SPV has issued tradeable debt securities.

Sale/Purchase of NPAs

Guidelines on sale/purchase NPAs were issued in July 2005.

The guidelines are applicable to banks, FIs and NBFCs purchasing/selling NPAs from/to others banks, FIs and NBFCs (excluding Reconstructions Companies/Securitisation Companies).

Capital Adequacy

The Narasimham Committee also recommended the introduction of capital adequacy requirements based on risk-weighted assets. The loans and advances (other than those guaranteed by the Government) carried a risk weight of 100 per cent, while investments in government and other approved securities carried zero risk weight. This might have prompted the shift of bank funds towards government securities, which were deemed risk-free.

The State Bank of India and the Associate Banks and 11 other nationalised banks reached the prescribed 8 per cent capital to risk asset ratio in 1995-96.

Based on the recommendations of the Narasimham Committee (II 1998) report, the Union Budget (1998-99) proposed to raise the minimum Capital to Risk-weighted Asset Ratio (CRAR) from the existing level of 8 per cent to 10 per cent in phases. Accordingly, the Reserve Bank decided to raise the CRAR to 9 per cent by March 31, 2000. Out of the 27 public sector banks, 26 banks attained the stipulated 8 per cent CRAR by March 31, 1998. By this date, 19 public sector banks attained CRAR exceeding 10 per cent. This was mainly facilitated by the recapitalisation of the banks.

As on March 31, 1999, the CRAR of public sector banks as a whole was 11.2 per cent. A number of banks have entered the capital market to satisfy the capital adequacy norms.

Table No. 7.10

CRAR Position of Scheduled Commercial Banks

Year	*Public Sector Banks*		*Private Sector Banks*		*Foreign Banks*	*Total No. of banks*
	SBI Group (No. of Banks)	*Nationalised banks (No. of Banks)*	*Old No. of Banks*	*New No. of Banks*	*No. of Banks*	
1995-96						
Below 4%	—	5	3	—	—	8
4 % to 8%	—	3	3	—	3	9
8 % to 10%	6	7	7	1	12	33
Above 10%	2	4	12	8	16	42
1996-97						
Below 4%	—	2	3	—	—	5
4 % to 8%	—	—	1	—	—	1
8 % to 10%	3	6	8	—	13	30
Above 10%	5	11	13	9	26	64
1997-98						
Below 4%	—	1	2	—	—	3
4% to 8%	—	—	2	—	—	2
8% to 10%	1	6	6	2	12	27
Above 10%	7	12	15	7	30	71
1998-99						
Below 4%	—	1	2	—	—	3
4 % to 9%	—	—	2	—	—	2
9% to 10%	—	—	—	—	—	23
Above 10%	8	14	18	7	29	76

1999-2000						
Below 4%	—	1	2	—	—	3
4% to 9%	—	—	2	—	—	2
9% to 10%	—	—	—	—	—	—
Above 10%	8	14	18	7	37	84
2000-01						
Below 4%	—	1	2	—	—	3
4% to 9%		1	1	—	—	2
9% to 10%		2	4	1	4	11
Above 10%	8	15	16	7	38	84
2001-02						
Below 4%	—	1	—	—	—	1
4% to 9%	—	1	—	1	—	2
9% to 10%	—	2	2	1	2	7
Above to 10%	8	15	19	6	33	81
2002-03						
Below 4%	—	—	—	2	—	2
4% to 9%	—	—	—	—	—	—
9% to 10%	—	1	2	1	—	4
Above 10%	8	18	19	6	36	87
2003-04						
Below 4%	—	—	—	1	—	1
4% to 9%	—	—	—	1	—	1
9% to 10%	—	—	—	—	—	1
Above 10%	8	18	20	8	33	87
2004-05						
Below 4%	—	—	1	—	—	1
4% to 9%	—	—	1	—	—	1
9% to 10%	—	2	3	2	1	8
Above 10%	8	18	15	7	30	78
2005-06						
Below 4%	—	—	3	—	—	3
4% to 9%	—	—	—	—	—	—
9% to 10%	—	—	1 } 17	1	2	4
Above 10%	8	20	16	7	27	78
2006-07						
Below 4%	—	—	1	—	—	1
4% to 9%	—	—	—	—	—	—
9% to 10%	—	—	2	—	—	2
10% to 12%	3 } 8	8 } 20	5 } 14	4 } 8	7 } 29	27 } 79
Above 12%	5	12	9	4	22	52
2007-08						
Below 4%	—	—	—	—	—	—
4% to 9%	—	—	—	—	—	—
9% to 10%	—	—	1	—	1	2
10% to 12%	2 } 8	11 } 20	3 } 14	2 } 8	3 } 27	21 } 77
Above 12%	6	9	11	6	24	56
2008-09						
Below 4%	—	—	—	—	—	—
4% to 9%	—	—	—	—	—	—
9% to 10%	—	1	—	—	—	1
10% to 12%	7	19	15	7	30	78
Above 12%	—	—	—	—	—	—

Scheduled Commercial Banks and CRAR

	2000 (March-end)	2005 (March-end)	2008 (March-end)
Total No. of SCBs	89	88	79
SCBs with CRAR above 10%	84	78	77
9% to 10%	—	8	2
4% to 9%	2	1	—
below 4%	3	1	—

	Public Sector Banks		Private Sector Banks		Foreign Banks	
	1999-00	*2004-05*	*1999-00*	*2004-05*	*1999-00*	*2004-05*
CRAR						
above 10%	22	26	25	22	37	30
9% to 10%	—	2	—	5	—	1
4% to 9%	—	—	2	1	—	—
below 4%	1	—	2	1	—	—

Exposure Norms and Risk Weights

Risk weight on bank's exposure to

Commercial real estate sector: Risk weight increased

July 2005 : 100% to 125%

April 2006 : 150%

Capital market exposures: risk weight increased

July 2005 : 100% to 125%

April 2006 : bank's exposure to venture capital funds as a part of its capital market exposure.

Risk weight increased to 150% to such exposures

Basel II accord (of 1998): New capital adequacy norms

For Basel II accord regarding New Capital adequacy framework to come into effect in India in 2007, all scheduled commercial banks (except RRBs) and financial institutions are required to implement capital adequacy norms with effect from March 31, 2007. With a view to monitor the progress of implementation by the banks, RBI issued guidelines on January 25, 2006 for raising capital to meet market as well as credit risks and advised banks to take up measures from April 2006 towards making smooth shift to Basel II.

Basel II framework has 3 major elements:

(1) minimum capital requirements: closely aligned to economic risks.
(2) supervisory review: bank supervision with minimum regulation.
(3) market improvement in the areas of disclosure: market discipline and standards of transparency.

In this regard, banks are required to have: (a) suitable risk management framework (b) risk-based supervision, and (c) internal capital adequacy assessment programme in alignment with the business plans.

To raise capital for capital adequacy as per the norms, banks were advised in January 2006 that they could augment their capital funds by issuing additional instruments such as perpetual debt instrument preference shares (cumulative and non-cumulative).

For the adoption of Basel II norms, RBI had earlier indicated March 31, 2007 as specified date for the banks. It has now been extended to March 31, 2008 in respect of foreign banks operating in India and Indian banks having presence outside the country and to March 2009, for all other scheduled commercial banks.

Bank Supervision and Regulation

Lack of financial discipline and absence of clarity regarding internationally comparable accounting systems resulted in no control on working of banks. For the healthy growth of the banks, such supervision was necessary.

The details of these supervisory provisions of the banks are as follows:

The Board for financial supervision has been given the main supervisory issues relating to on-site and off-site supervision of the banks. The on-site supervision system for banks is an annual cycle and is based on the 'CAMELS' model. It focuses on core assessments in accordance with the statutory mandate, *i.e.,* solvency, liquidity, operational soundness and management prudence. Banks are rated on the basis of this assessment.

In respect of off-site supervision, the aim is to note 'early warning signals' from off-site monitoring to avoid any financial crisis, of the nature of East Asian or Latin American crisis. In this respect, detailed guidelines have been issued by the apex bank on asset-liability management and risk management system. The recent trend towards financial integration, globalisation and technological upgradation is that such supervision is necessary.

Standing Committee on International Financial Standards and Codes:

For aligning India's standards and practices to the evolving International Standards, RBI appointed in Dec. 1999 a Standing Committee which appointed 10 Advisory Groups to examine the feasibility and time frame of compliance.

Advisory Groups on:

(i)	Banking Supervision	(ii)	Bankruptcy Laws
(iii)	Corporate Governance	(iv)	Fiscal Transparency
(v)	Data Dissemination	(vi)	Insurance Regulation
(vii)	International Accounting and Auditing	(viii)	Transparency in Monetary and Fiscal Policies
(ix)	Payments and Settlement System	(x)	Securities Market Regulation

The Advisory Groups have submitted their reports.

Advisory Group on Banking Supervision

Chairman: M.S. Verma

The Group assessed the position of the Indian banking system *vis-a-vis* the principles laid down by the Basel Committee on banking supervision. The Group has concluded that the overall level of compliance with the standards and codes is of a high order. The Group felt that there was an urgent need to: *(i)* follow best practices in the constitution and functioning of bank boards and *(ii)* strengthen management information systems.

Board for Financial Supervision (BFS): Constituted by RBI in Nov. 1994: Focus of BFS supervisory strategy:

(1) On-site inspection
(2) On-site surveillance
(3) Monitoring asset quality, capital adequacy measures and other prudential norms of banks.
(4) Strengthen management information systems and fraud monitoring procedure.

BFS is entrusted with supervision of commercial banks, select AIFIs, NBFCs, Primary Dealers (PDs) and Clearing Corporation of India Ltd. (CCIL).

During 2001-02, BFS held 12 meetings and reviewed 126 inspection reports. BFS met 13 times during 2005-06.

Risk-based Supervision (RBS)

It is intended to take up risk profiling of banks which would document various financial and non-financial risks confronting the banks and draw up a supervisory programme.

The instruments of RBS are:

(i) on-site examination
(ii) off-site monitoring, and
(iii) market intelligence mechanism.

RBS consists of
(i) Development of risk profile.
(ii) Designing supervisory action plan based on risk profile for each bank.
(iii) To target high risk areas and areas of supervisory concern.
(iv) Strengthening quality assurance and enforcement functions.

The implemention of RBS includes:

(a) setting up comprehensive risk management systems.
(b) adopting risk-focussed internal audit system.
(c) upgrading management information system.
(d) setting up compliance units.
(e) human resources and skills development.

RBI would switch over to RBS of banks by 2003.

Policy Changes: Flow of Credit from Banks

Stepping up, Credit to SME sector:

Banks were advised in August 2005 to enhance the flow of credit to Small and Medium Enterprises (SME) sectors. Financing of Small Scale (SSI) is included in the priority sector. Medium Enterprises: units with investment in plant and machinery beyond SSI limit and upto ₹ 10 crore.

Measures included in the policy package were communicated in August 2005 to all banks — private, foreign banks, RRBs and Local Area Banks (LABs).

Credit to agriculture and allied activities

Year	*Target*	*Disbursement by banks, RRBs and co operative banks*
2004-05	₹ 1,05,000 crore	₹ 1,15,243 crore
2005-06	₹ 1,42,000 crore	₹ 1,57,480 crore

Implementing the recommendation of the Advisory Committee (Chairman Prof. V.S. Vyas), RBI took up measures to increase the flow of credit to agriculture and allied activities.

Export Credit

SCBs were advised in February 2006 to review their procedure for export credit. Banks should give priority for the foreign currency export credit requirements over foreign currency loans to non-exporter borrowers.

General Credit Card 'GCC' Scheme

- Scheme to be implemented for the rural and semi-urban areas.
- Guideliness on GCC issued in December 2005.

Supervision and Regulation:

- On-site Monitoring and Surveillance:

June 2005: the time limit for submission of monthly returns reduced to 15 days for monthly returns and 21 days for quarterly returns.

Credit Card Operation

- Working Group on Regulatory Mechanism for Credit Cards was set up in October 2004.
- Guidelines on Credit Card Operations of banks was issued in November 2005.
- Monitoring of Frauds:

Fraud Reporting and Monitoring System (FRMS) introduced in 2003 Separate Fraud Monitoring Cell constituted in June 2004 FRMS revised in January 2006.

Cases of Frauds: 2004-05: 10,450 cases amounting ₹ 779 crore
2005-06: 13,914 cases amounting ₹ 1381 crore

2005-06: Irregularities in IPOs: Cornering the retail portion of IPOs by some individuals.
'IPO Scam': ● 10 commercial banks were involved. Penalties were imposed in these banks.
December 2005 Proceeds of A/c payee cheques were credited by banks to third party accounts.

Prompt Corrective Action

A scheme of prompt corrective action is being developed as a supervisory tool. The scheme aims at taking action at the early stages of weaknesses in banks. The tasks would be to identify the problem banks, to monitor the behaviour of troubled banks so as to prevent failure or limit losses.

Strengthening the Banking System

- *Disclosure of Information about Defaulters:*

The details of information about borrowers with outstandings aggregating ₹ 1 crore and above, classified as doubtful and loss as on March 31, and Sept. 30 every year are disseminated to banks and FIs.

- *Credit Information Bureaus (CIB)*

A Working Group under the chairmanship of Shri S.R. Iyer was constituted by RBI in Dec. 2001 to examine the possibility of CIB for collecting and disseminating information on the suit-filed accounts and the list of defaulters. The Report of the Working Group was submitted in Jan. 2002.

Credit Information Bureau (India) Ltd. (CIBIL) has been set up by SBI in collaboration with HDFC Ltd., and other two Foreign Technology partners in Jan. 2001. The purpose of CIBIL is to serve as an effective mechanism for exchange of information between banks and FIs for curbing the growth of NPAs.

- *Banks Investment Norms*

— Banks investments in non-SLR securities through private palcement:

Guidelines issued in June 2001 regarding undertaking of due diligence, obtaining disclosures and credit risk regarding privately placed investments.

— *Investment Fluctuation Reserve (IFR)*

Banks are advised to follow more prudent policy regarding:

— utilising the gains realised on the sale of investment in securities.

— building up adequate reserves to guard against any possible reversal of interest rate environment. Banks have to achieve an IFR at a minimum of 5.0 per cent of all investments held in for trading and available for sale categories within 5 years.

Rehabilitation of Public Sector Banks

There were large proportions of non-performing assets in the banking system in 1991. Many public sector banks made huge losses and the net profit to asset ratio varied between minus 6.8 per cent and plus 0.5 per cent.

The Narasimham Committee had recommended setting up of the Asset Reconstruction Fund (ARF) so that the banks could transfer their bad assets to it at a discount or at book value. The Government did not approve it. But the banks were given legal support in their recovery efforts and special recovery tribunals had been set up to avail of the related benefits.

A working group on the restructuring of weak public sector banks was set up by the Reserve Bank in February 1999 under the chairmanship of M.S. Verma. The group suggested measures for revival of weak public sector banks in India.

Seven parameters covering three areas have been identified by this group. These are —

- Solvency
  (i) Capital adequacy ratio and
  (ii) Coverage ratio
- Earning Capacity
  (iii) Return on assets and
  (iv) Net interest margin
- Profitability
  (v) Ratio of operating profit to average working funds
  (vi) Ratio of cost to income and
  (vii) Ratio of staff cost to net interest income + all other incomes.

These seven parameters can be used to judge the weaknesses of the banks in future.

Restructuring of weak banks should be a two-stage operation in the opinion of this group.

The first stage involves operational, organisational and financial restructuring aimed at restoring competitive efficiency and the second stage covers options of privatisation and/or merger.

Working Group under the Chairmanship of Shri M.S. Verma identified three weak banks. On the lines suggested by Verma Working Group, it was announced in Feb. 2000 that a Financial Restructuring Authority (FRA) be instituted in respect of any bank which is considered potentially weak.

Lack of Competition

Upto 1991, there was little competition in the banking sector. Competition among the banks was mainly lacking due to regulated interest rates. The public sector banks which had more than 90 per cent share in banking field also had no incentive to complete among themselves. Non-price competition also was completely missing.

The Narasimham Committee not only suggested the injection of competition in the banking system but also recommended financial autonomy for the public sector banks. It also recommended opening up of the banking business to the private sector. Subsequently, 10 new private sector banks started functioning.

The policy changes regarding deregulation of interest rates and dilution of consortium lending requirements also have been made. Now, the banks also have to compete with the non-banking financial intermediaries, by widening their activities and by operating more efficiently.

Competition among the banks has been fostered by adopting two different policy measures. Firstly, with the amendment of the Nationalisation Act, state-owned banks were allowed to access the market to raise funds from the public. This resulted in increased accountability and made the banks more conscious to run more efficiently and earn profits. Secondly, new banks in the private sector were allowed to be set up and the entry of foreign banks was liberalised. The decision to allow setting up of local area banks was taken with the purpose of creating a more competitive environment in both rural and semi-urban areas.

Competition among commercial banks has increased in the recent years. In 1993, guidelines were issued for the entry of new private sector banks and now 8 new private sector banks are in operation. As against the stipulation of 8 branches, the foreign banks have been permitted in 1998-99 to open 12 branches. The guidelines on Local Area Banks were announced by RBI in 1996. Presently, 4 Local Area Banks are functioning, one each in the states of Andhra Pradesh, Punjab, Gujarat and Karnataka. Still, the structure of banking sector in the country is oligopolistic, being dominated by a few large banks.

Increased Expenditure

The accelerated growth of bank expenditures due to the proliferation of unremunerative branches in rural and semi-urban areas, overstaffing, low level of efficiency of the employees, lack of discipline and work culture among the staff — all this reduced the profitability of the banks.

The working group on restructuring the weak public sector banks suggested measures in this respect as 30 per cent to 35 per cent reduction in staff cost, offering voluntary retirement scheme etc. These measures were recommended particularly for three weak banks identified by the group.

Thus, in the first half of the nineties, there was an emphasis on liberalisation and deregulation of the banking sector guided primarily by the recommendations of the committee on financial system (under the chairmanship of M. Narasimham-1991). The major issues of these recommendations related to reduction in the statutory pre-emption levels, dismantling the complex administered interest rate structure, laying down of capital adequacy requirements, introduction of prudential norms relating to income recognition, asset classification and provisioning and liberalisation of entry norms for both domestic and foreign banks.

The measures aimed at deregulation were those of lowering of statutory pre-emptions, deregulation of interest rates and greater operational autonomy. The liberalisation of the banking sector marked the end of a detailed regime of interest rates on term deposits of varied maturities and various categories of loans. Banks were allowed to decide the interest rates on the loans they grant, subject to certain limitations.

During the late 1990s, there was increasing awareness on part of the policymakers of the dangers associated with inadequate regulation and supervision of banks.

The Second Narasimham Committee which submitted its report April 1998, suggested prudential measures like increase in the Capital to Risk-weighted Assets Ratio (CRAR) to 10 per cent within a stipulated time period, the introduction of market risks on government securities, the stricter non-performing asset norms and provisioning requirements and the introduction of asset-liability management guidelines and of risk management guidelines.

The banks have been directed to bring in more transparency in respect of financial information and the extent of disclosures has been increased so as to give a clear picture of their balance sheet to the people. Hence, from the year ending March 31, 2000, banks operating in India have been directed to disclose in their published accounts information relating to maturity pattern of loans and advances, investment securities, deposits and borrowings, foreign currency assets and liabilities, movements in non-performing assets and provisions and lending to sensitive sectors as defined by the Reserve Bank from time to time. Such transparency of operations will facilitate the effective monitoring of banks.

7.6 ASSETS AND LIABILITIES OF SCHEDULED COMMERCIAL BANKS

Bank Assets

The assets of the banks are: (a) Cash in hand and the balance with RBI, (b) Balances with other banks, (c) Investments in Government Securities and other approved securities, and (d) Bank Credit.

The most important assets of the banks are, the bank credit and investment in the government securities.

As on March 31, 2002, the bank advances constituted a share of over 42 per cent while the investments accounted for a share of 38.3 per cent in the total assets of scheduled commercial banks. The investment in Government and other approved securities constituted 77.1 per cent share of the total investments of the banks as on March 31, 2002 and 36.5% of their net demand and time liabilities by March-end 2002.

Table No. 7.11
Asset Portfolio of Scheduled Commercial Banks
(Five-yearly Averages)

(Per cent)

Item	*1969 to 1973*	*1974 to 1978*	*1979 to 1983*	*1984 to 1988-89*	*1989-90 to 1993-94*	*1994-95 to 1998-99*
1	2	3	4	5	6	7
1. Cash in Hand & Bal. with RBI	6.59	7.12	8.44	10.49	10.91	9.79
2. Balances with other banks	2.22	3.10	4.00	4.09	3.51	8.39
3. Govt. & other approved securities	23.14	21.63	20.80	22.22	25.37	26.83
4. Shares, B & D, others	1.11	0.80	0.66	1.21	3.04	6.80
5. Bills purchased/ discounted	9.83	8.86	6.78	4.90	4.98	4.54
6. Cash credit, etc. & Term loans	44.24	42.08	40.68	39.56	38.24	35.83

Source: Report on Currency and Finance, 1998-99.

Table No. 7.12

Assets Position of Scheduled Commercial Banks (as of March end)

(₹ in Crores)

Item	2001	% to total	2002	% to total	2003	% to total	2004	% to total	2005	% to total	2006	% to total
1. Cash	84,503	6.5	86,761	5.7	86,123	5.1	113246	5.7	1,18,075	5.0	1,14,461	5.2
2. Balance with other and Money at call	1,05,971	8.2	1,17,518	7.7	75,113	4.2	82,023	4.2	95,356	4.0	1,16,396	4.2
3. Investments	4,91,755	38.0	5,88,058	38.3	6,93,753	40.8	8,04,199	40.7	8,69,737	36.9	8,67.790	31.1
3.1 in Govt. securities	3,53,190	27.3	4,31,753	27.9	5,36,214	31.6	6,39,143	32.4	6,98,789	28.7	6,91.946	24.8
3.2 other approved Securities	23,801	1.8	21,753	1.4	19,281	1.1	1,81,000	0.9	16,291	0.7	13,948	0.5
3.3 in non-approved Securities	1,14,764	8.9	1,34,552	8.8	1,38,258	8.1	1,46,956	7.4	1,54,656	6.6	1,61,895	5.8
4. Loans and Advances	5,26,151	40.6	6,45,743	42.0	7,39,553	43.5	8,64,271	43.8	11,50,836	48.8	15,16,557	54.4
4.1 bills purchased and discounted	50,267	3.9	53,609	3.5	58,813	3.5	66,968	3.4	91,902	3.9	1,03,648	3.7
4.2 cash credits and overdrafts	2,85,852	22.0	3,21,726	21.0	3,54,768	20.9	3,72,207	18.9	4,37,018	18.5	5,68,965	20.4
4.3 Term loans	1,90,032	14.7	2,70,408	17.7	3,25,972	19.2	4,25,096	21.5	6,21,914	26.4	8,43,942	30.3
5. Fixed Assets	16,237	1.3	20,083	1.3	20,278	1.2	21,409	1.1	23,050	1.0	25,058	0.9
6. Other Assets	70,788	5.5	77,350	5.0	84,378	5.0	88,860	4.5	98,898	4.2	1,17,627	4.2
Total Assets	12,95,405	100.0	15,35,513	100.0	16,99,197	100.0	19,74,017	100.0	23,55,955	100.0	27,87,891	100.0

(Contd...)

(Contd...)

Item	2007	% to total	2008	% to total	2009	% to total
1. Cash	195264	5.6	322971	7.5	297263	5.7
2. Balance with other and Money at call	158298	4.6	109109	2.5	198581	3.8
3. Investments	950977	27.5	1177329	27.2	1479474	27.7
3.1 in Govt. securities			925723	21.4	1164444	22.2
3.2 other approved securities			10587	0.2	8153	0.2
3.3 in non-approved securities			241017	5.6	276876	5.3
4. Loans and Advances	1981235	57.3	2476936	57.3	3000876	57.3
4.1 bills purchased and discounted			150988	3.5	173910	3.3
4.2 cash credits and overdrafts			888882	20.5	1113556	21.2
4.3 Term loans			1437085	33.2	1713439	32.7
5. Fixed Assets	31363	0.9	42394	1.0	48361	0.9
6. Other Assets	142809	4.1	197425	4.6	246743	4.7
Total Assets	3459946	100.0	4326166	100.0	5241330	100.0

Source: Report on Trends and Progress of Banking in India: RBI 2005-06.

Between 2000-01 and 2008-09, the total assets have increased more than 4 times.

Table No. 7.13

Distribution of Outstanding Credit of Scheduled Commercial Banks
(According to type of account)

(₹ *in Crores)*

Year	*Cash Credit*	*Over Drafts*	*Demand Loans*	*Term Loans*	*Packing Credit*	*Export Bills Purchased/ Discounted/ Advanced against*	*Inland Bills Purch-ased/ Discoun-ted*	*Advances against Import Bills*	*Unclass-ified Others*	*Total**
1	*2*	*3*	*4*	*5*	*6*	*7*	*8*	*9*	*10*	*11*
1972	2,545	480	331	601	210	212	632	30	11	5,051
	(50.4)	(9.5)	(6.6)	(11.9)	(4.1)	(4.2)	(12.5)	(0.6)	(0.2)	(100.0)
1975	4,232	718	530	1,307	377	342	1,459	64	0	9,030
	(46.9)	(8.0)	(5.9)	(14.5)	(4.2)	(3.8)	(16.2)	(0.7)	(0.0)	(100.0)
1980	8,578	1,345	981	4,492	754	796	3,057	217	0	20.221
	(42.4)	(6.7)	(4.9)	(22.2)	(3.7)	(3.9)	(15.1)	(1.1)	(0.0)	(100.0)
1985	15,253	3,255	1,673	12,323	1,201	827	6,137	267	56	40,992
	(37.2)	(7.9)	(4.1)	(30.1)	(2.9)	(2.0)	(15.0)	(0.7)	(0.1)	(100.0)
1990	29,054	5,878	2,913	24,643	3,973	2,966	8,280	1,319	1,138	80,165
	(36.2)	(7.3)	(3.6)	(30.7)	(5.0)	(3.7)	(10.3)	(1.6)	(1.4)	(100.0)
1996	78,052	16,132	17,483	65,872	15,248	11,813	11,104	1,697	1,039	2,18,439
	(35.7)	(7.4)	(8.0)	(30.2)	(7.0)	(5.4)	(5.1)	(0.8)	(0.5)	(100.0)
1997	77,174	18,877	30,488	77,041	16,382	13,090	11,571	1,419	885	2,46,927
	(31.3)	(7.6)	(12.3)	(31.2)	(6.6)	(5.3)	(4.7)	(0.6)	(0.4)	(100.0)
1998	85,151	21,160	41,692	93,957	17,209	13,830	12,983	1,905	962	2,88,849
	(29.5)	(7.3)	(14.4)	(32.5)	(6.0)	(4.8)	(4.5)	(0.7)	(0.3)	(100.0)

Source: Report on Currency and Finance, 1998-99.

Figures in brackets indicate percentage to the total.

The five-year average share of liquid assets, *i.e.,* cash in hand balance with RBI and balances with other banks in the total commercial banks increased during 1969-99 period.

The average share of Government and other approved securities in total assets firstly declined and subsequently increased upto 26.83 per cent during 1994-95 to 1998-99.

Investment Pattern of Scheduled Commercial Banks

From 1970 to mid-1980s, the share of government securities in total investment declined, whereas the share of other approved securities increased.

Shares in % *(in total investment)*	*1970*	*1985*
• Government Securities	75.7 per cent	60.9 per cent
• Other approved securities	20.0 per cent	36.8 per cent

During 1990 and 1997 the share of Government Securities increased in the total investment; as against this, the shares of other approved securities declined.

Shares in % *(in total investment)*	*1990*	*1997*
• Government Securities	63.4	70.1
• Other approved securities	31.9	12.9

Outstanding Credit

Table 7.13 presents the outstanding credit of scheduled commercial banks according to the type of account.

Cash credit : The share of cash credit in the total loans decreased from 50.4 per cent in 1972 to 37.2 per cent in 1985 and then decreased further to 29.5 per cent in 1998.

Demand loans: Share declined

1972 : 6.6 per cent
1980 : 4.9 per cent
1990 : 3.6 per cent
then increased 1996 : 8.0 per cent
1998 : 14.4 per cent

Term loans: share increased consistently
1972: 11.9 per cent to 30.1 per cent in 1985 and 32.5 per cent in 1998

Bills purchased / discounted: 1972 : 12.5 per cent
Share declined: 1998 : 4.5 per cent.

Table No. 7.14
Pattern of Sectoral Deployment of Gross Bank Credit

(₹ *in Crores*)

	Priority Sector					*Non-food Credit*					
Year	*Food Credit*	*Agri-culture*	*Small-scale Industries*	*Others*	*Total (3+4+5)*	*Indus-tries*	*Other Whole-sale Trade*	*Other Sector*	*Total (7+8+9)*	*Non-food Gross Bank Credit (6+10)*	*Gross Bank Credit (2+11)*
1	*2*	*3*	*4*	*5*	*6*	*7*	*8*	*9*	*10*	*11*	*12*
1972	542 (9.9)	439 (8.0)	597 (10.9)	172 (3.1)	1,208 (22.0)	3,730* (68.1)			3,730 (68.1)	4,938 (90.1)	5,480 (100.0)
1975	564 (6.4)	785 (8.9)	1,043 (11.9)	322 (3.7)	2,150 (24.5)	6.072 (69.1)			6,072 (69.1)	8,222 (93.6)	8,728 (100.0)
1980	2,100 (9.9)	2,767 (13.0)	2,635 (12.4)	1,328 (6.3)	6,730 (31.7)	8,269 (38.9)	1,915 (9.0)	2,221 (10.5)	12,405 (58.4)	19,135 (90.1)	21,235 (100.0)
1985	5,665 (11.8)	7,660 (16.0)	6,612 (13.8)	4,137 (8.6)	18,409 (38.4)	15,939 (33.2)	2,649 (5.5)	5,294 (11.0)	23,882 (49.8)	42,291 (88.2)	47,956 (100.0)
1990	2,006 (2.0)	16,612 (16.2)	15,615 (15.2)	8,248 (8.0)	40,475 (39.4)	38,274 (37.2)	5,879 (5.7)	16,149 (15.7)	60,302 (58.7)	1,00,777 (98.0)	1,02,783 (100.0)
1994	10.907 (7.0)	21,208 (13.5)	22,620 (14.4)	10,047 (6.4)	53,875 (34.4)	57,872 (36.9)	7,334 (4.7)	26,848 (17.1)	92,054 (58.7)	1,45,929 (93.0)	1,56,836 (100.0)
1996	9,791 (4.2)	27,044 (11.7)	31,884 (13.8)	14,401 (6.2)	73,329 (31.6)	93,053 (40.1)	11,980 (5.2)	43,707 (18.9)	1,48,740 (64.2)	2,22,069 (95.8)	2,31,860 (100.0)
1998	12,485 (4.2)	34,869 (11.6)	43,508 (14.5)	21,130 (7.0)	99,507 (33.1)	1,17,530 (39.1)	13,217 (4.4)	57,544 (19.2)	1,88,291 (62.7)	2,87,798 (95.8)	3,00,283 (100.0)
1999	16,816 (4.9)	39,634 (11.6)	48,483 (14.2)	26,494 (7.7)	1,14,611 (33.5)	1,30,516 (38.2)	13,965 (4.1)	66,104 (19.3)	2,10,585 (61.6)	3,25,196 (95.1)	3,42,012 (100.0)

Table No. 7.14 (Contd.)
Pattern of Sectoral Deployment of Gross Bank Credit

(₹ in Crores)

Year	Priority Sector: Food Credit	Priority Sector: Agri-culture	Priority Sector: Small-scale Industries	Priority Sector: Others	Priority Sector: Total (3+4+5)	Industries	Whole-Trade	Other Sector	Total (7+8+9)	Non-food Gross Bank Credit (6+10)	Gross Bank Credit (2+11)
1	2	3	4	5	6	7	8	9	10	11	12
2000	25691	44381	52814	34632	131827	147319	16818	79163	243300	375127	400818
	(6.4)	(11.1)	(13.2)	(8.6)	(32.9)	(36.7)	(4.2)	(19.7)	(60.6)	(93.6)	
2001	39991	51922	56002	46490	154414	162837	17845	94066	247748	429162	469153
	(8.5)	(11.1)	(11.9)	(9.9)	(32.9)	(34.7)	(3.8)	(20.0)	(58.5)	(91.5)	
2002	53978	60761	57199	57299	175259	172334	20459	114707	307490	482749	536727
	(10.0)	(11.3)	(10.6)	(10.7)	(32.6)	(32.2)	(3.8)	(21.4)	(57.3)	(90.0)	
2003	49479	71609	60486	71704	203799	200335	22398	140895	363628	567427	616906
	(8.0)				(33.0)						(92.7)
	49479	73518	60394	77697	211609	235168	22578	150700	408446	620055	669534
	(7.4)				(31.6)						(92.6)
2004	35961	90541	65855	107438	263834	247210	24867	192511	464588	728422	764383
	(4.7)	(11.8)	(8.6)		(34.5)	(32.3)	(3.25)			(95.3)	
2005	41121	125250	74588	181638	381476	352304	32549	233459	618312	999788	1040909
	(4.0)				(36.7)					(96)	
2006	40691	173972	91212	245554	510738	459232	39691	395179	894102	1466366	1507077
	(2.7)				(33.9)						
2007	46521	230377	117910	287679	635966	579429	50143	535702	1165274	1884669	1931189
	(2.4)				(32.9)						
2008	44399	275342	194842	277196	747380	672033	55702	727775	1455510	2317515	2361914
	(1.9)				(31.6)						
2009	46211	338656	257027	320303	915886	797363	67425	821616	1686404	2729338	2775549
	(1.7)				(33.0)						

Source: (i) Report on Trends and Progress of Banking in India, RBI 2005-06.

(ii) Handbook of Statistics on Indian Economy, RBI 2005-06.

(Data for the year 2003-04 pertains to 47 banks and the years 2004-05 and 2005-06 pertains to 52 banks)

Between 2000 and 2009 the share of priority sector in Gross Bank Credit has gone up to 36.7% in 2005, but has ranged between 32 to 34%. The share of food procurement credit in Gross Bank Credit has fallen to less than 2%.

Table No. 7.15
Banking Indicators

(*₹ in Crores*)

Item	*1997*	*1998*	*1999*	*2000*	*2001*	*2002*	*2003*	*2004*	*2005*	*2006*	*2007*	*2008*	*2009*
1. Aggregate deposits (a + b)	499163	598485	714025	813344	962618	1103360	1280853	1504416	1700198	2109049	2611933	3196939	3834110
(a) Demand Deposits	90010 (18.0)	102513 (17.0)	117423 (10.4)	127366 (15.6)	142552 (14.8)	153048 (14.0)	170289 (13.3)	225022 (15.00)	248028	3644640	429731	524310	523085
(b) Time Deposits	409153 (82.0)	495972 (83.0) (21.2)	596602 (83.4) (20.3)	685978 (85.2) (15.0)	820066 (86.0) (19.5)	950312 (86.0)	110564 (86.7)	1279394 (85.00)	1452171	1744409	2182203	2672630	3311025
Certificate of deposits (CDs)	12134	14296	3717	1227	771	1576	908	4461	—	—	—	—	—
2. Aggregate deposits (excluding CDs)	487029	584189	710308	812117	961847	1101784	—	—	—	—	—	—	—
3. Borrowing from RBI	560	395	2894	6491	3896	3616	79	—	50	1488	6245	4000	11728
4. Liability to banks	21193	32287	45204	53838	77088	53902	62346	54487	67049	75165	88545	98145	100116
5. Bank credit (a + b)	270805	324079 (19.7)	368837 (13.8)	435958 (18.7)	511434 (17.3)	589723 (15.3)	729215	840785	1100428	1507077	1931189	2361914	2775549
(a) Food credit	7597 (2.8)	12485 (3.8) (64.3)	16816 (4.5) (34.7)	25691 (5.9) (52.8)	39991 (7.8) (55.7)	53978 (9.2) (35.0)	49479 (6.8)	35961 (4.3)	41121	40691	46521	44399	46211
(b) Non-food credit	263208 (97.2)	311594 (96.0) (18.4)	352021 (95.5) (13)	410267 (94.1) (16.5)	471443 (92.2) (14.9)	535745 (90.8) (13.6)	679736 (93.2)	804824 (95.7)	1059308	1466386	1884669	2317515	2729338
6. Investments (a + b)	190514	218705 (14.8)	254594 (16.4)	308944 (21.3)	370160 (19.8)	438269 (18.4)	547546	677588	739154	717454	791516	971715	1166410
(a) Government securities	158890 (83.4)	186957 (85.3) (17.7)	223217 (87.7) (19.4)	278456 (90.1) (24.7)	340035 (91.9) (22.1)	411176 (93.8) (12.0)	523417 (95.6)	654758 (96.6)	718982	700742	776058	958661	1155786
(b) Other approved securities	31624 (16.6)	31748 (14.5) (0.4)	31377 (12.3) (–0.13)	30488 (9.9) (–0.8)	30125 (9.1) (–1.2)	27093 (6.2) (–10.0)	24129 (4.4)	22830 (3.4)	20172	16172	15458	13053	10624
7. Cash balances (a + b)	53195	61306	67910	62749	65202	68647	65902	76895	94577	140107	196361	275166	258476
(a) Cash in hand	3347	3608	4362	5330	5658	6245	7567 (11.5)	7898 (10.3)	6472	13046	16139	18044	20281
(b) Balance with RBI	49848	57698	63548	57419	59544	62402	58335 (88.5)	68997 (88.7)	88105	127061	180222	257122	238195
Credit-Deposit Ratio	54.2	54.1	51.7	53.6	53.1	53.4	56.9	55.9	64.7	71.5	73.9	73.9	72.4
Investment-Deposit Ratio	38.1	36.5	35.7	38.0	38.5	39.7	42.7	45.0	43.5	34.0	30.3	30.4	30.4

Source: Handbook of Statistics on Indian Economy, RBI 2008-09.
Handbook of Statistics on Indian Economy: RBI 2003-04.

Note: Figures in brackets **below** indicate % increase over the previous year and those on the **right side** indicate proportionate share in item total.

Figures in brackets indicate % share in the item total.

Table No. 7.16
Liabilities Position of Schedule Commercial Banks (as of March-end)

(₹ *in Crores*)

Item	2001		2002		2003		2004		2005		2006		2007		2008		2009	
	Amount	*% to total*	*Amount*	*% to total*	*Amount*	*% to total*	*Amount*	*% to total*	*Amount*	*% to total*	*Amount*	*% to total*	*Amount*	*% to total*	*Amount*	*% to total*	*Amount*	*% to total*
1. Capital	19,095	1.5	21,473	1.4	21,594	1.3	22,348	1.1	25,904	1.1	25,203	0.9	29559	0.85	39963	0.9	44037	0.8
2. Reserve and Surplus	48,645	3.8	62,687	4.1	76,288	4.5	94,240	4.8	1,23,704	5.3	1,57,909	5.7	189616	5.5	275524	6.4	324218	6.2
3. Deposits	10,55,386	81.5	12,02,699	78.3	13,55,654	79.8	15,75,143	79.8	18,37,557	78.0	21,64,477	77.6	2696934	77.9	3320061	76.6	4063203	77.5
3.1 Demand deposits	1,39,733	10.8	1,53,070	10.0	1,64,366	9.7	2,03,142	10.3	2,34,528	10.0	2,92,932	10.5			442056	10.2	472578	9.0
3.2 Saving Bank deposits	2,18,713	16.9	2,55,598	16.7	3,02,303	17.8	3,73,077	18.9	4,44,839	18.9	5,42,830	10.5			744051	17.2	874539	16.7
3.3 Term deposits	6,96,941	53.8	7,94,032	55.7	8,58,984	52.3	9,98,324	50.5	11,58,197	49.2	13,28,714	47.7			2133953	49.3	2716084	51.8
4. Borrowings	55,515	4.3	1,07.180	7.0	87,469	5.1	96,490	4.9	1,68,086	7.1	2,05,433	7.4	243008	7.0	302629	7.0	323184	6.2
5. Other Liabilties and Provision	1,16,765	9.0	1,41,474	9.2	1,58,192	9.3	1,86,798	9.5	2,00,701	8.5	2,34,866	8.4	300834	8.7	387987	9.0	486085	9.3
Total Liabilities	12,95,403	100.0	15.35,513	100.0	16,99,197	100.0	19,75,020	100.0	23,55,955	100.0	27,87,891	100.0	3459946	100.0	4326166	100.0	5241330	100.0

Report on Trends and Progress of Banking in India, RBI 2005-06.

Table No. 7.17
Bank Group-wise Total Deposits (as of March-end)

(₹ *in Crores)*

Bank Group	2001		2002		2003		2004		2005		2006	
	Amount	*% share*	*Amount*	*% share*	*Amount*	*% share*	*Amount*	*% share*	*Amount*	*% share*	*Amount*	*% share*
I. SBI Group	3,12,118.45	28.6	3,51,076.64	28.2	3,91,086.36	27.9	4,32,80.61	26.5	5,05,649.41	26.8	5,42,409.12	24.5
II. Nationalised Banks	5,47,343.50	50.1	6,17.672.63	49.6	6,88,081.00	49.0	7,93,946.95	48.6	9,15,788,47	48.6	10,54,071.06	47.7
III. Private Sector Banks	1,36,634.57	12.5	1,69,439.60	13.6	2,07,173.56	14.8	2,68,549.30	16.5	3,14,629.74	16.7	4,28,251.56	19.4
IV. Foreign Banks	59,289.91	5.4	64,510.55	5.2	69,313.07	4.9	79,756.42	4.9	86,389.16	4.6	1,13,744.99	5.1
V. RRBs	37,637.00	3.4	43,220.00	3.4	48,346.00	3.4	57,010.00	3.5	62,143.00	3.3	71,329.00	3.2
Total	10,92,413.43	100.0	12,45,919.42	100.0	14,03,999.99	100.0	16,32,153.28	100.0	18,84,599.78	100.0	22,09,811.07	100.0

Source: (i) Report on Trends and Progress of Banking in India, RBI 2005-06.

(ii) Handbook of Statistics on Indian Economy, RBI 2005-06.

In regard to deposit mobilisation, the shares of SBI Group and of nationalised bank have fallen during 2005-06 and the share of private sector banks was 12.5% in 2001, and has risen consistantly to reach 19.4% in 2005-06.

Sectoral Deployment of Bank Credit

Table 7.14 gives the sectoral deployment of gross bank credit for the selected years from 1992 to 2004.

In regard to credit allocation, one important feature since 1969 has been the improved sectoral spread of bank finance.

Share of priority sector:	1980 : 31.7%	1990 : 39.4%	
	2000 : 33%	2004 : 34.5%	
Industry (medium and large):	1970s : 68%	2002 : 32.2%	2004 : 32.3%
Small-scale Industries	1990s : 14 to 15%	2002 : 10.6%	2004 : 8.6%
Agriculture	1990 : 16.2%	2000 : 11.1%	2004 : 11.8
Food Credit	1990 : 2.0%	2000 : 6.4%	2004 : 4.7%

Banking Indicators:

Table 7.15 gives some important banking indicators in the recent years; 1997 to 2004.

Bank Deposits

The Aggregate Deposits (Demand and Time) constitute the main liabilities of the banks. The aggregate deposits by March-end 2004 were ₹ 15,04,416 crore, having increased by 17.45 per cent over the previous year. Of these, demand deposits were 15 per cent and 85 per cent were time deposits. Between 1997 and 2004, the share of demand deposits in the aggregate deposits has fallen from 18 per cent to 14 per cent in 2002 but improved to 15 per cent in 2004. The share of time deposits has increased from 80 per cent to 86 per cent in 2002 and 85 per cent in 2004.

The aggregate deposits of scheduled commercial banks were ₹ 908 crore in 1951 which increased to ₹ 5,173 crore in 1969, ₹ 1,74,823 crore in 1990 and further to ₹ 8,13,344 crore in 2000. Thus, there has been massive expansion of bank deposits.

The share of different sectors in the aggregate bank deposits of ₹ 7,14,025 crore by March-end 1999 were:

Sector	%
Government	10.2
Private Corporate Sector (non-financial)	4.1
Financial Sector	8.8
Household Sector	65.3
Foreign Sector	11.6

Between 1995 and 1999, the share of Household sector in the aggregate bank deposits declined from 69.2 per cent to 65.3 per cent.

As could be seen from Table 7.16, the share of deposits in the total liabilities of SCBs has fallen from 81.5% in 2001 to 79.8% by March-end 2004. The share of current (demand), saving and time deposits in the bank deposits were respectively 10.3 per cent, 18.9 per cent and 50.5 per cent by March-end 2004.

Among the liabilities, the other components are the liabilities to other banks, and the borrowings from RBI were at the level of ₹ 6,491 crore in 2000 but have fallen significantly since then, being only ₹ 79 crore in 2003 and Nil in 2004. The liabilities to other banks were ₹ 77,088 crore in 2001 but have come down since then to ₹ 54,487 by March-end 2004.

Financial Performance of Scheduled Commercial Banks

Table No. 7.18
Operating and Net Profits of SCBs

(₹ in Crores)

Year	*Operating Profits*	*% increase over the previous year*	*Net Profits*	*% increase over the previous year*
1999-2000	18307	—	7245	—
2000-01	19757	7.9	6403	–11.6
2001-02	29837	51.0	11576	80.8
2002-03	40682	36.3	17077	47.5
2003-04	52671	29.5	22271	30.4
2004-05	51023	–3.0	20958	–5.9
2005-06	56560	10.9	24592	17.3
2006-07	65977	64.6	31203	64.6
2007-08	83590	60.2	42726	62.2
2008-09	111349	60.2	52771	65.2

Source: Report on Trends and Progress of Banking in India, RBI 2008-09.

Operating Profits

As against, the decline of 3 per cent in the operating profits of SCBs during 2004-05, the operating profits increased by 10.9 per cent in the year 2005-06. The increase in operating profits have been mainly due to increase in interest income.

The share of public sector banks in the operating profits have been as under:

Year	*%*
2000-01	69.8
2001-02	72.7
2002-03	73.0
2003-04	74.9
2004-05	76.0
2005-06	69.2
2006-07	64.6
2007-08	60.2
2008-09	60.2

Net Profits

The Net Profits of SCBs declined by 11.6% during 2000-01. In case of public sector banks, the decline in net profits was 15.6 per cent. The decline was at 15 per cent for old private sector banks. As against this, the net profits of new private sector banks showed an increase of 12.3 per cent during 2000-01.

The increase in Net Profits during 2001-02 at 80.8 per cent is quite significant when viewed against the decline of 11.6 per cent in Net Profits of SCBs during 2002-03 and 2003-04 showed an increase at a slower rate when compared with the preceding years.

The shares of Public Sector banks in the Net Profits of SCBs have been:

Year	% Share
2001-02	92.3
2202-03	72.0
2003-04	74.3
2004-05	73.7
2005-06	67.3
2006-07	64.6
2007-08	62.2
2008-09	65.2

Table No. 7.19
Income and Expenditure of SCBs

(*₹ in Crores)*

Year	*Income*	*% increase over the previous year*	*Expenditure*	*% increase over the previous year*
1999-2000	1,14,930	—	1,07,685	—
2000-01	1,32,076	14.9	1,25,672	16.7
2001-02	1,51,032	14.3	1,39,456	11.0
2002-03	1,72,345	14.1	1,55,268	11.3
2003-04	1,83,861	6.7	1,61,590	3.8
2004-05	1,90,236	3.5	1,69,278	4.8
2005-06	2,22,209	16.8	1,97,616	16.7
2006-07	2,74,716	23.6	2,43,514	23.2
2007-08	3,68,873	34.3	3,26,147	33.9
2008-09	4,63,837	25.7	4,11,066	26.0

Source: Report on Trends and Progress of Banking in India, RBI 2008-09.

As the interest income and non-interest income of SCBs increased during 2005-06, the income showed an increase of 16.8 per cent against an increase of only 3.5 per cent during the previous year.

7.7 CO OPERATIVE BANKING IN INDIA — STRUCTURE AND PERFORMANCE

The beginning of the co operative sector in India dates back to 1904. The institutional source of credit for agriculture and related activities was very inadequate at that time. The moneylenders provided the funds required and charged exorbitantly high rates of interest. The co operative banks were expected to take place of such unorganised money market agencies and provide short-term and long-term institutional credit at reasonable rates of interest. It was expected that they would co ordinate the activities of the unorganised and organised segments of Indian Money Market.

Subsequent to the adoption of economic planning in 1951, co operative banks were assigned to play a crucial role in achieving agricultural and rural development. Before nationalisation of the commercial banks, the co operative banks were the only substitute for moneylenders and other informal sector lenders. After nationalisation of commercial banks and the setting up of Regional Rural Banks (RRB) and NABARD, the relative share of co operative banks in institutional lending declined from 80 per cent in 1969 to 40 per cent in 1990.

The co operative banks perform all the main banking functions of deposit mobilisation, supply of credit and provision of remittance facilities. Some of the co operative banks are Scheduled banks and many of them are non-scheduled banks. Under the Banking Regulation Act, 1949, only Urban Co operative Banks, State Co-operative Banks and District Central Co-operative Banks are qualified to be called as banks in the co-operative sector.

The co operative banks accept short-term and long-term deposits and some of them also mobilise funds through the issue of debentures. Besides this, the resources of the co-operative banks significantly consists of borrowings from institutions like NABARD and from RBI and the government.

As could be seen from the chart, the Primary Agricultural Credit Societies (PACS) at the village level, Central Co operative Banks (CCBs) at the district level and the State Co-operative Banks (StCBs) at the state level provide short/medium term loans and the long-term lending is done by the 'Development Banks.' The Urban Co-operative Banks (UCBs) meet both the working capital as well as fixed capital requirements. The minimum lending rate of UCBs has been reduced from 13 per cent to 12 per cent from March 2002.

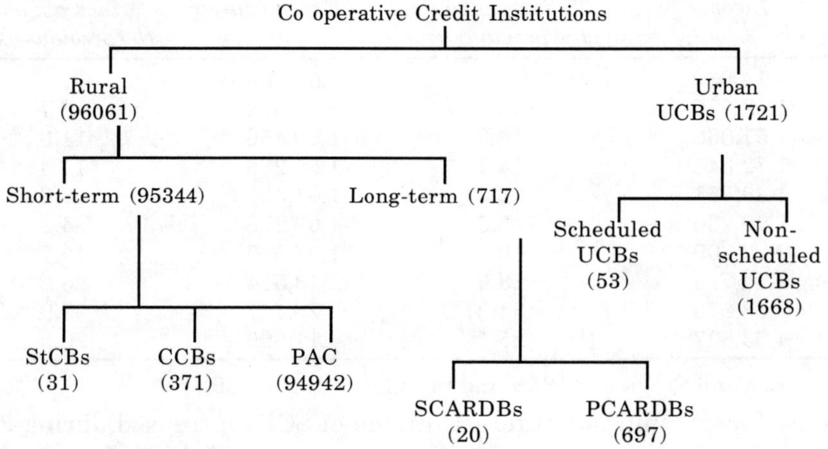

Note: Figures in the brackets indicate the number of respective institutions.
Source: Report on Trend and Progress of Banking in India.

StCB: State Co operative Bank.
CCB: Central Co operative Bank (district level).
PACs: Primary Agricultural Credit Societies (village level).
UCBS: Urban Co operative Banks.
SCARDBs: State Co operative Agricultural and Rural Development Banks.
PCARDBs: Primary Co operative Agricultural and Rural Development Banks.

Progress of Co operative Credit Institutions

(₹ *in Crores)*

Type of Institution	*Item*	*2002-03*	*2003-04*	*2004-05*	*2005-06*
1. Urban Co-op Banks (UCBs)	No	1941	1926	1872	1853
	Owned Funds	9830	12348	13604	13640
	Deposits	101546	110256	105021	112237
	Borrowings	1590	1484	1782	1799
	Loans outstanding	64830	67930	66874	70379
	CD Ratio	64	62	65	64

2. State Co op Banks (StCBs)	No	30	31	31	31
	Owned Funds	7550	8473	9495	NA
	Deposits	39384	43586	44316	45833
	Borrowings	13374	12457	14038	17054
	Working Capital	57134	57936	65879	NA
	Loans issued	38534	33961	44452	43837
	Loans outstanding	34754	35105	37346	39967
	Recovery performance	80	83	84	NA
	CD Ratio	83	81	84	87
3. District Central Co op. Banks (DCCBs)	No	367	365	367	365
	Owned Funds	14695	19131	20495	NA
	Deposits	73858	79153	82098	86855
	Borrowings	19641	20256	22568	24622
	Working Capital	106187	114702	111970	NA
	Loans issued	58802	58708	66266	64276
	Loans outstanding	64126	67152	73091	80090
	Recovery	61	63	71	NA
	CD Ratio	87	85	89	92
4. SCARDBs	No	20	20	20	20
	Owned Funds	3199	4403	5022	NA
	Deposits	501	524	566	502
	Borrowings	15904	16933	17118	16964
	Working Capital	20473	22038	23187	NA
	Loans issued	2959	2837	3292	2819
	Loans outstanding	15365	16263	17425	17895
	Recovery	49	44	44	NA
5. PCARDBs	No	768	768	727	697
	Owned funds	2729	3856	3494	NA
	Deposits	254	395	365	298
	Borrowings	11235	11879	12873	13238
	Working capital	15352	15812	17143	NA
	Loans issued	2177	2164	2509	2184
	Loans outstanding	10814	11311	12763	21792
	Recovery	44	44	51	NA

Source: Report on Trends and Progress of Banking in India, RBI 2005-06.

NA: Not Available

Urban Co operative Banks (UCBs)

Urban Co operative Banks have been set up with an objective of promoting banking habits among the lower and middle income strata of population. Earlier, *i.e.* prior to 1966, UCBs were exclusively under the purview of State Governments, being registered under the Co operative Societies Act of the respective State Governments. With effect from March 1, 1966, RBI has become the regulatory and supervisory authority of UCBs for their banking related operations.

Licensing: A Committee under the chairmanship of Shri K. Madhava Rao in 1999 recommended revisions in entry point norms for UCBs. An advisory committee has been constituted by RBI for licensing of UCBs. During 2001-02, RBI granted in principle approval to setting up of 7 new UCBs and 63 applications were rejected. The total number of UCBs was 2090 by March-end 2002.

Table No. 7.20
Financial Performance of UCBs
(as at March-end)

(₹ *in Crores)*

Item	*1999*	*2000*	*2001*	*2002*	*2003*	*2004 (P)*	*2005*	*2006*
No. of UCBs	1587	1784	1618	1854	1941	1926	1872	1853
Owned Funds	7314	9314	10826	13797	9830	12348	13604	13640
	(27.3)	(16.2)	(27.4)	(–28.7)	(–25.6)	(10.2)	(0.26)	(0.26)
Deposits	52617	71189	80840	93069	101546	110256	105021	112237
		(35.3)	(13.6)	(15.1)	(9.1)	(8.6)	(–5.15)	(6.9)
Loans outstanding	34172	45995	54389	62080	64880	67930	66874	70379
		(34.6)	(18.2)	(14.1)	(4.5)	(4.7)	(–1.55)	(5.2)
CD ratio (Credit deposit)	65	65	67	67	64	62	65	64

Note: Figures in brackets indicate % increase over the previous year. It may be noted that the number of UCBs (reporting) differs from year to year. Of the total 1853 UCBs, 55 UCBs are scheduled UCBs and 1798 are non-scheduled UCBs. Of these non-scheduled UCBs, 191 non-scheduled UCBs are with depsit size of ₹ 100 crore and above.

Among UCBs, there is a high level of diversity in regard to size, geographical spread, performance and financial status, extent of professional approach.

Urban Co operative Banks — Depositwise Structure

as on March-end 2006

Deposit Base (in ₹ crore)	*No. of UCBs*	*% of UCBs*	*Deposits (% to total)*
upto ₹ 100	1633	88.0	32.5
₹ 100 crore to ₹ 500	190	10.3	34.5
₹ 500 crore and more	30	1.7	33.0
Total	1853	100.00	100.00

as on March-end 2009

Deposit Base (in ₹ crore)	*No. of UCBs*	*% of UCBs*	*Deposits (% to total)*
upto ₹ 100	1429	83.04	23.6
₹ 100 crore to ₹ 500	245	14.23	31.1
₹ 500 crore and more	47	2.73	45.3
Total	1721	100.00	100.00

Over 83 per cent of UCBs in number (1429 out of 1721) accounted for 24 per cent of the total UCB deposits. Less than 3 per cent of UCBs accounted for over 45 per cent of the total UCB deposits in 2009.

UCBs Gradation

No. of UCBs

	2005	*2006*	*2007*	*2008*	*2009*
Grade I	807	716	652	748	845
Grade II	340	460	598	526	484
Grade III	497	407	295	258	219
Grade IV	228	270	268	238	173
Total	1872	1853	1813	1770	1721

The decline in number of UCBs was an outcome of the process of consolidation of this sector.

Grade I UCBs are sound banks.

Changing Profile of UCBs

Year (March-end)	*No. of UCBs*	*No. of UCBs in Grade*				*% of UCBs in Grade*
		I	*II*	*III*	*IV*	*III + IV*
2004	1919	880	307	529	203	38
2005	1872	807	340	497	228	39
2006	1853	716	460	407	270	37
2007	1813	652	598	295	268	31
2008	1770	748	526	258	238	26
2009	1721	845	484	219	173	23

There has been a decline in the number of UCBs in Grade III and IV taken together, from 725 as at March-end 2005 to 392 as at March-end 2009.

Profile of UCBs (As at March-end 2009)

(₹ in Crores)

Category	*No. of UCBs*	*Deposits*	*Loan & Advances*	*Assets*
All UCBs	1721	158733	97918	196395
Scheduled UCBs	53	67929 (42.8)	42234 (43.1)	84895 (43.7)
Non-Scheduled UCBs	1668	90804 (57.2)	55684 (56.9)	110500 (56.3)

At March end 2009, the No. of scheduled UCBs remained unchanged at 53, while the No. of non-scheduled UCBs was reduced to 1668 from 1717 in the previous year.

UCBs are termed as, weak banks due to unsatisfactory financial position in terms of CRAR, NPAs and net losses

Grade II	*Grade III*	*Grade IV*
— CRAR: 1% below norm or	— CRAR: below 75% of prescribed norm but above 50%	— CRAR less than 50% of the prescribed norm
— Net NPAs of 10% or more but below 15% or	— Net NPA of 10% or more but below 15%	— Net NPA of 15% or more

— Incurred net loss in the previous financial year	— Incurred net losses for 2 years of the last three years

Financial Performance of UCBs

Year	*No. of UCBs*	*UCBs Mating profits*
1999-00	1747	1497
2000-01	1618	1357
2001-02	1854	1629

Scheduled UCBs (55 in number)

The scheduled UCBs, together with non-scheduled UCBs with deposit size of ₹ 100 crore and more (191 in number) hold respectively 44 per cent and 28.2 per cent of the total assets of UCBs.

(₹ in Crores)

	Year	*Operating Profit*	*Net Profit*
Scheduled UCBs	2003-04	741	210
	2004-05	472	137
	2005-06	682	335
Non-scheduled UCBs with deposit size of ₹ 100 crore and more	2005-06	495	300

The accumulated losses of scheduled UCBs by March-end 2004 were ₹ 2,320 crore.

UCBs (as per size of advances)

Advances	*No.*	*% to total*	*Advances (% to total)*
Up to ₹ 100 crore	1841	89.5	32.0
₹ 100 crore to ₹ 500 crore	153	8.9	31.0
₹ 500 crore and Above	27	1.6	37.0

The pattern of advances of UCBs was similar to that of deposits.

Priority Sector Lending

UCBs are required to channelise 60 per cent of total loan and advances towards priority sector. The priority sector advances of UCBs were 63.5 per cent in 1998, 62.1 per cent in 2003, 64.2 per cent in 2004, but the share of priority sector in total advances was lower at about 54 per cent in 2005-06, but improved to 56.4% by the year 2008-09.

UCBs' Asset Quality

In the early 1990s, UCB sector showed rapid growth. In the recent years, UCBs have suffered from several weaknesses including improper lending, high loan default, absence of professional approach in decision-making. This resulted in the deterioration of assets reflected in the increasing level of non-performing assets NPAs.

Table No. 7.21
UCBs Gross NPAs
(as at March-end)

(₹ in Crores)

Year	*No. of UCBs Reporting*	*Gross NPAs*	*Gross NPA to Total Advances*	*Net NPAs*	*Net NPA to Net Advances*
1999	1474	3306	11.7		
2000	1748	4535	12.2		
2001	1942	9245	16.1		
2002	1937	13706	21.9		
2003	1941	12509	19.0	6428	
2004	1926	15406	22.7	8242	
2005	1872	15486	23.4	8257	
2006	1853	13871	19.7	6728	
2007	1813	14541	18.3	6235	8.8
2008	1770	14037	15.5	6083	7.7
2009	1221	13043	13.3	5318	6.1

The position regarding NPA worsened to 23.4 per cent of Gross advances in 2005, but the NPA ratio for UCBs declined between 2005 and 2009 reflecting the improving financial soundness of this sector.

Merger/Amalgamation of UCBs

In February 2005, RBI issued guidelines towards strengthening UCBs by way of merger/ amalgamation. RBI gave no objection certificate (NOC) in 17 cases out of 36 proposals received. 14 mergers have become effective.

State Level Task Force for UCBs

For UCBs, there is duality of command in the form of State/Central Registrar of co operative societies and RBI. For overcoming the problems faced by UCBs, RBI prepared a Vision Document in March 2005 which provided for reaching Memorandum of Understanding (MoU) between State Governments and RBI and formation of State Level Task Force for UCBs (TAFUCB) for examining the position of UCBs.

UCBs: Prudential Norms, Inspection: Weak Banks

Prudential norms: Introduction CRAR for UCBs: capital to Risk Assets Ratio.

Time frame	*CRAR for Scheduled UCBs*	*CRAR for Non-scheduled UCBs*
March 31, 2002	8 per cent	6 per cent
March 31, 2003	9 per cent	7 per cent
March 31, 2004	As applicable for commercial banks	9 per cent
March 31, 2005		As applicable for commercial banks

Scheduled UCB to achieve CRAR norms by March 2004, and non-scheduled UCBs by March 2005.

- Norms for recognising asset as NPA:

  present norms : if principal and/or interest remain overdue for 180 days.

  effective from March 31, 2005 : to be replaced by 90 days norm.

Certain categories of UCBs are permitted to classify loan accounts as NPA based on 180 days deliquency.

- Inspection: Scheduled UCBs: once a year

  Well managed non-scheduled UCBs: once in 3 years.

  Weak UCBs: Once a year.

  on the basis of supervisory ratings based on CAMELS (Capital adequacy, Asset quality, Management, Earnings, Liquidity and Systems).

Such supervisory ratings to be made applicable to UCBs:

- for scheduled UCBs by March 2003.
- to be extended to other UCBs in a phased manner.

Off-site Surveillance (OSS) for supervision

- designed to monitor compliance and obtain information
- applicable to scheduled UCBs from March 2001
- extended to non-scheduled UCBs with deposits of ₹ 100 crore and more from June 2004.

- Financial Audit : a key supervisory tool for monitoring implementation of various prudential norms.

  For UCBs supervision of audit — falls within the purview of the respective State Government.

  1995: — Committee to review the system of audit of UCBs.

  — recommended conduct of statutory audit by chartered accountants rather than government officials.

State Co operative Banks (StCBs)

State Co operative Banks are at the apex of the three/two tier co operative structure dispensing mainly short/medium term credit.

Table No. 7.22
Financial Performance of StCBs
(as at March-end)

(*₹ in Crores*)

Item	*1999*	*2000*	*2001*	*2002*	*2003*	*2004*	*2005*	*2006*	*2007*
Number	29	29	30	30	30	31	31	31	31
Owned Funds	4135	4911	5837	6712	7159	8473	9495	10549	10718
(Capital+Reserves)		(18.8)	(18.9)	(15.0)	(6.6)	(18.3)	(12.0)		
Deposits	25788	29557	32626	36191	36658	43486	44316	48560	52973
		(14.6)	(10.4)	(10.9)	(1.3)	(18.6)	(1.9)		(9.09% increase)
Loans issued	32834	44035	34307	34663	38642	39320	44452	—	57455
		(34.1)		(0.95)	(11.6)	(1.8)	(13.0)		
Loans outstanding	21909	25709	29861	32678	32798	35105	37346	47354	48228
		(17.3)	(16.1)	(9.4)	(0.4)	(7.0)	(6.4)		

Recovery performance as % of demand	81	83	84	82	79	83.3	83.5	85.7	84.6
CD ratio (credit deposit)	85	87	92	90	89	81	84	—	

Note: Figures in brackets indicate % increase over the previous year.

Out of the total number of StCBs (31), 23 StCBs earned profits amounting to ₹ 234 crore and 5 StCBs made losses of ₹ 49 crore during the year 2007-08. The accumulated losses of StCBs by March-end 2008 were ₹ 429 crore.

The deposits of StCBs showed a growth of over 18 per cent in the year 2004, but slowed down to an increase of less than 2% in the subsequent years. There was an increase of 13 per cent in the loans issued by StCBs during the year 2005. The recovery performance improved to over 83%.

Out of the total number of StCBs (31), 26 StCBs earned profits amounting to ₹ 328 crore, and 4 StCBs made losses of ₹ 37 crore. The accumulated losses of StCBs by March-end 2005 were ₹ 274 crore.

(₹ in Crores)

	Operating Profit	*Net Profit*	*Total Assets*
2003-04	1577	373	
2004-05	1455	291	
2006-07	777	275	85756
2007-08	557	185	90151

Operating profit to total assets

2003-04	2.3%
2004-05	2.03%
2006-07	0.9%
2007-08	0.6%

NPAs and NPAs as % of Loans Outstanding

Year	*Total NPAs*	*Total Loan Outstanding*	*Per cent*
2000-01	3859	29848	13.0
2001-02	4485	32111	14.0
2002-03	6284	32708	19.2
2003-04	6548	35105	18.7
2004-05	6072	37346	16.3
2005-06	6735	39084	17.0
2006-07	6704	47354	14.2
2007-08	6169	48228	12.8

The amount of NPAs has grown but has been lower than the rate of growth of loans outstanding.

Central Co operative Banks (CCBs)

Central Co operative Banks form the middle tier in the short-term credit structure of co operative credit institutions.

Table No. 7.23
Financial Performance of CCBs
(as at March-end)

(₹ *in Crores*)

Item	*1999*	*2000*	*2001*	*2002*	*2003*	*2004*	*2005*	*2006*	*2007*
Number	367	367	367	368	367	365	367	371	371
Owned Funds	7652	10116	12180	14141	16836	19131	20497	26180	24754
(Capital+Reserves)		(32.2)	(20.4)	(16.1)					
Deposits	40112	54248	61745	68181	73919	79153	82098	94529	102986
		(35.2)	(13.8)	(10.4)	(8.4)	(7.0)	(3.7)		
Loans issued	40397	46619	45016	55915	64665	48709	66266		93162
		(15.4)	(–3.4)	(22.6)	(17.1)	(–24.7)	(36.0)		
Loans outstanding	36949	44538	52478	59316	64214	67152	73091	89038	91374
		(20.5)	(17.8)	(13.0)	(8.2)	(4.6)	(8.8)		
Recovery Performance (as % of demand)	70	70	67	66	61	62.9	71.0	71	55.6
C.D. Ratio (credit deposit)	81	82	85	87	87	85			

Note: Figures in brackets indicate % increase over the previous year.

(₹ *in Crores*)

	Operating Profit *Amount*	*Net Profit* *Amount*
2003-04	2522	108
2004-05	3098	908
2006-07	2314	31
2007-08	1869	(–)65

Profits of CCBs have been on a decline falling rapidly from ₹ 971 crore in 2004-05 to (–) ₹ 65 crore in 2007-08.

Financial Performance

(₹ *in Crores*)

	Profit Making		*Loss Incurring*		*Accumulated Losses*
	No.	*Amount*	*No.*	*Amount*	
2003-04	263	864	102	756	5126
2004-05	296	1379	71	405	4723
March 08	234	760	88	– 825	– 6106

The number of profit-making CCBs had earlier gone up and their profits increased. The number of loss incurring CCBs had fallen and their losses showed a fall during 2004-05. In the recent years, their profits (Net) have been on the decline, resulting in an increase in accumulated losses.

NPAs and NPAs as % of Loans Outstanding

(₹ in Crores)

Year	*Total NPAs*	*Total loan outstanding*	*NPAs to loans outstanding (%)*
2000-01	9371	52491	17.9
2001-02	11838	59269	20.0
2002-03	13862	63198	21.9
2003-04	16144	67152	24.0
2004-05	14520	73125	19.9
2005-06	15709	79202	19.8
2006-07	16495	89037	18.5
2007-08	18728	91374	20.5

There has been deterioration in the asset quality of DCCBs.

Primary Agricultural Credit Societies (PACs)

Primary Agricultural Credit Societies are the grass-root level co-operative credit institutions playing a pivotal role in the disbursement of short-term credit.

Primary Agricultural Credit Societies (PACs)

No. of PACs (by March-end)

1998	:	92 thousand
2001	:	1 lakh
2003	:	1.12 lakh
2004	:	1.06 lakh
2005	:	1.09 lakh
2007	:	97224
2008	:	94942

Membership (by March-end)

2001	:	10.0 crore
2002	:	10.2 crore
2003	:	12.4 crore
2004	:	13.5 crore
2005	:	12.7 crore
2006	:	12.5 crore
2007	:	12.6 crore
2008	:	13.2 crore

Deposits (₹ in Crore)

2001	:	13,481
2002	:	14,846
2003	:	19,120
2004	:	18,143
2005	:	18,976
2006	:	19,549

2007	:	23,484	
2008	:	25,449	

Outstanding Loans (₹ in Crore) % of overdues to loans outstanding

2001	:	34,522	
2002	:	40,779	
2003	:	42,411	
2004	:	43,873	
2005	:	48,785	
2006	:	51,779	
2007	:	58,620	26.9
2008	:	65,666	36.6

During 2007-08, PACs had a high borrower to member ratio of 60 per cent as compared to only 38 per cent during the previous year.

During 2004-05

Profit Making		*Loss Incuring*		
No.	*Amount*	*No.*	*Amount*	*Net losses*
47015	₹ 728 crore	61323	₹ 1989 crore	₹ 1261 crore

As at March-end 2008

(*₹ in Crores*)

Profit Making		*Loss Incurring*		*Overall Loss*
No.	*Amount*	*No.*	*Amount*	
38307	2230	48520	5711	–3481

Total over dues	:	₹ 24004 crore
As % of loan outstanding	:	36.6
Recovery of loans to demand	:	64.3%

The PACs are exposed to serious financial problems due to high defaults and low recovery.

State Co-operative Agricultural and Rural Development Banks (SCARDBs)

The SCARDBs are at the top level of the long-term credit structure of the co-operatives. Earlier, the long-term lending co-operatives were known as Land Development Banks and they had a two-tier structure of State Land Development Banks and the Primary Land Development Banks.

As of March-end 2008, the deposits of 20 SCARDBs amounted to ₹ 645 crore. Over the years, the loans outstanding have increased from ₹ 17,422 crore by March-end 2005 to ₹ 18,217 crore by March-end 2008. The recovery performance of SCARDBs has been 49 per cent in 2008 as against 43.7% in 2004-05.

Table No. 7.24
Financial Performance of SCARDBs
(as at March-end)

(₹ *in Crores)*

Item	*1999*	*2000*	*2001*	*2002*	*2003*	*2004*	*2005*	*2007*	*2008*
Number	19	19	20	20	20	20	20 (864 branches	20	20
Owned Funds	2353	2702	3034	2984	2892	4403	5022	2931	3713
Deposits	240	422	536	571	546	524	566	605	645
Borrowings	11051	12390	13413	14846	15910	16933	17180	16662	15843
Loans outstanding	10441	11565	12553	14147	15385	16263	17422	18644	18217
Recovery Performance (as % of demand)	62	62	58	55	49	43.8	43.7	43.9	49.0

Source: Report on Trends and Progress of Banking in India, RBI 2005-06.
Note: Figures in brackets indicate % increase over the previous year.

Financial Performance of SCARDBs

(₹ *in Crores)*

Year	*Operating Profit* *Amount*	*Net Profit* *Amount*	*Accumulated Loss*
2003-04	433	119	2004 : ₹ 856 crore
2004-05	564	163	2005 : ₹ 1098 crore
2006-07	757	89	
2007-08	310	–247	2008 : ₹ 1257 crore

NPAs and NPAs as % of Loans Outstanding

2003-04		*2004-05*		*2006-07*		*2007-08*	
Amount	*%*	*Amount*	*%*	*Amount*	*%*	*Amount*	*%*
4336	27	5437	31	5642	30.3	6292	34.5

Working Results of SCARDBs

(₹ *in Crores)*

Year	*Profit Making*		*Loss Making*	
	No.	*Amount*	*No.*	*Amount*
2000-01	10	90	9	129
2001-02	9	85	11	180
2002-03	8	62	12	163
2003-04	10	97	9	210
2004-05	10	81.4	9	243

Performance of SCARDBs (March 2008).

Profit-making institutions : 9 : Amount ₹ 151 crore.
Loss-incurring institutions : 8 : Amount ₹ 398 crore.

Primary Co operative Agriculture and Rural Development Banks(PCARDBs)

PCARDBs are at the lowest level of the long-term credit co operative structure. PCARDBs are also depending on borrowings for their lending activities.

Table No. 7.25
Financial Performance of PCARDBs
(as at March-end)

(₹ *in Crores)*

Item	*1999*	*2000*	*2001*	*2002*	*2003*	*2004*	*2005*	*2006-07*	*2007-08*
Number	745	755	732	768	768	766	727	697	697
Owned Funds	1167	1379	1628	2494	2730	3856	3494	3596	3039
Deposits	166	218	210	256	222	395	365	341	331
		(31.3)							
Borrowings	6777	7647	8294	10334	11217	11879	12873	12751	10206
		(12.3)	(8.5)	(24.6)	(8.5)	(5.9)	(8.4)		
Loans Outstanding	6778	7611	8295	9982	10775	11311	12763	12114	9529
		(12.3)	(9.0)	(20.3)	(7.9)	(5.0)	(12.8)		
Recovery Performance	60	58	53	48	44	43.9	50.6	52.0	44.0

Source: Report on Trend and Progress of Banking in India, 2005-06.
Note: Figures in brackets indicate % increase over the previous year.

Table No. 7.25(A)
Financial Performance of SCARDBs and PCARDBs

SCARDBs (₹ *in Crores)*

Year	*Profit-making*		*Loss-making*		*Accumulated Losses*
	No.	*Amount*	*No.*	*Amount*	*Amount*
2000-01	10	99	9	129	907
2001-02	9	85	11	182	492
2002-03	8	62	11	164	681
2003-04	10	97	9	210	856
2004-05	10	81	9	243	1098

PCARDBs

Year	*Profit-making*		*Loss-making*		*Accumulated Losses*
	No.	*Amount*	*No.*	*Amount*	*Amount*
2000-01	273	49	459	165	1157
2001-02	191	47	577	294	1944
2002-03	236	54	542	330	2325
2003-04	282	77	489	335	2788
2004-05	262	665	465	274	2475

Source: Report on trends and progress of Banking in India: RBI 2005-06
Note: Figures in brackets indicate % increase over the previous year.

Financial Performane of PCARDBs

(₹ *in Crores)*

Year	*Operating Profit*	*Net Profit*	*Accumulated loss*
2003-04	354	-258	2003-04 : ₹ 2788 crore
2004-05	913	391	2004-05 : ₹ 2475 crore
2006-07	867	(–)147	—
	2007-08	189	(–)346 (–)3214

NPAs and NPAs as % to Loans Outstanding

2003-04		*2004-05*		*2007*		*2008*	
Amount	*%*	*Amount*	*%*	*Amount*	*%*	*Amount*	*%*
41016	35.8	4056	31.9	4318	35.4	5113	53.7

Working Results of PCARDBs

(*₹ in Crores*)

Year	*Profit Making*		*Loss Making*	
	No.	*Amount*	*No.*	*Amount*
2000-01	273	49	459	165
2001-02	191	47	577	294
2002-03	226	54	542	330
2003-04	282	77	489	335
2004-05	262	665	465	274
2006-07	350	419	342	566
2007-08	199	170	271	516

(470 reporting out of a total of 697 PCARDBs)

The NPAs of PCARDBs, both in absolute terms and as % of loan increased significantly. PCARDBs recorded an overall losses of ₹ 346 crore, reflecting the poor incidence and extent of profitability.

The deposits of PCARDBs having increased to ₹ 395 crore in the year 2004, showed decline in the year 2005. The borrowing, however, increased by 8.4 per cent in 2005. The recovery performance improved significantly to over 50 per cent. Though the number of PCARDBs has fallen in year 2005, the amount of profit has stood up to ₹ 665 crore as against ₹ 77 crore in the previous year. This performance resulted in the Net Profit of ₹ 391 crore in 2005 as against the Net Loss recorded in the previous year and thereby the accumulated losses of PCARDBs declined from ₹ 2788 crore in 2004 to ₹ 2,475 crore in the year 2005.

Table No. 7.26

(Gross) NPAs of StCBs CCBs, SCARDBs

(As on March 31, 2001)

(Gross)	*StCBs*		*CCBs*		*SCARDBs*	
NPA-as % to Outstanding loan	*No.*	*% to total*	*No.*	*% to total*	*No.*	*% to total*
0-10%	9	31	97	27	4	21
10-15	7	24	35	10	1	5
15-20	1	3	45	12	2	11
20-25	2	7	26	7	1	5
25-30	1	3	27	7	0	0
Above 30	9	31	136	37	11	58
No. reporting	29	100	366	100	19	100

By March-end 2001, the shares of rural co operative credit institutions with regard to NPAs above 30 per cent were 31% for StCBs, 37 per cent for CCBs and 58 per cent for SCAARDBs. The problem of NPAs appears to be more serious among long-term co operative credit institutions.

Table No. 26 (A)

Asset Quality: NPAs (Gross) of StCBs, CCBs, SCRADBs, PCARDBs

(₹ *in Crores)*

	StCBs			*CCBs*		
Assets	*2003*	*2004*	*2005*	*2003*	*2004*	*2005*
Substandard	3544	3288	2961	7595	8428	6468
Doubtful	2540	3010	1975	5073	6068	6053
Loss	210	250	1136	1213	1648	1999
Total NPAs	6294	6548	6072	13881	16147	14520
NPAs to Loan Outstanding	18.2	18.7	16.3	21.6	24.0	19.9
	SCARDBs			*PCARDBs*		
Substandard	2107	2630	3288	1975	2079	2161
Doubtful	1089	1686	2129	1565	1890	1845
Loss	22	20	20	29	47	50
Total NPAs	3218	4336	5437	3569	4016	4056
NPAs to Loan Outstanding	21.0	26.7	31.3	35.5	35.8	31.9

Report on Trends and Progress of Banking in India: RBI 2005-06.

Table No. 26 (B)

NPAs (Gross) to Loans Outstanding (%)

		Short-term		*Long-term*	
Year	*StBs*	*CCBs*	*PACs*	*SCARDBs*	*PCARDBs*
1999-00	10.7	17.2	35.4	18.7	20.0
200-01	13.0	17.9	34.9	20.5	24.3
2001-02	13.4	19.9	32.5	18.5	30.2
2002-03	18.2	21.2	37.9	20.9	33.8
2003-04	18.7	24.0	36.8	26.7	35.8
2004-05	16.3	19.9	33.6	31.3	31.9
2005-06	16.8	19.7	30.4	32.7	35.6
2006-07	14.2	18.5	26.9	23.0	43.3
2007-08	12.7	18.7			

Source: Handbook of Statistics on Indian Economy: RBI 2005-06.

A Profile of Rural Co operative Credit Institutions

(As at March-end 2008)

(₹ *in Crores)*

	Short-term			*Long-term*		*Total*
	St CBs	*DCCBs*	*PACs*	*SCARDBs*	*PCARDBs*	
No. of Co operative Bank	31	371	94942	20	697	96061
Owned Funds	10718	24754	10984	3713	3039	53208
Deposits	52973	102986	25449	645	331	182384
Borrowing	22164	26096	47848	15843	10206	122157
Loan & advances issued	57455	93162	57643	2226	1773	212259
Loans & advances outstanding	48228	913774	65666	18217	9529	233014
Investments	29060	44419	-	2526	752	76757
Total Liabilities/Assets	90151	161932	88107	24403	18209	382802
Institutions makin gprofit No.	23	234	38307	9	203	38776

Amount	234	760	2230	151	170	3545
Institutions incurring Loss No.	5	88	48520	8	258	48879
Amount	-49	-825	-5711	-398	-516	-7499
Accumulated loss	-429	-6106		-1257	-3214	-11006
NPAs: Amount	6169	18728	24004	6292	5114	60307
As % to loans outstanding	12.8	20.5	36.6	34.5	53.7	25.9
Recovery of loans to demand	84.6	55.6	64.3	49.0	44.0	

As could be seen from the above details, there is high level of loan deliquency as a problem among the short-term as well as long-term rural credit institutions.

Problems of Co operative Credit Institutions: Policy Measures

A large number of problems faced by the Co operative Credit institutions include:

- high level of loan delinquency.
- erosion of capital base; existence of a number of weak banks due to non-adherence to norms and regulations.
- paucity of funds for fresh deployment, and high level of dependence on other agencies for funds due to poor repayment (recovery) performance.
- lack of professionalism in conduct and management resulting in deficiencies like high transaction costs.
- inadequate internal controls and governance structure.

High Level of Loan Delinquency:

The loan impairment expressed in terms of high proportion of Gross Non-performing Assets (NPAs) as per cent of loans and advances outstanding is significant in case of both urban and rural credit co operatives.

UCBs

The NPA position in case UCBs has deteriorated in recent years. The Gross NPAs increased from ₹ 4,535 crore in 2000 to ₹ 13,706 crore in the year 2002. Since then NPAs of UCBs have declined to ₹ 12,509 crore in 2003 and ₹ 11,922 crore in 2004. The percentage of Gross NPA to total advances has also fallen from 21.9% to 17.6 per cent during 2002 and 2004.

StCBs and CCBs

For the year 2002-03, the gross NPAs as percentage to loans outstanding stood at 18 per cent and 22 per cent in case of StBCs and CCBs respectively. The composition of Gross NPAs of StCBs and CCBs shows that over 56 per cent and 55 per cent are substandard assets and more than one-third are doubtful assets.

For NPAs of commercial banks, One-time Settlement scheme has been proposed by RBI. Similar guidelines have been suggested by NABARD for credit co operatives.

Erosion of Capital Base: Capital Adequacy : Prudential Norms

Some co operative banks and other co operative credit institutions have been conducting business contrary to the spirit of co-operation and have flouted specific norms in their transactions. As these credit co operatives do not comply with the minimum capital requirements, their own funds get eroded. As on March 31, 2002, 9 out of 30 StCBs and 139 out of 367 CCBs were not adhering to the minimum share capital requirement. The financial position of UCB is termed unsatisfactory on the extent of erosion of own funds. Besides this, the other criteria for categorising UCB as weak banks are limit in terms of CRAR (below 75 per cent of the minimum) or NPA or profitability (net losses for two years out of last three years).

To ensure financial stability, some of the prudential norms introduced for commercial banks have to be extended to co-operative banks. The prudential norms have been introduced for co-operative banks in 1996-97 and a definite time frame has been worked out with regard to (CRAR) Capital to Risk-weighted Assets Ratio for UCBs and measures have been taken up to ensure that the minimum capital requirements are met by rural co operative banks.

Conduct and Management of Co operative Credit Institutions

- The major irritant to effective working and their supervision and regulation is the duality/multiplicity of control of co operative banks. The co operative credit institutions are under the regulatory control of State Government, RBI and NABARD and in certain cases the Central Government. The duality/multiplicity of control has resulted in overlapping jurisdiction particularly between state governments and RBI and has affected the improvement efforts in this sector.
- *Restructuring of organisational set-up:*

  Two alternatives considered in this regard are: (i) merger of short-term and long-term structure, and (ii) delayering of the short-term structure. The first alternative was recommended by Dr. Hazari Committee in 1976. The integration of short-term and long-term structure was implemented in Andhra Pradesh in 1986. The Second Narasimham Committee (1998) recommended delayering of the short-term structure wherein one-tier either StCBs or CCBs could be skipped.

SHG — Bank Linkage, Self-Help Groups

In 1991, it was reported in the findings of All India Debt and Investment Survey that 36 per cent of rural households depended for funds on informal sources. A programme to strengthen the provision of credit in rural areas was launched in 1992 by forming Self-Help Groups (SHGs) and linking SHGs and the non-governmental organisations (NGOs) with the banking system. The rural poor are organised to form SHGs and are encouraged to save small amounts regularly. NGOs support SHGs in getting banks loans. Most of SHGs (90%) are formed by women.

NABARD, supported by RBI, plays a key role in the prorgramme, *i.e.,* in the development and promotion of SHGs. All credit institutions, *i.e.,* commercial banks, co-operative banks and RRBs along with NGOs are assoicated with the programme.

There are *three* types or Models of Credit linkage of SHGs with the banks.

1. formed are financed by banks
2. formed by formal agencies (NGOs/Government agencies) other than banks, but financed by banks
3. promoted by NGOs and financed by banks, using NGOs/formed agencies as financial intermediaries

SHG Programme

(₹ *in Crores)*

Year	*No. of SHGs (in 000s)*		*Bank Loan*		*Refinance*	
	During the year	*Cumulative*	*During the year*	*Cumulative*	*During the year*	*Cumulative*
1992-99	33	33	57	57	52	52
1999-2000	82	115	136	193	98	150
2000-01	149	264	288	481	245	395
2001-02	198	461	345	1026	395	790
2002-03	256	717	1022	2049	622	1413
2003-04	362	1079	1856	3904	705	2118
2004-05	539	1018	2994	6898	968	3086
2005-06	620	2239	4449	11397	1068	4154
2006-07	1106	2895	6570	12366	1293	5446
2007-08	1228	3626	8849	16999.90	1616	7062
2008-09	808	—	4585	—	2620	9682

By March-end 2008, 3.6 million SHGs have been formed and the cumulative assistance provided by the banks was ₹ 17000 crore, NABARD extended cumulative refinance to the banks amounting to ₹ 7062 crore.

The agency-wise details of credit flow under the scheme show by March-end 2009, the commercial banks are agency which have financed over 65 per cent of the SHGs amounting to over 67 per cent of the total bank credit provided to them.

Since then, the programme has progressed well and by March-end 2006, 2.2 million SHGs have been formed and the cumulative assistance provided by the banks by March-end 2006 was ₹ 11,398 crore. NABARD extended cumulative refinance to the banks amounting to ₹ 4,154 crore.

Earlier, the SHGs had come up mainly in Southern states like Andhra Pradesh, Tamil Nadu, Karnataka. NABARD has intensified the SHG-bank linkage programme in 13 identified priority states which account for 70 per cent of the rural poor population.

SHG-Bank Linkage: Type or Modelwise

(Number in 000s) (Bank loan in ₹ crores)

Model / Type	*2004*		*2005*		*2006*	
	No.	*Bank loan*	*No.*	*Bank loan*	*No.*	*Bank loan*
1. Promoted and financed by banks	218 (20)	550 (14)	343 (21.2)	1013 (14.7)	449 (20.1)	1637 (14.4)
2. Promoted by formal agencies other than banks but financed by banks	777 (72)	3165 (81)	1158 (71.8)	5529 (80.2)	1646 (73.5)	9200 (80.7)
3. Promoted by NGOs and financed by bank	84 (8)	189 (5)	117 (7.2)	356 (5.2)	143 (6.4)	361 (4.9)
Total (1 + 2 + 3)	1079	3904	1618	6898	2239	11398

Of the above three models/types, around 72-73 per cent of SHGs under type 2 have been beneficiaries of bank loan accounting for over 80 per cent of the total.

The agency-wise details of credit flow under the scheme show that by March-end 2006, the commercial banks are agency which have financed over the 53 per cent of SHGs amounting to 61 per cent of the total bank credit provided to them.

(No. in '000s) (Bank loan in ₹ in Crores)

Agency	*2006 (March-end)*		*2007-08*		*2008-09*	
	No.	*Bank loans*	*No.*	*Bank loans*	*No.*	*Bank loans*
Commercial Banks	1188 (53)	6957 (61)	2378 (65.6)	11475 (67.5)	2831	16149
RRB	740 (33)	3322 (29)	876 (24.2)	4421 (26.0)	978	5224
Credit Co operative Bank	310 (19)	1087 (10)	371 (10.2)	1103 (6.5)	415	1306
Total	2239	11398	3626	17000	4224	22680

'Microfinance' Programme

For promoting Microfinance institutions, a study group was appointed by RBI which submitted report in July 2005.The scheme Microfinance Institutions MFIs — bank linkages was announced by NABARD. Microfinance Development and Equity Fund has been set up by NABARD and the corpus of the fund has been increased from ₹ 100 crore to ₹ 200 crore. The programme is meant for reaching the banking system to the rural poor.

The banking sector extended loans to MFIs (Microfinance Institutions) for on-lending to SHGs. During the year 2008-09 bank loan amounting ₹ 3,732 crore was disbursed to 581 MFIs taking the total loans outstanding to ₹ 5009 crore to 1915 MFIs as on March 31, 2009.

7.8 BANKING SECTOR REFORMS

The Reforms for creating a resilient banking system were taken up by the Narasimham Committee in 1991 itself.

A reduction in the pre-emption of bank resources (due to high CRR and high SLR) and improvement and effectiveness in the directed credit programme (priority sector lending) were to be implemented for increasing the profitability of the commercial banks.

Major reforms in the banking sector are given below:

- Interest rates on deposits and advances of all co operative banks including urban co-operative banks deregulated. Similarly, interest rates on commercial bank loans above ₹ 2 lakh, and on domestic term deposits above two years, and Non-Resident (External) Rupee Accounts (NRNR) deposits decontrolled. The number of administered interest rates on commercial bank advances reduced from more than 20 in 1989-90 to 2 in 1994-95. Banks allowed to set their own interest rate on post-shipment export credit in rupees for over 90 days.
- The State Bank of India and other nationalised banks enabled to access the capital market for debt and equity.
- Prudential norms for income recognition, classification of assets and provisioning for bed debts for commercial banks, including regional rural banks and financial institutions introduced. They are required to adopt uniform and sound accounting practices in

respect of these matters, and the valuation of investments. Banks are required to mark to market the securities held by them.

- The Performance Obligations and Commitments (PO&C) obtained by RBI from each bank; they provide for essential quantifiable performance parameters which lay emphasis on increased but low-cost deposits, quality lending, generation of more income and profits, compliance with priority sectors and export lending requirements, improvement in the quality of investments, reduction in expenditure, and stepping up of staff productivity. The PO&C are meant to ensure a high level of portfolio quality so that problems such as heavy losses, low profits, erosion of equity to not recur. The non-fulfillment of PO&C entail penalty in the form of higher CRR/SLR, stoppage of RBI refinance facility, stoppage of further capital contribution by the government, etc.
- Banks required making their balance sheets fully transparent and making full disclosures in keeping with International Accounts Standards Committee.
- The perceived constraints on banks such as prior credit authorisation, inventory and receivables norms, obligatory consortium lending and curbs in respect of project finance relaxed.
- The budgetary support extended for recapitalisation of weak public sector banks.
- Banking Ombudsman Scheme 1995 introduced to appoint 15 ombudsmen (by RBI) to look into and resolve customers' grievances in a quick and inexpensive manner. Most of the recommendations of Goiporia Committee in connection with improving customer service by banks implemented.
- Banks set free to fix their own foreign exchange open position limit subject to RBI approval.
- Loan system introduced for delivery of bank credit. Banks required bifurcating the maximum permissible bank finance into loan component (short-term working capital loan) and cash credit component, and the policy of progressively increasing the share of the former introduced.
- Operational autonomy has been granted to public sector banks.
- Public ownership in public sector banks are reduced by allowing them to raise capital from equity market up to 49 per cent of paid-up capital.
- Transparent norms have been issued for entry of Indian private sector, foreign and joint-venture banks and insurance companies, permission for foreign investment in the financial sector in the form of foreign direct investment (FDI) as well as portfolio investment, permission to banks to diversify product portfolio and business activities.
- Roadmap has been developed for presence of foreign banks and guidelines are issued for mergers and amalgamation of private sector banks and banks and NBFCs.
- Guidelines on ownership and governance in private sector banks are developed.
- Sharp reduction in pre-emption through reserve requirement, market-determined pricing for government securities, disbanding of administered interest rates with a few exceptions and enhanced transparency and disclosure norms to facilitate market discipline.

- Introduction of pure inter-bank call money market, auction-based repos-reverse repos for short-term liquidity management, facilitation of improved payments and settlement mechanism.
- Significant advancement in dematerialisation and markets for securitised assets are being developed.
- Introduction and phased implementation of international best practices and norms on risk-weighted capital adequacy requirement, accounting, income recognition, provisioning and exposure.
- Measures to strengthen risk management through recognition of different components of risk, assignment of risk-weights to various asset classes, norms on connected lending, risk concentration, application of market-to-market principle for investment portfolio and limits on deployment of fund in sensitive activities.
- 'Know Your Customer' and 'Anti Money Laundering' guidelines, roadmap for Basel II, introduction of capital charge for market risk, higher graded provisioning of NPAs, guidelines for ownership and governance, securitisation and debt restructuring mechanisms norms, etc.
- Setting up of Lok Adalats (people's courts), debt recovery tribunals, asset reconstruction companies, settlement advisory committees, corporate debt restructuring mechanism, etc., for quicker recovery/restructuring.
- Promulgation of Securitisation and Reconstruction of Financial Assets and Enforcement of Securities Interest (SARFAESI) Act, 2002 and its subsequent amendment to ensure creditor rights.
- Setting up of Credit Information Bureau of India Limited (CIBIL) for information sharing on defaulters as also other borrowers.
- Setting up of Clearing Corporation of India Limited (CCIL) to act as central counter party for facilitating payments and settlement system relating to fixed income securities and money market instruments.
- Establishment of the Board for Financial Supervision as the apex supervisory authority for commercial banks, financial institutions and non-banking financial companies.
- Introduction of CAMELS supervisory rating system, move towards risk-based supervision, consolidated supervision of financial conglomerates, strengthening of off-site surveillance through control returns.
- Recasting of the role of statutory auditors, increased internal control through strengthening of internal audit.
- Strengthening corporate governance, enhanced due diligence on important shareholders, fit and proper tests for directors.
- Setting up of INFINET as the communication backbone for the financial sector, introduction of negotiated dealing system (NDS) for screen-based trading in government securities and real time gross settlement (RTGS) system.

KEY TERMS

Commercial Bank, Assets, Liabilities, CRR, SLR Directed Credit, Directed Investment, Non-performing Assets, Capital Adequacy Norms.

REVIEW QUESTIONS

1. What is a commercial bank ? Discuss the functions of commercial banks.
2. Discuss the progress of commercial banking in India before the nationalisation of banks.
3. Explain the performance of the commercial banks in the post-nationalisation period.
4. Discuss the banking sector reforms introduced in India after 1991.
5. Discuss the Assets and Liabilities of the scheduled commercial banks.
6. Explain the structure of the Co operative Credit Institutions in India.
7. Discuss the performance of Urban Co operative Banks.
8. Discuss the Self-help Groups – Bank Linkage.

REFERENCES

1. Chakrabarty T.K. (1986), "Profitability of Banks", RBI Occasional Papers, June.
2. Govt. of India (1998 April), Report of the Committee on Banking Sector Reforms (Narasimham Committee Report No. 2).
3. Reserve Bank of India: Report on Currency and Finance, Report on Trends and Progress of Banking in India, Annual Reports – Various Issues.

❑ ❑ ❑

8

Non-Bank Finance Companies (NBFCs)

INTRODUCTION

The Non-Bank Finance Companies (NBFCs) are the financial intermediaries which mobilise funds by way of deposits from the public and channelise them to meet the requirements of borrowers in different sectors by way of loans and advances, leasing, hire purchase etc. NBFCs are a large number of decentralised, privately owned and small-sized financial intermediaries which highly compete with the commercial banks, especially in the recent years. The RBI (Amendment) Act, 1997 has given the Reserve Bank of India regulatory powers to regulate and control the NBFCs operating in India. the NBFCs are broadly classified as –

- Equipment Leasing Company (ELC)
- Hire Purchase Finance Company (HPFC)
- Housing Finance Company (HFC) — supervised by NHB (National Housing Bank)
- Investment Company (IC) — Primary Dealers (PDs) included.
- Loan Company (LC)
- Mutual Benefit Financial Company (MBFC) 'Nidhis'
- Residuary Non-banking Company (RNBC)
- Miscellaneous Non-banking Company (MNBC) — Chit Fund Companies.

The number of operating NBFCs is very large (run into thousands) but only a small number of such companies regularly report to the RBI. Due to emergence of many multi-service companies, categorising them has become increasingly difficult. There are serious definitional and data availability problems which make the study and analysis of the NBFCs much difficult.

The chapter is divided in following sections and sub-sections:

8.1 Growth of NBFCs

8.2 Classification of NBFCs

8.3 Types of NBFCs

8.4 Performance and Financial Position of NBFCs

8.5 Regulatory Framework of NBFCs

8.6 NBFCs *vis-à-vis* Scheduled Commercial Banks

8.7 NBFCs and Monetary Policy

8.1 GROWTH OF NBFCs

Upto 1995-96:

The NBFCs have been operating in India since long but came into prominence in the recent years. The total assets/liabilities of NBFCs grew rapidly at an average annual rate of 20.9 per cent during 1981-91 and at the rate of 36.7 per cent during 1991-98. As a percentage of household sector saving in gross financial asset, the share of NBFC deposits increased from 3.1 percent in 1980-81 to 10.6 per cent during 1995-96 and further to 13.6 per cent in 1996-97.

	1984	*1996*
No. of NBFCs	4240	51929 (Only 10161, *i.e.*, 20% reported to RBI)
NBFC Deposits Outstanding	₹ 274 crore	₹ 38676.5 crore

Source: RBI Bulletin – Various Issues.

The number of NBFCs and deposits mobilised by them increased manifold as there were no entry barriers and the NBFCs faced relatively less regulations. The advantages of NBFCs are lower transaction costs, quick decision-making, customer orientation, and prompt provision of services.

The NBFCs attracted small savers as they offered high returns on the deposits. Although NBFCs grew very rapidly, the need for their regulation arose as the NBFCs involved themselves in indiscriminate investments in real estate and in unquoted shares.

After January 1997:

After Jan. 1997, the NBFCs came under the regulatory framework of RBI. NBFCs are not a homogeneous group but consists of entities engaged in a wide range of activities. NBFCs are regulated and supervised by the RBI leaving aside the housing finance companies which are supervised by the National Housing Bank (NHB).

Since Sept. 2003, the supervision and regulation of Mutual Benefit finance companies and Mutual Benefit companies has been taken over by Department of Company Affairs.

By March 2006, RBI received 38244 applications for grant of Certificate of Registration (CoR) as NBFCs of these the RBI approved 13141 applications including 423 applications of companies authorised to accept/hold public deposits.

Table No. 8.1

Reporting NBFCs

Year	*All NBFCs*	*NBFCs Reporting*	*NBFCs in Southern Region*	*No. of NBFCs in Chennai*	*NBFCs Accepting Public Deposit*
1999-2000	8451	1005	508	340	—
2000-01	13615	981	497	349	—
2001-02	14077	910	451	317	—
2002-03	13849	875	435	318	—
2003-04	13764	777	392	304	—
2004-05	13262	703	381	322	—

2005-06	13014	432	172	130	428 (3.3)
2006-07	12968	371	—	—	401 (3.1)
2007-08	12809	335	—	—	364 (2.8)
2008-09	12740	—	—	—	336 (2.6)

8.2 CLASSIFICATION OF NBFCs

NBFCs may be broadly classified into 3 (three) categories –

(i) NBFCs accepting public deposits

(ii) NBFCs not accepting deposits from the public

(iii) Core Investment Companies – those acquiring shares/securities of their group/holding/ subsidiary companies to the extent of not less than 90 per cent of the total assets.

The NBFCs fall under different categories on the basis of their activities or the main business conducted by them.

1. *Equipment Leasing Companies (ELC)* – any company whose principal business is the activity of leasing of equipment or the financing of such activities.
2. *Hire Purchase Finance Company (HPFC)* – any company carrying on as its principal business the hire purchase transactions or the financing of such transaction.
3. *Housing Finance Company (HFC)* – any company carrying on as its principal business, the financing of the acquisition or construction of houses including the acquisition of development of plots of land in connection therewith.
4. *Investment Company (IC)* – means any company which is carrying on as its principal business, the acquisition of securities.
5. *Loan Company (LC)* – means any company which is carrying on as its principal business, the providing of finance whether by making loans or advances, or otherwise for any activity other than its own (it does not include Equipment Leasing, Hire Purchase and Housing Finance Company).
6. *Mutual Benefit Financial Company (MBFC)* – means any company which is notified by the Central Government under Section 620A of the Companies Act 1956 (1 of 1956).
7. *Miscellaneous Non-banking Company (MNBC)* – means a company carrying on all or any of following types of business –
   (a) Managing, conducting or supervising as a promoter, foreman or agent of any transaction or arrangement by which the company enters into an agreement with a specified number of subscribers that every one of them shall subscribe a certain sum in installments over a definite period and that everyone of such subscribers shall be his turn, as determined by lot or by auction or by tender or in such other manner as may be provided for in the agreement be entitled to the prize amount.
   (b) Conducting any other loan or chit or kuri which is different from the type of business referred to above. Undertaking or carrying on or engaging in or executing any other business similar to the business referred to above.
8. *Residuary Non-banking Company (RNBC)* – means a company which receives any deposit under any scheme or arrangement, by whatever name called, in one lump sum or in installments by way of contributions or subscriptions or by sale of units or certificates or other instruments or in any other manner and which according to the

definitions constrained in the Non-banking Financial Companies CRBI Directions 1977, or as the case may be the Miscellaneous Non-banking Companies (Reserve Bank) Directions 1977 is not an insurance company or a company belonging to one to seven above.

8.3 TYPES OF NBFCs

(i) Equipment Leasing Finance Companies

A detailed note on 'Lease Finance' has been furnished separately in subsequent chapter. Presently, some information is recorded on equipment leasing finance companies.

The organisations engaged in lease financing include –

- Nationalised banks subsidiaries
- All-India financial institutions : ICICI, IIBI, IFCI, SIDBI Infrastructure Leasing and Financial Services Ltd. (IL and FS), HDFC
- Insurance Companies : LIC, GIC
- State level – SIDCs and SIICs
- Some private sector manufacturing companies
- NBFCs: Most of these companies are small private limited companies.

The main function of leasing companies is to lease out equipment on rent to industrial companies. Apart from their Net Owned Funds (NOF), the leasing companies raise funds in the form of deposits from other companies, banks and the financial institutions. Public deposits and inter-corporate deposits account for 74 per cent of their total funds.

In 1981, there were only two established leasing companies. For two years, *i.e.,* between 1983 and 1985, there was a boom in leasing and the number of companies increased to 400. This boom in leasing did not last long and the number of leasing companies fell down to 100 in 1987.

Leasing is a form of rental system. A lease is a contractual arrangement whereby the lessor grants the lessee the right to use an asset in return for periodical lease rent payments. There are two types of leases: (i) operating lease, and (ii) financial or capital lease.

The operating lease is a short-term lease which can be cancelled. Financial lease is a non-cancellable contractual commitment.

(ii) Hire Purchase Finance Companies

The sources of hire purchase finance are:

(a) Hire purchase finance companies

(b) Retails and wholesale traders, *i.e.,* sellers

(c) Banks and financial institutions –

- Hire purchase finance or credit is a system under which term loans for purchase of goods – producer goods or consumer goods – and services are advanced which have to be liquidated under an installment plan.
- Hire purchase finance companies are the public or private limited companies or partnership firms engaged in giving credit for acquiring durable goods.

The sources of funds for these companies are mainly the deposits from the public and other borrowings.

The terms of hire purchase credit may vary from product to product. The down payment ranges between 10 per cent to 25 per cent and may be as high as 40 per cent.

The period of credit is generally one to three years. The hire purchase credit is available for a wide range of products and services. A large part of hire purchase finance is made available for the purchase of commercial vehicles and the borrowers are the transport operators.

Under the hire purchase finance arrangement, the goods are invariably hypothecated to the lender.

The *retail and wholesale traders* are the other source of hire purchase finance. When the sellers provide hire purchase credit, their sources of funds are his own capital or borrowing from financial institutions. The financial institutions may finance the sellers or alternatively the buyers by providing installment loans.

Hire purchase finance, particularly for the purchase of commercial vehicles is also provided by the subsidiaries or associate concerns of vehicle manufacturers.

The banks and financial institutions including DFIs like IDBI, ICICI, SFCs and other institutions like NSIC, Agro Industries Corporation are the other agencies operating in the field of hire purchase finance.

The commercial banks undertake financing of sales or purchases of goods by way of instalment credit directly to the buyer or sellers or they refinance hire purchase finance companies and associate concerns of manufacturers. IDBI participates indirectly in hire purchase by rediscounting of usuance bills/promissory notes arising out of sales of indigenous machinery on deferred payment basis.

(iii) Housing Finance Companies

Finance is provided for housing as mortgage loans. Those who supply housing loans are :

- Specialised institutions
  - Housing boards in different states, the apex co-operative housing finance societies.
  - HUDCO: Housing & Urban Development Corporation
  - HDFC.
- Government: Central and State Governments
- Insurance Companies: LIC, GIC
- Commercial Banks
- Private Housing Finance Companies and Nidhis
  - The roles of other agencies including specialised institutions, governments, insurance companies commercial banks and National Housing Bank (NHB) is discussed separately and in details under the Heading 'Housing Finance'.

The housing finance companies undertake financing of the acquisition or construction of houses including acquisition or development of plot of land. These companies are supervised by NHB, which refinances housing loans by scheduled commercial banks, co operative banks, housing finance companies and the apex co-operative housing finance societies.

There are around 400 Housing Finance Companies in operation. More than 95 per cent of disbursements are accounted for by only 29 HFCs availing refinance facility from National Housing Bank (NHB).

Reserve Bank has stipulated that the housing finance companies should mobilise household savings in the form of deposits with maturities beyond two years.

(iv) Investment Companies

Most of the investment companies are controlled by large business or industrial groups and their investments are concentrated in the companies of industrial groups to which they belong. The principal business of these companies is acquiring securities and trading in such securities.

These companies are investment holding companies formed by business houses. As such, they provide finance mainly to companies associated with these business houses.

As against open-end investment companies or Mutual Funds / Units Trusts, these investment companies are close-end organisations, having a fixed amount of share capital.

Almost all prominent industrial groups have their own investment companies.

Primary Dealers (PDs)

Primary Dealers fall under Investment Companies Category of NBFCs. The system of PDs has been made functional in 1996. By March-end 2000, there were 15 approved PDs. The number has gone upto 18. There are now 17 PDs. The minimum Net Owned Fund (NOF) is ₹ 50 crore. PDs are meant to strengthen the securities market by dealing in government securities.

Purchases of Government Securities and Treasury Bills by PDs

Year	*Primary Market*	*Secondary Market*
1996-97	20,835	90,453
1999-2000	53,797	3,34,471

RBI prescribed new guidelines in January 2002 to improve the risk management system of PDs. PDs are required to maintain CRAR of 15 per cent. In view of the risks in accepting Inter-corporate Deposits (ICDs), PDs are advised to restrict acceptance of ICDs to 50% of NOF. Revised capital adequacy standards and risk management guidelines for PDs were issued in January 2004. The prudential guidelines on investment by PDs in non-government securities in both primary and secondary markets were prescribed in March 2004. In July, 2006, guidelines were issued allowing PDs to diversify their activities for which they should have NOF of ₹ 100 crore.

Core activities	:	dealing in government securities
Non-core activities	:	advisory services/merchant banking, investment in equity or units of Mutual Funds

In the year 2004-05, PDs' interest income declined and they reported trading losses. As against this, PDs' financial performance showed a turnaround during 2005-06, yielding Net Profit in case of 14 PDs out of the total number of 17 PDs.

As the RBI would not be playing the role of an underwriter from 2006-07, it has been proposed that the RBI's role in the primary market be replaced by a more active participation by PDs.

Satellite Dealers (SDs)

As second tier Dealers, SDs were introduced in Dec. 1996. 9 SDs registered to perform in government securities market. The response is limited as only 4 SDs are in operation. The Satellite Dealers' Scheme has been discontinued effective from May 31, 2002.

(v) Loan Companies

Loan companies are generally small partnership concerns which obtain funds in the form of deposits from the pubic and give loans to wholesale and retail traders, small-scale industries and self-employed persons. These companies attract deposits from the public by offering higher rates of interest along with various kinds of prizes, gifts etc. These companies give loans at relatively higher rates of interest.

The deposits accepted by these companies are mainly fixed deposits and their funds are partly kept in fixed deposits with banks and the remaining is used to make loans and advances. The borrowers of funds from these companies are those who cannot get adequate credit from commercial banks. The loans are usually unsecured loans and are granted on the basis of companies' knowledge of personal credit standing of the borrowers.

(vi) Mutual Benefit Financial Companies: Nidhis

The sources of funds for Nidhis are share capital, deposits from their members and deposits from the public.

Nidhis advance loans to their members for several purposes like house construction and repairs, marriages, redemption of old debts, meeting medical expenses etc. These loans are generally for consumption purposes and are mostly secured.

The main characteristics of Nidhis are their local character, easy approachability and the absence of cumbersome procedures.

Nidhis offer saving schemes and make credit available to those whose credit needs remain unmet by the commercial banks. Nidhis charge interest rates which are reasonable and are comparable to those of commercial banks.

Mutual Benefit Financial Companies MBFCs or Nidhis are exempted from the main provisions of RBI Act 1934.

As part of the implementation of the recommendations of the Expert Group on the functioning of Nidhis, the Government prescribed entry point norm, NOF, to deposits ratio, liquid asset requirement etc. The government announced guidelines in July 2001 which were amended in April 2002.

Chit Fund Companies – Chit Fund Companies came under the Investment Company.

The members of a chit fund make regular periodic subscriptions to the fund.

The chit fund company enters into an agreement with the subscribers that every one of them shall subscribe a certain sum in installments over a definite period and that every one of such subscribers shall in his turn, as determined by lot or by auction or by tender, be entitled to a prize amount. Each member is assured of his turn before any other gets it the second time.

The operations of chit fund companies are governed under the Chit Fund Act, 1982, which is administered by state governments. Their deposit taking activities are regulated by the Reserve Bank.

Chit Funds originated in India over a century ago in rural areas of South India. Tamil Nadu has about 6 thousand registered Chit operators. Tamil Nadu has a separate Act of 1961 in respect of Chit funds. Two leading names in the field are Shriram Chit Fund, Chennai, Margdarshi Chit Fund, Hyderabad.

Chit Fund business is done by small self-help groups and the chit funds units in the unorganised sector are 4 times of those in organised sector.

(vii) Residuary Non-banking Companies

These are companies which receive deposits and do not belong to any of the other categories of NBFCs. There are a number of unhealthy features of the operations of these companies: (i) negative or negligible NOF, (ii) understatement of their deposit liability, (iii) forfeiture of deposits, (iv) discontinuation of deposit certificates, (v) low or negligible rate of return on deposits, (vi) payment of high rates of commission and (vii) levy of service charges on the depositors etc.

The apex bank has taken up different measures to remove these features. Earlier, the deposit-taking activities of these companies were governed by the provisions of Residuary Non-Banking Companies Directions issued by the RBI in 1987. The compliance as RBI Directions by these companies has been low.

Under the new regulatory framework of RBI (amendment) Act 1997, the RBI has extended prudential norms to these companies, introduced compulsory registration requirement, specified minimum rates of interest payable on their deposits under different schemes. The RBI has stepped up the inspections and monitoring of the activities of these companies.

Table No. 8.2

Profile of RNBCs

Year (March-end)	*No. of Reporting RNBCs*	*Public Deposit (₹ crore)*	*NOF (₹ crore)*	*Aggregate Assets (₹ crore)*
2001	7	12625 (18034)	(-) 179	16244
2002	5	12889 (18822)	111	18458
2003	5	15065 (20100)	809	21104
2004	5	15327 (19644)	1002	20362
2005	3	16600 (20526)	1065	19057
2006	3	20175 (22842)	1183	21891
2007-08	2	22358	1718	22452
2008-09	2	19607	1870	20211

Note: Figures in brackets, indicate public deposits held by all NBFCs reporting.

At present, there are 2 companies which operate as RNBCs. Of these, two RNBCs, one is in Eastern region (Kolkata) and the other is in Central region. One RNBC, from Central region accounted for over 80 per cent of the public deposits held by RNBCs (₹ 18,056 crore out of ₹ 22,358 crore in 2008.

The aggregate deposits 7 RNBCs accounted for 91.6 per cent in 2008 and 91 per cent in 2009 of public depostis held by all NBFCs, as against a share of 88 per cent in 2006.

The public deposits held by the two RNBCs declined during the year 2008-09. The RNBCs have agreed that the companies would reduce their deposit liabilities to NIL by 2015.

In May 2004, the RBI appointed Working Group (Chairman: Shri N. Sadasivan) on DFIs report has expressed concern about the unrestricted growth of deposits in terms of NOF. It was mentioned that initially the capital may be stipulated at 16 times the NOF and then RNBCs would have to conform to the norms for raising of public deposits as applicable for NBFCs in general.

In order to reduce the overall risk and impart greater liquidity and safety to the investments, RBI has, in March 2006, revised the investment pattern of RNBCs, prescribing the manner in which RNBCs would invest their aggregate liability to investors (ALD).

RBI prescribes Investment Pattern of RNBCs as reviewed on March 31, 2006.

Investment Pattern as Against Aggregate Liability to Depositors (ALD)

ALD as on	*Investment prescribed*
Prior to June 2004	80% of ALD
April 1, 2005	90% of ALD
December 31, 2005	95%
Investment ALD beyond December 31, 2005	100%

From April 1, 2007, the entire amount of ALD invested as per prescribed pattern.

8.4 PERFORMANCE AND FINANCIAL POSITION OF THE NBFCs

Table No. 8.3

Aggregate Assets of NBFCs

(₹ *in Crores)*

	Assets	*No.of Reporting NBFCs*
March-end 2000 :	51324	1005
March-end 2001 :	53878	981
March-end 2002 :	58290	910
March-end 2003 :	53071	87.5
March-end 2004 :	50709	777
March-end 2005 :	55059	403
March-end 2006 :	57453	463
March-end 2008 :	74562	335
March-end 2009 :	75516	275

Between March-end 2000 and 2006, the aggregate assets of NBFCs have increased by nearly 12 per cent. It may be noted that the number of reporting NBFCs has been different over the years.

Table No. 8.4

Assets Profile of NBFCs (excluding RNBCs)

(₹ *in Crores*)

Year	*2002*		*2003*		*2004*		*2005*		*2006*		*2007-08*		*2008-09*	
Range	*No. of Reporting NBFCs*	*% of Assets*	*No. of Reporting NBFCs*	*% of Assets*	*No. of Reporting NBFCs*	*% of Assets*	*No. of Reporting NBFCs*	*% of Assets*	*No. of Reporting NBFCs*	*% of Assets*	*No.of Reporting NBFCs*	*% of Assets*	*No.of Reporting NBFCs*	*% of Assets*
Less than 0.50	139	0.1	139	0.1	132	0.1	129	0.1	63	—	68	-	21	-
0.50 to 2.00	383	1.0	354	1.0	317	1.0	258	0.7	187	0.6	119	0.2	107	0.2
2.00 to 10.00	247	2.7	245	3.0	209	2.9	185	2.1	132	1.7	91	0.5	85	0.5
10.00 to 50.00	74	4.0	68	3.7	69	4.9	77	5.2	49	3.3	38	1.0	36	1.0
50.00 to 100.00	19	3.4	19	3.5	13	2.6	18	3.6	8	1.6	10	0.8	10	0.9
100.00 to 500.00	23	15.0	28	17.2	17	11.7	16	8.7	11	5.4	9	2.8	4	1.7
Above 500.00	20	73.8	17	71.5	17	76.8	17	79.6	13	87.3	15	94.7	12	95.8
Total	905		870		774		700		463		350		275	

Between 2002 and 2009, the number of large-sized NBFCs has fallen from 43 to 16, but their share in the total assets held has gone up 89 per cent to nearly 96 to 97 per cent.

Table No. 8.5

NBFCs: Public Deposit Outstanding
(NBFCs inclusive of RNBCs)

(₹ in Crores)

Year (March-end)	*No. of NBFCs Reporting*	*Amount*	*Percentage of Deposits of SCBs*
2000	1005 (9)	19342	2.2
2001	981 (7)	18084	1.7
2002	910 (5)	18822 (12889)	1.0
2003	875 (5)	20100 (15065)	1.5
2004	777 (3)	19644 (15327)	1.2
2005	703 (3)	20526 (16600)	1.1
2006	432 (3)	22622 (20175)	1.0
2007	371 (3)	24697 (22622)	0.9
2008	335 (2)	24395 (22358)	0.73
2009	(2)	21548 (19607)	0.56

Note: Figures in brackets indicate No. of RNBCs and their share in deposits outstanding, which has gone up from 60 per cent to nearly 91 per cent during 2002 to 2009 period.

The public deposits outstanding in case of NBFCs have fluctuated over the years and their ratio with regard to deposits outstanding of scheduled commercial banks has ranged around 1 per cent to 2 per cent earlier but has fallen to 0.73 per cent by 2007-08, and further to 0.56 per cent at the end of June 2009.

The Net Owned Funds (NOF) is the total of paid-up capital and free reserves and hence indicates the capital cushion available to NBFCs.

Table No. 8.6

(₹ in Crores)

Year March-end	*NOF*	*Public Deposits*	*Public deposits to NOF*
2003	4950	20100	4:1
2004	5098	19644	3.8:1
2005	6101	20526	3.4:1
2006	6663	22842	3.4:1
2008	11921	24400	2.05:1
2009	13458	21548	1.6:1

The public deposits to NOF indicating public deposits as a multiple of NOF has been 3.4:1 in 2006, but has declined to 1.6:1 by 2009.

Table No. 8.7
Financial Performance of NBFCs

(₹ in Crores)

Item	*2002-03*	*2003-04*	*2004-05*	*2005-06*
Income	5084	4332	4582	4578
Expenditure	4491	3621	3657	4134
Operating profit	593	711	924	443
Net profit	339	531	572	152

The financial performance had improved resulting in increase in Net Profit between 2003 and 2004, but received a set back during 2005-06.

Table No. 8.8 (A)

NPAs of NBFCs

(₹ in Crores)

As at the end of	*Total credit*	*Assets* Standard	Sub-standard	Doubtful	Loss	*Gross Assets as % of total Credit*
Sept 1998	21,752	30,399	1,499	693	319	11.5
March 1999	22,184	31,658	1,623	465	465	12.9
Sept. 1999	21,309	29,159	1,362	388	388	12.2.

Table No. 8.8 (B)

NBFCs: Assets Quality: (NPAs) Non-performing Assets

NPAs of NBFCs as % to Advances (Credit)

Year (March-end)	*Gross NPA*	*Net NPA*
1999	10.2	7.0
2000	9.9	9.5
2001	11.5	5.6
2002	10.6	9.9
2003	8.8	2.7
2004	8.2	2.4
2005	5.7	2.5
2006	3.6	0.5
2007	2.2	0.2
2008	2.1	0*
2009	2.7	0*

The Gross and Net NPAs as % to Gross and Net advances in case of NBFCs have declined in recent period and came down sharply during 2005-06.

* Provision exceeds NPA : As against the trend during the last few years, Gross NPA ratio increased to 2.7% during the year 2008-09 from 2.1% in the previous year. Net NPA turned negative with provisions exceeding NPA.

It may be noted here that the maximum limit in respect of interest rate payable by NBFCs on their public deposits has been reduced from 16% to 14% on April 11, 2001. It has been further reduced to 12.5% with effect from Nov. 1, 2001 and to 11 per cent from March 4, 2003.

Maturity Period of Public Deposits held by NBFCs

The periods for which public deposits are to be held by NBFCs are:

NBFCs : 12 to 60 months

RNBCs : 12 to 84 months

Chit Funds : 6 to 36 months

There is a distinct shift in favour of composition of public deposits with shorter periods of maturity, *i.e.,* less than 1 year and between 1 to 3 years. [See Table No. 8.4(A)]

8.5 REGULATORY FRAMEWORK FOR NBFCs

In 1997, RBI Act 1934 was amended granting the apex bank (RBI) regulatory powers over NBFCs.

The regulation of deposit acceptance activities of NBFCs could be traced back to 1963 when the RBI had limited powers of issuing orders to NBFCs regarding limits, manner and conditions under which deposits could be accepted by NBFCs.

In 1977, RBI issued guidelines —

NBFC Acceptance of Deposits Directions for NBFCs

MBFC Directions 1977 for Nidhis.

In 1970s, two study groups B. Datta (1971) and J. Ray (1974) examined the subject of regulatory framework.

1981 : Chakravarty Committee recommended introduction of a system of licensing for NBFCs.

1991 : Narasimham Committee mentioned that the regulatory framework for NBFCs should be specified.

1992 : An in-depth study of the role of NBFCs was carried out by the working group appointed by RBI under the chairmanship of Dr. A.C. Shah. The working group made wide-ranging recommendations.

Objectives

The twin objectives of RBI in regulating the activities of NBFCs were safeguarding the depositor's interest and ensuring that they function on healthy lines and align better with the overall financial system in the country.

The number of defaulting NBFCs had risen as they failed to repay the matured deposits as per the terms of their acceptance. The interests of the depositors were adversely affected as there was absence of an efficient and expeditious system for the redressal of depositors' grievances.

RBI Act 1997 provided for:

- Entry Norms
- Compulsory Registration
- Prescription of Prudential Norms
- Submission of Periodical Returns
- Supervision
- Asset liquidity
- Punitive Action.

Entry Point Norms:

- Entry Point Norm of ₹ 25 lakh as the minimum Net Owned Fund (NOF).
- Requirement of minimum NOF was raised to ₹ 2 crore effective from April 20,1999. This stipulation applied to new NBFCs incorporated on or after April 20,1999.

Registration:

- The registration of NBFCs with RBI has been made mandatory.
- Certain types of financial companies, *viz.,* insurance companies, housing finance companies, stock broking companies, Chit Fund companies, Companies notified as Nidhis etc. have been exempted from the requirement of registration.

- As on June 30, 2002:

Applications for Registration:36,269

of which approved: 14,077	784 companies (5.6%) permitted to accept public deposits.
	13,293 companies not permitted to accept public deposits.

Applications rejected:19,111

Applications pending: 3,081

- By June-end 2004 Application for Registration 38050
  of which approved by RBI: 13671
  of these the Cos authorised to accept public deposits: 584

- By March-end 2006

Application received by RBI for registration : 38244
of which approved : 13141
of these companies authorised to accept/hold public deposits : 423

Table No. 8.9

Certificate of Registration issued to NBFCs

Year (June-end)	*Total No. of NBFCs*	*No. of NBFCs Accepting Public Deposits*
1999	7855	624
2000	8451	679
2001	13815	776
2002	14077	784
2003	13849	710
2004	13764	604
2005	13261	507
2006	13014	428

Source: Report on Trends and Progress of Banking in India, 2005-06.

The regulatory framework is primarily focussed on NBFCs accepting public deposits.

Large NBFCs not accepting/holding public deposit

The reporting system for the large NBFCs not accepting/holding public deposits was introduced in September 2004 and was reviewed in September 2005.

	As per September 2004 system	*As reviewed in September 2005*
• Submission of returns	Quarterly	Monthly
• Applicable to NBFCs with asset size	₹ 500 crore	₹ 100 crore

Investment in Liquid Assets by NBFCs

15 per cent of outstanding public deposits. (10 per cent in case of RNBCs) *of which*

(i) not less than 10 per cent in approved securities.

(ii) not more than 5 per cent in term deposits with scheduled commercial banks.

These liquid assets securities are to be lodged with a scheduled commercial bank or Stock Holding Corporation of India. The government securities are to be held in SGL account with a scheduled commercial bank or in demat account with depositories through a depository participant registered with SEBI.

Creation of Reserve Fund

NBFCs to create a Reserve Fund and transfer thereto not less than 20 per cent of Net Profits every year.

Capital Adequacy Ratio

Capital adequacy norms relating to CRAR were made applicable to NBFCs in 1998. NBFCs to achieve a minimum 12 per cent CRAR by March 1999.

Capital adequacy norms for NBFCs accepting/holding public/deposits

Equipment Leasing Companies/Hire Purchase Companies	*CRAR*
with credit rating	12 per cent
without credit rating	15 per cent
Loan/Investment Companies	15 per cent
RNBCs	12 per cent

Table No. 8.10

NBFCs : Interest Rates on Public Deposits (as % to total deposits)

Interest Rate Range	*1999-2000*	*2000-01*	*2002-02*	*2002-03*	*2003-04*	*2004-05*	*2005-06*	*2007-08*	*2008-09*
Upto 10%	0.3	1.8	6.0	23.3	43.9	68.7	83.4	73.0	30.1
10% to 12%	7.1	21.8	34.6	41.7	36.7	21.7	11.6	25.4	65.0
12% to 14%	44.4	42.7	39.2	22.6	11.7	5.0	1.0	1.6	4.9
14% to 16%	34.6	23.7	14.1	9.4	5.9	3.2	2.1	—	—
More than 16%	13.6	10.0	6.1	3.0	1.8	1.4	1.0	—	—

The share of public deposits on which NBFC paid interest up to 10 per cent has sharply declined in 2008-09. The share of public deposits on which interest paid was above 12 per cent significantly increased.

There has been a sharp increase in the share of public deposits on which NBFCs paid interest upto 10 per cent. Since 2002, the shares of public deposits carrying higher interest have declined for all interest ranges.

Table No. 8.10(A)

NBFCs : Maturity Period of Public Deposits Held

Period	*2000*	*2001*	*2002*	*2003*	*2004*	*2005*	*2006*	*2007-08*	*2008-09*
Less than year	15.9	26.7	25.0	23.9	27.3	30.8	39.8	29.9	36.0
1 to 3 years	48.9	58.5	60.9	62.9	60.6	58.6	48.5	56.5	56.7
3 to 5 years	14.6	13.0	13.1	12.3	11.4	10.2	11.5	10.3	4.3
5 years above	20.6	1.8	0.9	0.9	0.7	0.5	0.2	3.2	3.0

The share of public deposits with maturity period of less than 1 year has increased. The most common maturity period among public deposits held is between 1 and 3 years.

The equipment leasing and hire purchase companies without credit rating should disclose in their advertisement and the application form the fact that it is an unrated company.

Deposit Acceptance Norms: NBFCS Accepting Public Deposits

Net Owned Funds (NOF)	*Equipment Leasing Companies and Hire Purchase Companies*	*Loan Companies and Investment Companies*
₹ 25 lakh and above without credit rating	1.5 times of NOF or ₹ 10 crore which-ever is less provided the company has CRAR of 15%.	—
₹ 25 lakh and above with minimum invest-ment grade credit rating	4 times of NOF provided the company has CRAR of 12% or more	1.5 times of NOF, provided the com-pany has CRAR of 15 per cent.

Restrictions on Investments

- Creation of Assets by defaulting NBFCs: NBFC defaulting in repayment of the matured deposits prohibited from creating any further assets.
- Investments by NBFCs in real estate and unquoted shares:

  Investment in real estate, except for their own use — upto 10 per cent of NOF.

  Investment in unquoted shares:

  — equipment leasing and hire purchase companies : 10 per cent of NOF
  — loan companies and investment companies : 20 per cent of NOF

Credit and Investment Concentration Norms

Single borrower : 15 per cent of NOF
Borrower group : 25 per cent of NOF

Composite totality of loans and investment

Single borrower : 25 per cent of NOF
Group of borrowers : 40 per cent of NOF

Table No. 8.11

CRAR of NBFCs (Reporting)

Range	*2002 (March-end)*				*2003 (March-end)*				*2004 (March end)*				*2005 (March-end)*				*2006 (March-end)*			
	EL	*HP*	*LC/IC*	*Total*	*EL*	*HP*	*LC/IC*	*Total*	*EL*	*HP*	*LC/IC*	*Total*	*EL*	*HP*	*LC/IC*	*Total*	*EL*	*HP*	*LC/IC*	*Total*
Less than 12%	10	17	15	42	11	13	13	37	5	12	8	25	4	54	6	64	6	10	3	19
12 — 15%	1	8	1	10	—	2	1	3	1	4	1	6	—	1	1	2	—	3	—	3
15 — 20%	4	32	9	45	3	27	3	33	2	15	2	19	3	19	4	26	—	10	—	10
20 — 30%	9	54	11	74	9	52	13	74	6	38	7	51	6	32	3	41	5	30	3	38
Above 30%	32	334	121	489	37	321	96	454	28	300	55	383	28	219	33	280	22	211	19	252
	(57)	(75)	(77)	(74)	(62)	(77)	(76)	(76)	(67)	(81)	(75)	(79)	(67)	(67)	(70)	(68)	(66)	(80)	(76)	(78)
Total	56	445	157	658	60	415	126	601	42	389	73	484	41	325	47	413	33	264	25	322

Range	*2007-08*					*2008-09*				
	AFC	*EL*	*HP*	*LC/IC*	*TOTAL*	*AFC*	*EL*	*HP*	*LC/IC*	*TOTAL*
Less than 12%	19	4	15	9	47	0	2	4	3	9
12 — 15%	3	0	0	1	4	3	0	0	0	3
15 — 20%	5	0	0	3	8	4	0	0	2	6
20 — 30%	25	0	1	3	29	17	0	2	2	21
Above 30%	117	10	66	46	239	99	8	34	26	168
Total	169	14	82	62	327	123	10	40	33	207

EL: Equipment Leasing HP: Hire Purchase LC/IC: Loan Co./Investment Co.

Note: Figures in brackets indicate % to the total.

During 2002-06 period, above 75 per cent of NBFC reported CRAR above 30 per cent

Loan Cos/Investment Cos : 70 to 77 per cent
Hire Purchase Cos. : 67 to 81 per cent
Equipment Leading Cos. : 57 to 67 per cent

The minimum regulatory CRAR is 12 per cent. The number of NBFCs with less than 12 per cent declined to 9 at March-end 2009 from 47 as at March 2008.

Disclosure Requirements

- Prudential Norms have been laid for NBFCs:

  Provisions for NPAs — Loans and Advances
  Provisions for NPAs — Equipment Lease and Hire Purchase Accounts

  NBFCs are required to separately disclose in their balance sheets the provisions made.

- Disclosure of dues from Group/connected companies.

Information relating to the exposure of NBFCs in the subsidiaries/companies in the group, other entities and the business ventures in which the directors and NBFCs are holding substantial interest.

Supervision of NBFCs

- The supervision is based on the three aspects: (a) size of NBFC, (b) type of activity and (c) whether it accepts/holds deposits from the public.
- The supervision consists of:

  (i) On-site supervision (ii) Off site monitoring
  (iii) Market intelligence (iv) Exception Reports of Statutory Auditors

The on-site supervision is structured on the basis of CAMELS model (Capital adequacy, Assets quality, Management, Earnings, Liquidity and Systems).

Companies with asset size of ₹ 100 crore and above : Annual inspection
Companies not holding public deposits : Once in 5 years.

To review the regulatory framework and supervision of NBFCs, the Government appointed a Task Force which submitted its report in Oct. 1998. The recommendations made by the Task Force covering different aspects like ceiling on public deposits, investments in real estate and unquoted shares, minimum NOF to be raised, registration and inspection disclosures have been implemented.

Flow of Credit from Banks to NBFCs

- Bank credit to NBFCs for their advances against commercial vehicles has been brought under the ambit of priority sector advances.

  It is reported that the Commercial Banks like ICICI Bank, IDBI Bank are posing challenge to NBFCs in regard to Commercial Vehicles Financing.

- The ceiling on bank lending to NBFCs (registered with RBI) has been removed.

Interest of Depositors: Depositor's Protection

RBI pursues with the State Governments the case for enacting legislation for protecting the interests of depositors in financial establishments. The state level legislations are:

- The Tamil Nadu Protection of Interests of Depositor (in financial establishments) Act 1997.
- Maharashtra Protection of Interests of Depositors (in financial establishments) Ordinance 1999.

The Governments in Andhra Pradesh, Gujarat, Himachal Pradesh, Assam and Haryana have already taken effective steps to introduce legislation on the same lines.

The Task Force in 1998 recommended that State Governments may set up cells at the State and District level to disseminate information relating to procedures for the redressal of depositors' grievances.

RBI has been conducting special seminars and training programmes related to the protection of depositors' interests.

Policy Developments

Prudential Regulation:

- NBFCs accepting/holding public deposits to maintain minimum prescribed CRAR at all times.
- The concept of 'past due' would be done way with in respect of the definition of NPAs of NBFCs effective from March 31, 2003.

Alignment of RBI Regulation with Companies (Amendment) Act, 2000

- RBI directions to NBFCs to align with these contained in the Companies Act 1956 as amended in 2000.
- All NBFCs to report to the Company Law Board the defaults, if any, in repayment of matured deposits or payment of interest to small depositors within 60 days of such default.
- NBFCs which were Private Limited Companies holding public deposits have become Public Limited Companies.

Liquid Asset Securities: Effective from Oct. 1, 2002

- All NBFCs to hold their investment in Government Securities either in — constituent SGL — account with a Scheduled Commercial Bank.

  — or Stock Holding Corporation of India.

  — or in a demat account with depositories. National Securities Depository Ltd. (NSDL)/ Central Depository Services (India) Ltd. (CDSL) through a participant registered with SEBI.
- Facility of holding government securities in physical form stands withdrawn. Government Securities held in physical form were to be dematerialised by Oct. 31, 2002.

Details of Different Types of NBFCs

Some further details on different categories of NBFCs are now furnished individually as next page:

Table No. 8.12

Profile of Different Categories of NBFCs (Exclusive of RNBCs)

(Amount of Public Deposits held in ₹ Crores)

Category of NBFC	*2002*		*2003*		*2004*		*2005*		*2006*	
	No.	*Amount*	*No.*	*Amount*	*No.*	*Amount*	*No.*	*Amount*	*No.*	*Amount*
Equipment Leasing	56 (6.2)	668 (11.2)	58 (6.7)	511 (10.1)	46 (5.9)	344 (8.0)	40 (5.7)	343 (8.7)	35 (7.6)	153 (5.7)
Hire Purchase	463 (51)	3709 (62.5)	439 (50.4)	3539 (70.3)	396 (51.1)	2963 (68.6)	336 (48)	2423 (61.7)	312 67.4)	2039 (76.4)
Investment Companies Loan Companies	231 (2.5)	1029 (17.3)	141 (16.2)	302 (6.0)	98 (12.7)	284 (6.6)	74 (10.6)	299 (7.6)	39 (8.4)	158 (5.9)
Other NBFCs	155 (17.1)	528 (11.3)	232 (26.7)	683 (13.5)	234 (30.2)	727 (16.8)	250 (35.7)	861 (21.9)	77 (16.6)	317 (12)
Total	905	5934	870	5035	774	4318	700	3926	463	2667

Note: Figures in brackets indicate % to the total. Other NBFCs include miscellaneous non-banking companies, Nidhis etc.

Hire purchase companies account for around 50% numberwise in the total and their share in the amount of public deposit held has gone up from 62 per cent to over 76 per cent between 2002 and 2006. The equipment leasing companies accounted for 6 to 8 per cent numberwise in the total, but their share in the public deposits held has fallen down from 11 per cent in 2002 to less than 6 per cent in 2006. The shares of Investment companies/Loan companies in the number and the public deposits held have fluctuated over the years.

8.6 NBFCs *vis-a-vis* SCHEDULED COMMERCIAL BANKS

The commercial banks are necessarily financial intermediaries as they mobilise savings of the people in the form of deposits and transfer these funds to the borrowers from trade, commerce and industry. The NBFCs are the non-bank financial institutions which also play the role of transferring funds from the lenders to the borrowers and yet are different from other non-bank financial intermediaries like insurance companies and mutual funds.

As the NBFCs and the commercial banks act as financial intermediaries, the question arises as to whether these NBFCs pose any competition for the commercial banks. The question gets its significance from the fact that there has been a manifold increase in the number of NBFCs in the recent years. The total number of non-bank financial companies was nearly 52,000 in 1996, *i.e.,* before the regulatory framework on NBFCs was introduced by amending the RBI Act in January 1997. To get the comparative picture of the growth of NBFCs and the commercial banks as the financial intermediaries, the shares of bank deposits and non-bank deposits in the gross savings of the household sector in the financial assets are presented in Table 8.9.

With regard to domestic savings, the household sector accounts for a major share. The household sector savings are held as financial assets and as real physical assets. The financial intermediaries play the role of channelising household sector savings into financial assets. There has been a perceptible rise in the recent years in the percentage share of non-bank deposits in the gross saving of the household sector in financial assets. Still, it could be said that the trends in the shares of bank deposits and non-bank deposits are not consistent as the share of bank deposits having fallen for a year or two has moved up again in the late 1990s.

Hence, it may not be possible to draw a clear simple conclusion by way of an answer to the question raised earlier. It has to be recognised that the business of NBFCs has undergone a fast growth in number as well as in volume. Still, these institutions have not gained the All-India status, as their activities have flourished in specific regions or states in the country. The NBFCs are playing a complementary role to that of banks. These institutions cater to the requirements of the borrowers whose needs have not been met by the banks. These institutions give loans for meeting even the consumption requirements.

The NBFCs have grown rapidly over the years and yet their activities have a number of unhealthy characteristics, exposing the depositors to a higher degree of risk. The NBFCs attract deposits from the people on account of higher interest rates and also due to other features like customer orientation, quick service etc.

It is not necessary to raise an issue of NBFCs being in competition with commercial banks as they can, under the new regulatory framework of RBI introduced in 1997, play their due role as financial intermediaries if they conduct their activities on healthy lines and align themselves better as complementary institutions to commercial banks in the overall financial system in the country.

Table No. 8.9

Financial Assets of Household Sector

(₹ in Crores)

	Financial Assets of Household Sector	*Bank Deposits*	*as % of Financial Assets*	*Non-bank Deposits*	*as % of Financial Assets*
1980-81	12118	5850	45.8	378	3.1
1985-86	25562	10603	41.5	1423	5.6
1990-91	58908	18777	31.9	1286	2.2
1995-96	124337	39941	32.1	13198	10.6
1996-97@	158519	50902	32.1	25930	16.4
1999-00	236214	82892	35.1	3844	1.6
2000-01	248394	94703	38.1	6911	2.8
2001-02	296581	112936	38.1	7912	2.7
2002-03	322583	123462	38.3	8788	2.7
2003-04	377387	141967	37.6	3803	1.0
2004-05	434318	156259	36.4	3370	0.8
2005-06	597867	274864	46.0	6130	1.0
2006-07	650412	311347	47.9	1516	0.2
2007-08	715994	360993	50.4	3751	0.5
2008-09	746864	409811	54.9	13453	1.8

Source: Handbook of Statistics on Indian Economy, 2008-09.

@ The regulatry framework on NBFCs was introduced in Jan. 1997.

Besides, the bank deposits and non-bank deposits, the other forms of the financial assets of the household sector include currency, LIC policies, PF and pension fund, claims on Government, shares and debentures, units of UTI.

In regard to the financial assets held by the Household Sector, the bank deposits attract a significantly higher share as against the relatively low share accounted for by the non-banking deposits.

8.7 NBFCs AND MONETARY POLICY

The monetary policy is formulated and acted upon by the Central Bank in pursuit of certain specified goals and objectives of the overall economic policy in the country. The monetary policy pertains to the regulation of the supply of money and credit and thereby influence the level of aggregate demand for goods and services.

In the context of economic planning in the country, the Reserve Bank of India, as a central bank, has a difficult task of harmonising or rather achieving a balance between the conflicting objectives of monetary policy of economic growth with stability and social justice. The apex bank has to promote the interests of rapid economic development, play a restrictive role of keeping the inflationary pressures under check, and also support measures and programmes aimed at reducing economic inequalities. It is not possible for the RBI to either liberalise credit so as to sustain the tempo of development by meeting the needs of production and trade and ignore the likely inflationary impact. It is also not appropriate to restrict credit and thereby jeopardise the growth rate.

In a continuous effort to strike a realistic and operational balance in the wake of conflicting objectives, the Central Bank has followed a policy of *'controlled expansion'* of bank credit and money supply. The main content of this policy of controlled expansion has been "selective credit control."

Reserve Bank transmits its monetary policy impulses in the economy through the use of its techniques of monetary and credit control over the banking sector, *i.e.,* commercial banks and co-operative banks. As an apex institution in the money market, RBI, apart from being the banker's bank, has the powers of control and supervision over the banking sector.

RBI made efforts to regulate the operations of NBFCs particularly those accepting deposits by issuing directions as given below:

Non-banking Financial Companies Directions: 1977

Miscellaneous Financial Companies Directions: 1977

Residuary Non-banking Companies Directions: 1989

Housing Finance Companies Directions: 1989.

These directives could not be effective as they provided services for very limited regulatory powers.

NBFCs remained nearly unregulated until 1997 when the RBI Act was amended to introduce the new regulatory framework providing for, particularly the NBFCs accepting public deposits, several measures of control and supervision mentioned earlier.

In the situation of being left relatively unregulated, the business of NBFCs has grown manifold, over the years, in number also in volume.

NBFCs attracted public deposits by offering relatively higher rates of interest but in many cases, failed to honour the terms and conditions regarding returns and repayment. The operations of NBFCs are considered a threat to the effective functioning of monetary policy, as the purposes for which they give loans and total quantum of lending and allocation runs counter to the credit control objectives of the policy. NBFCs often give loans to the borrowers whose proposals have been turned down by the banks, they give funds for financing margins fixed by banks under selective credit control, and to those who hoard scarce commodities. As a result, lending by the NBFCs reduce the overall effectiveness of credit planning and selective credit control objectives of the RBI policy.

Suggestions were made that the monetary controls should be extended over the NBFCs, particularly in terms of applying minimum reserve requirements to those NBFCs which accept public deposits.

In regard to the commercial banks and co operative banks, the RBI has, along with other powers, the powers to: (i) issue licences for the establishment of new banks and for setting up bank branches and (ii) prescribe minimum requirements regarding paid-up capital and reserves, transfer to reserve fund maintenance of cash reserves and other liquid assets. The Reserve Bank has the powers to inspect the working of banks in India and control their methods of operations.

The techniques and instruments of monetary and credit control used by RBI include — bank rate, open market operations, variable reserve ratio, moral suasion, selective and quantitative credit control. As the bank rate proved weak and ineffective, RBI took up regulating directly the interest rates on bank deposits and for lending. The cash reserve ratio refers to the cash which the banks have to maintain with the RBI. As such, the variable reserve ratio has become over the years an important and effective tool of directly regulating the lending capacity of banks. To serve the fund requirements of weaker sections of the society, the Reserve Bank directly influences credit allocation by bank by stipulating targets for the priority sector lending as high as 40 per cent of aggregate bank advances by mid-1980s. Under selective credit control, the flow of bank credit for certain purposes such as speculative hoarding of sensitive commodities like cereals, pulses, oilseeds etc. is regulated by: (i) fixing margin requirements, (ii) fixing minimum lending rates and (iii) fixing the ceiling on credit. This measure is, particularly meant for holding the inflationary trend.

As against this, the business of NBFCs has been exposed to relatively lower degree of regulation and had no entry barriers. They offered higher rates of return on deposits accepted and involved themselves in indiscriminate investment in certain sectors and in lending for purposes against the broader social interests like speculation and hoarding.

In view of their role for small depositors and small borrowers and for meeting the credit gaps as financial intermediaries, RBI has, on the one hand, taken in July 1996, the measures of liberalisation for NBFCs which were registered, rated and were complying with the prudential norms and, on the other, created new framework for effective regulation of NBFCs in March 1997. The measures of liberalisation grant freedom to NBFCs and yet expose them to a new regulatory framework so as to ensure their healthy growth in future.

KEY TERMS

Non-bank Finance Companies, Primary Dealers, Equipment Leasing Companies, Housing Finance Companies, Investment Companies, Loan Companies, Mutual Benefit Financial Company, Residuory Non-banking Company.

REVIEW QUESTIONS

1. Explain the classification and types of NBFCs.
2. Discuss the regulatory framework of the NBFCs.
3. Discuss the performance and financial position of the NBFCs in the recent years.
4. Explain the relation and difference between NBFCs and Commercial Banks.
5. 'The NBFCs are in close competition with the Commercial Banks.' Discuss.
6. What is the influence of the Monetary Policy of RBI as the NBFCs?

REFERENCES

1. Bhole L.M.
2. RBI Report on Trends and Progress of Banking in India, 2005-06.
3. RBI Bulletin, March, 1997.

❑❑❑

9

Development Finance Institutions

9.1 INTRODUCTION

The financial institutions in India could be broadly classified as:

All-India Financial Institutions (AIFIs):

State level Institutions

Other Institutions

All-India Financial Institutions

(a) Development institutions: IDBI, SIDBI, IIBI, IFCI
(ICICI has been merged with ICICI Bank)

(b) Specialised financial institutions: Export and Import Bank (EXIM Bank)
Tourism Finance Corporation of India (TFCI)
Infrastructure Development Finance Company Ltd. (IDFC)
Venture capital institutions of IFCI and ICICI

(c) Investment institutions: LIC, UTI, GIC

(d) Refinance institutions: NABARD, National Housing Bank (NHB)

All-India Financial Institutions are now classified as:

(i) Term Lending Institutions : IFCI, IIBI, EXIM Bank, TFCI, IDFC

(ii) Refinance Institutions: NABARD, SIDBI, NHB

(iii) Investment Institutions: LIC, GIC and its subsidiaries

State Level Institutions

State Finance Corporations (SFCs) and State Industrial Development Corporations (SIDCs)

Other Institutions such as Export Credit Guarantee Corporation (ECGC), Deposit Insurance and Credit Guarantee Corporation DICGC (to be converted as Bank Deposits Insurance Corporation (BDIC).

9.2 ALL-INDIA FINANCIAL INSTITUTIONS (AIFIs)

IFCI: The Industrial Financial Corporation of India (IFCI) was established in July 1948 under the Act of Parliament for providing medium and long-term funds to the industry. It was converted into a public limited company with effect from July 1, 1993. The corporation provides finance to a wide range of activities including mining, electric power generation and distribution, shipping and so on. Initially, the assistance of IFCI was meant only for the private sector but now it is extended to all public and joint sector activities.

Financial Resources

The paid-up capital of the IFCI was initially only ₹ 5 crore. Thereafter, it was raised a number of times and it stood at ₹ 352.81 crore as on March 28, 1997. The total reserves of IFCI as on March 28, 1996 was ₹ 1,350.86 crore. In addition to the paid-up capital and reserves, the major resources of IFCI are raised by issuing bonds and debentures. The total amount raised through bonds and debentures in 1998-99 was ₹ 3,545.5 crore. The IFCI also borrows funds from the government, the RBI and the IDBI. For granting loans to industrial concerns for the import of capital goods from abroad, the IFCI borrows from various foreign agencies. This borrowing from foreign agencies outstanding in terms of rupee equivalent as on March 28, 1997 was Rs. 3,197.52 crore.

Lending Activities

The Corporation provides rupee and foreign currency loans for setting up new industrial units besides focussing on the expansion, diversification, renovation and modernisation of existing units. It also underwrites and directly subscribes to industrial securities, provides financial guarantees, merchant banking services and lease finance. IFCI provides assistance for fixed assets which includes purchase of plant and machinery, construction of the factory building and purchase of land for the factory. It does not provide finance for the repayment of existing liabilities.

Before granting loans, the IFCI examines the technical and economic viability of the project, experience of the promoters and their contribution to the project cost and competence of the management regarding construction and operation of the project.

IFCI also considers the desirability of the project from the point of view of national priorities of development.

As on March 28, 1997, total cumulative financial assistance aggregated ₹ 25,106.6 crore. The share of foreign currency loans in the total loans sanctioned by the IFCI up to March 1997 was 15.3 per cent. The disbursements of IFCI in the year 1997-98 were ₹ 56,450.4 crore which declined to ₹ 4,749.5 crore in 1998-99.

Since the year 2001-02, there has been a significant decline in the sanctions and disbursement of IFCI, but has gone up in the recent years.

Table No. 9.1

Lending Pattern of IFCI

(₹ in Crores)

Year	*Sanctions*	*Disbursement*
2000-01	1417.9	2152.7
2001-02	698.0	1097.2
2002-03	1963.7	1783.6

2003-04	1394.6	281.2
2004-05	0	84
2005-06	0	187
2006-07	1050	550
2007-08	2550.5	2280.10
2008-09	4014.5	3311.5

The industries that have benefited most from IFCI lending are the traditional industries of sugar, cotton textiles, cement and paper. Followed by that, the chemical industries and fertilizers have received the maximum assistance.

The states of Maharashtra, Tamil Nadu, West Bengal and Gujarat have benefited most from the IFCI lending, accounting together for a 50 per cent share.

Appraisal of the performance of IFCI reveals that although its performance with regard to disbursement of assistance has been impressive, it is argued that IFCI lending encouraged concentration of wealth and capital. It has also not done anything to eliminate the regional imbalance. The IFCI has not succeeded in taking any disciplinary action against defaulting borrowers. Lastly, the IFCI has not paid enough attention to national priorities while granting assistance and it extended its assistance to the industrial concerns which could easily raise resources from the capital market.

9.2(A) IDBI

The Industrial Development Bank of India (IDBI) was established in 1964 by the Government under an Act of Parliament, the Industrial Development Bank of India Act (1964). IDBI was initially established as a wholly owned subsidiary of the Reserve Bank of India (RBI). In 1976, the ownership of IDBI was transferred to the Government of India. The IDBI Act was amended in October 1994, to permit IDBI to raise equity from the public, subject to the holding of the Government of India falling below 51 per cent of the issued capital.

There were a number of industrial financing institutions in India prior to the establishment of the IDBI. But there was no apex organisation to co-ordinate their activities. The IDBI was designated as an apex organisation in the field of development banking and it plays the role of a co-ordinator at all-India level. IDBI renders valuable services to other development institutions like IFCI, SFCs and so on as it provides refinance against loans granted to industrial concerns by them and rediscounts their machinery bills. IDBI also subscribes to the share capital and bond issues of the IFCI, SFCs and ICICI. The IDBI is an apex institution in the field of Industrial finance.

Resources

The total resources of the Industrial Development Bank of India in 1996-97 was, ₹ 50,329 crore. The main sources of funds are share capital, reserves, bonds and debentures issues, certificate of deposits and deposits from companies and borrowings from the Reserve Bank of India (RBI) and the Government of India. Through public issues of bonds and debentures, the IDBI raised ₹ 4,342 crore in 1998-99 and through private placement of bonds and debentures it raised ₹ 8,341 crore in 1998-99, adding up to ₹ 12,683 crore. To meet its foreign currency resource requirements, IDBI has been making periodic forays in international financial markets and has raised substantial resources through syndicated loans and floating rate bonds at cost effective rates of interest. The reserves of IDBI amounted to ₹ 8,033.7 crore and its total assets were worth ₹ 69,143.5 crore in 1998-99.

Subsidiary Organisations

To ensure focussed attention to the needs of the small-scale industry, IDBI had set up the Small Industries Development Bank of India (SIDBI) in 1990 as a wholly owned subsidiary. However, delinking of SIDBI from IDBI has been recently proposed by the Government.

Consequent to opening up of commercial banking to the private sector, IDBI set up a commercial bank, *i.e.,* IDBI Bank Ltd. which provides a complete range of banking facilities. The IDBI Bank has raised equity from the public and therefore the IDBI's shareholding in it is reduced to 57 per cent.

Assistance to Industry

IDBI provides financial assistance to all kinds of big, small and medium industrial enterprises and with regard to the size of loan, virtually there is no restriction. It provides direct financial assistance to industrial concerns in the form of loans, underwriting and direct subscription to shares, debentures and guarantees. The indirect assistance by IDBI takes the form of refinance of industrial loans, rediscounting of bills, subscription to shares and bonds of financial institutions and seed capital assistance. The IDBI's assistance to industries is often routed through some other financial institution such as SFCs. Prior to the establishment of the Export-Import Bank of India, the IDBI also provided export finance.

Apart from extending assistance to the industry the IDBI also undertakes promotional functions such as assistance to backward areas, to small-scale industry, to technicians, entrepreneurs and for modernisation under Soft loan scheme.

In the total disbursement of the IDBI, direct finance constitutes a major share of around 95 per cent. The following table shows the disbursement pattern of IDBI by the end of 1990s.

Table No. 9.2
Disbursements of IDBI

(₹ in Crores)

	1998-99	*1999-2000*
1. Direct finance	13797	15454
2. Refinance	102	229
3. Bill finance	476	528
4. Resource support to financial intermediaries	848	95
Total	14,470	17,059

In the total outstanding assistance of IDBI, the Iron and Steel industry received the largest share of 14.3 per cent followed by electricity generation with a share of 9.7 per cent.

The performance of IDBI right from the beginning has been very impressive. Over the years, not only the amount of assistance, but the range of activities undertaken also have expanded greatly.

Since the year 2001-02, there has been a significant decline in the sanctions and disbursement of IDBI.

(₹ in Crores)

Year	Sanctions	Disbursement
2000-01	26832.6	17476.9
2001-02	15867.9	11012.5
2002-03	5898.2	6614.9
2003-04	3937.7	4986.4
2004-05	10799	6183.3
2005-06	27442	12984

IDBI approached Government of India to corporatise IDBI by repealing IDBI Act. The Bill for corporatising IDBI is being put up to Parliament. To strengthen its capital, the World Bank loan outstanding in respect of IDBI has been transferred to Central Government and replaced with a long-term bond.

9.2(B) ICICI

The Industrial Credit and Investment Corporation of India was set up in 1955 as a public limited company under the sponsorship of the World Bank as an industrial financing institution. Unlike IFCI and IDBI, the ICICI is a privately owned institution with no participation by the Government in its share capital. The share capital of ICICI is partly owned by the Indian private sector and partly by foreign institutions. It was initially providing finance to the industrial units in the private sector only but later on, it extended its finance to the public and joint sector and also co operative projects. Apart from granting long and medium term loans to the industry, the ICICI has played a leading role in a number of activities such as underwriting, merchant banking and lease finance and so on. It also greatly contributed towards the establishment of Over The Counter Exchange, Credit Ratings Information Services of India Limited (CRISIL), Shipping and Investment Corporation of India (SCICI) and venture capital funds.

Resources of ICICI

The resources of ICICI are in the form of share capital, initial interest free loans by the Government of India, advances in foreign currency by the World Bank, rupee loans by the IDBI, borrowings from the Reserve Bank, lines of credit from the World Bank, bond issues in India and foreign capital markets, issue of shares to Indian public and reserves. At the time of its establishment, the initial share capital of ICICI was only ₹ 5 crore which increased to ₹ 550.33 crore in 1996-97. Its reserves stood at ₹ 3,900.21 crore in 1996-97. Through the issue of bonds and debentures, the total resources generated by the ICICI in 1998-99 was ₹ 7,866 crore. About 25 per cent resources of ICICI are in foreign currency.

Lending and Other Activities

The ICICI provides assistance in various forms such as long and medium term loans or equity participation, guaranteeing loans from other private investment sources, subscription to ordinary or preference capital, underwriting of new issues of securities, consultancy services to the Indian industry in the form of managerial and technical advice.

The total disbursements of the ICICI in 1997-98 stood at ₹ 15,806.9 crore which further increased to ₹ 19,225.1 crore in 1998-99. The cumulative assistance disbursed by ICICI at the end of March 1997 aggregated to ₹ 53,746.6 crore.

During the year 2001-02, there has been a significant decline in the sanctions and disbursement of ICICI.

(*₹ in Crores*)

Year	*Sanctions*	*Disbursement*
2000-01	55815.2	31664.6
2001-02	36229.1	25831.0

The ICICI sanctions foreign currency and loans for the import of foreign capital equipment.

The major share in the financial assistance of ICICI is that of non-traditional growth-oriented industries such as chemicals, petrochemicals, heavy engineering and metal products due to their large foreign currency loan requirements.

Maharashtra, Gujarat, West Bengal, Tamil Nadu and Karnataka are the five states that have benefited most from the ICICI lending.

The consortium of all-India development banks, comprising. IFCI, IDBI and ICICI has been extending assistance to cotton textile, jute, sugar, cement and engineering industries on soft terms for their modernisation.

The ICICI has been a pioneering institution in the field of underwriting business in India. Provision of foreign currency loans to the industrial units has been another distinguishing feature of the ICICI.

ICICI, however, has mainly extended its assistance only to the large-scale units, leading to the growth of monopoly power. It has fallen short in helping to remove the regional disparities, through its assistance.

The ICICI merger with ICICI Bank has been approved by RBI in April 2002.

9.2(C) Small Industries Development Bank of India (SIDBI)

The SIDBI was established in October 1989 as a wholly owned subsidiary of IDBI for strengthening the arrangements in order to provide larger flow of financial and non-financial assistance to the small-scale sector.

SIDBI had an initial paid-up capital of ₹ 250 crore which was subsequently raised to ₹ 450 crore. It also took over the outstanding portfolio of IDBI relating to the small-scale sector held under small industries development fund as on March 31, 1990.

Initially, the SIDBI's objectives were: (a) to initiate steps for technological upgradation and modernisation of the existing units, (b) to expand channels for the marketing of SSI sector products in India and abroad and (c) to promote employment-oriented industries in semi-urban areas and to check the migration of population to big cities.

SIDBI provides assistance to the small-scale units through the existing credit delivery system comprising state finance corporations, state industrial development corporations, commercial and co operative banks and RRBs.

A venture capital fund was established by SIDBI with an initial corpus of ₹ 10 crore for small-scale units that do not qualify for assistance under conventional modes.

In 1995-96, SIDBI disbursed a total sum of ₹ 4,585 crore which increased to ₹ 6,268.2 crore in 1998-99.

During last six years, the sanctions and disbursement of SIDBI were as under:

(₹ *in Crores)*

Year	*Sanctions*	*Disbursement*
2000-01	10820.6	6441.4
2001-02	9025.5	5919.3
2002-03	10903.5	6789.4
2003-04	8246.3	4414.2
2004-05	9091	6188
2005-06	11974.8	9099.8
2006-07	11102.3	10225.4
2007-08	16146.3	15099.3
2008-09	29644.9	28293.1

The major activities of SIDBI include refinance of loans and advances, discounting and rediscounting of bills, extension of seed capital or soft loans, granting direct assistance, provision of services such as factoring, leasing etc.

Reduction in interest rates, liberalising the terms of assistance widening the scope of some existing schemes, inclusion of new target groups for assistance and simplification of procedures are some of the new policy changes introduced by the SIDBI in recent years.

9.2(D) Industrial Investment Bank of India (IIBI)

To provide financial assistance to the sick units, the Industrial Reconstruction Corporation of India was established in 1971. In March 1985, it was converted into a statutory corporation called IRBI, *i.e.,* Industrial Reconstruction Bank of India. Again, the IRBI was reconstituted into the Industrial Investment Bank of India (IIBI) in March 1997.

Since the year 2001-02, the sanctions and disbursement of IIBI have been as under:

(₹ *in Crores)*

Year	*Sanctions*	*Disbursement*
2000-01	2102.3	1709.8
2001-02	1321.9	1068.0
2002-03	1206.5	1091.9
2003-04	2412.0	2252.2

9.2(E) National Bank for Agricultural and Rural Development (NABARD)

NABARD occupies a similar position in the field of rural and agricultural finance as that of IDBI in the field of industrial finance. NABARD came into existence in July 1982 and functions as an apex institution in the field of rural credit. It took over all the functions of RBI in this respect. The Agricultural Refinance and Development Corporation (ARDC) which was established in 1963 for meeting the long-term credit requirements in the rural areas also merged with NABARD.

Functions of NABARD

- Apex body in the field of rural credit.
- Supervise the functioning of the co-operative sector through its Agricultural Credit Department.
- Provision of short-term (18 months) credit to State Co operative Banks and medium-term credit (18 months to 7 years) to RRBs and state co operative banks.
- Provision of medium and long-term credit (not more than 25 years) for investment in agriculture.
- To undertake inspection of central and state co operative banks, RRBs and State Land Development Banks.
- Maintain a research and development fund to promote research in agriculture and rural development.

The major functions of NABARD are refinancing, institutional development and undertake inspection of client banks, but the refinance function has been the most prominent functions. NABARD does not deal directly with the farmers and other rural people. It extends assistance to them through co operative, commercial and regional rural banks.

NABARD provides credit for the development of agriculture, small-scale industries, cottage and village industries, handicrafts and other rural crafts and other economic activities in the rural areas.

The resources of NABARD comprise a line of credit from the RBI, loans from the Central Government, World Bank, other aid agencies, sale of bonds and debentures, direct borrowings, deposits, gifts, grants and so on.

Resources Raised by NABARD

(₹ in Crores)

Year	*Resources Raised*	*Outstanding*
2000-01	1472	3614
2001-02	2348	6078
2002-03	2988	8702
2003-04	5334	11883
2004-05	10642	26429
2005-06	8194	27303

9.2(F) Rural Infrastructure Development Fund (RIDF)

RIDF has been set up with NABARD by the Central Government in 1995-96. The Central Government contributes to the corpus of fund through budgetary provisions.

Purpose: assisting State Governments and state-owned corporations in expeditious completion of ongoing projects for the creation of rural infrastructure — minor and medium irrigation, soil conservation, watershed management, rural roads and bridges, market yards etc. Initially, irrigation projects were given a major thrust.

RIDF-II onwards — rural roads and bridges.

RIDF-V: Ambit of RIDF was extended to projects undertaken by Panchayati Raj institutions and projects in social sector covering primary education, health and drinking water.

Table No. 9.3
Loans Sanctioned and Disbursed under RIDF

(₹ in Crores)

RIDF	*Year*	*No. of Projects*	*Corpus*	*Sanction*	*Disbursement*	*Disbursement as % of Sanction*
I	1995	4168	2000	1906	1761	92.4
II	1996	8193	2500	2636	2398	91.0
III	1997	14345	2500	2733	2454	89.8
IV	1998	6171	3000	2903	2482	85.5
V	1999	12106	3500	3434	3055	89.0
VI	2000	43168	4500	4489	4071	90.7
VII	2001	24598	5000	4582	4053	88.5
VIII	2002	20887	5500	5950	5142	86.4
IX	2003	19548	5500	5639	4870	86.4
X	2004	17190	8000	7717	6198	80.3
XI	2005	29875	8000	8301	5728	69.0
XII	2006	42279	10000	10601	5771	54.4
XIII	2007	36948	12000	12749	5057	39.7
XIV	2008	85527	14000	14719	3013	20.5
Total		365000	86000	88359	56052	63.4

As regards the number of projects sanctioned under RIDF, there has been an increasing trend. However, loans disbursed as a percentage of loan sanctioned have shown a declining trend and has fallen sharply in the recent years. Since RIDF-VII with a view to encouraging the flow of credit to agriculture, the interest rate on banks' contribution to RIDF has been linked inversely to the extent of shortfall in agricultural lending *vis-a-vis* target of 18%.

RIDF-XII set up with a corpus of ₹ 10,000 crore. Nine states: Andhra Pradesh, Uttar Pradesh, Maharashtra, Tamil Nadu, Gujarat, Madhya Pradesh, West Bengal, Rajasthan and Karnataka accounted for 70 per cent of the total sanction and 72 per cent of the total disbursements.

Projects under RIDF I to XI

Projects	*% share*
Rural roads and bridges	45.2
Irrigation projects	39.0
Others (including power sector and social sector)	20.8

9.3 STATE LEVEL INSTITUTIONS

(a) State Financial Corporations (SFCs)

The State Financial Corporations were set up under the State Financial Corporations Act, 1951 by the respective state governments for the development of small and medium enterprises and for bringing about regionally balanced economic growth. They meet the long-term credit needs of small and medium enterprises. At present, there are 18 SFCs operating in different states.

The resources of SFCs come from share capital, reserves, bond issues, loans from the IDBI, RBI and the state government; refinance from SIDBI, IDBI and RBI; fixed deposits from the state governments, local authorities and the public and so on.

The lending operations of the SFCs were very small upto 1975 but expanded greatly thereafter. The financial assistance sanctioned and disbursed by all SFCs in 1997-98 were respectively ₹ 2,601.5 crore and ₹ 2,087.2 crore. During last four years, there has been a significant decline in sanctions and disbursement of all SFCs together.

(₹ in Crores)

Year	*Sanctions*	*Disbursement*
2000-01	2911.4	1979.0
2001-02	2210.2	1749.6
2002-03	1855.9	1454.0
2003-04	1133.8	856.8

Provision of assistance to small enterprises and the enterprises located in backward areas is an important aspect of the lending policy of the SFCs. The enterprises in the backward regions are given soft loans at concessional interest rates and at reduced service charge.

However, the performance of various SFCs has been far from satisfactory. Other than the soft loans they grant the interest rates on all other loans are very high. The increasing overdues due to delays in project implementation and industrial sickness have greatly squeezed away the resources of the SFCs. They have not met the demands of small and medium industries adequately.

(b) State Industrial Development Corporation (SIDCs)

Apart from the SFCs, there are 28 state industrial development corporations wholly owned by the respective state governments which are established for accelerating the pace of industrial development. The SIDCs provide assistance in the form of direct investment loans, extension for guarantee for loans and deferred payments, underwriting and subscribing to the issue of share, bonds and debentures.

9.4 PERFORMANCE OF FINANCIAL INSTITUTIONS

The Financial Institutions have been primarily engaged in providing medium and long-term loans. Besides this, the FIs have been providing risk capital, underwriting new issues, arranging for foreign currency loans, identifying investment projects and preparing and evaluating project reports.

(₹ in Crores)

Year	*Sanctions*	*Disbursement*
1999-00	101918	68594
2000-01	120548	75364
2001-02	75088	58735
2002-03	28311	26705
2003-04	46479	32875
2004-05	36818	25299
2005-06	65312	39552
2006-07	29964	37982
2007-08	55798	43512

Sanctions and disbursements have declined since 2001-02. However, financial assistance extended by All-India FIs has increased since 2005-06.

Table No. 9.4
Financial Parameters of FIs
(as on March 31, 2002)

(₹ in Crores)

FIs	*CRAR*	*Net NPA / Net Loans*	*Operating Profit / Working Funds*	*Return on Average Assets*	*Net Profit per Employee*
IDBI	17.86	13.40	1.72	0.61	0.15
IFCI	3.12	22.50	–4.17	–4.03	–1.06
IIBI	9.15	24.10	1.56	12.91	0.23
SIDBI	45.01	3.00	3.89	2.33	0.31
NABARD	36.92	–	4.35	3.58	0.28
Exim Bank	33.13	7.40	3.59	2.22	1.05
IDFC	56.86	—	6.62	5.91	1.61
TFCI	18.46	20.20	3.07	1.00	0.32
NHB	20.16	—	2.48	2.48	2.14

Source: Report on Trends and Progress of Banking in India, 2001-02.

Table No. 9.4 (A)
Financial Parameters of FIs

(₹ in Crores)

FI	*2003*		*2004*		*2005*		*2006*	
	Net NPA	*Net NPA net loan %*	*Net NPA*	*Net NPA net loan %*	*Net NPA*	*Net NPA net loan %*	*Net NPA*	*Net NPA net loan %*
IDBI	7157	15.8	8693	21.1	—	—	—	—
IFCI	4559	29.5	3865	32.3	2688	28.0	667	9.1
IIBI	915	34.7	800	38.0	405	27.3	13.2	13.1
IFCI	153	26.4	144	21.1	68	11.0	15	3.0
Exim Bank	184	2.3	129	1.3	109	0.9	105	0.6
NABARD	1	—	1	—	—	—	—	—
SIDBI	472	3.8	22.6	2.4	407	3.9	261	1.9
NHB	—	—	—	—	—	—	—	—

The ratio of net NPA to Net loans is significantly high in case of IIBI and IFCI. The ratio has been on higher side earlier for TFCI, but has now fallen. During 2005-06, the fall in Net NPA shows improvement in the asset quality of FIs.

Financial Performance of Select FIs

	2003	*2004*	*2005*	*2006*	*2007-08*	*2008-09*
(1) Operating Profit	2581	2211	1604	1993	2834	3782
(2) % to total asset	1.4	1.7	1.2	1.4	1.6	1.7
(3) Net Profit	1621	1545	1097	1402	1898	2592
(4) Net Profit to total assets	0.9	1.2	0.8	1.0	1.1	1.2

The combined net profit of 7 AIFIs declined in the recent years, but has improved since 2005-06.

Table No. 9.4 (B)

Financial Parameters of FIs

FI	*Net NPA/ net loans*			*Operating Profit Working Funds*			*Return on Average Assets*			*Net Profit Per Employee*		
	2004	*2005*	*2006*	*2004*	*2005*	*2006*	*2004*	*2005*	*2006*	*2004*	*2005*	*2006*
IDBI	21.1	—	—	2.9	—	—	0.5	—	—	0.12	—	—
IFCI	32.3	28.0	9.6	–1.9	1.8	6.7	–16.9	–2.2	–0.6	–5.34	–0.6	–0.2
IIBI	38.0	27.3	72.0	–4.9	–7.6	–1.4	—	—	—	–0.49	–0.8	–0.1
IFCI	21.1	11.0	3.9	3.1	3.6	4.0	1.6	2.0	1.9	0.39	0.4	0.4
Exim Bank	1.3	0.9	0.6	2.4	2.0	2.1	1.7	1.5	1.5	1.2	1.3	1.4
SIDBI	2.4	3.9	1.9	3.5	3.0	3.4	2.0	1.7	2.0	0.27	0.3	0.3
NABARD	—	—	—	3.6	3.2	2.1	2.8	1.8	1.8	0.28	0.2	0.2
NHB	—	—	—	2.2	0.5	1.1	2.2	0.3	0.5	2.35	0.3	0.3

IIBI continued to incur operating losses. Return on average assets ratio was negative for IFCI. Net profit per employee has been negative for IFCI and IIBI.

CRAR of FIs

FIs	*2000*	*2001*	*2002*	*2003*	*2004*	*2005*	*2006*
IFCI	8.8	6.2	3.1	1.0	–17.0	–23.4	–30.4
IIBI	9.7	13.9	9.2	–11.0	–20.1	–41.1	–46.2
TFCI	16.2	18.6	18.5	19.8	22.8	27.4	34.9
Exim Bank	24.4	23.8	33.1	26.9	23.5	21.6	18.4
SIDBI	27.8	28.1	45.0	44.0	51.6	50.7	43.2
NABARD	44.4	38.5	36.9	39.1	39.4	38.8	34.4
NHB	16.5	16.8	22.1	27.9	30.5	22.5	22.3

For FIs, the stipulated norm CRAR is 9 per cent (Capital Risk-weighted Asset Ratio) CRAR has turned negative in case of IFCI and IIBI. The causes for this are high NPAs, additional provisioning, continued losses resulting in erosion of capital.

Table No. 9.5

Assets and Liabilities of Select FIs

(as at March-end)

(₹ in Crores)

Item	*2001*	*2002*	*2003*	*2004*	*2005*	*2006*	*2008*	*2009*
Liabilities								
1. Capital	7866	6811	6784	6131	5331	5431	4000	4200
	(3.2)	(3.9)	(3.7)	(4.7)	(4.0)	(3.7)		
2. Reserves	39147	31137	18221	13499	14074	15211	17137	19069
	(15.9)	(17.7)	(9.9)	(10.4)	(10.5)	(10.5)		
3. Bond and Debentures	126155	81717	89640	50545	60150	67145	57741	52390
	(51.2)	(46.6)	(48.8)	(38.8)	(44.7)	(46.2)		
4. Deposits	17846	14240	20144	17946	13355	14520	36296	65501
	(7.2)	(8.1)	(11.0)	(13.8)	(9.9)	(10.0)		
5. Borrowings	37204	27146	21862	18360	17421	18950	33716	41663
	(151)	(18.5)	(11.9)	(14.1)	(13.0)	(13.0)		
6. Other Liabilities	18308	14469	27062	23661	24105	24217	31000	35579
	(7.4)	(8.2)	(14.7)	(18.2)	(17.9)	(16.6)		
Total Liabilities	246526	175520	183714	130142	134436	145474	179912	217372
Assets								
1. Cash	8901	5577	8027	12146	16490	9915	15835	19430
	(3.6)	(3.2)	(4.4)	(9.3)	(12.3)	(6.8)		
2. Investment	29864	21945	21726	14298	13617	10423	6694	8156
	(12.1)	(12.5)	(11.8)	(11.0)	(10.1)	(7.2)		
3. Loans & Advances	182026	131599	136819	91613	91874	111441	147008	178595
	(73.8)	(75.0)	(74.5)	(70.4)	(68.3)	(76.6)		
4. Bills discounted	3641	2744	1605	1218	1048	1810	2044	2145
	(1.5)	(1.0)	(0.9)	(0.9)	(0.8)	(1.2)		
5. Fixed Assets	8152	2747	2975	1217	1145	1088	539	570
	(3.3)	(1.6)	(1.6)	(0.9)	(0.9)	(0.7)		
6. Other Assets	13942	10908	12362	9650	10262	10797	7792	8477
	(5.7)	(8.2)	(6.8)	(7.4)	(7.6)	(7.4)		
Total Assets	246526	175520	183714	130142	134436	145474	179912	217372

The bonds and debentures account for the major share in the total liabilities of FIs. The main component on the asset side is loans and advances, which has significantly increased in the recent years.

9.5 MONEY MARKET OPERATIONS OF FIs: RESOURCES RAISED

Effective from May 2001, the participation (lending) of non-bank institutions in the call/notice money market has been curtailed.

Select FIs raise resources by way of term money, term deposits and ICDs, certificates of deposit (CDs) and Commercial Papers (CPs).

Table No. 9.6

Money Market Operations of Select FIs

(₹ in Crores)

Item	*2000-01*	*2001-02*	*2002-03*	*2003-04*	*2004-05*	*2005-06*	*2006-07*	*2007-08*	*2008-09*
Term Money	999	1206	373	245	175	—	—	250	1184
Term Deposit	701	166	1548	2206	705	44	89	508	2222
Inter-corporate Deposits (ICDs)	5940	6526	3078	1329	477	—	—	—	—
CDs	2686	981	504	408	233	2	663	2286	5633
CPs	72	234	964	1847	1749	1931	2540	1414	6207
Total	10398	10112	6467	6035	3339	1977	3293	4458	15247

Resources raised by FIs from the money market increased significantly during the year 2008-09.

9.6 RESOURCES RAISED BY SELECT FIs FROM CAPITAL MARKET

IFCI and IIBI have been barred from mobilising fresh resources.

(₹ in Crores)

Select FI	*2003-04*		*2004-05*		*2005-06*		*2007-08*		*2008-09*	
	Long-term	*Short-term*	*Long term*	*Short-term*	*Long-term*	*Short-term*	*Long term*	*Short-term*	*Long-term*	*Short-term*
TFCI	102	70	23	—	71	—	—	—	—	—
Exim Bank	2025	1074	1480	1632	3260	1124	6825	2180	3197	8905
SIDBI	1429	1536	1607	799	2610	420	4531	461	5625	8811
NABARD	5334	—	10642	—	8195	—	12198	1422	4282	3494
NHB	2990	300	2419	1063	2631	199	3100	8016	3124	16881
Total							26654	12079	16198	38091

During 2008-09, there has been a significant rise in the short-term resources raised. The long-term resources raised and foreign currency resources declined in the year 2008-09 as compared with the previous year. NHB mobilised the largest amount of short-term resources during 2008-09, followed by Exim Bank and SIDBI.

Foreign Currency Resources

FI	*2003-04*	*2004-05*	*2005-06*	*2007-08*	*2008-09*
Exim Bank	3782	2189	2814	5553	3800
SIDBI	7	28	459	92	1381
Total				5645	5161

9.7 FINANCIAL ASSISTANCE TO FIs

IFCI: The Central Government provided support through subscription to the 20-year convertible bonds issued by IFCI for ₹ 400 crore and IDBI, SBI and LIC extended assistance of ₹ 200 crore each. (IDBI, SBI, LIC are major shareholders of IFCI).

Assistance from RBI

RBI transferred the assets on account of loans and advances worth ₹ 3792 crore to IDBI, SIDBI, Exim Bank and IIBI. These FIs issued 20-year convertible bonds in favour of the Government.

The practice of advancing loans by RBI to FIs has been discontinued.

RBI Assistance to SFCs

RBI sanctioned *ad hoc* borrowing limits amounting to ₹ 166 crore to 13 SFCs during 2001-02. In May 2004, RBI decided to discontinue the *ad hoc* borrowing facility to SFCs from 2004-05.

9.8 POLICY DEVELOPMENTS IN RESPECT OF FIs

Some of the policy developments are as under:

NPA of FIs

- An asset is NPA, if interest and/on instalment of principal remains overdue for more than 180 days instead of the overdue period of 365 days for the principal earlier.
- With effect from March-end 2006, an asset should be classified as NPA, if the interest and/or instalment of principal remain overdue for more than 90 days.
- An asset to be classified as 'doubtful' if it remains in the substandard category for more than 12 months *w.e.f.* from March 31, 2005.

Provisioning Requirement

- FIS are required to make for NPAs provisions on a graded basis as per the the age of NPA. With effect from March 2005, a graded higher provisioning for NPAs in 'doubtful' category for more than three years.
- Standard assets: Uniform provisioning requirement of 0.40 per cent with effect from December 2005 (earlier requirements: 0.25 per cent) except advances for agricultural and SME sector.
- *Projects under implementation:* Time Overrun

  RBI issued new guideline effective March 31,2002 under which a definite time frame has been evolved to ensure that loan assets relating to projects under implementation are appropriately classified and asset quality is correctly reflected.

Wilful defaulters

Working Group on Wilful defaulters (Chairman Shri S.S. Kohli) submitted its report in Nov. 2001 New definition: Wilful default would be deemed to have occurred: (a) the unit has defaulted in meeting its payment/repayment obligations to the lender, (b) the unit has not utilised the finance for the specific purposes for which the finance was availed of and (c) the unit has siphoned off the funds.

No additional facilities should be granted by any bank or FI to the listed wilful defaulters.

- Supervision of FIs

  On-site inspection : once in two years
  Effective March 31, 2001 : annual inspection.
  Off-site Surveillance : introduced in July 1999.
  Effective Sept. 2001 : FIs to submit returns on a 'quarterly' basis.
- Dematerialisation:

  June 30, 2001: CDs and CPs in demat form: all outstanding to be converted in demat form by Oct. 31, 2001.

  Fresh investments and bonds and debentures privately placed or otherwise in demat form by Oct. 31, 2001. Outstanding investment in scrip form to be converted in demat form by June 30, 2002.
- Additional Disclosures

  To enhance transparency in the annual reports of FIs, additional disclosures of certain parameter were made effective from the year 2001-02.
- Entry of FIs into Insurance business

  New guidelines have been issued for the entry of AIFIs into insurance business to ensure that risks involved in insurance business do not get transmitted to FIs and contaminate their principal business.
- Merger of ICICI with ICICI Bank Ltd. was approved by RBI in April 2002.

9.9 RESTRUCTURING OF FINANCIAL INSTITUTIONS

The significant feature of the ongoing reforms in the financial sector is the restructuring of financial institutions by way of their transformation into commercial banking institutions. As the line of demarcation between the functions of financial institutions and the banks become thinner giving rise to blurring of their functions over the years, the moves for the financial institutions to accept the model of a bank for their working gained ground. The financial institutions faced problems arising out of competition from the banks in their domain of project financing. The financial institutions also faced cash flow problems in providing finance to projects with longer gestation out of funds generated by borrowing with short-term commitments.

ICICI: The beginning of this transformation was when ICICI merged with ICICI Bank by the end of March 2002.

IDBI: The IDBI Act was repealed and the conversion of IDBI into a commercial bank — IDBI bank became effective since July 2004 vide IDBI (Transfer of Undertaking and Repeal) Act 2003 enacted in December 2003. On October 1, 2004 IDBI became IDBI Ltd. — a scheduled bank under RBI Act 1934. A Stressed Asset Stabilisation Fund (SASF) set up with a view to transfer the stressed assets of IDBI worth ₹ 9000 crore to SASF against a transfer of an equivalent amount of Government of India 20-year bonds issued.

IFCI: The Union Budget 2004-05 indicated restructuring of IFCI by effecting merger with a Public Sector Bank. The proposal for merging IFCI with Punjab National Bank has received the approval of the Boards of both the institutions.

DFIs in Post-reform Period

It is said that DFIs are fast losing ground as their role as an exclusive source of providing development finance has diminished during 1990s, *i.e.,* in post-reform period. DFIs have accumulated large NPAs and finding it difficult to remain viable.

In the post-independence period, the emphasis under economic planning was laid on bringing about a structural change in the country by way of rapid growth of industries. Beginning with IFCI in 1948, DFIs were set up for providing medium and long-term finance, *i.e.,* funding long-term industrial projects. In the pre-reform period, the DFIs were in an exclusive position and did not face much competition in respect of long-term finance. DFIs could draw upon funds at cheaper rates and could provide assistance to long gestation industrial projects.

Since 1991, *i.e.,* in post-reform period, the operational environment of DFIs changed exposing them to a set-up where they lost their exclusive status as providers of development finance and their access to concessional resources have been withdrawn.

The line of demarcation had already become thinner and DFIs and Banks become competitors as Banks took up project financing, besides their task of providing working capital.

In the post-reform period, there was an impact on DFIs' role in regard to both the demand side and supply side of their working.

On the demand side, DFIs had to face competitions from the banks and there has been a trend towards fall in the share of loans in project financing.

Shares of Loans and Equity in Project Financing (in %)

Year	*Loans*	*Equity*
1970-71 to 1974-75	53.5	28.5
1995-96 to 2000-01	43	53

On the supply side, DFIs suffered as they had to raise fund at high cost, the source of concessional funds being withdrawn.

Working Group on DFIs: Chairman: Shri N. Sadasivan

Working Group on DFIs under the chairmanship of Shri N. Sadasivan submitted its report on May 10, 2004.

Purpose: To review the experience and prospects of DFIs for transformation into banks

To assess the financial position and recommend regulatory framework for the existing Financial Institutions.

Recommendations:

Select All-India FIs:

- NABARD, NHB, SIDBI: Extend indirect finance by way of refinance. These are in sound financially health.
- Exim Bank, IDFC: Financially healthy.
- Remaining DFIs: Including IDBI, IFCI, IIBI are in poor financial health.

DFIs should scale down the proportion of project financing. Major Recommendations.

- On the basis of social cost-benefit analysis, Government should decide which institutions could continue as DFIs for the sectors which need development finance.
- The rest of DFIs should be converted either to a bank or NBFC.

SFCs

The main problems faced include centralised decision-making, lack of corporate culture, high transaction cost, poor appraisal skills etc. Recommendation: phasing out of SFCs.

NBFCs

There is a need to focus on all large-size NBFCs.

RBI has introduced quarterly reporting assessment for NBFCs not accepting public deposits and having asset size of ₹ 500 crore and above.

RNBCs

Recommendations:

- A cap in terms of NOF may be fixed for mobilisation of public deposits.
  Initial measure: 16 times the NOFs
  Within 5 years: a ceiling of 4 times or 1.5 times of NOF.
- Unlisted and unrated bonds should not form part of investments.

KEY TERMS

Refinance, Term Lending, Credit Guarantee.

REVIEW QUESTIONS

1. What are the different types of financial institutions in India?
2. Explain the role and pattern of lending of the IFCI.
3. Give an outline of the lending activities of the IDBI.
4. Write notes –
   (a) ICICI
   (b) SIDBI
   (c) Functions of NABARD
   (d) Role of SFCs
   (e) Restructuring of Financial Institutions
5. Discuss the performance of the financial institutions in the recent years.
6. Discuss the money market and capital market participation of financial institutions.
7. Explain the recent policy developments in the context of financial institutions and the financial assistance provided to them.

REFERENCES

1. RBI Reports on Trends and Progress of Banking in India, Various Issues.
2. RBI Reports on Currency and Finance, Various Issues.

❑ ❑ ❑

10

Investment Institutions: Insurance Companies and Mutual Funds

INTRODUCTION

This chapter is divided into two sections:

(A) Insurance Companies

(B) UTI and Mutual Funds

Section (A)

I. Nature of Insurance Companies

II. Economic and Social Relevance of Insurance

III. History of Indian Insurance Sector

IV. Insurance Sector Reforms

V. Progress of LIC and GIC in the Post-nationalisation Period

VI. Insurance Regulatory and Development Authority — IRDA

VII. Indian Insurance Scenario — Post 2000

Section (B)

I. Unit Trust of India

II. Mutual Funds

(A) INSURANCE COMPANIES

I. NATURE OF INSURANCE COMPANIES

Insurance Companies are financial intermediaries, as they collect and invest large amounts of premium. Insurance companies offer protection to the investors, provide means for accumulating savings and channelise funds to the government and other sectors. Insurance companies receive, mostly without fail, steady in flow of funds in the form of premiums or some regular contribution to the pension funds etc. Liquidity is not a problem for them as their liabilities are essentially of long-term. The policies are usually held for 3-40 or even longer years. Life insurance companies offer life cover to the investors (insured) and the rate of return specified in the insurance policies is generally low. Therefore, they do not have to obtain high rate of return on their investments and they mainly invest in long-term investments such as government securities, state and government authorities debts and corporate debentures/bonds.

Insurance companies operate in the fields of life, health and general insurance, pension schemes, mutual funds and so on.

Insurance business consists of spreading risks over time and sharing them between persons and organisations. The operations of life insurance business are governed by the law of mortality. In case of life insurance, the claim is fixed and certain but in case of non-life (or general) insurance the claim is uncertain, the amount of claim is variable and is ascertainable only sometime after the event. Pension schemes are very often linked with life insurance.

The insurance business has always been an important component of the Indian Financial System. Before independence, the insurance business was in the private sector and competitive market. After independence, the life insurance business was nationalised (1956) and non-life insurance business was nationalised in 1972. After 2000, the insurance sector has been opened to the entry of private domestic and foreign companies.

II. ECONOMIC AND SOCIAL RELEVANCE OF INSURANCE

Insurance reduces risks associated with life and property. It provides social security and promotes individual welfare. It raises productivity in the economy as the insurance companies mobilise large funds and undertake large investments in long-term infrastructure development projects.

It provides the dependents of the main breadwinner of the family with some financial support in the event of his premature death.

III. HISTORY OF INDIAN INSURANCE SECTOR

Life Insurance:

Phases of Insurance Business

1818 to 1956	Competitive Market & 245 private companies in business
1956 to 2000	Nationalisation of LIC was established as a state monopoly in 1956 and functioned as a monopoly till 2000.
After 2000	Private domestic and foreign companies entered business.

General (Non-life) Insurance:

1850 - 1972	107 private companies operated in competitive environment.
1972 - 2000	General Insurance Corporation of India (GIC) was established in 1972 with its 4 subsidiaries.
After 2000	Competitive market and entry allowed for domestic and private players.

The first life insurance company, namely Oriental Life Insurance Company was established in 1818 in Calcutta and the first general insurance company, Tritan Insurance Company was established in 1850. Before independence, totally 352 insurance companies (245 life and 107 non-life) grew in numbers, volume of premium, investible resources. The Insurance Act 1938 was passed to regulate the insurance business in India. After the independence, in 1956 the Life Insurance Corporation of India (LIC) was established as a public sector (monopoly) insurance corporation by putting together the assets and the liabilities of 245 private (Indian and Foreign) life insurance companies. Similarly, in 1972 around 107 non-life insurers were put together to nationalise the general insurance business. The General Insurance Business (Nationalisation) Act 1972 was passed and five companies — National Insurance Company (NIC), New India Assurance Company (NIAC), Oriental Insurance Company (OIC), United India Insurance Company (VIIC) and General Insurance Corporation were established.

- Public Sector
  - Life
    - Life Insurance Corporation of India
    - Postal Life Insurance
  - Non-life
    - General Insurance Corporation of India and 4 Subsidiaries
- Private Sector
  - Life
  - Non-life

IV. INSURANCE SECTOR REFORMS

In consonance with the ongoing economic reforms, the Indian Government set the reform ball rolling in the insurance sector, taking the first step by appointing the Malhotra Committee in April, 1993 to suggest reforms for the nationalised insurance industry of India. The Committee submitted its report in the year 1994 and recommended opening up of the insurance sector to private participation and restructuring of the existing players. In the wake of the reform process and passing Insurance Regulatory Development Act (IRDA) through Indian Parliament in 1999, the Indian insurance business was opened up to private domestic and foreign players. **Malhotra Committee** in its report in 1994 stated that only 22% of the Indian population was covered by insurance. The poor reach of insurance in the country and the sheer numbers made India a market with tremendous potential.

The Terms of Reference of the Malhotra Committee –

- To examine the structure of the insurance industry as it has evolved within the existing framework and to assess its strength and weaknesses in terms of the objectives of creating an efficient and viable insurance industry providing a wide range of insurance services and a variety of insurance products with a high quality of service to the public and serving as an effective instrument for mobilisation of financial resources for development.
- To make recommendations for changes in the structure of insurance industry, as well as the general framework of policy, as may be appropriate for the pursuit of the above

objectives keeping in mind the structural changes currently underway in other parts of the financial system and in the economy.

- To make specific suggestions regarding LIC and GIC, which would help to improve the functioning of these organisations in the changing economic environment.
- To review the present structure of regulation and supervision of the insurance sector and to make recommendation for strengthening and modernisation of the regulatory system in the tune with changing requirements.
- To review and make recommendations on the role and functioning of surveyors, intermediaries like agents and other ancillaries of the insurance sector.
- To make recommendations on such other matters as the committee considers relevant for the health and long-term development of the insurance sector or which are consequential on other recommendations made by the committee, including changes in the legislations where necessary.

The Malhotra Committee made a number of important and far-reaching recommendations

- The LIC should be selective in the recruitment of LIC agents. Train these people after the identification of training needs.
- The committee suggested that the Federation of Insurance Institute, Mumbai should start new courses and diploma courses for intermediaries of the insurance sector.
- The LIC should use an MBA specialised in Marketing (a similar suggestion for the GIC subsidiaries).
- It suggested that settlement of claims were to be done within a specific time frame without delay.
- The committee has several recommendations on product pricing, vigilance, systems and procedures, improving customer service and use of technology.
- It also made a number of recommendations to alter the existing structure of the LIC and the GIC.
- The committee insisted that the insurance companies should pay special attention to the rural insurance business.
- In the case of liberalisation of the insurance sector, the committee made several recommendations, including entry to new players and the minimum capital level requirements for such new players should be ₹ 100 crore (about USD 24 million). However, a lower capital requirement could be considered for a co-operative sectors' entry in the insurance business.
- The committee suggested some norms relating to promoters' equity and equity capital by foreign companies, etc.

V. PROGRESS OF LIC AND GIC IN THE POST-NATIONALISATION PERIOD

In the post-nationalisation period, the growth of the insurance business was not very rapid in India. These governments owned (monopoly) companies were not very responsive to the needs of the customers. There were expectations of the customers for reduction of premium, for innovative products, for higher return on premium and much better quality of services. The LIC and the GIC could not fulfill these expectations of the customers for various reasons and the government decided to open up the insurance sector to the private insurers.

The weak areas of the insurance industry before 2000 were poor customer services, vast marketing and services network of the insurance companies, inadequately responsive to the customer's needs, low insurance awareness among the general public, high costs and low returns on insurance cover compared to other savings instruments due to excessive **government directed investments** of the insurance funds, inadequate technical knowledge of agents and development officers that prevented them from providing sufficient information in regard to the scope of available covers, delay in provision of essential services such as issue of policies and settlement of claims and lack of product innovation.

Growth of Life Insurance Business in India (1914-1948)

	1914	*1930*	*1940*	*1945*	*1948*
1. No. of insurers	44	68	195	215	209
(A) Indian	44	68	179	200	189
(B) Non-Indian	N.A.	N.A.	16	15	20
2. Total No. Policies in Force (in Million)	N.A.	0.7	1.6	2.7	3.0
3. Total Business in Force (₹ in Million)	224	2584	3040	5731	7127
4. Total Life Fund (₹ in Million)	63	205	624	1074	1504

Source: R.N. Jha (see references)

Life Insurance Business in India : Individual Insurance

Year	*New Business*			*Business in Force*		
	No. of Policies (in Million)	*Sum Assured (₹ in Billion)*	*First Year Premium Income (₹ in Billion)*	*No. of Policies (in Million)*	*Sum Assured (₹ in Billion)*	*First Year Premium Income (₹ in Billion)*
1957	0.932	3.280	0.131	5.417	13.75	0.820
1970-71	1.600	12.156	0.480	14.700	69.52	2.790
1980-81	1.954	28.827	1.422	22.758	209.23	8.882
1985-86	3.286	70.561	2.851	27.989	404.04	16.095
1990-91	8.645	281.391	11.920	45.508	1186.51	47.780
1991-92	9.238	320.644	13.988	50.863	1459.29	59.466
1992-93	9.958	359.568	16.092	56.612	1772.68	71.458
1993-94	10.726	418.138	18.906	60.800	2076.01	87.602
1994-95	10.875	552.285	20.454	65.452	2533.33	103.730
1995-96	11.021	518.155	23.211	70.878	2943.36	120.940
1996-97	12.268	567.405	28.020	77.666	3430.18	145.017
1997-98	13.311	636.177	32.841	84.915	3989.59	170.596
1998-99	14.844	735.163	39.749	91.637	4574.34	202.298
1999-00	16.977	912.143	49.449	101.298	5345.89	245.495
2000-01	19.657	1247.716	65.820	113.024	6432.41	307.172
2001-02	22.491	1925.723	99.585	125.799	8091.70	423.037

Source: Annual Reports (Various Issues), Life Insurance Corporation of India.

Milestones of Insurance Regulations in the 20th Century

Year	*Significant Regulatory Event*
1912	The Indian Life Insurance Company Act
1938	The Insurance Act: Comprehensive Act to regulate insurance business in India
1956	Nationalisation of Life insurance business in India
1972	Nationalised of general insurance business in India
1993	Setting up of Malhotra Committee
1994	Recommendations of Malhotra Committee
1995	Setting up of Mukherjee Committee
1996	Setting up of (interim) Insurance Regulatory Authority (IRA) Recommendations of the IRA
1997	Mukherjee Committee Report submitted but not made public
1997	The Government gives greater autonomy to LIC, GIC and its subsidiaries with regards to the restructuring of boards and flexibility in investment norms aimed at channeling funds to the infrastructure sector
1998	The cabinet decides to allow 40% foreign equity in private insurance companies – 26% to foreign companies and 14% to NRIs, OCBs and FIIs
1999	The Standing Committee headed by Murali Deora decides that foreign equity in private insurance should be limited to 26%. The IRA bill is renamed the Insurance Regulatory and Development Authority (IRDA) Bill
1999	Cabinet clears IRDA Bill
2000	President gives Assent to the IRDA Bill

Source: Tapen Sinha (see references)

Share of Life Insurance in the World Market in 2002

Country	*Rank*	*Premium Volume (US$)*	*Share of world market penetration (in %)*	*Insurance Penetration*	*Insurance Density*
United States	1	480452	31.28	4.60	1662.60
Japan	2	354553	23.08	8.64	2783.90
United Kingdom	3	159656	10.39	10.19	2679.40
France	4	80411	5.23	5.61	1349.50
Germany	5	60860	3.96	3.06	736.70
Italy	6	52444	3.41	4.39	904.90
South Korea	7	39272	2.56	8.23	821.90
PR China	8	25054	1.63	2.03	19.50
Spain	9	23840	1.55	3.65	588.00
Switzerland	10	22566	1.47	8.41	3099.70
Netherlands	11	20842	1.36	4.98	1296.10
Taiwan	12	20719	1.35	7.35	925.10
Canada	13	20697	1.35	2.81	657.30
Australia	14	19992	1.30	5.02	1010.40
South Africa	15	16622	1.08	15.92	360.50
Belgium	16	13878	0.90	5.57	1323.60
Ireland	17	12995	0.85	5.42	1712.20
India	18	12274	0.80	2.59	11.70

Source: Sigma, Swiss Re.

Share of Non-life Insurance in the World Market in 2002

Country	*Rank*	*Premium Volume (US$)*	*Share of world market (in %)*	*Insurance Penetration*	*Insurance Density*
United States	1	519858	47.66	4.98	1799.0
Japan	2	91028	8.35	2.22	714.7
United Kingdom	3	77026	7.06	4.56	1199.7
Germany	4	74911	6.87	3.7	891.1
France	5	44649	4.09	2.97	714.7
Italy	6	31616	2.90	2.58	530.5
Canada	7	28520	2.61	3.88	905.8
Spain	8	20415	1.87	3.12	503.5
Netherlands	9	18915	1.73	4.52	1176.3
South Korea	10	16143	1.48	3.38	337.8
Australia	11	13763	1.26	3.46	695.6
Switzerland	12	13269	1.22	4.95	1822.6
PR China	13	11834	1.08	0.96	9.2
Belgium	14	9999	0.92	2.86	679.3
Taiwan	15	7932	0.73	2.81	354.1
Brazil	16	7852	0.72	1.47	45.0
Mexico	17	6816	0.62	1.07	67.5
Austria	18	6589	0.60	3.23	803.4
Russia	19	6266	0.57	1.81	43.5
Ireland	20	5917	0.54	3.14	990.7
Sweden	21	4985	0.46	2.07	560.5
Denmark	22	4655	0.43	2.68	73.4
Norway	23	4506	0.41	1.96	838.0
Portugal	24	3827	0.35	3.14	830.8
Poland	25	3621	0.33	1.92	93.8
Israel	26	3431	0.31	3.34	521.8
India	27	3197	0.29	0.67	3.0
South Africa	28	2988	0.27	2.86	64.8

Source: Sigma, Swiss Re.

VI. INSURANCE REGULATORY AND DEVELOPMENT AUTHORITY— IRDA

On December 7, 1999 the Insurance Regulatory and Development Authority (IRDA) Act was passed by the government. This Act repealed the monopoly conferred to the Life Insurance Corporation in 1956 and the General Insurance Corporation in 1972. The IRDA has separated out life, non-life and the reinsurance business and therefore, a company has to obtain a separate license for each line of business with a separate own capital requirement as well.

Salient Features of Insurance Sector Reform Bill:

- The bill seeks to regulate; promote and ensure orderly growth of the insurance industry and provides for solvency norms and specifies that the funds of policyholders would be retained within the country.
- The minimum capital requirement for life and general insurance has been retained at ₹100 crore ($23.02 million) and for reinsurance firms at ₹ 200 crore ($46.04 million) as provided in the earlier IRA Bill.

- It has been stipulated that the aggregate foreign holding in an Indian insurance company shall not exceed 26 per cent of the paid-up equity. Moreover, to provide a level playing field, it has been proposed that the Indian promoters would also be required to bring down their equity holding to 26 per cent after a period of 10 years from the commencement of business.
- The Bill has proposed solvency margins of ₹ 50 crore (US $ 11.51 million) for life and general insurance and ₹ 100 crore (US $ 23.03 million) for reinsurance companies.
- IRDA, in addition to other functions, would supervise the functioning of the Tariff Advisory Committee (TAC) and specify the percentage of premium income of the insurers to be set aside to finance schemes for promoting and regulating professional organisations in the insurance sectors.
- The four amendments, made in the Insurance Bill by the Lok Sabha, are as under:
  - (i) The Insurance Regulatory and Development Authority (IRDA) should give priority to health insurance;
  - (ii) Policyholder's funds will be invested in the social sector and infrastructure. The per cent may be specified by the IRDA and such regulations will apply to all insurers operating in the country.
  - (iii) Insurers will be expected to undertake a certain per cent of business in rural areas, and cover workers in the unorganised and informal sectors and economically backward classes.
  - (iv) In the event of insurers failing to fulfill the social sector obligations, a fine of ₹ 25 lakh ($ 0.06 million) would be imposed the first time. Subsequent failures would result in cancellation of licenses.

Salient Features of the Insurance Regulatory and Development Authority Act (IRDAA) 1999 (as mentioned in the Economic Survey, [Govt. of India] 1999-2000):

- The insurance sector in India has been thrown open to the private sector. The second and third schedules of the Act provide for removal of exclusive privilege of existing corporations/companies to do life and general insurance business.
- An Indian insurance company is a company registered under the Companies Act, 1956, in which foreign equity does not exceed 26 per cent of the total equity shareholding, including the equity shareholding of Non-resident Indians (NRIs), Foreign Institutional Investors (FIIs) and Overseas Corporate Bodies (OCBs).
- After the commencement of an insurance company, the Indian promoters can hold more than 25 per cent of the total equity holding for a period of ten years, the balance shares being held by the non-promoter Indian shareholders which will not include equity of the foreign promoters, and shareholding of FIIs, NRIs and OCBs.
- After the permissible period of ten years, excess equity above the prescribed level of 26 per cent will be disinvested as per a phased programme to be indicated by IRDA. The Central Government is empowered to extend the period of ten years in individual cases and also to provide for higher ceiling on shareholding of Indian promoters in excess of which disinvestment will be required.
- On foreign promoters, the maximum of 26 per cent will always be operational. They will, thus, be unable to hold any equity beyond this ceiling at any stage.

- The Act gives statutory status for the interim Insurance Regulatory Authority (IRA) set up by the Central Government through resolution in January 1996.
- All the powers presently being exercised under the Insurance Act, 1938 by the Controller of Insurance (COI) will be transferred to the Insurance Regulatory and Development Authority (IRDA).
- The IRDA Act also provides for the appointment of the COI by the Central Government when the regulatory authority is superseded.
- The minimum amount of paid-up equity capital is ₹ 100 crore in case of life insurance as well as general insurance and ₹ 200 crore in case of reinsurance.
- Solvency margin (excess of assets over liabilities) is fixed at not less than ₹ 50 crore for life as well as general insurers, for reinsurance solvency margin stipulated at not less than ₹ 100 crore in each case.
- Insurance companies will deposit ₹ 10 crore as security deposit before starting their business.
- In the non-life sector, IRDA would give preference to companies providing health insurance.
- Safeguards for policyholders' funds include specific provision prohibiting investments of policyholders' funds outside India and provision for investment of funds in accordance with policy directions of the IRDA, including social and infrastructural investments.
- Every insurer shall provide life insurance or general insurance policies (including insurance for crops) to the persons residing in the rural sector, workers in the unorganised or informal sector or for economically vulnerable or backward classes of the society and other categories of persons as may be specified by regulations made by the IRDA.
- Failure to fulfill the social obligations would attract a fine of ₹ 25 lakh, in case the obligations are still not fulfilled, license would be cancelled.

Statutory Functions of IRDA are as follows:

- Issue to the applicant a certificate of registration, renew, modify, withdraw, suspend or cancel such registration.
- Protection of the interests of the policyholders in matters concerning assigning of policy, nomination by policyholders, insurable interest, settlement of insurance claim, surrender value of policy and other terms and conditions of contracts of insurance.
- Specifying requisite qualifications, code of conduct and practical training for intermediaries or insurance intermediaries and agents.
- Specifying the code of conduct for surveyors and loss assessors.
- Promoting efficiency in the conduct of insurance business.
- Promoting and regulating professional organisations connected with insurance and reinsurance business.
- Levying fees and other charges for carrying out the purposes of the Act.
- Calling for information from, undertaking inspection of, conducting enquiries and investigations including audit of the insurers, intermediaries, insurance intermediaries and other organisations connected with the insurance business.

- Control and regulation of rates, advantages, terms and conditions that may be offered by the insurers in respect of general insurance business not so controlled and regulated by the Tariff Advisory Committee under Section 64U of the Insurance Act 1938 (4 of 1938).
- Specifying the form and manner in which books of accounts shall be maintained and statements of accounts shall be rendered by insurers and other insurance intermediaries.
- Regulating investment of funds by insurance companies.
- Regulating maintenance of margin of solvency.
- Adjudication of disputes between insurers and intermediaries or insurance intermediaries.
- Supervising the functioning of the Tariff Advisory Committee.
- Specifying the percentage of the premium income of the insurer to finance schemes for promoting and regulating professional organisations referred to in the clause (f).
- Specifying the percentage of life insurance business and general insurance business to be undertaken by the insurers in the rural and social sector.
- Exercising such other powers as may be prescribed.

Policy Developments

Several policy initiatives were taken in the insurance sector during 2007. In the insurance sector, the major policy initiatives included are as follows:

(1) Detariffing of the general insurance industry. This measure was aimed at providing better choices to policyholders, differentiated rates consistent with the level of risks borne as well as overall improvement in risk management.

(2) Obligations towards the rural and social sectors. The IRDA Regulations, 2002, had laid down the obligations of the insurers for the first five years of operations. Amendments to the regulations incorporating the obligations of the insurers up to the tenth year and thereafter have been notified during 2007.

(3) IRDA had done away with the tariffs on the rates of general insurance products from January 1, 2007. IRDA has advised all insurance companies to furnish details of the initiatives taken to promote micro insurance as a viable business opportunity, with particular reference to understanding the constraints faced by them. With a view to synergising the efforts of all state governments which are promoting the poverty alleviation programmes, the IRDA has requested the state governments to publicise the concept of micro insurance through their various agencies.

(4) While permitting foreign participating in the ventures set up by the private sector, the government restricted participation of the foreign joint venture partner through the FDI route to 26 per cent of the paid-up equity of the insurance company.

(5) Every insurer is required to maintain a required solvency margin as per Section 64VA of the Insurance Act 1938. Every insurer shall maintain an excess of the value of assets over the amount of liabilities of not less than an amount prescribed by the IRDA, which is referred to as a required solvency margin. In case of life insurers, the required solvency margin is the higher of an amount of ₹ 50 crore and a sum which is based on a formula given in the said regulations. In case of general insurers, the required solvency

margin, shall be maximum of the following amounts: Fifty crore of rupees (one hundred crore of rupees in case of re-insurer); or a sum equivalent to twenty per cent of net premium income; or a sum equivalent to thirty per cent of net incurred claims, subject to credit for reinsurance in computing net premiums and net incurred claims being actual but a percentage, determined by the regulations, not exceeding fifty per cent. IRDA has set a working solvency margin ratio (ratio of actual solvency margin to the required solvency margin) of 1.5 for all insurers.

As per the IRDA regulations, the insurer has to maintain a separate account relating to the fund of shareholders, and policyholders. The funds of policyholders have to be retained within the country but not the repatriation of profits and dividends. Insurance companies under the new regine have to follow the guidelines given in the context of investment in social sectors and capturing the rural markets. The foreign investment in insurance, as the bill states is crucial to financing infrastructure and better insurance cover. A key to success in opening up the insurance sector in India is regulation.

Some Details of the IRDA Bill

On July 14, 2000, the Chairman of the IRDA, Mr. N. Rangachary set forth a set of regulations in an extraordinary issue of the Indian Gazette that details of the regulation.

Regulations

The **first** covers the Insurance Advisory Committee that sets out the rules and regulation.

The **second** stipulates that the "Appointed Actuary" has to be a Fellow of the Actuarial Society of India. Given that there has been a dearth of actuaries in India with the qualification of a Fellow of the Actuarial Society of India, this becomes a requirement of tall order. As a result, some companies have not been able to attract a qualified Appointed Actuary (Dasgupta, 2001). The IRDA is also in the process of replacing the Actuarial Society of India by a newly formed institution to be called the Chartered Institute of Indian Actuarial (modeled after the Institute of Actuaries of London). Curiously, for life insurers the Appointed Actuary has to be an internal company employee, but he or she may be an external consultant if the company happens to be a non-life insurance company.

Third, the Appointed Actuary would be responsible for reporting to the IRDA a detailed account of the company.

Fourth, insurance agents should have at least a high school diploma along with training of 100 hours from a recognised institution. More than a dozen institutions have been recognised by the IRDA for training insurance agents.

Fifth, the IRDA has set up strict guidelines on asset and liability management of the insurance companies along with solvency margin requirements. Initial margins are set high (compared with developed countries). The margins vary with the lines of business (for example, fire insurance has a lower margin than aviation insurance).

Sixth, the disclosure requirements have been kept rather vague. This has been done despite the recommendations to the contrary by the Mukherjee Committee recommendations.

Seventh, all the insurers are forced to provide some coverage for the rural sector.

- In respect of a life insurer,
  - Five per cent in the first financial year;
  - Seven per cent in the second financial year;
  - Ten per cent in the third financial year;
  - Twelve per cent in the fourth financial year;
  - Fifteen per cent in the fifth year (of total policies written direct in that year).
- In respect of a general insurer.
  - Two per cent in the first financial year;
  - Three per cent in the second financial year;
  - Five per cent thereafter (of total gross premium income written direct in that year).

VII. INDIAN INSURANCE SCENARIO – POST 2000

As per the World Insurance Report published by the Reinsurance major Swiss Re, the global insurance premium for the calendar year 2009 was US $ 4066 billion which was 1.1 (inflation adjusted) per cent lower than US $ 4220 billion reported during the previous calendar year 2008. The share of life insurance business was 57 per cent in total premium collection. During 2009, the premium in the life insurance business fell by 2 per cent on account of double digit decline in premium collection in USA and UK.

The first year premium which is a measure of new business secured, underwritten by the life insurers in India, during 2009-10 was ₹ 1,09,894 crore as compared to ₹ 87,331 crore in 2008-09 registering a growth of 25.84 per cent against a negative growth rate of 6.81 per cent during 2008-09.

The total insurance premium underwritten by the life insurance sector in 2009-10 was ₹ 2,65,450 crore as against ₹ 221785 in the financial year 2008-09, registering a growth rate of 19.69 per cent (which was 10.15 per cent in 2008-09). Private sector insurers recorded 23.06 per cent growth in 2009-10 (against growth rate of 25.09 per cent in 2008-09) in their premium income and LIC recorded 18.30 per cent growth (against 5.01 per cent growth in 2008-09).

Registered Insurers in India

Since opening of the sector, the number of participants in the insurance business has gone up from six insurers (including Life Insurance Corporation of India, four public sector non-life insurers and the General Insurance Corporation as the national insurer) in the year 2000 to 48 insurers operating in life, non-life and reinsurance segments (including specialised insurers, *viz.*, Export Credit Guarantee Corporation and Agriculture Insurance Company). Three of the non-life insurance companies, *viz.*, Star Health and Alliance Insurance Company, Apollo Munich and Health Insurance Company and Max Bupa Health insurance Company function as stand-alone health insurance companies. Of the twenty-two private Insurance companies which have set up operations in the life segment, post opening up of the sector twenty are in joint venture with foreign partners. Of the seventeen insurers (including all three health insurers) who have commenced operation in non-life segment, sixteen are in collaboration with foreign partners.

Table No. 10.1

Registered Insurers in India (As on 30th September 2010)

Type of Business	*Public Sector*	*Private Sector*	*Total*
Life Insurance	1	22	23
Non-life Insurance	6*	18**	24
Reinsurance	1	0	1
Total	8	40	48

* Includes specialised insurance companies Export Credit Guarantee Corporation of India Ltd., and Agricultural Insurance Company of India Ltd.

** Includes 3 Stand-alone Health Insurance Companies — Star Health and Allied Insurance Co., Apollo Munich Health Insurance Co., and Max Bupa Health Insurance Co. Includes L&T General Insurance Co. Ltd which was granted registration in 2010-11.

Unit Linked Insurance

Unit linked products (ULIPs) witnessed 27.44 per cent increase in premium income from ₹ 90,647 crore in 2008-09 to ₹ 1,15,521 crore in 2009-10. On the other hand, the growth of premium income in traditional products was lower at 14.33 per cent with premium income increasing to ₹ 1,49,929 crore as against ₹ 1,31,138 crore in 2008-09. The share of unit linked products in total premium increased to 43.52 per cent in 2009-10 as against 40.87 per cent in 2008-09.

Table No. 10.2

Insurance Penetration and Density in India

Year	*Life*		*Non-life*		*Industry*	
	Density (US $)	*Penetration (%)*	*Density (US $)*	*Penetration (%)*	*Density (US $)*	*Penetration (%)*
2001	9.1	2.15	2.4	0.56	11.5	2.71
2002	11.7	2.59	3.0	0.67	14.7	3.26
2003	12.9	2.26	3.5	0.62	16.4	2.88
2004	15.7	2.53	4.0	0.64	19.7	3.17
2005	18.3	2.53	4.4	0.61	22.7	3.14
2006	33.2	4.10	5.2	0.60	38.4	4.80
2007	40.4	4.00	6.2	0,60	46.6	4.70
2008	41.2	4.00	6.2	0.60	47.4	4.60
2009	47.7	4.60	6.7	0.60	54.3	5.20

Insurance Density and Insurance Penetration in India

The potential and performance of the insurance sector is universally assessed with reference to two parameters, *viz.*, **insurance penetration and insurance density.**

Insurance Penetration is defined as the ratio of premium underwritten in a given year to the Gross Domestic Product (GDP) and **Insurance Density** is defined as the ratio of premium underwritten in a given year to the total population (measured in US $ for convenience of comparison).

Since opening up of Indian insurance sector for private participation, India has reported increase in both, insurance density and penetration and the increase has been entirely contributed by the life insurance sector. The insurance density of life insurance sector has gone up from

US $ 9.1 to 47.7 in 2009 and the insurance penetration of the life insurance sector has gone up from 2.15 per cent in 2001 to 4.60 per cent in 2009.

Table No. 10.3

Investment of Life Insurers: Instrument-wise (As on 31st March)

(₹ in Crores)

Form of Investment	*Amount*	*Percentage*	*Amount*	*Percentage*	*Amount*	*Percentage*
1. Central Govt. Securities	296687.46	46.88	316010	42.50	361520	41.39
2. State Government and Other Approved Securities	85198.11	13.46	107190	14.41	136998	15.68
3. Housing and Infrastructure	63262.13	10.00	66673	8.97	72439	8.29
4. Approved Investments	145553.71	22.99	202469	27.23	245987	28.16
5. Other Investments	42190.44	6.67	51260	6.89	56592	6.48
A Total (1+2+3+4+5)	**632891.85**	**100**	**743602**	**100.00**	**873536**	**100.00**
ULIP Funds						
6. Approved Investments	111629.43	83.88	151490	87.69	293114	88.30
7. Other Investments	21448.05	16.12	21273	12.31	38505	11.61
B Total (6+7)	**133077.48**	**100**	**172763**	**100.00**	**331619**	**100.00**
Gross Total (A+B)	**765969.33**		**916365**		**1205155**	

The Market Share

The share of LIC of India in total life insurance business has been declining gradually from 100 per cent in 2000-01 to 85.57 per cent in 2005-06 and to around 70 per cent for two consecutive years 2008-09 and 2009-2010.

Table No. 10.4

Market Share of Life Insurers

Insurer		*2005-06*	*2006-07*	*2007-08*	*2008-09*	*2009-10*
Regular Premium	LIC	64.59	65.89	47.77	38.77	43.13
	PVT. SECTOR	35.41	34.11	52.23	61.23	56.87
	TOTAL	**100.00**	**100.00**	**100.00**	**100.00**	**100.00**
Single Premium	LIC	84.35	86.96	86.99	90.44	92.19
	PVT. SECTOR	15.85	13.04	13.01	9.56	7.81
	TOTAL	**100.00**	**100.00**	**100.00**	**100.00**	**100.00**
First Year Premium	LIC	73.52	74.32	64.02	61.12	65.08
	PVT. SECTOR	26.48	25.68	35.98	38.88	34.92
	TOTAL	**100.00**	**100.00**	**100.00**	**100.00**	**100.00**

Renewal Premium	LIC	92.82	89.02	83.42	77.24	73.64
	PVT. SECTOR	7.18	10.98	16.58	22.76	26.36
	TOTAL	**100.00**	**100.00**	**100.00**	**100.00**	**100.00**
Total Premium	LIC	85.75	81.90	74.39	70.92	70.10
	PVT. SECTOR	14.25	18.10	25.61	29.8	19.29
	TOTAL	**100.00**	**100.00**	**100.00**	**100.00**	**100.00**

Source: IRDA Annual Report 2008-09, p. 11, 2009-10, p. 16

Table No. 10.5

New Policies Issued by Life Insurers (In Lakh)

Insurer	*2008-09*	*2009-10*
LIC	359.13 (- 4.52)	388.63 (8.21)
Private sector	150.11 (13.19)	143.62 (- 4.32)
Total	509.24 (0.10)	532.25 (4.52)

Table No. 10.6

Total Investments of Life Insurers – Investment-wise

	31-03-2008		*31-03-2009*	
Traditional Products	*Annual*	*Percentage*	*Annual*	*Percentage*
1. Central Government Securities	296687.46	46.88	**316009.75**	**42.50**
2. State Government and Other Approved Securities	85198.11	13.46	**107189.59**	**14.41**
3. Housing & Infrastructure	63262.13	10.00	**66673.33**	**8.97**
4. Approved Investments	145553.71	22.99	**202468.97**	**27.23**
5. Other Investments	42190.44	6.67	**51260.39**	**6.89**
A. Total (1+2+3+4+5)	**632891.85**	**100.00**	**743602.02**	**100.00**
ULIP Funds				
6. Approved Investments	111629.43	83.88	**151489.89**	**87.69**
7. Other Investments	21448.05	16.12	**21272.87**	**12.31**
B. Total (6+7)	**133077.48**	**100.00**	**172762.76**	**100.00**
Grand Total (A +B)	**765969.33**		**916364.78**	

Table No. 10.7

Financial Savings of the Household Sector and Share of Insurance

	2003-04	*2004-05*	*2005-06*	*2006-07*	*2007-08*	*2008-09*
Financial Savings (Gross)	100.0 (13.8)	100.0 (13.9)	100.0 (16.7)	100.0 (15.8)	100.0 (15.2)	100.0 (14.0)
1. Currency	11.2 (1.5)	8.5 (1.2)	8.9 (1.5)	10.2 (1.6)	11.40 (1.7)	12.50 (1.8)
2. Deposits	38.3 (5.3)	37.2 (5.2)	47.0 (7.8)	49.1 (7.7)	52.2 (7.9)	58.5 (8.2)
(a) With Banks	**37.4**	36.5	46.0	47.8	50.4	54.9
(b) With Non-banking companies	**1.0**	0.8	0.1	0.2	0.5	1.8

(c) With co operative banks and societies	**0.0**	0.0	0.0	0.0	0.0	0.0
(d) Trade debt (net)	**0.0**	0.0	0.0	1.0	1.3	1.8
3. Shares and Debentures	0.1	1.1	5.1	9.0	12.4	2.6
	(0.0)	(0.4)	(1.9)	(1.4)	(1.9)	(0.4)
(a) Pvt. corporate business	**1.1**	1.4	1.3	3.7	4.4	4.2
(b) Banking	**0.0**	0.1	0.1	0.0	0.1	0.1
(c) Units of UTI	**-2.3**	-0.7	-0.1	0.0	0.0	-0.4
(d) Bonds of Public Sector Undertakings	**0.0**	0.0	0.0	0.0	0.0	0.1
(e) Mutual fund (other than UTI)	**1.2**	0.4	3.8	5.3	7.9	-1.4
4. Claims on Government	23	24.5	14.6	3.0	-4.0	-3.1
	(3.2)	(3.4)	(2.4)	(0.5)	(- 0.6)	(-0.4)
(a) Investment in Govt. securities	**7.5**	4.9	2.4	0.3	-2.1	-4.5
(b) Investment in Small savings etc.	**15.5**	19.6	12.2	2.7	-1.9	1.4
5. Insurance Funds	13.7	15.7	14.0	17.7	18.0	20.1
	(1.9)	(2.2)	(2.3)	(2.8)	(2.7)	(2.8)
(a) Life Insurance Funds	**13**	15.1	13.4	17.1	17.4	19.5
(b) Postal Insurance	**0.3**	0.3	0.3	0.3	0.4	0.3
(c) State Insurance	**0.5**	0.2	0.3	0.3	0.2	0.3
6. Provident and Pension Funds	13.6	13.0	10.5	11.1	9.9	9.5
	(1.9)	(1.8)	(1.7)	(1.7)	(1.5)	(1.3)

Table No. 10.8

Life Insurance Premium – First Year (Including Single Premium)

(₹ in Crores)

Insurer	*2003-04*	*2004-05*	*2005-06*	*2006-07*	*2007-08*	*2008-09*	*2009-10*
LIC	17347.62	20653.06	28515.87	56223.56	59996.57	53179.08	71521.90
	(8.58)	(19.05)	(38.07)	(97.17)	(6.71)	(-11.36)	(34.49)
ING Vaisya	72.10	282.42	283.98	467.66	704.44	688.95	642.43
HDFC Standard	209.33	486.15	1042.65	1648.85	2685.37	2651.11	3257.51
Birla Sun	449.86	621.31	678.12	882.72	1965.01	2823.91	2960.01
ICICI Prudential	750.84	1584.34	2602.50	5162.13	8034.75	6483.92	6334.09
Kotak Mahindra	125.51	373.99	396.06	614.94	1106.62	1343.03	1333.98
TATA AIG	181.59	297.55	464.53	644.82	964.51	1142.67	1322.01
SBI Life	207.05	484.85	827.82	2563.84	4792.82	5386.64	7040.74
Bajaj Allianz	179.55	857.45	2716.77	4302.74	6674.48	4491.43	4451.10
Max New York	137.28	233.63	471.36	912.11	1597.83	1842.91	1849.08
Metlife	23.41	57.52	148.53	340.44	825.35	1144.70	1061.85
Reliance	27.21	91.83	193.56	932.11	2751.05	3513.98	3920.78
Aviva	76.96	192.29	407.12	721.35	1053.98	724.56	798.37
Sahara	—	1.74	26.34	43.00	122.12	134.01	124.83
Shriram Life	—	—	10.33	181.17	309.99	314.47	419.50
Bharati Axa	—	—	7.78	113.24	292.93	437.43	
Future Generali	—	—	—	—	2.49	149.97	486.08
IDBI Forties	—	—	—	—	11.93	316.78	400.56
Kanara HSBC	—	—	—	—	—	296.41	622.62
DLF Pramerica	—	—	—	—	—	3.37	150.37
Aegon Religare	—	—	—	—	—	31.21	37.38
Star Union Dai Ichi	—	—	—	—	—	50.19	519.87

India First		—	—	—	—	—	201.59
Private sector	2440.71	5564.57	10269.67	19425.65	33715.95	33827.15	201.59
	(152.74)	(127.99)	(84.55)	(88.84)	(73.56)	(0.33)	(12.36)
Total	19788.33	26217.64	38785.54	75649.21	93712.52	87006.23	109894.02
	(16.80)	(32.49)	(47.94)	(94.96)	(23.88)	(-7.16)	25.84

Note: 1 Figures in the bracket represent the growth over the previous year in per cent.
2 Represents business not started.

Profits of Life Insurers

The experience of the insurance market globally indicates that the companies in the life sector take seven to ten years to break-even.

Out of the 23 life insurers in operation during 2009-10, eight companies reported profits, *viz.,* LIC, ICICI Prudential, Kotak Mahindra, SBI, Metlife, Baja Allianz, Sahara India and Aegon Religare.

Life insurance industry requires infusion of capital at regular intervals to fund the new business strain and to expand their infrastructure base, including expenses on initial operations, training costs for development of the distribution channels, creating niche markets and achieving reasonable levels of persistency.

LIC of India reported net profit of ₹ 1,061 crore in 2009-10, an increase of 10.80 per cent over ₹ 957 crore in 2008-09. ICICI Prudential reported a net profit of ₹ 258 crore after incurring losses for eight consecutive years, after setting up operations. Kotak Mahindra has reported a profit for last two years (*i.e.,* 2008-09 and 2009-10), SBI Life for last three years, Metlife for last two years and Aegon Religare also has reported profit for last two years

Dividends paid by the life insurers

Insurer	*2008-09*	*2009-10*
Public	929.12	1030.92
Private	—	—
Total	929.12	1030.92

(B) UNIT TRUST OF INDIA AND MUTUAL FUNDS

I. UTI

The importance of unit trusts in mobilising savings of small savers was recognised in early twentieth century and the need for setting up these trusts was stressed by the Shroff Committee in 1954. However, the Unit Trust of India (UTI) was set up only in 1964 as a public sector financial institution.

The unit trusts are highly popular in the UK, USA and Canada and they have mobilised great amounts of resources. They enable small savers to gain advantage and reap the benefit of professional management of portfolio which helps in earning a relatively higher rate of returns than what they would have otherwise earned if they had invested their small savings independently. Such trusts enable the small savers to have a diversified portfolio and pooling of individual risks. In addition to this, the higher degree of liquidity due to the redemption feature of units induces large number of small savers to purchase the units of the trust.

The prime objective of the UTI is to encourage and mobilise the savings of the community and channelise them into productive investments and thus help to promote growth and diversification of the economy.

Initial Capital

The initial capital of Unit Trust was statutorily fixed at ₹ 5 crore which was to be contributed by the Reserve Bank (₹ 2.5 crore), the LIC (₹ 0.75 crore), the SBI and the Associate banks (₹ 0.75 crore) and other financial institutions and banks (₹ 1.0 crore). In February 1976, the initial capital held by the RBI was transferred to the Industrial Development Bank of India (IDBI) and UTI became an associate institution of the IDBI.

Since the Trust does not have any share capital, it operates on the principle of *"no profit, no loss"* as all income and gains, net of all costs and development charges, ultimately go back to the investors of the respective schemes.

Unit Capital

The main source of the funds of the UTI is the unit capital raised from the sale of units to the public under various schemes. The most popular scheme of UTI is the Unit Scheme 1964 (US-64). Under this scheme, the units sold are of the face value ₹ 10 each but their market price is higher than this value and it is periodically determined.

Various Schemes of UTI

The Unit Trust of India sells units under various schemes, plans and funds. The total number of schemes or plans in operation were 84 in 1998-99 out of which 28 were open-ended and 51 close-ended. The Unit Scheme 1964 still continues to be the most popular scheme of the Trust. It has given as high as 26 per cent dividend to its investors in 1993, 1994 and 1995 and in the next two years it was 20 per cent each.

The UTI introduced a reinvestment plan in 1966-67 (for automatic reinvestment of dividends to US-64 unitholders).

In 1971, the UTI introduced a unique scheme combining the benefits of insurance with a steady growth in investment, called Unit Linked Insurance Plan (ULIP). It had a contractual period of 10 years initially, which was later extended to 15 years.

In the decade of 1980s, the UTI emerged as a large All-India financial institution. During 1981-84, it launched many new schemes. For example, an open-ended fund for charitable and religious trusts and registered societies (1981), open-ended capital gains unit scheme (1983) which provided tax shelter for income from capital gains.

Children's Gift Growth Fund (CGGF), an open-ended fund and Mastershare, a close-ended growth fund were launched in 1986. The Unit Trust of India also established Indian offshore funds.

Master Plus 1991, Master Equity Plan 1992 and the (MEP series) Master Gain 1992 were some other popular schemes of UTI.

The monthly income schemes also have become very popular over the years.

The 'Rajalakshmi Unit Scheme' 1992 for girls below the age of 5, senior citizen's unit plan for the people above the age of 58 are the schemes of UTI designed to cater to the needs of different age groups and their preferences.

The various schemes of the UTI are open-ended or closed-ended — like Growth schemes, Cumulative income schemes, Special purpose schemes and Tax saving schemes and so on.

The UTI now has many associate institutions which include UTI Securities Exchange Ltd., UTI Bank, UTI Investors Services Ltd., etc.

The major financial instrument introduced by UTI is 'Units', which are of two types: (a) ordinary unit with a face value of ₹ 10, and (b) capital unit with a face value of ₹ 100. These units are highly liquid as the UTI repurchases them at the declared price. These units are approved securities and are accepted by banks while granting loans.

The total assets of the Trust have increased manifold from ₹ 24 crore in 1964-65 to ₹ 59,618.64 crore in 1994-95. This is due to attractive dividends on certain schemes, launching of more and more new schemes, large marketing network and giving a number of tax benefits to the investors. Total outstanding unit capital of the UTI has grown from ₹ 19 crore in 1964-65 to ₹ 44,381 crore in 1995-96.

The table below shows some important indicators regarding expansion of the UTI business.

Table No. 10.9
Expansion in UTI Business

(₹ in Crores)

Year	*Sales*	*Repurchases*	*Outstanding Unit Capital*	*Investible Fund*	*Repurchases as % of Sales*
1970-71	18	3	92	105	17.78
1975-76	29	11	161	184	37.93
1979-80	58	14	391	468	24.81
1985-86	892	63	2,586	3,218	7.06
1990-91	4,543	1,081	16,409	21,376	23.74
1995-96	6,373	7,643	44,381	56,620	119.92

Investment Pattern of the UTI

The Government and the Securities Exchange Board of India (SEBI) have laid down some norms for Trust investment, such as the investment by the UTI in any one company should not exceed 5 per cent of its total investible funds or 10 per cent of the value of the outstanding securities of that company, whichever is lower. The UTI also cannot invest more than 5 per cent of its funds in the initial issue of any new company. This avoids the concentration of funds in a few companies and reduces risks of investment.

The UTI has been investing a major part of its funds in the private corporate sector. This ratio was as high as 90-95 per cent upto the mid-80s, and now it has come down to around 80 per cent.

The UTI investment in the government securities has varied between 10 per cent to 20 per cent. It had gone up to 24 per cent in 1990-91 which came down to 11 per cent in 1995-96.

In 1995-96, the proportion of UTI investment in corporate shares (equity and preference) was 50 per cent and that of debentures was around 25 per cent.

The other components of the UTI investment have been term loans, special deposits and other investments with the banks.

The Return on Investment

The return on the investments in various schemes of UTI has been very impressive. For example US-64 has given as high as 26 per cent dividends. But ups and downs have been quite sharp in certain years.

The ULIP has given a return on investment ranging between 10 per cent to 15 per cent plus life cover and tax benefits.

In 1998-99, the UTI had as many as 84 operating schemes and plans and it had 45 million outstanding units holding accounts.

Problems Faced: Government Intervention

UTI's US-64 scheme faced repeated problems and the Government took initiative to resolve the problems and protect the interests of investors. Government's financial interventions are accompanied by the structural improvements.

An analysis of the trends in market share of MFs reveals that UTI suffered significant loss in market share from around 85 per cent in 1996 to 50 per cent in 2001.

Resources Mobilisation by UTI

(₹ in Crores)

	1999-2000	*2000-01*	*2001-02*
Gross Inflow	13698	12413	
Redemption	9150	12090	
Net Inflow	4548	323	(–) 7284

Source: Economic Survey, Government of India.

Resources mobilisation by UTI declined in 2000-01 and further in 2001-02 registering an outflow of ₹7,284 crores. Government's Financial Interventions: Us 64 Scheme

1. Special Unit Scheme: One June 29,1999, Government of India did a buyback from UTI of PSU shares at book value, which was higher than the then prevailing market value. This effectively amounted to a transfer of ₹ 1,528 crore to the investors in US-64.

2. Limited Repurchase Facility (July 2001): Investors were given a window through which upto 3000 units (per investor) could be sold back to UTI at an administratively determined price, which started from ₹ 10 in August 2001, and would go by ₹ 0.1 per month till it reached ₹ 12 in May 2003. For each unit repurchased by UTI at a price above NAV, Government would make the difference to UTI so that the investors exiting would not do so at the expense of investors who did not exit. This programme covered roughly 40 per cent of the assets of US-64.

3. Extended Repurchase Facility (Dec. 2001): The limit of 3000 units was raised to 5000 units. In addition, investors above 5000 units were given an assurance that if they exited in May 2003, they would get the higher of NAV or ₹ 10. Government would make up the gap between repurchase price and NAV experienced by UTI.

Restructuring of UTI

Reform package: as approved by Government on Aug. 31, 2002.

- The Government would honour the redemption guarantee for US-64 unitholders. The liability in this account was estimated to be about ₹ 6,000 crore. In respect of the assured return schemes, interest will be reset at a lower level. The shortfall in these schemes was estimated to be about ₹ 8,561 crore.
- UTI would be divided into two parts:

  (a) UTI-I and (b) UTI-II

(i) UTI-I : US-64 for which assured repurchase prices have been announced.

(ii) UTI-II: all net asset value (NAV) based scheme.

- Government will meet its obligations annually to cover any deficit in UTI-I.
- UTI-I will be managed by a Government appointed administrator and a team of advisers nominated by Government.
- UTI-II will for the time being be managed by professional chairman and Board of Trustees and will be disinvested.
- UTI Act would be repealed and both UTI-I and UTI-II will be restructured as per SEBI regulations.
- The operational aspect including, but not limited to distribution of assets and liabilities between UTI-I and UTI-II etc., would be worked out by Government.

The following decisions were announced by Government on Sept. 3, 2002.

- All sales and purchase of stocks will take place in UTI-II based upon the market perception of its management.
- Fresh units of US-64 in its present form will not be issued by UTI-I.

Initiative undertaken by UTI

- making US-64 NAV-based effective Jan. 1, 2002.
- disclosure of portfolio for all schemes including US-64 on a monthly basis.
- daily announcement of NAVs.
- introduction of special repurchase facility with monthly increasing price support for investments upto 3000 units per investor from Aug. 1, 2001 and upto 5000 units for investor from Jan. 1, 2002.
- price support of ₹ 10 per unit from May 31, 2003 for holdings in excess of 5000 units per investor.
- issue of detailed investment manual and comprehensive delegation of powers.
- setting up of Risk Management Department.
- Setting up of Asset Reconstruction Fund for focussed effort for recovery of NPAs.
- performance linked incentivisation for officers.
- commissioning of Central Processing Centre and Central Data Centre and Centralisation of all back office functions.
- implementation of integrated front office automation system.

Source: Report on Trends and Progress of Banking in India, RBI 2001-02.

II. MUTUAL FUNDS

A mutual fund is an intermediary which buys and sells securities on behalf of the unit holders. It enables small and medium income earners to have high and secure rate of return on their savings.

Mutual Funds (MFs) can broadly be classified as public sector MFs and private sector MFs. The entry of private sector in Mutual Funds' industry was allowed in 1993. All the MFs, *i.e.,* UTI and those sponsored by the banks and the Financial Institutions are the Public Sector MFs. The MFs have schemes operating domestically and even offshore funds.

Mutual funds have now emerged as an important segment of financial markets in the country. They play a crucial role in channelising the savings of millions of individuals/households from different parts of the country into investments in both equity and debt instruments.

During the year 1998-99, three new private sector MFs were registered with SEBI, taking the total number of Mutual Funds (excluding UTI) registered with SEBI to 40 as on March 31, 1999. Of the 40 MFs registered with SEBI as many as 31 mutual funds were set up in the private sector during 1990s.

As per International rating agency — Moody's Investor Service, Indian MF market is beginning to mature with the entry of more number of players as under:

Banks and FIs: Banks: SBI, Canara Bank, Punjab National Bank, Bank of Baroda.
FIs: ICICI, IDBI.
Insurance Companies: GIC, LIC.

Business Houses in Private Sector: Reliance, Tata, Birla.

NBFCs: Sundaram, Cholamandalam.

Foreign Cos.: Pioneer, Cazenove, ING, Prudential, Sun, Morgan Stanley, Jardine Fleming, F&C, Templeton, Newton, Alliance, Standard Chartered, Dundee and Zurich.

Three new offshore funds launched in 1998-99.

India debt Fund : a 100 per cent fund

India PSU Fund : an equity fund investing exclusively in Public Sector units

India IT Fund : an equity fund investing predominantly in information technology sector.

Recently, there is a trend towards consolidation in MF industry through mergers and acquisitions to seek advantages of economies of scale in terms of enhanced ability to offer superior and wider range of products and invest in technology and resources for improved customer service.

Birla Sun Life : acquisition of Apple Mutual Fund

Zurich India : took over 20th century MF

Tata MF : acquisition of Indian Bank MF

The government and SEBI laid down certain norms for the investment of funds raised by MFs. To give stable, regular and growing income to the investors, the MFs devise a diversified portfolio.

Cumulative Net Assets of MFs (as on Dec. 31, 2001)

Sector	Amount (₹ in crore)	Per cent to total
Private	42,582	41.8
Public	8059	7.9
UTI	51,181	50.3
Total	1,01,822	100.0

(Rs. in Crores)

Date	Amount (Cumulative) (Public + Private Sector)	(Private Sector)	Share of Private Sector %
April 2002	1,02,831	44,185	42.9
April 2003	89,238	65,398	73.3
March 2004	1,43,688	1,11,492	77.6

Source: Economic Survey: Government of India, 2003-04.

The growth of MFs has a striking feature of a significant share of private sector. The overall assets of MFs now account for 5.10% of GDP.

Gold Exchange Trade Funds (GETFs)

ETF is a Mutual Fund Scheme that allows the investors to trade in gold. Gold can be viewed as investment vehicle as units of Gold ETF could be bought and sold on stock exchanges. Each unit represents 1 gm of pure gold. Two GETF have been launched — Benchmark GETF, UTI GETF.

Units traded on National Stock Exchange

April 23, 2007 : average 2500 units

May 21, 2007 : average 12000 units

Policy Developments

- SEBI tightened the disclosure norms for the MFs to help investors take more informed decisions. A common format was prescribed for all MF schemes to disclose their portfolio at half-yearly intervals. MFs are required to disclose investments in various types of instruments.
- SEBI laid down detailed investment and disclosure norms for employees of asset management companies and Trustee companies. All asset management companies are required to maintain records in support of each investment decision.
- Detailed guidelines on disclosure and reporting requirements issued to MFs for investment in foreign securities.
- SEBI decided to make mandatory for all MFs to appoint agents/distributors who have obtained Association of MFs of India (AMFI) certification.

A scheme of Money Market Mutual Funds (MMMFs) was introduced by the RBI in April 1992. The banks, financial institutions and also the institutions in private sector are allowed to set up MMMFs.

Table No. 10.9
Resources Mobilised by the Mutual Funds

(₹ *in Crores*)

Mutual Fund	*1993-94*	*1994-95*	*1995-96*	*1996-97*	*1997-98*	*1998-99*	*1999-00*	*2000-01*	*2001-02*	*2002-03*	*2003-04*	*2004-05*	*2005-06*	*2006-07*	*2007-08*	*2008-09*
I. Bank Sponsored (1 to 6)	148.1	765.5	113.3	5.9	236.9	–88.3	338.0	248	863	1033.4	4526.2	706.5	5365	3033	7786	4489
1. SBIMF	105.0	218.3	76.0	2.6	190.1	–71.8	659.0	251.5	613.7	686.4	1927.4	1024.3	5250	3208	7339	2617
2. Canbank MF	43.1	205.6	2.7	1.7	46.8	–16.5	–361.0	–5.4	140.2	237.2	494.9	–10.8	56	–96	295	1317
3. Indian bank MF	—	94.5	—	—	—	—	—	—	—	—	—	—	—	—	—	—
4. Bank of India MF	—	53.5	—	—	—	—	—	—	—	—	—	—	—	—	—	—
5. PNB MF	—	156.0	10.3	—	—	—	39.6	2.1	50.4	14.1	1841.1	—	—	—	—	—
6. BOB MF	—	37.8	24.3	1.6	—	—	1.7	–0.4	58.5	95.7	262.8	–307.0	29	–79	152	556
II. Financial Institution Sponsored (7 to 9)	238.6	576.3	234.8	136.9	2084	546.8	295.5	1272.8	406.8	861.5	1126.7		2112	4226	2178	5954
7. GIC MF	227.2	319.7	64.9	–32.4	-19.2	–12.1	–268.3	–43.4	–59.5	861.6	786.8	3383.5	—	—	—	—
8. LIC MF	11.4	69.0	116.5	169.3	99.8	348.4	284.5	566.0	640.4	–96.7	–146.7	32.5	2112	4226	2178	5984
9. IDBI MF	—	187.6	53.4	—	123.0	210.5	279.2	750.3	–177.9	578.0	933.5	3351.0	—	—	—	—
III. Unit Trust of India	9297	8611.0	–6314	–3043	2875	170.0	4548.0	322.0	–7284.0	380.3	—	—	3424	7326	10678	–4112
(UTI)				(-2877)	(–855)	(2592)	(1300)	(5762)	(1201.)	–9434.1	1049.9	–2467.2				
IV. Private Sector MF	1559.5	1321.8	133.0	863.6	748.6	2066.9	16937.4	9292.1	16134.1	12122.2	41509.8	7933.1	41581	79477	163356	–28685
Total I + II + III + IV	11243.2	11274.6	-5832.9	-2036.7	4063.9	2695.4	22116.8	11134.7	10119.7	4583.0	47872.0	2788.9	52482	94062	183998	–22355

Source: Handbook of Statistics on Indian Economy, RBI 2008-09.

All schemes of Indian Bank MF, Bank of India, MF PNB MF, GIC MF and IDBI MF are transferred to other MFs. In case of GICMF the schemes have been transferred to Canbank MF and in cases of PNB MF and IDBI MF the transfer has been to a private sector MF (Principal MF).

The MMMFs are those mutual funds which invest money primarily in money market instruments of very short maturity and high quality. The progress of MMMFs has not been impressive in India so far.

Recently, initiative was taken by the Government to resolve problems associated with US64 of Unit Trust of India and to liberalise tax treatment and to incomes earned through mutual funds. Some of the mutual funds have introduced limited cheque writing facility by allowing its unitholders to issue cheques against a savings account with a designated bank.

In the mutual fund business in India, UTI plays a very dominative role. In recent years, there has been a proliferation of mutual funds and their schemes. However, the mutual fund business is highly concentrated fund-wise and scheme-wise and the small savers have not really benefited greatly from the various schemes of the mutual funds. Although much larger funds are now available for investment in the corporate securities due to these mutual funds, proper regulation of these mutual funds is very necessary for a healthy financial system.

Resources mobilised by mutual funds declined sharply between 1992-93 and 1995-96 at an average annual rate of (–) 37.3 per cent. Resource mobilisation during 1996-97, 1997-98 an 1998-99 was only of the order of ₹ (–) 2,037 crore, ₹ 4,002 crore and ₹ 3,090 crore. It is however, significant to note that of the total resource mobilisation during 1998-99, nearly two-thirds was accounted for by the private sector mutual funds unlike in the past, when public sector mutual funds dominated.

There was an upsurge in resources mobilisation by Mutual Funds in the year 1999-2000 to reach ₹ 22,116.8 crore. Of this, over two-thirds amounting to ₹ 16,937.4 crore was accounted for by the private sector. There has been a decline in this trend in the subsequent years, but improved in the year 2003-04 and further to over Rupees Fifty Thousand Crores during 2005-06. Over 80 per cent of this is the share of private sector MFs.

KEY TERMS

IRDA, Life Insurance, Non-life Insurance, Malhotra Committee, UTI, Mutual Funds.

REVIEW QUESTIONS

1. What are the main segments of the Insurance Business in India?
2. What were the main recommendations of the Malhotra Committee on privatisation of insurance business in India?
3. Discuss the performance of the public and private life insurance companies operating in India in last one decade.
4. Discuss the progress of Non-life insurance business in India in post-privatisation period.
5. Discuss the role of UTI in mobilising savings in Indian financial system.
6. Explain the significance of the Mutual Funds and their performance in Indian financial system.
7. What policy reforms have been introduced in the Mutual fund business in India?

REFERENCES

1. IRDA Annual Reports 2006-07, 2007-08, 2008-09, 2009-10.
2. IRDA Journal, Various Issues.
3. LIC Annual Reports, Various Issues.
4. Yogakshema, Life Insurance Corporation of India.

❑❑❑

11

Small Savings, Provident Fund and Pension Plans

INTRODUCTION

Next to the commercial banks, small savings organisations mobilise the largest volumes of savings in India. They are even ahead of the co operative banks and the UTI in the mobilisation of savings. The small savings schemes are administered through the post offices widely scattered over the country including the large number of villages. Although large branch expansions of the commercial banks has taken place after nationlisation, the post office savings are most preferred by small savers with small incomes in the country.

Small savings are directly available to the Central Government as a part of its budgetary resources and they are shared with the state governments by the Centre. Upto 1970, the states used to receive two thirds of net collections raised in their respective areas as a loan for a period of 10 years. After 1970, for every 5 per cent of receipts obtained in excess of the national average of net or gross collection, the state governments have been getting 2.5 per cent as an additional loan. This is meant for inducing the states to raise more resources but there is no mechanism at present to ensure that the funds raised in a particular area would be spent only there.

In this chapter, following aspects of Small savings are discussed:

11.1 Role of Small Savings

11.2 Characteristics of Small Saving Instruments

11.3 Post Office Savings

11.4 Provident Funds Schemes

11.5 Norms regarding Investments of PFs

11.6 Pension Funds

11.1 ROLE OF SMALL SAVINGS

Small savings can be divided into two groups: (a) post office deposits and (b) saving certificates and bonds. The small savings organisations offer a great variety of financial assets to the people. These assets represent medium-term and long-term investment opportunities. These assets are liquid. For example, in case of recurring deposits, one withdrawal upto 50 per cent of deposit is permitted. The time deposit can be pledged for obtaining loans from banks for meeting a temporary need. The National Saving Certificates also can be pledged for obtaining loans. The Post Office saving bank deposits are as liquid as bank demand deposits. They can be withdrawn by cheque and there are no restrictions on the number of withdrawals. Therefore, they are included by the Reserve Bank as one of the constituents of money supply.

The unit-linked insurance plans and some other schemes provide good insurance coverage to the small savers.

Small savings offer excellent tax benefits for those who fall in the income tax brackets.

Some schemes offer reinvestment plans to those investors who can forgo their current income (and purchasing power) and thereby reduce the inflationary pressures in the economy.

These savings schemes are highly safe investments for the small savers.

11.2 CHARACTERISTICS OF SMALL SAVING INSTRUMENTS

1. Small savings represent medium-term and long-term investment opportunities with regard to maturity, liquidity, safety. They are a good substitute to bank deposits, debentures, government securities and units.
2. The reinvestment plans offer good opportunity to those investors who can forgo current income and are also desirable for mitigating inflation.
3. These assets are liquid for example, in case of Cumulative Time Deposits (CTDs), 50 per cent of the outstanding balance can be withdrawn twice which may be repaid in lump sum or in installments. In case of Recurring Deposits (RDs), one withdrawal upto 50% of deposits is permitted, similarly the National Saving Certificates are pledgeable.
4. Post Office Saving Bank Deposits are as liquid as bank demand deposits. They can be withdrawn by cheque and there are no restrictions on number of withdrawals. The RBI includes these deposits as constituents of money supply in the economy.
5. RD and CTD provide insurance cover to the investor.
6. It gives excellent income tax benefits to income tax payers.

The rate of interest on PF has been raised to 9 per cent per annum. The effective rate of return on provident fund is much higher due to income tax and wealth tax benefits on account of yearly contribution to PF, interest on PF and the wealth in the form of PF.

11.3 POST OFFICE SAVINGS

(i) Post Office Saving Bank Deposits (POSBD) –

This scheme is in operation since 1896. It pays 5.5 per cent rate of interest. The investment limits in case of single account are a minimum ₹ 20 and a maximum of ₹ 50,000 and in case of joint account, it is ₹ 1,00,000. The interest earned on the deposit is tax free but the amount of deposit itself is taxable. The amount of deposit upto ₹ 5 lakh is exempted from the wealth tax. The total outstanding amount in POSBD as on March 1995 was ₹ 5,504 crore.

(ii) Post Office Time Deposits (POTD) –

The post offices have been accepting time deposits of one, three and five year maturity since March 1970 and the deposits of two years maturity since August 1973. The rate of interest on these deposits ranges between 10.5 per cent to 12.5 per cent at present. The interest income is exempted from tax. The deposit amount is eligible form wealth tax exemption upto ₹ 5 lakh but not eligible for income tax rebate. There is no limit on investment in these deposits.

(iii) Post Office Recurring Deposits (PORD) –

This scheme was introduced in April 1970 with a maturity period of five years and carrying an interest rate of 12.5 per cent per annum. There is no limit on the investment in this scheme. (minimum amount ₹ 10). It is eligible for the same tax concessions as the above schemes. Total amount outstanding in PORDs as on March 1995 was ₹ 5320 crore.

(iv) National Savings Certificates (NSCs) –

Issues of seven-year NSCs II, III, IV in 1970 and V in 1974 were introduced earlier. Then two six-year NSC issues VI & VII were introduced in 1981-82. All these were later discontinued. Another six-year NSC issue VIII was introduced in May 1989 on which a compound rate of interest of 12 per cent is paid and unlimited amounts can be invested in it. The interest income from NSCs is not tax free but the amount invested in them qualified for deduction while calculating taxable income. Total amount outstanding in NSC VIII on March 1995 was ₹ 11,866 crores.

(v) Indira Vikas Patra (IVP) and Kisan Vikas Patra (KVP) –

These two schemes were introduced in 1986 and 1988 respectively. Both have a maturity period of 5½ years and give a compound interest rate of 13.43 per cent each.

There is no limit to investment in them but the investment does not enjoy any tax benefits.

In case of Indira Vikas Patra, the value doubles every 5½ years and its purchase price is half of its face value. It does not carry the name of the holder or buyer and it is transferable only by delivery.

The total amount outstanding in IVP and KVP on March 1995 were respectively ₹ 7,972 crore and ₹ 34,305 crore.

(vi) National Saving Scheme (NSS) –

It was introduced in April 1987. It carried 11 per cent interest per year and the maximum investment limit is ₹ 40,000. It carried 100 per cent tax benefit on the amount invested by an investor during a year.

(vii) Post Office Monthly Income Scheme (POMIS) –

This fixed deposit scheme was introduced in 1987, with a maturity period of six years and interest rate per annum 12 per cent. This interest is payable every month. Minimum and maximum investment limits are ₹ 5,000 and ₹ two lakh for a single account and maximum limit ₹ four lakh for a joint account. Interest income is eligible for tax rebate. A bonus of 10 per cent on the deposit amount is payable at the end of six years when total deposit matures. The total amount outstanding as at the end of March 1995 was ₹ 7,164 crore.

The yearly receipts as well as the outstandings of small savings have increased greatly over the years but they have facing a keen competition from the commercial banks especially in rural areas.

The interest on the various small savings schemes were lower than those offered by banks and private non-banking companies before 1970. Afterwards, the interest rates were made comparable and at present, they are more attractive than the rates on bank deposits. The interest rates on small savings are now altered along with the other interest rates in the economy.

As a pert of the need for moving to the low interest rate regime, the reduction by one percentage point in the administered interest rates on PPF and small savings seems to be most appropriate.

11.4 PROVIDENT FUNDS SCHEMES

Mostly salaried people put their savings in provident funds. But the Public Provident Fund (PPF) schemes enables even the non-salary earners to put their savings in this form. In provident fund, salaried people can save and pit small amounts on a regular basis to provide for old age or for the dependent family. The savings in Provident Fund is a contractual obligation and it does not aim at making nay profits or seek any capital growth.

There are a variety of provident fund schemes in operation in India:

(a) Employees' Provident Fund scheme (EPF) covering non-exempted (industrial) establishments.

(b) Provident funds of exempted industrial establishments.

(c) Central and State Government Employees (non-industrial) Provident Fund.

(d) Coal Mines Provident Fund.

(e) Assam Tea Plantations Provident Fund.

(f) Public Provident Fund (PPF).

The **Public Provident Fund** was introduced in 1968. It was earlier operated through the State Bank of India (SBI) and its subsidiaries but since January, 1979 a PPF account can be opened at head Post Offices. It was originally meant for self-employed persons or the general public but now salaried employees can also take advantage of it. Unlike the Employees' PF where a contribution is made by the employer, there is no such provision possible in the case of PPF.

The maturity period of PPF is 15 years. In case of EPF, the maturity period depends on the age at which the employee joins the fund.

In case of the PPF scheme, withdrawals to the extent of 50 per cent of the outstanding amount to the credit of the concerned person's account are allowed at the end of 7th, 11th and 15th years. During the first six years, it is possible to get a loan upto 25 per cent of the balance to one's credit (on completion of two years of opening the account). On the other hand, in the case of EPF, the withdrawal facilities are more restricted. An employee can withdraw a part of his contribution on completion of 50 years of his age. He can obtain a loan against his PF account which has to be repaid.

TABLE 11.1
Small Saving Schemes
(Position as of March-end 2003)

Scheme	*Maturity period (in years)*	*Interest rate (%)*				*Outstanding (₹ in crores)*
		April 1992	*Jan. 2000*	*Mar. 2001*	*Mar. 2003*	
Post Office Saving Bank deposit	—	5.50	4.50	3.50	3.50	11545
Post Office Time deposit	Rate graded as per no. of years 1, 2, 3 and 5 years	12 to 13.5	8.0 to 10.5	7.50 to 9.00	6.25 to 7.50	15440
Post Office Recurring Deposit	5 years	11.0	10.50	9.00	7.50	28084
National Saving Certificate VIII issue (NSC)	6 years	12.0	11.0	9.50	8.00	44524
Indira Vikas Patra (IVP)	5 years raised to 6 yrs in Jan. 99	14.87	Cumulative interest rate discontinued in July 1999			6009
Kisan Vikas Patra (KVP)	5 yrs raised to 6 1/2 yrs in Jan. 2000 7 yrs 3 month in March 2001 7 yrs 8 month in March 2002 8 yrs 7 month in March 2003	14.87	11.25	10.00	8.41	113658
National Saving Scheme	4 yrs	11.00	10.50	9.00	8.50	789
		Withdrawn w.e.f. November 2002				
Post Office Monthly Income Scheme	6 yrs	14.00	11.0	9.50	8.00	80915
PPF	15 yrs	12.00	11.0	9.50	8.00	10132

Note: The position under the schemes in regard to the maturity period, interest rate, outstanding amount as of March-end 2003.

Table No. 11.2

Small Saving Schemes (Position as of March-end 2006)

(₹ in Crores)

Scheme	*Outstanding (2006)*
Post Office	16476
Saving Bank Deposit	
P.O. Time Deposit	36861
P.O. Recurring Deposit	49957
National Saving Certificate	
VII issue (NSC)	58507
Kisan Vikas Patra (KVP)	14638
National Saving Scheme 1992 Scheme	
(withdrawn in 2002)	2153
P.O. Monthly Income Scheme	182540
PPF	16376
Senior Citizen Saving Scheme (9%)	14974

Small Saving Schemes (Position as of March-end 2009)

Scheme	*Maturity period (in years)*	*Interest rate (%)*	*Outstanding (2009) (₹ in Crores)*
Post Office Saving	—	—	22217
Bank Deposit			
Post Office Time Deposit	—	—	28331
Post Office Recurring Deposit	—	—	64822
National Saving Scheme	—	—	55465
VIII Issue NSC			
National Saving Scheme 1992	—	—	565
Indira Vikas Patra (IVP)	—	—	1072
Kisan Vikas Patra (KVP)	—	—	14784
Post Office Monthly Income Scheme	—	—	178270
PPF	—	—	21758
Senior Citizens Saving Scheme	5	—	20812

Table No. 11 .3

Employees Provident Fund Organisation

	2003-04	*2004-05*	*2005-06*
Members (lakhs)	400.92	411.10	429.59
Contribution of Members			
(1) Provident Fund	12355.97	12918.15	16576.56
(2) Pension Fund	5942.55	6511.85	6885.45
(3) Deposit-linked Insurance Fund	175.36	191.62	220.09
Investments			
(1) Provident Fund	10650.06	16869.18	18789.24
(2) Pension Fund	7698.66	9349.49	9612.00
(3) Deposit-linked Insurance Fund	419.01	502.02	546.79

Source: Ministry of Labour, Government of India.

11.5 NORMS REGARDING INVESTMENTS OF PFs

The Indian Trusts Act 1982 and Employees Provident Fund Act, 1952 have laid down norms regarding investments of PF. The funds mobilised through small savings and provident fund have to be invested either wholly or substantially in the central and state government securities and the securities guaranteed by these governments.

Table No. 11.4

Break-up of Investment of the Provident Fund as on 31st March, 2006

	Investment Categories	*Holding at Face Value*	*(₹ in crore) Percentage Holding*
1.	Central Govt. Securities	14,778.24	15.27
2.(a)	State Development Loans (SDL)	10,751.13	11.11
(b)	Govt. Guaranteed Securities (STG)	1,532.50	1.58
3.	Special Deposit Scheme (SDS)	52,230.93	53.97
4.	Public Sector Undertaking/ Financial Institutions (PSUs/PSFIs)	17,481.80	18.06
	Total	96,774.60	100

Source: Ministry of Labour, Govt. of India.

A number of factors have contributed to the growth of provident funds in India.

1. The adoption of statutory measures to make provident fund compulsory for industrial and other establishments.
2. An increase in the number of establishments covered under the statutory provisions.
3. An expansion of the industrial and service sector of the economy and a consequent increase in the number of salary earners.
4. Introduction of Public Provident Fund Scheme.
5. Provision of tax benefit given to the savers.
6. An increase in the minimum rate of contribution by the employees and employers.
7. Rise in the basic pay of the employees.
8. Rise in the level of money incomes.

11.6 PENSION FUNDS

In many developed countries, pension funds are important financial intermediaries. In India, a need for establishing private pension funds is being felt first investment based pension funds proposed by the Unit Trust of India was approved by the Government of India in1994.

This retirement benefit plan is meant to enable self-employed people to contribute to a pension fund to provide security in their old age.

Pension plans may be classified as –

(a) **Defined Benefits Pension Plan** – Under DBPP, the final pension is predefined based on the final salary and the period of service. Pension plans offered by public sector enterprises and the government as employer in India are of this type. It ensures a predictable amount of pension to the employees for all the years after their retirement and it is guaranteed by the state DBPP involves a considerable cost to the employer. A legally separate trust fund is established and the trustees invest employers' contribution in shares and bonds.

(b) Defined Contribution Pension Plan – It does not guarantee the amount of final benefit which the employees would get after they retire. Both the employees and the employer make a predetermined contribution each year and these funds are invested over the period of time till the retirement of employee whatever the value of these investments at the time of retirement, the employee gets a certain amount which he would use to purchase an annuity. DCPP is also regarded as money purchase pension plan.

Pay – As – You – Go Pension Plan –

Such plans are common in most of the European countries. Under this plan, current employees pay a percentage of their income to provide for the old and this, along with the contribution of the state, goes as a pension that sustain old persons.

At present, the pension coverage in India is very small.

KEY TERMS

Provident Fund, Pension Fund

REVIEW QUESTIONS

1. What are small savings, Explain the role of small savings.
2. What are the characteristics of small savings?
3. Explain the norms and pattern of Provident Fund investments?
4. What factors have contributed to the growth of Provident Funds in India?
5. What are different types of Pension funds?
6. Discuss different kinds of Post office saving schemes.
7. What are different types of Provident schemes operating in India?

REFERENCES

1. Economic Survey, Govt. of India, Various Issues.
2. RBI Report on Currency and Finance, Various Issues.

❑❑❑

12

Financial Services

It is proposed to describe in this chapter, the details in respect of specific financial services as under:

12.1 Merchant Banking

12.2 Lease Financing

12.3 Housing Finance

12.4 Venture Capital

12.5 Factoring

12.6 Credit Rating

12.1 MERCHANT BANKING

Merchant Banking as a financial service did not exist in Indian Financial System till early 1960s. The initiative in this regard was taken by the Foreign banks as Grindlays Bank introduced merchant bank in India in 1967 and other foreign banks like CITI Bank, Chartered Bank soon followed.

Presently, the number of Merchant Banks in the country has been put at 1200.

Merchant Banking services are mainly non-fund based activities related to management of public issue of equity capital. The corporate sector units raise capital for setting up new enterprises and for the expansion/diversification of existing units. The activities of Merchant Banks are related to all aspects of raising capital by the companies from the primary capital market through the sale of securities. In managing the public issue, the merchant bankers handle all aspects of the sale of securities — origination, underwriting and distribution. The merchant bankers free the promoters of the companies from the risks of low/inadequate subscription to capital issues by underwriting them. The merchant bankers often share such risks between themselves by forming syndicate to sell different issues. The merchant bankers perform like Issue Houses and render services like receiving application, allotment of shares, collecting amounts of money, sending share/debenture certificates etc.

Besides issue management, *i.e.,* marketing securities, guaranteeing their sale through underwriting and distribution of securities, the merchant bankers now render a comprehensive package of services including:

- Project Counselling: Identification of Project, Project Reports Preparation, Feasibility Report, Advising on Capital Structure etc.
- Issue Management:
- Project Finance: — Debt finance from financial institutions.
  — Working capital provision from banks.
  — Foreign currency loans.
- Advisory services to NRI, *i.e.,* portfolio management.
- Assignment as the bankers to the issue.

Merchant Banking services are rendered by:

- Foreign Banks: Grindlays Bank, CITI Bank, Chartered Bank.
- Commercial Banks: The Commercial banks establish separate divisions or create subsidiaries for merchant banking functions.

SBI took the lead and set up SBI Capital Markets Ltd. in 1972. The other commercial banks operating in this field are Bank of India, Central Bank of India, Bank of Baroda, Punjab National Bank, UCO Bank, Canara Bank.

- *Financial Institutions:* All-India Financial Institutions including ICICI (in 1974), IDBI, IFCI and IRBI (now IIBI).
- Technical Consultancy Organisations (TCOs) set up by All-India Financial institutions.
- *Private Consultancy Firms:* like DSP Financial Consultants Credit Capital Finance Corporation, J.M. Financial & Investment Services Ltd.
- *Professional Merchant Banks* like VMC Project Technologies.

The merchant bankers have to register themselves with SEBI and operate as per SEBI's guidelines, and the rules notified by SEBI — SEBI (Merchant Bankers) Regulations 1992. Merchant Banking Companies have been exempted from the provisions of the RBI Act 1934, provided they are registered with SEBI.

12.2 LEASE FINANCING

Leasing is a method of financing equipment and machinery purchases. A lease is a financing device utilised to acquire the use of assets — say machinery, equipment. The acquisition of the economic use of an asset is possible through a contractual commitment to make periodic lease payments to the lessor who owns the asset.

A lease is a contractual arrangement whereby 'lessor' grants the 'lessee' the right to use an asset in return for periodical lease rental payments. In this arrangement, the 'lessor' buys capital equipment for the use of the 'lessee' in accordance with the latter's requirements and specifications. Lease financing is quite advantageous to lessee as he acquires the use of asset-machinery, equipment with no initial cash outlay.

Contents of Lease Contracts

(i) Lease period.

(ii) The timing and amounts of rental payments.

(iii) Option to renew the lease or purchase the asset at the end of lease period.

(iv) Method of payment of the cost of maintenance and repairs taxes, insurance etc.

As the 'Hire purchase' is also a method of financing equipment/machinery purchases, it is necessary to distinguish between Leasing and Hire Purchase.

Hire Purchase

The hire purchases an asset and hirer agrees to pay in equal periodic instalments in specific time-length. The instalments cover interest and principal repayment.

Leasing	*Hire Purchase*
Distinguished from Lessee or Hirer's Point of View	
● The Lessee is not the owner of the asset. He cannot enjoy the salvage or terminal value of the asset.	● The hirer is the owner of the asset. He enjoys the salvage value of the asset.
● Depreciation on investment made cannot be claimed by the Lessee for tax purposes.	● The depreciation claimed by the hirer.
● The entire lease rental is a tax deductible expenses.	● Only the interest component of the hire purchase installment is tax deductible.

There are two types of leases:

Operating or service lease

Financial lease.

Financial Leases are:
- Direct lease
- Sale and lease back
- Leverage lease.

Operating Lease:
- Short-term lease, cancellable at short notice.
- Assets leased under operating arrangement include computers, air-conditioners, vehicles etc.
- The lessor is responsible for repair and maintenance, insurance, taxes etc.
- The lease rentals payable do not fully cover the cost of equipment.
- The lessor assumes the risk of obsolescence and underutilisation.

Financial Lease:
- It is medium to long-term, non-cancellable arrangement; period: 3/5/8 years.
- Leases in India are mostly financial leases. Assets leased, Machines, DG Sets, Aircraft, Land & Building.
- The lessee is responsible for maintenance, insurance and taxes.
- The lessee fully recovers through the lease rentals, his investment in equipment and also an acceptable rate of return.
- The lessee has the option to extend the lease for further period.
- The lessee assumes the risk of obsolescence and underutilisation.

Lease Financing in India

By 1981, there were only 2 leasing companies in the country:

- 20th Century Leasing (P) Ltd. (1979)
- Jaybharat Credit & Investment Co. (1981).

The boom in leasing field began in 1983 and by 1984 there were already over 100 companies in the line. In these years, the leasing companies were being set up at an outstanding rate and

Direct Leasing	*Sale & Lease back*	*Leverage Lease*
The supplier sells an asset to the lessor who leases it to the lessee who acquires the use of the asset without owning it.	A firm sells an asset it owns to a party who leases it back to the firm.	Involves 3 parties — lessor, lessee and the lender. * The lessor acquires the asset by financing partly say 25% and for the remaining part he borrows from the lender — say a bank or financial institution. * The lender is paid back by the lessee from the lease rentals. * After satisfying the claim of the lender, the surplus goes to the lessor.

the number of leasing companies reached 400 in 1985. The boom petered out soon and the number of leasing companies declined to 100 by 1987.

The major sector to avail of leasing is service sector inclusive of computer services, hospital services, transport operators etc.

Lease Financing Organisations

- NBFCs: Non-banking finance companies.
- LIC, GIC, HDFC.
- All-India Financial Institutions: ICICI, IFCI, IRBI (now IIBI), SIDBI
- Public sector banks — subsidiaries — like SBI Capital Markets Ltd.
- Private sector manufacturing companies.
- Infrastructure Leasing and Financial Services Ltd.
- Certain SIDCs/SIICs — state level institutions.

Infrastructure Leasing and Financial Services Ltd. has been jointly promoted by the Central Bank of India, UTI and HDFC. It provides innovative services in its areas of operations.

RBI has issued guidelines to encourage the healthy growth of financial leasing of equipments. As per these guidelines, equipment leasing companies are allowed to accept deposits for 6 to 36 month's period. Public deposits are a major source of funds for lease finance companies.

The All-India Financial Institutions like IFCI, ICICI and SIDBI and the Public Sector banks through their subsidiaries like SBI Capital Markets Ltd. are playing a significant role in developing Lease financing among the corporate and other clients in the country.

12.3 HOUSING FINANCE

Though 'housing' is one of the basic human necessities and hence there is ever growing need for housing provision, the arrangements for the supply of funds for house building activities particularly for the economically weaker sections of society have not been adequately developed. Though a prime need, the households with limited incomes are not in a position to raise resources from own savings as much as are required for building or shelter creation. As such, the need for the institutional arrangements for supplying finance for the purpose of 'housing' is far greater.

The demand for housing and hence for finance for housing has ever increasing dimensions. To cope up with this demand, it is necessary that the institutional finance is made accessible to families belonging to different sections of society at reasonable rates which they could afford. In the recent years, significant emphasis has been laid on creating an institutional set-up for the provision of housing finance in the form of specialised housing finance institutions and the general financial institutions extending housing finance like LIC, GIC, commercial banks and provident fund.

The institutions operating in housing finance need long-term funds and they extend mortgage loans for house building against the security of immovable property in land and buildings.

Those who supply funds for housing include:

- Specialised Institutions : HUDCO (Housing Urban Development Corporation, HDFC) and NHB at the apex level.
- Co operative Institutions : State Housing Finance Societies.
- Other Organisations : Insurance Companies: LIC, GIC, Central and State Governments, Housing Boards in different states, PF organisations.
- Commercial bank subsidiaries: mainly nationalised banks.
- Private Housing Finance companies and Nidhis.

HUDCO:
- Set up in 1970.
- Major portion of HUDCO loans are earmarked for economically weaker sections of society and low income groups.
- Provides mortgage loans to co-operative housing societies also.

State Housing Finance Societies

These societies in different states provide loans to the co-operative housing societies formed at the primary level for purchase of land and the construction of houses. The terms and conditions for advancing loans differ in different states. These societies draw their funds as: (i) investment in their share capital by State Governments and Co operative Institutions, (ii) loans from Government and LIC, (iii) Fixed deposit from individuals and institutions, and (iv) debentures issues, guaranteed by Government.

HDFC: Housing Development Finance Corporation.

- Set up by ICICI in 1977.
- The major part of loans are for individual homes. HDFC has different schemes for funding.
- Sources of funds are long-term funds from financial institutions, commercial banks and international institutions like World Bank, USAID and 10-year bonds.

Table No. 12.1
HDFC: Sanctions and Disbursements

	1990-91	1991-92	1992-93	1993-94	1994-95	1995-96	
Sanction	813.8	711.9	859.1	1024.8	1494.6	2071.5	
Disbursement	668.5	627.8	719.9	889.1	1211.7	1683.6	
Outstanding	1726.9	2129.9	2561.7	3071.2	3747.6	4740.7	
	1996-97	*1997-98*	*1998-99*	*1999-00*	*2000-01*	*2001-02*	*2002-03*
Sanction	2521.7	3251.3	4071.8	5305.1	6879.8	9041.3	11731.6
Disbursement	2100.8	2753.6	3424.3	4492.7	5803.0	7616.6	9950.9
Outstanding	5709.3	6944.1	8219.3	10063.0	13224.7	17169.2	21749.9
	2003-04	*2004-05*	*2005-06*	*2006-07*	*2007-2008*	*2008-2009*	
Sanction	15215.6	19715	25634	33332	42520	49166	
Disbursement	12696.8	16207	20679	26178	32875	39650	
Outstanding	27974.3	36011	44990	56512	72998	85198	

Housing Loans Sanctioned and Disbursed by HDFC

(*₹ in Crores*)

Year	*Loan Sanctioned*	*Loan Disbursed*	*Loans Outstanding*
1980-81	31.4	22.1	29.8
1985-86	186.4	145.7	351.8
1990-91	813.8	668.5	1726.9
1995-96	2071.5	1683.6	4740.7
1999-2000	5305.1	4492.7	10063.0
2000-01	6879.8	5803.0	13224.7
2001-02	9041.3	7616.6	17169.2
2002-03	11731.6	9950.9	21749.9
2003-04	15215.6	12698.8	27974.3
2004-05	19715.0	16207.0	36011.5
2005-06	25633.7	20679.2	44990.1
2006-07	33331.7	26178.4	56512.4
2007-08	42520.0	32875.0	72998.0
2008-09	49166.0	39650.0	85198.0

Source: RBI, Handbook of Statistics on the Indian Economy, 2002-03, p. 115 and 2006-07, p. 149.

It is reported that HDFC funding has helped creation of over 12 lakh housing units in the country.

Commercial Banks: As per RBI guidelines issued in 1988, the commercial banks have been allowed to step up the flow of their credit to housing particularly for economically weaker sections.

Apart from their own activities, the commercial banks, particularly public sector banks have set up their subsidiaries specially for housing finance.

Certain measures taken to enhance the commercial banks role in housing finance include ratio of incremental bank deposits earmarked for housing finance raised to 1.5%; restriction on the quantum of housing loan per individual removed, margin for banks housing loans fixed at 20% to 35%.

The commercial banks extend loans to individuals, housing finance institutions and private housing finance companies as per targets specified by RBI.

Subsidiaries: Canara Bank — Canfin Homes Ltd.
Punjab National Bank: PNB Housing Finance Ltd.
SBI: SBI Housing Finance Ltd.

LIC-GIC

LIC is the single largest institutional lender to the housing sector. LIC's investment in housing is indirect, *i.e.,* through agencies and institutions engaged in providing funds for housing and also housing including State Government, State Co-operative Housing Societies, Housing Boards, HUDCO, LIC has now made entry in the direct mortgage loans for housing. The LIC has set up its subsidiary in 1989 — LIC Housing Finance Ltd. which has various schemes of Housing loans. GIC has set up its subsidiary in 1990 — GIC Griha Vitta Ltd. as a joint venture of GIC, UTI, ICICI, HDFC, IFCI and SBI Capital Markets Ltd.

Private Housing Finance Companies

There are 400 housing finance companies. National Housing Bank is the regulatory authority for these companies. The disbursements from only 29 housing finance companies are eligible for NHB refinance. Special consideration is given by NHB to finance provided to rural areas by the Housing Finance Companies.

National Housing Bank (NHB)

RBI has set up National Housing Bank as a wholly owned subsidiary in 1988. As an apex level housing finance institution, NHB performs to promote housing finance institutions at the local and regional levels and in private and joint sector.

The main role of NHB is to provide financial and other support through its Refinance scheme to housing loans advanced by scheduled commercial banks, co operative banks, Housing finance companies and Apex Co-operative Housing finance societies.

Table No. 12.2
Refinance Scheme of NHB
(Disbursement and Outstanding)

(₹ in Crores)

Item	*1989-90*	*1990-91*	*1991-92*	*1992-93*	*1993-94*	*1994-95*	*1995-96*
Housing Finance	115	308	541	388	241	275	248
	(115)	(425)	(952)	(1284)	(1437)	(1604)	(1719)
Banks	9	23	68	53	9	3	22
	(9)	(29)	(80)	(127)	(137)	(135)	(102)
Others (Co-op Banks)	8	54	68	39	54	39	64
	(8)	(63)	(130)	(161)	(206)	(214)	(267)
Total	132	385	677	479	303	317	333
	(132)	(517)	(1162)	(1571)	(1780)	(1952)	(2088)

	1996-97	*1997-98*	*1998-99*	*1999-00*	*2000-01*	*2001-02*	*2002-03*
Housing Finance	828	381	545	651	762	719	1772
	(1893)	(2083)	(2444)	(2865)	(3344)	(3750)	(4629)
Banks	6	8	39	2	106	85	789
	(82)	(68)	(88)	(54)	(150)	(211)	(935)
Others	112	138	163	188	141	219	140
	(364)	(476)	(607)	(748)	(830)	(984)	(1044)
Total	445	528	747	842	1008	1024	2710
		(2339)	(2629)	(3139)	(3666)	(4325)	(4946)
(6607)							

	2003-04	*2004-05*	*2005-06*	*2006-07*	*2007-08*	*2008-09*
Housing Finance	1851	2623	1840	1210	1189	6045
	(4736)	(4928)	(4888)	(4915)	(4750)	(9373)
Banks	1284	5404	3791	4280	7398	3799
	(2259)	(6720)	(10425)	(14011)	(11758)	(6521)
Others	118	35	2	10	—	—
	(1056)	(819)	(952)	(348)	(268)	(166)
Total	3263	8062	5633	5500	8587	9844
	(8052)	(12467)	(16268)	(19274)	(16776)	(16060)

Note: Figures in brackets indicate amounts outstanding

Refinance Disbursed for NHB to Various Agencies

(*₹ in Crores*)

Year	*Housing Finance Companies*		*Banks*		*Others*		*Total*	
	D	*O*	*D*	*O*	*D*	*O*	*D*	*O*
1990-91	359	468	21	29	55	63	436	560
1995-96	248	1719	11	66	74	303	334	2088
1999-2000	652	2864	2	54	188	748	842	3686
2000-01	762	3376	101	146	141	830	1004	4352
2001-02	719	3750	86	207	219	986	1024	4941
2002-03	1772	4629	798	935	140	1044	2710	6807
2003-04	1851	4736	1284	2259	118	1056	3253	8052
2004-05	2623	4928	5704	6720	35	819	8062	12467
2005-06	1840	4888	3791	10428	2	952	5633	16268

Note: D = disbursements; O = outstanding
Source: RBI, Handbook of Statistics on the Indian Economy, 2002-03, p. 117 and 2006-07, p. 151.

12.4 VENTURE CAPITAL

Venture capital is equity support to fund new concepts that involve a higher risk and at the same time, have high growth and profit potential.

Venture capitalists finance innovations and ideas that have a potential for high growth, but are *unproven*.

Venture capital is capital provided to start new enterprises, particularly for small entrepreneurs with enthusiasm, but with — inadequate or lack of finance.

Venture capitalist focussed on *new projects 'seed capital'* — helping technocrat entrepreneurs to fill in gap in regard to promoter's contribution.

Start-up finance includes support for marketing and product development.

Technology and innovation: funding risky and unproven, but sophisticated technologies. Venture capitalist provides funds to new entrepreneur. Venture capital refers to investment of long-term equity finance in high risk projects with high reward possibilities. As such, the objective of venture capitalist is to achieve high returns on investment. Venture capital consists of—

- long-term investment in high risk, high-tech projects with longer gestation period.
- equity or quasi-equity form of investment.
- does not carry interest charge, but carries royalty linked to sales.

These are the projects which do not have access to conventional sources of capital due to high risk and the absence of suitable collateral.

Areas attracting venture capital funds —

Biotechnology	Health and Pharmaceutical
Medical services	Agricultural business
Communications	Retailing
Software companies	

Suppliers of Venture Capital Finance

Individual investors
Subsidiaries of banks and financial institutions
Private venture capital firms
Large manufacturing corporates — their subsidiaries/divisions.

There are 20 venture capital companies in public and private sector. In 1988, RBI issued guidelines on venture capital. By 1996-97, venture capital companies provided finance to 550 projects amounting to ₹ 450 crore.

Venture Capital Funds

All-India Financial Institutions:

ICICI — Technology Development & Investment Corporation of India (1986) — TDICI
IFCI — Risk Capital & Tech. Finance Corporation Ltd. (1985) (RCTFC)
UTI — Technology Development & Information Company of India Ltd. set up in 1989 in collaboration with ICICI
RCTC — Risk Capital Technology Corporation

Venture Capital Scheme of IDBI

Objective: To provide financial assistance to industrial concerns attempting commercial application of indigenous technologies and adoption of imported technologies for domestic application.

Source of finance: 5% cess levied and collected on all payments made for the import of technology. IDBI draws on funds collected under the cess.

Commercial Banks

Grindlays Bank: India Investment Fund
SBI SBI Capital Markets Ltd., Equity Development Scheme

Venture Capital Company in Private Sector: Credit Capital Venture Fund — First private sector company.

Recently, the limit of venture capital fund investing up to 40% equity base in high risk ventures has been removed. Venture capital fund can now invest in one company upto 25% of its capital base.

12.5 FACTORING

In case of business transactions between buyers and sellers which are not settled by cash payment, the sellers allow the buyers some time for making payments after goods have been received by them. The firms which sell the goods on credit may face problems in regard to the timely collection. For these firms particularly in small-scale sector, the book debts on the trade receivables lock up the funds if the firms are unable to manage timely collection. "Factoring" is a financial service designed to help firms in better management of their receivables. A factor is a debt collection service which buys out the supplier's book debts or account receivables. There is a credit risk associated with these accounts which is borne by the factor. *'Factoring'* involves 3 parties — the seller, the factor and the buyer and it takes the form of a contract between the factor and the seller as a client wherein the risk in respect of bad debts is either borne by the client or the factor.

Through the bills discounting facilities, the banks and financial institutions finance only a part of clients' book debts. The clients of the banks show high preference for cash credit and hence the efforts of RBI to popularise the commercial bills market have not yielded the desired results. Vaghul Working Group in 1987 recommended that banks should develop factoring services. In Jan. 1988, a Study Group was appointed by RBI to examine the feasibility of and the manner in which factoring could be introduced in India. In its Report submitted in Jan. 1989, the Study Group estimated the potential demand for factoring services in the country to be around ₹ 4,000 crore per year. The Report estimation was based on the following data:

	Output sold on credit
Large & Medium Scale Sector	50%
Small-scale Sector	64%
	Credit Sales for the factor to handle
Large & Medium Scale Sector	₹ 4,500 crore
SSI Sector	₹ 12,000 crore

The average collection period for the above categories was respectively 45 days and 90 days.

It is possible that the factors could be subsidiaries of banks or there could be a close inter-relationship between them in regard to sharing information on the creditworthiness of the parties. The book debts may be assigned by the suppliers to the factor who may borrow, in turn, from the banks.

There are certain types of Factoring services such as —

Recourse factoring : The credit risk in respect of bad debt is carried by the seller.

Without recourse factoring : Bad debts are borne by the factor.

Notified factoring : When the buyer is intimated about the assignment of debt to a factor.

Non-notified factoring (Confidential) : When the assignment of debt to a factor is not declared to the buyer.

The factor charges Fees/Commission as a percentage of the value of receivables.

Both Factoring and bills discounting provide finance at a discount to the suppliers against invoices. The factor buys the book debt at a discount and pays back the same, *i.e.,* discount amount to the client when the buyer makes the payment at the end of the credit period.

Four banks were chosen on a regional basis to set up factoring companies:

W. India : SBI

N. India : Punjab National Bank

E. India : Allahabad Bank

S. India : Canara Bank

Only SBI and Canara Bank have ventured into factoring.

'Forfaiting' is an arrangement by which the exporter surrenders export receivables to the forfaiting agency. Forfaiting is a source of finance enabling exporters to get funds from the forfaiter on transferring the right to recover debts from the importer.

Forfaiting is the non-recourse discounting of export receivables. By selling the export receivables to the forfaiter, the exporter is relieved of the risks involved in international trade.

Factoring is a service in regard to short-term trade finance; whereas Forfaiting pertains to export of capital goods on medium and long-term credit.

EXIM Bank has been authorised by RBI in Feb. 1992 to facilitate export financing through forfaiting.

Forfaiting originated in Germany and Switzerland in 1960s. London is the prominent centre of forfaiting.

12.6 CREDIT RATING

Investors always try to minimise or eliminate the risk of investment in different types of financial instruments. Credit Rating Service helps them in designing the strategies for the same. **Credit Rating** may be defined as an act of assigning values to credit instruments by estimating or assessing the solvency, *i.e.,* the ability of the borrower to repay debt and expressing them through predetermined symbols, such as AAA, AA, BBB, B, C, D etc. These symbols convey the grade of safety to the investor.

Ratings are classified into 3 grades, High Investment Grades, Investment Grades and Speculative Grades. The risks are classified into around 14 to 15 categories. For example, AAA, *i.e.,* Triple A denotes highest safety in terms of timely payment of interest and principal. The issuer is fundamentally strong and any adverse changes may not affect it. 'A' denotes adequate safety in terms of timely payment of interest and principal, but may get adversely affected by changing circumstances. After the financial sector reforms introduced in India, lot of new instruments, number of firms seeking savings of the investors has been growing very rapidly making it more and more difficult for an ordinary investor to understand and analyse them. Credit Rating Agencies have come into existence to assist the investors to make a choice out of large investment opportunities opened up to them.

Volume of Credit Rating Business in India

(₹ in Crores)

Agency/Instrument	1992-93		1993-94		1994-95		1995-96		Cumulative at end of March 1996	
	N	A	N	A	N	A	N	A	N	A
1. CRISIL										
(a) Debentures	-	-	77	6227	103	7641	161	13342	646	45700
(b) FDs	-	-	69	5116	97	9130	218	14513	543	38625
(c) CPs	-	-	211	4801	137	1629	21	3255	459	11415
(d) Others	-	-	9	527	47	6144	27	12336	88	19133
(e) Total	229	20011	366	16671	384	24544	427	43086	1736	114873
2. ICRA										
(a) Debentures	-	-	28	1999	45	1779	66	8224	223	18599
(b) FDs	-	-	42	1083	87	540	192	50507	360	52481
(c) CPs	-	-	69	1669	80	3023	35	17011	195	22299
(d) Total	86	5329	139	4750	212	5343	293	75742	778	93380
3. CARE										
(a) Debentures	-	-	-	-	34	3429	54	9330	93	13572
(b) CPs	-	-	-	-	112	1639	39	1692	179	3704
(c) FDs	-	-	-	-	38	3335	124	2887	173	6362
(d) Total	-	-	46	1326	184	8403	217	13909	445	23638
4. Grand Total										
(a) Debenture	-	-	105	8226	182	13629	281	30896	962	77871
(b) FDs	-	-	111	6159	222	13005	534	67547	1076	97468
(c) CPs	-	-	280	6470	329	6291	95	21958	833	37418
(d) Others	-	-	9	527	47	6144	27	12336	88	19133
(e) Total	315	25340	551	22748	780	38290	937	132737	2959	231891

Source: RBI, RCF, Vol. II, Various Issues. The comparable information for the later years is not available.
Notes: N = Number; A = Amount; FDs = Fixed Deposits; CPs = Commercial Papers.

PE and VC Investments in India

(US $ in million)

	2000	2001	2002	2003	2004	2005	2006	2007
Number of Deals	280	110	78	56	106	146	299	387
Value of Deals	1160	937	591	470	1671	2200	7500	142234

Source: TSJ Venture Intelligence.

Industry-wise Private Equity and Venture Capital Investments in 2007

(US $ in million)

Industry	IT	Energy	MANF	M&E	BFSI	S&L	E&C	TEL	HC&LS	OTH
Deals	91	25	61	19	50	20	30	13	29	49
Value of Deals	988	1101	1638	616	3979	658	1628	1839	478	1284

Source: TSJ Venture Intelligence.

Credit Rating refers to the assessment of a borrower's credit quality. Credit Rating performs the function of credit risk evaluation reflecting the borrower's expected capability to repay the debt as per the terms of issue.

The leading Credit Rating agencies in India are –

(i) Credit Rating Information Services of India Ltd. (CRISIL)

(ii) Investment Information and Credit Rating Agency of India Ltd. (ICRA)

(iii) Credit Analysis and Research Limited (CARE)

(iv) Fitch Rating India Private Ltd.

CRISIL was set up in Jan.1988 jointly by ICICI, UTI, LIC, GIC ADB as the first Credit Rating Agency of India. It major function is to rate, on request from companies, their debentures, fixed deposit programmes short-term borrowing instruments and preference shares. The CRISIL ratings are now asked for by the authorities, banks, UTI, merchant bankers when they assist companies. In addition to credit rating, the CRISIL provides corporate reports on a regular basis on companies (Public and Private) containing information on their financial, business and technical aspects. It also undertakes industry studies on requests covering topics such as structure of industry, basis of competition and demand supply estimates.

ICRA – It was established in 1991 and it primarily rates short, medium and long-term debt instruments. It undertakes equity rating for primary as well as secondary market, at the instance of the issuer and investor respectively.

CARE was set up by the IDBI in collaboration with some banks and financial service companies.

It is regarded as Securities and Exchange Bank of India (Credit Rating Agencies) Regulation 1999

1. Commercial banks, public financial institutions, foreign banks operating in India, Foreign Credit rating agencies and companies with a minimum net worth of ₹ 100 crore as per its audited annual accounts for the previous five years are eligible to promote rating agencies in India.
2. Rating agencies are required to have a minimum net worth of ₹ 5 crore.
3. Rating agencies cannot assess financial instruments of their promoters who have more than 10 per cent stake in them.
4. Rating agencies cannot rate a security issued by an entity which is a borrower of its promoter or a subsidiary of its promoter or an associate of its promoter if –
   (i) There are common chairman, directors between credit rating agency and these entities
   (ii) There are common employees
   (iii) There are common chairman, directors, and employees on the rating committee.
5. Rating agencies cannot rate a security issued by its associate or subsidiary, if the credit rating agency or its rating committee has a chairman, director or employee who is also a chairman, director or employee of any such entity.

6. A penalty of suspension of the certificate of registration or a penalty of cancellation of registration may be imposed on the rating agency if it fails to comply with any condition or contravenes any of the provisions of the Act.

Limitations of Credit Rating in India

The Credit Rating Activities in India suffer from certain weaknesses. It is estimated that around one-third of ratings done by CR agencies are not accepted by their clients. Bonds ratings have been characterised by variability, particularly a decline in ratings over time.

The methodology of rating has not always been consistent. Sometimes old bond ratings and not the current bond ratings are used and therefore such rating which has been made compulsory may not a actually help the investors.

KEY TERMS

Merchant Banking, Lease Finance, Hire Purchase Factoring, Credit Rating, Venture Capital.

REVIEW QUESTIONS

1. What is merchant banking? Explain its functioning in India.
2. What is a Lease contract? Distinguish between Leasing and Hire Purchase.
3. Explain different types of Lease and Lease Financing in India.
4. Explain the performance of Housing Finance Services in India.
5. Explain the role of Venture Capital in Financing Investments.
6. What is factoring?
7. What is Credit Rating? What is the need for credit rating in India?
8. Write a note on Credit Rating Agencies in India.
9. Discuss the progress and limitations of Credit Rating in India.

❑ ❑ ❑

13

Financial Markets in India

INTRODUCTION

Having focussed on 'Financial Institutions' as the constituents of Indian Financial System in the earlier chapters, our attention is now turned to describing 'Financial Markets and Financial Instruments.'

As explained earlier, financial institutions, financial markets and financial instruments are the main constituents of any financial system. These constituents are interrelated as the financial institutions operate in financial markets and deal with financial instruments.

Financial transactions involve the creation or transfer of financial assets. Financial transactions take place in the financial markets.

Financial markets are the centres or arrangements that provide facilities for buying and selling of financial claims (assets) and services. They perform an important function of mobilisation of savings and channelising them into the most productive uses. Financial market in India has the market segments as Money Market, Government Securities Market, Capital Market and Foreign Exchange Market.

It is proposed to describe the Indian financial markets on the following lines:

13.1 Money Market: Characteristic Features

13.2 Capital Market

13.3 Interlinking between Money Market and Capital Market

Financial markets and the financial market segments in India remained insufficiently developed for long due to certain inadequacies and deficiencies like limited number of participants limited volume of business, tight regulations, limited instruments etc.

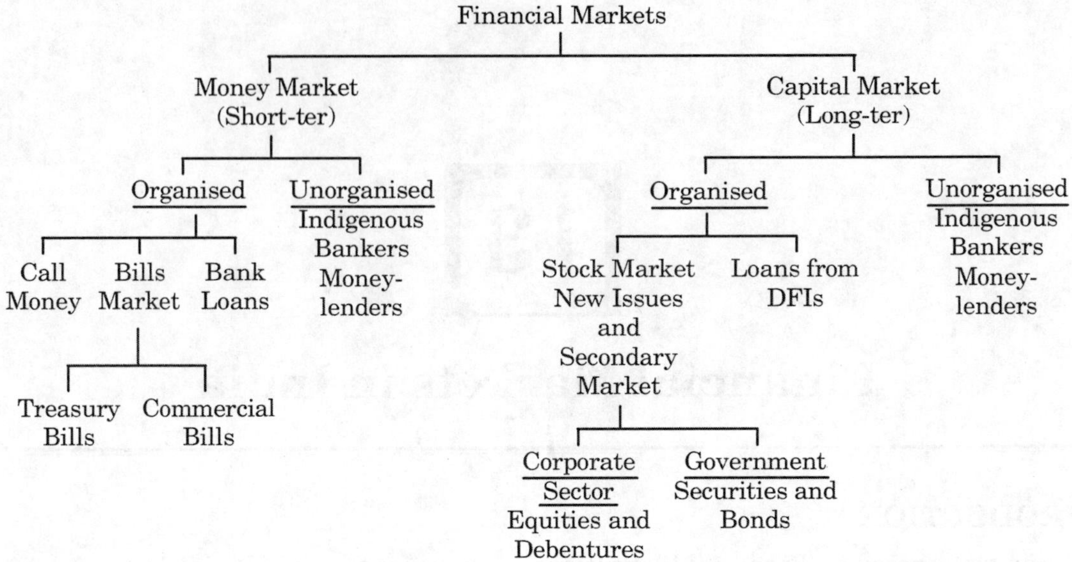

Financial Markets and their segments remained insufficiently developed for a long time in India due to certain inadequacies and deficiencies in terms of limited number of participants, limited volume of business, strict regulations and limited types of financial instruments.

13.1 MONEY MARKET: CHARACTERISTIC FEATURES

To put it briefly, the money market is a short-term credit market or a market for short-term funds. Money market deals in monetary assets whose period of maturity is less than or up to one year. As such, these monetary assets could be said to be relatively closer substitutes of money.

Money market is the centre for dealing in monetary assets of a short-term character, wherein transactions take place in short-term financial assets which are close substitutes for money.

To put it differently, money market provides an institutional set-up for transmission of monetary policy impulses by equilibriating the demand for and supply of funds at the short-end of the market.

It is necessary to consider and record certain common points:

The main factor which distinguishes money market from the capital market is the time length or the period of maturity of the financial assets. The money market deals with short-term assets and the capital market relates to the provision of medium and long-term funds.

The monetary assets dealt with in the money market are close substitutes of money, as these mature in short period, ranging from one day to one year.

The monetary policy pertains to monitoring the supply of money and credit in the country. The money market, which deals with monetary assets which are *'near-money'*, is quite significant in terms of its influence over demand for and supply of money/money substitutes.

The characteristic features of Indian money market are:

- ***Dualistic Character:*** The money market has two components — organised money market and unorganised money market. Organised money market consists of the apex institutions — Reserve Bank of India, the commercial banks and co operative banks. The unorganised money market has the indigenous bankers, agency houses, the moneylenders, the shroffs etc. The dualistic setting has made the Indian money market segmented, and not integrated.
- ***Seasonal Variation in Business:*** The business in the Indian money market is exposed to seasonal variations reflected in credit requirements and money supply in accordance with the seasons of agricultural operations and production. October-November to March-April is a busy season when there is increase in bank credit. RBI tries to moderate these seasonal changes and smoothen out the transition from one season to the other.
- ***Insufficiently Developed:*** The money market in India remained insufficiently developed having limited number of participants and limited number of instruments and being exposed to regulations. It was in the late 1980s when some reform measures were introduced in Indian money market in accordance with the recommendations of Chakravarty Committee (1985) and Vaghul Working Group (1987). The reform efforts pertaining to the Indian money market were sustained further in 1990s in terms of initiatives as proposed by Narasimham Committee (1991).

13.2 CAPITAL MARKET

Role of Capital market in Indian Economy and Industrial Growth

1. **Mobilising Saving and Acceleration of Capital Formation:**

   Different types of bonds and securities help in mobilising savings from various sections of population.

2. **Promotion of Industrial Growth:**

   Through the Capital market, savings of large number of people get channelised to productive sectors of the economy. In absence of such investment opportunities, these savings would have been allocated on real estate, bullion etc. Productive investment in capital market has brought about industrial growth in India.

3. **Raising Long-term Capital:**

   Stock exchanges enable companies to raise permanent capital. Shareholders buy and sell their securities but the capital once raised permanently or for a long time remains with the companies which raise them.

4. **Ready and Continuous Market:**

   Stock exchanges are a central place where buyers and sellers can sell and purchase securities any time they wish and with modern technological advancement in trading systems (online screen-based trading) it has much easier for the shareholders to do their transactions.

5. **Proper Channelisation of Funds:**

   Efficient stock exchanges lead to allocation of resources to proper channels. Prevailing market price and relative yield act as guiding forces for channelisation of funds.

6. Provision of a Variety of Services:

Along with the primary and secondary markets, capital market also brings about growth of specialised financial services such as merchant banking, underwriting, venture capital etc.

Capital market is a market for both medium and long-term funds. Capital market provides medium and long-term debt and equity finance for the government and the corporate sector. The Government or public sector and the private corporate sector as the *'deficit'* spenders who are unable to mobilise financial resources required by them for 'investment', *i.e.,* for acquiring fixed capital assets from 'within' or from internal sources, have to approach the 'savers' directly by inviting subscription to equity issues and/or seek debt finance from the financial institutions.

As against the fast increasing demand for long-term finance for rapid industrialisation in India during the post-Independence period, arrangements for the provision of long-term finance facilities were limited as the capital market in the country lacked in this regard. The Development Financial Institutions (DFIs) which have come up at All-India and the states level are an integral part of the Indian capital market and have played a very important role in financing investment for the growth of the industry sector.

The Constituents of the Indian Capital Market are:

- Development Financial Institutions (DFIs)
- Specialised Financial Institutions — TFCI, RCTC, and TDICI for specific activities like tourism, technology development, venture capital etc.
- Investment Institutions: LIC, GIC and Mutual Funds including UTI.
- Other specialised institutions for financial services like SEBI, SHCIL, Merchant Banking and institutions for credit rating etc.
- The capital market has two components of the stock market.

Primary Market: New Issues Market.

Secondary Market: Stock Exchanges including OTCEI and National Stock Exchange (NSE).

The capital market in India has also the unorganised sector consisting of indigenous bankers, nidhis and chit funds etc. and non-banking finance companies like investment companies, finance companies and hire purchase companies.

The securities or instruments dealt with in the capital market are:

Corporate Sector: New Issues: equity shares ordinary and preference.

Debt Instruments: Debentures/bonds.

Government / Public Sector: Government securities.

Debt Instruments: Bonds.

These include units of Mutual Funds including Unit Trust of India. Greater reliance on debt instruments as against equity is a significant feature of the Indian capital market.

Some measures were initiated to reform the capital market in India during the 1980s. These consisted of *institutionalisation of capital market* as under:

The Banking Regulation Act (1949) was amended in 1983, permitting banks to undertake non-banking functions like merchant banking and mutual funds. The banks started these operations in the capital market through their subsidiaries. The public sector banks made entry into the capital market through their mutual funds channelling small saving into the capital market.

The *merchant banking* services were started in India by foreign banks — Grindlays Bank, Citi Bank and Chartered Bank. The lead among Indian banks was taken by State Bank of India — SBI Capital Markets Ltd. The other banks which followed were Bank of India, Central Bank of India, Bank of Baroda, Punjab National Bank, UCO Bank and Canara Bank.

Until 1986, there was only one Mutual Fund UTI — operating in India. Between 1986 and 1990, 16 more mutual funds were set up in the country. In the year 1987, State Bank of India, Canara Bank and Indian Bank, in 1989, LIC mutual fund and in 1990, Punjab National Bank, Bank of India, GIC and Andhra Bank mutual funds were set up. Of these, 16 mutual funds set up during this period, 7 were overseas funds which collected subscriptions from the residents abroad.

On April 12, 1988, the Securities and Exchange Board of India was set up for the promotion of healthy growth in the securities market and for the protection for investor's interests. In 1987 Stock Holding Corporation of India (SHCIL) was set up to facilitate transfer of shares and render support services like clearing depository etc.

Soon after the submission of the Report by the Narasimham Committee on the Financial System in November 1991, major reforms have been initiated beginning with the year 1992 and during the next two decades.

Major Reforms in Indian Capital Market

1. SEBI was given a legal status and statutory powers under the SEBI Act in April 1992.
2. The Capital Issues (Control) Act, 1947 was repealed in May 1992
   — free entry into the capital market and free pricing of shares by the issuing companies. Interest rates on debentures also freed.
3. Institutionalisation of the capital market gained further momentum when mutual funds were allowed to be set up in the private sector. Of the 40 mutual funds registered with SEBI as at March-end 1999, 31 mutual funds were set up in the private sector.
4. The infrastructure of the primary capital market has become fairly diversified over the years with the setting up of a number of merchant bankers, investment and consultancy agencies, registrar to the issue etc.
5. Integrating Indian capital market with international capital markets: Foreign Institutional Investors (FIIs) allowed to operate in the market.
6. Indian companies allowed to raise capital from the international capital markets.
7. Secondary market: Stock Exchanges
   — open outcry trading system has been replaced by online screen-based electronic trading.
   — Trading and settlement cycles shortened from 14 days to seven days.
8. OTCEI started operations in 1992, National Stock Exchange in 1994.
9. Disinvestment by public sector undertakings of their equity shares to the public since 1991.
10. Settlement period reduced from T + 5 to T + 1.
11. Reduction in transaction costs.
12. Demutualisation of capital market.

The stock market in India has grown in size and presently it has 23 stock exchanges with 7500-8000 listed companies. Market capitalisation of equity shares quoted is estimated to be around 9% of GNP.

13.3 INTERLINKING BETWEEN MONEY MARKET AND CAPITAL MARKET

Both the money market and the capital market are the centres which arrange for the transfer of funds from the lenders or the suppliers of funds to the borrowers or users of funds. They differ, however, in regard to the time-lengths or the maturity periods of the financial assets created and dealt with for effecting the transfer funds. As mentioned earlier, money market arranges for short-term and capital market provides for medium and long-term funds. The time- length in respect of short-term funds is less than and upto one year.

These segments — money market and capital market remained insufficiently developed and segregated from each other as they operated under a regulated framework inclusive of tight entry restrictions.

One significant aspect of the interdependence of these markets is that the suppliers of funds to both the markets are the *'savers'* or the members of the household sector who exercise option in regard to assets holding, firstly between the real physical assets and financial assets and then between different types of financial assets. Their choice spreads over bank deposit, P.O. deposit, insurance policies or the direct purchase of primary securities.

The important aspect which interlinks these markets is that the banks operate and serve in both the markets. The commercial banks are the major source of short-term credit and hence constitute a major player in the money market. The banks mobilise savings in the form of deposits or secondary securities and provide credit, extend loans, even medium term loans and invest in primary securities issued by the Government and corporate sector. In other words, the performance of banks results in short-term funds being transformed into long-term funds and *vice versa.*

The role of commercial banks as an interlinking factor between money market and capital market was further activated during 1980s, when the Banking Regulation Act, 1949, was amended in 1983, permitting the banks to undertake non-banking functions like merchant banking and mutual fund. As a result, the banks started operating in the capital market through their subsidiaries. Between 1986 and 1990, the public sector banks made an entry into the field of mutual fund for channelling small savings into the capital market. The subsidiaries of State Bank of India and Canara Bank shared with Development Financial Institutions (DFIs) and Investment Institutions like LIC, GIC and UTI in promoting the Over the Counter Exchange of India — OTCEI in 1989.

During the 1990s, the reforms initiated have given rise to the entry of non-bank participants in the money market segments like call money, term money, bills rediscounting. All-India financial institutions shared in the paid-up capital while setting up the Discount and Finance House of India (DFHI) in 1988. Call money market is called inter-bank call and short notice market as the participants are the commercial banks and co operative banks as both the borrowers and lenders. Since October 1990, the DFIs, Mutual Funds including private sector mutual funds, *i.e.,* all institutions participating in the bills rediscounting market are allowed as the lenders in call money market.

Earlier, Reserve Bank had permitted scheduled commercial banks to rediscount genuine trade bills with other commercial banks, LIC, UTI, GIC and ICICI. In May 1990, the apex bank increased the number of participants in the bills rediscounting market by permitting All-India level Development Financial Institutions (DFIs), Mutual Funds and select urban co-operative banks.

In October 1993, the financial institutions like IDBI, ICICI, IFCI, IRBI (IIBI), SIDBI, EXIM Bank and NABARD were permitted to borrow from the term money market for three to six months maturity.

The Certificate of Deposits (CDs) are issued by the banks. In 1991-92, the All-India Financial Institutions have been allowed to issue CDs with maturity period of one to three years. In April 1998, Foreign Institutional Investors (FIIs) permitted to purchase and sell Treasury Bills.

The All-India financial institutions like IDBI, ICICI and UTI have set up their banks. The Narasimham Committee (II) in its report submitted in April 1998, has noted that the banks and DFIs are moving closer to each other in the scope of their activities. The All-India level DFIs have entered the area of working capital financing and the banks have taken up project financing. The Narasimham Committee (1998) has proposed that the DFIs should over a period of time, convert themselves into banks.

The interlinking of different market segments is a key factor in developing a better integrated financial system in the country. The measures to promote interlinking between the money market and the capital market since the 1980s have progressed further during 1990s.

KEY TERMS

Money Market, Capital Market.

REVIEW QUESTIONS

1. What are the main constituents of the Indian Financial Market?
2. What is money market? What are the characteristic features of India money market?
3. What is capital market? What are its main constituents?
4. What reforms have been introduced in the Indian Capital Market in last two decades?
5. Discuss the role of Capital market in the industrial development in India.
6. Discuss the interlink between Indian Money Market and Capital Market.

REFERENCES

1. RBI Bulletin, Various Issues.
2. RBI Report on Currency and Finance, Various Issues.

❑ ❑ ❑

14

Money Market

INTRODUCTION

A market for an overnight and short-term funds and instruments having a maturity period of upto and less than one year (14 days/90 days/180 days etc.) is regarded as money market. It is a market for financial assets that are close substitutes for money.

Money Market: sub-markets and instruments dealt with –

14.1 Call Money

14.2 Short Notice Money

14.3 Discount and Finance House of India (DFHI)

14.4 Term Money

14.5 Commercial Bills

14.6 Treasury Bills

14.7 Commercial Paper (CP)

14.8 Certificate of Deposit (CD)

14.9 Money Market Mutual Funds (MMMFs)

The main functions of money market are –

1. Provide a balancing mechanism to even out the demand for and supply of short-term funds.
2. Provide a focal point for central bank intervention for influencing liquidity and general level of interest rates in the economy.
3. Provide reasonable access to suppliers and users of short-term funds to fulfill their borrowings and investment requirements at an efficient market clearing price.
4. It provides a stable source of funds to banks in addition to deposits, it allows the banks to manage risks arising from interest rate fluctuations and to manage the maturity structure of their assets and liabilities.
5. It ensures an adequate flow of credit to the productive sectors of the economy.

Role of Money Market –

The money market performs as:

(i) a mechanism to equilibrate the demand for and the supply of short-term funds.

(ii) a market which enables borrowers and lenders of short-term funds to fulfill their borrowing and investment requirements.

(iii) an avenue for RBI to intervene and influence both quantity and cost of liquidity in the financial system, as such the effectiveness of the monetary policy depends on how efficiently the money market performs.

Progress of Money Market and Effectiveness of Monetary Policy

Monetary policy decisions are transmitted to the whole economy through changes in financial prices (e.g., interest rates, exchange rates, yields, asset prices, equity prices) and financial quantities (money supply, credit supply, supply of government bonds, foreign-denominated bonds).

All over the world, the interest rate channel is the key channel of monetary policy transmission.

During the controlled or administered regime, the management of liquidity was essentially done by the RBI through direct instruments such as varying cash reserve requirement, limit on refinance, administered interest rates and qualitative and quantitative restrictions on credit.

After 1991, in the liberalised regime interest rates are largely market-determined. The objective of the monetary policy is to make the interest rate regine more flexible and responsive to economic fundamentals.

The RBI influences the monetary conditions through market-based indirect instruments. For example, if the RBI wants to inject liquidity for a short period, it may resort to repos which may provide funds to the banks in exchange of securities of a predetermined interest rate and reversing the transaction at a predetermined time. Similarly if the reserve bank wants influence long lasting liquidity, it could resort to open market operations involving outright purchase (or sale) of securities.

The other instruments such as standing facilities provide limited liquidity to eligible market participants such as banks and the market-based discount window makes available reserves either through direct lending or through rediscounting or purchase of financial assets held by banks.

A well developed, liquid, efficient and vibrant money market which is also well integrated with the other segments of financial markets such as government securities market foreign exchange market is a prerequisite for the success of market-based indirect instruments of the monetary policy.

14.1 CALL MONEY

Call/Notice money market is the most active segment of the money market. The market is meant for the transfer of funds among the banks. It consists of an arrangement for making the surpluses of some banks available to other banks in temporary deficit of cash. Hence, it is known as inter-bank call/notice money market. The call loan is one day or overnight loan and the short notice loan is for a short period of upto 14 days. The borrowers in the market are the banks who are temporarily short of funds and the lenders who are temporarily in excess of cash.

The main centres at which call money markets are located are Mumbai, Kolkata, Chennai, Delhi and Ahmedabad.

Participants: The participants in the call/notice money market are the scheduled and non-scheduled commercial banks, foreign banks and co-operative banks.

In the past, the source of call money for banks also consisted of the funds placed on call with the banks by the individuals and companies with large short-term surpluses.

Earlier, the call/notice money market operated through brokers who as intermediaries, would bring the borrowing and lending banks together. From March 1978, banks have been prohibited by the apex bank from paying brokerage for arranging call loans for them.

As the financial institutions like LIC and UTI were allowed in 1970 to operate as lenders in the market, the participants in the call/notice money market upto 1987 were the banks as both borrowers and lenders and LIC and UTI as lenders. It was only after the Vaghul Working Group Report in 1987, there has been enlargement in the number of participants by allowing the non-banking institutions to function as lenders.

In April 1988, the Discount and Finance House of India (DFHI) was set up to oversee and supervise the money market operations and was allowed to borrow and lend and also arrange funds in the inter-bank call/notice money market.

In May 1990, financial institutions, IDBI, NABARD and GIC were allowed as lenders in the market. In October 1990, the list of participants as lenders increased to include all institutions participating in the commercial bills rediscounting market.

DFIs: IDBI, IFCI, ICICI, IRBI (now IIBI), NABARD, TFCI, NHB, EXIM Bank, SIDBI.

Insurance Companies: LIC, GIC.

Mutual Funds: UTI, SBI-MF, Canbank MF, LIC-MF, Select Urban Co operative Banks, M.S. Co-operative Bank.

April 1991: RBI allowed, as lenders, the entry to the corporate entities having bulk lendable resources. 17 corporate entities have been allowed to operate as lenders.

13 primary dealers (PDs) have been allowed to operate both as borrowers and lenders.

1994: Securities Trading Corporation of India (STCI) has been set up by the Reserve Bank of India. Though it has been set up to promote a secondary market for government securities, its operations include borrowing and lending in the call/notice money.

1998-99: 3 Private Sector Mutual Funds have been allowed to participate as lenders.

Call Money Rates

As the call money rates fluctuate widely, the call/notice money market is described as the most volatile market. The rates fluctuate depending on the demand and supply position of liquid funds with the banks. As explained earlier, the Indian money market and the business of the banks in particular is exposed to seasonal variations in terms of more demand of bank funds during the "busy" season and reduced requirement of bank credit in the slack position. In accordance with the seasonal changes, the market experiences tight liquidity conditions during the 'busy' season and the pressure of excess demand pushes the call rate up and the excess supply along with the reduced requirement of bank credit in the slack sensor pulls the rate down. The call money rate shot up as high as 30 per cent during December 1973. Thereupon, the Indian Banks' Association (IBA) intervened and fixed a ceiling at 15 per cent. The Association progressively brought the call rate down from 15 per cent in December 1973 to 10 per cent in 1980. Still, the ceiling imposed by IBA on the call money rates was observed more in breach. It was Vaghul Working Group on money markets in 1987 which recommended freeing of call money rates for inter-bank transactions, the ceiling on interest rates on call/notice money were withdrawn and the call rates were freed on May 1, 1989. The call rates were market-determined till 1973, the rates were exposed to the IBA which fixed ceiling during 1973-80 period and the rates have been freed again from May 1, 1989.

As borrowing from the RBI acts as an important source of liquid funds for banks, there exists a significant relationship between the bank rate and the call rate. The banks prefer to opt for call money depending upon how easy or restricted is their access to the discount window of the RBI.

Call Money Rates (Inter-bank)

Year	*Rates Variation*		*Average*	*Bank Rate*
	Minimum	*Maximum*		*(as March-end)*
1996-97	1.05	14.56	7.84	12.00
1997-98	0.24	52.19	8.89	10.50
1998-99	3.61	20.19	7.83	8.00
1999-00	0.10	35.00	8.87	8.00
2000-01	0.20	35.00	9.15	7.00
2001-02	3.61	22.00	7.16	6.50
2002-03	0.50	20.00	5.89	6.25
2003-04	1.00	12.00	4.33	6.00
2004-05	0.60	10.95	4.65	6.00
2005-06	0.60	8.25	5.60	6.00
2006-07	1.90	80.00	7.22	6.00
2007-08	0.10	55.00	6.07	6.00
2008-09	1.00	23.00	7.06	6.00

Need for Call Money

The banks borrow in the call money market to meet their temporary shortfall in funds.

Temporary Gap or Mismatch

Banks lend out of the deposits they mobilise. Still, the credit operations of the bank tend to go beyond their own resources, and/or there arises a mismatch creating a temporary gap.

CRR Requirements

Cash Reserve Ratio (CRR) denotes the cash reserves maintained by banks with the RBI. The banks report to the RBI their position regarding CRR every alternate Friday. The banks borrow funds from the call money market to meet their specific CRR requirements (specified percentage of their net demand and time liabilities) and their demand for call money is lower when requirements have been met on the reporting Friday. Inter-bank liabilities have been freed from reserve requirements in April 1997.

Funds Management by Banks

As a part of their funds management the banks undertake investments in financial assets which improve their earnings, but reduce their liquidity position. The banks take recourse to the call money market to ensure their liquidity status.

Developments in Call Money Market

The developments regarding: (i) the broadening of the market by allowing the non-banking institutions as lenders and (ii) Freeing of the call money rates have been already mentioned.

Though Reserve Bank does not participate in the market as the lender or borrower of funds, RBI intervenes in the call/notice money market through the two intermediary institutions: Discount & Finance House of India (DFHI) — (April 1988) and Securities Trading Corporation of India STCI — (May 1994).

Lending for Non-bank Participants: With a view to move towards a pure inter-bank call/notice money market, the limit on lending by the non-bank participants has been reduced. Non-bank participants allowed to lend on an average in a reporting fortnight:

May 2001	:	85 per cent
June 2003	:	75 per cent
Dec. 2003	:	60 per cent
June 2004	:	45 per cent
Jan. 2005	:	30 per cent

The percentage refers to their average daily lending in call/notice money market in 2000-01.

Inter-bank market

- The process of transforming the call/notice money market into a pure *inter-bank* market has been completed by August 2005.
- **Clearing Corpration of India(CCIL)** has been set up by RBI in 2001 to mitigate the risks in Indian Financial markets. CCIL developed a screen-based negotiated quote-driven system — NDS — for all deals in the call money and term money market in Sept. 2006.

NDS Call Sytem

- System developed by CCIL.
- A screen-based negotiated quote-driven system for dealing in call/notice and term money market.

Borrowing by PDs

Feb. 2004: PDs allowed to borrow in call/notice money market on an average, in a report fortnight, upto 200 per cent of NOF as at March-end of the preceding year.

During 2003-04, the average daily turnover of call notice money market declined from ₹ 17,338 crore in April 2003 to ₹ 12,916 crore in April 2004 on account of abundant liquidity.

14.2 SHORT NOTICE MONEY: REPOs

REPO is a repurchase agreement, *i.e.*, selling a security under an agreement to repurchase at a predetermined date and rate. Repo is a money market instrument which enables short-term borrowing and lending through sale/purchase operation.

REPO: Selling a security on a spot (ready) basis to repurchase the same on a forward basis.

- Repo introduced in Dec. 1992.

Reverse REPO : Buying or acquiring a security an a spot basis with a commitment to resell on a forward basis.

- Reverse REPO introduced by RBI during 1994-95.

With effect from Oct. 29, 2004, the nomenclature of Repo and reverse Repo under LAF (Liquidity Adjustment Facility) has been changed to adopt the international usage in this regard. (Source: Report on Trend and Progress of Banking in India: RBI 2003-04).

Repo : to indicate buying securities for injecting liquidity.

Reverse Repo: to indicate selling securities for absorption of liquidity.

Reverse Repo and Repo Rates

Effective Since	*Reverse Repo Rates*	*Repo Rate*
March 5, 2002	6.00	8.50
March 28, 2002	6.00	8.00
June 27, 2002	5.75	8.00
October 30, 2002	5.50	8.00
November 12, 2002	5.50	7.50
March 3, 2003	5.00	7.50
August 25, 2003	4.50	7.00
March 31, 2004	4.50	6.00
October 27, 2004	4.75	6.00
April 29, 2005	5.00	6.00
October 26, 2005	5.25	6.25
January 24, 2006	5.50	6.50
June 9, 2006	5.75	6.75
July 25, 2006	6.00	7.00
October 31, 2006	6.00	7.25
Nov. 10, 2007	7.75	6.00
April 26, 2008	7.75	6.00
June 25, 2008	8.50	6.00
Oct. 20, 2008	8.00	6.00
Dec. 6, 2008	6.50	5.00
Jan. 17, 2009	5.50	4.00
April 21, 2009	4.75	3.25

Earlier

Repo: absorption of liquidity

Reverse Repo: injection of liquidity

With effect from October 29, 2004

Reverse Repo: absorption of liquidity

Repo: injection of liqudity

Source: Economic Survey, 2008-09.

Liquidity Adjustment Facility (LAF)

An interim LAF was introduced as a mechanism for liquidity management in April 1999. The mechanism consisted of a combination of: (i) repo operations, (ii) export credit refinance facilities and (iii) collateralised lending facilities supported by open market operations.

In June 2000, the facility was upgraded into a full-fledged LAF. The window allows RBI to manage market liquidity on a daily basis.

As per *earlier nomenclature,*

RBI absorbs liquidity through Repos and injects liquidity through reverse repos on daily basis.

New nomenclature w.e.f. Oct. 29, 2004.

Repo: indicates operations for injecting liquidity.

Reverse Repos: Selling securities for absorption of liquidity since 2001-02, LAF has been bearing much of the burden of sterilisation in view of the persistent capital (foreign exchange) inflows.

LAF has been revised with effect from March 29, 2004.

(i) 7 days Repo conducted daily. 14-days Repo to be phased out.

(ii) Earlier interest rate under LAF were allowed to emerge from the bids. RBI switched over to a fixed auction format.

Overnight fixed rate Repo conducted daily, reverse repo auction on overnight basis at a fixed rate.

LAF has now emerged as the principal operating instrument of monetary policy. LAF stabilises liquidity cycles by: (i) ironing out seasonal fluctuations, and (ii) by modulating sudden liquidity shocks.

With the introduction of market stabilisation scheme (MSS) in April 2004, the pressure on LAF window has to some extent come down. The outstanding reverse repo amount under LAF has fallen from ₹ 89,435 crore mid-April 2004 to ₹ 15,820 crore by Dec. 10, 2004.

Liquidity Management: Sterilisation Effects

2004-05
- higher accretion to Net Foreign Exchange Assets (NFA)
- extensive use of LAF and MSS operation by RBI

Outstanding balances: LAF : ₹ 19,330 crore

(March-end 2005) MSS : ₹ 64,211 crore

2005-06 : Slow-down in inflow of NFA

Lower order of sterilisation effort

Outstanding balance: LAF : ₹ 40,178 crore

(Jan/Feb 2006) MSS : ₹ 34,852 crore

Second LAF was introduced in November 2005

Participants in Repo Market

Repo transactions are effected between banks and financial institutions and among banks themselves. RBI also undertakes repo/reverse repo operations with scheduled commercial banks (SCBs) and primary dealers (PDs).

July 1999: Non-bank participants (maintaining SGL Account with RBI) in the money market have been allowed to access short-term liquidity through Repos on par with banks and PDs.

March 2003: To broaden the repo market, RBI enabled NBFCs, MFs, Housing Finance Companies and Insurance Companies not holding SGL Account to undertake Repo transactions.

Securities Transacted

Initially: Central Government Treasury bills and Government Securities created, converting some of treasury bills.

Now: All Central Government Securities and Treasury bills of all maturities.

Recently, State Government securities have been made eligible for Repos.

Tenor of Repos

Upto Feb. 1995	:	14-days Repos
Since Nov. 1996	:	3-4 days (minmum 3 days) Repo auctions conducted by RBI
Nov. 1997	:	Fixed rate repo auction on a daily basis Under LAF introduced on June 5, 2000.
March 29, 2004	:	Revised LAF scheme — 7-days fixed rate repo to be conducted daily in place of daily auctions — Overnight fixed rate reverse repo to be conducted daily.
Nov. 1, 2004	:	7-days and 14-days Repo/reverse repo have been discontinued. Revised LAF scheme, would be operated with overnight fixed rate repo and reverse repo.

Repo rate

Nov. 1997:	A fixed rate repo auction system.
Year 2000:	Aug 2000: 15 per cent, Sept. 2000: 10 per cent, Oct. 2000: 8 per cent
Year 2002:	June 2002: 5.75 per cent, Oct. 2002: 5.5 per cent
Year 2004:	Aug: 2004: overnight fixed rate reverse repo at 6.0 per cent Overnight fixed rate repo: 4.5 per cent Oct. 2004: fixed repo rate raised to 4.75 per cent

Volume of Repo Transactions

The volume of Repo transactions in Government securities and treasury bills have gone up from ₹ 97,648 crore in 1995-96 to ₹ 9,55,533 crore in the year 2003-04. RBI has set up Clearing Corporation of India Ltd. **(CCIL)** in April 2001. All Repo transactions have to be necessarily put through CCIL effective from Feb. 2002.

14.3 DISCOUNT AND FINANCE HOUSE OF INDIA (DFHI)

The Discount Finance House of India (DFHI) was set up RBI in April 1988 in accordance with recommendation made by Vaghul Working Group in 1987. The paid-up capital of DFHI of ₹ 150 crore is contributed by RBI, public sector banks. DFIs, *i.e.,* All-India Financial Institutions in the proportion of 5:3:2.

Earlier, the matter of setting up a discount house in India was discussed by Chore Working Group in 1979. DFHI is to oversee and supervise money market operations and intervene in the inter-bank call/notice market, commercial bills, treasury bills market and also Commercial Paper (CPs) and CDs market. The main goal of DFHI is to smoothen short-term liquidity imbalances by activating secondary money market.

Upto May 1994, DFHI performed in the money markets as well as in the government securities market which it took up only in 1992. In May 1994, when Securities Trading Corporation of India was set up, the work of Government securities trading was entrusted to STCI and DFHI continued to operate as money market intermediary with a developmental and stabilising role.

The developmental role consisting of developing secondary market for monetary instruments and the stabilising function relates to activating money markets so that short-run surpluses and deficits are equilibriated at market-related rates.

DFHI has refinance facilities from the Reserve Bank and a line of credit of ₹ 200 crore from public sector banks on a consortium basis.

The functions of DFHI consist of—

(i) Operations as both lender and borrower in the inter-bank call/notice money market.

(ii) Purchases and sales of treasury bills: 91-days, 182-days and 364-days (364-days treasury bills replaced 182-days Treasury Bills during 1992-93; 182-days treasury bills have now been reintroduced).

(iii) Discounting and rediscounting of commercial bills, CDs and CPs.

DFHI has been more active in call notice money market followed by 182-days Treasury Bills and then commercial bills markets. (See Table 14.2 on DFHI operations)

For the treasury bills and commercial bills, DFHI gives bid (buying) and offer (selling) discount rates. DFHI also quotes bid and offer rates for 'Repos', *i.e.,* buyback transactions. The Repos facility has a maximum limit of 14 days for banks and financial institutions.

Due to 'Repos' facility provided by the DFHI, the banks, financial institutions and mutual funds can invest money and also raise money for short periods. DFHI participates in 182-days treasury bill auctions. It quotes daily bid and offer rates for these bills. DFHI extends Repos facility and quotes bid and offer rates for 'Repos'.

Bill rediscounting is an important activity of the DFHI. It rediscounts commercial bills with commercial banks and other non-banking financial institutions like—

DFIs — IDBI, ICICI, IRBI (now IIBI), ECGC, New Insurance companies like LIC, GIC.

Mutual Funds: SBI Mutual Fund, Canbank Mutual Fund and select urban co-operative banks.

To widen the scope of the market, the other institutions including IFCI, NABARD, NHB, TFCI and EXIM bank were also granted entry.

To facilitate multiple rediscounting of bills, the derivative usance promissory notes were introduced in 1988 for imparting greater liquidity to the commercial bills. The interest rate ceiling of 12.5 per cent in respect of rediscounting of commercial bills was withdrawn on May 1, 1989.

14.4 TERM MONEY MARKET

The following measures have been taken to develop the Inter-bank term money market:

- Interest rate ceiling at 10.5% to 11.5% was withdrawn with effect from March 1, 1989.
- Select financial Institutions — IDBI, ICICI, IFCI, IRBI (now IIBI), SIDBI, EXIM Bank and NABARD permitted to borrow from term money market for three to six months maturity.
- Bank exempted from maintenance of CRR and SLR in regard to liabilities to the banking system: April 1997.
- No restriction on period for which *'repos'* can be undertaken: April 1999.

Term money borrowings by financial institutions	*(₹ in crore)*	*Term money deposits mobilised by financial institutions*	*(₹ in crore)*
March 1997	645	March 1997	406
Nov 1997	802	March 1998	908
March 1998	273	June 1998	909
Interest rates on borrowings (%)		*Interest rates on deposits (%)*	
March 1997	: 12.35 to 12.7	1996-97	: 13.5 to 14
Dec. 1997	: 9.0	1997-98	: 10.5 to 12
March 1998	: 13.0 to 15.25	June 1998	: 10.0 to 11.5
June 1998	: 12.25		

14.5 COMMERCIAL BILLS

A commercial bills market is the market for short-term bills generally of three months duration. The commercial bills are an important device for providing short-term finance to trade and industry. The commercial bills or the bills of exchange are used to finance the transactions in goods taking place between different firms. When the goods are sold on credit, the firms which receive the value in goods become liable to make payment on a specific date in future. The firms which sell the goods could wait till the specified date or make use of the monetary instrument — the bill of exchange. The seller of the goods draws the bill and the buyer, *i.e.,* the drawee accepts it. On being accepted, the bill becomes a marketable instrument. The bank comes into the picture when the drawer approaches the bank for getting the bill discounted. The discount rate is the rate of interest charged while discounting the bill and paying the drawer the face value of the bill. The bank exercises the option of getting the bills rediscounted with the Reserve Bank of India. The commercial bills are described as *'self-liquidating'* in nature as they have a fixed term to maturity called *usance* — during which the drawee is likely to recover the cost of goods from the sale enabling him to make payments when due.

Kinds of Bills: There are different kinds of commercial bills.

A *bill of exchange* is an instrument in writing containing an unconditional order by the maker, directing a specified person to pay a sum of money to the order or to the bearer of the bill.

An indigenous variety of the bill is known as 'Hundi', which has a long tradition of use, particularly financing the transactions pertaining to agricultural produce.

The bills are distinguished as —

● *Demand bills* Payable on demand or at sight	*Time bills (usance)* Payable after a definite period stipulated in the bills

A similar distinction is made in respect of Hundis — darshani (sight or demand) and Muddati (usance).

● *Trade bills* Bills carry with them papers pertaining to genuine trade transactions	*Finance bills* Do not carry any documents of sale of goods with them as these bills do not arise out of any genuine trade transaction. These are only accommodation bills. These are 'clear' bills, *i.e.,* without any consideration.

A large proportion of Hundis are finance bills.

- *Inland bills* — Used to finance inland trade.
- *Foreign bills* — Used to finance foreign trade
  Import bills: to finance imports
  Export bills: to finance exports.

The distinction is also made as the drawer bill and the drawees' bill depending on who presents the bill to the bank for discounting.

Status of Bills Market

It is widely known that the market for commercial bills in the country has not developed over the years inspite of several efforts made and measures taken by RBI including schemes introduced, committees/working groups appointed to study the reasons and suggest remedial action.

The main factor is whether and how far those engaged in trade and industry show a preference for financing their transactions in goods with the help of commercial bills as monetary instrument. This factor will influence the flow of bills in the market.

The other related factor is the preference of commercial banks to opt for commercial bills as a mode of providing credit. It is also necessary that the banks discounting the bills need not hold the bills till maturity. Apart from the facilities for rediscounting of bills with the central bank, the market should develop possibilities of the bills changing hands before they mature.

In India, there are certain factors which have caused slow growth or rather impeded the development of the bills market.

(1) Reluctance of Trading and Industry Sectors: The traders in the private sector and public sector organisations engaged in trading are reluctant to bind themselves by payment discipline involved in the bills market. In *'accepting'* the bills, the buyers of goods have to commit themselves to making payments on maturity.

(2) Alternative Forms of Bank Credit: With regard to banks lending, cash credit and overdraft are the main forms and account for much high shares in the aggregate bank credit. Likewise, the borrowers from the bank opt for cash credit and overdraft as being more convenient than bills financing.

As could be seen from the Table 14.1, the share of inland bills purchased/discounted in the aggregate bank credit has come down to less than 5 per cent in the recent years from 12.5 per cent in 1972 and around 15-16 per cent between 1975 and 1985.

The shares of cash credit and overdraft together in aggregate bank credit were 55-60 per cent during 1970s and 45-50 per cent during 1980s. During this period, the share of inland bills purchased/discounted ranged between 12 to 16 per cent. The shares of these forms have come down respectively to less than 40 per cent and less than 5 per cent in the recent years.

Bill Market Schemes

These schemes form part of the efforts made by the Reserve Bank to develop the Bills market in the country.

Scheme of 1952

Under the scheme, RBI would grant advances to scheduled banks against the security of trade bills or usance promissory notes having a maturity of 90 days.

The scheme provided for the lodgement of bills as security for loans from the RBI and not for being discounted by it.

As an inducement to banks to popularise the bill, RBI offered to make advances against bills at half per cent below the bank rate. This concession and also the other in regard to stamp duty were withdrawn in 1956.

The banks created bills by converting a portion of their cash credit/overdraft accounts into usance promissory notes. The apex bank gave demand loans to scheduled banks against these promissory notes supported by the security of bills.

Scheme of 1970

The scheme specified that the bills of exchange should be genuine trade bills.

The scheme is known as rediscounting scheme as it said that all scheduled banks are eligible for offering bills exchange to the RBI for rediscounting. The bills of exchange which arise out of sales of certain commodities, particularly those covered by selective credit controls are excluded from the purview of the scheme.

The drawback of the 1952 scheme was that it permitted conversion of cash credit/overdrafts into usance bills. The 1970 scheme made only genuine trade bills eligible for rediscounting with the RBI.

During 1970s and 1980s, a number of committees and working groups — including Tandon Committee, Chore Committee, Dahejia Committee, Chakravarty Committee and Vaghul Working Group studied the matter of lack of development in respect of the bills market. Based on the recommendations made by these committees, the RBI subsequently introduced different measures aimed at promoting the growth of bills market.

April 1988: DFHI has been set up by the RBI as a major financial institution for developing the money market.

September 1988: The Reserve Bank introduced *derivative usance promissory notes* to be issued by the discounting institution on the strength of underlying bills which have a tenor not more than 90 days. The derivative usance promissory notes have been exempted from stamp duty.

1st May 1989: *Bill Market Rates.*

Bill Finance Rate: The minimum rate fixed by the RBI at which commercial banks could discount bills pertains to bill finance rates. It was 12 per cent in June 1977, and was raised to 12.5 per cent in 1978. On May 1, 1989, the ceiling on discount rate in respect of commercial bills was withdrawn.

Table No. 14.1

Outstanding Credit of Scheduled Commercial Banks

(₹ in Crores)

Year	*Cash credit*	*Overdraft*	*Demand Loan*	*Term Loan*	*Packaging credit*	*Export bills purchased / discounted*	*Inland bills purchased / discounted*	*Import bills*	*Other*	*Total*
1972	2545	480	331	601	210	212	632	30	11	5051
	(5.0)	(9.5)	(6.6)	(11.0)	(4.1)	(4.2)	(12.5)	(0.6)	(0.2)	
1975	4232	718	530	1307	377	342	1459	64	0	9030
	(46.0)	(8.0)	(5.9)	(14.5)	(4.2)	(3.8)	(16.2)	(0.7)		
1980	8578	1345	981	4492	754	796	3057	217	0	20221
	(42.4)	(6.7)	(4.9)1	(22.2)	(3.7)	(3.9)	(15.1)	(1.1)		
1985	15253	3255	1673	12323	1201	827	6137	207	56	40992
	(37.2)	(7.0)	(4.1)	(30.1)	(2.9)	(2.0)	(15.0)	(0.7)	(0.1)	
1990	29054	5878	2913	24643	3973	2966	8280	1319	1138	80165
	(30.2)	(7.3)	(3.6)	(30.1)	(2.9)	(3.7)	(10.3)	(1.6)	(1.4)	
1996	78052	16132	17483	65872	15248	11813	11104	1697	1039	218439
	(35.1)	(7.4)	(8.0)	(30.2)	(7.0)	(5.4)	(5.1)	(0.8)	(0.5)	
1997	77074	18877	30488	77041	16382	13090	11571	1419	885	246927
	(31.3)	(7.6)	(12.3)	(31.2)	(6.6)	(5.3)	(4.7)	(0.6)	(0.4)	
1998	85151	21160	41692	93957	17200	13830	12983	1905	962	288849
	(29.5)	(7.3)	(14.4)	(32.5)	(6.0)	(4.8)	(4.5)	(0.7)	(0.3)	

Source: Report on Currency & Finance, RBI, 1998-99.

Note: Figures in brackets indicate percentage to the total.

May 1990: *Participants in rediscounting market.*

The following institutions permitted to participate in bills rediscounting are:

All scheduled commercial banks.

DFIs: IDBI, IFCI, ICICI, IRBI (now IIBI), NABARD, NHB, TFCI, SIDBI, EXIM Bank, ECGC, DFHI

Investment institutions: LIC, GIC, UTI

Mutual Funds: SBI Mutual Fund, Canbank Mutual Fund, Select Urban Co operative Banks — M.S. Co-operative Bank.

October 1997: To encourage the bills culture, the Reserve Bank advised banks that atleast 25 per cent of the inland credit purchases of their borrowers should be through the bills.

Though the commercial bills market as a segment of the money market has come up and developed in industrial countries, it has not made significant progress in India mainly due to the cash credit system of credit delivery, where the responsibility of cash management lies with the banks. The trade and industry sectors have also shown reluctance to submit themselves to the discipline of bill finance.

The share of bill finance in the total bank credit has been relatively low and has fallen below 5 per cent in the recent years.

Long-term Bills

IDBI introduced bills rediscounting scheme in 1965. The long-term bills arise out of the sale of machinery on deferred payment basis. These bills enable the manufacturer of machinery to get paid without delay. They enable the purchasers to pay the cost over the number of years.

IDBI can directly accept or discount these bills or it may rediscount them from banks and other institutions. The maturity of these bills is normally five years, which could be extended to seven years. The rediscounting facilities from IDBI are available *at rates of interest fixed by it.*

The Table 14.2 pertaining to the operational details of DFHI indicates the trend in its role of being a money market intermediary in respect of different money market instruments.

14.6 TREASURY BILLS

Treasury Bills are the main instrument of short-term borrowing by the government, (Government of India) issued to meet temporary need for funds.

For banks and financial institutions, Treasury Bills are instruments for short-term investment.

Upto 1986, the only treasury bills issued in India were 91 days Treasury Bill. In November 1986, a new instrument *182 days treasury bill* was introduced.

Table No. 14.2

Discount & Finance House of India: Operational Details

(₹ in Crores)

Market	*1990-91*	*1991-92*	*1992-93*	*1993-94*	*1994-95*	*1995-96*	*1996-97*	*1997-98*
Call Money	202792	294373	457013	584048	522154	548827	421870	415031
Notice Money	—			5386	7029	5168	6088	8807
Term Money	3532	5959	3797	1542	22	18	34	656
Treasury Bills	32329	23413	16019	19971	30921	12222	6489	5662
Commercial Bills	12675	6995	786	32	332	118	31	186
CDs	8	22	33	184	7	—	—	5
CPs	107	5	42	212	—	—	—	—
Government Dated Securities	—	—	18605	14388	12488	60077	16660	14906

Source: DFHI.

364 days Treasury Bills were introduced in April 1992. During the year 1992-93, 364 days Treasury Bill replaced 182-days Treasury Bill (discontinued April 1992).

14-days Treasury Bills introduced in June 1997

28-days Treasury Bills introduced in October 1997

182-days Treasury Bills were reintroduced in May 1999.

- Treasury Bills are highly liquid and have assured yield and no risk of default.
- They are issued by the RBI on behalf of the Central Government.
- Treasury Bills are issued at a discount. The discount is the difference between the price at which Treasury Bills are sold and their redemption value.

  The price is lower than its face value by the amount of interest due on the bill.

  They are bought and sold on 'discounted basis'.
- Treasury Bills were sold by tenders or at weekly auctions upto 1965. With effect from 12th July, 1965 Treasury Bills (91-days) are available *'on tap'* throughout the week.

All regular Treasury Bills are now sold on auction basis.

In case of 91-days Treasury Bills, selling through auctions was introduced in January 1993.

- There are two types of Treasury Bills.

  'Ordinary' or 'Regular' and

  'Ad hoc'.

The *ad hoc* Treasury Bills have a maturity period of 91-days. Ordinary Treasury Bills are 91-days Treasury Bills, which are issued to enable the government to meet the needs of short-term finance. *'Ad hoc'* Treasury Bills are issued in favour of the RBI and are purchased by the latter on tap. They are not marketable but are issued for providing investment outlet to state governments, semi-government departments and foreign central banks for their temporary surpluses. The holders of these bills, when in need of cash, can sell them back to the Reserve Bank.

The regular or ordinary Treasury Bills are sold to the public and the RBI and hence are marketable. Apart from RBI, they are purchased by commercial banks, state governments, semi-government bodies and the financial institutions like LIC, UTI. Annually, the RBI and banks taken together account for about 90 per cent of the sales of treasury bills. Still, the RBI is the only major holder of the Treasury Bills, as the banks purchase these bills using their surplus funds, but soon sell these to RBI.

In November 1986, RBI decided to recycle Treasury bills to reduce the size of its holding of these bills. The apex bank would sell back to banks the rediscounted Treasury bills and impose an additional early rediscounting fees.

Treasury Bill Rate

Treasury Bill rate is the rate of discount at which the Treasury Bills are sold by the Reserve Bank. In case of 91-days Treasury Bills, the rate is fixed by RBI and at such a low level as *4.6%* per annum since 1974. The rate in case of other Treasury Bills is not administered. It is market-determined, but RBI fixes the floor price.

The low Treasury Bill rate has kept the interest cost to the government in respect of Treasury bills debt very low. Due to low rate of return on Treasury Bills, the non-banking financial institutions, corporate and other firms are disinclined to invest their surpluses in these bills.

The Chakravarty Committee (1985) and Vaghul Working Group (1987) have recommended that the discount rate should be deregulated and the discount rate be suitably revised upwards.

Funding of Treasury Bills and Monetary Policy

'Funding' means extension in the maturity of government debt. The funding of Treasury bills in the country is confined to the *'ad hoc'* Treasury Bills only. Funding of Treasury bills means their conversion into government securities. It is argued that the funding may have a favourable impact on monetary policy to the extent government securities coming into being as a result of funding help to contract the credit creating capacity of the banks. Funding of auction Treasury Bills into fixed coupon dated securities introduced in April 1993.

The Reserve Bank has to purchase whatever *ad hoc* Treasury Bills are sold to it by the Government and also rediscount whatever amount of these bills are presented to its rediscounting window by banks and others. This has an effect of monetisation of government debt which is main source of excessive expansion in money supply. The large holdings of Treasury bills by banks result, on the one hand, in reduction in bank cash and thereby in their credit-creating capacity, but, on the other hand, indicate a potential danger for the monetary policy.

System of Automatic Monetisation of Deficits (Since July 1974)

Central Government Budgetary deficit and financing it through *'ad hoc'* Treasury Bills: To cover up the Budgetary deficit, the Central Government raises short-term finance through the sale of *'ad hoc'* Treasury Bills. The *'ad hoc'* Treasury bills are issued on 'tap' and are issued in favour of the Reserve Bank of India (RBI), against which the RBI adds to money supply resulting in 'automatic monetisation'.

Since April 1997, the practice of automatic monetisation of central government budget deficit through *'ad hoc'* treasury Bills (91-days) has been replaced by a scheme of 'ways and means' advances. The *ad hoc* Treasury bills and 'tap' 91-days Treasury Bills have been discontinued.

Table 14.3 gives the trend in central government budget deficit over the years which also expressed increase in outstanding Treasury Bills *(ad hoc)* and additions to government cash balances.

Table No. 14.3
Central Government Budgetary Deficit

(₹ in Crores)

Year	*Budgetary Deficit (Central Government)*
1980-81	2,477
1985-86	5,315
1990-91	11,347
1991-92	6,855
1992-93	12,312
1993-94	10,960
1994-95	961
1995-96	9,807
1996-97	13,184

Table No. 14.4

91-days Treasury Bills: Outstanding Amount (as of March-end)

(₹ *in Crores)*

As of March-end	*Reserve Bank of India*			*Banks*		*State Governments*		*Others Banks*		*Foreign*
	Tap Redis-counted	*Ad hoc*	*Auction*	*Tap*	*Auction*	*Tap*	*Auction*	*Tap*	*Auction*	*Auction*
1993	1,287	15,430	1,147	306	155	2,083	—	160	22	—
1994	2,108	21,730	605	72	3,428	2,296	—	541	935	—
1995	1,687	23,480	68	—	38	5969	618	394	77	—
1996	2,355	29,445	3,211	—	408	5026	2,285	465	595	—
1997	9,544	34,130	1,468	—	2,365	6,539	1,262	604	605	—
1998*	—	—	627	—	29	—	530	—	95	319

* As mentioned earlier, the practice of issuing *ad hoc* Treasury Bills (91 days) on 'tap' has been discontinued with effect from April 1997, and replaced by the scheme of 'ways and means' advances. In case of 91-days Treasury Bills, the selling through Auctions introduced in January 1993. In Sept. 1994, RBI and Government agreed to phase out the system of '*ad hocs*'.

182-days Treasury Bills

To widen the short-term money market, RBI introduced a new instrument 182-days Treasury Bill in November 1986. The first auction was held in that year and from July 1988 the 182-days Treasury Bills are sold in fortnightly auctions.

RBI does not purchase these bills. They cannot be purchased by the state governments and PF organisations.

These Bills are purchased by scheduled commercial banks, foreign banks, financial institutions, joint-stock companies, National Co operative Development Organisation and DFHI which purchases and sells these bills.

These bills were replaced by 364-days Treasury Bills during 1992-93, *i.e.,* April 1992 and were reintroduced in May 1999.

Table No. 14.4(A)

Profile of Treasury Bills

(*₹ in Crores*)

91-days Treasury Bills			
Year	*Gross Amount*	*Net Amount*	*Outstanding Amount*
2002-03	26402	4626	9627
2003-04	36789	2485	7139
2004-05	100592	20653	27992
	(67955)	(19500)	(19500)
2005-06	103424	–11474	18318
	(52057)	(–19500)	—
182-days Treasury Bills Auction reintroduced in April 2005			
	Gross Amount	*Net Amount*	*Outstanding Amount*
2005-06	26828	9771	9771
	(13078)	(3000)	(3000)
364-days Treasury Bills			
	Gross Amount	*Net Amount*	*Outstanding Amount*
2002-03	26126	6538	26126
2003-04	26136	10	26136
2004-05	47132	20997	47132
	(20981)	(20981)	
2005-06	45018	– 2114	45018
	(16000)	(– 4981)	(16000)

Note: Figures in brackets indicate issues under the MSS

The auctions of 182 days Treasury Bills discontinued from May 14, 2001 and reintroduced in April 2005.

The 182-days Treasury bills are issued at a rate of discount which is market-determined. These bills have a relatively attractive rate of return. Though discount rate is market-determined, the Reserve Bank fixes the floor price.

RBI has provided refinance facilities in April 1987 to the purchases and holders of these Treasury Bills and RBI extended the refinance facilities to DFHI in April 1988.

Role of DFHI: DFHI has contributed towards developing the secondary market for the 182-days Treasury Bills. DFHI actively participates in the primary auctions of these bills, purchases and sells these bills by quoting two-way prices, *i.e.,* bid (buying) and offer (selling) prices. DFHI also quotes bid and offer rates for 'repos', *i.e.,* buyback transactions as it extends 'repos' facility upto 14 days to banks and All-India Financial institutions. The role played by DFHI in Treasury Bills market could be seen from the Table 14.2 on the operational details of DFHI.

Trends in Treasury Bills Market

The total sales of Treasury bills increased from ₹ 25,013 crore in 1977-78 to ₹ 66,530 crore in 1988-89. The outstanding Treasury Bills with the public and the RBI increased from ₹ 8,619 crore to ₹ 14,273 crore during the same period. The total sales and outstanding amount during 1988-89 in respect of 182-days Treasury bills were respectively ₹ 1,489 crore and ₹ 1,106 crore. The outstanding amount at the beginning of 1992 was ₹ 3,986 crore.

364-days Treasury Bills

Introduced during 1992-93.

1995-96: Amount of issue ₹ 1,875 crore.

The gross mobilisation almost doubled from ₹ 8,241 crore in 1996-97 to ₹ 16,247 crores in 1997-98 During 1998-99, *i.e.,* upto Sept., end 1998, the gross issues aggregated to ₹ 2,500 crore.

14-days Treasury Bills:

Introduced on June 6, 1997.

During 1997-98, gross issues amounted to ₹ 69,237 crore. However, the amount outstanding declined sharply from ₹ 10,625 crore in mid-Sept to ₹ 240 crore by March-end.

The auctions of 14-days Treasury Bills discountinued from May 14, 2001.

The Reserve Bank now auctions 91-days Treasury Bills on a weekly basis and 182-days Treasury Bills and 364-days Treasury Bills on a fortnightly basis on behalf of the Central Government. To enable investors to acquire these bills in between the auction, primary dealers (PDs) quote their bid daily.

14.7 COMMERCIAL PAPER (CP)

As recommended by the Vaghul Working Group (1987), the Commercial Papers (CPs) was introduced by RBI in March 1989 and came into effect on January 1, 1990 when the guidelines were issued. This new money market instrument is intended to provide to the companies with good credit rating a source of short-term borrowing. The guidelines of RBI apply to non-banking financial companies and non-financial companies. The companies are allowed to borrow through the issue of CPs, subject to the fulfillment of conditions spelt out in the Guidelines. The conditions have been modified and also relaxed from time to time.

- The CPs are issued in the form of usance promissory notes by the companies with good credit rating.
- They are issued at a discount. The discount rate is market-determined.
- They are freely transferrable and negotiable.
- Any person, bank, company and other registered bodies — incorporated and unincorporated, NRIs can invest in CPs. NRIs can invest in CPs on a non-repatriable basis.

- The Primary Dealers (PDs) were also permitted in September 1996 to issue CPs.
- Effective from April 30,2001 the banks, FIs, PDs have been advised to make fresh investments and hold CPs in the dematerialised form.
- The timing and issue of CPs needed RBI approval. The need for prior approval of the RBI was withdrawn in April 1991.
- The companies issuing CPs may seek stand-by facility for their bankers for meeting the liabilities of CPs on maturity. The stand-by facility was withdrawn in October 1994.

Conditions: The company — private or public sector — has to satisfy the following conditions:

	Condition	*Modified / relaxed*
1.	Minimum tangible net worth: ₹ 10 crore.	Reduced to ₹ 5 crore.
2.	Current ratio of 1.33:1.	Minimum current ratio of 1.33:1 dispensed with in October 1997.
3.	Fund-based working capital limit of ₹ 25 crore or more.	Limit reduced to ₹ 10 crore.
4.	Should be listed on one or more stock exchanges.	—
5.	The maximum amount of CP a company can raise is limited to 20% of Maximum Permissible Bank Finance (MPBF).	CPs delinked from the cash credit component of MPBF.
6.	A company can issue CP to the extent of 30% working capital limit. (November 1996).	CPs can be issued by the companies to 100% of the working capital credit limits.
7.	Minimum Amount of CP was ₹ 1 crore.	Reduced to ₹ 50 lakh and then to ₹ 25 lakh to a single investor.
8.	Maturity period: 91 days to 182 days	Modified as 15 days to 1 year.
9.	Credit Rating norm was P_1^+ from CRISIL.	Credit Rating Norm relaxed to P_2.

Table No. 14.5

Trend in CPs Issue

Year (as of March-end)	*Interest Rate (%)*	*Outstanding Amount (₹ in Crores)*
1993	15.8 to 16	577
1994	11 to 12	3264
1995	14 to 15	604
1996	20.2	76
1997	11.3 to 12.3	646
1998	14.2 to 15.5	1500
1999	10.05 to 11.50	4770
2000	10.0 to 12.0	5663
2001	8.75 to 11.25	5846
2002	7.41 to 10.25	7224
2003	6.00 to 7.75	5749

2004	4.70 to 6.50	9131
July 2004	4.61 to 5.60	10848
Nov. 2004		10150
March-end 2005	5.20 to 7.25	14235
March-end 2006	6.69 to 9.25	12718
July, 31 2006	6.50 to 8.25	21110
Oct. 31, 2006	7.00 to 8.75	23171
March 31, 2007	10.25 to 13.00	17838
July 31, 2007	2.25 to 11.50	30031
Oct. 31, 2007	6.70 to 12.00	42183
March 31, 2008	9.50 to 14.25	32592
July 31, 2008	9.60 to 12.00	51569
Oct. 31, 2008	11.50 to 16.90	48442
March 31, 2009	6.40 to 12.50	44171
June 15, 2009	3.50 to 9.15	67239

Source: Handbook of Statistics on Indian Economy, RBI 2005-06.

The non-bank institutional investors like LIC, GIC, UTI are not substantial buyers of CPs. The major holders of CPs are banks. It is possible that the bankers may reduce a company's working capital limits by an amount equal to that raised through CPs. In that case, CP finance is not an additional finance.

The success of CPs and the development of the market for CPs depends on the growth of the secondary market. As could be seen from the Table 14.2 on the operational details, DFHI has not been effective in this regard.

Issuance of CPs has increased recently with greater interest shown by mutual funds and banks. During the year 2003-04, the outstanding amount under CPs has gone up by 52% from ₹ 5,994 crore in April 2003 to ₹ 9,131 crore in March 2004.

			₹ in Crore
Outanding amount under CPs	April 2004	:	9,706
	May 2004	:	10,328
	June 2004	:	10,910
	July 2004	:	10,848

Certain developments in regard to CPs are:

- Reduction in stamp duty on CPS in March 2004.
- Minimum maturity period reduced from 15 days to 7 days.

The most preferred maturities of CPs are upto 90 days and 181 days and above.

The minimum size of individual issue as well as individual investment has been reduced to ₹ 5 lakh.

A major reform to give a measure of independence to the CP market took place when the issuance of CP was delinked from the cash credit limit in Oct. 1997 and was converted into a 'stand-alone' product from Oct. 2000.

The companies have mobilised large volume of funds through CPs as there has been significant easing in discount rates recently.

Discount rates:	2000-01 :	8.75 to 11.25
	2001-02 :	7.41 to 10.35
	2002-03 :	6.00 to 7.75
	2003-04 :	5.25 to 8.15
	upto July 2004 :	4.70 to 6.50

Shares of Companies in Issuance of CPs (in %)

Year (March-end)	*Manufacturing Companies*	*FIs*	*Finance and Leasing Companies*
2002-03	35	24	41
2003-04	22	29	49
2004-05	20	20	60
2005-06	16	10	74

Source: RBI Annual Report 2003-04.

14.8 CERTIFICATE OF DEPOSITs (CDs)

A new short-term money market instrument — Certificate of Deposit — was introduced in June 1989 to widen the range of money market instruments as per the recommendations of the Vaghul Working Group (1987).

CDs are issued by banks against the deposits kept by individuals, companies and institutions. CDs were permitted to be issued by the All-India financial institutions such as IDBI, ICICI and IFCI during 1991-92

CDs are issued on discounted basis. The discount rate or interest rate is market-determined. They are a marketable and negotiable instrument.

Condition	*Modified / relaxed*
• Minimum size of a CD to a single investor: ₹ 1 crore	Reduced to ₹ 50 lakh then to ₹ 25 lakh. April 1997: reduced to ₹ 10 lakh. Oct., 1997: reduced to ₹ 5 lakh June 2002 : ₹ 1 lakh.
• Bank wise limit on issue of CD: permitted upto 1% of fortnightly average aggregate deposits.	Limit raised to 10% of fortnightly average aggregate deposits. Bankwise limits on issue of CD abolished in Oct., 1993.
• The maturity period of CDs is between 3 months and 1 year.	Minimum lock-in period is reduced to 30 days, further reduced to 15 days in May 1998. The minimum maturity period of CDs issued by banks lowered to 7-days in April 2005.

CDs can be issued to individuals, companies, corporations trusts, Funds, associations and NRIs can also subscribe to CDs on a non-repatriable basis.

Table No. 14.6

Trend in CD Issue

Year as at March-end	*Interest rate %*	*Outstanding Amount (₹ in crore)*
1993	12.5 to 16.5	9803
1994	7.0 to 12.2	5571
1995	10 to 15.0	8017
1996	12.0 to 22.3	16316
1997	7.0 to 14.3	12134
1998	7.2 to 26.00	14296
1999	8.0 to 12.50	3717
2000	7.50 to 12.00	1227
2001	5.50 to 11.00	771
2002	5.50 to 10.03	1576
2003	5.00 to 7.10	908
2004	3.87 to 5.16	4461
June-end 2004	3.96 to 6.75	5438
Nov. 2004	3.90 to 7.00	5425
March-end 2005	4.21 to 6.34	12078
March-end 2006	6.50 to 8.94	43568
July 21, 2006	4.35 to 8.21	59167
Oct. 27, 2006	6.00 to 8.50	65764
March 30, 2007	10.23 to 11.90	93272
July 20, 2007	5.50 to 10.82	105317
Oct. 26, 2007	6.85 to 10.00	124232
March 28, 2008	9.00 to 10.75	147792
July 18, 2008	8.92 to 10.95	164892
Oct. 24, 2008	8.80 to 12.90	158562
March 2009	6.00 to 11.50	192867
July 19, 2009	3.60 to 8.00	221491

Source: Handbook of Statistics on Indian Economy, RBI 2005-06.

The issue of CDs by the scheduled commercial banks during July 1990 - September 1999 broadly reflected the liquidity trends of the economy. The activity of the CDs has fluctuated widely during the 1990-99 period. CDs gained in importance during the credit upswing.

The scheme of CDs has not made much progress. The success of CDs depends on the existence of an active secondary market for its performance. This has not come up as the holders of CDs prefer to hold them till maturity. The Table 14.2 on operational details of DFHI clearly shows that DFHI involvement in CDs has been insignificant.

The current accounts of banks are getting somewhat depleted as funds are being diverted from these accounts to CDs. In other words, a part of CDs is in the form of substitution.

The recent decline in CDs is due to certain measures in respect of term deposits such as interest rate deregulation and the reduction in the maturity period to 15 days which have facilitated better management of liabilities by banks and hence reduced the need to issue CDs. The presence of stamp duty on CDs has also affected its growth.

There has been increased activity in the segment of CDs on account of certain developments —

- issuance of guidelines on investments by banks in non-SLR debt securities.
- reduction in stamp duty w.e.f. March 2004.
- a ban on premature closure of CDs.

There has been greater demand for investment in CDs by mutual funds.

Other Money Market Instruments

• **Participation Certificates (PCs):** PCs were introduced by the RBI in 1970. It is an instrument whereby a bank can sell to a third party, a part or the total loan made by the bank to a borrower. The banks were advised to reduce their recourse to PCs after 1979.

• **Inter-bank Participations (IBPs):** This was introduced by the RBI in October 1988 IBPs are of two types: risk-sharing basis; without risk sharing.

These are inter-bank instruments to even out the short-term liquidity within the banking system.

IBP with risk-sharing: Issued for 91-180 days, rate of interest fixed by the participatory banks, minimum 14%.

IBP without risk-sharing: Maturity not exceeding 90 days. Rate of interest ceiling of 12.5%. This ceiling was withdrawn on May 1989.

IBPs without risk are subject to CRR and SLR requirements.

IBPs with 3 months maturity and without risk sharing are preferred.

Collateralised Borrowing and Lending Obligation (CBLO): CBLO as a money market operationalised by CCIL in Jan. 2003.

Membership of CBLO segment: 79 (as in Oct., 2004)

Maturity: 1 day to 1 year.

Supplier of funds : Mutual funds, Co operative Banks, Insurance Companies.

Demand for funds : Public and private sector banks, co-operative banks, PDs.

CCIL is the central counterparty, *i.e.,* it does netting for CBLO.

CBLO can be viewed as borrowing backed by securities as collateral issued at a discount to face value. CBLOs always redeem at par. CBLO is structured in a manner which includes facilities for closing out of borrowing position prior to maturity.

Private firms, NBFCs etc., who are normally excluded from the OTC bond market are able to participate in CBLO market.

CBLO has been a remarkable success.

Average Daily Turnover: April 2003: ₹ 47 crore
April 2004: ₹ 2,506 crore
Nov. 2004: ₹ 9,651 crore

The importance of CBLO lies in the fact that it is the first successful use of anonymous electronic trading in the bond market in India.

14.9 MONEY MARKET MUTUAL FUNDS (MMMFs)

The scheduled commercial banks and the public financial institutions were allowed to set up; MMMFs in April 1992. In November 1995, the Reserve Bank permitted private sector mutual funds to set up MMMFs. The individuals and NRIs can subscribe to the schemes of MMMF.

The resources mobilised by MMMFs are to be invested in call/notice money, commercial bills, CDs, CPs, treasury bills and government dated securities having an unexpired maturity of and upto one year.

The Reserve Bank of India has taken up some measures to develop these funds.

October 1997: MMMFs permitted to invest in rated corporate bonds and debentures with a residual maturity of one year.

May 1998: Initially, the lock-in period was 46 days. Minimum lock-in period reduced from 30 days to 15 days. MMMFs permitted to offer cheque writing facility in a tie-up arrangement with a bank.

MMMFs have not picked up as yet, as only three funds are currently operational.

Progress of Money Market and Effectiveness of Monetary Policy

Monetary policy decisions are transmitted to the whole economy through changes in financial prices (e.g., interest rates, exchange rates, yields, asset prices, equity prices) and financial quantities (money supply, credit supply, supply of government bonds, foreign-denominated bonds).

All over the world, the interest rate channel is the key channel of monetary policy transmission.

During the controlled or administered regime, the management of liquidity was essentially done by the RBI through direct instruments such as varying cash reserve requirement, limit on refinance, administered interest rates and qualitative and quantitative restrictions on credit.

After 1991, in the liberalised regime, interest rates are largely market-determined. The objective of the monetary policy is to make the interest rate regime more flexible and responsive to economic fundamentals.

The RBI influences the monetary conditions through market-based indirect instruments. For example, if the RBI wants to inject liquidity for a short period, it may resort to repos which may provide funds to the banks in exchange of securities of a predetermined interest rate and reversing the transaction at a predetermined time. Similarly, if the Reserve Bank wants influence long lasting liquidity, it could resort to open market operations involving outright purchase (or sale) of securities.

The other instruments such as **standing facilities** provide limited liquidity to eligible market participants such as banks and the market-based discount window makes available reserves either through direct lending or through rediscounting or purchase of financial assets held by banks.

A well developed, liquid, efficient and vibrant money market which is also well integrated with the other segments of financial markets such as government securities market-foreign exchange market is a prerequisite for the success of market-based indirect instruments of the moretary policy.

KEY TERMS

Call Money, Commercial Bill, Treasury Bill, Repo.

REVIEW QUESTIONS

1. What is money market? Explain the role and functions of money market.
2. Explain the progress and recent developments in the Indian Call Money Market.
3. Explain the role of REPO and LAF (Liquidity Adjusted Facility) in Indian Money Market.
4. Explain the role of Discount and Finance House of India.
5. What measures have been taken up to develop the inter-bank term money market?
6. What is a Commercial Bill? Explain its different types.
7. Explain the recent developments in the Indian Commercial bill market and the measures introduced by the RBI to develop the commercial bill market.
8. Discuss the different types of Treasury bills and the progress of the Treasury bill market in India.
9. What is a Commercial Paper? What conditions have to be fulfilled by the companies issuing commercial paper?
10. Write short notes –
    (a) Certificate of Deposit
    (b) Money Market Mutual Funds (MMMFs)
    (c) Collateralised Borrowing and Lending Obligation
    (d) Term Money Market
    (e) Commercial Paper
    (f) Participation Certificate, Inter-bank Participation, CBLO
11. Explain the role of money market in effectiveness of monetary policy.

REFERENCES

1. Bhole L. M. and J. Mahakud (2009), Financial Institutions and Markets — Structure, Growth and Innovations, Tata McGraw-Hill, New Delhi.
2. Ghose A. (2001), Emerging Money Markets in India, Deep and Deep Publications, New Delhi.
3. Reddy Y.Y. (1999), Development of Money Market in India, RBI Bulletin, March, 1999, p. 387.
4. RBI Annual Reports.
5. RBI Reports on Currency and Finance.

❑ ❑ ❑

15

Government Securities Market: Internal Debt: Debt Trap

INTRODUCTION

Governments at centre and state spend huge amounts to perform various administrative, regulatory functions and also to provide large economic and social infrastructure. The governments also generate revenue in terms of Taxes and Incomes from the ownership of assets and productive activities. But to fill up the gap between revenue and expenditure an important source of borrowing funds to the governments is the Government Securities Market.

The Internal or domestic debt market consists of two segments: (i) Government Securities and (ii) other securities including private corporate debt, PSU bonds, DFI bonds. Of the two, Government securities market is predominant.

The details regarding the government securities market are discussed under the following headings:

15.1 Features of the Government Securities Market

15.2 Repos Market

15.3 Significance of the Market

15.4 Volume and Composition of Issues and Other Details

15.5 Secondary Market

15.6 Status of Market Prior to 1991

15.7 Reforms After the Mid-1990s

15.8 Internal Public Debt – Debt Trap and Fiscal Consolidation

15.1 FEATURES OF THE GOVERNMENT SECURITIES MARKET

(1) Participants

(i) Central and state governments.

(ii) Banking sector: RBI, SBI, other commercial banks, co operative banks.

(iii) Insurance companies.

(iv) PF organisations.

(v) Others: financial institutions, local authorities, trusts, joint-stock companies, NRIs.

(vi) Mutual funds especially the gilt funds dealing exclusively in government securities, primary dealers (PDs), Satellite Dealers (SDs) and NBFCs.

The banks have traditionally been the dominant investors in the government securities. The share of commercial bank holding was as high as 72.5 per cent at March-end 1994, but came down to 59.5 per cent by March-end 1999.

- The market consists of mainly the institutional investors.
- The individual-dealer activity in the market is quite limited.
- The market is over-the-counter, *i.e.,* through telephones, telex etc.

(2) Forms of Government Securities

- Stock certificates: entries in SGL Account. (SGL: Subsidiary General Ledger).
- Promissory notes
- Bearer Bonds

Government securities are mostly issued in the form of promissory notes.

(3) Position of RBI

- RBI occupies the key position in the market.
- Government securities are issued through the PDO of RBI. (PDO: Public Debt Office).
- RBI engages in selling and buying of government securities.

With effect from April 12, 2006, RBI no longer participates in primary issues of Central Government Securities.

(4) Securities are issued in the denomination of ₹ 100 or ₹ 1,000.

(5) Securities are issued by:

— *Central Government*

— *State Governments*

— *Semi-government authorities* consisting of local government authorities: City Corporations, Municipalities.

— *Autonomous Institutions:* Port Trusts, Improvement Trusts, State Electricity Boards, Metropolitan Authorities, Public Sector Corporation.

— *Other Government Agencies:* IDBI, IFCI, SFCs, NABARD, LDBs, Housing Boards.

(6) Purposes of Issues

- Refunding: conversion of maturing securities.
- Advance refunding: this is of securities that have not yet matured.
- Cash financing.

Other operations: 'grooming': acquiring securities nearing maturity to facilitate redemption. 'Switches': purchase of one security against the sale of the other.

The purpose of conversion is to lengthen the maturity structure of government debt, and to reduce cash repayment.

(7) Interest on Government Securities

- Government securities are liquid and safe. They are known as 'Gilt-edged' activities.
- Rate of interest on government securities is low and it is payable half-yearly.
- Rate of interest is low to minimise the cost of servicing.

(8) Method of Issuing

Earlier: The issues are notified a few days before they become open for subscription and they are kept open for subscription for two to three days.

The auction system for the sale of government securities was introduced in June 1992.

(9) 'Captive' Market

The market for government securities consists of institutions acting as financial intermediaries such as the commercial banks, insurance companies, PF organisations which mobilise savings of the people and transfer these savings to the government through their investments in government securities. These institutions have to undertake investments in government securities to abide by the specified statutory requirements. Besides these institutions, the local authorities, semi-government bodies and NRIs also invest to a great extent in government securities.

The central government and state governments, in any given year, raise funds separately through public borrowings as per budgeted amount for that year. As the issues are mostly bought by the institutional investors, funds are raised through a small number of large issues.

15.2 REPOs MARKET

'Repo': Repurchase Agreement: One party sells a security to another party agreeing to repurchase it in future at a specified date and time.

'Reverse Repos': The opposite of Repo, in which a party buys a security from another party with a commitment to sell it back to the latter at a specified date and time. For one party, the transaction is Repo and for the other party, it is reverse Repo.

(The nomenclature has changed w.e.f. Oct. 2004)

The maturity period is short-term — 1 to 14 days, 1 to 3 weeks or 1 to 6 months. Tenders for Repos have to be for a minimum amount of ₹ 1 crore.

Reserve Bank is the major participant in the Repos market Other participants are the dealers, commercial banks, co-operative banks, DFHI and STCI. Most of the deals in the Repo market are between the banks and RBI, and between banks and DFHI or Securities Trading Corporation of India (STCI).

RBI announced on 4th December 1992 a scheme for Repos auctions for central government securities. Repos transactions were banned after the scam in 1992. With effect from April 1997, Repos have been allowed in government securities and Treasury Bills of all maturities.

Securities Trading Corporation of India (STCI)

The Reserve Bank has set up STCI in May 1994 and it started operations in June 1994.

Authorised capital: ₹ 500 crore

Paid-up capital: ₹ 12.5 crore

Objective: to promote a secondary market in government securities.

STCI also operates in call/notice money, term money, treasury bills, commercial bills, CPs, and CDs. The operations of STCI during 1994-95 were:

Call / notice money: ₹ 26,418 crore

Treasury Bills: ₹ 310 crore

Government securities: ₹ 39,631 crore.

Primary Dealers (PDs)

There are six primary dealers operational in the government securities market. PDs were introduced in 1994 and became operational in March 1995. RBI has introduced certain guidelines for the enlistment of PDs. There are now 17 PDs.

Satellite Dealers (SDs)

Reserve Bank granted approval to 16 SDs in December 1996 for dealing and distribution arrangements in the government securities market.

The primary purpose in creating the system of PDs is to strengthen the infrastructure in government securities market and to provide secondary market.

The PDs can maintain clearing balances with the RBI and participate in securities auctions.

15.3 SIGNIFICANCE OF THE MARKET

The significance of government securities market has a bearing on both fiscal and monetary policies, in terms of activating internal debt management policy and for the more effective conduct of the monetary policy.

The operations of government securities market have to ensure that suitable and low cost finance is available to the government on an ongoing basis to meet the growing requirement of funds by the government.

In the context of an inflationary environment, an important aspect of the monetary policy is to control banking sector liquidity or credit-creating capacity through the active use of weapon like variations in the reserve ratio — the SLR. As the prime component of SLR is the banks holding in government securities, variations in SLR have a direct bearing on the demand side of the government securities market. The effectiveness of the monetary policy lies in the flexibility of using such techniques of monetary control. At the same time, such a flexibility should not go against the role of government securities market in achieving the objectives of debt management. RBI has been trying to strike a mean between these two aspects — objectives of debt management and inflation control. The reform measures initiated by the Government after 1991 are meant to bring about significant changes in this direction of developing the government securities market into a vibrant market.

15.4 VOLUME AND COMPOSITION OF ISSUES AND OTHER DETAILS

The size of government securities issues has gone up from ₹ 2,630 crore to ₹ 43,390 crore in the case of central government; and from ₹ 300 crore to ₹ 7,749 crore in the case of state governments during 1980-81 to 1997-98 period.

Table No. 15.1
Market Borrowings of Government of India and State Governments

(₹ in Crores)

Loan	Subscription accepted						
	Amt. of Issue	*Amt. sub-scribed*	*Cash*	*Conver-sion*	*Total*	*Amt. Repay-able in cash*	*Net Borrow-ing*
1	2	3	4	5	6 (4+5)	7	8 (4–7)
1980-81							
Central Government	2630	2871	2734	137	2871	131	2603
State Government	300	400	284	49	333	83	201
Total	2,930	3271	3018	186	3204	214	2804
1985-86							
Central Government	5325	5764	5554	210	5764	453	5101
State Government	1284	1414	1189	225	1414	216	973
Total	6609	7178	6743	435	7178	669	6074
1990-91							
Central Government	5325	5764	5554	210	5764	453	5101
State Government	1284	1414	1189	225	1414	216	973
Total	6609	7178	6743	435	7178	669	6074
1990-91							
Central Government	8988	8989	8531	458	8989	529	8001
State Government	2565	2569	2569	—	2569	—	2569
Total	11553	11558	11099	458	11558	529	10570
1995-96							
Central Government	38636	38636	38635	—	38635	5556	33079
State Government	6274	6274	6274	—	6274	343	5931
Total	44909	44909	44909	—	44909	5899	39010
1996-97							
Central Government	27911	27911	27911	—	27911	7921	26526
State Government	6536	6536	6536	—	6536	—	6536
Total	34447	34447	34447	—	34447	7921	26526
1997-98							
Central Government	43390	43390	43390	—	43390	10902	32448
State Government	7749	7749	7749	—	7749	557	7192
Total	51139	51139	51139	—	51139	11459	39680

Source: Report on Currency and Finance, RBI 1997-98.

It could also be seen that the central as well as state government loans were oversubscribed till year 1990-91.

The other point to be noted is that the government prefers fresh borrowings increasingly in terms of cash subscriptions.

During the year 1998-99, the Government securities issues amounted to ₹ 93,953 crore in case of Central government and ₹ 12,114 crore in case of state governments.

Table No. 15.1(A)

Market Borrowings of Central Government and State Government

Year	*Centre*		*State*		*Total (Centre and State)*	
	Gross	*Net*	*Gross*	*Net*	*Gross*	*Net*
1990-91	8989	8001	2569	2569	11558	10570
1994-95	38108	20074	5123	5123	43231	25197
1995-96	40509	26790	6274	5931	46783	32721
1996-97	36152	26356	6536	6536	42688	32892
1997-98	59367	40494	7749	7193	67386	47687
1998-99	93953	62903	12114	10700	106067	73603
1999-00	99630	73077	13706	12405	113336	85482
2000-01	115183	73787	13300	12880	128483	86667
2001-02	133801	92302	18707	17261	152508	109563
2002-03	151126	104118	30853	29064	181979	133182
2003-04	147636	88816	50521	46376	198157	135192
2004-05	106501	46050	39101	33978	145602	80026
2005-06	160018	98237	21729	15455	181747	113692
2006-07	179373	111275	20825	14274	200198	125549
2007-08	188205	109504	67779	56224	255984	165728
2008-09	175780	99000	59062	44737	234842	143737

Source: Handbook of Statistics on Indian Economy, RBI 2005-06.

Between 1994-95 and 2003-04, the (net) market borrowings of Central Government have gone up nearly 4½ times, in case of state Government more than 9 times, and their combined market borrowing (net) has increased nearly 5½ times.

Table No. 15.2

Ownership Pattern of Government Securities (in %)

Year (by March-end)	*Total (₹ in Crore)*	*RBI (%)*	*Commercial Banks %*	*Insurance Companies (%) (LIC)*	*PF/ EPF*	*Others (%)*
Central Government						
1991	70377	24.7	55.1	13.4	0.9	5.7
1992	76909	22.3	59.9	14.7	0.8	2.3
1993	81693	10.6	64.6	16.3	0.8	7.7
1994	110581	3.0	71.9	16.9	0.6	7.7
1995	137515	2.5	68.7	17.2	0.5	11.1
1996	169626	9.0	64.3	17.8	0.6	8.3
1997	192893	3.4	67.5	19.8	1.0	8.2
1998	249024	12.8	57.7	18.7	1.1	9.7
1999	311605	10.9	58.9	18.2	1.4	10.6
2000	381881	8.3	60.7	18.4	1.6	11.0
2001	453668	9.2	61.0	18.6	1.9	9.3
2002	536324	7.6	60.7	20.0	2.0	9.7
2003	674203	7.8	58.5	19.3	2.0	12.64
2004	824612	5.0	55.3	19.4	2.0	18.3
2005	929612	6.8	53.2	20.2	2.4	17.6
2006	1032296	6.05	45.8	21.6	2.7	22.2
2007	1147425	9.4	47.9	24.5	3.4	15.2

State Government						
1991	15644	—	78.6	6.9	2.6	11.9
1992	18971	—	79.1	7.8	2.3	10.8
1993	23646	—	72.7	9.0	2.0	16.4
1994	26087	—	74.8	11.1	2.0	12.1
1995	31208	—	73.0	11.8	2.0	13.2
1996	37931	—	67.7	12.2	2.2	18.0
1997	43582	—	66.3	13.5	2.9	17.3
1998	50828	—	64.8	14.5	3.4	17.3
1999	61531	—	62.4	16.2	3.9	17.5
2000	73885	—	61.9	16.1	4.4	17.6
2001	86765	—	60.8	16.6	4.6	18.0
2002	104026	—	60.3	17.6	6.2	15.9
2003	133089	—	59.0	19.5	5.9	15.7
2004	179465		59.8	19.8	5.6	14.9
2005	235173	—	49.0	21.3	5.9	23.8
2006	238056	—	47.6	24.3	7.6	16.1
2007	272779	—	43.5	21.7	9.5	25.0

Source: Handbook of Statistics on Indian Economy, RBI 2003-04.

The Reserve Bank does not hold state government securities and its absorption of issues has substantially declined in case of central government securities. The government securities are predominantly held by the banks and insurance companies together.

The *maturity structure* of government borrowing has significantly shifted in favour of medium and short-term pattern. [In case of government securities, short-term is 1-5 years and medium term is between 5 to 10 years and long-term is beyond 15 years]. The state government securities are generally medium term. In the recent years, central government securities have not been issued for long-term, and are issued with maturities not beyond 10 years.

The government securities are issued at a discount. The extent of discount has been greater in case of state government securities. The 'coupon' rate is the rate of interest paid on the face value of the security. The coupon rate which significantly increased over the years, has now been lower in recent period.

Table No. 15.3
Coupon Rates
Interest Rates % (Weighted Average)

Year	*Central Government*	*State Government*
1980-81	7.03	6.75
1985-86	11.08	9.75
1990-91	11.41	11.50
1994-95	11.91	12.50
1997-98	12.01	12.82
1998-99	11.86	12.35
199-2000	11.77	11.89
2000-01	10.95	10.99
2001-02	9.44	9.20
2002-03	7.34	7.49
2003-04	5.71	6.13
2004-05	6.11	6.45
2005-06	7.34	7.63
2006-07	7.89	8.10
2007-08	8.12	8.25

Source: Handbook of Statistics on Indian Economy, RBI 2003-04.

The interest rates have declined since 1996-97 from 13.67 per cent to 5.71 per cent in case of Central Government Securities and from 13.82 per cent to 6.13 for State Government Securities.

15.5 SECONDARY MARKET

The government securities are predominantly held by the institutional investors like banks, insurance companies, PF organisations, and public financial institutions. The institutional investors like PF, LIC, public financial institutions tend to hold securities till maturity. It is mainly banks and corporate holders that engage in the buying and selling of government securities on the stock exchanges. The secondary markets for government securities is therefore quite limited. The secondary market is mainly concentrated in Mumbai. The growth of secondary market is limited due to the significant refunding of debt undertaken by the Reserve Bank.

The turnover in Government Securities declined in 2005-06 as banks preferred to hold securities, than trade.

	2004-05	*2005-06*
Average daily turnover in government securities	₹ 4,826 crore	₹ 3,643 crore

There are no Repos transactions in state government securities and the extent of outright transactions is also very small. In the case of central government securities, Repos transactions earlier exceeded the outright transactions.

Table No. 15.4
Secondary Market Transactions in Government Securities

(₹ in Crores)

Year	*Outright*	*Repo*	*Total*
1994-95	21306	29263	50569
	(42.1)	(57.9)	
1995-96	29531	97648	127179
	(23.2)	(76.8)	
1996-97	93921	29021	122942
	(76.4)	(23.6)	
1997-98	161090	24619	185709
	(86.8)	(13.2)	
1998-99	187531	40697	228228
	(82.2)	(17.8)	
1999-00	456515	82739	539255
	(84.7)	(15.3)	
2000-01	572145	126001	698146
	(81.95)	(18.05)	
2001-02	1211942	361932	1573874
	(77.00)	(23.00)	
2002-03	1378158	563515	1941673
	(71.00)	(29.00)	
2003-04	1683711	955533	2639244
	(63.8)	(36.2)	
2004-05	1160632	1562989	2723621
	(42.6)	(57.4)	
2005-06	881652	1698769	2580421
	(34.2)	(65.8)	

Source: Handbook of Statistics on Indian Economy, RBI 2005-06.

Note: Figures in brackets indicate % share in the total.

After 1995-96, the outright transactions in Government Securities exceed Repo transactions. However, the share of outright transactions has been declining and that of Repo transactions has shown a rising trend over the years.

15.6 STATUS OF MARKET PRIOR TO 1991

In the pre-1991 period, the government securities market in India was not developed. The main constraints in this regard were: (i) relatively low coupon rates — in order to keep cost of government borrowing low, the coupon rates on government securities remained low — even negative in real terms for several years till about mid-1980s and (ii) absence of definite limits on the automatic monetisation of the central government budget deficits. During the 1980s, the volume of both long-term and short-term debt expanded considerably, due to automatic accommodation through the mechanism of *'ad hoc'* Treasury bills. The apex bank had little control over the facets of debt management, *i.e.,* volume and maturity structure of securities and structure of interest rates. The maturity structure of market loans was generally of longer term of more than 15 years. The market also had limited institutional infrastructure.

15.7 REFORMS AFTER THE MID-1997

1. Coupon Rate	The maximum coupon rate raised to near market rates: 13.05% in 1997-98.
2. Maturity period	Reduced to 10 years.
3. Auction System	The auction system for the sale of government securities introduced from June 3, 1992.
4. New Instruments	Zero coupon bonds, capital indexed bonds. Tap stocks and partly paid stocks introduced.
5. Conversion of auction	Treasury Bills into long-term securities from April, 1993.
6. Delivery vs. payment system	• System of settling transactions in government securities introduced in July 1995. • It synchronises transfer of securities with cash payment.
7. Primary Dealers (PDs) Satellite Dealers (SDs)	PDs in March 1995, SDs in December 1996 system made operational.
8. Permanent and Current Securities Share of current category of securities increased	*Permanent:* Securities intended to be held till maturity. *Current:* Securities which are intended to be traded Banks were allowed to hold permanent and current securities as 70 : 30 Modified in March 1999 as *Current:* Permanent — 70:30 in March 2000 as *Current:* Permanent — 75:25
9. DFHI & STCI	Made operational and given 'Repos' facility with RBI.
10. Liquidity support to mutual funds	RBI started in April 1996 giving liquidity support to Mutual Funds engaged exclusively in government securities investment.
11. Exemption from TDS	The interest income on government securities exempted from the provisions Tax Deduction at source from June, 1997.

12. FIIs	FIIs with 100 per cent debt funds have been from January 1997 permitted to invest in government securities . Other FIIs were also allowed to invest in government securities, subject to a ceiling of 30%.
13. SGL account	The transactions in government securities market which are recorded in Special General Ledger Account (SGL) are being published to attain transparency in the working of the market.
14. Settlement system	Under the 'Rolling' Settlement, the transactions made on a particular day result in delivery after a fixed number of days. Effective from May 11, 2005, the settlement system for transactions in Government securities was standardised to T + 1 cycle.
15. 'Intra-day' transactions	Banks and PDs are permitted in February 2006 to undertake sale of government securities that they do not own, subject to the same being covered by purchase of government securities from the secondary market on the same day.
16. 'When issued' transactions	Guidelines issued in May 2006. Transactions in security authorised for issuance, but not actually issued. Transactions to be settled if and when actually issued 'when issued' trading commenced from August 1, 2006.

15.8 INTERNAL PUBLIC DEBT: DEBT TRAP

Public debts are classified as *internal debts* and *external debts* depending on whether the loans are raised by the Government within the country and outside the country. The details furnished in this chapter pertain to loans raised by the Government of India, *i.e.,* Central Government.

Public debt is raised by the Government to meet its ever growing expenditure. Being unable to generate resources adequately, the government has to leave a gap or a deficit in the budget. The government borrows internally and externally to cover up the gap and mobilise resources needed to achieve the growth targets.

Components of Internal Public Debt

The main components of Internal public debt are:

- Market loans
- Treasury Bills
- Special securities issued to the RBI and International Financial Institutions
- Others — special bearer bonds, compensation and other bonds, special floating loans, gold bonds 1998
- 'Other Liabilities' are comprising of small savings, PFs, Reserve funds and deposits.

Table No. 15.5

Outstanding Liabilities (Public Debt) of the Central Government

(as at March-end)

(₹ *in Crores*)

Item	1980-81	1985-86	1990-91	1995-96	2000-01	2001-02	2002-03	2003-04	2004-05	2005-06 (RE)	2006-07	2007-08	2008-09	2009-10
1. Internal Debt of which	30864	71039	154004	307869	803698	913061	1020689	1141706	1275971	1389758	1544975	1808359	2014451	2356940
(i) Market Loans	15549	35241	70520	163986	428793	516517	619105	707965	758995	862370	972801	1092468	1358940	1766897
(ii) Treasury Bills	12851	26014	8031	45665	18172	24631	35795	33316	34486	52149	73427	71752	139430	139430
2. Small Savings + PF	10621	26078	61771	121425	96343	144511	226400	288378	390477	479761	539450	553620	556723	548467
3. Other Accounts	3332	10781	45336	92010	144020	164157	172374	168094	174107	186921	220160	236373	320508	329007
4. Reserve Fund + Deposit	3634	11433	23464	33680	58535	73133	80126	92376	92989	109492	131295	127043	1227759	123357
I. Total Internal Liabilities (1 + 2 + 3 + 4)	48451 (81)	119331	317714	554983 (89.6)	1102596 (91.5)	1294862	1499589	1690554	1933545	2165902	2435880	272595	3014441	3357771
II. External Liabilities	11298	18153	36948	51249	65945	71546	59612	46124	60877	94243	102716	112031	121634	137681
III. Total Liabilities	59749	137484	354662	606232	1168541	1365408	1559201	1736678	1994422	2260145	2538596	2837426	3136078	3495452

Source: Handbook of Statistics on Indian Economy, RBI 2005-06.

Public Debt (Total Liabilities)

As at end-March 2010, the total liabilities of the Central Government stood at ₹ 34,95,452 crore and if external liabilities are excluded the total internal liabilities amounted to ₹ 3,35,77,771 crore.

Public Debt (Total Liabilities)

As at the end of March 2006, the total liabilities of the Central Government stood at ₹ 21,95,387 crore and if the external liabilities are excluded, the total internal liabilities amounted to ₹ 21,26,995 crore. The total internal liabilities of the Central Government by March-end 1996 were ₹ 5,54,983 crore, constituting 60.2 per cent of the Gross Domestic Product GDP. The total internal liabilities by March-end 2006 now constitute over 66 per cent of the GDP.

Ownership Pattern: The bulk of the internal public debt in the country is owned by the commercial banks and the Life Insurance Corporation. In other words, the market for public debt is a captive market and limited in nature.

Table No. 15.6

Maturity Pattern : Government Securities

Year (March-end)	*Short-term Under 5 years*	*Between 5 and 10 years*	*Over 10 years*
1991	8.6	5.6	85.8
1992	7.4	16.8	75.8
1993	8.1	14.2	77.7
1994	21.4	22.3	56.3
1995	25.3	27.4	47.3
1996	38.4	30.3	31.3
1997	45.2	29.0	25.8
1998	41.0	40.8	18.2
1999	41.4	42.4	16.2
2000	37.4	38.7	23.9
2001	27.0	47.0	25.0
2002	30.6	35.6	33.8
2003	26.4	34.7	38.9
2003-04	22.4	30.9	46.7
2004-05	23.8	30.5	45.7
2005-06	23.8	29.8	46.4

In the recent years, the maturity pattern has shifted in favour of medium-term and long-term loans.

Table 15.7

Interest Payments

(*₹ in Crores*)

	1985-86	*1993-94*	*1994-95*	*1995-96*	*1996-97*	*1997-98 (₹)*
1. Interest Payments on Internal debt	3856	15588	19168	22179	27233	31459
of which Market loans	—	9358	13205	15400	19125	22824
2. Interest payment on external debt	530	3724	4026	4414	4223	4150
3. On small savings PF	2664	16936	20313	22531	27101	29047
4. On Reserve Funds	58	170	220	253	378	510
Total interest payments	7512	36741	44060	50045	59478	65700

The above table clearly shows how the interest burden has increased significantly over the years.

Table No. 15.7 (A)
Average Interest Rates on Outstanding Internal Liabilities of Central Government

(Per cent)

Year	*Market Loans*	*Small Savings*	*PF*	*Special deposit@*
1997-98	12.05	11.92	12.48	15.08
1998-99	13.09	10.34	11.93	14.05
1999-00	13.34	11.50	11.80	15.46
2000-01	12.99	11.60	10.54	13.01
2001-02	12.83	11.61	9.09	13.73
2002-03	12.11	11.56	8.53	8.82
2003-04	11.11	10.88	7.39	7.94
2004-05	9.87	9.37	7.99	7.65
2005-06 (RE)	8.76	8.91	8.15	7.49

Source: Annual Report, RBI 2003-04.

@ The Government has notified the freezing of the corpus of special deposit scheme as on June 30, 2003.

As could be seen from the above Table, the weighted average interest rate on the market loans has declined in the recent of years. The cost of resources raised through small savings and PF has also declined.

Table No. 15.8
Interest Payments and Revenue Receipts of Central Government

(₹ in Crores)

Year	*Revenue Receipts*	*Revenue Expenditure*	*Interest Payments*	*Interest Payments % Share in Revenue Expenditure*	*Interest Payments % Share in Revenue Receipt*
(1)	*(2)*	*(3)*	*(4)*	*(4/3)*	*(4/2)*
1990-91	54954	73516	21498	29.2	39.1
1991-92	66030	82292	26596	32.3	40.3
1992-93	74128	92702	31075	33.5	41.9
1993-94	75453	108169	36741	34.0	48.7
1994-95	91083	122112	44060	36.0	48.4
1995-96	110130	139861	50045	35.8	45.4
1996-97	126279	158933	59478	37.4	47.1
1997-98	133886	180335	65637	36.4	49.0
1998-99	149485	216461	77882	36.0	52.1
1999-00	181482	249078	90249	36.2	49.7
2000-01	192605	277839	99314	35.7	51.6
2001-02	201306	301468	107460	35.6	53.4
2002-03	230834	338713	117804	34.8	51.0
2003-04	263813	362074	124088	34.3	47.0
2004-05	305991	384329	126934	33.0	41.5
2005-06	347077	439376	132630	30.2	38.2
2006-07	434387	514609	150272	29.2	28.9
2007-08	541925	594494	171030	28.8	31.6
2008-09 (RE)	562173	803446	192694	24.0	34.3

Source: Economic Survey, Government of India 2008-09.

The increase in interest burden is also seen from the increase in the proportion of interest payments in the revenue expenditure from 22 per cent in 1985-86 to around 35 per cent to 36 per cent during 1990s. The above table reveals that the interest payments pre-empt nearly 45% to 49% per cent of the revenue receipts of the Central government. The pre-emption in case of the state governments amounts to about 20 per cent.

While assessing the burden of debt, it is necessary to take into account the *debt stock, i.e.,* debt outstanding and the *debt service, i.e.,* interest and principal repayments. The above details regarding the size of public debt, maturity pattern and interest payments have been furnished to highlight these two aspects of debt burden.

In view of the above details regarding the pace at which the domestic or internal public debt has been rising, the question is raised as to whether the country is moving towards a debt trap or already caught in the internal debt trap. This question needs to be analysed and answered strategically.

Debt Trap

The accumulation of internal debt of the Government has taken place in an explosive manner. The pace at which the internal debt has grown is expressed in terms of a rise in debt/GDP ratio. In the first half of 1980s, the debt/GDP ratio was 43.6%, it has risen to 56.5%. In the 1990s, the fiscal reforms or the fiscal correction initiatives taken by the government could result in some reduction in debt/GDP ratio with regard to central government liabilities, but achieved only a small reduction in debt/GDP ratio in cases of state government liabilities.

Central Government: 1991: 52.9% of GDP, 1999:46.6% of GDP.
State Governments: 1991: 20.6% of GDP, 1999 19.4% of GDP.

The issue is that the mounting debt burden cannot be serviced indefinitely by creating new debt, or otherwise, the interest burden on existing debt would be translated into a perpetual growth in the debt/GDP ratio. In simpler language, it would be a vicious circle of borrowing more to meet the liabilities of servicing and repayments of earlier loans.

The issue has been discussed as "Sustainability of Government Domestic Debt in India" in the Report on Currency and Finance, RBI — 1998-1999. Is the mounting growth in government domestic debt sustainable from the point of view of ensuring the stability of debt/GDP ratio?

The concerns on sustainability of public debt in India arise from: (i) high stock of domestic debt, (ii) changing composition from low cost to high cost constituents — the share of liabilities consisting small savings and PF in the combined government domestic debt has increased from 36.9 per cent in the early 1980s to 44.9 per cent during the 1991-99 period and (iii) interest rates on such borrowing, the interest rates on government securities being aligned to the market rates, the borrowings from the market are mobilised at higher interest rates.

The sustainability condition suggests that the real output growth should exceed the real interest rate for ensuring the stability of the debt/GDP ratio. The relationship between nominal growth in output and debt stock provides a broad measure of the sustainability of the debt accumulation process.

1980s: Nominal growth in domestic debt: 19.4%
Growth in nominal GDP: 14.9%
1990s: after
Fiscal consolidation measures: Debt Growth: 15.2%
GDP growth: 12.5%

The factor creating pressure on the fiscal front is that the growth in the nominal GDP is estimated to be lower than the growth in the combined domestic debt of the government.

It may be said that the present level of government debt is not consistent with the medium term sustainability of the fiscal policy. This is mentioned with regard to two aspects — debt servicing burden on the budgets and quality of government expenditure.

1980s: Crossover of debt growth over the GDP growth, though output growth was above real interest rates (Interest rates were administered).

1990s: Debt/GDP ratio — growth was somewhat lower; debts servicing burden reached high levels. Interest payments pre-empt 49% of revenue receipts of the Central Government and 20% in case of state governments.

The high level of interest payments curtail capital expenditure with advance implications for output growth.

Fiscal Consolidation:

- Bringing down Gross Fiscal Deficit (GFD):

  Central Government: by 1.9%
  State Government: by 0.4%
  Overall from 8.5% to 7.5%.

The main thrust of fiscal consolidation is on:

(i) *Strengthening resource mobilisation:* Tax reforms, tax revenue of government to GDP dropped down from 16.8% in 1980's to 14.7% in 1990s.

(ii) *Expenditure management:* Reduction in government current consumption expenditure on wages and salaries and interest payment obligations.

(iii) *Restructuring of public sector:*

Strengthening of strategic units

Privatising non-strategic units: disinvestment capital receipts through disinvestment.

The major concerns are —

- Persistence of significant budget deficits of the Government sector over the years.
- The growth in the nominal GDP is estimated to be lower than the growth in the combined domestic debt of the government.

What is to be achieved is the reduction in the combined government debt to a sustainable level in the medium time frame.

KEY TERMS

Government Securities, Repo, Reverse Repo SGL Account, Public Debt, Debt Trap, Treasury Bills, Fiscal Consolidation.

REVIEW QUESTIONS

1. Explain the features of Government Securities Market in India.
2. Explain the following –
   (a) Participants in the Government Securities Market
   (b) Repos Market in Government Securities
   (c) Securities trading corporation of India.
3. Explain the volume, composition and ownership pattern in the government securities market.
4. Write a note on Secondary Market Transactions in Government Securities.
5. What measures have been taken up to develop the Government Securities Market in last two decades?
6. What is Internal Public Debt? What are its major components?
7. Discuss the situation of Internal Debt Trap and sustainability of Public debt in India.
8. Write a note on fiscal consolidation.

REFERENCES

1. Economic Survey, Government of India, Various Issues.
2. RBI, Reports on Currency and Finance.

❑ ❑ ❑

16

Capital Market: New Issues (Primary Securities) Market and Derivatives Market

INTRODUCTION

A focus in this and the following chapter is on the two segments of the capital market. The two segments are mentioned below:

Primary Market: 'New Issues' market.

Secondary Market: Stock Exchanges.

The capital market deals in long-term securities inclusive of both government securities and corporate securities. The market for government securities has been already described in a separate chapter. Presently, it is intended to provide details on the market for industrial securities issued by the corporate sector units.

16.1 New Issues Market

- (i) Floating of New Issues
- (ii) Pricing of New Issues
- (iii) Types and Major Forms of New Issues
- (iv) Services Associated with New Issues
- (v) Recent Developments in the New Issues Market
- (vi) Resource Mobilisation in the New Issues Market
- (vii) Introduction of Innovative Instruments in the Capital Market

16.2 Derivative Market

- (i) Definition
- (ii) Need for Derivative
- (iii) Types of Derivatives
- (iv) Derivative Instruments
- (v) Uses of Derivatives
- (vi) L.C. Gupta Committee Report and Recommendation
- (vii) Recent Developments in Derivative Market

The primary market segment, *i.e.,* 'New Issues market' arranges for raising of capital through floating of new issues by the corporate units in the form of shares and debentures and bonds by the Public Sector Undertaking (PSUs). The secondary market segment or stock exchanges are engaged in trading, *i.e.,* buying and selling of existing securities. It could be said that the secondary market segment is an important adjunct of the primary market. The investors in new issues can buy securities in the primary market, and can buy and sell the existing securities in the secondary market.

16.1 'NEW ISSUES' MARKET

The New Issues market plays a role of attracting investible resources in the corporate sector. It enables the corporate sector units to raise capital for setting up new enterprises or for the expansion and diversification of the existing ones.

The funds are raised in the market by the corporate sector units by issuing industrial securities and by PSUs through bonds. The funds are mobilised from the savers directly or through the institutions like commercial banks, co-operative banks, financial institutions, insurance companies, mutual funds including Unit Trust of India and other non-banking finance companies.

(i) Floating of New Issues

Prior to 1992, *the Capital Issues (Control) Act 1947* regulated the primary or New Issues market. The Act was administered by the Controller of Capital Issues, (CCI). The Act required prior approval or consent for issues of capital to the public and pricing of issues. The timing of new issues, composition of securities and other aspects of the issues were also regulated.

1992: The Capital Issues (Control) Act, 1947 was repealed, allowing issuers of securities to raise capital from the market without requiring any consent from any authority either for floating the issues or for pricing it. The other restrictions on Rights and Bonus issues, interest rates on debentures etc. have also been removed.

1992 and After: The new issue of capital has been brought under SEBI's purview and the issuers are required to meet SEBI's guidelines for disclosure and investor protection.

Ways of Floating New Issues

There are three main ways of floating new issues:

(i) By the issue of prospectus to the public: It is an open invitation to the public to subscribe to the issue by giving the details in the prospectus regarding the company, the issue, the underwriters etc.

(ii) By private placement: The issue is not offered to the public for subscription but placed privately with a few big financiers — including brokers who may sell them to clients or to the public.

(iii) By the right issue to the existing shareholders of the company: Invitation to the existing shareholders to subscribe to a part or whole of the new issue.

There are other methods including offer for sale and bonus issues.

(ii) Pricing of New Issues or Issuing Mechanism

Earlier, floating of new issues or issuing was by way of *fixed price* mechanism.

Free Pricing Regime

In 1992, the Capital Issues (Control) Act 1947 was repealed and all controls relating to raising of resources from the market were removed. The promoters (issuers of securities) no longer required concert of any authority either for floating the issue or pricing it. The restrictions on Rights and Bonus issues, interest rates on debentures etc. also were removed. The promoter and the merchant banker could together decide the price of the issue. Both new and established companies could freely decide the price of their issue.

Under the free pricing regime malpractices of some promoters and their merchant bankers brought out very attractive but unreal projects and old shares at very high premiums. Their unreal projections never materialised and led to crash in prices. In the early days of free pricing companies with negative bottom line announced repeated rights issues at a premium. This spoilt the primary market. Most of these issues were quoted below their offer price on the day they were listed on the stock exchange. Later, the new issues of capital were brought under SEBI's purview and the issuers were required to meet SEBI's guidelines for disclosure and investor protection. But by then the small investors had suffered greatly and driven away from the market. The promoters of issue are now required to justify the issue price in the prospectus and make material disclosures about the risk factors in the offer document.

Book Building – In 1995

Under the fixed price method, investor's demand is not taken into account. But the book building method explicitly uses investors' demand for shares at various prices as an important input to arrive at an offer price. Globally book building is used as a mechanism of capital raising.

In 1995, an alternative mechanism, *i.e., book building* was introduced. Book building denotes offer price, *i.e.,* Initial Offer Price (IPO) for assessing investor's demand. The guidelines regarding book building were modified in 1999. As per modified guidelines, issuer is given an option to either book build 90 per cent or 75 per cent of the net offer to the public, leaving the balance to be offered at a fixed price.

Book building, as per the guidelines of SEBI is defined as a process undertaken by which a demand for the securities proposed to be issued by a corporate body is elicited and built up and the price for such securities is assessed for the determination of the quantum of such securities to be issued by means of a notice, circular, advertisement, document or information, memoranda or offer document.

Book building, basically means auction of shares. A chart (on NSE or BSE) shows the bid price and the number of shares being bid for. It helps the investor to know the market price.

In the recent past, the method of Book Building (BB) is being increasingly used for new issues of corporate and government securities. As indicated earlier also, BB process or mechanism invites subscription from the eligible investors to a public offer of securities through a tendering process. The lead manager to the issue invites bids from individual and institutional investors for the number and price of shares for the purpose of investment by them. At the end of cut-off period, the price at which demand is sufficient to match the size of the issue, the lead manager then decides the price at which demand is sufficient to match the size of the issue. The lead manager then decides the price at which the issue will be subscribed, and proceeds to allot shares to investors who have bid at or above the price fixed by him. Book building can be undertaken for issuing equity shares, debentures, government securities, etc. In the case of government securities, only the institutional investors are eligible for bidding in book building. In case of equity, SEBI has prescribed that at least 60 per cent of the issue shall be allocated to qualified institutional buyers, not less than 15 per cent of the issue shall be available for allocation to non-institutional high network investors, and not less than 25 per cent of issue shall be reserved for retail investors, who are defined as those applying for 1000 shares or less. In respect of institutional investor quota, the lead manager is free to use his discretion in allotting shares. The bids for book-building can be paced with book running lead manager who is a merchant banker or any person authorised by the lead manager to receive the bids.

SEBI defines BB as, "a process undertaken by which a demand for the securities proposed to be issued by a body corporate is elicited and built up and the price for such securities is assessed for the determination of the quantum of such securities to be issued by means of a notice, circular, advertisement, information memoranda, and offer documents." It is used in Initial Public Offer (IPO) for efficient price discovery. During the period IPO is open, bids are collected from investors at various prices which are equal to or above the floor price. The offer price is determined after the bid closing date.

The SEBI has stipulated that the public issue through BB route should consist of two portions:

(a) the Book Built Portion (BBP) and (b) the Fixed Price Portion (FPP). The FPP is conducted like a normal public issue after the BBP during which the issue price is determined. The mechanism of these two types of public issues is given in the table.

Book Building Process in India

Issue Type	*Office Price*	*Demand*	*Payment*	*Reservations*
Fixed Price Issues	Price at which the securities are offered and would be allotted is made known in advance to the investors	Demand for the securities offered is known only after the closure of the issue	100% advance payment is required to be made by the investors at the time of application	50% of the shares offered are reserved for applications below ₹ 1 lakh and the balance for higher amount applications
Book Building Issues	A 20% price band is offered by the issuer within which investors are allowed to bid and the final price is determined by the issuer only after closure of the bidding	Demand for the securities offered, and at various prices, is available on a real time basis on the BSE website during the bidding period	10% advance payment is required to be made by the QIBs along with the application, while other categories of investors have to pay 100% advance along with the application	50% of shares offered are reserved for QIBS, 35% for small investors and the balance for all other investors

Reverse Book Building on the other hand is a price discovery mechanism for companies who want to delist their shares or buy back shares from the shareholders.

Book building is beneficial to an issuer due to the price and demand behaviour and the issue gets presold, eliminating the chance of any under subscription. The procedure is simple and if reduces the cost and time involved in making a public process in India is much different from that adopted in the USA and other developed countries. In India, the number of investors invited to apply are limited and it is the peer pressure and reputation which ensures that there are no defaults and the process is still dependent on good faith. Book building relies much on interaction among the firms, merchant bankers and investors which is not there in India.

In India, still there is lack of transparency at critical steps of book building and there is lack of strong regulation.

The Primary Market Advisory Committee's Recommendations on Book Building Guidelines:

- Hiking the allocation for retail investors to 35% (as voracious appetite displayed for public offering).
- The bid amount defining a retail investor to ₹ 1 lakh, reducing the bid period and more data disclosure and communication between the NSE and the BSE while maintaining the book.
- The committee has also come out against a price band for listed companies coming out with a fresh public offering. It has also suggested that the relatively unused 75 per cent book building option be dispensed with the offer document should disclose the parameters on which QIBs are allotted shares. Better communication between the two exchanges and category wise display of the bio-data will give investors a better idea of the kind and level of subscription.

Green Shoe Option

The SEBI amendments of Aug. 2003 permitted the green shoe option in book building issues. It is also referred to as an over allotment option. It is a mechanism to provide post-listing price stability to an initial public offering. The name green shoe option is derived from the name of the company — Green Shoe Company that used this option for the first time.

A Green Shoe option means an option of allocating shares in excess of the shares included in the public issue and operating a post-listing price stabilizing mechanism for a period not exceeding 30 days in accordance with the provision of Chapter VIII A of the DIP guidelines as given below:

- A company desirous of availing the option should seek authorisation in the general meeting for allotment of the additional shares to the stabilising agent (SA) at the end of the stabilisation period.
- The company should appoint one of the merchant bankers or book runners as the SA who will be responsible for the price stabilisation process, if required. The SA should enter into an agreement with the Issuer Company, prior to filing of offer document with the SEBI, clearly stating all the terms and conditions relating to this option including fees charged/expenses to be incurred by the SA for this purpose.
- The SA should also enter into an agreement with the promoter(s) who will lend their shares. The agreement should specify the maximum number of shares that may be borrowed from the promoters or the shareholders which should not be in excess of 15 per cent of the total issue size. The details of the agreements shall be disclosed in the

draft prospectus, the draft Red Herring Prospectus, the Red Herring Prospectus and the final prospectus.

- The promoters and pre-issue shareholders, of both unlisted and listed company, holding more than 5 per cent shares should lend the shares for the purpose of green shoe option.
- The allocation of these shares should be on pro-rata basis to all the applicants. The stabilisation mechanism should be made available for not more than 30 days from the date when trading is permitted on the exchange(s).

A stabilising agent (SA) steps in and buys the shares from the market when the share price falls below the offer price. He has the discretion to decide the timing, the quantity and the price at which to buy shares for stabilising the post-listing price. To ensure the post-listing price, the SA may either buy the issuer's equity shares from institutional shareholders or purchase them from the market but not in excess of 15 per cent of the issue size. The issuer may set up a separate stabilising fund account to keep the funds as well as the shares for purpose of stabilisation. The stabilising measure serves as a cushion against temporary volatility in stock. The SA is also responsible for meeting the excess demand after the commencement of the trading activity. On expiry of the stabilisation period, in case the SA does not buy shares to the extent of shares over allotted by the company from the market, the issuer company shall allot shares to the extent of the shortfall in dematerialised form.

The first-ever exercise of a green shoe option in the course of a public issue was carried out by the ICICI Bank. The Life Insurance Corporation became the first institution to lend shares in the primary market. It provided 16 million shares to the DSP Merill Lynch to ensure the post-listing price.

The green shoe option is an investor protection measure - especially for protection of small investors during the post-listing period. This option benefits the underwriters in both bullish and bearish conditions. In a bull market, underwriters will opt for additional allotment of 15 per cent due to index riding high. In such a scenario, the post-listing price will be automatically maintained and sometimes even higher than the offer price, enabling underwriters to make larger profits. However, in a bearish market, the underwriting option may not be exercised or the underwriters may buy up to 15 per cent at prices lower than the issue price from the market.

Earlier, the green shoe option could be exercised only in book built IPOs. Now it can be exercised in all IPOs. This measure is expected to mitigate volatility and enhance investor confidence.

Online IPOs

The online issue of shares is carried out *via* the electronic network of the stock exchanges. The guidelines for online issue of shares are incorporated in a new chapter in the SEBI (Disclosure and Investor Protection) Guidelines, 2000. The guidelines clearly state that public issue can be made either through the online system or through the existing banking channels. The company proposing to make a public issue through the online system of stock exchange has to comply with Sections 55-68A of the Companies Act, 1956 and Disclosure and Investor Protection (DIP) guidelines. The issuer company is required to enter into an agreement with stock exchanges which have the requisite system for an online offer and has to appoint brokers and registrars to the issue having electronic connectivity with stock exchanges.

This system reduces the time taken for the issue process and securities get listed within 15 days from the closure of the issue, thereby enabling faster access to funds. The new norms prescribe that the allotment of securities should be made not later than 15 days from the closure of the issue, failing which interest at the rate of 15 per cent should be paid to investors. Corporate planning an IPO can reduce their stationary, printing, and other expenses. The investor also benefits as the system eliminates refunds accept in case of direct application.

The SEBI, in its endeavour to bring the Indian stock market on par with its global counterparts, has issued guidelines for the online issue of shares by corporate. The salient features of the guidelines are as follows:

- The company will have to first enter into an agreement with a stock exchange for the online offer of securities.
- The company will have to appoint a registrar to the issue having electronic connectivity with the stock exchange.
- The stock exchange, in turn, will appoint the SEBI-registered brokers for accepting applications and placing orders for shares.
- Then broker will collect the money from clients. In case, the client fails to pay for the shares collected, the broker will have to pay the amount.
- The broker shall accept orders from clients to send the application with payment to the registrar to the issue or place the order to subscribe through a broker under the on-line system.
- In case a client fails to pay the application money, the broker, through whom the client placed the order, will have to bring in the money. If the broker fails to pay, he will be declared a defaulter.
- During the period the issue is given to the public for subscription, applicants may approach brokers of the stock exchange through which the securities are offered under the online system to place an order for subscribing to the share.
- In the case of public issues of ₹ 10 crore or more, the registrar to the issue shall open centres for collection of applications in New Delhi, Chennai, Kolkata and Mumbai.
- The broker shall open a separate bank account (escrow account) with the clearing house for primary market issue and the amount collected by the broker from his clients as margin money shall be deposited in this account.
- The prospectus should list the names of all the brokers appointed for the issue along with the names of other intermediaries like lead managers and registrars to the issue.
- The company shall have the option of listing its securities on any other exchange(s) other than the exchange through which it offers its securities to the public through the online system.

Primary Issues

- Public Issue
  - Initial Public Offering (IPO) A first time offer of sale of securities by an unlisted company
  - Follow-up Public Offering (FPO) An offer of sale of securities by a listed company
- Rights Issue
  - An offer of sale of securities existing to shareholders
- Private Placement
  - Private Placement (Unlisted companies) Direct sale of securities to some selected people or to financial institutions
  - Referential Issue
    - Allotment of shares to some select group of persons under Section 81 of the Companies Act
  - Qualified Institutions Placement (For listed companies)

Resources Mobilisation from Primary Market

(₹ in Crores)

	1999-2000		*2000-01*	
	No.	*Amount*	*No.*	*Amount*
IPO	51	2719	114	2722
Others	14	3538	10	2656
Total	65	6257	124	5378

(iii) Types and Major Forms of New Issues

Types: Initial issues: issues of the new companies.

Further issues: issues by the existing companies.

Initial capital is raised by issuing ordinary and preference shares.

Further capital can be raised by issuing ordinary shares, preference shares and debentures.

Major Forms of New Issues

Depending on the raising of capital of ownership or debt , the new issues may take the form of equity shares — ordinary shares, preference shares and debentures.

Ordinary Shares: These are ownership securities. These involve permanent investment, but could be viewed as liquid by exercising the option of selling these in the secondary market.

Preference Shares: It is an ownership security, but carries a fixed rate of return.

Debentures / Bonds: A creditorship security with a fixed rate of return and fixed maturity period.

(iv) Services associated with New Issues

(i) Origination
(ii) Underwriting
(iii) Distribution.

These services are rendered by the intermediaries like brokers, merchant bankers who mediate between the issuers of securities and the individual savers and the institutional investors willing to subscribe to the issues.

Origination: The proposal of the company raising capital through new issues needs to be evaluated by investigating viability and the prospects of the new project. A careful scrutiny of new issues proposal in technical, financial and marketing aspects improves the acceptability by the public and institutional investors.

Underwriting: The underwriting is to ensure the success of new issues by guaranteeing subscription of a stipulated amount of new issues. The part of the public issue which is not subscribed by the public is taken up by the underwriter. It may be undertaken through outright purchases of issues, or mostly on a commission basis. Mostly, underwriting is done by a group of underwriters, and the principal underwriter may get the issue sub-underwritten.

All the three forms of issues — ordinary shares, preference shares and debentures are underwritten.

The agencies rendering underwriting services include brokers, private investment companies, commercial banks and the term lending institutions.

Distribution Merchant Banks: The basic function of merchant banks is marketing corporate and other securities. They handle all the three aspects — origination, underwriting and distribution of the sale of industrial securities. The merchant bankers offer services to those who raise capital and also to those who subscribe to the capital issues.

The *'underwriting'* as a service has became significant after 1960.

In the underwriting business, the commercial banks and the DFIs — IDBI, ICICI, IFCI and the investment institutions — LIC, UTI play a significant role.

The level of subscription to the new capital issues or the extent of public response to the new issues decides how much of the amount underwritten would devolve on the underwriters. The public response to the new capital issues would improve depending on whether or not the underwriter generates confidence among the investors.

Cost of Issues

The cost of issues includes underwriting commission, brokerage and other expenses such as printing, registration, advertisement and legal expenses. As per Companies Act 1956, the overall limits have been prescribed as a certain proportion of the nominal values of shares and debentures.

Overall limit: 5 per cent and 2.5 per cent of the nominal values of shares and debentures respectively.

(v) Recent Developments in New Issues Market

It is intended to trace the developments in regard to New Issues Market during the 1980s and 1990s and further.

1. ***Dilution of foreign equity holdings:*** Under Foreign Exchange Regulation Act 1973 (FERA), the Government gave guidelines to foreign companies to bring down their foreign shareholding. For the purpose of dilution of foreign equity holding under FERA,

a number of foreign companies went in for Indianisation through additional equity share issues or disinvestment of foreign holdings. In 1976 and onwards, the primary capital market got encouragement through increase in capital issues.

2. ***Mid-1980s:*** Liberalisation policies in the spheres of industry, export-import, inflow of foreign capital-foreign collaboration gave an impetus to industrial activities and in turn, to new issues market for raising capital through capital issues.
3. ***Public sector bonds introduced in 1985-86:*** The entry of public sector bonds in the New Issues market has been an important development which enhanced resources mobilisation.
4. ***Introduction of a variety of new instruments:*** Along with the introduction of a new variety of preference shares — Cumulative Convertible Preference Share (CCPs) in 1985, there were, in the decade of 1980s, other varieties of debentures introduced and also the public sector bonds.
5. ***1988 Onwards:***
   - Increase in the inflow of NRI funds.
   - Relaxation in the norms of foreign investment/collaboration and equity participation.
   - Companies encouraged the participation of employees in their equity capital.
   - RBI allowed greater participation of banks in the form of increase of their investment in corporate shares and debentures.
6. ***Mutual Funds:*** UTI: In the recent years, the institutional investors like mutual funds including Unit Trust of India have, with huge resources at their command, gained a position of significance in terms of their role in both the segments of capital market.

   Resource mobilisation by mutual funds increased sharply in the 1980s and during the first two years of the 1990s. Resources mobilised by mutual funds during the period 1981-82 and 1991-92 grew at an average annual rate of 71 per cent.
7. ***1990s: Abolition of control over capital issues and free pricing of issues:*** These reform measures gave rise to an upsurge of activity in the primary capital market from 1992-93 to 1994-95.

   One significant factor in this regard was a spurt in equity issues with *"premium"*.

   1995-96 to 1997-98: The primary capital market experienced depressed conditions and resources mobilisation declined.
8. ***Primary Market-IPO mechanism***

   The primary market consists of:

   IPO : initial public offering

   SEO : seasoned equity offering

   The number of IPOs per year has gone up significantly from 2002 onwards. The IPO market has switched over from fixed price offerings to price discovery through a screen-based auction.

   Misuse of IPO process: Cornering of retail portion of IPOs by a few individuals: IPO Scam in December 2005.

   : individual investors placing multiple bids in the IPO auction.

: some banks (10 banks) credited the proceeds of individual A/c payee cheques to third party accounts instead of accounts of respective payees.

9. Mutual Funds registered with SEBI have been provided effective September 2005 — a specific quota of 5 per cent under the category (QIBs) qualified institutional buyers for IPO mechanism.
10. Rationalisation of Disclosures:

at present : disclosure framework was same for unlisted companies doing an IPO or listed companies doing an SEO

rationalised : disclosure requirements for an SEO have been considerably eased.

(vi) Resource Mobilisation in the New Issues Market

Private Placement: There has been rapid growth in private placements in the recent years and resources mobilisation from private placements increased significantly from ₹ 13,361 crore in 1995-96 to ₹ 49,664 crore in 1998-99.

Table No. 16.1
Resource Mobilisation from the Primary Capital Market

Year	*Prospectus & Rights*			*Private Placement*			*Total*
	Non-Government Public Ltd. Co.	*Government Companies*	*Banks & FI in Public Sector*	*Public Sector*	*Private Sector*	*PSU*	
(1)	*(2)*	*(3)*	*(4)*	*(5)*	*(6)*	*(7)*	*(8)*
1983-84	838	—	—	—	—	—	838
1984-85	1,056	—	—	—	—	—	1,056
1985-86	1,745	—	—	—	—	354	2,099
1986-87	2,581	—	—	—	—	1,674	4,255
1987-88	1,788	—	—	—	—	2,,334	4,122
1988-89	3,225	—	—	—	—	2,868	6,093
1989-90	6,510	—	—	—	—	4,229	10,739
1990-91	4,312	—	—	—	—	5,663	9,975
1991-92	6,193	—	—	—	—	5,710	11,903
1992-93	19,803	430	356	—	—	1,062	21,651
1993-94	19,330	819	3,843	—	—	5,586	29,578
1994-95	26,417	888	425	—	—	3,070	30,800
1995-96	16,075	1,000	3,465	9,290	4,071	—	33,901
1996-97	10,410	650	4,352	12,573	2,493	50	30,528
1997-98	3,138	43	1,476	20,896	9,202	—	34,755
1998-99 (p)	5,013	—	4,352	32,681	16,983	—	59,029

Col. 7. PSU Bonds: Up to 1994-95, bonds floated through prospectus and on private placement. 1995-96 onwards - privately placed PSU bonds are shown included in private placement data for the public sector.

Table No. 16.1(A)

(1)	*(2)*	*(3)*	*(4)*		*(2+3+4)*	*(5)*	*(6)*	*(5+6)*	*Total*
2002-03	1878	—	2989	—	4867	41871	25077	66948	71815
	(9)		(8)		(17)	(267)	(877)	(1144)	(1161)
2003-04					7851			63901	71752
2004-05					21892			83405	105297
2005-06					26940			96368	123308

Note: Figures in brackets indicate no. of issues.

During 2003-04, four public sector banks floated equity issues amounting to ₹ 950 crore and there were 6 bond issues floated: 3 issues by IDBI — ₹ 2930 crore and 3 issues by ICICI banks worth ₹ 1251 crore aggregate to ₹ 4181 crores.

As against the previous year, the private placement resources mobilisation declined during 2003-04. (Sept. 2003: SEBI prescribed disclosure norms.)

Table No. 16.1(B)

Private Placement Market

(₹ in Crores)

Year	*Private Sector*	*Public Sector*	*Total*
1995-96	4071	9290	13361
1996-97	2493	12573	15066
1997-98	9202	20896	30098
1998-99	16998	32681	49679
1999-00	19403	41856	61259
2000-01	23106	44731	67837
2001-02	28620	36256	64876
2002-03	25077	41871	66948
2003-04	18760	45140	63901
2004-05	35794	47611	83405
2005-06	41191	55282	96473
2006-07	81841	64025	145866
2007-08	129677	83048	212725
2008-09	93036	109709	202745

Equity Issues with Premium:

The sharp increase in resource mobilisation was due to the spurt in equity issues with *"premium"*.

		Amount	*% of the total*
1991-92	56 issues with premium	₹ 237 crore	12.4
1992-93	325 issues with premium	₹ 5,154 crore	51.8
1993-94	381 issues with premium	₹ 4,299 crore	43.2
1994-95	628 issues with premium	₹ 8,420 crore	48.4

(vii) Introduction of Innovative Instruments in the Capital Market

New instruments:

- Secured premium notes with detachable warrants.
- Non-convertible debentures with detachable equity warrants.
- Zero-interest equity shares with detachable equity warrants.
- Fully convertible cumulative, redeemable preference shares.

The resources raised through the innovative new instruments amounted to ₹ 4,703 crore in 1993-94 and ₹ 5,460 crore in 1994-95.

Capital Market Instruments

Long-term capital is raised by the corporate sector units from the stock market either in the form of ownership capital equity shares and preference shares and debt capital like debentures and bonds. The other sources of long-term capital for corporate sector units are the borrowings or term loans from the financial institutions and the deposits from the public. Of the above sources, the equity shares, preference shares, debentures and bonds are tradable and transferable.

The financial markets, inclusive of the capital market segment in India remained insufficiently developed on account of a number of deficiencies. Limited number of instruments has been one of these deficiencies. Over the years, particularly during the last two decades of 1980s and 1990s, the instrumental innovations have been attempted in the form of an introduction of a variety of new instruments with flexible features.

Ownership Securities

These consists of primary securities issued by the corporate sector units, known as *'equities'*: They are Ordinary shares and Preference shares.

Ordinary Shares

Though investment in the ordinary shares of a company is of a permanent nature, these shares possess *'liquidity'* as they could be turned into cash through the secondary capital market.

The holder of ordinary shares exposes himself to high risks, but as an owner he can participate in the earnings and the wealth of the company. The holders enjoy voting rights.

For the company, it is however, not mandatory to pay dividends on ordinary shares.

Preference Shares

Preference shares are ownership securities which carry a fixed rate of return.

As compared to ordinary shares, the preference shares with certainty of a fixed income are described as 'less risky.'

The preference shareholders have voting rights of a limited nature on issues affecting rights attached to the shares.

There are different types of preference shares:

(a) Cumulative and non-cumulative.

(b) Convertible and non-convertible.

(c) Redeemable and non-redeemable.

(d) Participating and non-participating.

Table No. 16.2

New Capital Issues by Non-Government Public Ltd. Companies

(₹ in Crores)

Year	Equity Shares		Preference Shares		Debentures: Convertible		Debentures: Non-convertible		Debentures: Total for Debentures		Total Issues	
	No.	Amount	No.	Amount	No.	Amount	No.	Amount	No.	Amount	No.	Amount
(1)	(2)	(3)	(4)	(5)	(6)	(7)	(8)	(9)	(10)	(11)	(12)	(13)
1993-94	983	9959.7	1	0.3	127	8146.3	22	1224.0	149	9370.3	1133	19330.3
	(381)	(4299.2)									(381)	(4299.2)
1994-95	1548	17414.4	9	131.4	100	7643.0	21	1227.9	121	8870.9	1678	26416.7
	(628)	(8420)									(628)	(8420)
1995-96	1598	11997.3	9	150.1	48	3438.4	15	561.7	63	3970.9	1670	16917.5
	(458)	(4856.4)									(458)	(4856.4)
1996-97	805	6116.0	5	74.9	20	527.4	12	3705.8	32	4234.2	842	10424.1
	(127)	(1464.8)									(127)	(1464.8)
1997-98	89	1162.4	1	4.3	10	1471.6	2	500.0	12	1971.6	102	3138.3
	(22)	(653.5)									(29)	(653.5)
1998-99	33	2562.70	3	59.7	5	190.6	7	2200.0	12	2390.6	48	5013.0
1999-00	69	2752.56	—	—	2	50.78	8	2350.0	10	2400.78	79	5153.34
2000-01	128	2607.51	2	142.18	1	36.26	8	3032.09	9	3068.60	139	5818.30
2001-02	6	860.2	—	—	3	518.12	10	4313.85	13	4831.97	19	5692.3
	(3)	(654.3)										
2002-03	(5)	460.2	—	—	1	217.48	3	1200.00	4	1417.48	9	1877.7
	(5)	(391.3)										
2003-04	24	1958.8	—	—	—	—	3	1250.91	3	1250.91	27	3209.7
	(17)	(1240.3)										
2004-05	51	12004.10	—	—	—	—	3	1478.0	3	1478.0	54	13482.10
2005-06	128	20899.0	1	10	1	127	1	118.0	2	245.0	131	21154.0
2006-07	115	30753	—	—	—	—	3	847	3	847	118	91600
2007-08	111	63848	1	5481	1	206	2	1103	3	1309	115	70638
2008-09	45	14671	—	—	—	—	—	—	—	—	45	14671

Note: Figures in brackets indicate data in respect of premium on capital issues which are indicated in respective totals.

After the strong growth recorded during the year 2006 and 2007, the number of new issues declined sharply during the year 2008.

Cumulative and Non-cumulative

Cumulative: If the company skips dividend in a period/periods, it has to be paid subsequently once the company makes profit.

Non-cumulative: No right of accumulation of arrears.

Convertible and Non-convertible

Convertible: They can be converted into ordinary shares as per terms and conditions generally after 3 to 5 years.

Redeemable and Non-redeemable

Redeemable: These are to be redeemed out of profits or capital raised for the purpose. The redemption has to be after after 9-12 years. The non-redeemable preference shares were abolished in 1988.

Participating and Non-participating

Participating: They have a provision for sharing in profits, *i.e.,* earn dividend higher than the fixed return, if the company makes good profits.

Cumulative Convertible Preference Shares (CCPs)

These shares are convertible into equity after 3 to 5 years. They were introduced in 1985.

Being cumulative, dividend has to be paid in arrears in a cumulative manner. They are not redeemable.

Bonus Shares

The issues of bonus shares are out of free reserves. These could be issued out of general reserves. The bonus shares can be issued under certain conditions such as —

- They are permitted if all the existing shares are fully paid and are not in lieu of a dividend.
- Total amount permitted to be capitalised for bonus shares issue should not exceed the total paid-up equity of the company.
- Residual reserves after the issue of bonus shares should be atleast 40% of the increased paid up capital.
- A resolution for the proposed capitalisation should be approved by the general body of the shareholders.

Debentures/Bonds: Creditorship Securities

Debentures

Being creditorship securities, the debentures represent loans taken by the company form the public. Debentures have a fixed maturity period and promise a fixed rate of return. The maturity period is upto 12 years. The debentures which are listed on Indian Stock Exchanges are mortgage registered debentures. The most common maturity period of debentures is seven years.

There are different types of debentures:

- Registered and unregistered (bearer).
- Convertible and non-convertible.
- Redeemable and non-redeemable.

- Partially convertible debentures.
- Perpetual debentures.
- Right debentures.

The private corporate sector is not permitted to issue non-redeemable debentures and the unregistered debentures, *i.e.,* bearer bonds.

Registered Debentures: Registered holders of debentures are those whose names appear in the registers of companies. These debentures are transferable.

Redeemable Debentures: are those which are repaid after a fixed period, normally seven years.

Convertible Debentures: These debentures are convertible into equity in part, in full or in instalments spread over a number of years.

Partly Convertible Debentures (PCDs): PCDs is a new instrument introduced in 1989. It has a maturity period of five years and the issuing company provides buyback facility in respect of the residual non-convertible portion. The PCDs have two portions ownership capital (convertible) and creditor capital.

Non-convertible Debentures (NCDs): These debentures have a buyback facility after a lock-in period of 1 year. The companies are allowed to retain 50 per cent of over subscribed amount to convert NCDs into equity shares.

"Linked" NCDs: Ordinary shares issued with NCDs.

Right Debentures

They are not issued to the public, but are issued on a right basis to the existing shareholders in a certain ratio to the ordinary shares held by them.

The maturity period is 12 years. These debentures are mostly non-convertibles.

Bonds

- **Public Sector Bonds (PSU Bonds)**

Guidelines for the issue of public sector bonds were issued in September 1985.

— Maximum maturity period is 10 years.
— Not redeemable before the expiry of seven years.
— These bonds are traded on stock exchange.
— These bonds are transferable.

- **Capital Gains Bonds**

— Institutions like IDBI, NHB, HUDCO have issued these bonds. Maturity period is three years.
— These bonds are meant for investment of capital gains for the purpose of exemption.

- **NRI Bonds**

The first series of these bonds were issued in 1988. These are US dollar-denominated instruments in the form of promissory notes offered by State Bank of India to NRI.

New Instruments

Discount Bonds and Deep Discount Bonds: These are sold at a discount to secure the face value after the specified period.

'Zero' Coupon Bonds: No interim coupon payments. It is like cumulative fixed deposit on maturity, the principal and accumulated interest is paid.

Zero Coupon Convertible Bonds: Bonds Convertible into equity at the end of three years.

Floating Rate Bonds (Sept. 1995)

Capital Indexed Bonds (1997).

Other New Instruments

Secured Premium Notes (SPN): Raised debt which can be converted into equity after 3 to 5 years.

Loyalty Coupons: Holder of debt for 2 to 3 years to exchange into equity shares.

Warrants: These are entitlements to buying an equity after 2 to 3 years.

- Non-voting Equity shares.
- Zero interest equity shares with detachable equity warrants.
- Non-convertible debentures with detachable equity warrants.
- Fully convertible cumulative, redeemable preference shares.
- The corporate financing pattern shows greater reliance on debt instruments as against equity. During 1980s, and 1990s the share of borrowing in the total sources of capital has been on an average around 36 per cent.

16.2 DERIVATIVE MARKET

Within a relatively short span of time in the recent past, there has been a substantial progress with regard to the introduction of 'Derivatives', *i.e.,* the development of financial derivatives market in the country. *The Patel Committee on the Review of System of Carry Forward Transactions* in 1995 had expressed a view that — 'The time is not yet ripe in our country for experimenting with financial derivatives fearing greater likelihood of derivatives being used for speculation rather than for risk management. Being concerned about investor protection, SEBI appointed a committee under Shri L.C. Gupta, which submitted its Report in December 1997 regarding the development of an appropriate regulatory framework on derivatives trading in India. Among the measures pertaining to the capital market, the Central Government in the Budget for the year 1998-99 proposed to bring forward necessary amendments to the Securities Contracts (Regulation) Act (SCRA) 1956 to enable trading in derivative instruments. As recorded in Economic Survey 1999-2000, The Securities Law (Amendment) Bill 1999, proposing expanded definition of securities including derivatives to facilitate development and regulation of markets for derivatives as securities has been passed by the Parliament in December 1999.

It has been clearly stated that the Securities Contracts (Regulation) Act, (SCRA) 1956 is the basis for regulation of Securities contracts and the Stock Exchanges in India. In 1995, SCRA was amended to delete *'prohibition of options.'** SCRA is now (in 1999) amended to include 'derivatives' as securities, defined earlier, quite inclusively under the Act. In view of these developments, it is necessary to be informed about 'Derivatives' as a new instrument in the Indian financial system.

It is proposed to describe 'Derivatives' as under:

- What are derivatives: Background and concept.
- Need for Derivatives: Risk Management
- Types of Derivatives: Financial Derivatives, Credit Derivatives
- Derivative Instruments: Forwards, Futures, Swap, Options etc.
- Uses of Derivatives: Hedging, Speculation, etc.

- L.C. Gupta Committee Report: recommendations.
- Further developments about derivatives.

Derivatives

Derivatives are recognised as a way of hedging risks in commercial and financial transactions. The risks arise in these transactions as the probable changes in future in regard to say, commodity prices, stock prices and exchange rates between currencies are not known to the decision-makers who participate in the markets for commodities, securities and currencies.

They are the financial contracts (written) between the two parties — one party willing to reduce or minimise the risk of negative price movements through hedging and the other ready to be counterparty to the hedger. Derivatives draw their value from the value of underlying marketable assets such as commodities, currencies and financial instruments and intangible things like price indices for commodities, securities. Obviously, the counterparties to these contracts are those other than the holders of the underlying assets.

Derivatives are also known as "deferred delivery or deferred payment instruments." The transactions are 'cash' or 'spot' transactions when delivery is immediate or against payment. In practice, however, the execution in respect of transactions agreed today is deferred till some specific date in future. Derivatives are the hedging mechanism offering possibilities of curtailing risks carried pertaining to transactions.

One significant aspect of *'Derivatives'* is that these are *off-balance sheet instruments.* When the derivatives are traded between parties, the actual delivery of the underlying assets is not involved. When the investor buys say an 'option' to purchase shares, the balance sheet is unaffected unless and until the shares are bought and paid for.

Need for Derivatives

The need for derivatives is for protecting the interests of the investors. The derivatives are viewed by the investors — both the individual and institutional as the *'hedging mechanism', i.e.,* ways and means of minimising the risks accompanying mainly the volatile market fluctuations. The fluctuations refer to movements in the asset values like changing prices of securities and commodities, interest rates and exchange rates between currencies which may mismatch with expectations.

To minimise the risk, the Forward Contracts have been in practice in markets for commodities and financial instruments. In case of forward contracts, the execution of the contract, *i.e.,* the delivery of commodities and payment thereof is deferred to a specific date in future, at the terms and conditions and contract price agreed today.

Types of Derivatives

The derivatives are financial derivatives and credit derivatives. As the hedging mechanism, the financial and credit derivatives are the ways and means of mitigating the risks, *i.e.,* the risks associated with volatile market fluctuations in case of the former, *i.e.,* financial derivatives and the credit risks in case of the latter, *i.e.,* credit derivatives. Credit risks arise in case of loans extended by the banks and financial institutions/companies with regard to the quality of the borrowers. The lenders are exposed to risk — credit risk when the corporate sector raises funds as debts, and the government in form of bonds.

The financial derivatives are further classified as equity derivatives, interest derivatives, currency derivatives on the basis of the underlying assets consisting of financial instruments, currencies etc. or indices of asset values.

Derivative Instruments

Though there are a wide variety of derivatives, the most common derivate instruments are forward contracts or forwards, futures, swaps, options warrants and convertible etc.

Forwards

Forwards are the contracts which are tailor-made as per specific needs of the two contracting parties. As these are not standardised, the forwards are not tradeable. Forwards are used for covering currency risks, commodity prices fluctuations, *i.e.*, risks.

Futures: Futures as contracts are standardised instruments in respect of several aspects like size, expiry date etc. As such, the futures one transferrable legal agreements between parties for the transactions at a price today, but actually taking place at some fixed future date. The period for which deferred could be some months, say 3 months and more. In futures trading what is exchanged is contract notes.

The futures trading is presently in practice on the Stock Exchanges in group A securities (specified securities actually traded) as they are permitted to be carried forward from settlement to settlement without taking deliveries of shares.

Swaps: Swaps are agreements between two parties for the exchange of assets or for the exchange of future streams of payments, *i.e.*, set of financial obligations or a series of cash flows for a specified period. A swap deal involves simultaneous spot deal and a matching forward deal in the opposite direction. The common swap deals are currency swaps, interest rate swaps, credit swaps, debt-equity swaps etc. An interest rate swap is a transaction between two parties for an exchange of one stream of interest payments for another. A currency swap refers to contract exchanging foreign currency in a spot market with a simultaneous transaction in the forward market in the opposite direction.

RBI issued guidelines on Interest Rate Swaps (IRS) and Forward Rate Agreements (FRAs) in July 1999.

Options are contracts between two parties — one who creates an option and obligates to sell and the other who is the buyer who gets entitled without obligation to buy a particular asset at a contracted price within a specified period. The buyers have to pay one-time non-refundable premium to the sellers. There are a number of types of options — currency options, stock index options, stock options etc.

Call Option: is a contract giving the owner the right to buy a particular asset at a fixed price at any time or before a given date.

Put Option: is a contract giving the owner the right to sell a particular asset at a fixed price at any time on or before a given date.

Cross-currency Option

- Introduced in 1994
- Gives the holder the right but not the obligation to buy or sell on underlying currency at an agreed exchange rate.
- Option holder has a right to rescind the contract.
- An instrument which provides access to foreign currency at a predetermined exchange rate.

Warrants and Convertibles

Warrant is a contract between the issuing company and the warrant holder by way of the right to purchase or subscribe to the equity shares at a predetermined price within a specified period. Warrants are issued attached to bond debentures and equity issues to attract subscription and ensure success.

Convertibles: Bonds/debentures, preference shares are 'convertible' when they can be fully or partially converted into equity of the issuing company on a specified terms.

Uses of Derivatives

Derivatives are useful for the services rendered by them:

(1) Derivatives are a useful tool of risk management. As a hedging mechanism, they reduce the risks and help markets in absorbing the risk.

(2) Derivatives serve as barometers of future trends in prices.

(3) Derivatives help in smoothening out price fluctuations.

(4) They enhance liquidity in markets for underlying assets.

(5) They enable investors — individuals and institutions to devise proper asset allocation.

Besides being used as a hedging mechanism, Derivatives are likely to facilitate speculative buying and selling resulting in the trading volume of derivatives being much higher than the values of the underlying assets. SEBI appointed a committee to make recommendations on the regulatory framework for derivatives.

L.C. Gupta Committee on Derivatives

The Gupta Committee on Derivatives appointed by SEBI submitted its report in December 1997.

The terms of reference were mainly to develop an appropriate regulatory framework for derivatives trading in India.

The committee recommended that the equity derivatives market should be developed in phases. According to the committee, the *stock index futures* are the most popular and hence the preferred type of equity derivatives.

There could be a separate exchange for futures trading or initially permission for derivatives trading could be granted to existing stock exchanges. The minimum requirement suggested was 50 members for starting derivatives trading.

The regulations of derivatives trading should be at two levels in the form of SEBI rules and Stock Exchange level rules as approved by the SEBI. The more stringent requirements recommended by Gupta Committee for derivative market included strict entry rules for brokers/dealers, independent clearing corporation, regulation of sales practices and disclosures etc.

The committee suggested bye-laws for regulation and control of trading an settlement of derivative contracts.

Further Developments Regarding Derivatives

Earlier, SEBI (Mutual Fund) regulations prohibited the use of derivatives by the Mutual Funds. The Gupta committee recommended the withdrawal of the prohibition on the use of derivatives by the Mutual Funds.

As per SEBI guidelines recently released, the Mutual Funds have been allowed to trade in derivatives for the purpose of hedging their portfolios.

SEBI has given the green signal for the introduction of 'Index Futures' trading on the two premier exchanges in the country — Bombay Stock Exchange and National Stock Exchange (NSE).

The committees differed in their views on whether the time is ripe enough for the introduction of derivatives market in the country. The focus of the debate on the subject is regarding the speculative dimension of derivatives and their likely impact towards further enhancing the speculative character of the Indian stock market.

This debate apart, all measures have been taken for developing the derivatives market in the country.

Introduction of IRS and FRA in July 1999

IRS: interest rate swap; FRA: Forward Rate Agreement. IRS, FRA introduced to enable banks, PDs, and FIs to hedge interest rate risks.

FRA: One party agrees that on a specified future date that party would lodge a nominal deposit with the other for a specified sum of money for a specified period of time at a specified rate of interest.

The party that has agreed to make a notional deposit has sold FRA and other party has bought it.

IRS: IRS is a contract between two counterparties for exchanging interest payment for a specified period based on a notional principal amount. The notional principal amount is used to calculate interest payment but not exchanged. Only the interest payment streams are exchanged. As in Nov. 2000, there were 928 outstanding IRS deals amounting to ₹ 12,620 crore of notional principal.

Transaction in FRAs/IRS Market

Month and Year	*No. of Contract*	*Outstanding Notional Principal Amount (₹ crore)*
April 6, 2001	1615	22865
March-end 2002	4379	86749
Sept. 2002	5675	131898
April 4, 2003	9363	242983
March 19, 2004	19867	518260
May 28, 2004	23331	611595
April 2005		1358487
March 2006		2194637

The participants in the market include public sector banks, PDs, foreign banks and private sector banks.

Though there has been a significant increase in the number and amount of contracts, participation is restricted mainly to select foreign and new private sector banks and PDs.

Introduction of Equity Derivatives

Trading Equity Derivatives began in India in the year 2000, when stock index futures trading on Bombay Stock Exchange (BSE) and National Stock Exchange (NSE) was allowed in June 2000.

BSE: Bombay Stock Exchange 'Sensex' comprising 30 scrips.

NSE: National Stock Exchange 'Nifty' comprising 50 scrips.

- Stock Index futures: Standardised exchange traded contracts asset: Stock index
  An agreement between buyer and seller
  at a specific future date: one/two/three months maturity
  at a price: agreed upon at the time of contract.

Till Nov. 2000, BSE and NSE combined turnover was ₹ 1,210 crore (NSE: ₹ 752 crore)

- Stock index option: introduced in Jan. 2001.

  Contract between buyer and seller:

  One who creates option has an obligation to sell at a specific future date at a price agreed upon.

  Buyer has a right to buy without obligation to buy. Buyer has to pay premium to the seller

  Seller: has an obligation to sell.
- 'Individual Stock' Option: introduced in July 2001.
- Individual Stock Futures: introduced in Nov. 2001.

  Derivatives trading is allowed in 31 stocks in both BSE and NSE. SEBI has now allowed trading in 31 additional scrips on NSE taking the total to 62 stock.
- 'Interest Rate' Derivatives: SEBI approval in June 2003 NSE introduced trading in interest rate futures on June 24, 2003.

The derivatives market segment continues to attract larger volumes particularly on National Stock Exchange as the growth in this regard on BSE has remained at low level. On NSE, the turnover in the derivatives market has outpaced the turnover in cash market.

In the recent years, there has been distinctly significant growth in equity derivatives market.

Table No. 16.3

Equity Market Turnover

(₹ in Crores)

Year	2002	2003	2004	2005	2006	2007	2008
(i) NSE Spot	624322	907882	1170298	1888112	1916227	3093982	3188510
(ii) BSE Spot	332913	409373	529704	701025	961563	1414727	1324083
(iii) Total Spot (i + ii)	957235	1317255 (37.6)	1700002 (29.0)	2589137	2877790	4508709	4512563
(iv) NSE Derivatives	345443	1350610	2586738	3926843	7046665	11940877	11654375
(v) BSE Derivatives	928	9103	19173	1965	18071	219824	75178
(vi) Total Derivatives (iv + v)	346371	1359713 (292.6)	2605911 (91.7)	3928808	7064736	12160701	11730553
Total Equity	1303508	2757287 (111.5)	4314322 (56.5)	6517945	9942526	16669410	16243116

Source: Economic Survey, Government of India 2005-06.

Note: Figures in brackets indicate % increase over the previous year.

Between 2002 and 2003, the equity spot market turnover grew at 37.6 per cent, but the equity derivatives market recorded three times increase in the turnover. In the subsequent years 2004 and 2005 the growth in turnover of spot and derivatives market was slower. The share of BSE in the derivatives market has been quite low as against that of NSE.

Table No. 16.4
Turnover in Derivatives Market *vis-a-vis* Cash market

(₹ in Crores)

Year	*On NSE Derivatives*	*Cash*
2001-02	1,01,927	5,13,167
2002-03	4,39,855	6,17,989
2003-04	21,30,612	10,99,535
2004-05 (April to Nov.)	14,61,088	7.11,702

Table No. 16.5
Turnover in Equity Derivatives Market

(₹ in Crores)

Year	*BSE*				*NSE*			
	Index Futures	*Index Option*	*Stock Future*	*Stock Option*	*Index Future*	*Index Option*	*Stock Future*	*Stock Option*
2001-02	1276.30	78.30	451.50	115.51	21482	3766	51516	25163
2002-03	1810.99	1.98	644.30	21.17	43952	9247	286532	100133
2003-04	6571.52	0.03	5171.05	331.61	554466	52816	1305939	217207
2004-05	13600	2297	213	3	772147	121943	1484056	168836
2005-06	6	3	1	0	1513755	338469	2791697	180253

Between June 2003 and March-end 2004, NSE has attained a turnover of ₹ 202 crore in interest rate futures.

As could be seen from the above Table 16.5, the single stock futures account for a sizeable proportion in trading in derivatives market. There has also been rapid growth in index derivatives. Index derivatives in April 2002 accounted for only 9.4% share in the total equity derivatives turnover. The same has gone up to 33 per cent by Jan. 2004.

Commodity Future Market

As a commodity futures exchange, National Commodity Derivatives Exchange (NCDEX) has come up. The turnover under commodity futures market rose to a level of ₹ 13.87 lakh crore in 2005.

Like stock markets, the derivatives' markets in the country are heavily dependent on a few instruments.

In developed markets, trading volumes in the derivatives segment are thrice as large as in the cash market. In India, derivative markets have a long way to go.

KEY TERMS

New Issues Market, Underwriting, Merchant Banking, Initial Public Offering (IPO), Private Placement. Shares – Ordinary and Preference, Debentures, Bonds, Derivatives Forwards, Futures, Swaps Shares, Options, Interest Rate Swaps, Forward Rate Agreements, Commodity Future Market.

REVIEW QUESTIONS

1. Discuss the pattern of growth Indian Capital Market since 1947.
2. What is New Issues or Primary Market? What are different ways of floating new issue?
3. Explain the following in the context of Primary (New Issues) market -
   (a) Book Building
   (b) Green Shoe Option
   (c) Online IPOs
4. What are the services associated with new issues?
5. Discuss the recent developments (post 1991) in the new issues market.
6. What different instruments have been introduced in the Indian Capital Market?
7. Give the definition of financial derivative and explain the need for it.
8. What are the different types of derivatives?
9. Explain the different types of derivative instruments.
10. What are the uses of derivatives?
11. Discuss the L.C. Gupta Committee Report and Recommendations on financial derivatives.
12. Discuss the recent developments in the derivatives market.

REFERENCES

1. Bhole L.M. & Mahakud J. (2009), Financial Institutions and Markets — Structure, Growth and Innovations, Tata McGraw-Hill Education Private Limited, New Delhi.
2. RBI – (a) Report on Currency and Finance, Various Issues
   (b) Handbook of Statistics on Indian Economy
3. SEBI – (a) Handbook of Statistics on the Indian Securities Market, Various Issues
   (b) Annual Report, Various Issues

❑❑❑

17

Secondary Capital Market: Stock Exchanges

INTRODUCTION

Having discussed the Primary (New Issues) Market, we intend to discuss the secondary capital markets in this chapter.

The chapter is divided into following sections and sub-sections –

17.1 Definition and Meaning of Stock Exchange

17.2 Functions, Legal Framework and Organisation of Stock Exchanges

17.3 Growth of Stock Exchanges

17.4 Stock Market Development Ratios

17.5 Bombay (Mumbai) Stock Exchange, Performance Market Capitalisation, Turnover, Sensex

17.6 Drawbacks of Stock Exchanges

17.7 Secondary Capital Market Reforms

17.8 Foreign Institutional Investors and Secondary Capital Market

17.9 Institutional Developments in Secondary Capital Market –

(i) Securities and Exchange Board of India (SEBI)

(ii) Securities Holding Corporation of India Ltd. (SHCIL)

(iii) Over the Counter Exchange of India Ltd. (OTCEI)

(iv) National Stock Exchange (NSE)

Stock Exchanges are organisations making a market for buying and selling of existing securities — government securities and corporate securities. Government securities are traded outside the trading ring in the form of over-the-counter sales and purchase.

Stock Exchange is defined as *'any body or individuals whether incorporated or not, constituted for the purpose of assisting, regulating or controlling in the business of buying, selling or dealing in securities'.*

As a market, the Stock Exchange provides facilities for exchange of shares into money and *vice versa.* It is an association which performs through member brokers who assist, facilitate and regulate trading in securities.

There are at present 23 Stock Exchanges in India recognised under the Securities Contract (Regulation) Act, 1956, including Over the Counter Exchange of India (OTCEI) and National Stock Exchange (NSE).

OTCEI was set up in 1992 and the National Stock Exchange started its operations in 1994. The number of 'listed' companies was 9877 by the year 1998-99. The 'listed' securities are securities that appear on the approved lists of stock exchanges. Bombay Stock Exchange is the leading exchange distinguished by its size, its share in the listed companies and market capitalisation, *i.e.,* the market value of the issues listed.

Secondary Capital Market

Stock Exchanges (21)	*Over The Counter Exchange of India (OTCEI)*	*National Stock Exchange (NSE)*
For big companies with paid-up capital of ₹ 5 crore and more from 1995 (in 1989: ₹ 3 crore) Membership: around 6000 members in 1995. (membership in mid-1980s was 1200).	• Smaller companies with paid-up capital of ₹ 30 lakh to ₹ 25 crore. • Computerised trading.	• Computerised trading. • Nationwide trading facilities. • Fully automated screen-based trading.

Functions of Stock Exchanges

Stock Exchanges help the corporate sector in raising funds-equity and debt-from the market. Stock Exchanges extend facilities for trading, *i.e.,* buying and selling in corporate securities and public sector bonds. Stock Exchanges impart liquidity to the capital market instruments so that investors can disinvest while new savers can invest and enter the market.

The prime function of a stock exchange is to offer 'liquidity' to the existing securities.

Stock Exchanges provide an opportunity to all concerned to invest in securities as and when they like. This opens a way for the continuous inflow of funds into the market. Investment in new issues is facilitated greatly by operations of the secondary market.

Legal Framework

The Securities Contracts (Regulations) Act 1956 is the basis for the operations of stock exchanges in India. The objective of the Act is to regulate the working of stock exchanges with a view to prevent undesirable transactions or speculations in securities and thereby build up a healthy and strong investment market in which the public could invest with confidence.

Under the Act, the Government is empowered to recognise and derecognise the stock exchanges, stipulate laws and bye-laws for their functioning and make the listing of securities on stock exchanges by the public limited companies mandatory.

Securities Contract (Regulation) Rules 1957 give effect to the objects of the Act in terms of a code of standardised regulations uniformly applicable to all the recognised stock exchanges.

Organisation of Stock Exchanges

Though the stock exchanges differ in their organisational set-up, there is a broad uniformity as the rules and their constitution is approved by the Government.

Type of Organisation	*Stock Exchanges*
(1) Non-profit Making Associations	Mumbai, Ahmedabad, Indore
(2) Joint-stock Companies limited by shares	Calcutta, Delhi, Bangalore, Cochin, Kanpur, Ludhiana, Guwahati
(3) Companies Limited by Guarantee	Chennai, Hyderabad, Pune.

- ***Governing Body:*** Subject to government approval, the Governing body of stock exchanges has powers to make amend and suspend the operations of the rules, bye-laws and regulations of the Exchanges. It has full jurisdiction over all members.
- ***Recognition:*** A stock exchange is recognised only after the government is satisfied that its rules and bye-laws conform to the conditions prescribed for ensuring fair dealings and ensuring protection to investors.

Stock Exchange: Growth

The growth in the stock exchanges activity is expressed in terms of increase in: (a) the number of listed companies, (b) market capitalisation, *i.e.,* market value of the securities of listed companies and (c) turnover.

The growth is also indicated in terms of ratios: (i) market capitalisation ratio, (ii) the total value traded ratio, and (iii) turnover ratio.

Table No. 17.1

Some Important Indicators: Stock Exchanges

Year	*No. of Listed Companies*	*Market Capitalisation (₹in Crore)*	*Turnover (₹ in Crore)*
1984-85	3883	13381	—
	(1295)	(10219)	
1985-86	4344	24302	—
	(1529)	(20378)	
1986-87	4744	27572	—
	(1911)	(21636)	
1987-88	5560	35521	—
	(2095)	(25937)	(7912)
1988-89	5841	51379	—
	(2240)	(45519)	(20562)
1989-90	5968	70521	—
	(2247)	(65206)	(29386)
1990-91	6229	1,10,279	—
	(2471)	(90836)	(36012)
1991-92	6480	354106	—
	(2601)	(323363)	(71777)
1992-93	6925	228780	—
	(2903)	(188146)	(45696)

1993-94	7811 (3585)	400077 (368071)	203703 (84536)
1994-95	9077 (4802)	473349 (435481)	162905 (67748)
1995-96	9100 (5603)	572257 (526476)	227368 (50064)
1996-97	9890 (5832)	488332 (463915)	646116 (124284)
1997-98	9833 (5853)	589816 (560325)	908681 (207383)
1998-99	9877 (5848)	574064 (545361)	1023382 (311999)

Note: Figures in brackets indicate figures pertaining to Bombay Stock Exchange
— : Not Available

No. of listed companies: 1980s — growth at 10.6%
1990s — growth at 6.1%

Market capitalisation: 1980s — grew at 38.5%
1990s — grew at 37.9%

Table No. 17.1(A)

Some Important Indicators: Stock Exchanges

(₹ in Crores)

Year	*No. of Listed Companies*	*Market Capitalisation*		*Turnover*	
1999-00	9871	BSE NSE	912842 1020426	BSE NSE All India	685028 839050 2067031
2000-01	9954	BSE NSE	571553 657847	BSE NSE All India	1000032 1339910 2880990
2001-02	9644	BSE NSE	612224 636861	BSE NSE All India	307292 513167 895818
2002-03	9413 (5650)	BSE NSE	572198 537133	BSE NSE All India	394073 617988 968909
2003-04	— (5528)	BSE NSE	1201207 1120976	BSE NSE All India	502620 1099535 1603934
2004-05		BSE NSE	1698426 1585585	BSE NSE	518717 1140071
2005-06 (March)		BSE NSE	3022191 2813201	BSE NSE	816074 1569556
2006-07 (March)		BSE NSE	3545041 3367350	BSE NSE	956165 1945285

2007-08 (March)	BSE	5138015	BSE	1578856
	NSE	4858122	NSE	3551038
2008-09 (March)	BSE	3086076	BSE	1100074
	NSE	2896194	NSE	2752023

Note: Figures in brackets indicate figures pertaining to Bombay Stock Exchange. The sotck market turned buoyant in 2003-04, after remaining subdued for over three years since Feb. 2000.

Table No. 17.2
Turnover of Stock Exchanges

(₹ *in Crores)*

Year	*BSE*	*NSE*	*Others*	*All India*
1990-91	36012	—	—	—
1991-92	71777	—	—	—
	(99.3)	—	—	—
1992-93	45696	—	—	—
	(–36.3)			
1993-94	84536	—	119167	203703
	(85.0)			
1994-95	67748	1728	93429	162905
	(–19.9)		(–21.6)	(–20.5)
1995-96	50064	68141	109163	227368
	(–26.1)	(3843.3)	(16.3)	(39.6)
1996-97	124284	294504	227328	646116
	(148.3)	(332.2)	(108.2)	(184.2)
1997-98	207383	369934	331364	908681
	(66.9)	(25.6)	(45.8)	(40.6)
1998-99	311999	414383	297000	1023382
	(50.4)	(12.0)	(–10.4)	(12.6)
1999-2000	685028	839052	542951	2067031
	(119.6)	(10.25)	(82.8)	(102.0)
2000-01	1000032	1339910	—	2880990
2001-02	307292	513167	—	895818
2002-03	314073	617988	—	963909
2003-04	502620	1099535	—	1603934
2004-05	518717	1140071	—	—
2005-06	816074	1569556	—	—

Source: Report on Currency & Finance RBI, 1999-2000.

Average Annual Growth rate	*BSE*	*NSE*	*Others*	*All India*
1990-91 to 1994-95	30.13	—	—	—
1995-96 to 1999-2000	71.81	863.13	48.66	75.8

Note: ● BSE: Bombay Stock Exchange; NSE; National Stock Exchange; Others: Other Stock Exchanges in the country.
● Figures in brackets indicate % change over the previous year.

Table No. 17.2(A)
Turnover of Stock Exchange

(₹ in Crores)

Year	*BSE*	*NSE*
2001-02	3,07,292	5,13,167
2002-03	3,14,073	6,17,989
2003-04	5,02,620	10,99,535
2004-05	5,18,717	11,40,071
2005-06	8,16,074	15,69,556

Source: RBI Annual Report, 2005-06.

Stock Market Development Ratios

- market capitalisation ratio is market capitalisation /GDP
- total value traded ratio is total value traded/GDP
- turnover ratio is value of total shares traded/market capitalisation.

Table No. 17.3
Stock Market Development Ratios

Year	*Market Capitalisation Ratio*	*Traded Value Ratio*	*Turnover Ratio*
1984	5.8	—	—
1985	9.3	—	—
1986	9.4	—	—
1987	10.7	—	—
1988	13.0	—	—
1989-90	15.4	—	—
1990-91	20.6	—	—
1991-92	57.4	—	—
1992-93	32.4	—	—
1993-94	45.6	23.2	50.9
1994-95	45.6	15.7	34.4
1995-96	47.0	18.7	39.7
1996-97	34.6	45.8	132.3
1997-98	37.7	58.1	154.1
1998-99	—	58.1	178.3
1999-2000	—	—	215.1

The market capitalisation ratio has significantly gone up in the early 1990s; the Traded Value Ratio and Turnover Ratio have risen in the second half of 1990s.

Bombay Stock Exchange

The Bombay Stock Exchange is the premier Stock Exchange in India and it was the first to be recognised on a permanent basis in 1957. An organisation named 'The Native Share & Stock Brokers' Association formed in 1875, is viewed as the forerunner of the present-day Bombay Stock Exchange. This was soon followed by a stock exchange being set up at Ahmedabad in 1894.

Bombay Stock Exchange is organised as voluntary non-profit making association.

Governing Body: The Governing body of Bombay Stock Exchange consists of both the elected and the nominated members. The members (on roll) elect 16 members to be Directors on the Governing Board, who in turn elect a President, Vice-President and Treasurers. The Executive Director is appointed by the Government to be the Chief Administrator. The nominated members of Governing Board consist of those representing Government, SEBI and RBI.

Performance of Bombay (Mumbai) Stock Exchange

No. of Listed Companies: As could be seen from Table No. 17.1, the number of listed companies has gone up from 1295 in 1984-85 to 5848 in 1998-99. The number of Listed Companies on BSE were 5874 by March-end 2001. The share of BSE in regard to the number of listed companies on all Stock Exchanges in the country has risen from around 33 per cent in 1984-85 to 40 per cent in 1990-91 and nearly 60 per cent in 1998-99.

Market Capitalisation

The market capitalisation on BSE in 1984-85 amounted to ₹ 10,219 crore accounting for over 75 per cent of market capitalisation on all stock exchanges in the country. The market capitalisation on Bombay Stock Exchange is of the order of ₹ 5,45,361 crore in 1998-99 accounting for 95 per cent of the market capitalisation on all Stock Exchanges in the country. The market capitalisation on BSE by March-end 2001 was ₹ 625, 553 crore.

Turnover

The Turnover of BSE was ₹ 7,912 crore in the year 1987-88 and has gone up to ₹ 3,11,999 crore in 1998-99. As could be seen from Table 17.1, there was a sudden spurt in Turnover in 1991-92 and a downward slide in the following year i.e., 1992-93. Again, there was a spurt in Turnover during 1993-94 followed by a distinct fall in the year 1994-95. The share of BSE Turnover in all the Stock Exchanges Turnover in the country was nearly 42 per cent in 1994-95. Since then it had fallen to less than 20 per cent in 1996-97; but has improved to around 33 per cent during 1999-2000. (See Table No. 17.3). The declining share of BSE Turnover in the total turnover of stock exchanges in the country in the recent years needs to be viewed with the rapidly grown share of National Stock Exchange (NSE) since 1995-96.

The growth in the working of BSE is presented in Market Capitalisation and Turnover as % GDP at Current prices.

Table No. 17.4
Market Capitalisation and Turnover on BSE

(Per cent)

As at the end of	*Market Capitalisation (as % of GDP at Current Prices)*	*Turnover*
Dec. 1980	3.8	1.5
Dec. 1985	7.4	2.2
March 1990	13.4	6.0
March 1991	16.0	6.3
March 1992	49.5	11.0
March 1993	28.2	6.1
March 1994	42.8	9.8
March 1995	43.1	6.7
March 1996	44.5	4.2
March 1997	34.1	9.1
March 1998	37.0	13.7
March 1999	30.9	17.7
March 2000	46.8	35.1
2005-06	92.0	24.9
2006-07	93.8	25.3
2007-08	84.0	50.4
2008-09	62.5	22.3

Source: Report on Currency and Finance, RBI 1999-2000.

The Market capitalisation of BSE as a percentage of GDP (as at the end of March) has gone up from 13.4 per cent in 1990, 46.8 per cent in year 2000 to 93.8 per cent in the year 2006-07.

The Turnover of BSE as a percentage of GDP was low at 6 per cent in 1990, but gone up to over 35 per cent in the year 2000 and to over 50 per cent in the year 2007-08.

Sensex

The BSE index is value-weighted index with 1979-100 as base and consisting of 30 companies which account from around one-fifth of the market capitalisation of BSE.

- The number of deals put through on BSE on daily basis range between 70 to 80 thousand.
- The shares listed are classified into 2 groups:

  Group A : around 150 shares of companies (specified shares) with large capital base and steady dividend record.

  Group B : (non-specified shares)

- Open outcry system

  Floor-trading: an arrangement under which buyers and sellers transacted face to face using a variety of signals.

  BSE switched over from the outcry system to the screen-based system in 1995.

- The analysis of market capitalisation and turnover of 50 top companies listed on BSE during 1990s indicates that:

Traditionally, manufacturing companies — cement, steel etc. and financial services constituted the bulk of market capitalisation and turnover at the Stock Exchange. In the recent years, the relative importance of the traditional sectors has declined, while that of the Information Technology (IT), pharmaceuticals and fast moving consumer goods sectors has increased.

Drawbacks of Stock Exchanges

(1) The trading in stock exchanges is thin and restricted. The number of listed securities in which active trading takes place is quite small.

(2) Institutional investors: A large component of the shares of good companies are held by the financial institutions and mutual funds. The public holding of these shares is limited.

(3) The whole activity on the stock exchanges and the share prices do not reflect the performance in the industries sector or the real performance of the economy. The share prices are influenced by other extraneous factors and also speculation.

(4) The working of the stock exchange is characterised by malpractices and hence the interests of small investors are not protected.

(5) The standards of services poor, suffering from delays.

Patel Committee: In May 1984, a committee under the chairmanship of Shri G.S. Patel, former Chairman of UTI was appointed by the Government to make a comprehensive review of the functioning of Stock Exchanges. The committee submitted its report in Dec. 1985.

Secondary Capital Market: Reform Measures during 1990-2010

1. Open outcry trading system replaced by online screen-based electronic trading. 23 stock exchanges have 8000 trading terminals.
2. Trading and settlement cycles

   The account period settlement system allowed the positions of brokers to be accumulated till the end of the period, giving rise to increased possibilities of default. The period of trading cycle was shortened from 14 days to 7 days.

   An alternative system - *Rolling Settlement* - was introduced in Jan. 2000 in select 10 scrips. Under the system, the transactions made on a particular day result in delivery after a fixed number of days *i.e.,* T + 5. In May 2000, 153 more scrips were brought under rolling settlement system. By Dec.-end 2001, all scrips listed on BSE were brought under compulsory rolling settlement. The rolling settlement cycle of T + 5 has been shortened to T + 3 from April 1, 2002 to T + 2 subsequently.
3. 1992: Regulation of Insider Trading — SEBI formulated the Insider trading regulations prohibiting insider trading.
4. Structural changes:
   — boards of various stock exchanges have been made broad-based to represent different interests.

   — permitted corporate and institutional members and also a member to be a member of another stock exchange.
5. Process of dematerialisation of securities through depository system and their transfer through electronic book entry : Depositories Act, 1996 passed to provide legal framework for the establishment of depositories to record ownership details in book entry form and to facilitate the dematerialisation of securities.

By March-end 2000, 93 per cent of securities delivered for settlement at BSE and NSE together were in demat form. By March-end 2001, 98 per cent of scrips traded on all exchanges were to be in demat form.

6. Transaction Costs

   Changes including automated trading, dematerialisation, increased competition in the supply of brokerage services resulting in reduction of brokerage fees have led to significant reduction in transaction costs.

   1994 : 4.75 per cent of selling/buying price

   1999 : 0.6 per cent of selling/buying price.

   This indicates improvement in the overall market efficiency.

7. Disclosure standards have been strengthened:
   — disclosure of information having a bearing on the performance/operations of a company is required to be made available to the public.
   — the stock exchanges have to disclose carry forward position — scriptwise and brokerwise at the beginning of carry forward session (transactions of stock exchanges are carried out on either cash basis or carry forward basis.

8. Setting up Trade/Settlement Guarantee fund:
   — to ensure timely completion of settlements.
   — 10 stock exchange have set up trade/settlement guarantee funds.

9. Integration with international capital markets: Permission given to Foreign Institutional Investors (FIIs) to operate in the primary and secondary segments of the Indian capital market.

   Integration of Securities Market: The Interconnected Stock Exchange of India Ltd. has been set up as an interconnected system for the integration of various regional stock exchanges.

10. Indian companies have been allowed to raise capital from international capital markets — in the form of instruments such as Global Depository Receipts (GDRs), American Depository Receipts (ADRs), Foreign Currency Convertible bonds (FCCBs) and External Commercial Borrowings (ECBs).

Table No. 17.5
Resource Mobilisation from International Capital Markets

(₹ in Crores)

	Euro-Issues				
Year	*GDR (including ADR)*	*FCCB*	*Total*	*ECB*	*Total*
1	*2*	*3*	*4 (2+3)*	*5*	*(5+6)*
1990-91	—	—	—	4,034	4,034
1991-92	—	—	—	3,807	3,807
1992-93	251	—	251	(–)1,095	(–) 844

1993-94	4,324	3,130	7,454	1,905	9,359
1994-95	5,027	1,083	6,110	3,238	9,348
1995-96	496	—	496	4,548	5,044
1996-97	1,625	1,651	3,275	10,003	13,278
1997-98	4,330	48	4,287	14,557	18,936
1998-99	2,105	—	2,105	3,485	5,589
1999-00 (April to Sept.)	482	—	482	—	—

11. Companies allowed to buy back their own shares for capital restructuring.

Table No. 17.5 (A)
Euro Issues

(₹ *in Crores*)

Year	*No. of Issues*	*Amount*
1993-94	27	7898
1994-95	31	6743
1995-96	5	1297
1996-97	16	5594
1997-98	7	4009
1998-99	3	1148
1999-00	6	3487
2000-01	13	4197
2001-02	5	2385
2002-03	11	3426
2003-04	18	3098
2004-05	15	3353
2005-06	49	11358
2006-07	40	17005
2007-08	26	26556
2008-09	13	4788

Source: Handbook of Statistics on Indian Economy, RBI 2005-06.

FII Trends in Secondary Capital Market

Trends in share prices: The volatility in share prices declined sharply to 23.4% in 1990s in comparison with 45.9% in the 1980s.

Trend in FII Investments: FIIs play a significant role in the market and the share prices are influenced by the behaviour of FIIs.

Table No. 17.6
Trend in FII Investments

(₹ *in Crore*)

Year	*Net Investments*
1993-94	5445
1994-95	4777
1995-96	6721
1996-97	7386
1997-98	–729
1999-00	9765
2000-01	9683

	2001-02	8273
	2002-03	2659
	2003-04	44000
	2004-05	41416
	2005-06	48650
	2006-07	23754
	2007-08	62584
	2008-09	(–) 43338
No. of FIIs in India	2002 : 489 2003 : 517 2004 : 637 2005 : 837 and sub-accounts: 2273	

	Net Investments in Equity	*Net Investments in Debt*
2001-02	8067	685
2002-03	2528	162
2003-04	39959	5805

FII were permitted to invest in Indian securities markets in Sept. 1992. FII are required to register with RBI and SEBI.

The FII investments in India began in 1993. The number of FIIs in India has grown over the years to nearly 500. Some of the prominent names among FIIs operating in India are Morgan Stanley, Templeton, Capital International, CDC, Warburg and JFAM.

FII investments have steadily grown from about ₹ 2,595.30 crore in Dec. 1993 to a cumulative investment of ₹ 58,766.10 crore by December-end 2002.

Although the number of registered FIIs in the country is 500, the number of FIIs actively operating are 150 who have invested in about 100 companies with the bulk of investment being in 30 scrips.

Linkage between the Primary and Secondary Market

The primary and secondary segments of the capital market are mutually dependent. Securities issued in the primary market are traded in the secondary market.

A two-way relationship exists between the two segments of the capital market.

Secondary market conditions influence the firm's decision to go for new capital issues.

A buoyant economy creates favourable conditions for the secondary market by increasing profits and market prices of the existing shares and also creates the need for raising fresh capital for financing new projects and expansion and modernisation of existing projects.

A favourable trend in secondary market induces the investing public to subscribe to new issues as the investors will invest in new issues if they perceive that they would be able to gain financially by selling in the secondary market.

A buoyant secondary market is indispensable for a vibrant primary market.

Institutional Development in Secondary Capital Market

It is necessary to mention the setting up of specific institutions during the 1990s as measures to promote the healthy and orderly growth of the secondary capital market.

(i) Securities and Exchange Board of India (SEBI)

The Securities and Exchange Board of India (SEBI) was set up in 1988 as a non-statutory body. It was given statutory powers under the Act in 1992.

Twin objectives: orderly development of the capital market and investor protection.

The Capital Issues (Control) Act 1947 was repealed in 1992 and the new issue of capital has been brought under the purview of SEBI.

Prior to the establishment of SEBI, there was a set-up of multiple regulatory bodies for the capital market.

Companies Act, 1956

The Act formulated specific provisions to regulate —

(a) issue of capital, (b) capital structure of companies, (c) dividend distribution, (d) inter-corporate investment, (e) shareholders' meetings, voting rights of shareholders and (f) procedure for allotment of shares issue of share at premium or discount, issues of share certificates etc.

Securities Contracts (Regulation) Act, 1956

To regulate the working of stock exchanges.

Capital Issues (Control) Act, 1947

- Prior consent for the issue of capital to the public.
- To regulate new issues — timing, composition, dividend rates, prior allotment, premium on securities etc.

The basis for the creation on of SEBI is that every aspect of the securities market is entrusted to a single and independent organisation backed up by an Act.

The Board has the twin task of regulation and development.

Objectives: To regulate stock exchange and securities market and to promote their orderly functioning.

To protect the rights and interests of investors, particularly individual investors.

To prevent trading malpractices.

To achieve a balance between self-regulation and the statutory regulation of the securities market.

To facilitate efficient mobilisation and allocation of resources through the securities market, stimulating competition and encouraging innovation.

Powers of SEBI

Powers to regulate — (i) depositories and participants, (ii) custodians, (iii) debentures trustees and trust deals, (iv) FIIs, (v) insider trading, (vi) merchant bankers, (vii) mutual funds, (viii) portfolio managers, investment advisers, (ix) registrar to issue and share transfer agents, (x) stock brokers, (xi) underwriters and (xii) bankers to issues, acquisition of shares, takeovers, venture capital funds.

Issue Guidelines on:

(i) Information disclosure, operational transparency

(ii) Investor protection

(iii) Development of financial institutions
(iv) Allotment and transfer of shares among promoters
(v) Pricing of issues
(vi) Bonus issues
(vii) Preferential issues
(viii) Financial instruments

Power to Register: Any agency or intermediary associated with securities market.

SEBI's Performance

New Issues Market

- The standards of disclosure in public issues: efforts made to raise the standards.
- Companies making first public issue: they have to have three years of dividend paying track record preceding the issue.
- The companies not meeting this requirement should get their projects appraised by banks or financial institutions.

Secondary Market

- Governing boards of stock exchanges have been restuctured, broad-based and recognised.
- Corporate membership of stock exchange is allowed. 1917 corporate members by March-end 1996.
- Computerised, screen-based trading, stock exchanges directed to establish a clearing house.
- Carried forward trading system: Stock Exchanges can introduce forward trading only with the permission of SEBI.
- Dual registration of brokers with SEBI and the stock exchange.
- Listing agreements have been amended by stock exchanges to provide shareholders with the cash flow statement and the balance sheet and profit and loss statement.
- Registration of:

  Registrar to Issues: 209 by March 1996

  Merchant Bankers: 1012 by March 1996

  Classification of merchant bankers abolished in September 1997.

  Mutual Funds: 40 by March 1999

  UTI has been brought under SEBI jurisdiction since July 1994.

  FIIs: March 1996 : 367
  March 1997 : 439
  March 1998 : 496
  Sept. 1998 : 533
  Nov. 2000 : 551

Investor Protection Measures

An automated complaints handling system introduced to deal with investor complaints.

Non-receipt of refund orders/allotment letters/stock investments.

Non-receipt of dividend.

Non-receipt of share certificates/bonus shares.

Non-receipts of debenture certificates/interest on debentures/ redemption amount of debentures etc.

Non-receipt of annual reports, right issue forms etc.

SEBI has accorded recognition to genuine investor associations.

SEBI issues fortnightly press releases to enlighten investors on their rights and remedies.

(ii) Stock Holding Corporation of India Ltd. (SHCIL)

- SHCIL was set up in 1987 by
  DFIs: IDBI, IFCI, ICICI, IRBI (now IIBI)
  Investment Institutions: LIC, GIC, UTI
- SHCIL is a company offering post-trading and custodial service to institutional investors, particularly its own promoter institutions with services now extended to banks and mutual funds etc.
- SHCIL started operations in 1988.
- *Objects:*
  - To provide infrastructural facilities for post-trading clearing services, depository and other support services.
  - To facilitate quicker share transfers.
- Services rendered:

(a) clearing services, (b) depository services, (c) support services, (d) management/ information services and (e) development services.

During 1991-92, SHCIL commenced its work of setting up of a National Clearing and Depository system.

Clearing Services: Post-trading work, *i.e.,* it receives and/or delivers the securities on behalf of the institutions.

The computerised book entry transfer system: SHCIL has eliminated paperwork by replacing the physical transfer of shares by passing the necessary receipts.

SHCIL ensures that the securities are duly and in time transferred.

Depository Services

A 'depository' is a custodial service where the securities are kept in an electronic form. It is meant for eliminating paper ownership and minimising paperwork in trading and transfer of shares.

The investors hand over their shares for 'dematerialisation', they operate their accounts in the same way as bank accounts. Securities are credited in the electronic holdings of the investors. Securities account balances are maintained and the status of their holdings is intimated to them from time to time.

SHCIL has provided a custodial service for securities and related services to the institutions while the securities are in its custody.

Services include collection of dividend warrants, interest cheques, redemption and collection of bonus and rights and privileges attached to securities.

Support Services: to monitor interest/dividend payments due to institutions.

Information System: regarding safe custody, trade monitoring, details of interest/dividend due and of redemption conversion/rights etc.

Developmental Services: Extension of services to new clients.

The SHCIL business turnover comprises of processing of purchases and sales orders.

1993-94: Sales orders worth ₹ 1,645 crore

Purchases orders worth ₹ 5,442 crore

Business turnover: 1996-97: ₹ 10,247 crore

1997-98: ₹ 13,153 crore.

Collected dividends, interests and redemption benefits:

1992-93: ₹ 1,180 crore

1993-94: ₹ 1,850 crore

1997-98: ₹ 4,160 crore

SHCIL handled 127 crore certificates and 101 crore transfer deeds as on January 2, 1999, and 508 crore shares having a total value of ₹ 70,333 crore were dematerialised.

(iii) Over the Counter Exchange of India Limited (OTCEI)

- OTCEI was set up with the approval under the Securities Contracts (Regulation) Act in August 1989. It started operations in October 1992.
- OTCEI is promoted by

  DFIs: IDBI, IFCI, ICICI

  Investment Institutions: LIC, GIC, UTI

  Bank subsidiaries: SBI Capital Markets Ltd.

  Canbank Financial Services Ltd.
- OTCEI is a recognised stock exchange with automated screen-based ringless trading system.
- Small and medium-sized companies with a paid up capital between ₹ 30 lakh and ₹ 25 crore can be enlisted.
- The number of listed companies:

  (March-end) 1994: 34

  " 1995: 49

  " 1996: 90

  " 1997: 108

  " 1998: 146

- *Objectives:*
    - To help companies in raising capital at cheap costs.
    - To provide investors a convenient access to the capital market.
    - To cater to companies which cannot be listed on other stock exchanges.
    - To eliminate problems of delayed settlement, unfair prices etc.
- Types of securities traded:

  'Listed': The company appoints a member of OTCEI as a sponsor.

Permitted: not listed but permitted

Initiated: initiated debentures.

OTCEI is a market for small investors and small companies. The focus of its activity is shifting to the bigger 'permitted' securities.

- *Members of OTCEI:* scheduled banks, mutual funds, banking subsidiary, financial institution, merchant bankers, venture capital funds, NBFCs other than finance and leasing companies can become members.

The OTCEI has two players — members and dealers. They perform the functions of broking and trading on their own accounts and market making. By 1994-95, there were 94 members and 235 dealers. The market maker who may be the sponsor, initiates trading by quoting two way prices (bid and offer rates) for the security for which he wants to create a market.

The trading and settlement system ensures deliveries vs. payment — all trading done on any day is settled on the same day itself.

The activity level of OTCEI has not picked up and has actually slowed down over the years. The average monthly volume of business recorded a decline from 1.2 crore shares in 1994 to 4.5 lakh shares in 1996. SEBI appointed two committees to study the working of OTCEI and suggest appropriate measures (Malegam Committee, and Dave Committee). As per the recommendations of Dave Committee, OTCEI relaunched the trading in *'permitted'* scrips and moved over to a weekly settlement cycle. The volume of trade transactions of OTCEI increased by 29.5 per cent from ₹ 218.5 crore during 1996-97 to ₹ 283 crore in the year 1997-98. The turnover was as high as ₹ 365 crore in 1994-95 but declined to ₹ 120 crore in 1995-96 and ₹ 142 crore in 1998-99.

(iv) National Stock Exchange (NSE)

- Pherwani Committee Report on national market system in 1991.
- NSE was set up in November 1992 and started operations in 1994, debt trading in June 1994 and equity trading in November 1994.
- NSE is promoted by

  DFIs: IDBI, ICICI.

  Investment Institutions: LIC and GIC.
- Commercial banks including SBI-SBI Capital Markets Ltd. NSE is a fully automated screen-based trading system. There is no trading floor.

- **Objectives:**
    - To establish nationwide trading facilities for equities and debt instruments.
    - To provide access to investors all over the country.
- *NSE has two segments:*
    - — Capital market segment trading in equities, debentures.
    - — Wholesale debt market segment — trading in debt instruments — including PSU bonds, government securities, treasury bills, CPs and CDs.
- NSE has participating trading members — trading on their own behalf, intermediary trading members — trading on behalf of the clients.

Debt market component has the trading members and participants.

More than 600 companies are already listed on the NSE.

Medium-sized companies and PSUs are listed on the NSE.

Wholesale Debt Market Segment (WDM)

No. of listed securities (by March-end)	1996-97: 307 1997-98: 418
Turnover	1996-97: ₹ 42,277 crore 1997-98: ₹ 1,11,263 crore

Capital Market Segment

No. of scrips listed	1995-96: 422 1996-97: 550 1997-98: 612
Turnover:	1995-96 ₹ 67,287 crore 1996-97: ₹ 2,94,504 crore 1997-98: ₹ 3,70,193 crore

Table No. 17.7
Turnover of Stock Exchanges: Percentage Shares

Year	*BSE*	*NSE*	*Others*	*All India*
1995-96	22	30	48	100
1996-97	19.2	45.6	35.2	100
1997-98	22.8	40.7	36.5	100
1998-99	30.5	40.5	29.0	100
1999-2000	33.1	40.6	26.3	100

As could be seen from the above Table, the share of NSE Turnover in the Turnover of all Stock Exchanges in the country has shot up to over 40 per cent. As seen from Table 17.7, the average annual growth rate in NSE Turnover during second half of 1990s is 863.13.

NSE's Subsidiary — National Securities Clearing Corporation has been permitted to open Subsidiary Ledger Account (SGL) to be used for holding government securities and treasury bills. Trading in new instruments like deep discount bonds, PSU infrastructure bonds was introduced in the WDM segment of the National Stock Exchange during 1997-98.

NSE ensures total transparency in transactions.

NSE practices order-driven trading as against the quote-driven trading prevalent at other exchanges.

Types of Credit Rating Institutions

• Credit Rating

Credit Rating is a symbolic indicator of an expert opinion by a rating agency on the relative willingness and ability of the issuer of a debt instrument to meet the debt servicing obligations in time and in full.

Equities are not rated as their risk is not measurable and the equityholders as the owners have to bear the residual risk.

Debt instruments are rated.

- *Capital Market Instruments:* Bonds, debentures not converted into equity within 18 months, preference shares and different types of debt instruments.
- *Money Market Instruments:* CPs, short-term instruments of less than one year, Fixed deposits of one to three years.

A credit rating is specific to a particular debt instrument. It is intended to grade different debt instruments in terms of credit risks associated with the particular instruments.

Ratings are matters of opinion and they still carry weight and play a useful role for the investors.

Ratings need to be updated.

Rating helps companies with good rating to enter the capital market confidently. It enables the investors to take calculated risks.

Ratings are classified as: High Investment Grade
Investment Grade
Speculative Grade
Poor Grade

Though credit rating institutions use different symbols, their interpretations are identical.

Key factors considered: in credit rating
(a) Business Analysis
(b) Financial Analysis
(c) Management Evaluation
(d) Regulatory and Competitive Environment
(e) Fundamental Analysis

(a) Business Analysis

Industry Risk: Industry structure, market factors — competition, government policies.

Marketing Risk: Market share, selling and distribution network, customer service.

Operating Efficiency: Operating margins, locational advantages, labour aspect.

Legal: security offered, trust deed, trustees' reputation.

(b) Financial Analysis

Accounting quality, income recognition, treatment of bad debts

Earnings protection: profitability ratios, interest in relation to GP and NP, projection of future earnings, earnings per share (EPS).

Adequacy of Cash Flows: Current ratio, working capital management, inventory to sales.

Financial flexibility: Capital financing plans, flexibility in financing through alternative methods.

(c) Management Evaluation — Track Record of management
— Planning and control systems
— Goals, philosophy and strategies
— Capacity and foresight to meet adverse conditions.

(d) Regulatory and Competitive Environment — Operations of regulatory authorities.

For assessment of finance companies — regulatory framework of the financial system.

(e) Fundamental Analysis

Liquidity Management — matching of cash inflows and outflows,
Liquid assets — term matching of assets and liabilities receivables to current assets.
Asset Quality — Credit-risk management, systems for monitoring credit.
Profitability — Financial position, accretion to reserves, profit managing, spread on funds deployment.
Interest and Tax: Interest rate changes, tax law changes.

Credit Rating Institutions

CRISIL: Credit Rating Information Services of India Limited

- Promoted in 1987; first rating agency in India.
- Promoted by ICICI and UTI.
- Other shareholders include LIC, GIC, HDFC, foreign banks and Indian commercial banks.

Table No. 17.8
Credit Rating by CRISIL

(₹ in Crores)

Instrument	*1995-96*		*1996-97*		*19977-98*		*Cumulative upto March 1998*	
	No.	*Amt.*	*No.*	*Amt.*	*No.*	*Amt.*	*No.*	*Amt.*
Debentures	161	13342	174	12750	221	28649	1041	97099
Fixed Deposit Programme	218	14153	111	6118	35	4238	689	48981
CP Programme	21	3255	42	2690	262	6257	763	20362
Others	43	12336	24	3290	50	1213	304	23636
Total	443	43086	351	24848	568	50357	2797	1,90,078

Symbols

AAA/FAAA : Highest safety P1 : Very strong
AA/FAA : High safety P2 : Strong

A/FA : Adequate safety P3 : Adequate
BB/FB : Inadequate safety

CRISIL developed methodologies for rating bonds of public bodies engaged in water works. CRISIL has rated New India Assurance Company, which has been first one in the insurance sector to be rated.

ICRA: Investment Information and Credit Rating Agency of India Limited

ICRA has been set up by IFCI and other financial institutions in 1991.

ICRA ratings establish a link between risk and return.

The agency has carried out several studies for financial sector intermediaries, and specific studies for 13 PSUs.

It has been appointed as a consultant for the Disinvestment Commission.

Table No. 17.9
Credit Rating by ICRA

(₹ *in Crores*)

Instrument	*1995-96*		*1996-97*		*19977-98*		*Cumulative upto March 1998*	
	No.	*Amt.*	*No.*	*Amt.*	*No.*	*Amt.*	*No.*	*Amt.*
Debentures	66	82242	73	6672	109	25666.2	405	50937.9
Fixed Deposit Programme	192	50506.8	153	2946	94	24718.8	607	80145.7
CP Programme	35	17011	35	3231.7	110	4805.7	340	30336.7
Total	293	75742.0	261	12849.7	313	55190.7	1352	161420.3

CARE: Credit Analysis and Research Limited

CARE was set up in April 1993 and started the operations in October 1993.

CARE was promoted by IDBI, UTI, Canara Bank and other banks and financial services companies.

The agency completed credit analysis and assignments for rating parallel marketers of LPG and superior kerosene oil.

Table No. 17.10
Credit Rating by CARE

(₹ *in Crores*)

Instrument	*1996-97*		*1997-98*		*Cummulative*	
	No.	*Amt*	*No.*	*Amt.*	*No.*	*Amt.*
CP & other short-term instrument	39	1,331	97	3,309	315	8,344
Debenture/bonds	105	1,426	78	28,054	276	55,852
Fixed Deposits/CDs	104	4,192	23	5,026	300	15,580
Total	248	19,749	198	36,389	891	79,776

Credit Rating is mandatory for the issuance of certain debt instruments.

Debentures/bonds with conversion/redemption period exceeding 18 months.

CPs.

Fixed deposits programmes of all non-banking finance companies.

Symbols

CARE			*ICRA*	
			CPs	
AAA	AAAFD	Best Quality	A1	Highest Safety
AA	AAFD	High Quality	A2	High Safety
A	AFD	Adequate Quality Safety	A3	Adequate Safety
BBB	BBB(FD)	Moderate Safety	A4	Risk Prone
BB	BB(FD)	Inadequate Safety	*Debenture*	
B	B (FD)	Risk Prone	LAAA	Highest Safety
B	C (FD)	High Risk	LAA	High Safety
D	D (FD)	Default	LA	Adequate Safety
			LBBB	Moderate Safety
PR1	Superior		LBB	Inadequate Safety
PR2	Strong		LB	Risk Prone
PR3	Adequate		LC	Substantial Risk
PR4	Risk Prone		LD	Default
PR5	Default		CDs	4 Fixed Deposits
			MAAA	Highest Safety
			MAA	High Safety
			MA	Adequate Safety
			MB	Inadequate Safety
			MC	Risk Prone

KEY TERMS

Stock Exchange, Market Capitalisation, Transaction Costs SEBI, SHCIL, OTCEI, NSE.

REVIEW QUESTIONS

1. Give definition and meaning of stock exchange.
2. Explain the functions, legal framework and organisation of stock exchanges.
3. Discuss the growth of stock exchanges in recent years.
4. What are stock market development ratios?
5. Write a note on the following –
   (a) Bombay (Mumbai) Stock Exchange
   (b) Sensex
6. What are the drawbacks of stock exchanges?

7. Explain the Reforms in Indian Capital Markets.
8. Discuss the influence of Foreign Institutional Investors on Indian Capital Market.
9. Discuss the role of SEBI in Indian Capital Market.
10. Write short notes –
    (a) Securities Holding Corporation of India Ltd. (SHCIL)
    (b) Over the Counter Exchange of India Ltd. (OTCEI)
    (c) National Stock Exchange (NSE)

REFERENCES

1. National Stock Exchange of India, Derivatives Core Module Workbook.
2. Pathak B.V. (2008), 'The Indian Financial System — Markets, Institutions and Services', Pearson Edition.
3. Rao, J.N. (2001), 'Indian ADRs: The Resurgence Chartered Financial Analyst', June 2001.
4. RBI, Handbook of Statistics on Indian Economy, Various Issues.
5. Shah, Ajay (1997), 'Securities Markets, Towards 'Greater Efficiency' in K.S. Parikh (ed.), Indian Development Report 1997, Oxford University Press, Delhi.

❑ ❑ ❑

18

Foreign Exchange Market

In this chapter, we shall discuss what is –

18.1 Foreign Exchange

18.2 Foreign Exchange Market

18.3 Exchange Rate

18.4 Measures Taken to Widen and Deepen the Foreign Exchange Market in India

18.5 Exchange Control

18.6 Exchange Rate Management

18.7 Foreign Exchange Market Turnover

18.8 International Dimensions of Financial Market

18.9 Indian Companies – Resource Mobilisation Abroad – GDR, ADR, Euro Currency, Euro Dollar, Euro Swiss, Franc Loan, Euro Bonds

18.10 FII and FDI

18.1 FOREIGN EXCHANGE

Business on the global level between any two countries is conducted using currencies of the two countries respectively.

A country has the domestic monetary unit and the currencies of other countries are foreign monetary units. The foreign monetary units are the *Foreign Exchange*. The transactions take place between the residents of different countries. As a result, the residents of a country have some receipts from and payments to foreign countries. All payments and receipts denominated in foreign currencies are foreign exchange. Foreign exchange includes coins, notes, bank deposits and claims denominated in foreign exchange.

18.2 FOREIGN EXCHANGE MARKET

Foreign exchange market is a market for currencies of various countries to be bought and sold. There is a Foreign Exchange market in every country. A market in which domestic monetary units or claims are exchanged for foreign monetary units is known as Foreign Exchange market.

The market provides for exchange of domestic currency as against all foreign currencies with which the country has dealings.

In the 'retail' segment of the foreign exchange market, the exchange of bank notes, bank drafts, currency and traveller's cheques takes place between the private customers, tourists and the banks. In the wholesale segment of the market, the banks trade in currencies which does not involve physical transfer of currency, but only a bookkeeping entries among banks. The inter-bank transactions are mostly conducted though the exchange brokers.

The demand for and supply of foreign currencies arises when—

— the importers need foreign exchange and the exporters hold foreign exchange and they approach their banks as authorised dealers,

— the residents of the country receive from or make payments to foreign countries.

There are 86 scheduled commercial banks which are the authorised dealers licensed to engage in the buying and selling of foreign exchange. The foreign exchange transactions take place between the public and the banks, between the banks and between the banks and the Reserve Bank of India (RBI), as RBI does not deal in foreign exchange directly with the public, but through the banks as authorised dealers.

The banks as authorised dealers sell foreign currencies to the public in exchange of rupee and purchase foreign currencies from the public also against the rupee.

When the bank *sells* foreign currencies, it receives rupees for say dollars and when the bank buys say dollars, it will pay rupees for the dollars. Bank quotes twoway price — a price at which it buys and a price at which it sells the currency.

In the foreign exchange market, the currencies of various countries are bought and sold either on *'spot'* basis or *'forward'* basis.

'Spot' transaction: When foreign exchange is bought and sold for *immediate delivery.*

'Spot'rate: rate at which transaction takes place.

'Forward' transaction: transaction takes place today at a price, *i.e.,* forward rate, for the delivery in future.

Besides these transactions, the derivative instruments including futures, options are traded and payments between currencies are exchanged as Swaps.

A *currency future* is a commitment to deliver or take delivery of a given amount of currency on a specific future date at a price fixed on the date of contract. Futures differ from Forward contracts as the Forwards result in delivery whereas Futures may not result in effective delivery as they are settled through reverse operations.

Currency options is a financial instrument that gives its holder a right but no obligation to buy or sell a currency sometime in future.

Call option — The buyer, *i.e.,* holder of a call option acquires a right to buy currency 'A' against currency 'B' at a certain price.

Put option — The buyer, *i.e.,* holder of a put option acquires a right to sell currency 'A' against currency 'B' at a pre-fixed price.

The foreign exchange market deals with foreign exchange transactions arising in respect of:

— Trade relations between different countries, *i.e.*, exports and imports of goods.

— Financial transactions, *i.e.,* receipts and payments between different countries not directly related to trade. These transactions pertain to 'invisibles' including services like transportation, insurance and foreign travel and tourism, investment income, transfer payments etc, and also arise in terms of capital inflows and outflows which influence the exchange rate.

The Foreign Exchange transactions are *trade-based* and those which are *not directly related to trade.* The transactions not directly related to trade are on account of capital transfers, arbitrage, speculation etc. Barely 5% of foreign exchange transactions reflect international trade. The Foreign exchange transactions are *'merchant'* transactions and *'inter-bank'* transactions with inter-bank transactions accounting for 85 to 90 per cent of the foreign exchange market turnover. Spot transactions dominate merchant segment and forward transactions in the interbank segment.

During 1999-2000, spot transactions accounted for about 55 per cent of total merchant turnover, and forward transactions formed 40 per cent of total inter-bank turnover.

18.3 EXCHANGE RATE

The three main kinds of exchange rate system are **(i) floating or freely fluctuating, (ii) fixed, and (iii) pegged or managed.**

Under *floating* exchange rates, the exchange rates are left purely to the market mechanism, whereas under the *'fixed'* system, the central banks seeks to maintain the exchange rate within a specific margin of predetermined value in other currency. The term 'floating' indicates that the currency has no fixed relationship with any other currency. Under the pegged/or managed system, the currency is pegged or linked to a single currency or a *'basket'* of currencies, with discretionary intervention by the central banks to attain stability of exchange rates.

Exchange rate is the rate at which one currency is converted into another.

'Direct' Rate: When the value of foreign currency say dollar is expressed in domestic currency rupee, *i.e.,* \$ 1 = ₹ ......

Indirect Rate: When the value of domestic currency is expressed in foreign currency, say ₹ 100 = \$ ....

Hence, it is determined by the supply and demand for foreign exchange. The export and import of goods and services and the capital flows between nations give rise to the supply and demand for foreign exchange and influence the exchange rate.

Till 1971, the exchange rate system consisted of fixed exchange rate regime when the exchange rate was maintained within specific limits of the par values of the currencies. The par value of the rupee was expressed in gold and exchange rate in terms of pound sterling. From 1971 to 1975, the RBI buying and selling rate of pound sterling (intervention currency) was adopted.

Between 1975 and 1992, the basket-linked exchange rate policy was followed. The exchange value of the rupee was linked with a basket of a selected number of currencies which were major trading partners of India. The Reserve Bank performed the market clearing role towards the obligation of buying and selling unlimited amounts of the intervention currency — the pound sterling — on a day-to-day basis.

The *intervention currency* is the currency — the pound sterling used by the apex bank in transactions taken up to structure the *exchange rate.*

After 1991, the exchange rate regime in India shifted from basket-linked managed float and moved towards market-determined exchange rate. Between March 1992 and February 1993, there was a phase of dual exchange rates, which gave way to unified exchange rate with effect from March 1, 1993.

18.4 MEASURES TAKEN TO WIDEN AND DEEPEN THE FOREIGN EXCHANGE MARKET IN INDIA

(i) Banks have been allowed to take trading position in the overseas markets.

(ii) Banks have been given freedom to determine the interest rates of NRI deposits.

(iii) Authorised dealers are allowed to borrow abroad upto 15% of their unimpaired capital or $10 million whichever is higher.

(iv) Corporate entities have been provided significant freedom in managing their foreign exchange exposures.

The foreign exchange market in the country consists of customers including merchants, authorised dealers (commercial banks) and RBI. In the recent years, there has been significant increase in the merchant transactions including those of PSUs like IOC and the FII have emerged as the major players in the market.

18.5 EXCHANGE CONTROL

In a developing country like India, the major constraint faced in regard to foreign exchange is the inadequacy of the foreign exchange reserves. The shortage of foreign exchange reserves would not emerge if the exports would earn enough foreign exchange to pay for imports. The demand for foreign exchange on account of imports when it exceeds the supply of foreign exchange, it has to be met by: (a) drawing upon foreign exchange reserves, (b) from the net receipts on '*invisibles*' account, (c) net receipts on capital account and (d) receipts by way of external assistance.

Foreign exchange control is adopted to regulate the demand for foreign exchange so as to be within the limits set by limited supply. For regulating and allocating foreign exchange, a scheme of priorities is formulated.

Under the Defence of India Rules (DIR), the Exchange Control was imposed in India in 1939. The Foreign Exchange Regulation Act of 1947 (FERA) as amended in 1973, placed exchange control on statutory basis. This Act was administered by the Reserve Bank.

The apex bank supervised and controlled the foreign exchange market. RBI decided the exchange rate of rupee in terms of pound sterling on day-to-day basis and was obliged to buy and sell foreign exchange against the rupee on demand without any limit to maintain the exchange rate. It also regulated the amount of and the purposes for which foreign exchange was made available. It would sell pound sterling against specific demand and would also buy US dollar pound sterling, German mark and Japanese Yen.

In March 1992, the dollar replaced pound sterling as the intervention currency. Hence, RBI would sell only dollar and would continue buying the four currencies specified earlier.

In the post-1991 period, the system of exchange control was relaxed and the intervention of the RBI in the foreign exchange market is limited only to ensure rupee stability against selected foreign currencies. Under the unified exchange rate system introduced with effect from March 1, 1993, the exchange rates are market-determined, *i.e.,* floating rates as per demand-supply influences and the RBI has intervention rates, *i.e.,* rates for buying and selling intervention currency, *i.e.,* dollar. The other development was the rupee being made convertible for current account transactions in August 1994. The foreign exchange market has shifted out of the exchange control regime and has moved towards liberalisation in terms of developments in the exchange rate regime, current account convertibility, replacement of FERA of 1973 by Foreign Exchange Management Act (FEMA) 1999, and the measures taken by way of implementation of the recommendations of the Tarapore Committee on capital account convertibility.

18.6 EXCHANGE RATE MANAGEMENT

As a part of the structural reforms undertaken during 1990s, the external sector reforms introduced growing openness in the Indian economy. The exchange rate was administered earlier. As exchange rate became market-determined under liberalisation process, RBI intervened by making purchase and sales of foreign currency to ensure orderly conditions in the foreign exchange market.

Exchange rate management is meant for —

(i) Careful monitoring of the exchange rate.

(ii) Flexibility in exchange rate alongwith intervention if and when necessary.

(iii) Building a higher level of foreign exchange reserves.

With the progressive opening of the economy, there has been a sustained increase in the capital (foreign exchange) flows in the country, giving rise to large balance of payments surplus. Capital flows have become the main influence on the exchange rate movements on a day-to-day basis. Apart from the sustained increase in the capital flows, the characteristic feature of these capital flows is their 'volatility.'

The capital flows till 1980s were mainly as aid flows and were relatively stable. Since 1990s, *i.e.,* since liberalisation, the main source of capital flows being 'private', the capital flows have increased, but are associated with volatility. Among the private capital flows, the direct investment flows are relatively stable, but the portfolio and debt flows are highly volatile.

India's exchange rate policy is directed towards allowing demand and supply conditions to determine exchange rate movement in an orderly way and yet focusing on managing volatility, by taking initiatives and measures to meet temporary demand-supply gaps.

FEMA-1999: As the change in the title of the Act suggests, the emphasis has moved away from *'regulation'* to *'management'* in regard to foreign exchange. Under FERA, it was necessary to obtain Reserve Bank's permission in respect of most of the regulations under the Act. Under FEMA, except for Section 3 which relates to dealing in foreign exchange, no other provision of FEMA stipulates obtaining RBI's permission. To facilitate external trade and payments, the restrictions on drawals of foreign exchange for the purpose of current account transactions have been removed. The two key aspects of FEMA are the relaxation of foreign exchange controls and the move towards capital account convertibility. FEMA has indicated that the RBI shall not impose any restriction on the drawal of foreign exchange for payments due on account of amortisation of loans or for depreciation of direct investments.

18.7 FOREIGN EXCHANGE MARKET: TURNOVER

The combined turnover of merchant and inter-bank transactions in the foreign exchange market has increased more than sixfold between 1987-88 and 1998-99 and three times between 1998-99 and 2005-06.

Average monthly turnover:	1987-88 : US $17 billion
	1993-94 : US $50 billion
	1998-99 : US $110 billion
	2003-04 : US $173.8 billion
	2005-06 : US $339.6 billion
Current account transaction:	increased from US $62 billion to US $124 billion.
Capital account transaction:	increased from US $38 billion to US $69 billion in 1997-98.

18.8 INTERNATIONAL DIMENSIONS OF FINANCIAL MARKET

It is observed that during the last two decades, *i.e.,* during the 1980s and more particularly during 1990s, the capital markets in different countries are getting more integrated and a global capital market has begun to emerge. It need not be stressed that the growing integration of capital markets across national boundaries has been considerably facilitated by the technological developments in electronic payments system and communication systems. Easy and quick facilities for contacts and payments through the global network has enhanced cross-border mobility of funds and thereby reduced arbitrage opportunities.

The industrially advanced countries are capital rich and generate surplus investible resources which search for potential markets. The capital scarce developing countries try to attract international capital to supplement their domestic resources. The international capital is being welcomed by the developing countries in the form of Foreign Direct Investment (FDI) and Foreign Institutional Investment (FII) either directly in the equity markets or indirectly through mutual funds.

18.9 INDIAN COMPANIES: RESOURCE MOBILISATION ABROAD

The importance of international capital markets from the point of view of resource mobilisation has certainly increased during the 1990s. Indian companies have been able to garner substantial funds from the international markets by way GDRs/ADRs, Foreign Currency Convertible Bonds (FCCBs) and External Commercial Borrowings (FCBs). (See Table 17.5 in Chapter 17.)

(i) Global Depository Receipts

Raising capital by issuing fresh shares in euro markets and transferring to a depository which issues receipts which is quoted and traded at any stock exchange abroad where it is listed, this is called Global Depository Receipt (GDR).

(ii) American Depository Receipts (ADRs): Similar to GDR

It involves floating issues in USA.

The depository issues — ADR which is listed on New York Stock Exchange.

GDRs are generally used when a country's capital markets are not fully open to foreign investors. GDRs have remained popular even after the Indian stock markets have been opened to FIIs in 1993.

It is necessary to refer now briefly to euro-currency and euro-currency market.

(iii) Euro-currency

When short-term financial instruments denominated in a particular currency, say US dollar are traded outside the country (USA) of that currency. This pertains to euro-currency.

It is the location that matters and not the ownership of the instruments.

Initially, it was US dollars in Europe. Now, it includes leading West European currencies — German Mark, Swiss Francs.

Euro-currency Market

Banks making up the euro-currency market are located mainly in Europe.

Now, it involves banks outside Europe.

(iv) Eurodollar

Dollar-denominated bank deposits or loans arranged in a country other than USA — say an American owns a bank deposit with the London branch of an American bank.

(v) Euro Swiss Franc Loan

A Swiss Franc loan by a German bank in Frankfurt, *i.e.,* to say, a French borrower.

(vi) Euro Bonds

There are a number of bonds, *viz.,* Eurobonds, Yankee bonds, Samurai bonds which are listed in stock exchanges abroad and sold in European, US and Japanese markets respectively. Euro-market instruments include Euro-equity (GDR/ADR), Euro-debt (Bonds), and Euro-convertible bonds etc.

In 1992, Reliance Industries Ltd. (RIL) sold $150 million worth GDRs. It was the first Indian company to access the international capital market. In 1993, Essar Gujarat became the first Indian to issue euro-convertible bonds. The successful ADR issues in the year 1997-98 include ICICI, Infosys Technologies and Satyam Infosys Ltd.

18.10 FII AND FDI

FII Investments

In 1993, FIIs commenced their operations in the Indian stock markets. Since then, their investments have grown substantially. (See Table 16.6 of Chapter 16) except the year 1998-99 during which the net FII investments turned negative. The cumulative net FII investments as on October-end 1999 stood at ₹ 32,155 crore (US $ 9432.35 million).

It is proposed to broad-base FII category by including insurance/reinsurance companies, investment managers, investment advisors, international or multilateral organisations, foreign governmental agencies and foreign Central banks in the eligibility list.

Foreign Direct Investment (FDI)

As mentioned in Economic Survey 1999-2000, several initiatives have been taken to enhance the flow of FDIs into the country.

A Foreign Investment Implementation Authority has been established to ensure that the approvals of foreign investments are quickly translated into actual investments inflows and that the proposals become successful projects.

Table No. 18.1
FDI Inflows

(₹ in Crores)

Year	*FDI*
1990-91	174
1991-92	316
1992-93	965
1993-94	1838
1994-95	4126
1995-96	7172
1996-97	10015
1997-98	13220
1998-99	10358
1999-00	9338
2000-01	18406
2001-02	29240
2002-03	24637
2003-04	19860
2004-05 (P)	25395
2005-06 (P)	34316

Source: Handbook of Statistics on Indian Economy, RBI 2003-04.

Note: Data on FDI have been revised since 2000-01 and hence are not comparable with FDI data for earlier years.

Table No. 18.1(A)
Composition of Capital Inflows

(US $ in million)

Year	*Total Capital Inflows (Net)*
1990-91	7056
1995-96	4089
1996-97	12006
1997-98	9844
1998-99	8435
1999-00	10444
2000-01	10916
2001-02	8551
2002-03	10840
2003-04	16736
2004-05	31027
2005-06	24893

Composition of Inflows

(in %)

	FDI	*Portfolio Investment*	*Debt Creating Inflows*	*Other Capital*
1990-91	1.4	0.1	83.3	15.2
1995-96	52.4	65.1	57.7	–75.2
1996-97	23.7	27.6	61.7	–13.0
1997-98	36.2	18.6	32.4	–7.2
1998-99	29.4	-0.8	54.4	17.0
1999-00	20.7	29.0	23.1	27.2
2000-01	40.2	27.6	59.4	–27.2
2001-02	71.6	23.6	12.4	–7.6
2002-03	46.5	9.0	–12.3	56.8
2003-04	25.8	67.9	–6.0	12.3
2004-05	18.0	28.7	30.6	22.7
2005-06	31.1	50.6	29.9	–11.6

Source: Annual Report, RBI 2005-06.

Data on FDI have been revised since 2000-01. As such data from 2000-01 onwards are not comparable with those in earlier years.

'Other capital' includes loans to NRIs, Indian investment abroad. India's subscription to international institutions and quota payments to IMF.

The foreign capital utilisation ratio has been small particularly in the case of FDI.

Table No. 18.2

Actual Inflows as Percentage of Approvals (in US $ terms)

	1991	*1992*	*1993*	*1994*	*1995*	*1996*	*1997*	*1998*	*1991-98*
(in %)	47.7	13.1	16.1	22.1	18.7	21.4	21.1	32	21.7

During 1998, the ratio was at 32%. The ratio has been below 22 per cent for the 1991-98 period.

KEY TERMS

Foreign Exchange, Foreign Exchange Market, Exchange Rate, Exchange Rate Management, FEMA, GDRs, ADRs, FII, FDI.

REVIEW QUESTIONS

1. What is foreign exchange?
2. What is Foreign Exchange Market?
3. Explain the operations in the Foreign Exchange Market?
4. What are the different types of exchange rates?
5. What measures have been introduced to widen and deepen the foreign exchange market in India?

6. What is Exchange Control?
7. Discuss the recent developments in the field of exchange control in India.
8. What is the significance of Exchange Rate Management?
9. Write a note on FEMA 1999.
10. What is the volume of turnover as the Foreign Exchange Market?
11. What is meant by International dimension of Financial Market?
12. Explain how India Companies have been raising funds from abroad in the recent years.
13. Explain the Financial Instruments that enable Indian Companies to raise capital from International Financial Market.
14. Discuss the participation of FII and FDI in Indian Financial Market.

REFERENCES

1. Batliwala C.J. (1992), 'Foreign Exchange Auction Markets; Evidence and Issues', Indian Council for Research in International Economic Relations, Allied Publisher, New Delhi.
2. Reserve Bank of India, Report of the Expert Group on Foreign Exchange Market in India (Sodhani Group), Mumbai, 1995.
3. Reserve Bank of India, Report on Foreign Exchange Reserves, 2007.

❑❑❑

19

International Financial Markets

INTRODUCTION

Before going ahead with describing the International or global financial markets, it would be more appropriate to explain the term 'Euro' as the Euro currency markets based in London since 1950s were earlier the only markets which were global in operations. The origin of Euro currency market dates back to 1950s when the Soviet government agencies maintained currency deposits in dollars in the banks in London. The term 'Euro' means external indicating the market wherein the banks accept deposits and make loans denominated in currencies other than that of a country in which the bank is located. What matters is the location of a bank. 'Eurodollar' is a dollar deposited in a bank outside USA. A French Company taking a dollar loan from a bank located in London is Eurodollar loan. In other words, the ownership of a bank or that of the deposit is not significant. Since then, the Euro-currency markets have developed and expanded and hence no longer restricted to London but spread to other places like Paris, Rome, Luxembourg, Tokyo, Singapore and Hong Kong. It is said that the prefix 'Euro' is now outdated since such deposits and loans are regularly traded outside Europe. What Euro market signifies is really the 'offshore' market as distinguished from the 'domestic' segment. The participants in the market come from all over the world — the borrower is from one country and the funding is from the other country.

In this chapter the following components of the International Financial Markets have been discussed.

19.1 Euro or Offshore Market

19.2 Major Global Markets –

(i) US Dollar Market

(ii) Japanese Yen Market

(iii) Deutsche Mark Market

(iv) Swiss Franc Market

(v) Australian Dollar Market

(vi) Sterling Market

19.3 Financing Instruments in International Financial Market –

(i) Debt Instruments

(a) Bonds – domestic, External, Foreign, Euro Bonds and Bonds with Option, Sinking Fund bonds, Zero coupon bonds, Warrants.

(b) Floating Rate Notes (FRNs)

(c) Euro Medium Term Notes (EMTNs)

(d) Note Issuing Facility (NIFs)

(e) Syndicated Bank Loans

(f) Euro Commercial Paper (Euro CPs)

(g) Euro Certificate Deposits (Euro CDs)

(ii) Equity Instruments –

Global Depository Receipts

American Depository Receipts

European Depository Receipts

Foreign Currency Convertible Borrowings

19.4 Multilateral Financial Institutions and Asian Development Bank – Organisation, Goals and Operations

The globalisation of financial markets, *i.e.,* emergence of financial markets transcending national boundaries is the development of post-1980s period. Prior to 1980s, the financial markets in different countries were largely independent of each other and the operations of the financial intermediaries in different countries were limited within their boundaries.

The dominant trend after 1980s is towards globalisation of financial markets and a vast international financial market has emerged transcending national boundaries in the form of a large volume of cross-border financial flows. A number of factors has given rise to this trend towards globalisation of financial markets.

For their developmental efforts, the developing countries are unable to mobilise resources adequately from within and hence look to external sources for funds to bridge their resources gap. As the volume of concessional aid and lending from official bilateral and multilateral agencies including World Bank, Asian Development Bank (ADB) etc. falls short, the developing countries have to resort to international financial markets for the provision of funds.

The other factor is the significant easing of restrictions and regulations governing the operations of the financial markets in different countries as the process of liberalisation/globalisation initiated. These restrictions included exchange control, restrictions on financial institutions regarding the services they can render, kind of securities they can issue and hold and barriers to foreign entities accessing national markets. The emergence of a vast international financial market has been to a significant extent facilitated by the dismantling of barriers and easing of regulations/restrictions introduced in different countries.

In the recent years, the investors have opted for international diversification and showed increasing preference for developing asset portfolios in the diverse financial markets.

19.1 EURO OR OFFSHORE MARKETS

The Euro or offshore markets are a large international source of funds for the borrowers — corporates, MNCs and others all over the world and a significant avenue for the investors with surplus to direct their funds to the markets transcending their national boundaries.

Euro market is primarily an inter-bank money market in time deposits and short-term loans. Over the years, however, these markets have evolved a variety of financial instruments like Euro bonds, Floating rate loans, Euro CDs, Euro CPs etc. (The details of financing instruments have been given separately in the chapter).

The key significance of Euro markets is that they represent 'unregulated' markets. Euro banks are free from regulatory provisions such as reserve requirements, deposit insurance etc. and Euro bonds are free from rating and disclosure requirements.

Euro bonds' market is the market for the internationally sold bonds in countries other than the country of the currency in which the issue is denominated.

Euro credit market is the market for loans in currencies which are not native to the country in which the bank making loan is located. MNCs and the governments are the main borrowers in the market.

Interest rates on deposits and loans in Euro currencies are tied to the rates in respective domestic markets of these currencies. Interest rates on Euro market instruments are tied to the benchmark or reference rate. The commonly used benchmark is LIBOR — London Inter-bank Offer Rate.

International Equity Markets, *i.e.,* new issues equity markets with cross-border equity investments developed during and after 1980s, when institutional investors in advanced countries like USA, UK and Japan directed their funds into foreign equities. It was only in 1992 that an Indian firm Reliance Industries approached global capital market to raise equity financing. In September 1992, Government of India allowed entry of foreign institutional investors (FIIs) in the domestic capital markets.

Multiple Deposit Expansion

As has been mentioned earlier, the Euro market is primarily an inter-bank money market in time deposits and short-term loans. As in case of the domestic banking system in any country, the Euro banks can generate multiple expansion of Euro deposits on receiving a fresh deposit of cash. The cash reserve ratio for the banks in the domestic monetary system is statutorily fixed. There is no statutory reserve requirement for Euro banks, they do keep voluntarily prudential reserves.

Suppose a bank in London receives a deposit of $ 1000 from a firm and the bank maintains 3% reserves against Euro deposits. The bank lends $ 970 to a customer. If the borrower deposits the dollars with another Euro bank, the chain continues and the total amount of Euro deposits created could be a multiple of initial deposit as under:

$$1000 + 1000\,(0.97) + 1000\,(0.97)^2 + 1000\,(0.97)^3 + \ldots$$

International Banking – The International banks have —

The International banks have multinational presence at important financial centres in different countries in the forms such as correspondent banking, Resident representatives, Bank agencies, Foreign branches, Foreign subsidiaries and consortium banks.

Euro currency markets exist outside the borders of the country of the underlying currency concerned. For each major currency like US dollar, German Mark, Japanese Yen etc. there is the domestic segment and the offshore or Euro segment. In case of US dollar, the market in dollar assets in USA is domestic segment and the market in US dollar assets outside USA, *i.e.,* in London, Singapore etc. is the offshore segment.

The distinction between the two segments domestic and offshore lies in the degree and nature of regulatory supervision exercised by the authorities. The domestic segments are tightly regulated and closely monitored. The absence of regulatory aspects like reserve requirements, deposit insurance on deposits etc. characterise the Euro markets.

19.2 MAJOR GLOBAL MARKETS

(i) US Dollar Market

(ii) Japanese Yen Market

(iii) Deutsche Mark Market

(iv) Swiss Franc Market

(v) Australian Dollar Market

(vi) Sterling Market

(i) US Dollar Market

US Financial market is the largest market due to its versatile nature and its importance is linked with the dominant role played by US dollar as the convertible currency.

The financial system in USA consists of commercial banks — domestic and foreign, investment banks and a variety of non-bank financial institutions, insurance companies, pension funds, mutual funds etc.

The domestic segment of US dollar market is subject to strict regulation and supervision. The banks and the capital markets in USA. are subject to regulation of authorities like Federal Reserve Board and Securities Exchange Commission (SEC).

The financing instruments for foreign borrowers in the US dollar domestic markets are Foreign bonds (Yankee bonds), Medium Term Notes and CPs. These borrowers have to be top rated with good credit reputation.

The Eurodollar market has rapidly grown due to the favourable factors of absence of restrictions and the distinctive role of US dollar as the convertible currency. The foreign branches of American banks could offer better rates to depositors. The non-US entities raised their loans in the form of Eurodollar bonds, Floating rate notes (FRNs) and the Note Issuing Facility (NIFs). The US multinationals finance their foreign operations in the form of Eurodollar loans.

(ii) Japanese Yen Market

Upto 1970s Japanese financial markets were strictly regulated. Since then there has been deregulation of certain segments.

The funding options available to foreign borrowers are Yen bonds issued by, non-resident entities in Japanese market known as 'Samurai' bonds and Shibosai bonds for private placement. The Euro-Yen bond market became accessible to non-Japanese entities in 1984.

(iii) Deutsche Mark (DM) Market in Germany

The entire financial system is dominated by banks. The DM bond market is very large in size. The Euro DM banks and Euro DM bonds market are quite free from controls imposed on domestic segments.

(iv) Swiss Franc Market

Switzerland has a highly developed banking system. The major form of financing in Swiss Franc segment is bond issues. International Swiss Franc bonds are foreign bonds.

(v) Australian Dollar Market

The bond issues in offshore markets with Australian dollar as a currency of denomination have been popular.

(vi) Sterling Market

Upto World War II, London was the leading international capital market. Since then its importance declined but emerged as Euro sterling market after 1979 when exchange controls were lifted. The main instruments in Euro Sterling market are bonds with different time-lengths, FRNs and Equity linked convertible bonds. The borrowers are corporates, financial institutions and sovereign governments.

19.3 FINANCING INSTRUMENTS IN INTERNATIONAL FINANCIAL MARKET

The financing instruments in the International Financial markets, *i.e.,* offshore or Euro markets are:

(A) Debt Instruments:	External bonds, *i.e.,* Foreign bonds,
	Euro bonds, Floating Rate Notes (FRNs), Euro Medium Term Notes (EMTNs), Note Issuing Facility (NIF), Euro CPs and Euro CDs etc.
(B) Equity Instruments:	Depository Receipts.
	Foreign Currency Convertible Borrowing (FCCB).

The Euro markets have been primarily inter-bank money markets in time deposits and short-term loans. These markets have, over the years, evolved a wide variety instruments consisting of both — debt instruments and equity instruments.

(A) Debt Instruments

1. Bonds

The bonds could be distinguished as: (i) Domestic bonds, and (ii) External bonds. The External bonds consists of Foreign bonds and Euro bonds.

(i) ***Domestic bonds***: bonds issued by a resident issuer in the country of residence and denominated in the currency of that country.

- Indian Company issuing rupee-denominated bonds in India.

(ii) ***External bonds:*** Some examples of External bonds are:

Yankee bonds: dollar-denominated bonds issued by a foreign borrower in USA.

Bulldog bonds: bonds-denominated in Dutch currency and sold in Netherlands.

Samurai bonds: Yen-denominated bonds issued in Japanese market ONGC issued Samurai bonds in 1988.

Shibosai bonds: Yen-denominated private placement bonds. IDBI made Shibosai issue in 1984.

(iii) Foreign bonds: Bonds issued by a non-resident entity and denominated in the currency of that country.

- Indian company issuing dollar denominated bonds in USA.

(iv) Euro bonds: Bonds denominated in currency other than the currency of the country of issue.

- A dollar-denominated bond issued outside USA or say a DM bond issued outside Germany.
- Straight bonds:

A straight bond is a debt instrument with fixed maturity and fixed coupon rate. The face value of a bond is repaid in one go at maturity. The coupon payments are made annually, semi-annually or quarterly.

A bond is said to be selling at par: purchase price is same as face value

Selling at discount: purchase price is lower than face value.

Selling at premium: purchase price is higher than face value.

A straight bond may have a maturity of as long as 50 years. Bonds with shorter maturity (7 to 10 years) are known as Notes.

***(v)* Bonds with Option**

Callable bonds: can be called back or redeemed by the *issuer* before the date of maturity.

Puttable bonds: allows the investor to sell back bond to the issuer before the date of maturity.

(vi) Sinking Fund bond: Repayment of face vlaue is not made as a single payment at maturity, but a part of the principal is redeemed every year.

- *Zero coupon bond:* Interim coupon payments are not made. Interest earned every year is reinvested at coupon rate. The principal and accumulated interest is paid at maturity.
- *Warrants:* Along-with the bond issued an option is given allowing the holder to purchase at a future date more bonds or equity shares.

  Unlike convertible bond, the warrant holder has a choice not to exercise the option at the given date.

  The warrant gives a right to buy a share on a given date. In case it is not profitable for him, the warrant holder may not exercise his right.

2. Floating Rate Notes (FRNs)

FRN is a bond with varying coupon over its life, coupon rate is reset every six months. The rate is generally indexed with LIBOR (London Inter-bank Offer Rate).

3. Euro Medium Term Notes (EMTNs)

EMTNs are issued in several tranches. Each tranche may carry same or different coupons and maturity dates. These may be issued in different currencies.

4. Note Issuing Facility (NIFs)

NIF is a medium (5 to 7 years maturity) term debt instrument. The borrower, however, issues a short-term paper which is rolled over. The interest rate on NIF is set with a spread over LIBOR.

5. Syndicated Bank Loans

Earlier, this has been the most common form of cross-border lending as the developing country borrowers relied heavily on this source. Euro syndicated loan has one of the participating bank acting as an agent bank. The loan has a fixed maturity (say 5 to 10 years), a floating rate of interest and a specific repayment schedule. The interest is typically reset every six months with reference to LIBOR.

6. Euro Commercial Papers (Euro CPs)

Euro CPs are a short-term Euro rates issued by corporates on a discount basis. The investors in Euro CPs are insurance companies, pension funds and other corporates.

7. Euro Certificates of Deposits (Euro CDs)

Euro CDs are issued by London banks. The CDs could be fixed rate and floating rate CDs.

(B) Equity Instruments (see Table 16.5 on page 367 for Finance raised by Indian Companies from Euro-equity markets)

Depository Receipts:

(i) *like GDR: Global Depository Receipts*

(ii) *ADR: American Depository Receipts limited to US markets*

(iii) *EDR: European Depository Receipts limited to European markets*

(iv) *FCCB: Foreign Currency Convertible Borrowings* are in the form of deferred equity consisting of convertible bonds which can be exchanged for equity shares at some later date after the issue. The number of shares that each bond will give is equal to the bond issue price divided by conversion price.

Some of the Indian Companies that made ECCB include Reliance Industries, TISCO, Sterlite, ICICI, Gujarat Ambuja Cement and Reliance Petroleum Ltd.

Global Depository Receipts (GDRs)

GDR made its appearance in the international financial markets in 1991.

As against ADR which is limited to US markets, the term 'global indicates that more markets than one are tapped simultaneously.

A depository receipt represent a claim on a specified number of equity shares. A GDR is denominated in a convertible currency say US dollar. A depository receipt being negotiable instrument can be traded freely.

The shares issued by a company are held by a large international bank called 'depository.' The bank, *i.e.*, depository issues depository receipts to investors. The issuing company pays dividends in home currency to the depository who, in turn converts it into the currency of investors; say US dollars.

The major advantage of GDR is that the issuing company does not bear any exchange risk. The dividend outflow is in home currency.

The parties involved in GDR issue are:

- Issuing company: Company deciding to raise financing from foreign markets.
- Lead managers: appointed by issuing company.

They collect and evaluate information about the issuing company and present the correct picture about the company.

- Depository: An international bank appointed by the company.
- Custodian: A bank appointed by the depository for keeping the custody of shares and certificates.
- Clearing House arrangement: Registrars who keep records of particulars of GDRs and investors.

DTC: Depository Trust Company in USA.

CEDEL: in London

Euroclear: a clearing house located in Brussels.

Reliance Industries was the first Indian company to go to Euro market in May 1992 to raise $100 million. The other Indian companies that issued GDR of more than $100 million include Grasim, Sterlite, Arvind Mills, Indo Gulf Fertilizers, Indian Rayon, GE shipping, Hindalco, Ranbaxy, TELCO, Bajaj Auto, Century Textiles, L&T, IPCL and ICICI.

19.4 MULTILATERAL FINANCIAL INSTITUTIONS AND ASIAN DEVELOPMENT BANK

The developing countries like India have in their developmental tasks, significantly availed of the financial assistance in the form of: (i) funds from multilateral financial institutions such as World Bank, International Development Agency (IDA), International Finance Corporation (IFC) and Asian Development Bank (ADB), and (ii) bilateral government to government concessional financing. The World Bank mainly extends project finance with maturity period upto 20 years. IDA is the 'soft loan' window of the World Bank which provides financial assistance as interest free loans (with small service charge) of very long maturity period upto 50 years and with substantial grace periods. The assistance is provided to projects in areas like agriculture, forestry, livestock, development, irrigation etc., with emphasis on employment generation. The IFC is an institution which promotes private sector development in the member developing countries by: (i) financing private sector projects, (ii) investing in the share capital of Development Finance

Institutions (DFIs); and (iii) providing technical and other advisory services. The role played by ADB is dealt with later in the chapter.

The multilateral financial institutions and the bilateral inter-governmental provision of funds has been an important source of meeting financing needs in case of developing countries like India. The dominant trend in the recent years is resorting to international financial markets, *i.e.,* to draw upon cross-border financial flows in offshore markets.

Asian Development Bank (ADB)

Asian Development Bank was established in 1966.

The Headquarters of ADB is in Manila, Philippines.

ADB is a multilateral development finance institution dedicated to reducing poverty in Asia and the Pacific.

There are 23 offices of ADB around the world.

- 15 resident missions in Asia
- A regional mission for the Pacific in Vanuatu
- A country office in the Philippines
- Representative offices in:

  Frankfurt to Europe

  Tokyo for Japan

  Washington D.C. for N. America
- A special office in Timor
- Extended missions in Gujarat, India and Papua, New Guinea.

Organisation of ADB

There are 61 member countries. Each member country nominates one Governor and an alternate Governor.

ADB is managed by a Board of Governers, a Board of Directors, a President, three Vice-Presidents and the Heads of Departments and officers.

The Board of Governors elects 12 Directors (each with an alternate) — eight representing countries within the Asian Pacific region and four representing outside the region.

The Board of Governors also elects the President for a term of 5 years.

Table No. 19.1

India's External Borrowing

(Multilateral, Bilateral and Commercial Borrowing)
(as at March-end)

(US $ in million)

Type	*1994*	*1995*	*1996*	*1997*	*1998*	*1999*	*2000*	*2001*	*2002*	*2003*	*2004*	*2005*	*2006*	*2007*	*2008*	*2009*
Multilateral	26263	28542	28616	29218	29553	30534	31438	31105	31899	30002	29288	31744	32620	35337	39490	39566
(A + B)									(155633)	(142720)	(131089)	(138897)	(145503)	(154053)	(157901)	(201565)
A. Government	24158	26127	26059	26369	26344	26967	27584	27414	28290	27271	26826	29204	29996	32514	36171	25728
Borrowing									(138023)	(129727)	(120073)	(127782)	(133800)	(141746)	(144627)	(181997)
B. Non-Government	2105	2415	2557	2849	3209	3567	3854	3691	3609	2731	2462	2540	2624	2823	3319	3841
Borrowing									(17610)	(12993)	(10996)	(11115)	(11703)	(12307)	(13274)	(19568)
Bilateral	17450	20270	19213	17494	16969	17499	18175	15974	15323	16802	17278	17034	15761	16065	19701	20587
(A + B)									(74762)	(79918)	(77085)	(74530)	(70302)	(70034)	(76776)	(104882)
A. Government	14519	16841	15535	13652	12998	13447	13966	12176	11540	12664	12988	13132	12239	12344	14853	14655
Borrowing									(56302)	(60242)	(58121)	(57458)	(54593)	(53810)	(59391)	(74662)
B. Non-Government	2931	3429	3678	3842	3971	4052	4209	3798	3783	4138	4290	3902	3522	3721	4848	5932
Borrowing									(18460)	(19676)	(18964)	(17072)	(15709)	(16224)	(19385)	(30220)
Commercial	11643	12363	12991	13873	16986	20978	19943	24215	23226	22530	22101	26405	26452	41443	62337	62676
Borrowing									(113451)	(107119)	(96016)	(115533)	(117991)	(180669)	(249255)	(319302)

Source: Handbook of Statistics on Indian Economy, RBI 2008-09.

Note: Figures in brackets indicate amounts expressed in ₹ crore.

The Departments of ADB are:

- South Asia Department
- East and Central Asia Department
- Southeast Asia Department
- Mekong Department
- Pacific Department
- Private Sector Operations Department

Activities of ADB

ADB operations include:

- Lending
- Technical Assistance
- Capacity building
- Economic and sector work
- Donor co-ordination
- Policy dialogue.

Goal: The overarching goal of ADB is poverty reduction in Asia and Pacific region.

Strategy

1. Pro-poor sustainable economic growth based on policies and programmes that facilitate employment and income generation for the poor.
2. Social development: which can enable the poor to make full use of opportunities to improve their living standards and programmes that directly address the severity of poverty, 3 good governance to ensure that the poor have better access to basic services and greater voice and participation in the decisions affecting them.

Promoting Economic Growth

Economic Growth Projects include those which support economic growth through —

- Infrastructure development : Energy projects
  : Transport and Communications.
- Industry and Finance

Finance: to support reform in the finance sector by improving financial intermediation and broadening and deepening the capital markets.

- Supporting Agriculture and Natural resources.

In addition, technical assistance provided for capacity building, strategic planning and institutional innovations.

In 1999, ADB lent $2.9 billion for 23 public sector — financed projects with economic growth as the primary objective.

Supporting Human Development

The main human development objective of ADB is to reduce poverty by improving the health, living standards and livelihood of people in developing member countries.

This is done by strengthening institutions, building capacity, reforming policy and providing loans and technical assistance in education, health and nutrition, water supply and sanitation in the urban sectors.

ADB and education: Lending and technical assistance: Education rehabilitation, secondary education, skills development, teacher training and higher education.

ADB and health: ADB's updated health sector policy adopted in Feb. 1999, re-emphasises primary health care, including reproductive health, family planning and selected nuitrition innerventions.

Water supply and sanitation: Lending to reduce pollution, improve the environment and projects of water resources management. Technical assistance for projects in the water supply and sanitation.

Urban Development

ADB approved 3 loans totalling $200 million in 1999 to assist the Government of India in developing urban and environmental infrastructure, meeting basic human needs and improving the quality of life of urban residents. An integrated urban development project loan of $175 million is helping Karnataka, India meet basic human needs by developing urban services, building capacity, and supporting community participation at the state and local levels.

Technical assistance in the urban sector approved for a number of member countries.

Projects Assisted by ADB in 1999 (Illustrative List)

Energy		
● Power sector restructing programme	Indonesia	$ 380 million
● Upgrading power system	Dhaka, Bangladesh	$ 157 million
● Rural electrification	Nepal	$ 50 million
Transport and Communications		
● Primary road system	Republic of China	2 projects $ 250 million each.
● Road linking	Mongolia	$ 25 million
● Upgrading and maintaining of roads	Papua New Guinea	$ 63 million
● Corridor road project	Vietnam	$ 25 million
Industry and Finance		
● To support reforms in the finance sector	Kyrgyz Republic	$ 36 million
● Industry sector	Pakistan	$ 307 million
● State-owned enterprise Reforms:	Vietnam	$ 100 million

Agriculture and Natural Resources

- Loans amounting to \$ 430.4 million for six projects in 5 countries
- Technical assistance of \$ 28.4 million

Supporting Education

Secondary education Improvement	Bangladesh	\$ 60 million
Employment oriented skills development:	Papua New Guinea	\$ 20 million
Skills development	Sri Lanka	\$ 18.8 million
Social sector rehabilitation	Tajikistan	\$ 20 million
Higher education	Thailand	\$ 59.3 million
Teacher training	Tajikistan	\$ 20 million

Primary Health Care

Health care	Marshall Islands	\$ 9.3 million
Women's health	Pakistan	\$ 47 million
Social sector rehabilitation	Tajikistan	\$ 20 million

Water Supply and Sanitation

Reducing pollution	Republic of China	\$ 300 million
Water supply system	Cambodia	\$ 20 million
Water supply	Lao Republic	\$ 20 million

Table No. 19.2
Utilisation of ADB Assistance in India

(₹ in Crores)

Year	*Loans*	*Grants*	*Total*
1990-91	381.1	—	381.1
1997-98	2230.0	—	2230.0
1998-99	2581.0	—	2581.0
1999-00	2641.7	—	2641.7
2000-01	2146.9	—	2146.9
2001-02	1911.7	—	1911.7
2002-03	2467.8	120.3	2588.1
2003-04	2743.0		2743.0
2004-05	2148.6		2148.6

Source: Economic Survey: Government of India, 2005-06.

KEY TERMS

Euro (Offshore) Market, US Dollar Market, Debt Instruments, Equity Instruments.

REVIEW QUESTIONS

1. What is Euro or Offshore market?
2. What are the major global financial markets?
3. What are the financing instruments in the international financial market?
4. Explain different Debt and Equity instruments in International Financial Market?
5. Discuss the organisation, goals and operations of the Asian Development Bank?

REFERENCES

1. Purfield Catriona, Hiroko Oura, Charles F. Cramer and Andreas Jobst, "Asian Equity Markets; Growth, Opportunities and Challenges", IMF Working Paper, WP/06/266. December, 2006.
2. Rajwade, A.V., (1990), Foreign Exchage and International Finance, NSB Publications, Mumbai.
3. Reddy Y.Y., "Foreign Exchange Reserves; New Realities and Opinions", RBI Bulletin, October, 2006d.

❑ ❑ ❑

![20]

Financial Inclusion — Microfinance

INTRODUCTION

A new mode of credit delivery has been evolved by RBI in the form of "Microfinance" the dominent forms of microfinance in the country are — Self-help Groups and Microfinance Institutions.

The details of SHGs-Bank Linkage Programme have been separately given in the chapter on banking. This chapter gives further details on the issues like Financial Exclusion and measures taken for Financial Inclusion.

This chapter intends to discuss:

20.1 Extent of Financial Exclusion in India

20.2 Financial Inclusion – Definition, Meaning and Techniques of Financial Inclusion

20.3 National Rural Financial Inclusion Plan (NRFIP)

20.4 SHG, SHG and Bank Linkage, Impact and Limitations of SHG

20.5 Joint Liability Groups (JLGs)

20.6 Microfinance – Definition and Meaning, History of Microfinance in India

20.7 Demand for and Supply of Microfinance Services

20.1 EXTENT OF FINANCIAL EXCLUSION IN INDIA

Financial Inclusion

Financial services needed by people include credit, savings, insurance, payments and remittance facilities and also financial counselling/advisory services. It is expected that the access to these facilities should be easy and at reasonable cost. As against the earlier 'informal' managements of traditional society for extending these services consisting of friends and relatives and money lenders, the 'formal' set-up such as co operative outlets, the banks came up in the form of a network of institutions. The benefits of this change have to reach all sections of society. 'Financial Exclusion' has taken place because vast sections of people in the country who live on low income and are even illiterate could not access the services rendered by the formal financial institutions. Those who are excluded consist of:

- Marginal farmers
- Landless labourers
- Oral lessees
- Self-employed
- Unorganised sector enterprises/employees
- Migrants
- Ethnic minorities
- Socially excluded groups
- Senior citizens and women.

As per NSS (National Sample Survey) data, there are 203 million households in the country, including 147 million in rural areas and 56 million in urban areas. Of those in rural areas, 89.3 million are farmer households, 45.9 million, *i.e.,* 51.4 per cent of the farmer households have no access to formal or informal sources of credit. Farm households' not accessing credit from formal sources is high in North Eastern, Eastern and Central regions of the country. The poor the group, the greater is the exclusion.

The government as a custodian of broader social interest and the RBI as an apex body over viewing the functioning and activities of other institutions undertook different programmes to extend the out reach of the formal network of financial institutions to bring in their fold the poor and the disadvantaged segments of society in the rural and urban areas. Still, the vast sections of low income vulnerable groups remained away and outside their ambit. Marginal farmers who account for 66 per cent of all farm holdings remained excluded from the formal financial system. Incidence of financial exclusion among the non-cultivation households has been estimated at over 78%.

A number of reasons have been cited for Financial Exclusion with the blame lying on both demand and supply side. The poor and low income groups have remained outside the ambit of the formal financial institutions.

Many of them are either illiterate and/or are not aware of the services rendered. They do not have assets to support nor the base of adequate incomes. As against the documentation and procedures of the formal institutions, they prefer to opt for easy availability of informal credit.

Even with the creation of extensive network of branches in rural areas, the branch offices remain geographically distant and their timings unsuitable. It is said that only about 1 (one) bank branch exists in rural areas per 100 sq.kms. The insensitiveness of indifferent staff at the bank branches affects the level and nature of services rendered. For rendering services to low income groups particularly in rural areas, the bank staff with proper attitudes and motivation is essential. The poor and low income groups find the nature and the type of financial services rendered by the formal institutions not shifted well with what and how frequently they need.

A new mode of credit delivery was evolved by RBI in the form of 'Microfinance' to extend the scope of activities of the organised financial system to include within its ambit people with low incomes. The two dominant forms of microfinance in the country are now – Self-help Groups and Microfinance Institutions (SHGs and MFIs details given separately). Prior to making explicitly 'Financial Inclusion' as a policy objective in 2005, RBI had taken several steps towards extending the reach of the formal financial institutions to the poor and excluded groups of people, such as spread of co operative outlets, expansion of bank branches particularly in rural areas, establishment of Regional Rural Banks (RRBs) directed credit priority sector. The Government implemented subsidised credit programme for the poor through banks under Integrated Rural Development Programme (IRDP). The efforts for including the low income segments of population received stimulus in 1980s when Self-help Groups were formed by Non- Government Organisations (NGOs). In early, 1990s the movement was strengthened when NABARD launched a programme of linking SHGs and NGOs with the banks for the provision of credit in rural areas. NGOs initiated setting up Microfinance Institutions (MFIs) to meet the credit needs of the poor.

20.2 FINANCIAL INCLUSION – DEFINITION, MEANING AND TECHNIQUES OF FINANCIAL INCLUSION

As mentioned earlier, RBI has made since 2005, the 'Financial Inclusion' as a specific policy objective. One common measure of Financial Inclusion is the percentage of adult population having bank account. On all India basis, 59% of the adult population in the country have bank account. In other words, 41% are unbanked. In a research work "Building Inclusive Financial Sector for Development" called Blue book, UN raised in 2006 a basic question – Why are so many bankable people unbanked ? The approach to financial inclusion in the developing country like India has to focus on the vast sections of vulnerable groups who are excluded. In the Annual Policy of RBI announced for 2004-05, it was mentioned that — "While commercial considerations are no doubt important, the banks should be obliged to provide banking services to all segments of the population on equitable basis." The 11th Five Year Plan (2007-12) of the Government emphasises the initiatives on financial inclusion having focus on inclusive growth.

Inclusive growth is desired from the point of view of equity as well as efficiency. It is imperative for the institutions in the formal financial system to have concern for taking their services as and where needed by all segments of society. The process of economic growth in the country would be in a position to sustain if the large number of those who are excluded for want of opportunities including access to credit are made eligible to perform better and efficiently.

The *objective of* financial inclusion is to extend the scope of activities of the organised financial system to include within its ambit people with low income. The ultimate objective is of abolishing the state of 'social exclusion' by way of empowerment of the people, *i.e.,* making them creditworthy.

Financial inclusion denotes delivery of financial services at an affordable cost to the vast sections of the disadvantaged and low income groups.

Definition

Financial inclusion is the process of ensuring access to financial services and adequate credit where needed by vulnerable groups such as weaker sections and low income groups at an affordable cost.

Financial inclusion:
(i) delivery of financial services;
(ii) at an affordable cost;
(iii) extending financial services by formal institutional set-up to cover weaker segments of people.

Microfinance Institutions (MFIs) have been established to fulfil a mission of reaching credit and financial services to the poor who are not reached by the mainstream financial institutions.

In June 2006, the Government of India constituted a 'Committee on Financial Inclusion' under the Chairmanship of Dr. C. Rangarajan. The committee submitted its report in Jan. 2008. Along with making recommendations, the committee suggested that financial inclusion must be taken up as a mission and formulated 'National Rural Financial Inclusion Plan'.

20.3 NATIONAL RURAL FINANCIAL INCLUSION PLAN (NRFIP)

- **By 2012:** to provide access to comprehensive financial services to at least 50% of the excluded rural cultivation and non-cultivation households.
- **By 2015:** the remaining households to be covered.
- State Level Rural Financial Inclusion Plan (SLRFIP) shall be prepared by the State Level Bankers' Committee and NABARD.
- **Financial Inclusion Funds:**

  Two Funds : Initial :

  Corpus : ₹ 250 crore each

  Financial Inclusion Promotion and Development Fund

  Financial Inclusion Technology Fund
- NABARD in consultation with RBI may prepare detailed guidelines for operating the funds.
- Resource centers to be set up by NGOs, banks, Government Departments.

Business Facilitators (BFs) / Business Correspondents (BCs)

As per the circular issued in Jan. 2006, RBI has permitted banks to utilise the services of NGOs, SHGs, MFIs and other social organisation as intermediaries in providing financial services through BFs and BCs.

It is being noticed that small value clients particularly in remote locations get little preference in accessing financial services. Banks are unwilling to increase their physical presence in remote locations.

Earlier, insurance agents could acts BFs. Later on, retired Government servants like poster masters, school teachers and headmistress have been made eligible to act as BFs. Besides these, the complete list is given below:

Business Facilitators (BFs)

NGOs, farmers, clubs, co operatives

Community-based organisations,

IT-enabled rural outlets of corporate bodies,

Panchayats, village knowledge centres,

Agri-clinics, argi-business centres,

Krishi Vigyan Kendras, KVIC/KVIB units.

Services to be rendered by BFs

Identification of borrowers,

Collection of loan applications,

Processing and submission of application to banks,

Post-sanction monitoring,

Creation of awareness about savings and other products,

Promotion and nurturing of SHGs/JLGs,

Follow-up for recovery.

Business Correspondents

NGOs/MFIs set up under the Societies/Trust Act,

Mutually Addied Co operative Societies,

Sec. 25 Companies,

NBFCs not accepting public deposits,

Post offices.

Services to be rendered by BCs

In addition to the activities listed in respect of BFs, the activities of BCs also include –

Disbursal of small value credit,

Collection of small value deposits,

Recovery of principal/collection of interest,

Receipt and delivery of small value remittances,

Sale of micro insurance/pension products etc.

By having a BC touch point in wide spread villages and in remote locations, the banks can cater to a large number of clients with low value transactions.

In practice, however, the response of the banking system to BFs and BCs is low key due to lack of clarity regarding certain procedural complexities.

Though the banks have provided access to small depositors, the supply of savings for the poor households falls short of the need. In case of supply of insurance services, the usage is limited due to low awareness among the poor.

Micro Insurance

It may be noted that less than is per cent of the country's population is insured. As against the vulnerability to various risks being highest for the poor, there is a huge gap in respect of insurance services available to the poor. The major block in the progress of micro insurance is that the poor are unable to meet with the expectations of insurance companies in regard to insurance contacts and the paperwork.

At present, micro insurance service have been extended mainly as credit – Life insurance, *i.e.,* bundled with micro credit. As a stand-alone product micro insurance is not easy as it has to be 'pushed' being faced with low level of awareness among the poor.

Under Insurance Regulation and Development Act (IRDA), provisions were made in 2005 to encourage both insurers and micro insurance distributors to actively promote micro insurance. As per rural and social obligations stipulated under the IRDA, insurance companies are required to achieve a certain number of policies for the rural and social sector. The IRDA provides for SFGs, Societies and Co operatives to function as micro insurance agents.

Livestock Insurance

As against, 284 million cattle in the country, only 6 per cent, *i.e.,* 18 million cattle are insured.

Credit-Life Insurance

Under Credit-Life Insurance, *i.e.,* bundled with micro credit it is convenient for the borrowers to pay the insurance premium in small monthly installments to the insurance company along with their loan repayments.

Health Insurance

As per the compilation of micro health insurance programme carried out by ILO, about 9 million are insured under 90 Micro Health Insurance programmes in the country.

To scale up and develop micro insurance apart from offering subsidy to the poor for their premiums, programmes have to be undertaken to educate on the benefits of insurance.

As regards the reach of microfinance services to the needy poor households, the problems arise in case of the financial institutions involved like commercial banks and also the MFIs.

The financial institutions continue to consider their involvement in microfinance services as a 'social obligation' and not as a business proposition. The rendering of microfinance services by these institutions involve documentation, delays and higher transaction cost. As such, the provision of credit by these institutions does not suit properly with the needs of poor.

Historically, the MFIs were looked upon as 'not-for-profit' organisation and did not have adequate financial structure. MFIs now have undergone *transformation* and opted alternative forms which would enable them to improve their financial sustainability. MFIs lack, proper governance and accountability. MFIs in the newer organisational forms would result in improvising the quality of governance also.

There are certain restrictions in regard to the support by the financial institutions to MFIs.

SIDBI extends loans to MFIs only for the non-farm sector. HUDCO can lend for housing only. NABARD cannot refinance MFIs which lend in urban areas, or to MFIs registered as NBFCs.

Technology for Financial Inclusion

RBI has set up an advisory group for IT-enabled financial inclusion to facilitate development of IT solutions for delivery of banking services. For extending the banking outreach for the 'excluded', RBI Annual Policy 2007-08 advises banks to scale up their efforts for IT-based financial inclusion.

To meet the costs of technology adoption, a financial inclusion technology fund has been constituted with NABARD having an initial corpus of ₹ 500 crore.

FINO is a company set up by ICICI to offer technology solutions to MFIs. FINO provides technology platform to MFIs to manage their data electronically. In view of the recent developments in banking technologies and expansion in Telecommunication Network, a proper use of information and communication technologies can be very beneficial to MFIs.

For software development, the smaller organisations can ill-afford developing in-house facilities. For them it is better to source software externally. Larger organisations can opt for either developing in-house or outsourcing.

The prime aspect of the application of new technologies in microfinance is that it will help institutions to introduce MIS — management information system and in creating a national data-base. This will facilitate promoting financial inclusion further using the existing banking infrastructure and NGOs.

One significant obstacle to financial inclusion is that the transaction costs are high. Technology can play a major role in reducing cost of availing financial services in terms of solutions –

(i) Portable devices that can electronically capture transactions,

(ii) Rural ATMs – IIT Chennai and ICICI Bank have developed a suitable low cost ATM,

(iii) Mobile phones based solutions,

(iv) **Smart Cards** with Near Field Communication (NFC) enabled chips on them allowing transfer of small amounts.

(v) SBI launched a project in Dec. 2006.

(vi) Social security through Smart Cards in Andhra Pradesh introduced in April 2007.

In the recent period, an ordinance was passed by Andhra Pradesh regulating the operations and working of Microfinance Sector in the state. It is reported that the states of Odisha and West Bengal are likely to move in the same direction. Microfinance sector (Development of Regulations) Bill 2007 has been introduced in Lok Sabha and referred to standing committee of finance. The report is awaited of the committee appointed by RBI-known as Malegam. Committee to look into the issues related to the working of Microfinance institutions sector. Among other things, the issues pertaining to the functioning of microfinance institutions related to two main aspects –

(i) High interest rates charged — Microfinance Institutions (Companies) charge 24 per cent to 232 per cent.

(ii) Recovery methods adopted – It is alleged that Microfinance Institutions use strong-arm collection tactics.

Of late, the microfinance sector faced a trouble when CRISIL – the credit rating agency issued a credit alert on MFI sector. CRISIL has put the following 12 MFIs on rating watch with negative implications:

Asmitha Microfin
Bhartiya Samrudhi Finance
Diagamber Capfin
Equitas Microfinance
Grameen Financial Services
Sanghmitra Rural Financial
Shri Kshetra Dharmasathla Rural Dev.
SKS Microfinance
South Sunderban Janakalyan Sangha
Spandana Spoorthy Financial
Dijivan Financial Services
Vedika Credit Capital.

The MFIs have landed into trouble as their collections have come down to about 20% from the earlier phase of over 90 per cent recovery.

20.4 SELF-HELP GROUPS (SHGs)

Self-help Groups (SHGs) are small groups of about 15 to 20 people (rural and urban) bonding together to form savings and credit organisations. SHGs comprise mostly, *i.e.,* 90% of women. The number of households linked to 1 (one) SHG is set at an average of 17.

In 1980s, *i.e.,* in the early stages, NGOs (Non-government Organisations) played a key role in initiating and setting up SHGs, by lending to SHG.

In 1991, it was reported in the findings of All India Debt and Investment surveys that 36 per cent of rural households depending for funds on informal source. Institutional sources; including Government, Co operative Societies, Banks, *Informal* (Non-institutional Sources); Money-lenders, relatives and friends, professionals – doctors, lawyers. It has to be noted here that as per the Survey Report, the dependence of the rural poor on informal sources had declined from 83.7 per cent in 1961 to 36 per cent in 1991. A programme to strengthen the provision of credit in rural areas was launched in 1992 by linking SHGs and NGOs with the banking system. NABARD launched the pilot phase of SHG-bank linkage programme. NGOs support SHGs in getting bank loans, against guarantees of groups members. Initially, there was not much response by the banks. The pilot project was reviewed in 1995 and RBI advised commercial banks to consider lending to SHGs as part of their rural credit operations. During 1992-99, *i.e.* by March end 1999 the banks financed ₹ 57 crore to nearly 33,000 SHGs all over the country.

SHGs are like micro banks who manage loans. Internal loans are based on savings of the members having Savings Accounts with bank. External loans are from the banks *via* NGOs. SHGs usually meet every week to collect savings, repayments and deposit this collection in the banks. Every SHG has a group elected President, Secretary and Treasurer. In SHGs, the hold of caste is powerful both economically and socially.

After the slow progress initially, there has been a huge expansion in terms of the number of SHGs being formed and in the number of households linked to them.

Year	*No. of SHGs (in thousands)*
1999-2000	115
2000-2001	264
2001-2002	461
2002-2003	717
2003-2004	1079
2004-2005	1618

By March-end 2005, there were nearly 2 million SHGs in the country.

2005-06	2238
2006-07	2925

By March-end 2009, SHGs were linking to 40 million households.

By March-end 2008, there were 3.6 million SHGs.

With the spread of SHGs, SHG Federations were formed registering themselves as societies, mutual benefit trusts, and mutually aided co operative societies. About 15 to 20 SHGs make up a cluster. Several clusters come together to form an apex body – SHG federation. While SHGs are informal, SHG federations are formal institutions.

Regional Imbalance

Earlier, the SHGs had come up mainly in Southern States like Andhra Pradesh, Tamil Nadu, Karnataka. In March 2001, 71% of the bank-linked SHGs were from the southern region consisting of Andhra Pradesh, Karnataka, Kerala and Tamil Nadu. The uneven spread of SHGs in different regions has been on account of various factors like socio-cultural factors, hilly terrain of N.E. region, better performance of SHGs, active support from NGOs, and the role of state governments. NABARD intensified the SHGs linking with banks in 13 identified priority states which accounted for 70 per cent of the rural poor population.

SHGs-Bank Linkage Programme

NABARD, supported by RBI plays a key role in SHGs-bank linkage programme. Commercial banks, co operative banks and RRBs along with NGOs are associated with the programme. NABARD provides refinance and promotional support to these credit institutions involved in the programme.

There are three types of credit linkage of SHGs with the banks:

1. Formed and financed by banks.
2. Formed by formal agencies (NGOs/Government agencies) other than banks, but financed by banks.
3. Promoted by NGOs and by banks, using NGOs/formal agencies as financial intermediaries.

The financial needs of SHGs are catered to by 498 credit institutions through their network/ outlets of branches –

	No. of Institutions	*No. of branches / outlets*
Commercial Banks	50	33,000
RRBs	96	14,000
Co operative Banks	352	94,000

SHG – Programme – Bank Loan

(₹ *in Crores*)

Year	*Bank Loan (Cumulative)*
1999-2000	193
2000-2002	481
2001-2002	1026
2002-2003	2049
2003-2004	3094
2004-2005	6898
2005-2006	11398

By March-end 2008, the amount of outstanding bank loan to SHGs was ₹17,000 crore.

The financial agency-wise details of credit flow under the scheme shows that by March-end 2007, the commercial banks financed 54% and RRBs – 31% of SHGs.

As per the study conducted by NABARD in 2005, 1.44 million SHGs had bank loans outstanding of ₹ 4,200 crore, 2.63 million SHGs had saving accounts with the banks, and savings outstanding amounted to ₹ 2,391 crore.

Interest Rates: While the average rate of interest on bank's lending to SHGs is around 12%, most SHGs charge interest rates of around 22% to 24% to members.

One of the significant aspects of SHG-bank linkage has been high one-time recovery, which as on June, 2005 was 90% in commercial banks, 87% in RRBs and 86% in co-operative banks.

Impact of SHGs

It could be said that through SHGs there has been greater outreach of financial services to the poor. Poverty reduction by way of improvement in livelihoods of members is a matter of prime concern of SHGs. The livelihoods of the rural poor are linked with various goods and services activities such as agriculture, farming, animal husbandry, dairy etc. SHGs have rendered help to their members in starting enterprises related to these activities.

It is significant to note the impact of SHGs in both the financial as well as other than financial areas. The foremost among the non-financial aspect is that SHGs empower their members who are mainly women, and inspire them to play powerful political role. At present, the compositions of SHGs are often consisting of members belonging to one particular social group. It may be said that over the years SHGs may give rise to mixed membership and bridge the social distances. As against the few instances, at present, of SHGs making some contribution in resolving community problems, SHGs with the village level support would be able to play active role in community development.

Limitations

The sustainability of SHGs is closely linked with the financial aspects, and in this regard SHGs are generally in the state of average to weak financial management.

The major issue for the SHGs and their federations is the challenge of functioning with improved governance and standard management practices. SHGs need a strong governance system and accountability.

Support

In respect of the above two aspects, what is required is building the capacities of staff with SHGs for carrying out activities such as bookkeeping and accounting, governance, organisational structure etc. SHGs being unable to acquire the suitable human resources on their own, the role of NGOs to provide support for this purpose is essential. At the same time, there is a need for both SHGs and SHG Federation to attain standards following the best practices.

It is said that, the further development of SHGs is associated with how far they provide 'livelihood' finance. Livelihood is improved when the people, particularly in rural areas, are exposed to better facilities for education, health care and for reaching markets. Investment by government in providing effectively functioning public systems and improved infrastructure like roads and bridges could be said to be essential for enriching the livelihood of the poor. State Government intervention can help SHG members in getting increased cash flows to the extent they can bypass middlemen and sell their goods at markets.

20.5 JOINT LIABILITY GROUPS (JLGs)

During 2004-05, NABARD introduced a pilot project of JLGs through RRBs in 8 states. There are certain segments of the poor such as share croppers, tenant farmers, oral lessees whose loan requirements do not fit into the traditional financing approaches of the banking system. Under the pilot project, a scheme of financing JLGs of tenant farmers and oral lessees has been evolved for implementation by the commercial banks, RRBs and co operatives.

A JLG is an informal group of 4 to 10 individuals coming together for the purposes of availing bank loan against mutual guarantee. The JLG members are expected to engage in similar type of economic activities.

20.6 MICROFINANCE

Microfinance refers to small-scale financial service for both credits and deposits extended to the poor in rural and urban areas. Inspite of the efforts made since 1969, *i.e.,* in the post-nationalisation of banks period, to direct funds towards meeting the credit needs of the poor, these disadvantaged sections of society remained beyond reach of the formal financial system in the country. Microfinance wave began with the formation of Self-help Groups (SHGs) in 1980s. The share of formal financial sector in total rural credit in 1980s was 56.6% and that of informal sources consisting mainly of moneylenders was nearly 40 per cent.

Microfinance programme was launched in 1992. In late 1990s (1999), NABARD appointed Task Force which defined Microfinance as – "provision of thrift, credit and other financial services and products of very small amounts to the poor in rural, semi-urban and urban areas for enabling to raise their income levels and improve their living standards."

Microfinance is meant for reaching those people (including women, small and marginal farmers, rural artisans etc.) who –

- Farm, or fish or herd,
- Operate small or micro enterprise where goods are produced, recycled, repaired or tracked,
- Provide services, work for wages or commission,
- Gain income from renting small amounts of land, vehicles, draft animals or machine tools.

Microfinance – Definition

"Providing financial assistance to an undivided or eligible client either directly or through as group mechanism for an amount not exceeding ₹ 50,000/- in aggregate (₹ One Lakh Fifty Thousand for housing purposes). About 60 million households in the country are living below poverty line or just above the line. In this context, provision of microfinance to the poor assumes significance as it is argued that provision of funds at reasonable cost to the poor can bring about a reduction in poverty.

In April 1999, RBI set up Micro Credit Special Cell for Microfinance Sector.

Microfinance Institutions (MFIs) have come up to meet the needs of the poor for micro credit. Since 1997, RBI has tightened up deposit taking activity and hence MFIs being not allowed to take deposits, a large part of Microfinance activity, at present, is confined to credit only.

The Microfinance Institutions (MFIs) are classified as:

(1) NGOs engaged in promoting Self-help Groups (SHGs) and their federations and linking SHGs with banks;

(2) NGOs directly lending to borrowers organised as SHGs. NGOs get funds from SIDBI and borrow from various donors.

(3) MFIs organised as co operatives – Mutually aided co operative societies.

(4) MFIs organised as Non-banking Finance Companies (NBFCs).

It is estimated that there are about 1000 NGO-MFIs and more than 20 companies MFIs. The company MFIs account for over 80% of microfinance loans portfolio. The mainstream financial institutions involved in extending microfinance are –

- NABARD – NABARD refinance MFIs engaged in microfinance,
- Small Industries Development Bank of India (SIDBI),
- Housing Development Finance Corporation (HDFC),
- Commercial Banks,
- Regional Rural Banks (RRBs),
- Co operative Credit Societies.

For promoting MFIs, a study group was appointed by RBI which submitted its report in July 2005. Year 2005 was declared as International Year of Micro Credit.

The three segments of the rural and urban poor who need microfinance are –

(1) The segment at the rock bottom consists of –
  - landless and engaged in agricultural work
  - manual labourers in forestry, mining, household industries, construction and transport.

(2) Small and marginal farmers,
Rural artisans, weavers,

Self-employed in urban informal sector as hawkers, vendors, workers in household enterprises.

(3) Small and medium farmers

Those engaged in dairying, poultry, fishing etc.

Though the share of institutional credit for rural households has gone up, the household at the rock bottom level continued to be dependent on non-institutional sources with a share of debt from these informal agencies at 58 per cent, as against an overall share of 36% for the rural poor.

Large MFIs *(Gross Loan Portfolio of ₹10 lakh & more)*

	Name	*Location (State)*	*Form of Organisation*
1.	Share Microfin Ltd.	A.P.	NBFC
2.	Spandana Spporthy Financial Services Ltd.	A.P.	NBFC
3.	SKS Microfinance (P) Ltd.	A.P.	NBFC
4.	KAS Foundation	Orissa	Company
5.	Shree Kshetra Dharmsthala Rural Development	Karnataka	Trust
6.	BASIX	A.P.	NBFC
7.	SE Investments Ltd.	U.P.	NBFC
8.	Bandhan Kannagan	W.Bengal	Co operative Society

The other prominent MFIs are Asmitha, Cashpor India, Micro Credit India, Sadhana, Samrudhi, SKS Microfinance (P) Ltd., was launched in 1998 and has branches in 19 states in the country. SKS India is the fastest growing MFI.

Some of the leading microfinance institutions are –

Name	*State*
SEWA Bank	Gujarat
Serva Jana Seva Koshi Ltd.	Tamil Nadu
Association for Social Development (ASA)	Tamil Nadu
Care	Andhra Pradesh
Sanghmitra (Myrada)	Karnataka
Sakhi Samiti	Rajasthan
Adithi	Bihar
Rashtriya Gramin Vikas Nidhi	Assam

History of Microfinance in India

Co operative: The early efforts of the government to offer substitute for exploiting moneylenders and provide microfinance to the rural poor through the formal set-up have been in the form of Co operative institutions. The co operative banks were assigned to play a crucial role in achieving agricultural and rural development. In 1967, Hazare Committee on Industrial Policy observed that most of the bank funds were being diverted to the urban-based industrial sector and very little funds was made available to the farmers and other weaker sections of society.

Nationalisation of Commercial Banks: 1969 onwards –

(i) Banking network underwent expansion in terms of rural bank branches -

	Year	*No.*
Average population per bank branch	1969	64,000
	1991	13,711
	2001	12,000

The rural bank branches by June 2009 were 31,727, *i.e.,* 39.7 per cent (as against 1860 in 1969), of the total bank branches.

(ii) Directed Credit Programme : Target set for the banks to provide 40% of loan funds to the priority sector (including agriculture, small-scale units etc.)

Regional Rural Banks (RRBs): In 1975, Regional Rural Banks were established to extend further the efforts of the banking sector in reaching the rural poor. RRBs were set up with the objective of providing credit and deposit facilities to the small and marginal farmers, agricultural laborers artisans and small entrepreneurs.

Integrated Rural Development Programme (IRDP): IRDP was launched by Government in 1980 for providing subsidised credit through the banks to the poor.

As a result of these efforts and programmes, there came up in the country a large network of institutions in the formal sector to reach the poor and low income groups for meeting their credit needs. Still, the exclusion of these sections of society from the reach of the formal set-up was large.

It is estimated that the total MFI loan portfolio is over ₹ 25,000 crore, and MFIs have made loans accessible to about 2.8 crore rural poor – 4.72 crore poor households have gained access to microfinance.

It is said that MFIs achieve success in the initial period but do not sustain themselves primarily due to lack of commercial orientation. A vast majority of MFIs in the country are non-profit NGOs, registered as Societies or Trusts. NGOs doee not have the appropriate financial structure for carrying out microfinance activities on long-term as sustainable basis, as the major source of funds of NGOs are grants which are always limited. These not-for-profit organisations are 'public purpose' entities working on the basis of donor money. When microfinance scaled up, MFIs underwent **transformation** since 2002 from 'not-for profit' to 'for profit' organisations by opting for alternative forms of a co-operative or company. Co operatives are subject to political interference and pose a challenge of continuously raising capital from the members. The other option for MFIs was being incorporated as a Company – an NBFC, *i.e.,* Non-banking Financial Company which has entry level capital requirement of minimum ₹ 2 crore. Recently, MFI sector in the country is seen to be attracting private equity investments – (i) SKS: $ 11.5 million and (ii) SHARE: $ 25 million.

The other limitation of MFIs is the lack of proper governance and accountability. A number of MFI have started taking effective steps towards improving sustainability by: (a) increasing interest rates, atleast, to cover their costs and (b) transformation, *i.e.,* converting themselves into 'for-profit' organisations which would improve the quality of governance also.

20.7 DEMAND FOR AND SUPPLY OF MICROFINANCE SERVICES

Demand for Microfinancial Services:

Around 300 million people or about 60 million households are living below the poverty line in the country. The annual credit usage of all poor families has been put at over ₹ 45,000 crore, of which 80 per cent is met by informal sources and only about 20 per cent have access to credit from the formal sector. The demand for savings services and for insurance services is quite high because the incomes of the poor are not only low but are also highly variable.

Supply of Microfinance Services:

Over the years, a large network of formal institutions has been created in the country consisting of nearly 50,000 commercial bank outlets, over 14 thousand RRBs and 1.09 lakh primary agricultural co-operative societies. Nearly 43 per cent of the commercial banks and RRB branches are located in rural areas. Along with expansion in terms of bank branches, the commercial banks laid emphasis on lending to small borrowers. Still, the dependence of poor households for meeting their credit needs on the informal non-institutional sources continued to be significant.

Share of Debt from Institutional and Non-institutional Sources

Household classified by asset holding

Household Assets (in ₹) ('ooo)	*Share of debt (in %)*	
	Institutional Agency	*Non-institutional Agency*
Less than 5	42	58
5 – 10	47	53
10 – 20	44	56
20 – 30	68	32
30 – 50	55	45

50 – 70	53	47
70 – 100	61	39
100 – 150	61	39
150 – 200	68	32
250 and above	81	19
All Classes	64	36

Source: Rural Microfinance & Employment : Working Paper 2009.

It could be seen from the above Table that the households with negligible or low asset holding relied mostly on the non-institutional agencies for the provision of credit.

As against a common perception that MFIs and SHGs can improve Financial Inclusion, there are very few borrowers who are being serviced by MFIs and SHGs.

Credit: 93 per cent borrow from sources other than SHGs and only 6% borrow from SHGs.

70% per cent of the borrowing population in rural areas and 63% of the borrowing population from urban areas who are SHG members have not borrowed from SHGs but have done so from the non-institutional sources.

Saving: It is said that SHGs encourage savings. Actually, only 60% of rural households save. Of these, 36% do not save in SHGs at all. In case of 24% who save in SHGs, less than 1 per cent save exclusively in SHGs. Households who save in SHGs have other methods of savings.

The reach of microfinance in the country has remained limited due to certain **obstacles** to financial inclusion. MFIs and SHGs continue to be of lesser significance than the moneylenders.

	Households Without Bank Account (in %)	*Households Without Life Insurance*	*Households Without Health Insurance*
Rural	59.59	68.3	98.58
Urban	36.67	45.4	94.72
All-India	52.41 (52)	61.10 (61)	97.39 (97)

It is possible that households choose not to deal with formal financial institutions for the reasons: (i) lack of awareness and (ii) ineffective financial services that do not address their specific requirements. About 61 per cent of the households do not have insurance because it is too costly.

KYE TERMS

Financial Exclusion, Financial Inclusion, Microfinance, Self-help Groups.

REVIEW QUESTIONS

1. Discuss the extent of financial exclusion in India.
2. Define and explain the term Financial Inclusion and the techniques of Financial Inclusion.

3. What are SHGs? Discuss the link between SHGs and Banks.
4. Write short notes —
   (a) National Rural Financial Inclusion Plan
   (b) Business Facilitators and Business Correspondents
   (c) Joint Liability Groups
   (d) Micro Insurance
   (e) Demand for and Supply of Microfinance
5. What is Microfinance?
6. Give a brief history of Microfinance in India.

REFERENCES

1. RBI Annual Reports.
2. MFIs: Newspaper Media Coverage.

❑ ❑ ❑

ANNEXURE

Report of the RBI Committee on MFI Sector (Report released in Jan. 2011)

Report of the RBI committee under the chairmanship of Shri. Y.H. Malegam on MFI sector.

Terms of Reference

1. To review MFIs for the purpose of regulation of NBFCs undertaking microfinance by the RBI.
2. To examine the prevalent practices of MFIs in regard to interest rates, lending and recovery practices.
3. To delineate the objectives and scope of regulation of NBFCs undertaking microfinance by the RBI.
4. To examine the applicability of money lending legislation of the states.
5. To examine the role of MFIs in enhancing transparency disclosure and best practices.
6. A grievance redressal machinery to be put in place.
7. To examine the conditions under which loans to MFIs can be classified as priority sector lending.

Specific Areas of 'Concern'

(i) Unjustified high rates of interest
(ii) Lack of transparency in interest rates and other charges
(iii) Multiple lending
(iv) Upfront collection of security deposits
(v) Overborrowing
(vi) Ghost borrowers
(vii) Coercive methods of recovery.

Need for Regulation of NBFCs Operating in MFI Sector

1. The borrowers in MFI sector represent a vulnerable section of society.
2. NBFCs operating in the MFIs sector compete among themselves.
3. Credit to the MFI sector is an important plank in the scheme for financial inclusion.
4. The finance obtained by NBFCs operating in the MFI sector is provided by banks and financial institution including SIDBI.

Recommendations

1. A separate category be created for NBFCs operating in the microfinance sector to be designated as NBFC-MFIs.

   NBFC-MFIs extend loan satisfying the following criteria:

   (a) the loan is given to a borrower who is a member of a household whose annual income does not exceed ₹ 50,000.

(b) Amount of loan, not to exceed ₹ 25,000.

(c) Teure of the loan:

12 months : loans upto ₹ 15,000

24 months : other cases

(d) Loan is without collateral.

(e) Loans given for income generation purposes not less than 75% of the total loan given by MFIs.

(f) Loan is repayable by weekly, fortnightly or monthly instalments.

2. Interest rate control

Margin cap for MFI loan portfolio (outstanding)

10%	₹ 100 crore
12%	not exceeding ₹ 100 crore
24%	on individual loans

3. Transparency in interest charges

- MFI should levy only:

  Processing fee — not exceeding 1% of the gross loan amount

  Interest charge

  Insurance premium.

- MFI should provide to the borrowers a loan card.
- There should be a standard form of loan agreement.

4. Multiple lending, overborrowing and Ghost borrowers

- Not more than two MFI should lend to the same borrower.
- MFIs should lend to an individual borrower only as a member of JLG.
- A borrower cannot be a member of more than 1 SHG/JLG.
- A Credit Information Bureau be established.

5. Coercive methods of recovery

- The primary responsibility for the prevention of coercive methods of recovery should rest with the MFI.
- For resorting to coercive methods of recovery, severe penalties must be levied on the MFIs and their managements.
- MFI to establish a proper Grievance Redresal procedure.
- Client Protection Code: It should be mandatory for MFIs to accept and observe such a code.

Other recommendations

6. Support to SHGs/JLGs

Greater resources be devoted to professional inputs for:

(a) the formation of SHGs/JLGs.

(b) The imparting of skill development and training.

7. Corporate size: All NBFC-MFIs should have a minimum net worth of ₹ 15 crore. (presently NBFCs required to have a minimum capital of ₹ 2 crore.)

8. Good Systems of Corporate Governance

Disclosures to be made — analysis of overdues

Geographic distribution of loan portfolio

The average effective rate of interest, the average cost of funds, and the average margin earned.

Outstanding loans by nature of purpose.

Composition of shareholding.

9. Maintenance of Solvency

(a) MFI should maintain on aggregate provision for loan losses

1% of the outstanding loan portfolio

50% of loan installments overdue for 90 days to 180 days.

100% of loan installments overdue for 180 days or more.

(b) MFIs to maintain capital adequacy ratio of 15%.

10. Need for competition: Within the MFIs and from other agencies operating in MFIs sector (SHG-Bank Linkage Programme).

11. Priority Sector Status

Bank advances to MFIs should continue to enjoy priority sector lending status.

12. Funding of MFIs: To widen the base from which MFIs are funded:

'Domestic Social Capital Fund' to be established: Targeted towards 'Social Investors' who are willing to accept returns 10% to 12%.

MFIs to issue preference capital with a coupon rate 10% to 12%.

13. Monitoring of Compliance: The responsibility be shared by –

The primary responsibility for compliance must rest with the MFI itself.

The industry association to assume greater responsibility.

Banks which lend funds to MFIs.

RBI.

14. Money Lending Acts

There are Acts in several states governing money lending.

NBFC-MFIs should be exempted from the provisions of the Money Lending Acts.

15. The Microfinance (Development & Regulation) Bill 2010

It is recommended that

The proposed Act should provide for all entities to be registered with RBI (except those where aggregate loan portfolio does not exceed ₹ 10 crore).

If NABARD is designated as the regulator, there must be close co-ordination between NABARD and RBI.